Programming C#

Other Microsoft .NET resources from O'Reilly

Related titles

C# Cookbook

C# Language Pocket Reference

C# in a Nutshell

C# and VB.NET Conversion Pocket Reference

Learning C# .NET Framework Essentials

Mono: A Developer's Notebook

Programming .NET Windows Applications

Programming Visual Basic .NET

.NET Books Resource Center

dotnet.oreilly.com is a complete catalog of O'Reilly's books on .NET and related technologies, including sample chapters and code examples.

ONDotnet.com provides independent coverage of fundamental, interoperable, and emerging Microsoft .NET programming and web services technologies.

Conferences

O'Reilly brings diverse innovators together to nurture the ideas that spark revolutionary industries. We specialize in documenting the latest tools and systems, translating the innovator's knowledge into useful skills for those in the trenches. Visit *conferences.oreilly.com* for our upcoming events.

Safari Bookshelf (*safari.oreilly.com*) is the premier online reference library for programmers and IT professionals. Conduct searches across more than 1,000 books. Subscribers can zero in on answers to time-critical questions in a matter of seconds. Read the books on your Bookshelf from cover to cover or simply flip to the page you need. Try it today with a free trial.

FOURTH EDITION

Programming C#

Jesse Liberty

O'REILLY®

Beijing · Cambridge · Farnham · Köln · Paris · Sebastopol · Taipei · Tokyo

Programming C#, Fourth Edition

by Jesse Liberty

Copyright © 2005, 2003, 2002, 2001 O'Reilly Media, Inc. All rights reserved.
Printed in the United States of America.

Published by O'Reilly Media, Inc., 1005 Gravenstein Highway North, Sebastopol, CA 95472.

O'Reilly books may be purchased for educational, business, or sales promotional use. Online editions are also available for most titles (*safari.oreilly.com*). For more information, contact our corporate/institutional sales department: (800) 998-9938 or *corporate@oreilly.com*.

Editor:	Brian Jepson
Production Editor:	Mary Anne Weeks Mayo
Cover Designer:	Ellie Volckhausen
Interior Designer:	David Futato

Printing History:

July 2001:	First Edition.
February 2002:	Second Edition.
May 2003:	Third Edition.
February 2005:	Fourth Edition.

Nutshell Handbook, the Nutshell Handbook logo, and the O'Reilly logo are registered trademarks of O'Reilly Media, Inc. *Programming C#*, the image of an African crowned crane, and related trade dress are trademarks of O'Reilly Media, Inc.

Many of the designations used by manufacturers and sellers to distinguish their products are claimed as trademarks. Where those designations appear in this book, and O'Reilly Media, Inc. was aware of a trademark claim, the designations have been printed in caps or initial caps.

While every precaution has been taken in the preparation of this book, the publisher and author assume no responsibility for errors or omissions, or for damages resulting from the use of the information contained herein.

 This book uses RepKover,™ a durable and flexible lay-flat binding.

ISBN-10: 0-596-00699-3
ISBN-13: 978-0-596-00699-0
[M]

Table of Contents

Part I.   The C# Language

Part II. Programming with C#

Part III.   The CLR and the .NET Framework

Preface

Every 10 years or so, a new technology arrives that changes the way we think about application development. In the early 1980s, the new technologies were Unix, which could be run on a desktop, and a powerful new language called C, developed by AT&T. The early '90s brought Windows and C++. Each development represented a sea change in the way we approached programming. In 2000, .NET and C# were the next wave, and .NET 2.0 completes the transition.

Microsoft has "bet the company" on .NET. When a company of its size and influence spends billions of dollars and reorganizes its entire corporate structure to support a new platform, programmers take notice. It turns out that .NET represents a major change in the way you'll think about programming. It is, in short, a new development platform designed to facilitate object-oriented Internet development. The programming language of choice for this platform is C#, which builds on the lessons learned from C (high performance), C++ (object-oriented structure), Java™ (garbage collection, high security), and Visual Basic (rapid development) to create a new language ideally suited for developing component-based, *n*-tier distributed web applications.

C# 2.0, the language of choice for .NET 2005, comes with updated tools and a powerful new development environment. It is the crowning achievement of Microsoft's R&D investment. It is wicked cool.

About This Book

This book is a tutorial, both on C# and on writing .NET applications with C#.

If you are a proficient C# 1.1 programmer, and all you want to know is what is new in C# 2.0, put this book down, and buy *Visual C# 2005: A Developer's Notebook* (O'Reilly Media, Inc.).

If, on the other hand, you want to brush up on your C# skills, or you are proficient in another programming language like C++ or Java, or even if this is your first programming language, then this book is for you.

What You Need To Use This Book

Starting with the Beta release of Visual Studio Whidbey (2005), Microsoft has made it much easier for you to get access to their works-in-progress. There are several options available to you: just as Visual Studio comes in many flavors, the prerelease versions of .NET 2.0 and Visual Studio 2005 come in many forms:

Download the SDK
> The Beta SDK, which includes command-line compilers, documentation, and other tools, is available as a free download from *http://msdn.microsoft.com/ netframework/downloads/updates/default.aspx*. This is a small download, but you'll need to bring your own code editor (anything from Notepad to SharpDevelop will do).

Express Editions
> Microsoft has released stripped-down versions of Visual Studio that are small downloads, so you can get up and running quickly. You can download the Express Editions from *http://lab.msdn.microsoft.com/vs2005/*. Use Visual C# Express for most of the examples in this book. You'll need Visual Web Developer Express for some of the examples, and you'll need to install SQL Server Express or MSDE (Microsoft Data Engine) for some of the ADO.NET examples.

Beta and Community Tech Preview
> Microsoft has also made full versions of Visual Studio 2005 available for download. These come in two forms: Community Technology Preview (CTP), which are somewhat rough around the edges, and full-fledged beta releases. At the time of this writing, CTPs is available to MSDN subscribers for Visual Studio Professional, Standard, and Team System. Beta 1 of Visual Studio Professional is also available to MSDN subscribers and to nonsubscribers for the cost of shipping. For more information, see *http://lab.msdn.microsoft.com/vs2005/get/default.aspx*.

Mono
> The Mono Project is an open source development platform based on .NET. It's sponsored by Novell, and runs on Linux, Mac OS X, and other operating system. Although the current version is targeted at .NET 1.1, you can choose to install it with support for some .NET 2.0 features. For more information, see *http://www.mono-project.com/about/index.html*.

Programming C#, Fourth Edition, will work with any of these environments. However, because each one is at a slightly different version level, some screenshots may differ from what you see. In short, your mileage may vary.

How the Book Is Organized

Part I focuses on the details of the language, Part II discusses how to write .NET programs, and Part III describes how to use C# with the .NET Common Language Runtime and Framework Class Library.

Part I, The C# Language

Chapter 1, *C# and the .NET Framework*, introduces you to the C# language and the .NET platform.

Chapter 2, *Getting Started: "Hello World"*, demonstrates a simple program to provide a context for what follows, and introduces you to the Visual Studio IDE and a number of C# language concepts.

Chapter 3, *C# Language Fundamentals*, presents the basics of the language, from built-in datatypes to keywords.

Classes define new types and allow the programmer to extend the language so that he can better model the problem he's trying to solve. Chapter 4, *Classes and Objects*, explains the components that form the heart and soul of C#.

Classes can be complex representations and abstractions of things in the real world. Chapter 5, *Inheritance and Polymorphism*, discusses how classes relate and interact.

Chapter 6, *Operator Overloading*, teaches you how to add operators to your user-defined types.

Chapters 7 and 8 introduce *Structs* and *Interfaces*, respectively, both close cousins to classes. Structs are lightweight objects that are more restricted than classes, and that make fewer demands on the operating system and on memory. Interfaces are contracts: they describe how a class will work so that other programmers can interact with your objects in well-defined ways.

Object-oriented programs can create a great many objects. It is often convenient to group these objects and manipulate them together, and C# provides extensive support for collections. Chapter 9, *Arrays, Indexers, and Collections*, explores the collection classes provided by the Framework Class Library, the new Generic collections, and how to create your own collection types using Generics.

Chapter 10, *Strings and Regular Expressions*, discusses how you can use C# to manipulate text strings and regular expressions. Most Windows and web programs interact with the user, and strings play a vital role in the user interface.

Chapter 11, *Handling Exceptions*, explains how to deal with exceptions, which provide an object-oriented mechanism for handling life's little emergencies.

Both Windows and web applications are event-driven. In C#, events are first-class members of the language. Chapter 12, *Delegates and Events*, focuses on how events are managed and how *delegates* (object-oriented type-safe callback mechanisms) are used to support event handling.

Part II, Programming with C#

Part II details how to write .NET programs: both desktop applications with Windows Forms and web applications with Web Forms. In addition, Part II describes database interactivity and how to create web services.

On top of the .NET infrastructure sits a high-level abstraction of the operating system, designed to facilitate object-oriented software development. This top tier includes ASP.NET and Windows Forms. ASP.NET includes both Web Forms, for rapid development of web applications, and web services, for creating web objects with no user interface. A web service is a distributed application that provides functionality via standard web protocols, most commonly XML and HTTP.

C# provides a Rapid Application Development (RAD) model similar to that previously available only in Visual Basic. Chapter 13, *Building Windows Applications*, describes how to use this RAD model to create professional-quality Windows programs using the Windows Forms development environment.

Whether intended for the Web or for the desktop, most applications depend on the manipulation and management of large amounts of data. Chapter 14, *Accessing Data with ADO.NET*, explains the ADO.NET layer of the .NET Framework and how to interact with Microsoft SQL Server and other data providers.

Chapter 15, *Programming ASP.NET Applications and Web Services* focuses on the two parts of ASP.NET technology: Web Forms and Web Services.

Chapter 16, *Putting It All Together,* combines a number of the skills taught in Part II to show you how to build a set of integrated applications.

Part III, The CLR and the .NET Framework

A runtime is an environment in which programs are executed. The *Common Language Runtime* (CLR) is the heart of .NET. It includes a data-typing system that is enforced throughout the platform and that is common to all languages developed for .NET. The CLR is responsible for processes such as memory management and reference counting of objects.

Another key feature of the .NET CLR is *garbage collection*. Unlike with traditional C/C++ programming, in C# the developer isn't responsible for destroying objects. Endless hours spent searching for memory leaks are a thing of the past; the CLR cleans up after you when your objects are no longer in use. The CLR's garbage collector checks the heap for unreferenced objects and frees the memory used by these objects.

The .NET platform and class library extend upward to the middle-level platform, where you find an infrastructure of supporting classes, including types for interprocess communication, XML, threading, I/O, security, diagnostics, etc. The middle tier also includes the data-access components collectively referred to as ADO.NET.

Part III of this book discusses the relationship of C# to the CLR and the Framework Class Library.

Chapter 17, *Assemblies and Versioning*, distinguishes between private and public assemblies and describes how assemblies are created and managed. In .NET, an *assembly* is a collection of files that appears to the user to be a single dynamic link library (DLL) or executable file. An assembly is the basic unit of reuse, versioning, security, and deployment.

.NET assemblies include extensive metadata about classes, methods, properties, events, and so forth. This metadata is compiled into the program and retrieved programmatically through reflection. Chapter 18, *Attributes and Reflection*, explores how to add metadata to your code, how to create custom attributes, and how to access this metadata through reflection. It goes on to discuss dynamic invocation, in which methods are invoked with late (runtime) binding.

The .NET Framework was designed to support web-based and distributed applications. Components created in C# may reside within other processes on the same machine or on other machines across the network or across the Internet. *Marshaling* is the technique of interacting with objects that aren't really there, while *remoting* comprises techniques for communicating with such objects. Chapter 19, *Marshaling and Remoting*, elaborates.

The Framework Class Library provides extensive support for asynchronous I/O and other classes that make explicit manipulation of threads unnecessary. However, C# does provide extensive support for *Threads and Synchronization*, discussed in Chapter 20.

Chapter 21 discusses *Streams*, a mechanism not only for interacting with the user, but also for retrieving data across the Internet. This chapter includes full coverage of C# support for *serialization*: the ability to write an object graph to disk and read it back again.

Chapter 22, *Programming .NET and COM*, explores interoperability, the ability to interact with COM components that are created outside the managed environment of the .NET Framework. It's possible to call components from C# applications into COM and to call components from COM into C#. Chapter 22 describes how this is done.

The book concludes with an appendix of C# keywords.

Who This Book Is For

Programming C#, Fourth Edition, was written for programmers who want to develop applications for the .NET platform. No doubt many of you already have experience in C++, Java, or Visual Basic (VB). Other readers may have experience with other programming languages, and some readers may have no specific programming experience but perhaps have been working with HTML and other web technologies. This book is written for all of you, though if you have no programming experience at all, you may find some of it tough going.

If you're migrating from C, C++, VB 6, or Java, the following sections should give you some basic comparisons with C#. More importantly, keep an eye out for notes specifically for you throughout the book.

C# 2.0 Versus C# 1.1

There have been many changes to C# and to the development environment and the .NET Framework since 1.1. All are designed to minimize the amount of "plumbing" you have to write, and to help you focus on building robust applications.

This book integrates the changes and isn't intended to be a guide for the proficient C# 1.1 programmer looking only for the changes in C# 2.0. That said, I do try to flag what is new in C# 2.0 as we go along.

C# Versus Visual Basic .NET

The premise of the .NET Framework is that all languages are created equal. To paraphrase George Orwell, however, some languages are more equal than others. C# is an excellent language for .NET development. You will find it is an extremely versatile, robust, and well-designed language. It is also currently the language most often used in articles and tutorials about .NET programming.

It is possible that many VB 6 programmers will choose to learn C# instead of upgrading their skills to VB.NET. The transition from VB 6 to VB.NET is, arguably, nearly as difficult as from VB 6 to C#, and, whether it's fair or not, historically, C-family programmers have had higher earning potential than VB programmers. As a practical matter, VB programmers have never gotten the respect or compensation they deserve, and C# offers a wonderful chance to make a potentially lucrative transition.

In any case, if you do have VB experience, welcome! This book was designed with you in mind too, and I've tried to make the conversion easy.

C# Versus Java

Java programmers may look at C# with a mixture of trepidation, glee, and resentment. It has been suggested that C# is somehow a "rip-off" of Java. I won't comment on the religious war between Microsoft and the "anyone but Microsoft" crowd, except to acknowledge that C# certainly learned a great deal from Java. But then Java learned a great deal from C++, which owed its syntax to C, which in turn was built on lessons learned in other languages. We all stand on the shoulders of giants.

C# offers an easy transition for Java programmers: the syntax is very similar and the semantics are familiar and comfortable. Java programmers will probably want to focus on the differences between Java and C# to use the C# language effectively. I've tried to provide a series of markers along the way (see the notes to Java programmers within the chapters).

C# Versus C and C++

While it is possible to program in .NET with C or C++, it isn't easy or natural. Frankly, having worked for 10 years as a C++ programmer and written a dozen books on the subject, I'd rather have my teeth drilled than work with managed C++. Perhaps it is just that C# is so much friendlier. In any case, once I saw C#, I never looked back.

Be careful, though; there are a number of small traps along the way, and I've been careful to mark these with flashing lights and yellow cones.

Conventions Used in This Book

The following font conventions are used in this book:

Italic is used for:

- Pathnames, filenames, and program names
- Internet addresses, such as domain names and URLs
- New terms where they are defined

`Constant Width` is used for:

- Command lines and options that should be typed verbatim
- Names and keywords in program examples, including method names, variable names, and class names

`Constant Width Italic` is used for:

- Replaceable items, such as variables or optional elements, within syntax lines or code

Constant Width Bold is used for:

- Emphasis within program code

Pay special attention to notes set apart from the text with the following icons:

This is a tip. It contains useful supplementary information about the topic at hand.

This is a warning. It helps you solve and avoid annoying problems.

Support

As part of my responsibilities as author, I provide ongoing support for my books through my web site:

http://www.LibertyAssociates.com

You can also obtain the source code for all the examples in *Programming C#* at my site. You will find access to a book-support discussion group with a section set aside for questions about C#. Before you post a question, however, please check the FAQ (Frequently Asked Questions) and errata files. If you check these files and still have a question, please go ahead and post to the discussion center.

The most effective way to get help is to ask a very precise question or even to create a small program that illustrates your area of concern or confusion. You may also want to check the various newsgroups and discussion centers on the Internet. Microsoft offers a wide array of newsgroups, and DevelopMentor (*http://discuss.develop.com*) has wonderful .NET email discussion lists.

We'd Like to Hear from You

We have tested and verified the information in this book to the best of our ability, but you may find that features have changed (or even that we have made mistakes!). Please let us know about any errors you find, as well as your suggestions for future editions, by writing to:

O'Reilly Media, Inc.
1005 Gravenstein Highway North
Sebastopol, CA 95472
(800) 998-9938 (in the United States or Canada)
(707) 829-0515 (international or local)
(707) 829-0104 (fax)

We have a web page for the book that lists examples and any plans for future editions. You can access this information at:

http://www.oreilly.com/catalog/progcsharp4

To comment or ask technical questions about this book, send email to:

bookquestions@oreilly.com

For more information about our books, conferences, Resource Centers, and the O'Reilly Network, as well as additional technical articles and discussion on C# and the .NET Framework, see the O'Reilly web site:

http://www.oreilly.com

and O'Reilly's ONDotnet:

http://www.ondotnet.com

Safari Enabled

 When you see a Safari® Enabled icon on the cover of your favorite technology book, it means the book is available online through the O'Reilly Network Safari Bookshelf.

Safari offers a solution that's better than e-books. It's a virtual library that lets you easily search thousands of top tech books, cut and paste code samples, download chapters, and find quick answers when you need the most accurate, current information. Try it for free at *http://safari.oreilly.com*.

Acknowledgments

Before I say anything else, I must give special thank to Ian Griffiths, who provided extensive technical editing and expertise and is one of the nicer and smarter guys around.

This is the fourth edition of *Programming C#*, and too many friends and readers have helped me improve the book to possibly name them all, but I must make special mention of Donald Xie, Dan Hurwitz, Seth Weiss, Sue Lynch, Cliff Gerald, Tom Petr, Jim Culbert, Mike Woodring, Eric Gunnerson, Rob Howard, Piet Obermeyer, Jonathan Hawkins, Peter Drayton, Brad Merrill, Ben Albahari, Susan Warren, Brian Bischof, and Kent Quirk.

John Osborn signed me to O'Reilly, for which I will forever be in his debt. Valerie Quercia, Claire Cloutier, and Tatiana Diaz did tremendous work on previous versions, and the upgrade to C# 2.0 was shepherded by Brian Jepson. Rob Romano created a number of the illustrations and improved the others. Tim O'Reilly provided support and resources, and I'm grateful.

Many readers have written to point out typos and minor errors in the first three editions. Their effort is very much appreciated, with special thanks to Peter Adams, Sol Bick, Brian Cassel, Steve Charbonneau, Ronald Chu, John Corner, Duane Corpe, Kevin Coupland, Randy Eastwood, Glen Fischer, Larry Fix, Andy Gaskall, Dave Fowler, Vojimir Golem, David Kindred, Steve Kirk, Bob Kline, Theron LaBounty, Aron Landy, Jeremy Lin, Chris Linton, Mark Melhado, Harry Martyrossian, Jason Mauss, Stephen Nelson, Harold Norris, Tim Noll, Mark Phillips, Marcus Rahilly, Paul Reed, Christian Rodriguez, David Solum, Paul Schwartzburg, Erwing Steininger, Fred Talmadge, Steve Thomson, Greg Torrance, Ted Volk, John Watson, Walt White, and Seen Sai Yang.

We've worked hard to fix all of these errors in this fourth edition. We've scoured the book to ensure that no new errors were added, and that all the code compiles and runs properly with Visual Studio 2005. That said, if you do find errors, please check the errata on my web site (*http://www.LibertyAssociates.com*) and if your error is new, please send me email at *jliberty@libertyassociates.com*.

PART I

The C# Language

CHAPTER 1

C# and the .NET Framework

The goal of C# 2.0 is to provide a simple, safe, modern, object-oriented, Internet-centric, high-performance language for .NET development. C# is now a fully mature language, and it draws on the lessons learned over the past three decades. In much the way that you can see in young children the features and personalities of their parents and grandparents, you can easily see in C# the influence of Java, C++, Visual Basic (VB), and other languages, but you can also see the lessons learned since C# was first introduced.

The focus of this book is the C# language and its use as a tool for programming on the .NET platform, specifically and especially with Visual Studio .NET 2005 (full or Express Edition).

Many of the programs in this book are written as console applications (rather than as Windows or web applications) to facilitate concentrating on features of the language instead of being distracted by the details of the user interface.

If you are using Mono or other non-Microsoft versions of C#, you should find that all of the programs in this book work just fine, though we have not tested on anything other than the Microsoft authorized version.

This chapter introduces both the C# language and the .NET platform, including the .NET Framework.

The .NET Platform

When Microsoft announced C# in July 2000, its unveiling was part of a much larger event: the announcement of the .NET platform. C# 2.0 represents the maturation of that language and coincides with the release of the next generation of tools for .NET.

The .NET platform is a development framework that provides a new application programming interface (API) to the services and APIs of classic Windows operating systems while bringing together a number of disparate technologies that emerged from Microsoft during the late 1990s. This includes COM+ component services, a commitment to XML and object-oriented design, support for new web services protocols such as SOAP, WSDL, and UDDI, and a focus on the Internet, all integrated within the Distributed interNet Applications (DNA) architecture.

Microsoft has devoted enormous resources to the development of .NET and its associated technologies. The results of this commitment to date are impressive. For one thing, the scope of .NET is huge. The platform consists of three product groups:

- A set of languages, including C# and VB, a set of development tools including Visual Studio .NET, a comprehensive class library for building web services and web and Windows applications, as well as the Common Language Runtime (CLR) to execute objects built within this framework
- Two generations of .NET Enterprise Servers: those already released and those to be released over the next 24–36 months
- New .NET-enabled non-PC devices, from cell phones to game boxes

The .NET Framework

Microsoft .NET supports not only language independence, but also language integration. This means that you can inherit from classes, catch exceptions, and take advantage of polymorphism across different languages. The .NET Framework makes this possible with a specification called the *Common Type System* (CTS) that all .NET components must obey. For example, everything in .NET is an object of a specific class that derives from the root class called System.Object. The CTS supports the general concept of classes, interfaces, and delegates (which support callbacks).

Additionally, .NET includes a *Common Language Specification* (CLS), which provides a series of basic rules that are required for language integration. The CLS determines the minimum requirements for being a .NET language. Compilers that conform to the CLS create objects that can interoperate with one another. The entire Framework Class Library (FCL) can be used by any language that conforms to the CLS.

The .NET Framework sits on top of the operating system, which can be any flavor of Windows,* and consists of a number of components, currently including:

- Five official languages: C#, VB, Visual C++, Visual J#, and JScript.NET
- The CLR, an object-oriented platform for Windows and web development that all these languages share
- A number of related class libraries, collectively known as the Framework Class Library

---

* Because of the architecture of the CLR, the operating system can be any variety of Unix or another operating system altogether.

Figure 1-1 breaks down the .NET Framework into its system architectural components.

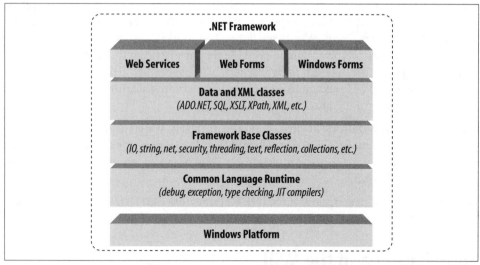

Figure 1-1. NET Framework architecture

The most important component of the .NET Framework is the CLR, which provides the environment in which programs are executed. The CLR includes a virtual machine, analogous in many ways to the Java virtual machine. At a high level, the CLR activates objects, performs security checks on them, lays them out in memory, executes them, and garbage-collects them. (The Common Type System is also part of the CLR.)

In Figure 1-1, the layer on top of the CLR is a set of framework classes, followed by an additional layer of data and XML classes, plus another layer of classes intended for web services, Web Forms, and Windows Forms. Collectively, these classes make up the FCL, one of the largest class libraries in history and one that provides an object-oriented API for all the functionality that the .NET platform encapsulates. With more than 4,000 classes, the FCL facilitates rapid development of desktop, client/server, and other web services and applications.

The set of Framework base classes, the lowest level of the FCL, is similar to the set of classes in Java. These classes support input and output, string manipulation, security management, network communication, thread management, text manipulation, reflection and collections functionality, etc.

Above this level is a tier of classes that extend the base classes to support data management and XML manipulation. The data classes support persistent management of data that is maintained on backend databases. These classes include the Structured Query Language (SQL) classes to let you manipulate persistent data stores through a standard SQL interface. The .NET Framework also supports a number of classes to let you manipulate XML data and perform XML searching and translations.

Extending the Framework base classes and the data and XML classes is a tier of classes geared toward building applications using three different technologies: web services, Web Forms, and Windows Forms. Web services include a number of classes that support the development of lightweight distributed components, which will work even in the face of firewalls and NAT software. Because web services employ standard HTTP and SOAP as underlying communications protocols, these components support Plug and Play across cyberspace.

Web Forms and Windows Forms allow you to apply Rapid Application Development (RAD) techniques to building web and Windows applications. Simply drag and drop controls onto your form, double-click a control, and write the code to respond to the associated event.

For a more detailed description of the .NET Framework, see *.NET Framework Essentials* (O'Reilly).

Compilation and the MSIL

In .NET, programs aren't compiled into executable files; they are compiled into assemblies that consist of *Microsoft Intermediate Language* (MSIL) instructions, which the CLR then converts into machine code and executes. The MSIL (often shortened to IL) files C# produces are nearly identical to the IL files other .NET languages produce; the platform is language-agnostic. A key fact about the CLR is that it is common: the same runtime supports development in C# as well as in VB.NET.

C# code is compiled into IL when you build your project. The IL is saved in a file on disk. When you run your program, the IL is compiled again, using the *Just In Time* (JIT) compiler (a process often called *JITing*). The result is machine code, executed by the machine's processor.

The standard JIT compiler runs *on demand*. When a method is called, the JIT compiler analyzes the IL and produces highly efficient machine code, which runs very fast. As the application runs, compilation happens only as needed, and once JIT-compiled, the code is cached for future use. As .NET applications run, they tend to become faster and faster, as the already compiled code is reused.

The CLS means that all .NET languages produce very similar IL code. As a result, objects created in one language can be accessed and derived from another. Thus it is possible to create a base class in VB.NET and derive from it in C#.

The C# Language

The C# language is disarmingly simple, with only about 80 keywords and a dozen built-in datatypes, but it's highly expressive when it comes to implementing modern programming concepts. C# includes all the support for structured, component-based, object-oriented programming that you expect of a modern language built on the shoulders of C++ and Java, and now with Version 2.0, many of the most important missing ingredients, such as generics and anonymous methods, have been added.

 C++ programmers take note: generics are the C# equivalent to Templates, though it turns out that C# generics are a bit simpler and more efficient than C++ templates; they reduce code bloat by reusing shared code at runtime, while giving up a bit of the flexibility available with C++ templates.

The C# language was developed by a small team led by two distinguished Microsoft engineers, Anders Hejlsberg and Scott Wiltamuth. Hejlsberg is also known for creating Turbo Pascal, a popular language for PC programming, and for leading the team that designed Borland Delphi, one of the first successful integrated development environments for client/server programming.

At the heart of any object-oriented language is its support for defining and working with classes. Classes define new types, allowing you to extend the language to better model the problem you are trying to solve. C# contains keywords for declaring new classes and their methods and properties, and for implementing encapsulation, inheritance, and polymorphism, the three pillars of object-oriented programming.

In C#, everything pertaining to a class declaration is found in the declaration itself. C# class definitions don't require separate header files or Interface Definition Language (IDL) files. Moreover, C# supports a new XML style of inline documentation that simplifies the creation of online and print reference documentation for an application.

C# also supports *interfaces*, a means of making a contract with a class for services that the interface stipulates. In C#, a class can inherit from only a single parent, but a class can implement multiple interfaces. When it implements an interface, a C# class in effect promises to provide the functionality the interface specifies.

C# also provides support for *structs*, a concept whose meaning has changed significantly from C++. In C#, a struct is a restricted, lightweight type that, when instantiated, makes fewer demands on the operating system and on memory than a conventional class does. A struct can't inherit from a class or be inherited from, but a struct can implement an interface.

C# provides full support of *delegates*: to provide invocation of methods through indirection. In other languages, such as C++, you might find similar functionality (as in pointers to member functions), but delegates are type-safe reference types that encapsulate methods with specific signatures and return types.

C# provides component-oriented features, such as properties, events, and declarative constructs (such as *attributes*). Component-oriented programming is supported by the storage of metadata with the code for the class. The metadata describes the class, including its methods and properties, as well as its security needs and other attributes, such as whether it can be serialized; the code contains the logic necessary to carry out its functions. A compiled class is thus a self-contained unit. Therefore, a hosting environment that knows how to read a class' metadata and code needs no other information to make use of it. Using C# and the CLR, it is possible to add custom metadata to a class by creating custom attributes. Likewise, it is possible to read class metadata using CLR types that support reflection.

When you compile your code you create an assembly. An *assembly* is a collection of files that appear to the programmer to be a single dynamic link library (DLL) or executable (EXE). In .NET, an assembly is the basic unit of reuse, versioning, security, and deployment. The CLR provides a number of classes for manipulating assemblies.

A final note about C# is that it also provides support for:

- Directly accessing memory using C++ style pointers
- Keywords for bracketing such operations as unsafe
- Warning the CLR garbage collector not to collect objects referenced by pointers until they are released

CHAPTER 2

Getting Started: "Hello World"

It is a time-honored tradition to start a programming book with a "Hello World" program. In this chapter, we create, compile, and run a simple "Hello World" program written in C#. The analysis of this brief program will introduce key features of the C# language.

Example 2-1 illustrates the fundamental elements of a very elementary C# program.

Example 2-1. A simple "Hello World" program in C#

```
class Hello
{
    static void Main()
    {
        // Use the system console object
        System.Console.WriteLine("Hello World");
    }
}
```

Compiling and running this code displays the words "Hello World" at the console. Before we compile and run it, let's first take a closer look at this simple program.

Classes, Objects, and Types

The essence of object-oriented programming is the creation of new types. A *type* represents a thing. Sometimes the thing is abstract, such as a data table or a thread; sometimes it is more tangible, such as a button in a window. A type defines the thing's general properties and behaviors.

If your program uses three instances of a button type in a window—say, an OK, a Cancel, and a Help button—each button will have a size, though the specific size of each button may differ. Similarly, all the buttons will have the same behaviors (draw, click), though how they actually implement these behaviors may vary. Thus, the details might differ among the individual buttons, but they are all of the same type.

As in many object-oriented programming languages, in C# a type is defined by a *class*, while the individual instances of that class are known as *objects*. Later chapters explain that there are other types in C# besides classes, including enums, structs, and delegates, but for now the focus is on classes.

The "Hello World" program declares a single type: the Hello class. To define a C# type, you declare it as a class using the class keyword, give it a name—in this case, Hello—and then define its properties and behaviors. The property and behavior definitions of a C# class must be enclosed by open and closed braces ({}).

 C++ programmers take note: there is no semicolon after the closing brace.

Methods

A class has both properties and behaviors. Behaviors are defined with member methods; properties are discussed in Chapter 3.

A *method* is a *function* owned by your class. In fact, member methods are sometimes called *member functions*. The member methods define what your class can do or how it behaves. Typically, methods are given action names, such as WriteLine() or AddNumbers(). In the case shown here, however, the class method has a special name, Main(), which doesn't describe an action but does designate to the CLR that this is the main, or first method, for your class.

 C++ programmers take note: Main() is capitalized in C# and must be a member of a class, not a global member. Main() can also return int or void.

The CLR calls Main() when your program starts. Main() is the entry point for your program, and every C# program must have a Main() method.*

Method declarations are a contract between the creator of the method and the consumer (user) of the method. It is likely that the creator and consumer of the method will be the same programmer, but this doesn't have to be so: it is possible that one member of a development team will create the method and another programmer will use it.

---

* It's technically possible to have multiple Main() methods in C#; in that case you use the /main command-line switch to tell C# which class contains the Main() method that should serve as the entry point to the program.

Java programmers take note: `Main()` is the entry point for every C# program, similar in some ways to the Java applet `run()` method or the Java program's `main()` method.

To declare a method, you specify a return value type followed by a name. Method declarations also require parentheses, whether the method accepts parameters or not. For example:

```
int myMethod(int size)
```

declares a method named `myMethod()` that takes one parameter: an integer that will be referred to within the method as `size`. This method returns an integer value. The return value type tells the consumer of the method what kind of data the method will return when it finishes running.

Some methods don't return a value at all; these are said to return void, which is specified by the void keyword. For example:

```
void myVoidMethod();
```

declares a method that returns void and takes no parameters. In C# you must always declare a return type or void.

Comments

A C# program can also contain comments. Take a look at the first line after the opening brace of the main method shown earlier:

```
// Use the system console object
```

The text begins with two forward slash marks (//). These designate a *comment*. A comment is a note to the programmer and doesn't affect how the program runs. C# supports three types of comments.

The first type, just shown, indicates that all text to the right of the comment mark is to be considered a comment, until the end of that line. This is known as a *C++ style comment*.

The second type of comment, known as a *C-style comment*, begins with an open comment mark (/*) and ends with a closed comment mark (*/). This allows comments to span more than one line without having to have // characters at the beginning of each comment line, as shown in Example 2-2.

Example 2-2. Illustrating multiline comments

```
namespace HelloWorld
{
    class HelloWorld
    {
        static void Main()
```

Example 2-2. Illustrating multiline comments (continued)

```
    {
        /* Use the system console object
           as explained in the text */
        System.Console.WriteLine("Hello World");
    }
  }
}
```

While you can't nest C++ style comments, it is possible to nest C++ style comments within C-style comments. For this reason, it is common to use C++ style comments whenever possible, and to reserve the C-style comments for "commenting-out" blocks of code.

The third and final type of comment that C# supports is used to associate external XML-based documentation with your code, and is illustrated in Chapter 13.

Console Applications

"Hello World" is an example of a *console* program. A console application typically has no graphical user interface (GUI); there are no list boxes, buttons, windows, and so forth. Text input and output are handled through the standard console (typically a command or DOS window on your PC). Sticking to console applications for now helps simplify the early examples in this book, and keeps the focus on the language itself. In later chapters, we'll turn our attention to Windows and web applications, and at that time we'll focus on the Visual Studio .NET GUI design tools.

All that the Main() method does in this simple example is write the text "Hello World" to the *standard output* (typically a command prompt window). Standard output is managed by an object named Console. This Console object has a method called WriteLine() that takes a *string* (a set of characters) and writes it to the standard output. When you run this program, a command or DOS screen will pop up on your computer monitor and display the words "Hello World."

You invoke a method with the dot operator (.). Thus, to call the Console object's WriteLine() method, you write Console.WriteLine(...), filling in the string to be printed.

Namespaces

Console is only one of a tremendous number of useful types that are part of the .NET FCL. Each class has a name, and thus the FCL contains thousands of names, such as ArrayList, Hashtable, FileDialog, DataException, EventArgs, and so on. There are hundreds, thousands, even tens of thousands of names.

This presents a problem. No developer can possibly memorize all the names that the .NET Framework uses, and sooner or later you are likely to create an object and give it a name that has already been used. What will happen if you purchase a Hashtable class from another vendor, only to discover that it conflicts with the Hashtable class that .NET provides? Remember, each class in C# must have a unique name and you typically can't rename classes in a vendor's code!

The solution to this problem is the use of *namespaces*. A namespace restricts a name's scope, making it meaningful only within the defined namespace.

 C++ programmers take note: C++ namespaces are delimited with the scope resolution operator (::), in C# you use the dot (.) operator.

Java programmers take note: namespaces provide many of the benefits of packages.

Assume that I tell you that Jim is an engineer[*]. The word "engineer" is used for many things in English, and can cause confusion. Does he design buildings? Write software? Run a train?

In English I might clarify by saying "he's a scientist," or "he's a train engineer." A C# programmer could tell you that Jim is a science.engineer rather than a train. engineer. The namespace (in this case, science or train) restricts the scope of the word that follows. It creates a "space" in which that name is meaningful.

Further, it might happen that Jim is not just any kind of science.engineer. Perhaps Jim graduated from MIT with a degree in software engineering, not civil engineering (are *civil* engineers especially polite?). Thus, the object that is Jim might be defined more specifically as a science.software.engineer. This classification implies that the namespace software is meaningful within the namespace science, and that engineer in this context is meaningful within the namespace software. If later you learn that Charlotte is a transportation.train.engineer, you will not be confused as to what kind of engineer she is. The two uses of engineer can coexist, each within its own namespace.

Similarly, if it turns out that .NET has a Hashtable class within its System.Collections namespace, and that I have also created a Hashtable class within a ProgCSharp.DataStructures namespace, there is no conflict because each exists in its own namespace.

In Example 2-1, the Console class' name is identified as being in the System namespace by using the code:

```
System.Console.WriteLine();
```

The Dot Operator (.)

In Example 2-1, the dot operator (.) is used both to access a method (and data) in a class (in this case, the method WriteLine()), and to restrict the class name to a spe-

---

[*] Apologies to our friends across the pond where the person who drives a locomotive is called a "train driver" rather than an "engineer."

cific namespace (in this case, to locate Console within the System namespace). This works well because in both cases we are "drilling down" to find the exact thing we want. The top level is the System namespace (which contains all the System objects that the FCL provides); the Console type exists within that namespace, and the WriteLine() method is a member function of the Console type.

In many cases, namespaces are divided into subspaces. For example, the System namespace contains a number of subnamespaces such as Data, Configuration, Collections, and so forth, while the Collections namespace itself is divided into multiple subnamespaces.

Namespaces can help you organize and compartmentalize your types. When you write a complex C# program, you might want to create your own namespace hierarchy, and there is no limit to how deep this hierarchy can be. The goal of namespaces is to help you divide and conquer the complexity of your object hierarchy.

The using Keyword

Rather than writing the word System before Console, you could specify that you will be using types from the System namespace by writing the directive:

```
using System;
```

at the top of the listing, as shown in Example 2-3.

Example 2-3. The using keyword

```
using System;
class Hello
{
    static void Main()
    {
        //Console from the System namespace
        Console.WriteLine("Hello World");
    }
}
```

Notice the using System directive is placed before the Hello class definition. Visual Studio .NET 2005 defaults to including three using statements in every console application (System, System.Collections.Generic, System.Text).

Although you can designate that you are using the System namespace, you can't designate that you are using the System.Console object, as you can with some languages. Example 2-4 won't compile.

Example 2-4. Code that doesn't compile (not legal C#)

```
using System.Console;
class Hello
{
    static void Main()
    {
        //Console from the System namespace
```

Example 2-4. Code that doesn't compile (not legal C#) (continued)

```
        WriteLine("Hello World");
    }
}
```

This generates the compile error:

```
error CS0138: A using namespace directive can only be applied
to namespaces; 'System.Console' is a type not a namespace
```

> If you are using Visual Studio, you will know that you've made a mistake, because when you type using System followed by the dot, Visual Studio .NET 2005 will provide a list of valid namespaces, and Console won't be among them.

The using keyword can save a great deal of typing, but it can undermine the advantages of namespaces by polluting the scope with many undifferentiated names. A common solution is to use the using keyword with the built-in namespaces and with your own corporate namespaces, but perhaps not with third-party components.

> Some programming groups make it a policy to spell out the entire namespace path to the object (e.g., System.Console.WriteLine() and not Console.WriteLine()) as a form of documentation. This can become unworkable pretty quickly with deeply nested namespaces.

Case Sensitivity

C# is case-sensitive, which means that writeLine is not the same as WriteLine, which in turn is not the same as WRITELINE. Unfortunately, unlike in VB, the C# development environment will not fix your case mistakes; if you write the same word twice with different cases, you might introduce a tricky-to-find bug into your program.

> A handy trick is to hover over a name that is correct in all but case and then hit Ctrl-Space. The Autocomplete feature of Intellisense will fix the case for you.

To prevent such a time-wasting and energy-depleting mistake, you should develop conventions for naming your variables, functions, constants, etc. The convention in this book is to name variables with camel notation (e.g., someVariableName), and to name functions, constants, and properties with Pascal notation (e.g., SomeFunction).

The only difference between camel and Pascal notation is that in Pascal notation, names begin with an uppercase letter.

Microsoft has developed code style guidelines that make a very good starting point (and often are all you need). You can download them from:

http://msdn.microsoft.com/library/default.asp?url=/library/en-us/ cpgenref/html/cpconNETFrameworkDesignGuidelines.asp

The static Keyword

The `Main()` method shown in Example 2-1 has one more designation. Just before the return type declaration `void` (which, you will remember, indicates that the method doesn't return a value) you'll find the keyword `static`:

```
static void Main()
```

The `static` keyword indicates that you can invoke `Main()` without first creating an object of type `Hello`. This somewhat complex issue will be considered in much greater detail in subsequent chapters. One of the problems with learning a new computer language is you must use some of the advanced features before you fully understand them. For now, you can treat the declaration of the `Main()` method as tantamount to magic.

Developing "Hello World"

There are at least two ways to enter, compile, and run the programs in this book: use the Visual Studio .NET Integrated Development Environment (IDE), or use a text editor and a command-line compiler (along with some additional command-line tools to be introduced later).

Although you *can* develop software outside Visual Studio .NET, the IDE provides enormous advantages. These include indentation support, Intellisense word completion, color coding, and integration with the help files. Most important, the IDE includes a powerful debugger and a wealth of other tools.

This book tacitly assumes that you'll be using Visual Studio .NET. However, the tutorials focus more on the language and the platform than on the tools. You can copy all the examples into a text editor such as Windows Notepad or Emacs, save them as text files with the extension *.cs*, and compile them with the C# command-line compiler that is distributed with the .NET Framework SDK (or a .NET-compatible development toolchain such as Mono or Microsoft's Shared Source CLI). Note that some examples in later chapters use Visual Studio .NET tools for creating Windows Forms and Web Forms, but even these you can write by hand in Notepad if you are determined to do things the hard way.

Editing "Hello World"

To create the "Hello World" program in the IDE, select Visual Studio .NET from your Start menu or a desktop icon, and then choose File → New → Project from the menu toolbar. This will invoke the New Project window. (If you are using Visual Studio for the first time, the New Project window might appear without further prompting.) Figure 2-1 shows the New Project window.

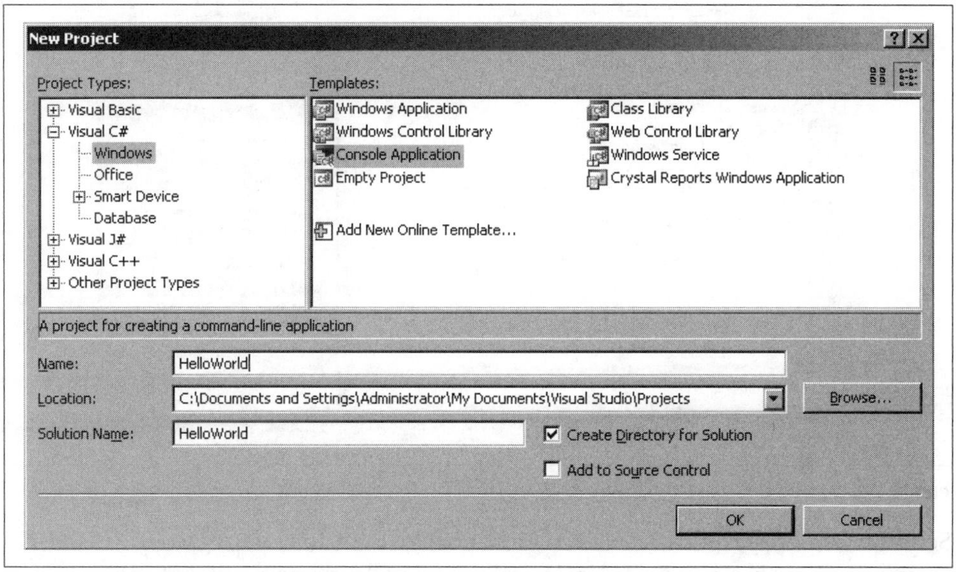

Figure 2-1. Creating a C# console application in Visual Studio .NET

To open your application, select Visual C# in the Project Types window, and choose Console Application in the Templates window (if you use the Express Edition of Visual C#, you don't need to perform that first step; go directly to the Console Application).

You can now enter a name for the project and select a directory in which to store your files. Click OK, and a new window will appear in which you can enter the code in Example 2-1, as shown in Figure 2-2.

Notice that Visual Studio .NET creates a namespace based on the project name you've provided (HelloWorld), and adds a using directive for System, System.Collections.Generic, and System.Text because nearly every program you write will need types from those namespaces.

Visual Studio .NET creates a class named Program, which you are free to rename. When you rename the class, it's a good idea to rename the file as well (*Class1.cs*). If you rename the file, Visual Studio will automatically rename the class for you. To reproduce Example 2-1, for instance, rename the *Program.cs* file (listed in the

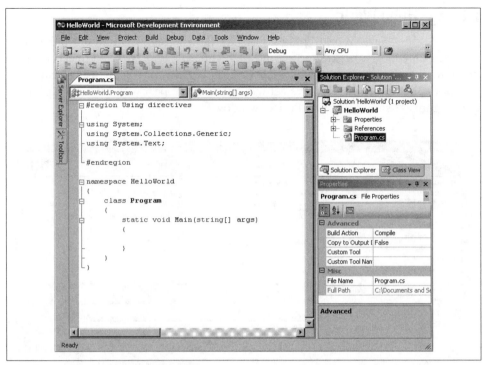

Figure 2-2. The editor, opened to your new project

Solution Explorer window) to *hello.cs* and change the name of Program to HelloWorld (if you do this in the reverse order, Visual Studio will rename the class to hello).

Finally, Visual Studio 2005 creates a program skeleton to get you started. To reproduce Example 2-1, remove the arguments (string[] args) from the Main() method. Then copy the following two lines into the body of Main():

```
// Use the system console object
System.Console.WriteLine("Hello World");
```

If you aren't using Visual Studio .NET, open Notepad, type in the code from Example 2-1, and save the file as a text file named *hello.cs*.

Compiling and Running "Hello World"

There are many ways to compile and run the "Hello World" program from within Visual Studio. Typically you can accomplish every task by choosing commands from the Visual Studio menu toolbar, by using buttons, and, in many cases, by using key-combination shortcuts.

Keyboard shortcuts can be set by going to Tools → Options → Keyboard. This book assumes you have chosen the default settings.

For example, to compile the "Hello World" program, press Ctrl-Shift-B or choose Build → Build Solution. As an alternative, you can click the Build button on the Build toolbar (you may need to right-click the toolbar to show the Build toolbar). The Build toolbar is shown in Figure 2-3; the Build button is leftmost and highlighted.

Figure 2-3. Build toolbar

To run the "Hello World" program without the debugger, you can press Ctrl-F5 on your keyboard, choose Debug → Start Without Debugging from the IDE menu toolbar, or press the Start Without Debugging button on the IDE Build toolbar, as shown in Figure 2-4 (you may need to customize your toolbar to make this button available). You can run the program without first explicitly building it; depending on how your options are set (Tools → Options), the IDE will save the file, build it, and run it, possibly asking you for permission at each step.

Figure 2-4. Start Without Debugging button

I strongly recommend that you spend some time exploring the Visual Studio 2005 development environment. This is your principal tool as a .NET developer, and you want to learn to use it well. Time invested up front in getting comfortable with Visual Studio will pay for itself many times over in the coming months. Go ahead, put the book down and look at it. I'll wait for you.

Use the following steps to compile and run the "Hello World" program using the C# command-line compiler that comes with the .NET Framework SDK, Mono (*http://www.mono-project.com*), or Shared Source CLI (*http://msdn.microsoft.com/net/sscli/*):

1. Save Example 2-1 as the file *hello.cs*.
2. Open a .NET command window (Start → Programs → Visual Studio .NET → Visual Studio Tools → Visual Studio Command Prompt. If you're on Unix, you should start at a text console, xterm, or something that gives you a shell prompt.

3. From the command line, use this command if you are using the .NET or Shared Source CLI C# compiler:

```
csc /debug hello.cs
```

Use this command if you are using Mono:

```
mcs -debug hello.cs
```

This step builds the EXE file. If the program contains errors, the compiler reports them in the command window. The /debug command-line switch inserts symbols in the code so that you can run the EXE under a debugger or see line numbers in stack traces. (You'll get a stack trace if your program generates an error that you don't handle.)

4. To run the program under .NET, enter:

```
hello
```

Use this command with the Shared Source CLI:

```
clix hello.exe
```

and this command with Mono:

```
mono hello.exe
```

You should now see the venerable words "Hello World" appear in your command window.

Just in Time Compilation

Compiling *hello.cs* using *csc* creates an EXE file. Keep in mind, however, that the *.exe* file contains op-codes written in MSIL, which is introduced in Chapter 1.

Interestingly, if you write this application in VB.NET or any other language compliant with the .NET CLS, you will have compiled it into more or less the same MSIL. By design, IL code created from different languages is virtually indistinguishable.

In addition to producing the IL code (which is similar in spirit to Java's bytecode), the compiler creates a read-only segment of the *.exe* file in which it inserts a standard Win32 executable header. The compiler designates an entry point within the read-only segment; the operating system loader jumps to that entry point when you run the program, just as it would for any Windows program.

The operating system can't execute the IL code, however, and that entry point does nothing but jump to the .NET JIT compiler (also introduced in Chapter 1). The JIT produces native CPU instructions, as you might find in a normal *.exe*. The key feature of a JIT compiler, however, is that functions are compiled only as they are used, just in time for execution.

Using the Visual Studio .NET Debugger

Arguably, the single most important tool in any development environment is the debugger. The Visual Studio debugger is very powerful and it will be well worth whatever time you put into learning how to use it well. That said, the fundamentals of debugging are very simple. The three key skills are:

- How to set a breakpoint and how to run to that breakpoint
- How to step into and over method calls
- How to examine and modify the value of variables, member data, and so forth

This chapter doesn't reiterate the entire debugger documentation, but these skills are so fundamental that it does provide a crash (pardon the expression) course.

The debugger can accomplish the same thing in many ways, typically via menu choices, buttons, and so forth. The simplest way to set a breakpoint is to click in the left margin. The IDE marks your breakpoint with a red dot, as shown in Figure 2-5.

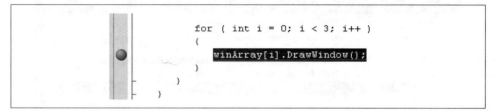

Figure 2-5. A breakpoint

 Discussing the debugger requires code examples. The code shown here is from Chapter 5, and you aren't expected to understand how it works yet (though if you program in C++ or Java, you'll probably get the gist of it).

To run the debugger, you can choose Debug → Start or just press F5. The program then compiles and runs to the breakpoint, at which time it stops, and a yellow arrow indicates the next statement for execution, as in Figure 2-6.

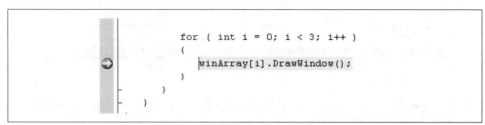

Figure 2-6. The breakpoint hit

After you've hit your breakpoint it is easy to examine the values of various objects. For example, you can find the value of the variable i just by putting the cursor over it and waiting a moment, as shown in Figure 2-7.

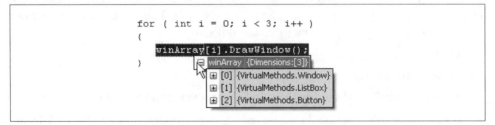

Figure 2-7. Showing a value

The debugger IDE also provides a number of useful windows, such as a Locals window that displays the values of all the local variables (see Figure 2-8).

Locals			
Name	Value	Type	
◆ counter	0	int	
⊞ ◆ win	{VirtualMethods.Window}	VirtualMethods.Window	
⊞ ◆ lb	{VirtualMethods.ListBox}	VirtualMethods.ListBox	
⊞ ◆ b	{VirtualMethods.Button}	VirtualMethods.Button	
⊞ ◆ winArray	{Dimensions:[3]}	VirtualMethods.Window[]	

Autos Locals Watch 1

Figure 2-8. Locals window

Intrinsic types such as integers simply show their value (see i earlier), but objects show their type and have a plus (+) sign. You can expand these objects to see their internal data, as shown in Figure 2-9. You'll learn more about objects and their internal data in upcoming chapters.

Locals			
Name	Value	Type	
⊞ ◆ b	{VirtualMethods.Button}	VirtualMethods.Button	
⊟ ◆ winArray	{Dimensions:[3]}	VirtualMethods.Window[]	
⊞ ◆ [0]	{VirtualMethods.Window}	VirtualMethods.Window	
⊟ ◆ [1]	{VirtualMethods.ListBox}	VirtualMethods.Window {VirtualMet	
⊞ ◆ [VirtualMethods.ListBox]	{VirtualMethods.ListBox}	VirtualMethods.ListBox	
◆ left	4	int	
◆ top	3	int	
⊞ ◆ [2]	{VirtualMethods.Button}	VirtualMethods.Window {VirtualMet	

Autos Locals Watch 1

Figure 2-9. Locals window object expanded

You can step into the next method by pressing F11. Doing so steps into the DrawWindow() method of the Window class, as shown in Figure 2-10.

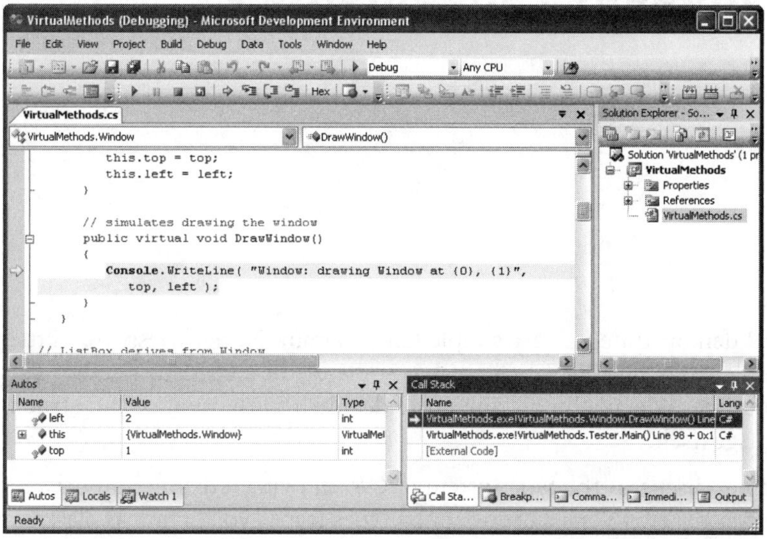

Figure 2-10. Stepping into a method

You can see that the next execution statement is now WriteLine() in DrawWindow(). The Autos window has updated to show the current state of the objects.

There is much more to learn about the debugger, but this brief introduction should get you started. You can answer many programming questions by writing short demonstration programs and examining them in the debugger. A good debugger is, in some ways, the single most powerful teaching tool for a programming language.

CHAPTER 3

C# Language Fundamentals

Chapter 2 demonstrated a very simple C# program. Nonetheless, that little program was complex enough that I had to skip some of the pertinent details. This chapter illuminates these details by delving more deeply into the syntax and structure of the C# language itself.

This chapter discusses the type system in C#, drawing a distinction between built-in types (int, bool, etc.) versus user-defined types (types you create as classes and interfaces). The chapter also covers programming fundamentals such as how to create and use variables and constants. It then goes on to introduce enumerations, strings, identifiers, expressions, and statements.

The second part of the chapter explains and demonstrates the use of flow control statements, using the if, switch, while, do...while, for, and foreach statements. Also discussed are operators, including the assignment, logical, relational, and mathematical operators. This is followed by an introduction to namespaces and a short tutorial on the C# precompiler.

Although C# is principally concerned with the creation and manipulation of objects, it is best to start with the fundamental building blocks: the elements from which objects are created. These include the built-in types that are an intrinsic part of the C# language as well as the syntactic elements of C#.

Types

C# is a strongly typed language. In a strongly typed language you must declare the type of each object you create (e.g., integers, floats, strings, windows, buttons, etc.), and the compiler will help you prevent bugs by enforcing that only data of the right type is assigned to those objects. The type of an object signals to the compiler the size of that object (e.g., int indicates an object of 4 bytes) and its capabilities (e.g., buttons can be drawn, pressed, and so forth).

C# 1.1 programmers take note: until Version 2, .NET was strongly typed in everything except collections. With the addition of generics, however, it is now easy to create strongly typed collection classes, as shown in Chapter 9.

Like C++ and Java, C# divides types into two sets: *intrinsic* (built-in) types that the language offers and *user-defined* types that the programmer defines.

C# also divides the set of types into two other categories: *value* types and *reference* types.* The principal difference between value and reference types is the manner in which their values are stored in memory. A value type holds its actual value in memory allocated on the stack (or it is allocated as part of a larger reference type object). The address of a reference type variable sits on the stack, but the actual object is stored on the heap.

 C and C++ programmers take note: in C#, there is no explicit indication that an object is a reference type (i.e., no use of the & operator). Also, pointers aren't normally used (but see Chapter 22 for the exception to this rule).

If you have a very large object, putting it on the heap has many advantages. Chapter 4 discusses the various advantages and disadvantages of working with reference types; the current chapter focuses on the intrinsic value types available in C#.

 In C#, the size and format of the storage for different intrinsic types (e.g., int) are platform-independent and consistent across all .NET languages.

C# also supports C++ style *pointer* types, but these are used only when working with unmanaged code. Unmanaged code is created outside of the .NET platform (for example, COM objects; working with COM objects is discussed in Chapter 22).

Working with Built-in Types

The C# language offers the usual cornucopia of intrinsic (built-in) types one expects in a modern language, each of which maps to an underlying type supported by the .NET CLS. Mapping the C# primitive types to the underlying .NET type ensures that objects created in C# can be used interchangeably with objects created in any other language compliant with the .NET CLS, such as VB.NET.

---

* All the intrinsic types are value types except for Object (discussed in Chapter 5) and String (discussed in Chapter 10). All user-defined types are reference types except for structs (discussed in Chapter 7) and enumerated types (discussed in Chapter 3).

Java programmers take note: C# has a broader range of basic types than Java. The C# decimal type is notable, and is useful for financial calculations.

Each type has a specific and unchanging size. Unlike with C++, a C# int is always 4 bytes because it maps to an Int32 in the .NET CLS. Table 3-1 lists the built-in value types offered by C#.

Table 3-1. C# built-in value types

Type	Size (in bytes)	.NET type	Description
byte	1	Byte	Unsigned (values 0-255).
char	2	Char	Unicode characters.
bool	1	Boolean	True or false.
sbyte	1	SByte	Signed (values -128 to 127).
short	2	Int16	Signed (short) (values -32,768 to 32,767).
ushort	2	UInt16	Unsigned (short) (values 0 to 65,535).
int	4	Int32	Signed integer values between -2,147,483,648 and 2,147,483,647.
uint	4	UInt32	Unsigned integer values between 0 and 4,294,967,295.
float	4	Single	Floating-point number. Holds the values from approximately +/-1.5 * 10^{-45} to approximately +/-3.4 * 10^{38} with seven significant figures.
double	8	Double	Double-precision floating point. Holds the values from approximately +/-5.0 * 10^{-324} to approximately +/-1.8 * 10^{308} with 15-16 significant figures.
decimal	16	Decimal	Fixed-precision up to 28 digits and the position of the decimal point. This is typically used in financial calculations. Requires the suffix "m" or "M."
long	8	Int64	Signed integers from -9,223,372,036,854,775,808 to 9,223,372,036,854,775,807.
ulong	8	UInt64	Unsigned integers ranging from 0 to 0xffffffffffffffff.

 C and C++ programmers take note: in C#, Boolean variables can only have the values true or false. Integer values don't equate to Boolean values in C# and there is no implicit conversion.

In addition to these primitive types, C# has two other value types: enum (considered later in this chapter) and struct (see Chapter 4). Chapter 4 also discusses other subtleties of value types, such as forcing value types to act as reference types through a process known as *boxing*, and that value types don't "inherit."

The Stack and the Heap

A *stack* is a data structure used to store items on a last-in first-out basis (like a stack of dishes at the buffet line in a restaurant). *The* stack refers to an area of memory supported by the processor, on which the local variables are stored.

In C#, value types (e.g., integers) are allocated on the stack—an area of memory is set aside for their value—and this area is referred to by the name of the variable.

Reference types (e.g., objects) are allocated on the *heap*. The heap is an area of memory used to allocate space for objects. When an object is allocated on the heap, its address is returned, and that address is assigned to a reference.

Objects on the stack are destroyed when they go out of scope. Typically a stack frame is defined by a function. Thus, if you declare a local variable within a function (as explained later in this chapter), the objects you place on the stack within that function will be destroyed when the function ends.

Objects on the heap are garbage-collected sometime after the final reference to them is destroyed.

C and C++ programmers take note: C# manages all memory with a garbage collection system—there is no delete operator.

Choosing a built-in type

Typically you decide which size integer to use (short, int, or long) based on the magnitude of the value you want to store. For example, a ushort can only hold values from 0 through 65,535, while a uint can hold values from 0 through 4,294,967,295.

That said, memory is fairly cheap, and programmer time is increasingly expensive; most of the time you'll simply declare your variables to be of type int, unless there is a good reason to do otherwise.

Integers are often faster than smaller types because modern CPUs are optimized for dealing with them. Further, because of padding inserted for alignment, there's often no space gain to be had from smaller datatypes.

Float, double, and decimal offer varying degrees of size and precision. For most small fractional numbers, float is fine. Note that the compiler assumes that any number with a decimal point is a double unless you tell it otherwise. To assign a literal float, follow the number with the letter f* (assigning values to literals is discussed in detail later in this chapter):

---

* You need to use the f suffix for a float, however there are no suffixes required for other types.

```
float someFloat = 57f;
```

The char type represents a Unicode character. char literals can be simple, Unicode, or escape characters enclosed by single quote marks. For example, A is a simple character while \u0041 is a Unicode character. Escape characters are special two-character tokens in which the first character is a backslash. For example, \t is a horizontal tab. The common escape characters are shown in Table 3-2.

Table 3-2. Common escape characters

Char	Meaning
\'	Single quote
\"	Double quote
\\	Backslash
\0	Null
\a	Alert
\b	Backspace
\f	Form feed
\n	Newline
\r	Carriage return
\t	Horizontal tab
\v	Vertical tab

Converting built-in types

Objects of one type can be converted into objects of another type either implicitly or explicitly. Implicit conversions happen automatically; the compiler takes care of it for you. Explicit conversions happen when you "cast" a value to a different type. The semantics of an explicit conversion are "Hey! Compiler! I know what I'm doing." This is sometimes called "hitting it with the big hammer" and can be very useful or very painful, depending on whether your thumb is in the way of the nail.

 VB6 programmers take note: in VB6 you can easily mix strings and the character datatype; a character is treated as a string with a length of 1. But C# is type-safe. To assign a literal character to a char variable, you must surround it with single quotes.

Note also that the VB6 functions to convert between a character and its ASCII equivalent (Chr() and Asc()) don't exist in C#. To convert a char to its ASCII equivalent, cast it as an int (integer):

```
(int)'A'
```

To convert a number to a char, cast the number as a char:

```
(char)65
```

Implicit conversions happen automatically and are guaranteed not to lose information. For example, you can implicitly cast from a short int (2 bytes) to an int (4 bytes). No matter what value is in the short, it is not lost when converting to an int:

```
short x = 5;
int y = x; // implicit conversion
```

If you convert the other way, however, you certainly can lose information. If the value in the int is greater than 32,767, it will be truncated in the conversion. The compiler will not perform an implicit conversion from int to short:

```
short x;
int y = 500;
x = y;  // won't compile
```

You must explicitly convert using the cast operator:

```
short x;
int y = 500;
x = (short) y;   // OK
```

All the intrinsic types define their own conversion rules. At times it is convenient to define conversion rules for your user-defined types, as discussed in Chapter 5.

Variables and Constants

A *variable* is a storage location with a type. In the preceding examples, both x and y are variables. Variables can have values assigned to them, and those values can be changed programmatically.

WriteLine()

The .NET Framework provides a useful method for writing output to the screen. The details of this method, System.Console.WriteLine(), will become clearer as we progress through the book, but the fundamentals are straightforward. Call the method as shown in Example 3-1, passing in a string that you want printed to the console (the command prompt or shell window) and, optionally, parameters that will be substituted. In the following example:

```
System.Console.WriteLine("After assignment, myInt: {0}", myInt);
```

the string "After assignment, myInt:" is printed as is, followed by the value in the variable myInt. The location of the substitution parameter {0} specifies where the value of the first output variable, myInt, is displayed—in this case, at the end of the string. You'll see a great deal more about WriteLine() in coming chapters.

Create a variable by declaring its type and then giving it a name. You can initialize the variable when you declare it, and you can assign a new value to that variable at any time, changing the value held in the variable. This is illustrated in Example 3-1.

Example 3-1. Initializing and assigning a value to a variable

```
#region Using directives

using System;
using System.Collections.Generic;
using System.Text;

#endregion

namespace InitializingVariables
{
    class Values
    {
        static void Main()
        {

            int myInt = 7;
            System.Console.WriteLine("Initialized, myInt: {0}",
                myInt);

            myInt = 5;
            System.Console.WriteLine("After assignment, myInt: {0}",
                myInt);

        }
    }
}

Output:
Initialized, myInt: 7
After assignment, myInt: 5
```

 Visual Studio 2005 creates a namespace and using directive (as well as a using region) for every program. To save space, these are left out of most of the code examples, though they are shown in the example code you can download from O'Reilly or LibertyAssociates.com.

Here we initialize the variable myInt to the value 7, display that value, reassign the variable with the value 5, and display it again.

 VB6 programmers take note: in C#, the datatype comes before the variable name.

Definite Assignment

C# requires definite assignment: that is, variables must be initialized or assigned to before they are used. To test this rule, change the line that initializes myInt in Example 3-1 to:

```
int myInt;
```

and save the revised program shown in Example 3-2.

 C and C++ programmers take note: C# requires that every variable must be assigned a definite value before use; this is checked by the compiler.

Example 3-2. Using an uninitialized variable

```
#region Using directives

using System;
using System.Collections.Generic;
using System.Text;

#endregion

namespace UninitializedVariable
{
   class UninitializedVariable
   {
      static void Main(string[] args)
      {
         int myInt;
         System.Console.WriteLine
         ("Uninitialized, myInt: {0}", myInt);
         myInt = 5;
         System.Console.WriteLine("Assigned, myInt: {0}", myInt);

      }
   }
}
```

When you try to compile this listing, the C# compiler will display an error message as shown in Figure 3-1.

	Description	File	Line	Column
❌ 1	Use of unassigned local variable 'myInt'	UninitializedVariable.cs	17	33

Figure 3-1. Error message resulting from using an unassigned variable

Double-clicking the error message will bring you to the problem in the code.

It isn't legal to use an uninitialized variable in C#. So, does this mean you must initialize every variable in a program? In fact, no. You don't actually need to initialize a variable, but you must assign a value to it before you attempt to use it. Example 3-3 illustrates a correct program.

Example 3-3. Assigning without initializing

```
#region Using directives

using System;
using System.Collections.Generic;
using System.Text;

#endregion

namespace AssigningWithoutInitializing
{
    class AssigningWithoutInitializing
    {
        static void Main(string[] args)
        {
            int myInt;
            myInt = 7;
            System.Console.WriteLine("Assigned, myInt: {0}", myInt);
            myInt = 5;
            System.Console.WriteLine("Reassigned, myInt: {0}", myInt);

        }
    }
}
```

Constants

A *constant* is a variable whose value can't be changed. Variables are a powerful tool, but there are times when you want to manipulate a defined value, one whose value you want to ensure remains constant. For example, you might need to work with the Fahrenheit freezing and boiling points of water in a program simulating a chemistry experiment. Your program will be clearer if you name the variables that store the values FreezingPoint and BoilingPoint, but you don't want to permit their values to be reassigned. How do you prevent reassignment? The answer is to use a constant.

Constants come in three flavors: *literals*, *symbolic constants*, and *enumerations*. In this assignment:

```
x = 32;
```

the value 32 is a literal constant. The value of 32 is always 32. You can't assign a new value to 32; you can't make 32 represent the value 99 no matter how you might try.

Symbolic constants assign a name to a constant value. You declare a symbolic constant using the const keyword and the following syntax:

```
const type identifier = value;
```

A constant must be initialized when it is declared, and once initialized it can't be altered. For example:

```
const int FreezingPoint = 32;
```

In this declaration, 32 is a literal constant and FreezingPoint is a symbolic constant of type int. Example 3-4 illustrates the use of symbolic constants.

Example 3-4. Using symbolic constants

```
#region Using directives

using System;
using System.Collections.Generic;
using System.Text;

#endregion

namespace SymbolicConstants
{
   class SymbolicConstants
   {
      static void Main(string[] args)
      {
         const int FreezingPoint = 32;    // degrees Fahrenheit
         const int BoilingPoint = 212;

         System.Console.WriteLine("Freezing point of water: {0}",
             FreezingPoint);
         System.Console.WriteLine("Boiling point of water: {0}",
             BoilingPoint);

         //BoilingPoint = 22;

      }
   }
}
```

Example 3-4 creates two symbolic integer constants: FreezingPoint and BoilingPoint. As a matter of style, constant names are written in Pascal notation, but this is certainly not required by the language.

These constants serve the same purpose as always using the *literal* values 32 and 212 for the freezing and boiling points of water in expressions that require them, but because these constants have names, they convey far more meaning. Also, if you decide to switch this program to Celsius, you can reinitialize these constants at compile time, to 0 and 100, respectively; all the rest of the code ought to continue to work.

To prove to yourself that the constant can't be reassigned, try uncommenting the last line of the program (shown in bold). When you recompile, you should receive the error shown in Figure 3-2.

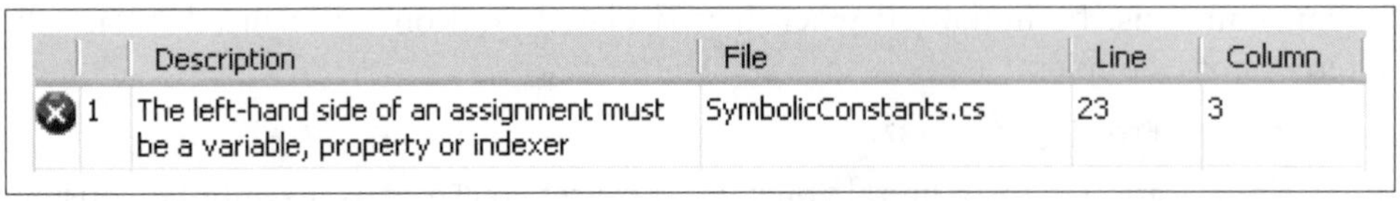

	Description	File	Line	Column
✖ 1	The left-hand side of an assignment must be a variable, property or indexer	SymbolicConstants.cs	23	3

Figure 3-2. Warning that occurs when you try to reassign a constant

Enumerations

Enumerations provide a powerful alternative to constants. An enumeration is a distinct value type, consisting of a set of named constants (called the *enumerator list*).

In Example 3-4, you created two related constants:

```
const int FreezingPoint = 32;
const int BoilingPoint = 212;
```

You might wish to add a number of other useful constants to this list, such as:

```
const int LightJacketWeather = 60;
const int SwimmingWeather = 72;
const int WickedCold = 0;
```

This process is somewhat cumbersome, and there is no logical connection between these various constants. C# provides the *enumeration* to solve these problems:

```
enum Temperatures
{
    WickedCold = 0,
    FreezingPoint = 32,
    LightJacketWeather = 60,
    SwimmingWeather = 72,
    BoilingPoint = 212,
}
```

Every enumeration has an underlying type, which can be any integral type (integer, short, long, etc.) except for char. The technical definition of an enumeration is:

```
[attributes] [modifiers] enum identifier
    [:base-type] {enumerator-list};
```

The optional attributes and modifiers are considered later in this book. For now, let's focus on the rest of this declaration. An enumeration begins with the keyword enum, which is generally followed by an identifier, such as:

```
enum Temperatures
```

The base type is the underlying type for the enumeration. If you leave out this optional value (and often you will), it defaults to int, but you are free to use any of the integral types (e.g., ushort, long) except for char. For example, the following fragment declares an enumeration of unsigned integers (uint):

```
enum ServingSizes :uint
{
    Small = 1,
```

```
        Regular = 2,
        Large = 3
    }
```

Notice that an enum declaration ends with the enumerator list. The enumerator list contains the constant assignments for the enumeration, each separated by a comma.

Example 3-5 rewrites Example 3-4 to use an enumeration.

Example 3-5. Using enumerations to simplify your code

```
#region Using directives

using System;
using System.Collections.Generic;
using System.Text;

#endregion

namespace EnumeratedConstants
{
    class EnumeratedConstants
    {

        enum Temperatures
        {
            WickedCold = 0,
            FreezingPoint = 32,
            LightJacketWeather = 60,
            SwimmingWeather = 72,
            BoilingPoint = 212,
        }

        static void Main(string[] args)
        {
            System.Console.WriteLine("Freezing point of water: {0}",
                (int)Temperatures.FreezingPoint);
            System.Console.WriteLine("Boiling point of water: {0}",
                (int)Temperatures.BoilingPoint);
        }
    }
}
```

As you can see, an enum must be qualified by its enumtype (e.g., Temperatures. WickedCold). By default, an enumeration value is displayed using its symbolic name (such as BoilingPoint or FreezingPoint). When you want to display the value of an enumerated constant, you must cast the constant to its underlying type (int). The integer value is passed to WriteLine, and that value is displayed.

Each constant in an enumeration corresponds to a numerical value—in this case, an integer. If you don't specifically set it otherwise, the enumeration begins at 0 and each subsequent value counts up from the previous.

If you create the following enumeration:

```
enum SomeValues
{
    First,
    Second,
    Third = 20,
    Fourth
}
```

the value of `First` will be 0, `Second` will be 1, `Third` will be 20, and `Fourth` will be 21.

Enums are formal types; therefore an explicit conversion is required to convert between an enum type and an integral type.

 C++ programmers take note: C#'s use of enums is subtly different from C++'s, which restricts assignment to an enum type from an integer but allows an enum to be promoted to an integer for assignment of an enum to an integer.

Strings

It is nearly impossible to write a C# program without creating strings. A string object holds a string of characters.

You declare a string variable using the `string` keyword much as you would create an instance of any object:

```
string myString;
```

A string literal is created by placing double quotes around a string of letters:

```
"Hello World"
```

It is common to initialize a string variable with a string literal:

```
string myString = "Hello World";
```

Strings are covered in much greater detail in Chapter 10.

Identifiers

Identifiers are names programmers choose for their types, methods, variables, constants, objects, and so forth. An identifier must begin with a letter or an underscore.

The Microsoft naming conventions suggest using camel notation (initial lowercase such as `someName`) for variable names and Pascal notation (initial uppercase such as `SomeOtherName`) for method names and most other identifiers.

Microsoft no longer recommends using Hungarian notation (e.g., iSomeInteger) or underscores (e.g., Some_Value).

Identifiers are case-sensitive, so C# treats myVariable and MyVariable as two different variable names.

Expressions

Statements that evaluate to a value are called *expressions*. You may be surprised how many statements do evaluate to a value. For example, an assignment such as:

```
myVariable = 57;
```

is an expression; it evaluates to the value assigned, which, in this case, is 57.

Note that the preceding statement assigns the value 57 to the variable myVariable. The assignment operator (=) doesn't test equality; rather it causes whatever is on the right side (57) to be assigned to whatever is on the left side (myVariable). All the C# operators (including assignment and equality) are discussed later in this chapter (see "Operators").

Because myVariable = 57 is an expression that evaluates to 57, it can be used as part of another assignment operator, such as:

```
mySecondVariable = myVariable = 57;
```

What happens in this statement is that the literal value 57 is assigned to the variable myVariable. The value of that assignment (57) is then assigned to the second variable, mySecondVariable. Thus, the value 57 is assigned to both variables. You can therefore initialize any number of variables to the same value with one statement:

```
a = b = c = d = e = 20;
```

Whitespace

In the C# language, spaces, tabs, and newlines are considered to be "whitespace" (so named because you see only the white of the underlying "page"). Extra whitespace is generally ignored in C# statements. You can write:

```
myVariable = 5;
```

or:

```
myVariable       =                         5;
```

and the compiler will treat the two statements as identical.

The exception to this rule is that whitespace within strings isn't ignored. If you write:

```
Console.WriteLine("Hello World")
```

each space between "Hello" and "World" is treated as another character in the string.

Most of the time the use of whitespace is intuitive. The key is to use whitespace to make the program more readable to the programmer; the compiler is indifferent.

However, there are instances in which the use of whitespace is quite significant. Although the expression:

```
int x = 5;
```

is the same as:

```
int x=5;
```

it is not the same as:

```
intx=5;
```

The compiler knows that the whitespace on either side of the assignment operator is extra, but the whitespace between the type declaration int and the variable name x is *not* extra, and is required. This is not surprising: the whitespace allows the compiler to parse the keyword int rather than some unknown term intx. You are free to add as much or as little whitespace between int and x as you care to, but there must be at least one whitespace character (typically a space or tab).

 VB programmers take note: in C# the end-of-line has no special significance; statements are ended with semicolons, not newline characters. There is no line-continuation character because none is needed.

Statements

In C# a complete program instruction is called a *statement*. Programs consist of sequences of C# statements. Each statement must end with a semicolon (;). For example:

```
int x;      // a statement
x = 23;     // another statement
int y = x; // yet another statement
```

C# statements are evaluated in order. The compiler starts at the beginning of a statement list and makes its way to the bottom. This would be entirely straightforward, and terribly limiting, were it not for branching. There are two types of branches in a C# program: *unconditional branching* and *conditional branching*.

Program flow is also affected by looping and iteration statements, which are signaled by the keywords for, while, do, in, and foreach. Iteration is discussed later in this chapter. For now, let's consider some of the more basic methods of conditional and unconditional branching.

Unconditional Branching Statements

An unconditional branch is created in one of two ways. The first way is by invoking a method. When the compiler encounters the name of a method, it stops execution in the current method and branches to the newly "called" method. When that method returns a value, execution picks up in the original method on the line just below the method call. Example 3-6 illustrates.

Example 3-6. Calling a method

```
#region Using directives

using System;
using System.Collections.Generic;
using System.Text;

#endregion

namespace CallingAMethod
{
    class CallingAMethod
    {
        static void Main()
        {
            Console.WriteLine("In Main! Calling SomeMethod()...");
            SomeMethod();
            Console.WriteLine("Back in Main().");
        }
        static void SomeMethod()
        {
            Console.WriteLine("Greetings from SomeMethod!");
        }
    }
}
Output:
In Main! Calling SomeMethod()...
Greetings from SomeMethod!
Back in Main().
```

Program flow begins in Main() and proceeds until SomeMethod() is invoked (invoking a method is sometimes referred to as "calling" the method). At that point, program flow branches to the method. When the method completes, program flow resumes at the next line after the call to that method.

The second way to create an unconditional branch is with one of the unconditional branch keywords: goto, break, continue, return, or throw. Additional information about the first three jump statements is provided later in this chapter; the return statement returns control to the calling method; the final statement, throw, is discussed in Chapter 11.

Conditional Branching Statements

A conditional branch is created by a conditional statement, which is signaled by keywords such as if, else, or switch. A conditional branch occurs only if the condition expression evaluates true.

 C and C++ programmers take note: unlike C and C++, in which any expression can be used in a conditional, C# requires that all conditional expressions evaluate to a Boolean value.

if...else statements

if...else statements branch based on a condition. The condition is an expression, tested in the head of the if statement. If the condition evaluates true, the statement (or block of statements) in the body of the if statement is executed.

if statements may contain an optional else statement. The else statement is executed only if the expression in the head of the if statement evaluates false:

```
if (expression)
    statement1
[else
    statement2]
```

This is the kind of if statement description you are likely to find in your compiler documentation. It shows you that the if statement takes a *Boolean expression* (an expression that evaluates true or false) in parentheses, and executes statement1 if the expression evaluates true. Note that statement1 can actually be a block of statements within braces.

You can also see that the else statement is optional, as it is enclosed in square brackets. Although this gives you the syntax of an if statement, an illustration will make its use clear. See Example 3-7.

Example 3-7. if...else statements

```
using System;
class Values
{
    static void Main()
    {
        int valueOne = 10;
        int valueTwo = 20;

        if ( valueOne > valueTwo )
        {
            Console.WriteLine(
              "ValueOne: {0} larger than ValueTwo: {1}",
                    valueOne, valueTwo);
        }
        else
```

Example 3-7. if...else statements (continued)

```
    {
       Console.WriteLine(
         "ValueTwo: {0} larger than ValueOne: {1}",
              valueTwo,valueOne);
    }

    valueOne = 30; // set valueOne higher

    if ( valueOne > valueTwo )
    {
       valueTwo = valueOne++;
       Console.WriteLine("\nSetting valueTwo to valueOne value, ");
       Console.WriteLine("and incrementing ValueOne.\n");
          Console.WriteLine("ValueOne: {0}  ValueTwo: {1}",
              valueOne, valueTwo);
    }
    else
    {
       valueOne = valueTwo;
       Console.WriteLine("Setting them equal. ");
          Console.WriteLine("ValueOne: {0}  ValueTwo: {1}",
              valueOne, valueTwo);
    }
  }
}
```

In Example 3-7, the first if statement tests whether valueOne is greater than valueTwo. The relational operators such as greater than (>), less than (<), and equal to (==) are fairly intuitive to use.

The test of whether valueOne is greater than valueTwo evaluates false (because valueOne is 10 and valueTwo is 20, so valueOne is *not* greater than valueTwo). The else statement is invoked, printing the statement:

```
ValueTwo: 20 is larger than ValueOne: 10
```

The second if statement evaluates true and all the statements in the if block are evaluated, causing two lines to print:

```
Setting valueTwo to valueOne value,
and incrementing ValueOne.

ValueOne: 31  ValueTwo: 30
```

Nested if statements

It is possible, and not uncommon, to nest if statements to handle complex conditions. For example, suppose you need to write a program to evaluate the temperature, and specifically to return the following types of information.

Statement Blocks

You can substitute a statement block anywhere that C# expects a statement. A *statement block* is a set of statements surrounded by braces.

Thus, where you might write:

```
if (someCondition)
    someStatement;
```

you can instead write:

```
if(someCondition)
{
    statementOne;
    statementTwo;
    statementThree;
}
```

- If the temperature is 32 degrees or lower, the program should warn you about ice on the road.

- If the temperature is exactly 32 degrees, the program should tell you that there may be ice patches.

There are many good ways to write this program. Example 3-8 illustrates one approach, using nested if statements.

Example 3-8. Nested if statements

```
#region Using directives

using System;
using System.Collections.Generic;
using System.Text;

#endregion

namespace NestedIf
{
    class NestedIf
    {
        static void Main()
        {
            int temp = 32;

            if ( temp <= 32 )
            {
                Console.WriteLine( "Warning! Ice on road!" );
                if ( temp == 32 )
                {
                    Console.WriteLine(
                        "Temp exactly freezing, beware of water." );
```

Example 3-8. Nested if statements (continued)

```
        }
        else
        {
            Console.WriteLine( "Watch for black ice! Temp: {0}", temp );
        }       // end else
    }           // end if (temp <= 32)
  }             // end main
 }              // end class
}               // end namespace
```

The logic of Example 3-8 is that it tests whether the temperature is less than or equal to 32. If so, it prints a warning:

```
if (temp <= 32)
{
    Console.WriteLine("Warning! Ice on road!");
```

The program then checks whether the temp is equal to 32 degrees. If so, it prints one message; if not, the temp must be less than 32 and the program prints the second message. Notice that this second if statement is nested within the first if, so the logic of the else is "since it has been established that the temp is less than or equal to 32, and it isn't equal to 32, it must be less than 32."

All Operators Aren't Created Equal

A closer examination of the second if statement in Example 3-8 reveals a common potential problem. This if statement tests whether the temperature is equal to 32:

```
if (temp == 32)
```

In C and C++, there is an inherent danger in this kind of statement. It's not uncommon for novice programmers to use the assignment operator rather than the equals operator, instead creating the statement:

```
if (temp = 32)
```

This mistake would be difficult to notice, and the result would be that 32 was assigned to temp, and 32 would be returned as the value of the assignment statement. Because any nonzero value evaluates to true in C and C++, the if statement would return true. The side effect would be that temp would be assigned a value of 32 whether or not it originally had that value. This is a common bug that could easily be overlooked—if the developers of C# had not anticipated it!

C# solves this problem by requiring that if statements accept only Boolean values. The 32 returned by the assignment is not Boolean (it is an integer) and, in C#, there is no automatic conversion from 32 to true. Thus, this bug would be caught at compile time, which is a very good thing, and a significant improvement over C++, at the small cost of not allowing implicit conversions from integers to Booleans!

---

switch statements: an alternative to nested ifs

Nested if statements are hard to read, hard to get right, and hard to debug. When you have a complex set of choices to make, the switch statement is a more readable alternative. The logic of a switch statement is "pick a matching value and act accordingly."

```
switch (expression)
{
    case constant-expression:
        statement
        jump-statement
    [default: statement]
}
```

As you can see, like an if statement, the expression is put in parentheses in the head of the switch statement. Each case statement then requires a constant expression; that is, a literal or symbolic constant or an enumeration.

If a case is matched, the statement(s) associated with that case is executed. This must be followed by a jump statement. Typically, the jump statement is break, which transfers execution out of the switch. An alternative is a goto statement, typically used to jump into another case, as illustrated in Example 3-9.

Example 3-9. The switch statement

```
#region Using directives

using System;
using System.Collections.Generic;
using System.Text;

#endregion

namespace SwitchStatement
{
    class SwitchStatement
    {
        static void Main( string[] args )
        {
            const int Democrat = 0;
            const int LiberalRepublican = 1;
            const int Republican = 2;
            const int Libertarian = 3;
            const int NewLeft = 4;
            const int Progressive = 5;

            int myChoice = Libertarian;

            switch ( myChoice )
            {
                case Democrat:
                    Console.WriteLine( "You voted Democratic.\n" );
                    break;
```

Example 3-9. The switch statement (continued)

```
        case LiberalRepublican:  // fall through
        //Console.WriteLine(
        //"Liberal Republicans vote Republican\n");
        case Republican:
            Console.WriteLine( "You voted Republican.\n" );
            break;
        case NewLeft:
            Console.WriteLine( "NewLeft is now Progressive" );
            goto case Progressive;
        case Progressive:
            Console.WriteLine( "You voted Progressive.\n" );
            break;
        case Libertarian:
            Console.WriteLine( "Libertarians are voting Republican" );
            goto case Republican;
        default:
            Console.WriteLine( "You did not pick a valid choice.\n" );
            break;
    }

    Console.WriteLine( "Thank you for voting." );
    }
  }
}
```

In this whimsical example, we create constants for various political parties. We then assign one value (Libertarian) to the variable myChoice and switch on that value. If myChoice is equal to Democrat, we print out a statement. Notice that this case ends with break. break is a jump statement that takes us out of the switch statement and down to the first line after the switch, on which we print "Thank you for voting."

> *VB6 programmers take note:* the equivalent of the C# switch statement is the VB6 Select Case statement. Also, while VB6 allows you to test a range of values using a single Case statement, C# syntax doesn't provide for this contingency. The following two Case statements are syntactically correct in VB6:
>
>   Case Is > 100
>   Case 50 to 60
>
> However, these statements aren't valid in C#. In C#, you can test only a single constant expression. To test a range, you must test each value independently and "fall through" to a common case block.

The value LiberalRepublican has no statement under it, and it "falls through" to the next statement: Republican. If the value is LiberalRepublican or Republican, the Republican statements execute. You can "fall through" in this way only if there is no body within the statement. If you uncomment WriteLine() under LiberalRepublican, this program won't compile.

C and C++ programmers take note: you can't fall through to the next case unless the case statement is empty. Thus, you can write this:

```
case 1: // fall through ok
case 2:
```

In this example, case 1 is empty. You can't, however, write this:

```
case 1:
    TakeSomeAction();
        // fall through not OK
case 2:
```

Here case 1 has a statement in it, and you can't fall through. If you want case 1 to fall through to case 2, you must explicitly use goto:

```
case 1:
    TakeSomeAction();
    goto case 2; // explicit fall through
case 2:
```

If you do need a statement but you then want to execute another case, you can use the goto statement, as shown in the NewLeft case:

```
goto case Progressive;
```

It is not required that the goto take you to the case immediately following. In the next instance, the Libertarian choice also has a goto, but this time it jumps all the way back up to the Republican case. Because our value was set to Libertarian, this is just what occurs. We print out the Libertarian statement, go to the Republican case, print that statement, and then hit the break, taking us out of the switch and down to the final statement. The output for all of this is:

```
Libertarians are voting Republican
You voted Republican.

Thank you for voting.
```

Note the default case, excerpted from Example 3-9:

```
default:
    Console.WriteLine(
     "You did not pick a valid choice.\n");
```

If none of the cases match, the default case will be invoked, warning the user of the mistake.

Switch on string statements

In the previous example, the switch value was an integral constant. C# offers the ability to switch on a string, allowing you to write:

```
case "Libertarian":
```

If the strings match, the case statement is entered.

Iteration Statements

C# provides an extensive suite of iteration statements, including for, while and do...while loops, as well as foreach loops (new to the C family but familiar to VB programmers). In addition, C# supports the goto, break, continue, and return jump statements.

The goto statement

The goto statement is the seed from which all other iteration statements have been germinated. Unfortunately, it is a semolina seed, producer of spaghetti code and endless confusion. Most experienced programmers properly shun the goto statement, but in the interest of completeness, here's how you use it:

1. Create a label.
2. goto that label.

The label is an identifier followed by a colon. The goto command is typically tied to a condition, as illustrated in Example 3-10.

Example 3-10. Using goto

```
#region Using directives

using System;
using System.Collections.Generic;
using System.Text;

#endregion

namespace UsingGoTo
{
   class UsingGoTo
   {
      static void Main( string[] args )
      {
         int i = 0;
      repeat:            // the label
         Console.WriteLine( "i: {0}", i );
         i++;
         if ( i < 10 )
            goto repeat;  // the dastardly deed
         return;
      }
   }
}
```

If you were to try to draw the flow of control in a program that makes extensive use of goto statements, the resulting morass of intersecting and overlapping lines might look like a plate of spaghetti; hence the term "spaghetti code." It was this phenomenon that led to the creation of alternatives, such as the while loop. Many programmers feel

that using goto in anything other than a trivial example creates confusion and diffi-
cult-to-maintain code.

The while loop

The semantics of the while loop are "while this condition is true, do this work." The
syntax is:

```
while (expression) statement
```

As usual, an expression is any statement that returns a value. While statements
require an expression that evaluates to a Boolean (true/false) value, and that statement can, of course, be a block of statements. Example 3-11 updates Example 3-10,
using a while loop.

Example 3-11. Using a while loop

```
#region Using directives

using System;
using System.Collections.Generic;
using System.Text;

#endregion

namespace WhileLoop
{
    class WhileLoop
    {
        static void Main( string[] args )
        {
            int i = 0;
            while ( i < 10 )
            {
                Console.WriteLine( "i: {0}", i );
                i++;
            }
            return;
        }
    }
}
```

The code in Example 3-11 produces results identical to the code in Example 3-10,
but the logic is a bit clearer. The while statement is nicely self-contained, and it reads
like an English sentence: "while i is less than 10, print this message and increment i."

Notice that the while loop tests the value of i before entering the loop. This ensures
that the loop will not run if the condition tested is false; thus if i is initialized to 11,
the loop will never run.

The do...while loop

A while statement may never execute if the condition tested returns false. If you want to ensure that your statement is run at least once, use a do...while loop:

```
do statement while expression
```

An *expression* is any statement that returns a value. Example 3-12 shows the do... while loop.

Example 3-12. The do...while loop

```
#region Using directives

using System;
using System.Collections.Generic;
using System.Text;

#endregion

namespace DoWhile
{
    class DoWhile
    {
        static int Main( string[] args )
        {
            int i = 11;
            do
            {
                Console.WriteLine( "i: {0}", i );
                i++;
            } while ( i < 10 );
            return 0;
        }
    }
}
```

Here i is initialized to 11 and the while test fails, but only after the body of the loop has run once.

The for loop

A careful examination of the while loop in Example 3-11 reveals a pattern often seen in iterative statements: initialize a variable (i = 0), test the variable (i < 10), execute a series of statements, and increment the variable (i++). The for loop allows you to combine all these steps in a single loop statement:

```
for ([initializers]; [expression]; [iterators]) statement
```

The for loop is illustrated in Example 3-13.

Example 3-13. The for loop

```
#region Using directives

using System;
using System.Collections.Generic;
using System.Text;

#endregion

namespace ForLoop
{
    class ForLoop
    {
        static void Main( string[] args )
        {
            for ( int i = 0; i < 100; i++ )
            {
                Console.Write( "{0} ", i );

                if ( i % 10 == 0 )
                {
                    Console.WriteLine( "\t{0}", i );
                }
            }
            return ;
        }
    }
}
```

Output:
```
0       0
1 2 3 4 5 6 7 8 9 10     10
11 12 13 14 15 16 17 18 19 20    20
21 22 23 24 25 26 27 28 29 30    30
31 32 33 34 35 36 37 38 39 40    40
41 42 43 44 45 46 47 48 49 50    50
51 52 53 54 55 56 57 58 59 60    60
61 62 63 64 65 66 67 68 69 70    70
71 72 73 74 75 76 77 78 79 80    80
81 82 83 84 85 86 87 88 89 90    90
91 92 93 94 95 96 97 98 99
```

This for loop makes use of the modulus operator described later in this chapter. The value of i is printed until i is a multiple of 10:

```
    if ( i % 10   == 0)
```

A tab is then printed, followed by the value. Thus, the 10s (20, 30, 40, etc.) are called out on the right side of the output.

VB6 programmers take note: in C#, looping variables are declared within the header of the for or foreach statement (rather than before the statement begins). This means that they are in scope only within the block, and you can't refer to them outside the loop. The foreach statement is covered in detail in Chapter 9.

The individual values are printed using Console.Write(), which is much like WriteLine() but which doesn't enter a newline character, allowing the subsequent writes to occur on the same line.

A few quick points to notice: in a for loop, the condition is tested before the statements are executed. Thus, in the example, i is initialized to 0, then it is tested to see if it is less than 100. Because i < 100 returns true, the statements within the for loop are executed. After the execution, i is incremented (i++).

Note that the variable i is *scoped* to within the for loop (that is, the variable i is visible only within the for loop). Example 3-14 will not compile.

Example 3-14. Scope of variables declared in a for loop

```
#region Using directives

using System;
using System.Collections.Generic;
using System.Text;

#endregion

namespace ForLoopScope
{
    class ForLoopScope
    {
        static void Main( string[] args )
        {
            for ( int i = 0; i < 100; i++ )
            {
                Console.Write( "{0} ", i );

                if ( i % 10 == 0 )
                {
                    Console.WriteLine( "\t{0}", i );
                }
            }

            Console.WriteLine( "\n Final value of i: {0}", i );
        }
    }
}
```

The line shown in bold fails, as the variable i is not available outside the scope of the for loop itself.

Whitespace and Braces

There is much controversy about the use of whitespace in programming. For example, this for loop:

```
for (int i=0;i<100;i++)
{
    if (i%10 == 0)
    {
        Console.WriteLine("\t{0}", i);
    }
}
```

can be written with more space between the operators:

```
for ( int i = 0; i < 100; i++ )
{
    if ( i % 10 == 0 )
    {
        Console.WriteLine("\t{0}", i);
    }
}
```

Much of this is a matter of personal taste. Visual Studio 2005 allows you to set your preference for the use of whitespace by setting the various options under Tools → Options → TextEditor → C# → Formatting → Spacing.

The foreach statement

The foreach statement is new to the C family of languages; it is used for looping through the elements of an array or a collection. Discussion of this incredibly useful statement is deferred until Chapter 9.

The continue and break statements

There are times when you would like to return to the top of a loop without executing the remaining statements in the loop. The continue statement causes the loop to skip the remaining steps in the loop.

The obverse side of that coin is the ability to break out of a loop and immediately end all further work within the loop. For this purpose the break statement exists.

 break and continue create multiple exit points and can make for hard-to-understand, and thus hard-to-maintain, code. Use them with some care.

Example 3-15 illustrates the mechanics of continue and break. This code, suggested to me by one of my technical reviewers, Donald Xie, is intended to create a traffic signal processing system. The signals are simulated by entering numerals and uppercase characters from the keyboard, using Console.ReadLine(), which reads a line of text from the keyboard.

The algorithm is simple: receipt of a 0 (zero) means normal conditions, and no further action is required except to log the event. (In this case, the program simply writes a message to the console; a real application might enter a timestamped record in a database.) On receipt of an abort signal (here simulated with an uppercase "A"), the problem is logged and the process is ended. Finally, for any other event, an alarm is raised, perhaps notifying the police. (Note that this sample doesn't actually notify the police, though it does print out a harrowing message to the console.) If the signal is "X," the alarm is raised, but the while loop is also terminated.

Example 3-15. Using continue and break

```csharp
#region Using directives

using System;
using System.Collections.Generic;
using System.Text;

#endregion

namespace ContinueBreak
{
    class ContinueBreak
    {
        static void Main( string[] args )
        {
            string signal = "0";       // initialize to neutral
            while ( signal != "X" )        // X indicates stop
            {
                Console.Write( "Enter a signal: " );
                signal = Console.ReadLine();

                // do some work here, no matter what signal you
                // receive
                Console.WriteLine( "Received: {0}", signal );

                if ( signal == "A" )
                {
                    // faulty - abort signal processing
                    // Log the problem and abort.
                    Console.WriteLine( "Fault! Abort\n" );
                    break;
                }

                if ( signal == "0" )
                {
```

Example 3-15. Using continue and break (continued)

```
                    // normal traffic condition
                    // log and continue on
                    Console.WriteLine( "All is well.\n" );
                    continue;
                }

                    // Problem. Take action and then log the problem
                    // and then continue on
                    Console.WriteLine( "{0} -- raise alarm!\n",
                        signal );
            }       // end while
        }           // end main
    }               // end class
}                   // end namespace
```

```
Output:
Enter a signal: 0
Received: 0
All is well.

Enter a signal: B
Received: B
B -- raise alarm!

Enter a signal: A
Received: A
Fault! Abort

Press any key to continue
```

The point of this exercise is that when the A signal is received, the action in the `if` statement is taken and then the program *breaks* out of the loop, without raising the alarm. When the signal is 0, it is also undesirable to raise the alarm, so the program *continues* from the top of the loop.

Operators

An *operator* is a symbol that causes C# to take an action. The C# primitive types (e.g., int) support a number of operators such as assignment, increment, and so forth.

The Assignment Operator (=)

The section titled "Expressions," earlier in this chapter, demonstrates the use of the assignment operator. This symbol causes the operand on the left side of the operator to have its value changed to whatever is on the right side of the operator.

Mathematical Operators

C# uses five mathematical operators: four for standard calculations and a fifth to return the remainder in integer division. The following sections consider the use of these operators.

Simple arithmetical operators (+, -, *, /)

C# offers operators for simple arithmetic: the addition (+), subtraction (-), multiplication (*), and division (/) operators work as you might expect, with the possible exception of integer division.

When you divide two integers, C# divides like a child in fourth grade: it throws away any fractional remainder. Thus, dividing 17 by 4 returns the value 4 (17/4 = 4, with a remainder of 1). C# provides a special operator (modulus, %, which is described in the next section) to retrieve the remainder.

Note, however, that C# does return fractional answers when you divide floats, doubles, and decimals.

The modulus operator (%) to return remainders

To find the remainder in integer division, use the modulus operator (%). For example, the statement 17%4 returns 1 (the remainder after integer division).

The modulus operator turns out to be more useful than you might at first imagine. When you perform modulus n on a number that is a multiple of *n*, the result is 0. Thus 80%10 = 0 because 80 is an even multiple of 10. This fact allows you to set up loops in which you take an action every *n*th time through the loop, by testing a counter to see if %n is equal to 0. This strategy comes in handy in the use of the for loop, as described earlier in this chapter. The effects of division on integers, floats, doubles, and decimals are illustrated in Example 3-16.

Example 3-16. Division and modulus

```
#region Using directives

using System;
using System.Collections.Generic;
using System.Text;

#endregion

namespace DivisionModulus
{
    class DivisionModulus
    {
        static void Main( string[] args )
        {
            int i1, i2;
```

Example 3-16. Division and modulus (continued)

```
        float f1, f2;
        double d1, d2;
        decimal dec1, dec2;

        i1 = 17;
        i2 = 4;
        f1 = 17f;
        f2 = 4f;
        d1 = 17;
        d2 = 4;
        dec1 = 17;
        dec2 = 4;
        Console.WriteLine( "Integer:\t{0}\nfloat:\t\t{1}",
            i1 / i2, f1 / f2 );
        Console.WriteLine( "double:\t\t{0}\ndecimal:\t{1}",
            d1 / d2, dec1 / dec2 );
        Console.WriteLine( "\nModulus:\t{0}", i1 % i2 );

    }
  }
}
```

```
Output:
Integer:      4
float:        4.25
double:       4.25
decimal:      4.25

Modulus:      1
```

Now consider this line from Example 3-16:

```
    Console.WriteLine("Integer:\t{0}\nfloat:\t\t{1}\n",
        i1/i2, f1/f2);
```

It begins with a call to `Console.WriteLine()`, passing in this partial string:

```
    "Integer:\t{0}\n
```

This will print the characters `Integer:`, followed by a tab (`\t`), followed by the first parameter (`{0}`), followed by a newline character (`\n`). The next string snippet:

```
    float:\t\t{1}\n
```

is very similar. It prints `float:`, followed by two tabs (to ensure alignment), the contents of the second parameter (`{1}`), and then another newline. Notice the subsequent line, as well:

```
    Console.WriteLine("\nModulus:\t{0}", i1%i2);
```

This time the string begins with a newline character, which causes a line to be skipped just before the string `Modulus:` is printed. You can see this effect in the output.

Increment and Decrement Operators

A common requirement is to add a value to a variable, subtract a value from a variable, or otherwise change the mathematical value, and then to assign that new value back to the same variable. You might even want to assign the result to another variable altogether. The following two sections discuss these cases respectively.

Calculate and reassign operators

Suppose you want to increment the mySalary variable by 5,000. You can do this by writing:

```
mySalary = mySalary + 5000;
```

The addition happens before the assignment, and it is perfectly legal to assign the result back to the original variable. Thus, after this operation completes, mySalary will have been incremented by 5,000. You can perform this kind of assignment with any mathematical operator:

```
mySalary = mySalary * 5000;
mySalary = mySalary - 5000;
```

and so forth.

The need to increment and decrement variables is so common that C# includes special operators for self-assignment. Among these operators are +=, -=, *=, /=, and %=, which, respectively, combine addition, subtraction, multiplication, division, and modulus with self-assignment. Thus, you can alternatively write the previous examples as:

```
mySalary += 5000;
mySalary *= 5000;
mySalary -= 5000;
```

The effect of this is to increment mySalary by 5,000, multiply mySalary by 5,000, and subtract 5,000 from the mySalary variable, respectively.

Because incrementing and decrementing by 1 is a very common need, C# (like C and C++ before it) also provides two special operators. To increment by 1, use the ++ operator, and to decrement by 1, use the -- operator.

Thus, if you want to increment the variable myAge by 1 you can write:

```
myAge++;
```

The prefix and postfix operators

To complicate matters further, you might want to increment a variable and assign the results to a second variable:

```
firstValue = secondValue++;
```

The question arises: do you want to assign before you increment the value, or after? In other words, if secondValue starts out with the value 10, do you want to end with both firstValue and secondValue equal to 11, or do you want firstValue to be equal to 10 (the original value) and secondValue to be equal to 11?

C# (again, like C and C++) offers two flavors of the increment and decrement operators: *prefix* and *postfix*. Thus, you can write:

```
firstValue = secondValue++;   // postfix
```

which will assign first, and then increment (firstValue=10, secondValue=11). You can also write:

```
firstValue = ++secondValue;   // prefix
```

which will increment first, and then assign (firstValue=11, secondValue=11).

It is important to understand the different effects of prefix and postfix, as illustrated in Example 3-17.

Example 3-17. Prefix versus postfix increment

```
#region Using directives

using System;
using System.Collections.Generic;
using System.Text;

#endregion

namespace PrefixPostfix
{
    class PrefixPostfix
    {
        static void Main( string[] args )
        {
            int valueOne = 10;
            int valueTwo;
            valueTwo = valueOne++;
            Console.WriteLine( "After postfix: {0}, {1}", valueOne,
            valueTwo );
            valueOne = 20;
            valueTwo = ++valueOne;
            Console.WriteLine( "After prefix: {0}, {1}", valueOne,
            valueTwo );

        }
    }
}

Output:
After postfix: 11, 10
After prefix: 21, 21
```

Relational Operators

Relational operators are used to compare two values, and then return a Boolean (true or false). The greater-than operator (>), for example, returns true if the value on the left of the operator is greater than the value on the right. Thus, 5 > 2 returns the value true, while 2 > 5 returns the value false.

The relational operators for C# are shown in Table 3-3. This table assumes two variables: bigValue and smallValue, in which bigValue has been assigned the value 100 and smallValue the value 50.

Table 3-3. C# relational operators (assumes bigValue = 100 and smallValue = 50)

Name	Operator	Given this statement	The expression evaluates to
Equals	==	bigValue == 100 bigValue == 80	true false
Not equals	!=	bigValue != 100 bigValue != 80	false true
Greater than	>	bigValue > smallValue	true
Greater than or equals	>=	bigValue >= smallValue smallValue >= bigValue	true false
Less than	<	bigValue < smallValue	false
Less than or equals	<=	smallValue <= bigValue bigValue <= smallValue	true false

Each relational operator acts as you might expect. However, take note of the equals operator (==), which is created by typing two equals signs (=) in a row (i.e., without any space between them); the C# compiler treats the pair as a single operator.

The C# equality operator (==) tests for equality between the objects on either side of the operator. This operator evaluates to a Boolean value (true or false). Thus, the statement:

```
myX == 5;
```

evaluates to true if and only if myX is a variable whose value is 5.

> It is not uncommon to confuse the assignment operator (=) with the equals operator (==). The latter has two equals signs, the former only one.

Use of Logical Operators with Conditionals

If statements (discussed earlier in this chapter) test whether a condition is true. Often you will want to test whether two conditions are both true, or whether only one is true, or none is true. C# provides a set of logical operators for this, as shown in Table 3-4. This table assumes two variables, x and y, in which x has the value 5 and y the value 7.

Table 3-4. C# logical operators (assumes x = 5, y = 7)

Name	Operator	Given this statement	The expression evaluates to
and	&&	(x == 3) && (y == 7)	false
or	||	(x == 3) || (y == 7)	true
not	!	! (x == 3)	true

The and operator tests whether two statements are both true. The first line in Table 3-4 includes an example that illustrates the use of the and operator:

```
(x == 3) && (y == 7)
```

The entire expression evaluates false because one side (x == 3) is false.

With the or operator, either or both sides must be true; the expression is false only if both sides are false. So, in the case of the example in Table 3-4:

```
(x == 3) || (y == 7)
```

the entire expression evaluates true because one side (y==7) is true.

With a not operator, the statement is true if the expression is false, and vice versa. So, in the accompanying example:

```
! (x == 3)
```

the entire expression is true because the tested expression (x==3) is false. (The logic is "it is true that it is not true that x is equal to 3.")

Operator Precedence

The compiler must know the order in which to evaluate a series of operators. For example, if I write:

```
myVariable = 5 + 7 * 3;
```

there are three operators for the compiler to evaluate (=, +, and *). It could, for example, operate left to right, which would assign the value 5 to myVariable, then add 7 to the 5 (12) and multiply by 3 (36)—but of course then it would throw that 36 away. This is clearly not what is intended.

The rules of precedence tell the compiler which operators to evaluate first. As is the case in algebra, multiplication has higher precedence than addition, so 5+7*3 is equal to 26 rather than 36. Both addition and multiplication have higher precedence than assignment, so the compiler will do the math, and then assign the result (26) to myVariable only after the math is completed.

In C#, parentheses are also used to change the order of precedence much as they are in algebra. Thus, you can change the result by writing:

```
myVariable = (5+7) * 3;
```

Short-Circuit Evaluation

Consider the following code snippet:

```
    int x = 8;
.   if ((x == 8) || (y == 12))
```

The `if` statement here is a bit complicated. The entire `if` statement is in parentheses, as are all `if` statements in C#. Thus, everything within the outer set of parentheses must evaluate true for the `if` statement to be true.

Within the outer parentheses are two expressions (x==8) and (y==12), which are separated by an or operator (||). Because x is 8, the first term (x==8) evaluates true. There is no need to evaluate the second term (y==12). It doesn't matter whether y is 12, the entire expression will be true. Similarly, consider this snippet:

```
    int x = 8;
    if ((x == 5) && (y == 12))
```

Again, there is no need to evaluate the second term. Because the first term is false, the and must fail. (Remember, for an and statement to evaluate true, both tested expressions must evaluate true.)

In cases such as these, the C# compiler will short-circuit the evaluation; the second test will never be performed.

Grouping the elements of the assignment in this way causes the compiler to add 5+7, multiply the result by 3, and then assign that value (36) to `myVariable`. Table 3-5 summarizes operator precedence in C#.

Table 3-5. Operator precedence

Category	Operators
Primary	`(x) x.y x->y f(x) a[x] x++ x-- new typeof sizeof checked unchecked stackalloc`
Unary	`+ - ! ~ ++x -- x (T)x *x &x`
Multiplicative	`* / %`
Additive	`+ -`
Shift	`<< >>`
Relational	`< > <= >= is as`
Equality	`== !=`
Logical AND	`&`
Logical XOR	`^`
Logical OR	`|`
Conditional AND	`&&`
Conditional OR	`||`

Table 3-5. Operator precedence (continued)

Category	Operators
Conditional	?:
Assignment	= *= /= %= += -= <<= >>= &= ^= |=

In some complex equations you might need to nest your parentheses to ensure the proper order of operations. Let's assume I want to know how many seconds my family wastes each morning. It turns out that the adults spend 20 minutes over coffee each morning and 10 minutes reading the newspaper. The children waste 30 minutes dawdling and 10 minutes arguing.

Here's my algorithm:

```
(((minDrinkingCoffee  + minReadingNewspaper )* numAdults ) +
((minDawdling + minArguing) * numChildren)) * secondsPerMinute.
```

Although this works, it is hard to read and hard to get right. It's much easier to use interim variables:

```
wastedByEachAdult = minDrinkingCoffee  +  minReadingNewspaper;
wastedByAllAdults =  wastedByEachAdult * numAdults;
wastedByEachKid = minDawdling  + minArguing;
wastedByAllKids =  wastedByEachKid * numChildren;
wastedByFamily = wastedByAllAdults + wastedByAllKids;
totalSeconds =  wastedByFamily * 60;
```

The latter example uses many more interim variables, but it is far easier to read, understand, and (most important) debug. As you step through this program in your debugger, you can see the interim values and make sure they are correct.

The Ternary Operator

Although most operators require one term (e.g., myValue++) or two terms (e.g., a+b), there is one operator that has three: the ternary operator (?:):

```
conditional-expression ? expression1 : expression2
```

This operator evaluates a *conditional expression* (an expression that returns a value of type bool), and then invokes either expression1 if the value returned from the conditional expression is true, or expression2 if the value returned is false. The logic is "if this is true, do the first; otherwise do the second." Example 3-18 illustrates.

Example 3-18. The ternary operator

```
#region Using directives

using System;
using System.Collections.Generic;
using System.Text;

#endregion
```

Example 3-18. The ternary operator (continued)

```
namespace TernaryOperator
{
    class TernaryOperator
    {
        static void Main( string[] args )
        {
            int valueOne = 10;
            int valueTwo = 20;

            int maxValue = valueOne > valueTwo ? valueOne : valueTwo;

            Console.WriteLine( "ValueOne: {0}, valueTwo: {1}, maxValue: {2}",
                valueOne, valueTwo, maxValue );

        }
    }
}
```

```
Output:
ValueOne: 10, valueTwo: 20, maxValue: 20
```

In Example 3-18, the ternary operator is being used to test whether valueOne is greater than valueTwo. If so, the value of valueOne is assigned to the integer variable maxValue; otherwise the value of valueTwo is assigned to maxValue.

Preprocessor Directives

In the examples you've seen so far, you've compiled your entire program whenever you compiled any of it. At times, however, you might want to compile only parts of your program—for example, depending on whether you are debugging or building your production code.

Before your code is compiled, another program called the *preprocessor* runs and prepares your program for the compiler. The preprocessor examines your code for special preprocessor directives, all of which begin with the pound sign (#). These directives allow you to define identifiers and then test for their existence.

Defining Identifiers

#define DEBUG defines a preprocessor identifier, DEBUG. Although other preprocessor directives can come anywhere in your code, identifiers must be defined before any other code, including using statements.

C and C++ programmer take note: the C# preprocessor implements only a subset of the C++ preprocessor and doesn't support macros.

You can test whether DEBUG has been defined with the #if statement. Thus, you can write:

```
#define DEBUG

//... some normal code - not affected by preprocessor

#if DEBUG
   // code to include if debugging
#else
   // code to include if not debugging
#endif

//... some normal code - not affected by preprocessor
```

When the preprocessor runs, it sees the #define statement and records the identifier DEBUG. The preprocessor skips over your normal C# code and then finds the #if - #else - #endif block.

The #if statement tests for the identifier DEBUG, which does exist, and so the code between #if and #else is compiled into your program—but the code between #else and #endif is *not* compiled. That code doesn't appear in your assembly at all; it is as if it were left out of your source code.

Had the #if statement failed—that is, if you had tested for an identifier that did not exist—the code between #if and #else would not be compiled, but the code between #else and #endif would be compiled.

 Any code not surrounded by #if/#endif is not affected by the preprocessor and is compiled into your program.

Undefining Identifiers

Undefine an identifier with #undef. The preprocessor works its way through the code from top to bottom, so the identifier is defined from the #define statement until the #undef statement, or until the program ends. Thus, if you write:

```
#define DEBUG

#if DEBUG
   // this code will be compiled
#endif

#undef DEBUG

#if DEBUG
   // this code will not be compiled
#endif
```

the first #if will succeed (DEBUG is defined), but the second will fail (DEBUG has been undefined).

#if, #elif, #else, and #endif

There is no switch statement for the preprocessor, but the #elif and #else directives provide great flexibility. The #elif directive allows the else-if logic of "if DEBUG then action one, else if TEST then action two, else action three":

```
#if DEBUG
    // compile this code if debug is defined
#elif TEST
    // compile this code if debug is not defined
    // but TEST is defined
#else
   // compile this code if neither DEBUG nor TEST
   // is defined
#endif
```

In this example, the preprocessor first tests to see if the identifier DEBUG is defined. If it is, the code between #if and #elif will be compiled, and the rest of the code until #endif will not be compiled.

If (and only if) DEBUG is not defined, the preprocessor next checks to see if TEST is defined. Note that the preprocessor will not check for TEST unless DEBUG is not defined. If TEST is defined, the code between the #elif and the #else directives will be compiled. If it turns out that neither DEBUG nor TEST is defined, the code between the #else and the #endif statements will be compiled.

#region

The #region preprocessor directive marks an area of text with a comment. The principal use of this preprocessor directive is to allow tools such as Visual Studio .NET to mark off areas of code and collapse them in the editor with only the region's comment showing.

For example, when you create a Windows application (covered in Chapter 13), Visual Studio creates a region for code generated by the designer. When the region is expanded, it looks like Figure 3-3. (Note: I've added the rectangle and highlighting to make it easier to find the region.)

You can see the region marked by the #region and #endregion preprocessor directives. When the region is collapsed, however, all you see is the region comment (Windows Form Designer generated code), as shown in Figure 3-4.

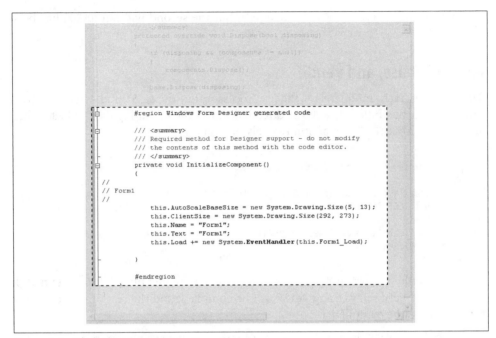

Figure 3-3. Expanding the Visual Studio code region

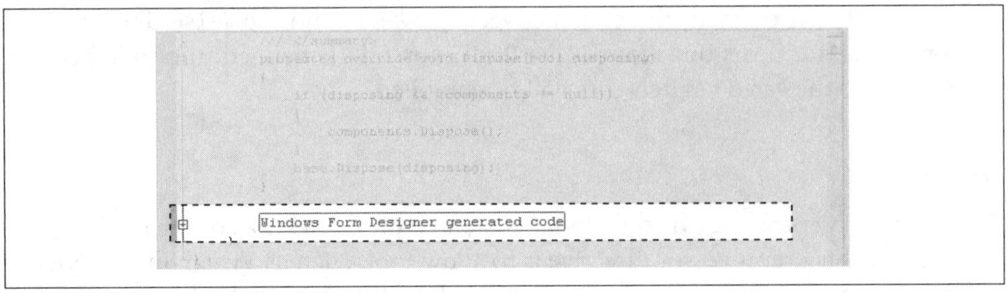

```
         Windows Form Designer generated code
```

Figure 3-4. Code region is collapsed

CHAPTER 4

Classes and Objects

Chapter 3 discussed the myriad primitive types built into the C# language, such as int, long, and char. The heart and soul of C#, however, is the ability to create new, complex, programmer-defined types that map cleanly to the objects that make up the problem you are trying to solve.

It is this ability to create new types that characterizes an object-oriented language. You specify new types in C# by declaring and defining classes. You can also define types with interfaces, as you will see in Chapter 8. Instances of a class are called *objects*. Objects are created in memory when your program executes.

The difference between a class and an object is the same as the difference between the concept of a dog and the particular dog who is sitting at your feet as you read this. You can't play fetch with the definition of a dog, only with an instance.

A Dog class describes what dogs are like: they have weight, height, eye color, hair color, disposition, and so forth. They also have actions they can take, such as eat, walk, bark, and sleep. A particular dog (such as my dog Milo) has a specific weight (62 pounds), height (22 inches), eye color (black), hair color (yellow), disposition (angelic), and so forth. He is capable of all the actions of any dog (though if you knew him you might imagine that eating is the only method he implements).

The huge advantage of classes in object-oriented programming is that they encapsulate the characteristics and capabilities of an entity in a single, self-contained, and self-sustaining *unit of code*. When you want to sort the contents of an instance of a Windows listbox control, for example, tell the listbox to sort itself. How it does so is of no concern; *that* it does so is all you need to know. Encapsulation, along with polymorphism and inheritance, is one of three cardinal principles of object-oriented programming.

An old programming joke asks, how many object-oriented programmers does it take to change a light bulb? Answer: none, you just tell the light bulb to change itself. (Alternate answer: none, Microsoft has changed the standard to darkness.)

This chapter explains the C# language features that are used to specify new classes. The elements of a class—its behaviors and properties—are known collectively as its *class members*. This chapter will show how methods are used to define the behaviors of the class, and how the state of the class is maintained in member variables (often called *fields*). In addition, this chapter introduces *properties*, which act like methods to the developer of the class but look like fields to clients of the class.

Defining Classes

To define a new type or class, first declare it, and then define its methods and fields. Declare a class using the class keyword. The complete syntax is as follows:

```
[attributes] [access-modifiers] class identifier [:base-class [,interface(s)]]
{class-body}
```

Attributes are covered in Chapter 8; access modifiers are discussed in the next section. (Typically, your classes will use the keyword public as an access modifier.) The identifier is the name of the class that you provide. The optional base-class is discussed in Chapter 5. The member definitions that make up the class-body are enclosed by open and closed curly braces ({}).

C and C++ programmers take note: a C# class definition doesn't end with a semicolon, though if you add one, the program will still compile.

In C#, everything happens within a class. So far, however, we've not *instantiated* any instances of that class; that is, we haven't created any objects. What is the difference between a class and an instance of that class? To answer that question, start with the distinction between the *type* int and a *variable* of type int. Thus, while you would write:

```
int myInteger = 5;
```

you wouldn't write:

```
int = 5;
```

You can't assign a value to a type; instead, you assign the value to an object of that type (in this case, a variable of type int).

When you declare a new class, you define the properties of all objects of that class, as well as their behaviors. For example, if you are creating a windowing environment, you might want to create screen widgets (more commonly known as controls in Windows programming) to simplify user interaction with your application. One control of interest might be a listbox, which is very useful for presenting a list of choices to the user and enabling the user to select from the list.

Listboxes have a variety of characteristics—for example, height, width, location, and text color. Programmers have also come to expect certain behaviors of listboxes: they can be opened, closed, sorted, and so on.

Object-oriented programming allows you to create a new type, ListBox, which encapsulates these characteristics and capabilities. Such a class might have member variables named height, width, location, and text_color, and member methods named sort(), add(), remove(), etc.

You can't assign data to the ListBox type. Instead you must first create an object of that type, as in the following code snippet:

```
ListBox myListBox;
```

Once you create an instance of ListBox, you can assign data to its fields.

Now consider a class to keep track of and display the time of day. The internal state of the class must be able to represent the current year, month, date, hour, minute, and second. You probably would also like the class to display the time in a variety of formats. You might implement such a class by defining a single method and six variables, as shown in Example 4-1.

Example 4-1. Simple Time class

```
#region Using directives

using System;
using System.Collections.Generic;
using System.Text;

#endregion

namespace TimeClass
{
    public class Time
    {
        // private variables
        int Year;
        int Month;
        int Date;
        int Hour;
        int Minute;
        int Second;

        // public methods
        public void DisplayCurrentTime()
        {
            Console.WriteLine(
                "stub for DisplayCurrentTime" );
        }
    }

    public class Tester
```

Example 4-1. Simple Time class (continued)

```
{
    static void Main()
    {
        Time t = new Time();
        t.DisplayCurrentTime();
    }
}
}
```

 You will receive warnings when you compile this class that the member variables of Time (Year, Month, etc.) are never used. Please ignore these warnings for now (though it is generally not a good idea to ignore warnings unless you are certain you understand what they are and why they can be ignored). In this case, we are *stubbing out* the Time class and if this were a real class, we would make use of these members in other methods.

The only method declared within the Time class definition is DisplayCurrentTime(). The body of the method is defined within the class definition itself. Unlike other languages (such as C++), C# doesn't require that methods be declared before they are defined, nor does the language support placing its declarations into one file and code into another. (C# has no header files.) All C# methods are defined inline as shown in Example 4-1 with DisplayCurrentTime().

The DisplayCurrentTime() method is defined to return void; that is, it will not return a value to a method that invokes it. For now, the body of this method has been stubbed out.

The Time class definition ends with the declaration of a number of member variables: Year, Month, Date, Hour, Minute, and Second.

After the closing brace, a second class, Tester, is defined. Tester contains our now familiar Main() method. In Main(), an instance of Time is created and its address is assigned to object t. Because t is an instance of Time, Main() can make use of the DisplayCurrentTime() method available with objects of that type and call it to display the time:

```
    t.DisplayCurrentTime();
```

Access Modifiers

An *access modifier* determines which class methods of other classes can see and use a member variable or method within this class. Table 4-1 summarizes the C# access modifiers.

Table 4-1. Access modifiers

Access modifier	Restrictions
public	No restrictions. Members marked public are visible to any method of any class.
private	The members in class A that are marked private are accessible only to methods of class A.
protected	The members in class A that are marked protected are accessible to methods of class A and also to methods of classes *derived from* class A.
internal	The members in class A that are marked internal are accessible to methods of any class in A's assembly.
protected internal	The members in class A that are marked protected internal are accessible to methods of class A, to methods of classes *derived from* class A, and also to any class in A's assembly. This is effectively protected OR internal. (There is no concept of protected AND internal.)

It is generally desirable to designate the member variables of a class as private. This means that only member methods of that class can access their value. Because private is the default accessibility level, you don't need to make it explicit, but I recommend that you do so. Thus, in Example 4-1, the declarations of member variables should have been written as follows:

```
// private variables
private int Year;
private int Month;
private int Date;
private int Hour;
private int Minute;
private int Second;
```

The Tester class and DisplayCurrentTime() method are both declared public so that any other class can make use of them.

It is good programming practice to explicitly set the accessibility of all methods and members of your class. Although you can rely on the fact that class members are declared private by default, making their access explicit indicates a conscious decision and is self-documenting.

Method Arguments

Methods can take any number of parameters.[*] The parameter list follows the method name and is encased in parentheses, with each parameter preceded by its type. For example, the following declaration defines a method named MyMethod(), which returns void (that is, which returns no value at all) and which takes two parameters: an integer and a button.

---

[*] The terms "argument" and "parameter" are often used interchangeably, though some programmers insist on differentiating between the parameter declaration and the arguments passed in when the method is invoked.

```
void MyMethod (int firstParam, Button secondParam)
{
  // ...
}
```

Within the body of the method, the parameters act as local variables, as if you had declared them in the body of the method and initialized them with the values passed in. Example 4-2 illustrates how you pass values into a method—in this case, values of type int and float.

Example 4-2. Passing values into SomeMethod()

```
#region Using directives

using System;
using System.Collections.Generic;
using System.Text;

#endregion

namespace PassingValues
{
    public class MyClass
    {
        public void SomeMethod( int firstParam, float secondParam )
        {
            Console.WriteLine(
                "Here are the parameters received: {0}, {1}",
                firstParam, secondParam );
        }
    }

    public class Tester
    {
        static void Main()
        {
            int howManyPeople = 5;
            float pi = 3.14f;
            MyClass mc = new MyClass();
            mc.SomeMethod( howManyPeople, pi );
        }
    }
}
```

The method SomeMethod() takes an int and a float and displays them using Console. WriteLine(). The parameters, which are named firstParam and secondParam, are treated as local variables within SomeMethod().

VB6 programmers take note: C# methods don't allow you to declare optional arguments. Instead, you have to use method overloading to create methods that declare different combinations of arguments. For more information, see the section "Overloading Methods and Constructors" later in this chapter.

In the calling method (Main), two local variables (howManyPeople and pi) are created and initialized. These variables are passed as the parameters to SomeMethod(). The compiler maps howManyPeople to firstParam and pi to secondParam, based on their relative positions in the parameter list.

Creating Objects

In Chapter 3, a distinction was drawn between value types and reference types. The primitive C# types (int, char, etc.) are value types, and are created on the stack. Objects, however, are reference types, and are created on the heap, using the keyword new, as in the following:

```
Time t = new Time();
```

t doesn't actually contain the value for the Time object; it contains the address of that (unnamed) object that is created on the heap. t itself is just a reference to that object.

VB6 programmers take note: while there is a performance penalty in using the VB6 keywords Dim and New on the same line, in C# this penalty has been removed. Thus, in C# there is no drawback to using the new keyword when declaring an object variable.

Constructors

In Example 4-1, notice that the statement that creates the Time object looks as though it is invoking a method:

```
Time t = new Time();
```

In fact, a method *is* invoked whenever you instantiate an object. This method is called a *constructor*, and you must either define one as part of your class definition or let the CLR provide one on your behalf. The job of a constructor is to create the object specified by a class and to put it into a *valid* state. Before the constructor runs, the object is undifferentiated memory; after the constructor completes, the memory holds a valid instance of the class type.

The Time class of Example 4-1 doesn't define a constructor. If a constructor is not declared, the compiler provides one for you. The default constructor creates the object but takes no other action.

Member variables are initialized to innocuous values (integers to 0, strings to null, etc.).* Table 4-2 lists the default values assigned to primitive types.

Table 4-2. Primitive types and their default values

Type	Default value
numeric (int, long, etc.)	0
bool	false
char	'\0' (null)
enum	0
reference	null

Typically, you'll want to define your own constructor and provide it with arguments so that the constructor can set the initial state for your object. In Example 4-1, assume that you want to pass in the current year, month, date, and so forth, so that the object is created with meaningful data.

To define a constructor, declare a method whose name is the same as the class in which it is declared. Constructors have no return type and are typically declared public. If there are arguments to pass, define an argument list just as you would for any other method. Example 4-3 declares a constructor for the Time class that accepts a single argument, an object of type DateTime.

Example 4-3. Declaring a constructor

```
#region Using directives

using System;
using System.Collections.Generic;
using System.Text;

#endregion

namespace DeclaringConstructor
{
    public class Time
    {

        // private member variables
        int Year;
        int Month;
        int Date;
        int Hour;
```

---

* When you write your own constructor you'll find that these values have been initialized before the constructor runs. In a sense, there are two steps to building new objects—some CLR-level magic that zeros out all the fields and does whatever else needs to be done to make the thing a valid object, and then the steps in the constructor you create (if any).

Example 4-3. Declaring a constructor (continued)

```
        int Minute;
        int Second;

        // public accessor methods
        public void DisplayCurrentTime()
        {
            System.Console.WriteLine( "{0}/{1}/{2} {3}:{4}:{5}",
                Month, Date, Year, Hour, Minute, Second );
        }

        // constructor
        public Time( System.DateTime dt )
        {

            Year = dt.Year;
            Month = dt.Month;
            Date = dt.Day;
            Hour = dt.Hour;
            Minute = dt.Minute;
            Second = dt.Second;
        }
    }

    public class Tester
    {
        static void Main()
        {
            System.DateTime currentTime = System.DateTime.Now;
            Time t = new Time( currentTime );
            t.DisplayCurrentTime();
        }
    }
}
```

Output:
11/16/2005 16:21:40

In this example, the constructor takes a DateTime object and initializes all the member variables based on values in that object. When the constructor finishes, the Time object exists and the values have been initialized. When DisplayCurrentTime() is called in Main(), the values are displayed.

Try commenting out one of the assignments and running the program again. You'll find that the member variable is initialized by the compiler to 0. Integer member variables are set to 0 if you don't otherwise assign them. Remember, value types (e.g., integers) can't be *uninitialized*; if you don't tell the constructor what to do, it will try for something innocuous.

In Example 4-3, the DateTime object is created in the Main() method of Tester. This object, supplied by the System library, offers a number of public values—Year, Month,

Day, Hour, Minute, and Second—that correspond directly to the private member variables of the Time object. In addition, the DateTime object offers a static member property, Now, which is a reference to an instance of a DateTime object initialized with the current time.

Examine the highlighted line in Main(), where the DateTime object is created by calling the static property Now. Now creates a DateTime value which, in this case, gets copied to the currentTime variable on the stack.

The currentTime variable is passed as a parameter to the Time constructor. The Time constructor parameter, dt, is a copy of the DateTime object.

Initializers

It is possible to initialize the values of member variables in an *initializer*, instead of having to do so in every constructor. Create an initializer by assigning an initial value to a class member:

```
private int Second  = 30;  // initializer
```

Assume that the semantics of our Time object are such that no matter what time is set, the seconds are always initialized to 30. We might rewrite the Time class to use an initializer so that no matter which constructor is called, the value of Second is always initialized, either explicitly by the constructor or implicitly by the initializer. See Example 4-4.

 Example 4-4 uses an *overloaded* constructor, which means there are two versions of the constructor that differ by the number and type of parameters. Overloading constructors is explained in detail later in this chapter.

Example 4-4. Using an initializer

```
#region Using directives

using System;
using System.Collections.Generic;
using System.Text;

#endregion

namespace Initializer
{
    public class Time
    {
        // private member variables
        private int Year;
        private int Month;
        private int Date;
        private int Hour;
```

Example 4-4. Using an initializer (continued)

```csharp
    private int Minute;
    private int Second = 30;  // initializer

    // public accessor methods
    public void DisplayCurrentTime()
    {
        System.DateTime now = System.DateTime.Now;
        System.Console.WriteLine(
        "\nDebug\t: {0}/{1}/{2} {3}:{4}:{5}",
        now.Month, now.Day, now.Year, now.Hour,
            now.Minute, now.Second );

        System.Console.WriteLine( "Time\t: {0}/{1}/{2} {3}:{4}:{5}",
            Month, Date, Year, Hour, Minute, Second );
    }

    // constructors
    public Time( System.DateTime dt )
    {

        Year = dt.Year;
        Month = dt.Month;
        Date = dt.Day;
        Hour = dt.Hour;
        Minute = dt.Minute;
        Second = dt.Second;    //explicit assignment

    }

    public Time( int Year, int Month, int Date,
            int Hour, int Minute )
    {
        this.Year = Year;
        this.Month = Month;
        this.Date = Date;
        this.Hour = Hour;
        this.Minute = Minute;
    }

}

public class Tester
{
    static void Main()
    {
        System.DateTime currentTime = System.DateTime.Now;
        Time t = new Time( currentTime );
        t.DisplayCurrentTime();

        Time t2 = new Time( 2005, 11, 18, 11, 45 );
        t2.DisplayCurrentTime();
```

Example 4-4. Using an initializer (continued)

```
        }
    }
}
```

```
Output:
Debug    : 11/27/2005 7:52:54
Time     : 11/27/2005 7:52:54

Debug    : 11/27/2005 7:52:54
Time     : 11/18/2005 11:45:30
```

If you don't provide a specific initializer, the constructor will initialize each integer member variable to zero (0). In the case shown, however, the Second member is initialized to 30:

```
private int Second = 30;  // initializer
```

If a value is not passed in for Second, its value will be set to 30 when t2 is created:

```
Time t2 = new Time(2005,11,18,11,45);
t2.DisplayCurrentTime();
```

However, if a value is assigned to Second, as is done in the constructor (which takes a DateTime object, shown in bold), that value overrides the initialized value.

The first time we invoke DisplayCurrentTime(), we call the constructor that takes a DateTime object, and the seconds are initialized to 54. The second time the method is invoked, we explicitly set the time to 11:45 (not setting the seconds), and the initializer takes over.

If the program didn't have an initializer and did not otherwise assign a value to Second, the value would be initialized by the CLR to 0.

 C++ programmers take note: C# doesn't have a copy constructor, and the semantics of copying are accomplished by implementing the ICloneable interface.

The ICloneable Interface

The .NET Framework defines an ICloneable interface to support the concept of a copy constructor. (Interfaces are covered in detail in Chapter 8.) This interface defines a single method: Clone(). Classes that support the idea of a copy constructor should implement ICloneable and then should implement either a shallow copy (calling MemberwiseClone) or a deep copy (e.g., by calling the copy constructor and hand-copying all the members).

```
class SomeType: ICloneable
{
   public Object Clone()
   {
```

```
        return MemberwiseClone(); // shallow copy
    }
}
```

The this Keyword

The keyword this refers to the current instance of an object. The this reference (sometimes referred to as a *this pointer*[*]) is a hidden reference passed to every non-static method of a class. Each method can refer to the other methods and variables of that object by way of the this reference.

The this reference is typically used in a number of ways. The first way is to qualify instance members otherwise hidden by parameters, as in the following:

```
public void SomeMethod (int hour)
{
    this.hour = hour;
}
```

In this example, SomeMethod() takes a parameter (hour) with the same name as a member variable of the class. The this reference is used to resolve the name ambiguity. While this.hour refers to the member variable, hour refers to the parameter.

The argument in favor of this style is that you pick the right variable name and then use it for both the parameter and the member variable. The counter argument is that using the same name for both the parameter and the member variable can be confusing.

The second use of the this reference is to pass the current object as a parameter to another method. For instance:

```
class myClass
{
    public void Foo(OtherClass otherObject)
    {
        otherObject.Bar(this);
    }
}
```

Let's unpack this example. Here we have a method named myClass.Foo. In the body of this method, you invoke the Bar method of the OtherClass instance, passing in a reference to the current instance of myClass. This allows the Bar method to fiddle with the public methods and members of the current instance of myClass.

The third use of this is with indexers, covered in Chapter 9.

---

[*] A pointer is a variable that holds the address of an object in memory. C# doesn't use pointers with managed objects. Some C++ programmers have become so used to talking about a this pointer that they've carried the term over (incorrectly) to C#. We'll refer to the this reference, and pay a $0.25 fine to charity each time we forget.

The fourth use of the this reference is to call one overloaded constructor from another, for example:

```
class myClass
{
    public myClass(int i) { //... }
    public myClass() : this(42) { //... }
}
```

In this example, the default constructor invokes the overloaded constructor that takes an integer, by using the this keyword.

The final way that the this keyword is used is to explicitly invoke methods and members of a class, as a form of documentation:

```
public void MyMethod(int y)
{
    int x = 0;
    x = 7;        // assign to a local variable
    y = 8;        // assign to a parameter
    this.z = 5;   // assign to a  member variable
    this.Draw(); // invoke member method
}
```

In the cases shown, the use of the this reference is superfluous, but may make the intent of the programmer clearer and does no harm (except, arguably, to clutter the code).

Using Static Members

The members of a class (variables, methods, events, indexers, etc.) can be either *instance members* or *static members*. Instance members are associated with instances of a type, while static members are considered to be part of the class. You access a static member through the name of the class in which it is declared. For example, suppose you have a class named Button and have instantiated objects of that class named btnUpdate and btnDelete.[*] Suppose as well that the Button class has a static method SomeMethod(). To access the static method, you write:

```
Button.SomeMethod();
```

rather than:

```
btnUpdate.SomeMethod();
```

In C#, it is not legal to access a static method or member variable through an instance, and trying to do so will generate a compiler error (C++ programmers, take note).

---

[*] As noted earlier, btnUpdate and btnDelete are actually variables that refer to the unnamed instances on the heap. For simplicity we'll refer to these as the names of the objects, keeping in mind that this is just short-hand for "the name of the variables that refer to the unnamed instances on the heap."

Some languages distinguish between class methods and other (global) methods that are available outside the context of any class. In C# there are no global methods, only class methods, but you can achieve an analogous result by defining static methods within your class.

> VB6 programmers take note: don't confuse the static keyword in C# with the Static keyword in VB6 and VB.NET. In VB, the Static keyword declares a variable that is available only to the method it was declared in. In other words, the Static variable is not shared among different objects of its class (i.e., each Static variable instance has its own value). However, this variable exists for the life of the program, which allows its value to persist from one method call to another.
>
> In C#, the static keyword indicates a class member. In VB, the equivalent keyword is Shared.

Static methods act more or less like global methods, in that you can invoke them without actually having an instance of the object at hand. The advantage of static methods over global, however, is that the name is scoped to the class in which it occurs, and thus you don't clutter up the global namespace with myriad function names. This can help manage highly complex programs, and the name of the class acts very much like a namespace for the static methods within it.

In addition, static methods may be passed instance members as parameters (or may create such instances themselves within the static method). Because they are scoped to the class, instead of being scoped globally, they have access to the private members of the instances.

> Resist the temptation to create a single class in your program in which you stash all your miscellaneous methods. It is possible but not desirable and undermines the encapsulation of an object-oriented design.

Invoking Static Methods

The Main() method is static. Static methods are said to operate on the class, rather than on an instance of the class. They don't have a this reference, as there is no instance to point to.

> Java programmers take note: in C#, calling static methods through instance variables is not permitted.

Static methods can't directly access nonstatic members. For Main() to call a nonstatic method, it must instantiate an object. Consider Example 4-2 shown earlier.

`SomeMethod()` is a nonstatic method of `MyClass`. For `Main()` to access this method, it must first instantiate an object of type `MyClass` and then invoke the method through that object.

Using Static Constructors

If your class declares a static constructor, you are guaranteed that the static constructor will run before any instance of your class is created.*

 You can't control exactly when a static constructor will run, but you do know that it will be after the start of your program and before the first instance is created. Because of this, you can't assume (or determine) whether an instance is being created.

For example, you might add the following static constructor to the `Time` class from Example 4-4:

```
static Time()
{
    Name = "Time";
}
```

Notice that there is no access modifier (e.g., `public`) before the static constructor. Access modifiers aren't allowed on static constructors. In addition, because this is a static member method, you can't access nonstatic member variables, and so `Name` must be declared a static member variable:

```
private static string Name;
```

The final change is to add a line to `DisplayCurrentTime()`, as in the following:

```
public void DisplayCurrentTime()
{
    System.Console.WriteLine("Name: {0}", Name);
    System.Console.WriteLine("{0}/{1}/{2} {3}:{4}:{5}",
        Month, Date, Year, Hour, Minute, Second);
}
```

When all these changes are made, the output is:

```
Name: Time
11/27/2005 7:52:54
Name: Time
11/18/2005 11:45:30
```

---

* Actually, the CLR guarantees to start running the static constructor before *anything* else is done with your class. However, it only guarantees to *start* running the static constructor; it doesn't actually guarantee to *finish* running it. It is possible to concoct a pathological case where two classes have a circular dependency on each other. Rather than deadlock, the CLR can run the constructors on different threads so that it meets the minimal guarantee of at least starting to run both constructors in the right order.

(Your output will vary depending on the date and time you run this code.)

Although this code works, it isn't necessary to create a static constructor to accomplish this goal. You can, instead, use an initializer:

```
private static string Name = "Time";
```

which accomplishes the same thing. Static constructors are useful, however, for setup work that can't be accomplished with an initializer and that needs to be done only once.

 Java programmers take note: in C#, a static constructor will serve where a static initializer would be used in Java.

For example, assume you have an unmanaged bit of code in a legacy DLL. You want to provide a class wrapper for this code. You can call LoadLibrary in your static constructor and initialize the jump table in the static constructor. Handling legacy code and interoperating with unmanaged code is discussed in Chapter 22.

Static Classes

In C#, there are no global methods or constants. You might find yourself creating small utility classes that exist only to hold static members. Setting aside whether this is a good design, if you create such a class you won't want any instances created. Mark your class Static to ensure that no instance of the class may be created. Static classes are sealed, and thus you may not create derived types of a Static class. Note, however, that static classes may not contain nonstatic members or have a constructor.

Using Static Fields

A common way to demonstrate the use of static member variables is to keep track of the number of instances that currently exist for your class. Example 4-5 illustrates.

Example 4-5. Using static fields for instance counting

```
#region Using directives

using System;
using System.Collections.Generic;
using System.Text;

#endregion

namespace StaticFields
{
   public class Cat
   {
```

Example 4-5. Using static fields for instance counting (continued)

```
    private static int instances = 0;

    public Cat()
    {
        instances++;
    }

    public static void HowManyCats()
    {
        Console.WriteLine( "{0} cats adopted",
            instances );
    }
}

public class Tester
{
    static void Main()
    {
        Cat.HowManyCats();
        Cat frisky = new Cat();
        Cat.HowManyCats();
        Cat whiskers = new Cat();
        Cat.HowManyCats();
    }
}
}
```

```
Output:
0 cats adopted
1 cats adopted
2 cats adopted
```

The Cat class has been stripped to its absolute essentials. A static member variable called instances is created and initialized to 0. Note that the static member is considered part of the class, not a member of an instance, and so it can't be initialized by the compiler on creation of an instance. Thus, if you want to initialize a static member, you must provide an explicit initializer. When additional instances of Cats are created (in a constructor), the count is incremented.

Static Methods to Access Static Fields

It is undesirable to make member data public. This applies to static member variables as well. One solution is to make the static member private, as we've done here with instances. We have created a public accessor method, HowManyCats(), to provide access to this private member.

Destroying Objects

Since C# provides garbage collection, you never need to explicitly destroy your objects. However, if your object controls unmanaged resources, you will need to explicitly free those resources when you are done with them. Implicit control over unmanaged resources is provided by a *destructor*, which will be called by the garbage collector when your object is destroyed.

 C and C++ programmers take note: a destructor is not necessarily called when an object goes out of scope, but rather, when it is garbage-collected (which may happen much later). This is known as *nondeterministic finalization.*

The destructor should only release resources that your object holds on to, and should not reference other objects. Note that if you have only managed references, you don't need to and should not implement a destructor; you want this only for handling unmanaged resources. Because there is some cost to having a destructor, you ought to implement this only on methods that require it (that is, methods that consume valuable unmanaged resources).

You can't call an object's destructor directly. The garbage collector will call it for you.

How Destructors Work

The garbage collector maintains a list of objects that have a destructor. This list is updated every time such an object is created or destroyed.

When an object on this list is first collected, it is placed in a queue with other objects waiting to be destroyed. After the destructor executes, the garbage collector then collects the object and updates the queue, as well as its list of destructible objects.

The C# Destructor

C#'s destructor looks, syntactically, much like a C++ destructor, but it behaves quite differently. Declare a C# destructor with a tilde as follows:

```
~MyClass(){}
```

In C#, this syntax is simply a shortcut for declaring a `Finalize()` method that chains up to its base class. Thus, when you write:

```
~MyClass()
{
    // do work here
}
```

the C# compiler translates it to:

```
protected override void Finalize()
{
    try
    {
        // do work here.
    }
    finally
    {
        base.Finalize();
    }
}
```

Destructors Versus Dispose

It is not legal to call a destructor explicitly. Your destructor will be called by the garbage collector. If you do handle precious unmanaged resources (such as file handles) that you want to close and dispose of as quickly as possible, you ought to implement the IDisposable interface.* (You will learn more about interfaces in Chapter 8.) The IDisposable interface requires its implementers to define one method, named Dispose(), to perform whatever cleanup you consider to be crucial. The availability of Dispose() is a way for your clients to say, "Don't wait for the destructor to be called, do it right now."

If you provide a Dispose() method, you should stop the garbage collector from calling your object's destructor. To do so, call the static method GC.SuppressFinalize(), passing in the this pointer for your object. Your destructor can then call your Dispose() method. Thus, you might write:

```
using System;
class Testing : IDisposable
{
    bool is_disposed = false;
    protected virtual void Dispose(bool disposing)
    {
        if (!is_disposed) // only dispose once!
        {
            if (disposing)
            {
                Console.WriteLine(
                    "Not in destructor, OK to reference other objects");
            }
            // perform cleanup for this object
            Console.WriteLine("Disposing...");
```

---

* Most of the time you will not write classes that deal with unmanaged resources such as raw handles directly. You may, however, use wrapper classes like FileStream or Socket, but these classes do implement IDisposable, in which case you ought to have your class implement IDisposable (but not a finalizer). Your Dispose method will call Dispose on any disposable resources that you're using.

```
      }
      this.is_disposed = true;
    }

    public void Dispose()
    {
      Dispose(true);
      // tell the GC not to finalize
      GC.SuppressFinalize(this);
    }

    ~Testing()
    {
      Dispose(false);
      Console.WriteLine("In destructor.");
    }
  }
}
```

Implementing the Close() Method

For some objects, you may prefer to have your clients call a method named Close().
(For example, Close() may make more sense than Dispose() for file objects.) You can
implement this by creating a private Dispose() method and a public Close() method
and having your Close() method invoke Dispose().

The using Statement

To make it easier for your clients to properly dispose your objects, C# provides a
using statement that ensures that Dispose() will be called at the earliest possible
time. The idiom is to declare the objects you are using and then to create a scope for
these objects with curly braces. When the close brace is reached, the Dispose()
method will be called on the object automatically, as illustrated in Example 4-6.

Example 4-6. The using statement

```
#region Using directives

using System;
using System.Collections.Generic;
using System.Drawing;
using System.Text;

#endregion

namespace usingStatement
{
   class Tester
   {
      public static void Main()
      {
         using ( Font theFont = new Font( "Arial", 10.0f ) )
```

Example 4-6. The using statement (continued)

```
      {
          // use theFont

      }   // compiler will call Dispose on theFont

      Font anotherFont = new Font( "Courier", 12.0f );

      using ( anotherFont )
      {
          // use anotherFont

      } // compiler calls Dispose on anotherFont
    }
  }
}
```

In the first part of this example, the Font object is created within the using statement. When the using statement ends, Dispose() is called on the Font object.

In the second part of the example, a Font object is created outside of the using statement. When we decide to use that font, we put it inside the using statement; when that statement ends, Dispose() is called once again.

This second approach is fraught with danger. If an exception is thrown after the object is created but before the using block is begun, the object will not be disposed. Second, the variable remains in scope after the using block ends, but if it is accessed it will fail.

The using statement also protects you against unanticipated exceptions. Regardless of how control leaves the using statement, Dispose() is called. An implicit try-finally block is created for you. (See Chapter 11 for details.)

Passing Parameters

By default, value types are passed into methods by value. (See the section entitled "Method Arguments," earlier in this chapter.) This means that when a value object is passed to a method, a temporary copy of the object is created within that method. Once the method completes, the copy is discarded. Although passing by value is the normal case, there are times when you will want to pass value objects by reference. C# provides the ref parameter modifier for passing value objects into a method by reference, and the out modifier for those cases in which you want to pass in a ref variable without first initializing it. C# also supports the params modifier, which allows a method to accept a variable number of parameters. The params keyword is discussed in Chapter 9.

Passing by Reference

Methods can return only a single value (though that value can be a collection of values). Let's return to the Time class and add a GetTime() method, which returns the hour, minutes, and seconds.

 Java programmers take note: in C#, there's no need for wrapper classes for basic types like int (integer). Instead, use reference parameters.

Because we can't return three values, perhaps we can pass in three parameters, let the method modify the parameters, and examine the result in the calling method. Example 4-7 shows a first attempt at this.

Example 4-7. Returning values in parameters

```
#region Using directives

using System;
using System.Collections.Generic;
using System.Text;

#endregion

namespace ReturningValuesInParams
{
    public class Time
    {
        // private member variables
        private int Year;
        private int Month;
        private int Date;
        private int Hour;
        private int Minute;
        private int Second;

        // public accessor methods
        public void DisplayCurrentTime()
        {
            System.Console.WriteLine( "{0}/{1}/{2} {3}:{4}:{5}",
                Month, Date, Year, Hour, Minute, Second );
        }

        public int GetHour()
        {
            return Hour;
        }

        public void GetTime( int h, int m, int s )
        {
            h = Hour;
            m = Minute;
```

Example 4-7. Returning values in parameters (continued)

```
            s = Second;
        }

        // constructor
        public Time( System.DateTime dt )
        {

            Year = dt.Year;
            Month = dt.Month;
            Date = dt.Day;
            Hour = dt.Hour;
            Minute = dt.Minute;
            Second = dt.Second;
        }
    }

    public class Tester
    {
        static void Main()
        {
            System.DateTime currentTime = System.DateTime.Now;
            Time t = new Time( currentTime );
            t.DisplayCurrentTime();

            int theHour = 0;
            int theMinute = 0;
            int theSecond = 0;
            t.GetTime( theHour, theMinute, theSecond );
            System.Console.WriteLine( "Current time: {0}:{1}:{2}",
                    theHour, theMinute, theSecond );
        }
    }
}
```

```
Output:
11/17/2005 13:41:18
Current time: 0:0:0
```

Notice that the Current time in the output is 0:0:0. Clearly, this first attempt did not work. The problem is with the parameters. We pass in three integer parameters to GetTime(), and we modify the parameters in GetTime(), but when the values are accessed back in Main(), they are unchanged. This is because integers are value types, and so are passed by value; a copy is made in GetTime(). What we need is to pass these values by reference.

Two small changes are required. First, change the parameters of the GetTime() method to indicate that the parameters are ref (reference) parameters:

```
    public void GetTime(ref int h, ref int m, ref int s)
    {
        h = Hour;
```

```
        m = Minute;
        s = Second;
    }
```

Second, modify the call to GetTime() to pass the arguments as references as well:

```
    t.GetTime(ref theHour, ref theMinute, ref theSecond);
```

If you leave out the second step of marking the arguments with the keyword ref, the compiler will complain that the argument can't be converted from an int to a ref int.

The results now show the correct time. By declaring these parameters to be ref parameters, you instruct the compiler to pass them by reference. Instead of a copy being made, the parameter in GetTime() is a reference to the same variable (theHour) that is created in Main(). When you change these values in GetTime(), the change is reflected in Main().

Keep in mind that ref parameters are references to the actual original value: it is as if you said, "Here, work on this one." Conversely, value parameters are copies: it is as if you said, "Here, work on one *just like* this."

Overcoming Definite Assignment with out Parameters

C# imposes *definite assignment*, which requires that all variables be assigned a value before they are used. In Example 4-7, if you don't initialize theHour, theMinute, and theSecond before you pass them as parameters to GetTime(), the compiler will complain. Yet the initialization that is done merely sets their values to 0 before they are passed to the method:

```
    int theHour = 0;
    int theMinute = 0;
    int theSecond = 0;
    t.GetTime( ref theHour, ref theMinute, ref theSecond);
```

It seems silly to initialize these values because you immediately pass them by reference into GetTime where they'll be changed, but if you don't, the following compiler errors are reported:

```
    Use of unassigned local variable 'theHour'
    Use of unassigned local variable 'theMinute'
    Use of unassigned local variable 'theSecond'
```

C# provides the out parameter modifier for this situation. The out modifier removes the requirement that a reference parameter be initialized. The parameters to GetTime(), for example, provide no information to the method; they are simply a mechanism for getting information out of it. Thus, by marking all three as out parameters, you eliminate the need to initialize them outside the method. Within the called method, the out parameters must be assigned a value before the method returns. The following are the altered parameter declarations for GetTime().

```
public void GetTime(out int h, out int m, out int s)
{
    h = Hour;
    m = Minute;
    s = Second;
}
```

and here is the new invocation of the method in Main():

```
t.GetTime( out theHour, out theMinute, out theSecond);
```

To summarize, value types are passed into methods by value. ref parameters are used to pass value types into a method by reference. This allows you to retrieve their modified value in the calling method. out parameters are used only to return information from a method. Example 4-8 rewrites Example 4-7 to use all three.

Example 4-8. Using in, out, and ref parameters

```
#region Using directives

using System;
using System.Collections.Generic;
using System.Text;

#endregion

namespace InOutRef
{
    public class Time
    {
        // private member variables
        private int Year;
        private int Month;
        private int Date;
        private int Hour;
        private int Minute;
        private int Second;

        // public accessor methods
        public void DisplayCurrentTime()
        {
            System.Console.WriteLine( "{0}/{1}/{2} {3}:{4}:{5}",
                Month, Date, Year, Hour, Minute, Second );
        }

        public int GetHour()
        {
            return Hour;
        }

        public void SetTime( int hr, out int min, ref int sec )
        {
            // if the passed in time is >= 30
            // increment the minute and set second to 0
```

Example 4-8. Using in, out, and ref parameters (continued)

```
        // otherwise leave both alone
        if ( sec >= 30 )
        {
            Minute++;
            Second = 0;
        }
        Hour = hr; // set to value passed in

        // pass the minute and second back out
        min = Minute;
        sec = Second;
    }

    // constructor
    public Time( System.DateTime dt )
    {
        Year = dt.Year;
        Month = dt.Month;
        Date = dt.Day;
        Hour = dt.Hour;
        Minute = dt.Minute;
        Second = dt.Second;
    }
}

public class Tester
{
    static void Main()
    {
        System.DateTime currentTime = System.DateTime.Now;
        Time t = new Time( currentTime );
        t.DisplayCurrentTime();

        int theHour = 3;
        int theMinute;
        int theSecond = 20;

        t.SetTime( theHour, out theMinute, ref theSecond );
        System.Console.WriteLine(
            "the Minute is now: {0} and {1} seconds",
                theMinute, theSecond );

        theSecond = 40;
        t.SetTime( theHour, out theMinute, ref theSecond );
        System.Console.WriteLine( "the Minute is now: " +
            "{0} and {1} seconds",
                theMinute, theSecond );
    }
}
```

Example 4-8. Using in, out, and ref parameters (continued)

```
Output:
11/17/2005 14:6:24
the Minute is now: 6 and 24 seconds
the Minute is now: 7 and 0 seconds
```

SetTime is a bit contrived, but it illustrates the three types of parameters. theHour is passed in as a value parameter; its entire job is to set the member variable Hour, and no value is returned using this parameter.

The ref parameter theSecond is used to set a value in the method. If theSecond is greater than or equal to 30, the member variable Second is reset to 0 and the member variable Minute is incremented.

 You must specify ref on both the call and the destination when using reference parameters.

Finally, theMinute is passed into the method only to return the value of the member variable Minute, and thus is marked as an out parameter.

It makes perfect sense that theHour and theSecond must be initialized; their values are needed and used. It is not necessary to initialize theMinute, as it is an out parameter that exists only to return a value. What at first appeared to be arbitrary and capricious rules now make sense; values are required to be initialized only when their initial value is meaningful.

Overloading Methods and Constructors

Often you'll want to have more than one function with the same name. The most common example of this is to have more than one constructor. In the examples shown so far, the constructor has taken a single parameter: a DateTime object. It would be convenient to be able to set new Time objects to an arbitrary time by passing in year, month, date, hour, minute, and second values. It would be even more convenient if some clients could use one constructor, and other clients could use the other constructor. Function overloading provides for exactly these contingencies.

The *signature* of a method is defined by its name and its parameter list. Two methods differ in their signatures if they have different names or different parameter lists. Parameter lists can differ by having different numbers or types of parameters. For example, in the following code the first method differs from the second in the number of parameters, and the second differs from the third in the types of parameters:

```
void myMethod(int p1);
void myMethod(int p1, int p2);
void myMethod(int p1, string s1);
```

A class can have any number of methods, as long as each one's signature differs from that of all the others.

Example 4-9 illustrates our Time class with two constructors: one that takes a DateTime object, and the other that takes six integers.

Example 4-9. Overloading the constructor

```
#region Using directives

using System;
using System.Collections.Generic;
using System.Text;

#endregion

namespace OverloadedConstructor
{
    public class Time
    {
        // private member variables
        private int Year;
        private int Month;
        private int Date;
        private int Hour;
        private int Minute;
        private int Second;

        // public accessor methods
        public void DisplayCurrentTime()
        {
            System.Console.WriteLine( "{0}/{1}/{2} {3}:{4}:{5}",
                Month, Date, Year, Hour, Minute, Second );
        }

        // constructors
        public Time( System.DateTime dt )
        {
            Year = dt.Year;
            Month = dt.Month;
            Date = dt.Day;
            Hour = dt.Hour;
            Minute = dt.Minute;
            Second = dt.Second;
        }

        public Time( int Year, int Month, int Date,
            int Hour, int Minute, int Second )
        {
            this.Year = Year;
            this.Month = Month;
            this.Date = Date;
            this.Hour = Hour;
```

Example 4-9. Overloading the constructor (continued)

```
            this.Minute = Minute;
            this.Second = Second;
        }
    }

    public class Tester
    {
        static void Main()
        {
            System.DateTime currentTime = System.DateTime.Now;

            Time t1 = new Time( currentTime );
            t.DisplayCurrentTime();

            Time t2 = new Time( 2005, 11, 18, 11, 03, 30 );
            t2.DisplayCurrentTime();

        }
    }
}
```

As you can see, the Time class in Example 4-9 has two constructors. If a function's signature consisted only of the function name, the compiler would not know which constructors to call when constructing t1 and t2. However, because the signature includes the function argument types, the compiler is able to match the constructor call for t1 with the constructor whose signature requires a DateTime object. Likewise, the compiler is able to associate the t2 constructor call with the constructor method whose signature specifies six integer arguments.

When you overload a method, you must change the signature (i.e., the name, number, or type of the parameters). You are free, as well, to change the return type, but this is optional. Changing only the return type doesn't overload the method, and creating two methods with the same signature but differing return types will generate a compile error (see Example 4-10).

Example 4-10. Varying the return type on overloaded methods

```
#region Using directives

using System;
using System.Collections.Generic;
using System.Text;

#endregion

namespace VaryingReturnType
{
    public class Tester
    {
        private int Triple( int val )
```

Example 4-10. Varying the return type on overloaded methods (continued)

```
    {
       return 3 * val;
    }

    private long Triple( long val )
    {
       return 3 * val;
    }

    public void Test()
    {
       int x = 5;
       int y = Triple( x );
       System.Console.WriteLine( "x: {0}  y: {1}", x, y );

       long lx = 10;
       long ly = Triple( lx );
       System.Console.WriteLine( "lx: {0}  ly: {1}", lx, ly );

    }
    static void Main()
    {
       Tester t = new Tester();
       t.Test();
    }
  }
}
```

In this example, the Tester class overloads the Triple() method, one to take an integer, the other to take a long. The return type for the two Triple() methods varies. Although this is not required, it is very convenient in this case.

Encapsulating Data with Properties

Properties allow clients to access class state as if they were accessing member fields directly, while actually implementing that access through a class method.

This is ideal. The client wants direct access to the state of the object and doesn't want to work with methods. The class designer, however, wants to hide the internal state of his class in class members, and provide indirect access through a method.

By decoupling the class state from the method that accesses that state, the designer is free to change the internal state of the object as needed. When the Time class is first created, the Hour value might be stored as a member variable. When the class is redesigned, the Hour value might be computed or retrieved from a database. If the client had direct access to the original Hour member variable, the change to computing the value would break the client. By decoupling and forcing the client to go through a method (or property), the Time class can change how it manages its internal state without breaking client code.

Properties meet both goals: they provide a simple interface to the client, appearing to be a member variable. They are implemented as methods, however, providing the data-hiding required by good object-oriented design, as illustrated in Example 4-11.

Example 4-11. Using a property

```
#region Using directives

using System;
using System.Collections.Generic;
using System.Text;

#endregion

namespace UsingAProperty
{
    public class Time
    {
        // private member variables
        private int year;
        private int month;
        private int date;
        private int hour;
        private int minute;
        private int second;

        // public accessor methods
        public void DisplayCurrentTime()
        {

            System.Console.WriteLine(
                "Time\t: {0}/{1}/{2} {3}:{4}:{5}",
                month, date, year, hour, minute, second );
        }

        // constructors
        public Time( System.DateTime dt )
        {
            year = dt.Year;
            month = dt.Month;
            date = dt.Day;
            hour = dt.Hour;
            minute = dt.Minute;
            second = dt.Second;
        }

        // create a property

        public int Hour
        {
```

Example 4-11. Using a property (continued)

```
        get
        {
           return hour;
        }

        set
        {
           hour = value;
        }
     }
   }

   public class Tester
   {
      static void Main()
      {
         System.DateTime currentTime = System.DateTime.Now;
         Time t = new Time( currentTime );
         t.DisplayCurrentTime();

         int theHour = t.Hour;
         System.Console.WriteLine( "\nRetrieved the hour: {0}\n",
            theHour );
         theHour++;
         t.Hour = theHour;
         System.Console.WriteLine( "Updated the hour: {0}\n", theHour );
      }
   }
}
```

To declare a property, write the property type and name followed by a pair of braces. Within the braces you may declare get and set accessors. Neither of these has explicit parameters, though the set() accessor has an implicit parameter value, as shown next.

In Example 4-11, Hour is a property. Its declaration creates two accessors: get and set:

```
   public int Hour
   {
      get
      {
         return hour;
      }

      set
      {
         hour = value;
      }
   }
```

Each accessor has an accessor body that does the work of retrieving and setting the property value. The property value might be stored in a database (in which case the accessor body would do whatever work is needed to interact with the database), or it might just be stored in a private member variable:

```
private int hour;
```

The get Accessor

The body of the get accessor is similar to a class method that returns an object of the type of the property. In the example, the accessor for Hour is similar to a method that returns an int. It returns the value of the private member variable in which the value of the property has been stored:

```
get
{
    return hour;
}
```

In this example, a local int member variable is returned, but you could just as easily retrieve an integer value from a database, or compute it on the fly.

Whenever you read the property the get accessor is invoked:

```
Time t = new Time(currentTime);
int theHour = t.Hour;
```

In this example, the value of the Time object's Hour property is retrieved, invoking the get accessor to extract the property, which is then assigned to a local variable.

The set Accessor

The set accessor sets the value of a property and is similar to a method that returns void. When you define a set accessor, you must use the value keyword to represent the argument whose value is passed to and stored by the property:

```
set
{
    hour = value;
}
```

Here, again, a private member variable is used to store the value of the property, but the set accessor could write to a database or update other member variables as needed.

When you assign a value to the property, the set accessor is automatically invoked, and the implicit parameter value is set to the value you assign:

```
theHour++;
t.Hour = theHour;
```

The two main advantages of this approach are that the client can interact with the properties directly, without sacrificing the data-hiding and encapsulation sacrosanct in good object-oriented design, and that the author of the property can ensure that the data provided is valid.

Property Access Modifiers

It is possible to set an access modifier (protected, internal, private) to modify access to either the get or set accessor. To do so, your property must have both a set and a get accessor, and you may modify only one or the other. Also, the modifier must be more restrictive than the accessibility level already on the property or the indexer (thus, you may add protected to the get or set accessor of a public property but not to a private property):

```
public string MyString
{
    protected get { return myString; }
             set { myString = value; }
}
```

In this example, access to the get accessor is restricted to methods of this class and classes derived from this class, while the set accessor is publicly visible.

 Note that you may not put an access modifier on an interface (see Chapter 8) nor on explicit interface member implementation. In addition, if you are overriding a virtual property or index (as discussed next), the access modifier *must* match the base property's access modifier.

readonly Fields

You might want to create a version of the Time class that is responsible for providing public static values representing the current time and date. Example 4-12 illustrates a simple approach to this problem.

Example 4-12. Using static public constants

```
#region Using directives

using System;
using System.Collections.Generic;
using System.Text;

#endregion

namespace StaticPublicConstants
{
    public class RightNow
```

Example 4-12. Using static public constants (continued)

```
    {
        // public member variables
        public static int Year;
        public static int Month;
        public static int Date;
        public static int Hour;
        public static int Minute;
        public static int Second;

        static RightNow()
        {
            System.DateTime dt = System.DateTime.Now;
            Year = dt.Year;
            Month = dt.Month;
            Date = dt.Day;
            Hour = dt.Hour;
            Minute = dt.Minute;
            Second = dt.Second;
        }
    }

    public class Tester
    {
        static void Main()
        {
            System.Console.WriteLine( "This year: {0}",
                    RightNow.Year.ToString() );
            RightNow.Year = 2006;
            System.Console.WriteLine( "This year: {0}",
                    RightNow.Year.ToString() );
        }
    }
}
```

```
Output:
This year: 2005
This year: 2006
```

This works well enough, until someone comes along and changes one of these values. As the example shows, the RightNow.Year value can be changed, for example, to 2006. This is clearly not what we'd like.

We'd like to mark the static values as constant, but that is not possible because we don't initialize them until the static constructor is executed. C# provides the keyword readonly for exactly this purpose. If you change the class member variable declarations as follows:

```
    public static readonly int Year;
    public static readonly int Month;
    public static readonly int Date;
```

```
public static readonly int Hour;
public static readonly int Minute;
public static readonly int Second;
```

then comment out the reassignment in Main():

```
// RightNow.Year = 2006; // error!
```

the program will compile and run as intended.

CHAPTER 5

Inheritance and Polymorphism

The previous chapter demonstrated how to create new types by declaring classes. The current chapter explores the relationship between objects in the real world and how to model these relationships in your code. This chapter focuses on *specialization*, which is implemented in C# through *inheritance*. This chapter also explains how instances of more specialized classes can be treated as if they were instances of more general classes, a process known as *polymorphism*. This chapter ends with a consideration of *sealed* classes, which can't be specialized; *abstract* classes, which exist only to be specialized; and a discussion of the root of all classes, the class Object.

 VB6 programmers take note: like VB.NET, C# provides full object-oriented technology, including inheritance, polymorphism, and encapsulation. These are relatively new topics for VB6 programmers. You should study them carefully; they affect your class and application design.

Specialization and Generalization

Classes and their instances (objects) don't exist in a vacuum, but rather, in a network of interdependencies and relationships, just as we, as social animals, live in a world of relationships and categories.

The *is-a* relationship is one of *specialization*. When we say that a dog *is-a* mammal, we mean that the dog is a specialized kind of mammal. It has all the characteristics of any mammal (it bears live young, nurses with milk, has hair), but it specializes these characteristics to the familiar characteristics of *canine domesticus*. A cat is also a mammal. As such, we expect it to share certain characteristics with the dog that are generalized in mammals, but to differ in those characteristics that are specialized in cats.

The specialization and generalization relationships are both reciprocal and hierarchical. They are reciprocal because specialization is the obverse side of the coin from generalization. Thus, dog and cat specialize mammal, and mammal generalizes from dog and cat.

These relationships are hierarchical because they create a relationship tree, with specialized types branching off from more generalized types. As you move up the hierarchy, you achieve greater *generalization*. You move up toward mammal to generalize that dogs and cats and horses all bear live young. As you move down the hierarchy, you specialize. Thus, the cat specializes mammal in having claws (a characteristic) and purring (a behavior).

Similarly, when you say that ListBox and Button *are* Controls you indicate that there are characteristics and behaviors of Controls that you expect to find in both of these types. In other words, Control generalizes the shared characteristics of both ListBox and Button, while each specializes its own particular characteristics and behaviors.

About the Unified Modeling Language

The Unified Modeling Language (UML) is a standardized "language" for describing a system or business. The part of the UML that is useful for the purposes of this chapter is the set of diagrams used to document the relationships between classes.

In the UML, classes are represented as boxes. The name of the class appears at the top of the box, and (optionally) methods and members can be listed in the sections within the box. In the UML, you model (for example) specialization relationships as shown in Figure 5-1. Note that the arrow points from the more specialized class up to the more general class.

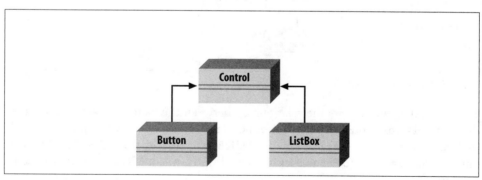

Figure 5-1. An is-a relationship

It is common to note that two classes share functionality, and then to factor out these commonalities into a shared base class. This provides you with easier-to-maintain code and greater reuse of common code. For example, suppose you started out creating a series of objects as illustrated in Figure 5-2.

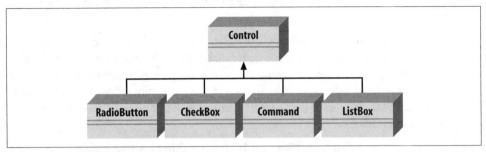

Figure 5-2. Deriving from Control

After working with RadioButtons, CheckBoxes, and Command buttons for a while, you realize that they share certain characteristics and behaviors that are more specialized than Control but more general than any of the three. You might factor these common traits and behaviors into a common base class, Button, and rearrange your inheritance hierarchy as shown in Figure 5-3. This is an example of how generalization is used in object-oriented development.

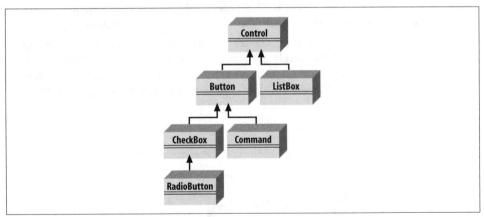

Figure 5-3. A more factored hierarchy

This UML diagram depicts the relationship between the factored classes and shows that both ListBox and Button derive from Control, and that Button is in turn specialized into CheckBox and Command. Finally, RadioButton derives from CheckBox. You can thus say that RadioButton is a CheckBox, which in turn is a Button, and that Buttons are Controls.

This is not the only, or even necessarily the best, organization for these objects, but it is a reasonable starting point for understanding how these types (classes) relate to one another.

Actually, although this might reflect how some widget hierarchies are organized, I'm very skeptical of any system in which the model doesn't reflect how I perceive reality. When I find myself saying that a RadioButton is a CheckBox, I have to think long and hard about whether that makes sense. I suppose a RadioButton *is* a kind of checkbox. It is a checkbox that supports the idiom of mutually exclusive choices. That said, it is a bit of a stretch and might be a sign of a shaky design.

Inheritance

In C#, the specialization relationship is typically implemented using inheritance. This is not the only way to implement specialization, but it is the most common and most natural way to implement this relationship.

Saying that ListBox inherits from (or derives from) Control indicates that it specializes Control. Control is referred to as the *base* class, and ListBox is referred to as the *derived* class. That is, ListBox derives its characteristics and behaviors from Control and then specializes to its own particular needs.

Implementing Inheritance

In C#, you create a derived class by adding a colon after the name of the derived class, followed by the name of the base class:

```
public class ListBox : Control
```

This code declares a new class, ListBox, that derives from Control. You can read the colon as "derives from."

C++ programmers take note: C# has no private or protected inheritance.

The derived class inherits all the members of the base class, both member variables and methods.

Polymorphism

There are two powerful aspects to inheritance. One is code reuse. When you create a ListBox class, you're able to reuse some of the logic in the base (Control) class.

What is arguably more powerful, however, is the second aspect of inheritance: *polymorphism*. *Poly* means many and *morph* means form. Thus, polymorphism refers to being able to use many forms of a type without regard to the details.

When the phone company sends your phone a ring signal, it doesn't know what type of phone is on the other end of the line. You might have an old-fashioned Western Electric phone that energizes a motor to ring a bell, or you might have an electronic phone that plays digital music.

As far as the phone company is concerned, it knows only about the "base type" Phone and expects that any "instance" of this type knows how to ring. When the phone company tells your phone to *ring*, it simply expects the phone to "do the right thing." Thus, the phone company treats your phone polymorphically.

Creating Polymorphic Types

Because a ListBox *is-a* Control and a Button *is-a* Control, we expect to be able to use either of these types in situations that call for a Control. For example, a form might want to keep a collection of all the instances of Control it manages so that when the form is opened, it can tell each of its Controls to draw itself. For this operation, the form doesn't want to know which elements are listboxes and which are buttons; it just wants to tick through its collection and tell each to "draw." In short, the form wants to treat all its Control objects polymorphically.

Creating Polymorphic Methods

To create a method that supports polymorphism, you need only mark it as virtual in its base class. For example, to indicate that the method DrawWindow() of class Control in Example 5-1 is polymorphic, simply add the keyword virtual to its declaration as follows:

```
public virtual void DrawWindow()
```

Now each derived class is free to implement its own version of DrawWindow(). To do so, simply override the base class virtual method by using the keyword override in the derived class method definition, and then add the new code for that overridden method.

In the following excerpt from Example 5-1 (which appears later in this section), ListBox derives from Control and implements its own version of DrawWindow():

```
public override void DrawWindow()
{
    base.DrawWindow();  // invoke the base method
    Console.WriteLine ("Writing string to the listbox: {0}",
        listBoxContents);
}
```

The keyword override tells the compiler that this class has intentionally overridden how DrawWindow() works. Similarly, you'll override this method in another class, Button, also derived from Control.

In the body of Example 5-1, you'll first create three objects: a Control, a ListBox, and a Button. You'll then call DrawWindow() on each:

```
Control win = new Control(1,2);
ListBox lb = new ListBox(3,4,"Stand alone list box");
Button b = new Button(5,6);
win.DrawWindow();
lb.DrawWindow();
b.DrawWindow();
```

This works much as you might expect. The correct DrawWindow() object is called for each. So far, nothing polymorphic has been done. The real magic starts when you create an array of Control objects. Because a ListBox *is-a* Control, you are free to place a ListBox into a Control array. You can also place a Button into an array of Control objects because a Button is also a Control:

```
Control[] winArray = new Control[3];
winArray[0] = new Control(1,2);
winArray[1] = new ListBox(3,4,"List box in array");
winArray[2] = new Button(5,6);
```

What happens when you call DrawWindow() on each object?

```
for (int i = 0;i < 3; i++)
{
    winArray[i].DrawWindow();
}
```

All the compiler knows is that it has three Control objects and that you've called DrawWindow() on each. If you had not marked DrawWindow as virtual, Control's DrawWindow() method would be called three times. However, because you did mark DrawWindow() as virtual, and because the derived classes override that method, when you call DrawWindow() on the array, the compiler determines the runtime type of the actual objects (a Control, a ListBox, and a Button) and calls the right method on each. This is the essence of polymorphism. The complete code for this example is shown in Example 5-1.

This listing uses an array, which is a collection of objects of the same type. Access the members of the array with the index operator:

```
// set the value of the element
// at offset 5
MyArray[5] = 7;
```

The first element in any array is at index 0. The use of the array in this example should be fairly intuitive. Arrays are explained in detail in Chapter 9.

Example 5-1. Using virtual methods

```
#region Using directives

using System;
using System.Collections.Generic;
using System.Text;

#endregion

namespace VirtualMethods
{
    public class Control
    {
        // these members are protected and thus visible
        // to derived class methods. We'll examine this
        // later in the chapter
        protected int top;
        protected int left;

        // constructor takes two integers to
        // fix location on the console
        public Control( int top, int left )
        {
            this.top = top;
            this.left = left;
        }

        // simulates drawing the window
        public virtual void DrawWindow()
        {
            Console.WriteLine( "Control: drawing Control at {0}, {1}",
                top, left );
        }
    }

// ListBox derives from Control
    public class ListBox : Control
    {
        private string listBoxContents;  // new member variable

        // constructor adds a parameter
        public ListBox(
            int top,
            int left,
            string contents ):
        base(top, left)  // call base constructor
        {

            listBoxContents = contents;
        }

// an overridden version (note keyword) because in the
        // derived method we change the behavior
```

Example 5-1. Using virtual methods (continued)

```
      public override void DrawWindow()
      {
         base.DrawWindow();   // invoke the base method
         Console.WriteLine( "Writing string to the listbox: {0}",
            listBoxContents );
      }
   }

   public class Button : Control
   {
      public Button(
         int top,
         int left ):
      base(top, left)
      {
      }


// an overridden version (note keyword) because in the
      // derived method we change the behavior
      public override void DrawWindow()
      {
         Console.WriteLine( "Drawing a button at {0}, {1}\n",
            top, left );
      }
   }

   public class Tester
   {
      static void Main()
      {
         Control win = new Control( 1, 2 );
         ListBox lb = new ListBox( 3, 4, "Stand alone list box" );
         Button b = new Button( 5, 6 );
         win.DrawWindow();
         lb.DrawWindow();
         b.DrawWindow();

         Control[] winArray = new Control[3];
         winArray[0] = new Control( 1, 2 );
         winArray[1] = new ListBox( 3, 4, "List box in array" );
         winArray[2] = new Button( 5, 6 );

         for ( int i = 0; i < 3; i++ )
         {
            winArray[i].DrawWindow();
         }
      }
   }
}
```

Example 5-1. Using virtual methods (continued)

```
Output:
Control: drawing Control at 1, 2
Control: drawing Control at 3, 4
Writing string to the listbox: Stand alone list box
Drawing a button at 5, 6

Control: drawing Control at 1, 2
Control: drawing Control at 3, 4
Writing string to the listbox: List box in array
Drawing a button at 5, 6
```

Note that throughout this example we've marked the new overridden methods with the keyword override:

> **public override void DrawWindow()**

The compiler now knows to use the overridden method when treating these objects polymorphically. The compiler is responsible for tracking the real type of the object and for handling the "late binding" so that it is `ListBox.DrawWindow()` that is called when the `Control` reference really points to a `ListBox` object.

 C++ programmers take note: you must explicitly mark the declaration of any method that overrides a virtual method with the keyword override.

Calling Base Class Constructors

In Example 5-1, the new class `ListBox` derives from `Control` and has its own constructor, which takes three parameters. The `ListBox` constructor invokes the constructor of its parent (`Control`) by placing a colon (:) after the parameter list and then invoking the base class with the keyword base:

```
public ListBox(
    int theTop,
    int theLeft,
    string theContents):
        base(theTop, theLeft)  // call base constructor
```

Because classes can't inherit constructors, a derived class must implement its own constructor and can only make use of the constructor of its base class by calling it explicitly.

If the base class has an accessible default constructor, the derived constructor is not required to invoke the base constructor explicitly; instead, the default constructor is called implicitly. However, if the base class doesn't have a default constructor, every derived constructor *must* explicitly invoke one of the base class constructors using the base keyword.

As discussed in Chapter 4, if you don't declare a constructor of any kind, the compiler will create a default constructor for you. Whether you write it yourself or you use the one provided "by default" by the compiler, a default constructor is one that takes no parameters. Note, however, that once you do create a constructor of any kind (with or without parameters), the compiler doesn't create a default constructor for you.

Controlling Access

The visibility of a class and its members can be restricted through the use of access modifiers, such as public, private, protected, internal, and protected internal. (See Chapter 4 for a discussion of access modifiers.)

As you've seen, public allows a member to be accessed by the member methods of other classes, while private indicates that the member is visible only to member methods of its own class. The protected keyword extends visibility to methods of derived classes, while internal extends visibility to methods of any class in the same assembly.*

The internal protected keyword pair allows access to members of the same assembly (internal) *or* derived classes (protected). You can think of this designation as internal *or* protected.

Classes as well as their members can be designated with any of these accessibility levels. If a class member has an access designation that is different from that of the class, the more restricted access applies. Thus, if you define a class, myClass, as follows:

```
public class myClass
{
    // ...
    protected int myValue;
}
```

the accessibility for myValue is protected even though the class itself is public. A *public class* is one that is visible to any other class that wishes to interact with it. Often, classes are created that exist only to help other classes in an assembly, and these classes might be marked internal rather than public.

Versioning with the new and override Keywords

In C#, the programmer's decision to override a virtual method is made explicit with the override keyword. This helps you release new versions of your code; changes to

---

* An assembly (discussed in Chapter 1) is the unit of sharing and reuse in the CLR (a logical DLL). Typically, an assembly is created from a collection of physical files, held in a single directory that includes all the resources (bitmaps, *.gif* files, etc.) required for an executable, along with the IL and metadata for that program.

the base class will not break existing code in the derived classes. The requirement to use the keyword override helps prevent that problem.

Here's how: assume for a moment that the Control base class of the previous example was written by Company A. Suppose also that the ListBox and RadioButton classes were written by programmers from Company B using a purchased copy of the Company A Control class as a base. The programmers in Company B have little or no control over the design of the Control class, including future changes that Company A might choose to make.

Now suppose that one of the programmers for Company B decides to add a Sort() method to ListBox:

```
public class ListBox : Control
{
    public virtual void Sort() {...}
}
```

This presents no problems until Company A, the author of Control, releases Version 2 of its Control class, and it turns out that the programmers in Company A have also added a Sort() method to their public class Control:

```
public class Control
{
    // ...
    public virtual void Sort() {...}
}
```

In other object-oriented languages (such as C++), the new virtual Sort() method in Control would now act as a base method for the virtual Sort() method in ListBox. The compiler would call the Sort() method in Control when you intend to call the Sort() in ListBox. In Java, if the Sort() in Control has a different return type, the class loader would consider the Sort() in ListBox to be an invalid override and would fail to load.

C# prevents this confusion. In C#, a virtual function is always considered to be the root of virtual dispatch; that is, once C# finds a virtual method, it looks no further up the inheritance hierarchy. If a new virtual Sort() function is introduced into Control, the runtime behavior of ListBox is unchanged.

When ListBox is compiled again, however, the compiler generates a warning:

```
...\class1.cs(54,24): warning CS0114: 'ListBox.Sort()' hides
inherited member 'Control.Sort()'.
To make the current member override that implementation,
add the override keyword. Otherwise add the new keyword.
```

To remove the warning, the programmer must indicate what he intends. He can mark the ListBox Sort() method new, to indicate that it is *not* an override of the virtual method in Control:

```
public class ListBox : Control
{
    public new virtual void Sort() {...}
```

This action removes the warning. If, on the other hand, the programmer does want to override the method in Control, he need only use the override keyword to make that intention explicit:

```
public class ListBox : Control
{
    public override void Sort() {...}
```

 To avoid this warning, it might be tempting to add the keyword new to all your virtual methods. This is a bad idea. When new appears in the code, it ought to document the versioning of code. It points a potential client to the base class to see what you aren't overriding. Using new scattershot undermines this documentation. Further, the warning exists to help identify a real issue.

Abstract Classes

Every subclass of Control *should* implement its own DrawWindow() method—but nothing requires that it do so. To require subclasses to implement a method of their base, you need to designate that method as *abstract*.

An abstract method has no implementation. It creates a method name and signature that must be implemented in all derived classes. Furthermore, making one or more methods of any class abstract has the side effect of making the class abstract.

Abstract classes establish a base for derived classes, but it is not legal to instantiate an object of an abstract class. Once you declare a method to be abstract, you prohibit the creation of any instances of that class.

Thus, if you were to designate DrawWindow() as abstract in the Control class, you could derive from Control, but you could not create any Control objects. Each derived class would have to implement DrawWindow(). If the derived class failed to implement the abstract method, that class would also be abstract, and again no instances would be possible.

Designating a method as abstract is accomplished by placing the keyword abstract at the beginning of the method definition, as follows:

```
abstract public void DrawWindow();
```

(Because the method can have no implementation, there are no braces; only a semicolon.)

If one or more methods are abstract, the class definition must also be marked abstract, as in the following:

```
abstract public class Control
```

Example 5-2 illustrates the creation of an abstract Control class and an abstract DrawWindow() method.

Example 5-2. Using an abstract method and class

```
#region Using directives

using System;
using System.Collections.Generic;
using System.Text;

#endregion

namespace abstractmethods
{
    using System;

    abstract public class Control
    {
        protected int top;
        protected int left;

        // constructor takes two integers to
        // fix location on the console
        public Control( int top, int left )
        {
            this.top = top;
            this.left = left;
        }

        // simulates drawing the window
        // notice: no implementation

        abstract public void DrawWindow();

    }

// ListBox derives from Control
    public class ListBox : Control
    {
        private string listBoxContents;  // new member variable

        // constructor adds a parameter
        public ListBox(
            int top,
            int left,
            string contents ):
        base(top, left)  // call base constructor
        {

            listBoxContents = contents;
        }
```

Example 5-2. Using an abstract method and class (continued)

```
      // an overridden version implementing the
      // abstract method

      public override void DrawWindow()
      {

         Console.WriteLine( "Writing string to the listbox: {0}",
            listBoxContents );
      }

   }

   public class Button : Control
   {
      public Button(
         int top,
         int left ):
      base(top, left)
      {
      }

      // implement the abstract method

      public override void DrawWindow()
      {
         Console.WriteLine( "Drawing a button at {0}, {1}\n",
            top, left );
      }

   }

   public class Tester
   {
      static void Main()
      {
         Control[] winArray = new Control[3];
         winArray[0] = new ListBox( 1, 2, "First List Box" );
         winArray[1] = new ListBox( 3, 4, "Second List Box" );
         winArray[2] = new Button( 5, 6 );

         for ( int i = 0; i < 3; i++ )
         {
            winArray[i].DrawWindow();
         }
      }
   }
}
```

In Example 5-2, the Control class has been declared abstract and therefore can't be
instantiated. If you replace the first array member:

```
   winArray[0] = new ListBox(1,2,"First List Box");
```

with this code:

```
winArray[0] = new Control(1,2);
```

the program generates the following error:

```
Cannot create an instance of the abstract class or interface 'abstractmethods.
Control'
```

You can instantiate the `ListBox` and `Button` objects because these classes override the abstract method, thus making the classes *concrete* (i.e., not abstract).

Limitations of Abstract

Although designating `DrawWindow()` as abstract does force all the derived classes to implement the method, this is a very limited solution to the problem. If we derive a class from `ListBox` (e.g., `DropDownListBox`), nothing forces that derived class to implement its own `DrawWindow()` method.

 C++ programmers take note: in C#, it is not possible for `Control. DrawWindow()` to provide an implementation, so we can't take advantage of the common `DrawWindow()` routines that might otherwise be shared by the derived classes.

Finally, abstract classes should not just be an implementation trick; they should represent the idea of an abstraction that establishes a "contract" for all derived classes. In other words, abstract classes describe the public methods of the classes that will implement the abstraction.

The idea of an abstract `Control` class ought to lay out the common characteristics and behaviors of all `Control`s, even if we never intend to instantiate the abstraction `Control` itself.

The idea of an abstract class is implied in the word "abstract." It serves to implement the abstraction "control" that will be manifest in the various concrete instances of `Control`, such as browser window, frame, button, listbox, or drop-down menu. The abstract class establishes what a `Control` is, even though we never intend to create a control *per se*. An alternative to using `abstract` is to define an interface, as described in Chapter 8.

Sealed Class

The obverse side of the design coin from abstract is *sealed*. Although an abstract class is intended to be derived from and to provide a template for its subclasses to follow, a sealed class doesn't allow classes to derive from it at all. Placed before the class declaration, the `sealed` keyword precludes derivation. Classes are most often marked `sealed` to prevent accidental inheritance.

Java programmers take note: a *sealed* class in C# is the equivalent of a *final* class in Java.

If the declaration of Control in Example 5-2 is changed from abstract to sealed (eliminating the abstract keyword from the DrawWindow() declaration as well), the program will fail to compile. If you try to build this project, the compiler will return the following error message:

```
'ListBox' cannot inherit from sealed class 'Control'
```

among many other complaints (such as that you can't create a new protected member in a sealed class).

The Root of All Classes: Object

All C# classes, of any type, are treated as if they ultimately derive from System. Object. Interestingly, this includes value types.

A base class is the immediate "parent" of a derived class. A derived class can be the base to further derived classes, creating an inheritance "tree" or hierarchy. A root class is the topmost class in an inheritance hierarchy. In C#, the root class is Object. The nomenclature is a bit confusing until you imagine an upside-down tree, with the root on top and the derived classes below. Thus, the base class is considered to be "above" the derived class.

 C++ *programmers take note:* C# uses single inheritance with a monolithic class hierarchy: every class inherits from a base class of Object, and multiple inheritance is not possible. However, C# interfaces provide many of the benefits of multiple inheritance. (See Chapter 8 for more information.)

Object provides a number of virtual methods that subclasses can and do override. These include Equals() to determine if two objects are the same; GetType(), which returns the type of the object (discussed in Chapter 8); and ToString(), which returns a string to represent the current object (discussed in Chapter 10). Table 5-1 summarizes the methods of Object.

Table 5-1. The methods of Object

Method	What it does
Equals()	Evaluates whether two objects are equivalent.
GetHashCode()	Allows objects to provide their own hash function for use in collections (see Chapter 9).
GetType()	Provides access to the type object (see Chapter 18).
ToString()	Provides a string representation of the object.

Table 5-1. The methods of Object (continued)

Method	What it does
Finalize()	Cleans up nonmemory resources; implemented by a destructor (see Chapter 4).
MemberwiseClone ()	Creates copies of the object; should never be implemented by your type.
ReferenceEquals()	Evaluates whether two objects refer to the same instance.

Example 5-3 illustrates the use of the ToString() method inherited from Object, as well as the fact that primitive datatypes such as int can be treated as if they inherit from Object. Note that the DisplayValue method expects an object, but works perfectly fine if you pass in an integer.

Example 5-3. Inheriting from Object

```
#region Using directives

using System;
using System.Collections.Generic;
using System.Text;

#endregion

namespace InheritingFromObject
{
    public class SomeClass
    {
        private int val;

        public SomeClass( int someVal )
        {
            val = someVal;
        }

        public override string ToString()
        {
            return val.ToString();
        }
    }

    public class Tester
    {
        static void DisplayValue( object o )
        {
            Console.WriteLine(
                "The value of the object passed in is {0}", o.ToString() );
        }

        static void Main()
        {
            int i = 5;
            Console.WriteLine( "The value of i is: {0}", i.ToString() );
            DisplayValue( i );
```

Example 5-3. Inheriting from Object (continued)

```
        SomeClass s = new SomeClass( 7 );
        Console.WriteLine( "The value of s is {0}", s.ToString() );
        DisplayValue( s );
    }
  }
}
```

```
Output:
The value of i is: 5
The value of the object passed in is 5
The value of s is 7
The value of the object passed in is 7
```

The documentation for Object.ToString() reveals its signature:

```
    public virtual string ToString();
```

It is a public virtual method that returns a string and that takes no parameters. All the built-in types, such as int, derive from Object and so can invoke Object's methods.

Example 5-3 overrides the virtual function for SomeClass, which is the usual case, so that the class' ToString() method will return a meaningful value. If you comment out the overridden function, the base method will be invoked, which will change the output to:

```
    The value of s is SomeClass
```

Thus, the default behavior is to return a string with the name of the class itself.

Classes don't need to explicitly declare that they derive from Object; the inheritance is implicit.

Boxing and Unboxing Types

Boxing and *unboxing* are the processes that enable value types (e.g., integers) to be treated as reference types (objects). The value is "boxed" inside an Object, and subsequently "unboxed" back to a value type.

 Java programmers take note: in Java, wrapping basic types in objects requires the explicit use of wrapper types like Integer and Float. In C#, the boxing mechanism takes care of all of this for you automatically; wrapper types are unnecessary.

Boxing Is Implicit

Boxing is an implicit conversion of a value type to the type Object. Boxing a value allocates an instance of the boxed type and copies the value into the new object instance, as shown in Figure 5-4.

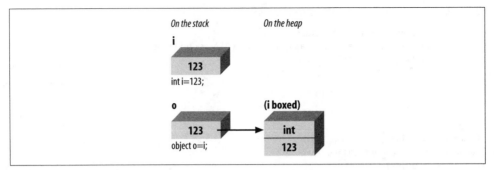

Figure 5-4. Boxing reference types

Boxing is implicit when you provide a value type where a reference is expected. For example, if you assign a primitive type, such as an integer to a variable of type Object (which is legal because int derives from Object), the value is boxed, as shown here:

```
using System;
class Boxing
{
    public static void Main()
    {
        int i = 123;
        Console.WriteLine("The object value = {0}", i);
    }
}
```

Console.WriteLine() expects an object, not an integer. To accommodate the method, the integer type is automatically boxed by the CLR, and ToString() is called on the resulting object. This feature allows you to create methods that take an object as a parameter; no matter what is passed in (reference or value type), the method will work.

Unboxing Must Be Explicit

To return the boxed object back to a value type, you must explicitly unbox it. You should accomplish this in two steps:

1. Make sure the object instance is a boxed value of the given value type.
2. Copy the value from the instance to the value-type variable.

Figure 5-5 illustrates.

For the unboxing to succeed, the object being unboxed must be of the appropriate type for the variable you are assigning it to. Boxing and unboxing are illustrated in Example 5-4.

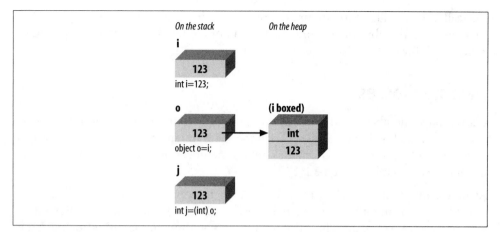

Figure 5-5. Boxing and then unboxing

Example 5-4. Boxing and unboxing

```
#region Using directives

using System;
using System.Collections.Generic;
using System.Text;

#endregion

namespace boxing
{
   public class UnboxingTest
   {
      public static void Main()
      {
         int i = 123;

         //Boxing
         object o = i;

         // unboxing (must be explicit)
         int j = ( int ) o;
         Console.WriteLine( "j: {0}", j );
      }
   }
}
```

Example 5-4 creates an integer i and implicitly boxes it when it is assigned to the object o. The value is then explicitly unboxed and assigned to a new int whose value is displayed.

Typically, you will wrap an unbox operation in a try block, as explained in Chapter 11. If the object being unboxed is null or a reference to an object of a different type, an InvalidCastException is thrown.

Nesting Classes

Classes have members, and it is entirely possible for the member of a class to be another user-defined type. Thus, a Button class might have a member of type Location, and a Location class might contain members of type Point. Finally, Point might contain members of type int.

At times, the contained class might exist only to serve the outer class, and there might be no reason for it to be otherwise visible. (In short, the contained class acts as a helper class.) You can define the helper class within the definition of the outer class. The contained, inner class is called a *nested* class, and the class that contains it is called, simply, the *outer* class.

Nested classes have the advantage of access to all the members of the outer class. A method of a nested class can access private members of the outer class.

> In addition, the nested class can be hidden from all other classes—that is, it can be private to the outer class.

Finally, a nested class that is public is accessed within the scope of the outer class. If Outer is the outer class, and Nested is the (public) inner class, refer to Nested as Outer.Nested, with the outer class acting (more or less) as a namespace or scope.

> *Java programmers take note:* nested classes are roughly equivalent to static inner classes; there is no C# equivalent to Java's nonstatic inner classes.

Example 5-5 features a nested class of Fraction named FractionArtist. The job of FractionArtist is to render the fraction on the console. In this example, the rendering is handled by a pair of simple WriteLine() statements.

Example 5-5. Using a nested class

```
#region Using directives

using System;
using System.Collections.Generic;
using System.Text;
```

Example 5-5. Using a nested class (continued)

```csharp
#endregion

namespace NestedClasses
{
    public class Fraction
    {
        private int numerator;
        private int denominator;

        public Fraction( int numerator, int denominator )
        {
            this.numerator = numerator;
            this.denominator = denominator;
        }

        public override string ToString()
        {
            return String.Format( "{0}/{1}",
                numerator, denominator );
        }

        internal class FractionArtist
        {
            public void Draw( Fraction f )
            {
                Console.WriteLine( "Drawing the numerator: {0}",
                    f.numerator );
                Console.WriteLine( "Drawing the denominator: {0}",
                    f.denominator );
            }
        }
    }

    public class Tester
    {
        static void Main()
        {
            Fraction f1 = new Fraction( 3, 4 );
            Console.WriteLine( "f1: {0}", f1.ToString() );

            Fraction.FractionArtist fa = new Fraction.FractionArtist();
            fa.Draw( f1 );
        }
    }
}
```

The nested class is shown in bold. The FractionArtist class provides only a single member, the Draw() method. What is particularly interesting is that Draw() has access to the private data members f.numerator and f.denominator, to which it wouldn't have had access if it weren't a nested class.

Notice in Main() that to declare an instance of this nested class, you must specify the type name of the outer class:

```
Fraction.FractionArtist fa = new Fraction.FractionArtist();
```

FractionArtist is scoped to within the Fraction class.

CHAPTER 6

Operator Overloading

It is a design goal of C# that user-defined classes can have all the functionality of built-in types. For example, suppose you have defined a type to represent fractions. Ensuring that this class has all the functionality of the built-in types means that you must be able to perform arithmetic on instances of your fractions (e.g., add two fractions, multiply, etc.) and convert fractions to and from built-in types such as integer (int). You could, of course, implement methods for each operation and invoke them by writing statements such as:

```
Fraction theSum = firstFraction.Add(secondFraction);
```

Although this will work, it is ugly and not how the built-in types are used. It would be much better to write:

```
Fraction theSum = firstFraction + secondFraction;
```

Statements like this are intuitive and consistent with how built-in types, such as int, are added.

In this chapter, you will learn techniques for adding standard operators to your user-defined types. You will also learn how to add conversion operators so that your user-defined types can be implicitly and explicitly converted to other types.

Using the operator Keyword

In C#, you implement operators by creating static methods whose return values represent the result of an operation and whose parameters are the operands. When you create an operator for a class you say you have "overloaded" that operator, much as you might overload any member method. Thus, to overload the addition operator (+), you would write:

```
public static Fraction operator+(Fraction lhs, Fraction rhs)
```

It is my convention to name the parameters lhs and rhs. The parameter name lhs stands for "lefthand side" and reminds me that the first parameter represents the lefthand side of the operation. Similarly, rhs stands for "righthand side."

The C# syntax for overloading an operator is to write the word operator followed by the operator to overload. The operator keyword is a method modifier. Thus, to overload the addition operator (+), write operator+.

When you write:

```
Fraction theSum = firstFraction + secondFraction;
```

the overloaded + operator is invoked, with the first Fraction passed as the first argument, and the second Fraction passed as the second argument. When the compiler sees the expression:

```
firstFraction + secondFraction
```

it translates that expression into:

```
Fraction.operator+(firstFraction, secondFraction)
```

The result is that a new Fraction is returned, which in this case is assigned to the Fraction object named theSum.

 C++ programmers take note: it is not possible to create nonstatic operators, and thus binary operators must take two operands.

Supporting Other .NET Languages

C# provides the ability to overload operators for your classes, even though this is not, strictly speaking, in the CLS. Other .NET languages, such as VB.NET, might not support operator overloading, and it is important to ensure that your class supports the alternative methods that these other languages might call to create the same effect.

Thus, if you overload the addition operator (+), you might also want to provide an add( ) method that does the same work. Operator overloading ought to be a syntactic shortcut, not the only path for your objects to accomplish a given task.

Creating Useful Operators

Operator overloading can make your code more intuitive and enable it to act more like the built-in types. It can also make your code unmanageable, complex, and obtuse if you break the common idiom for the use of operators. Resist the temptation to use operators in new and idiosyncratic ways.

For example, although it might be tempting to overload the increment operator (++) on an employee class to invoke a method incrementing the employee's pay level, this can create tremendous confusion for clients of your class. It is best to use operator overloading sparingly, and only when its meaning is clear and consistent with how the built-in classes operate.

Logical Pairs

It is quite common to overload the equality operator (==) to test whether two objects are equal (however equality might be defined for your object). C# insists that if you overload the equals operator, you must also overload the not-equals operator (!=). Similarly, the less-than (<) and greater-than (>) operators must be paired, as must the less-than or equals (<=) and greater-than or equals (>=) operators.

 C and C++ programmers take note: many C++ libraries require the implementation of only the < operator or the = operator, and other operations are derived from these. C# requires the implementation of both halves of these paired operators.

The Equality Operator

If you overload the equality operator (==), it is recommended that you also override the virtual Equals() method provided by object and route its functionality back to the equals operator. This allows your class to be polymorphic and provides compatibility with other .NET languages that don't overload operators (but do support method overloading). The FCL classes will not use the overloaded operators but will expect your classes to implement the underlying methods. The object class implements the Equals() method with this signature:

```
public virtual bool Equals(object o)
```

By overriding this method, you allow your Fraction class to act polymorphically with all other objects. Inside the body of Equals(), you will need to ensure that you are comparing with another Fraction, and if so you can pass the implementation along to the equals operator definition that you've written:

```
public override bool Equals(object o)
{
    if (! (o is Fraction) )
    {
        return false;
    }
    return this == (Fraction) o;
}
```

The is operator is used to check whether the runtime type of an object is compatible with the operand (in this case, Fraction). Thus, o is Fraction will evaluate true if o is in fact a type compatible with Fraction.

 The compiler will also expect you to override GetHashCode, as explained next.

Conversion Operators

C# converts int to long implicitly, and allows you to convert long to int explicitly. The conversion from int to long is *implicit* (it happens without requiring any special syntax) and is safe because you know that any int will fit into the memory representation of a long. The reverse operation, from long to int, must be *explicit* (using a cast operator) because it is possible to lose information in the conversion:

```
int myInt = 5;
long myLong;
myLong = myInt;        // implicit
myInt = (int) myLong;  // explicit
```

You must have the same functionality for your fractions. Given an int, you can support an implicit conversion to a fraction because any whole value is equal to that value over 1 (e.g., 15==15/1).

Given a fraction, you might want to provide an explicit conversion back to an integer, understanding that some value might be lost. Thus, you might convert 9/4 to the integer value 2.

When implementing your own conversions, the keyword implicit is used when the conversion is guaranteed to succeed and no information will be lost; otherwise explicit is used.

 Make sure to use implicit whenever you don't use explicit!

Example 6-1 illustrates how you might implement implicit and explicit conversions, and some of the operators of the Fraction class. (Although I've used Console. WriteLine() to print messages illustrating which method we're entering, the better way to pursue this kind of trace is with the debugger. You can place a breakpoint on each test statement, and then step into the code, watching the invocation of the constructors as they occur.) When you compile this example, it will generate some warnings because GetHashCode() is not implemented (see Chapter 9).

Example 6-1. Defining conversions and operators for the fraction class operators

```
public class Fraction
{
    private int numerator;
    private int denominator;

    public Fraction(int numerator, int denominator)
    {
        Console.WriteLine("In Fraction Constructor(int, int)");
        this.numerator=numerator;
        this.denominator=denominator;
    }

    public Fraction(int wholeNumber)
    {
        Console.WriteLine("In Fraction Constructor(int)");
        numerator = wholeNumber;
        denominator = 1;
    }

    public static implicit operator Fraction(int theInt)
    {
        Console.WriteLine("In implicit conversion to Fraction");
        return new Fraction(theInt);
    }

    public static explicit operator int(Fraction theFraction)
    {
        Console.WriteLine("In explicit conversion to int");
        return theFraction.numerator /
            theFraction.denominator;
    }

    public static bool operator==(Fraction lhs, Fraction rhs)
    {
        Console.WriteLine("In operator ==");
        if (lhs.denominator == rhs.denominator &&
            lhs.numerator == rhs.numerator)
        {
            return true;
        }
        // code here to handle unlike fractions
        return false;
    }

    public static bool operator !=(Fraction lhs, Fraction rhs)
    {
        Console.WriteLine("In operator !=");

        return !(lhs==rhs);
    }

    public override bool Equals(object o)
    {
```

Example 6-1. Defining conversions and operators for the fraction class operators (continued)

```
            Console.WriteLine("In method Equals");
            if (! (o is Fraction) )
            {
                return false;
            }
            return this == (Fraction) o;
        }

        public static Fraction operator+(Fraction lhs, Fraction rhs)
        {
            Console.WriteLine("In operator+");
            if (lhs.denominator == rhs.denominator)
            {
                return new Fraction(lhs.numerator+rhs.numerator,
                    lhs.denominator);
            }

            // simplistic solution for unlike fractions
            // 1/2 + 3/4 == (1*4) + (3*2) / (2*4) == 10/8
            int firstProduct = lhs.numerator * rhs.denominator;
            int secondProduct = rhs.numerator * lhs.denominator;
            return new Fraction(
                firstProduct + secondProduct,
                lhs.denominator * rhs.denominator
            );
        }

        public override string ToString()
        {
            String s = numerator.ToString() + "/" +
                denominator.ToString();
            return s;
        }
    }

public class Tester
{
    static void Main()
    {
        Fraction f1 = new Fraction(3,4);
        Console.WriteLine("f1: {0}", f1.ToString());

        Fraction f2 = new Fraction(2,4);
        Console.WriteLine("f2: {0}", f2.ToString());

        Fraction f3 = f1 + f2;
        Console.WriteLine("f1 + f2 = f3: {0}", f3.ToString());

        Fraction f4 = f3 + 5;
        Console.WriteLine("f3 + 5 = f4: {0}", f4.ToString());

        Fraction f5 = new Fraction(2,4);
        if (f5 == f2)
```

Example 6-1. Defining conversions and operators for the fraction class operators (continued)

```
        {
            Console.WriteLine("F5: {0} == F2: {1}",
                f5.ToString(),
                f2.ToString());
        }
    }
}
```

The Fraction class begins with two constructors. One takes a numerator and denominator, the other takes a whole number. The constructors are followed by the declaration of two conversion operators. The first conversion operator changes an integer into a Fraction:

```
public static implicit operator Fraction(int theInt)
{
    return new Fraction(theInt);
}
```

This conversion is marked implicit because any whole number (int) can be converted to a Fraction by setting the numerator to the int and the denominator to 1. Delegate this responsibility to the constructor that takes an int.

The second conversion operator is for the explicit conversion of Fractions into integers:

```
public static explicit operator int(Fraction theFraction)
{
    return theFraction.numerator /
        theFraction.denominator;
}
```

Because this example uses integer division, it will truncate the value. Thus, if the fraction is 15/16, the resulting integer value will be 0. A more sophisticated conversion operator might accomplish rounding.

The conversion operators are followed by the equals operator (==) and the not equals operator (!=). Remember that if you implement one of these equals operators, you must implement the other.

You have defined value equality for a Fraction such that the numerators and denominators must match. For this exercise, 3/4 and 6/8 aren't considered equal. Again, a more sophisticated implementation would reduce these fractions and notice the equality.

Include an override of the object class' Equals() method so that your Fraction objects can be treated polymorphically with any other object. Your implementation is to delegate the evaluation of equality to the equality operator.

A Fraction class would, no doubt, implement all the arithmetic operators (addition, subtraction, multiplication, division). To keep the illustration simple, implement only addition, and even here you simplify greatly. Check to see if the denominators are the same; if so, add the following numerators:

```
public static Fraction operator+(Fraction lhs, Fraction rhs)
{
    if (lhs.denominator == rhs.denominator)
    {
        return new Fraction(lhs.numerator+rhs.numerator,
            lhs.denominator);
    }
}
```

If the denominators aren't the same, cross multiply:

```
int firstProduct = lhs.numerator * rhs.denominator;
int secondProduct = rhs.numerator * lhs.denominator;
return new Fraction(
    firstProduct + secondProduct,
    lhs.denominator * rhs.denominator
);
```

This code is best understood with an example. If you were adding 1/2 and 3/4, you can multiply the first numerator (1) by the second denominator (4) and store the result (4) in firstProduct. You can also multiply the second numerator (3) by the first denominator (2) and store that result (6) in secondProduct. You add these products (6+4) to a sum of 10, which is the numerator for the answer. You then multiply the two denominators (2*4) to generate the new denominator (8). The resulting fraction (10/8) is the correct answer.[*]

Finally, you override ToString() so that Fraction can return its value in the format numerator/denominator:

```
public override string ToString()
{
    String s = numerator.ToString() + "/" +
        denominator.ToString();
    return s;
}
```

With your Fraction class in hand, you're ready to test. Your first tests create simple fractions, 3/4 and 2/4:

```
Fraction f1 = new Fraction(3,4);
Console.WriteLine("f1: {0}", f1.ToString());

Fraction f2 = new Fraction(2,4);
Console.WriteLine("f2: {0}", f2.ToString());
```

The output from this is what you would expect—the invocation of the constructors and the value printed in WriteLine():

---

[*] To recap: 1/2=4/8, 3/4=6/8, 4/8+6/8=10/8. The example doesn't reduce the fraction, to keep the code simple.

```
In Fraction Constructor(int, int)
f1: 3/4
In Fraction Constructor(int, int)
f2: 2/4
```

The next line in Main() invokes the static operator+. The purpose of this operator is to add two fractions and return the sum in a new fraction:

```
Fraction f3 = f1 + f2;
Console.WriteLine("f1 + f2 = f3: {0}", f3.ToString());
```

Examining the output reveals how operator+ works:

```
In operator+
In Fraction Constructor(int, int)
f1 + f2 = f3: 5/4
```

The operator+ is invoked, and then the constructor for f3, taking the two int values representing the numerator and denominator of the resulting new fraction.

The next test in Main() adds an int to the Fraction f3 and assigns the resulting value to a new Fraction, f4:

```
Fraction f4 = f3 + 5;
Console.WriteLine("f3 + 5: {0}", f4.ToString());
```

The output shows the steps for the various conversions:

```
In implicit conversion to Fraction
In Fraction Constructor(int)
In operator+
In Fraction Constructor(int, int)
f3 + 5 =  f4: 25/4
```

Notice that the implicit conversion operator was invoked to convert 5 to a fraction. In the return statement from the implicit conversion operator, the Fraction constructor was called, creating the fraction 5/1. This new fraction was then passed along with Fraction f3 to operator+, and the sum was passed to the constructor for f4.

In your final test, a new fraction (f5) is created. Test whether it is equal to f2. If so, print their values:

```
Fraction f5 = new Fraction(2,4);
if (f5 == f2)
{
    Console.WriteLine("F5: {0} == F2: {1}",
        f5.ToString(),
        f2.ToString());
}
```

The output shows the creation of f5, and then the invocation of the overloaded equals operator:

```
In Fraction Constructor(int, int)
In operator ==
F5: 2/4 == F2: 2/4
```

CHAPTER 7

Structs

A *struct* is a simple user-defined type, a lightweight alternative to a class. Structs are similar to classes in that they may contain constructors, properties, methods, fields, operators, nested types, and indexers (see Chapter 9).

There are also significant differences between classes and structs. For instance, structs don't support inheritance or destructors. More important, although a class is a reference type, a struct is a value type. (See Chapter 3 for more information about classes and types.) Thus, structs are useful for representing objects that don't require reference semantics.

The consensus view is that you ought to use structs only for types that are small, simple, and similar in their behavior and characteristics to built-in types.

> *C++ programmers take note:* the meaning of C#'s struct construct is very different from C++'s. In C++ a struct is exactly like a class, except that the visibility (public versus private) is different by default. In C#, structs are value types, while classes are reference types, and C# structs have other limitations as described in this chapter.

Structs are somewhat more efficient in their use of memory in arrays (see Chapter 9). However, they can be less efficient when used in some collections. Collections that take objects expect references, and structs must be boxed. There is overhead in boxing and unboxing, and classes might be more efficient in some large collections.

In this chapter, you will learn how to define and work with structs, and how to use constructors to initialize their values.

Defining Structs

The syntax for declaring a struct is almost identical to that for a class:

```
[attributes] [access-modifiers] struct identifier [:interface-list]
{ struct-members }
```

Example 7-1 illustrates the definition of a struct. Location represents a point on a two-dimensional surface. Notice that the struct Location is declared exactly as a class would be, except for the use of the keyword struct. Also notice that the Location constructor takes two integers and assigns their value to the instance members, xVal and yVal. The x and y coordinates of Location are declared as properties.

Example 7-1. Creating a struct

```
#region Using directives

using System;
using System.Collections.Generic;
using System.Text;

#endregion

namespace CreatingAStruct
{
    public struct Location
    {
        private int xVal;
        private int yVal;

        public Location( int xCoordinate, int yCoordinate )
        {
            xVal = xCoordinate;
            yVal = yCoordinate;
        }

        public int x
        {
            get
            {
                return xVal;
            }
            set
            {
                xVal = value;
            }
        }

        public int y
        {
            get
            {
                return yVal;
            }
            set
            {
                yVal = value;
            }
        }
```

Example 7-1. Creating a struct (continued)

```
    public override string ToString()
    {
        return ( String.Format( "{0}, {1}", xVal, yVal ) );
    }

}

public class Tester
{
    public void myFunc( Location loc )
    {
        loc.x = 50;
        loc.y = 100;
        Console.WriteLine( "In MyFunc loc: {0}", loc );
    }
    static void Main()
    {
        Location loc1 = new Location( 200, 300 );
        Console.WriteLine( "Loc1 location: {0}", loc1 );
        Tester t = new Tester();
        t.myFunc( loc1 );
        Console.WriteLine( "Loc1 location: {0}", loc1 );
    }
}
}
```

```
Output:
Loc1 location: 200, 300
In MyFunc loc: 50, 100
Loc1 location: 200, 300
```

Unlike classes, structs don't support inheritance. They implicitly derive from object (as do all types in C#, including the built-in types) but can't inherit from any other class or struct. Structs are also implicitly *sealed* (that is, no class or struct can derive from a struct). Like classes, however, structs can implement multiple interfaces. Additional differences include the following.

No destructor or custom default constructor

Structs can't have destructors, nor can they have a custom parameterless (default) constructor. If you don't have a constructor, the CLR will initialize your structure and zero out all the fields. If you do provide a nondefault constructor, the CLR initialization will not occur, and so you must initialize all the fields explicitly.

No initialization

You can't initialize an instance field in a struct. Thus, it is illegal to write:

```
    private int xVal = 50;
    private int yVal = 100;
```

though that would have been fine had this been a class.

Structs are designed to be simple and lightweight. While private member data promotes data-hiding and encapsulation, some programmers feel it is overkill for structs. They make the member data public, thus simplifying the implementation of the struct. Other programmers feel that properties provide a clean and simple interface, and that good programming practice demands data-hiding even with simple lightweight objects. With the new refactoring ability in Visual Studio, it's easy to turn your previously public variables into private variables with associated public properties. Just right-click on the variable, and choose Refactor → Encapsulate Field. Visual Studio will change your public variable to private and create a property with get and set accessors.

Creating Structs

Create an instance of a struct by using the new keyword in an assignment statement, just as you would for a class. In Example 7-1, the Tester class creates an instance of Location as follows:

```
Location loc1 = new Location(200,300);
```

Here the new instance is named loc1 and is passed two values, 200 and 300.

Structs as Value Types

The definition of the Tester class in Example 7-1 includes a Location object[*] struct (loc1) created with the values 200 and 300. This line of code calls the Location constructor:

```
Location loc1 = new Location(200,300);
```

Then WriteLine() is called:

```
Console.WriteLine("Loc1 location: {0}", loc1);
```

WriteLine() is expecting an object, but, of course, Location is a struct (a value type). The compiler automatically boxes the struct (as it would any value type), and it is the boxed object that is passed to WriteLine(). ToString() is called on the boxed object, and because the struct (implicitly) inherits from object, it is able to respond polymorphically, overriding the method just as any other object might:

```
Loc1 location: 200, 300
```

---

[*] Throughout this book, I use the term *object* to refer both to reference types and to value types. There is some debate in the object-oriented world about this, but I take solace in the fact that Microsoft has implemented the value types as if they inherited from the root class Object (and thus you may call all of Object's methods on any value type, including the built-in types such as int).

You can avoid this boxing by changing the preceding snippet to:

```
Console.WriteLine("Loc1 location: {0}",
    loc1.ToString());
```

You avoid the box operation by calling ToString directly on a variable of a value type where the value type provides an override of ToString.

Structs are value objects, however, and when passed to a function, they are passed by value—as seen in the next line of code, in which the loc1 object is passed to the myFunc() method:

```
t.myFunc(loc1);
```

In myFunc(), new values are assigned to x and y, and these new values are printed out:

```
Loc1 location: 50, 100
```

When you return to the calling function (Main()) and call WriteLine() again, the values are unchanged:

```
Loc1 location: 200, 300
```

The struct was passed as a value object, and a copy was made in myFunc(). Try changing the declaration to class:

```
public class Location
```

and run the test again. Here is the output:

```
Loc1 location: 200, 300
In MyFunc loc: 50, 100
Loc1 location: 50, 100
```

This time the Location object has reference semantics. Thus, when the values are changed in myFunc(), they are changed on the actual object back in Main().*

Creating Structs Without new

Because loc1 is a struct (not a class), it is created on the stack. Thus, in Example 7-1, when the new operator is called:

```
Location loc1 = new Location(200,300);
```

the resulting Location object is created on the stack.

The new operator calls the Location constructor. However, unlike with a class, it is possible to create a struct without using new at all. This is consistent with how built-in type variables (such as int) are defined, and is illustrated in Example 7-2.

---

* Another way to solve this problem is to use the keyword ref (as explained in the "Passing by Reference" section in Chapter 4), which allows you to pass a value type by reference.

A caveat: I am demonstrating how to create a struct without using new because it differentiates C# from C++ and also differentiates how C# treats classes versus structs. That said, however, creating structs without the keyword new brings little advantage and can create programs that are harder to understand, more error-prone, and more difficult to maintain. Proceed at your own risk.

Example 7-2. Creating a struct without using new

```
#region Using directives

using System;
using System.Collections.Generic;
using System.Text;

#endregion

namespace StructWithoutNew
{
    public struct Location
    {
        public int xVal;
        public int yVal;

        public Location( int xCoordinate, int yCoordinate )
        {
            xVal = xCoordinate;
            yVal = yCoordinate;
        }
        public int x
        {
            get
            {
                return xVal;
            }
            set
            {
                xVal = value;
            }
        }

        public int y
        {
            get
            {
                return yVal;
            }
            set
            {
                yVal = value;
            }
        }
```

Example 7-2. Creating a struct without using new (continued)

```
    public override string ToString()
    {
       return ( String.Format( "{0}, {1}", xVal, yVal ) );
    }
  }

  public class Tester
  {
     static void Main()
     {

         Location loc1;           // no call to the constructor

         loc1.xVal = 75;          // initialize the members
         loc1.yVal = 225;
         Console.WriteLine( loc1 );
     }
  }
}
```

In Example 7-2, you initialize the local variables directly, before calling a method of loc1 and before passing the object to WriteLine():

```
loc1.xVal = 75;
loc1.yVal = 225;
```

If you were to comment out one of the assignments and recompile:

```
static void Main()
{
    Location loc1;
    loc1.xVal = 75;
 //   loc1.yVal = 225;
    Console.WriteLine(loc1);
}
```

you would get a compiler error:

```
Use of unassigned local variable 'loc1'
```

Once you assign all the values, you can access the values through the properties x and y:

```
static void Main()
{
    Location loc1;
    loc1.xVal = 75;          // assign member variable
    loc1.yVal = 225;         // assign member variable
    loc1.x = 300;            // use property
    loc1.y = 400;            // use property
    Console.WriteLine(loc1);
}
```

Be careful when using properties. Although they allow you to support encapsulation by making the actual values private, the properties themselves are actually member methods, and you can't call a member method until you initialize all the member variables.

CHAPTER 8

Interfaces

An *interface* is a contract that guarantees to a client how a class or struct will behave. When a class (or struct) implements an interface, it tells any potential client "I guarantee I'll support the methods, properties, events, and indexers of the named interface." (See Chapter 4 for information about methods and properties, Chapter 12 for information about events, and Chapter 9 for coverage of indexers.)

An interface offers an alternative to an abstract class for creating contracts among classes and their clients. These contracts are made manifest using the interface keyword, which declares a reference type that encapsulates the contract.

When you define an interface, you may define methods, properties, indexers, and/or events that will be implemented by the class that implements the interface.

Interfaces are often compared to abstract classes. An abstract class serves as the base class for a family of derived classes, while interfaces are meant to be mixed in with other inheritance trees.

 For the rest of this chapter, wherever you see the word *class*, assume the text applies equally to structs, unless noted otherwise.

When a class implements an interface, it must implement all the parts of that interface (methods, properties, etc.); in effect, the class says "I agree to fulfill the contract defined by this interface."

 Java programmers take note: C# doesn't support the use of constant fields (member constants) in interfaces. The closest analog is the use of enumerated constants (enums).

You will remember from Chapter 5 that inheriting from an abstract class implements the *is-a* relationship. Implementing an interface, on the other hand, defines a different relationship that we've not seen until now, called (not surprisingly) the implements relationship. These two relationships are subtly different. A car *is-a* vehicle, but it might *implement* the CanBeBoughtWithABigLoan capability (as can a house, for example).

Mix-ins

In Somerville, Massachusetts, there was, at one time, an ice cream parlor where you could have candies and other goodies "mixed in" with your chosen ice cream flavor. This seemed like a good metaphor to some of the object-oriented pioneers from nearby MIT who were working on the fortuitously named SCOOPS programming language. They appropriated the term "mix in" for classes that mixed in additional capabilities. C++ includes a number of mix-in classes as well. These mix-in or capability classes serve much the same role as interfaces do in C#.

In this chapter, you will learn how to create, implement, and use interfaces. You'll learn how to implement multiple interfaces, and how to combine and extend interfaces, as well as how to test whether a class has implemented an interface.

Defining and Implementing an Interface

The syntax for defining an interface is as follows:

```
[attributes] [access-modifier] interface interface-name[:base-list] {interface-body}
```

Don't worry about attributes for now; they're covered in Chapter 18.

Access modifiers, including public, private, protected, internal, and protected internal, were discussed in Chapter 4.

The interface keyword is followed by the name of the interface. It is common (but not required) to begin the name of your interface with a capital I (thus, IStorable, ICloneable, IClaudius, etc.).

The base-list lists the interfaces that this interface extends (as described in the next section, "Implementing More Than One Interface").

The interface-body describes the methods, properties, and so forth that must be implemented by the implementing class.

Suppose you wish to create an interface that describes the methods and properties a class needs, to be stored to and retrieved from a database or other storage such as a file. You decide to call this interface IStorable.

In this interface you might specify two methods: Read() and Write(), which appear in the interface-body.

```
interface IStorable
{
    void Read();
    void Write(object);
}
```

The purpose of an interface is to define the capabilities that you want to have available in a class.

For example, you might create a class, Document. It turns out that Document types can be stored in a database, so you decide to have Document implement the IStorable interface.

To do so, use the same syntax as if the new Document class were inheriting from IStorable—a colon (:), followed by the interface name:

```
public class Document : IStorable
{
    public void Read() {...}
    public void Write(object obj) {...}
    // ...
}
```

It is now your responsibility, as the author of the Document class, to provide a meaningful implementation of the IStorable methods. Having designated Document as implementing IStorable, you must implement all the IStorable methods, or you will generate an error when you compile. This is illustrated in Example 8-1, in which the Document class implements the IStorable interface.

Example 8-1. Using a simple interface

```
#region Using directives

using System;
using System.Collections.Generic;
using System.Text;

#endregion

namespace SimpleInterface
{
// declare the interface

    interface IStorable
    {
        // no access modifiers, methods are public
        // no implementation
        void Read();
        void Write( object obj );
        int Status { get; set; }

    }
```

Example 8-1. Using a simple interface (continued)

```csharp
// create a class which implements the IStorable interface
   public class Document : IStorable
   {

      // store the value for the property
      private int status = 0;

      public Document( string s )
      {
         Console.WriteLine( "Creating document with: {0}", s );
      }

      // implement the Read method
      public void Read()
      {
         Console.WriteLine(
            "Implementing the Read Method for IStorable" );
      }

      // implement the Write method
      public void Write( object o )
      {
         Console.WriteLine(
            "Implementing the Write Method for IStorable" );
      }

      // implement the property
      public int Status
      {
         get
         {
            return status;
         }

         set
         {
            status = value;
         }
      }
   }

// Take our interface out for a spin
   public class Tester
   {

      static void Main()
      {
         // access the methods in the Document object
         Document doc = new Document( "Test Document" );
         doc.Status = -1;
         doc.Read();
         Console.WriteLine( "Document Status: {0}", doc.Status );
```

Example 8-1. Using a simple interface (continued)

```
        }
    }
}
```

```
Output:
Creating document with: Test Document
Implementing the Read Method for IStorable
Document Status: -1
```

Example 8-1 defines a simple interface, IStorable, with two methods (Read() and Write()) and a property (Status) of type integer. Notice that the property declaration doesn't provide an implementation for get() and set(), but simply designates that there *is* a get() and a set():

```
    int Status { get; set; }
```

Notice also that the IStorable method declarations don't include access modifiers (for example, public, protected, internal, private). In fact, providing an access modifier generates a compile error. Interface methods are implicitly public because an interface is a contract meant to be used by other classes. You can't create an instance of an interface; instead you instantiate a class that implements the interface.

The class implementing the interface must fulfill the contract exactly and completely. Document must provide both a Read() and a Write() method and the Status property. *How* it fulfills these requirements, however, is entirely up to the Document class. Although IStorable dictates that Document must have a Status property, it doesn't know or care whether Document stores the actual status as a member variable or looks it up in a database. The details are up to the implementing class.

Implementing More Than One Interface

Classes can implement more than one interface. For example, if your Document class can be stored and it also can be compressed, you might choose to implement both the IStorable and ICompressible interfaces. To do so, change the declaration (in the base list) to indicate that both interfaces are implemented, separating the two interfaces with commas:

```
    public class Document : IStorable, ICompressible
```

Having done this, the Document class must also implement the methods specified by the ICompressible interface (which is declared in Example 8-2):

```
    public void Compress()
    {
        Console.WriteLine("Implementing the Compress Method");
    }

    public void Decompress()
```

```
    {
        Console.WriteLine("Implementing the Decompress Method");
    }
```

Extending Interfaces

It is possible to extend an existing interface to add new methods or members, or to modify how existing members work. For example, you might extend ICompressible with a new interface, ILoggedCompressible, which extends the original interface with methods to keep track of the bytes saved:

```
interface ILoggedCompressible : ICompressible
{
    void LogSavedBytes();
}
```

> Effectively, by extending ICompressible in this way, you are saying that anything that implements ILoggedCompressible must also implement ICompressible.

Classes are now free to implement either ICompressible or ILoggedCompressible, depending on whether they need the additional functionality. If a class does implement ILoggedCompressible, it must implement all the methods of both ILoggedCompressible and ICompressible. Objects of that type can be cast either to ILoggedCompressible or to ICompressible.

Combining Interfaces

Similarly, you can create new interfaces by combining existing interfaces and, optionally, adding new methods or properties. For example, you might decide to create IStorableCompressible. This interface would combine the methods of each of the other two interfaces, but would also add a new method to store the original size of the precompressed item:

```
interface IStorableCompressible : IStorable, ILoggedCompressible
{
    void LogOriginalSize();
}
```

Example 8-2 illustrates extending and combining interfaces.

Example 8-2. Extending and combining interfaces

```
#region Using directives

using System;
using System.Collections.Generic;
using System.Text;
```

Example 8-2. Extending and combining interfaces (continued)

```
#endregion

namespace ExtendAndCombineInterface
{
    interface IStorable
    {
        void Read();
        void Write( object obj );
        int Status { get; set; }

    }

// here's the new interface
    interface ICompressible
    {
        void Compress();
        void Decompress();
    }

// Extend the interface
    interface ILoggedCompressible : ICompressible
    {
        void LogSavedBytes();
    }

// Combine Interfaces
    interface IStorableCompressible : IStorable, ILoggedCompressible
    {
        void LogOriginalSize();
    }

// yet another interface
    interface IEncryptable
    {
        void Encrypt();
        void Decrypt();
    }

    public class Document : IStorableCompressible, IEncryptable
    {

        // hold the data for IStorable's Status property
        private int status = 0;

        // the document constructor
        public Document( string s )
        {
            Console.WriteLine( "Creating document with: {0}", s );

        }
```

Example 8-2. Extending and combining interfaces (continued)

```csharp
// implement IStorable
public void Read()
{
    Console.WriteLine(
        "Implementing the Read Method for IStorable" );
}

public void Write( object o )
{
    Console.WriteLine(
        "Implementing the Write Method for IStorable" );
}

public int Status
{
    get
    {
        return status;
    }

    set
    {
        status = value;
    }
}

// implement ICompressible
public void Compress()
{
    Console.WriteLine( "Implementing Compress" );
}

public void Decompress()
{
    Console.WriteLine( "Implementing Decompress" );
}

// implement ILoggedCompressible
public void LogSavedBytes()
{
    Console.WriteLine( "Implementing LogSavedBytes" );
}

// implement IStorableCompressible
public void LogOriginalSize()
{
    Console.WriteLine( "Implementing LogOriginalSize" );
}

// implement IEncryptable
public void Encrypt()
```

Example 8-2. Extending and combining interfaces (continued)

```
        {
            Console.WriteLine( "Implementing Encrypt" );

        }

        public void Decrypt()
        {
            Console.WriteLine( "Implementing Decrypt" );

        }
    }

    public class Tester
    {

        static void Main()
        {
            // create a document object
            Document doc = new Document( "Test Document" );

            // cast the document to the various interfaces
            IStorable isDoc = doc as IStorable;
            if ( isDoc != null )
            {
                isDoc.Read();
            }
            else
                Console.WriteLine( "IStorable not supported" );

            ICompressible icDoc = doc as ICompressible;
            if ( icDoc != null )
            {
                icDoc.Compress();
            }
            else
                Console.WriteLine( "Compressible not supported" );

            ILoggedCompressible ilcDoc = doc as ILoggedCompressible;
            if ( ilcDoc != null )
            {
                ilcDoc.LogSavedBytes();
                ilcDoc.Compress();
                // ilcDoc.Read();
            }
            else
                Console.WriteLine( "LoggedCompressible not supported" );

            IStorableCompressible isc = doc as IStorableCompressible;
            if ( isc != null )
            {
                isc.LogOriginalSize();  // IStorableCompressible
                isc.LogSavedBytes();    // ILoggedCompressible
```

Example 8-2. Extending and combining interfaces (continued)

```
            isc.Compress();        // ICompressible
            isc.Read();            // IStorable

        }
        else
        {
            Console.WriteLine( "StorableCompressible not supported" );
        }

        IEncryptable ie = doc as IEncryptable;
        if ( ie != null )
        {
            ie.Encrypt();
        }
        else
            Console.WriteLine( "Encryptable not supported" );
    }
  }
}

Output:
Creating document with: Test Document
Implementing the Read Method for IStorable
Implementing Compress
Implementing LogSavedBytes
Implementing Compress
Implementing LogOriginalSize
Implementing LogSavedBytes
Implementing Compress
Implementing the Read Method for IStorable
Implementing Encrypt
```

Example 8-2 starts by implementing the IStorable interface and the ICompressible interface. The latter is extended to ILoggedCompressible and then the two are combined into IStorableCompressible. Finally, the example adds a new interface, IEncryptable.

The Tester program creates a new Document object and then uses it as an instance of the various interfaces. You are free to cast:

```
ICompressible icDoc = doc as ICompressible;
```

But this is unnecessary. The compiler knows that doc implements ICompressible and so can make the implicit cast for you:

```
ICompressible icDoc = doc;
```

On the other hand, if you are uncertain whether your class does implement a specific interface, you can cast using the as operator (described in detail later in this chapter), and then test whether the cast object is null (indicating that the cast was not legal) instead of assuming the cast and risk raising an exception.

```
ICompressible icDoc = doc as ICompressible;
if ( icDoc != null )
{
    icDoc.Compress();
}
else
    Console.WriteLine( "Compressible not supported" );
```

Casting to extended interfaces

When the object is cast to ILoggedCompressible, you can use the interface to call methods on ICompressible because ILoggedCompressible extends (and thus subsumes) the methods from the base interface:

```
ILoggedCompressible ilcDoc = doc as ILoggedCompressible;
if (ilcDoc != null)
{
    ilcDoc.LogSavedBytes();
    ilcDoc.Compress();
    // ilcDoc.Read();
}
```

You can't call Read(), however, because that is a method of IStorable, an unrelated interface. And if you uncomment out the call to Read(), you will receive a compiler error.

If you cast to IStorableCompressible (which combines the extended interface with the Storable interface), you can then call methods of IStorableCompressible, ICompressible, and IStorable:

```
IStorableCompressible isc = doc as IStorableCompressible
if (isc != null)
{
    isc.LogOriginalSize();   // IStorableCompressible
    isc.LogSavedBytes();     // ILoggedCompressible
    isc.Compress();          // ICompressible
    isc.Read();              // IStorable
}
```

Accessing Interface Methods

You can access the members of the IStorable interface as if they were members of the Document class:

```
Document doc = new Document("Test Document");
doc.status = -1;
doc.Read();
```

You can also create an instance of the interface[*] by casting the document to the interface type, and then use that interface to access the methods:

```
IStorable isDoc = doc;
isDoc.status = 0;
isDoc.Read();
```

In this case, in Main() you *know* that Document is in fact an IStorable, so you can take advantage of that knowledge and not explicitly cast or test the cast.

As stated earlier, you can't instantiate an interface directly. That is, you can't say:

```
IStorable isDoc = new IStorable();
```

You can, however, create an instance of the implementing class, as in the following:

```
Document doc = new Document("Test Document");
```

You can then create an instance of the interface by casting the implementing object to the interface type, which in this case is IStorable:

```
IStorable isDoc = doc;
```

You can combine these steps by writing:

```
IStorable isDoc = new Document("Test Document");
```

Access through an interface allows you to treat the interface polymorphically. In other words, you can have two or more classes implement the interface, and then by accessing these classes only through the interface, you can ignore their real runtime type and treat them interchangeably. See Chapter 5 for more information about polymorphism.

Casting to an Interface

In many cases, you don't know in advance that an object supports a particular interface. Given a collection of objects, you might not know whether a particular object supports IStorable or ICompressible or both. You *can* just cast[†] to the interfaces:

```
Document doc = myCollection[0];

IStorable isDoc = (IStorable) doc;
isDoc.Read();

ICompressible icDoc = (ICompressible) doc;
icDoc.Compress();
```

If it turns out that Document implements only the IStorable interface:

```
public class Document : IStorable
```

---

[*] Or more accurately, a properly cast reference to the object that implements the interface.

[†] The explicit casts shown at the bottom of the page are used as documentation, and are not required.

the cast to ICompressible still compiles because ICompressible is a valid interface. However, because of the illegal cast, when the program is run, an exception is thrown:

```
An exception of type System.InvalidCastException was thrown.
```

Exceptions are covered in detail in Chapter 11.

The is Operator

You would like to be able to ask the object if it supports the interface, to then invoke the appropriate methods. In C# there are two ways to accomplish this. The first method is to use the is operator. The form of the is operator is:

```
expression is type
```

The is operator evaluates true if the expression (which must be a reference type) can be safely cast to type without throwing an exception.* Example 8-3 illustrates the use of the is operator to test whether a Document implements the IStorable and ICompressible interfaces.

 Java programmers take note: the C# is operator is the equivalent of Java's instanceof.

Example 8-3. Using the is operator

```
#region Using directives

using System;
using System.Collections.Generic;
using System.Text;

#endregion

namespace IsOperator
{
    interface IStorable
    {
        void Read();
        void Write( object obj );
        int Status { get; set; }

    }
// here's the new interface
    interface ICompressible
```

---

* Both the is and the as operator (described next) can be used to evaluate types through inheritance, in addition to evaluating implementation of interfaces. Thus, you can use is to check whether a dog is a mammal.

Example 8-3. Using the is operator (continued)

```
    {
        void Compress();
        void Decompress();
    }

// Document implements IStorable
    public class Document : IStorable
    {

        private int status = 0;

        public Document( string s )
        {
            Console.WriteLine(
                "Creating document with: {0}", s );

        }

        // IStorable.Read
        public void Read()
        {
            Console.WriteLine( "Reading...");
        }

        // IStorable.Write
        public void Write( object o )
        {
            Console.WriteLine( "Writing...");
        }

        // IStorable.Status
        public int Status
        {
            get
            {
                return status;
            }

            set
            {
                status = value;
            }
        }
    }

    // derives from Document and implements ICompressible
    public class CompressibleDocument : Document, ICompressible
    {
        public CompressibleDocument(String s) :
            base(s)
        { }
```

Example 8-3. Using the is operator (continued)

```csharp
    public void Compress()
    {
        Console.WriteLine("Compressing...");
    }
    public void Decompress()
    {
        Console.WriteLine("Decompressing...");
    }


}

public class Tester
{

    static void Main()
    {
        // A collection of Documents
        Document[] docArray = new Document[2];

        // First entry is a Document
        docArray[0] = new Document( "Test Document" );

        // Second entry is a CompressibleDocument (ok because
        // CompressibleDocument is a Document)
        docArray[1] =
          new CompressibleDocument("Test compressibleDocument");

        // don't know what we'll pull out of this hat
        foreach (Document doc in docArray)
        {
            // report your name
            Console.WriteLine("Got: {0}", doc);

            // Both pass this test
            if (doc is IStorable)
            {
                IStorable isDoc = (IStorable)doc;
                isDoc.Read();
            }

            // fails for Document
            // passes for CompressibleDocument
            if (doc is ICompressible)
            {
                ICompressible icDoc = (ICompressible)doc;
                icDoc.Compress();
            }
        }
    }
}
}
```

Example 8-3. Using the is operator (continued)

```
Output:
Creating document with: Test Document
Creating document with: Test compressibleDocument
Got: IsOperator.Document
Reading...
Got: IsOperator.CompressibleDocument
Reading...
Compressing...
```

Example 8-3 differs from Example 8-2 in that Document no longer implements the ICompressible interface, but a class derived from Document named CompressibleDocument does.

Main() checks whether each cast is legal (sometimes referred to as safe) by evaluating the following if clause:

```
if (doc is IStorable)
```

This is clean and nearly self-documenting. The if statement tells you that the cast will happen only if the object is of the right interface type.

The Document class passes this test, but fails the next:

```
if (doc is ICompressible)
```

but the CompressibleDocument passes both tests.

We put both types of documents into an array (you can imagine such an array being handed to a method which can't know its contents). Before you try to call the ICompressible methods, you must be sure that the type of Document you have does implement ICompressible. The is operator makes that test for you.

Unfortunately, this use of the is operator turns out to be inefficient. To understand why, you need to dip into the MSIL code that this generates. Here is a small excerpt (note that the line numbers are in hexadecimal notation):

```
IL_0023:  isinst     ICompressible
IL_0028:  brfalse.s  IL_0039
IL_002a:  ldloc.0
IL_002b:  castclass  ICompressible
IL_0030:  stloc.2
IL_0031:  ldloc.2
IL_0032:  callvirt   instance void ICompressible::Compress()
```

What is most important here is the test for ICompressible on line 23. The keyword isinst is the MSIL code for the is operator. It tests to see if the object (doc) is in fact of the right type. Having passed this test we continue on to line 2b, in which castclass is called. Unfortunately, castclass also tests the type of the object. In effect, the test is done twice. A more efficient solution is to use the as operator.

The as Operator

The as operator combines the is and cast operations by testing first to see whether a cast is valid (i.e., whether an is test would return true) and then completing the cast when it is. If the cast is not valid (i.e., if an is test would return false), the as operator returns null.

 The keyword null represents a null reference—one that doesn't refer to any object.

Using the as operator eliminates the need to handle cast exceptions. At the same time you avoid the overhead of checking the cast twice. For these reasons, it is optimal to cast interfaces using as.

The form of the as operator is:

```
expression as type
```

The following code adapts the test code from Example 8-3, using the as operator and testing for null:

```
static void Main()
{
    // A collection of Documents
    Document[] docArray = new Document[2];

    // First entry is a Document
    docArray[0] = new Document( "Test Document" );

    // Second entry is a CompressibleDocument (ok because
    // CompressibleDocument is a Document)
    docArray[1] = new CompressibleDocument("Test compressibleDocument");


    // don't know what we'll pull out of this hat
    foreach (Document doc in docArray)
    {
        // report your name
        Console.WriteLine("Got: {0}", doc);

        // Both pass this test
        IStorable isDoc = doc as IStorable;
        if (isDoc != null)
        {
            isDoc.Read();
        }

        // fails for Document
        // passes for CompressibleDocument
        ICompressible icDoc = doc as ICompressible;
        if (icDoc != null)
```

```
        {
            icDoc.Compress();
        }
    }
}
```

A quick look at the comparable MSIL code shows that the following version is in fact more efficient:

```
IL_0023:  isinst      ICompressible
IL_0028:  stloc.2
IL_0029:  ldloc.2
IL_002a:  brfalse.s   IL_0034
IL_002c:  ldloc.2
IL_002d:  callvirt     instance void ICompressible::Compress()
```

The is Operator Versus the as Operator

If your design pattern is to test the object to see if it is of the type you need, and if so to immediately cast it, the as operator is more efficient. At times, however, you might want to test the type of an operator but not cast it immediately. Perhaps you want to test it but not cast it at all; you simply want to add it to a list if it fulfills the right interface. In that case, the is operator will be a better choice.

Interface Versus Abstract Class

Interfaces are very similar to abstract classes. In fact, you could change the declaration of IStorable to be an abstract class:

```
abstract class Storable
{
  abstract public void Read();
  abstract public void Write();
}
```

Document could now inherit from Storable, and there would not be much difference from using the interface.

Suppose, however, that you purchase a List class from a third-party vendor whose capabilities you wish to combine with those specified by Storable. In C++, you could create a StorableList class and inherit from both List and Storable. But in C#, you're stuck; you can't inherit from both the Storable abstract class and also the List class because C# doesn't allow multiple inheritance with classes.

However, C# does allow you to implement any number of interfaces and derive from one base class. Thus, by making Storable an interface, you can inherit from the List class and also from IStorable, as StorableList does in the following example:

```
public class StorableList : List, IStorable
{
```

```
    // List methods here ...
    public void Read() {...}
    public void Write(object obj) {...}
    // ...
}
```

Some designers at Microsoft discourage the use of interfaces and prefer abstract base classes because the latter do better with versioning.

For example, suppose you design an interface and programmers in your shop start using it. You now want to add a new member to that interface. You have two bad choices: you can either change the interface and break existing code, or you can treat the interface as immutable and create, for example, IStore2 or IStorageExtended. If you do that often enough, however, you will soon have dozens of closely related interfaces and a mess on your hands.

With an abstract base class, you can just add a new virtual method with a default implementation. Hey! Presto! Existing code continues to work, but no new class is introduced into the namespace.

The best practice seems to be that if you are creating a class library that will be reused by many people (especially outside your company), you might want to favor abstract base classes. If you are creating classes for a single project, however, interfaces may make for easier-to-understand and more flexible code.

Overriding Interface Implementations

An implementing class is free to mark any or all of the methods that implement the interface as virtual. Derived classes can override these implementations to achieve polymorphism. For example, a Document class might implement the IStorable interface and mark the Read() and Write() methods as virtual. The Document might Read() and Write() its contents to a File type. The developer might later derive new types from Document, such as a Note or EmailMessage type, and he might decide that Note will read and write to a database rather than to a file.

Example 8-4 strips down the complexity of Example 8-3 and illustrates overriding an interface implementation. The Read() method is marked as virtual and implemented by Document. Read() is then overridden in a Note type that derives from Document.

Example 8-4. Overriding an interface implementation

```
#region Using directives

using System;
using System.Collections.Generic;
using System.Text;

#endregion
```

Example 8-4. Overriding an interface implementation (continued)

```
namespace overridingInterface
{
    interface IStorable
    {
        void Read();
        void Write();
    }

// Simplify Document to implement only IStorable
    public class Document : IStorable
    {
        // the document constructor
        public Document( string s )
        {
            Console.WriteLine(
                "Creating document with: {0}", s );

        }

        // Make read virtual

        public virtual void Read()
        {
            Console.WriteLine(
                "Document Read Method for IStorable" );
        }

        // NB: Not virtual!
        public void Write()
        {
            Console.WriteLine(
                "Document Write Method for IStorable" );
        }
    }

// Derive from Document
    public class Note : Document
    {
        public Note( string s ):
        base(s)
        {
            Console.WriteLine(
                "Creating note with: {0}", s );
        }

        // override the Read method

        public override void Read()
        {
            Console.WriteLine(
                "Overriding the Read method for Note!" );
        }
```

Example 8-4. Overriding an interface implementation (continued)

```csharp
      // implement my own Write method
      public new void Write()
      {
         Console.WriteLine(
            "Implementing the Write method for Note!" );
      }
   }
   public class Tester
   {

      static void Main()
      {
         // create a document reference to a Note object
         Document theNote = new Note( "Test Note" );
         IStorable isNote = theNote as IStorable;
         if ( isNote != null )
         {
            isNote.Read();
            isNote.Write();
         }

         Console.WriteLine( "\n" );

         // direct call to the methods
         theNote.Read();
         theNote.Write();

         Console.WriteLine( "\n" );

         // create a note object
         Note note2 = new Note( "Second Test" );
         IStorable isNote2 = note2 as IStorable;
         if ( isNote2 != null )
         {
            isNote2.Read();
            isNote2.Write();
         }

         Console.WriteLine( "\n" );

         // directly call the methods
         note2.Read();
         note2.Write();
      }
   }
}

Output:
Creating document with: Test Note
Creating note with: Test Note
Overriding the Read method for Note!
Document Write Method for IStorable
```

Example 8-4. Overriding an interface implementation (continued)

```
Overriding the Read method for Note!
Document Write Method for IStorable

Creating document with: Second Test
Creating note with: Second Test
Overriding the Read method for Note!
Document Write Method for IStorable

Overriding the Read method for Note!
Implementing the Write method for Note!
```

In this example, Document implements a simplified IStorable interface (simplified to make the example clearer):

```
interface IStorable
{
    void Read();
    void Write();
}
```

The designer of Document has opted to make the Read() method virtual, but not to make the Write() method virtual:

```
public virtual void Read()
```

In a real-world application, if you were to mark one as virtual, you would almost certainly mark both as virtual, but I've differentiated them to demonstrate that the developer is free to pick and choose which methods are made virtual.

The Note class derives from Document:

```
public class Note : Document
```

It's not necessary for Note to override Read(), but it is free to do so and has in fact done so here:

```
public override void Read()
```

In Tester, the Read and Write methods are called in four ways:

- Through the base class reference to a derived object
- Through an interface created from the base class reference to the derived object
- Through a derived object
- Through an interface created from the derived object

To accomplish the first two calls, a Document (base class) reference is created, and the address of a new Note (derived) object created on the heap is assigned to the Document reference:

```
Document theNote = new Note("Test Note");
```

An interface reference is created and the as operator is used to cast the Document to the IStorable reference:

```
IStorable isNote = theNote as IStorable;
```

You then invoke the Read() and Write() methods through that interface. The output reveals that the Read() method is responded to polymorphically and the Write() method is not, just as we would expect:

```
Overriding the Read method for Note!
Document Write Method for IStorable
```

The Read() and Write() methods are then called directly on the object itself:

```
theNote.Read();
theNote.Write();
```

and once again you see the polymorphic implementation has worked:

```
Overriding the Read method for Note!
Document Write Method for IStorable
```

In both cases, the Read() method of Note is called and the Write() method of Document is called.

To prove to yourself that this is a result of the overriding method, next create a second Note object, this time assigning its address to a reference to a Note. This will be used to illustrate the final cases (i.e., a call through a derived object and a call through an interface created from the derived object):

```
Note note2 = new Note("Second Test");
```

Once again, when you cast to a reference, the overridden Read() method is called. When, however, methods are called directly on the Note object:

```
note2.Read();
note2.Write();
```

the output reflects that you've called a Note and not an overridden Document:

```
Overriding the Read method for Note!
Implementing the Write method for Note!
```

Explicit Interface Implementation

In the implementation shown so far, the implementing class (in this case, Document) creates a member method with the same signature and return type as the method detailed in the interface. It is not necessary to explicitly state that this is an implementation of an interface; this is understood by the compiler implicitly.

What happens, however, if the class implements two interfaces, each of which has a method with the same signature? Example 8-5 creates two interfaces: IStorable and ITalk. The latter implements a Read() method that reads a book aloud. Unfortunately, this conflicts with the Read() method in IStorable.

Because both IStorable and ITalk have a Read() method, the implementing Document class must use *explicit implementation* for at least one of the methods. With explicit implementation, the implementing class (Document) explicitly identifies the interface for the method:

```
void ITalk.Read()
```

This resolves the conflict, but it creates a series of interesting side effects.

First, there is no need to use explicit implementation with the other method of Read():

```
public void Read()
```

Because there is no conflict, this can be declared as usual.

More important, the explicit implementation method can't have an access modifier:

```
void ITalk.Read()
```

This method is implicitly public.

In fact, a method declared through explicit implementation can't be declared with the abstract, virtual, override, or new modifiers.

Most important, you can't access the explicitly implemented method through the object itself. When you write:

```
theDoc.Read();
```

the compiler assumes you mean the implicitly implemented interface for IStorable. The only way to access an explicitly implemented interface is through a cast to an interface:

```
ITalk itDoc = theDoc;
itDoc.Read();
```

Explicit implementation is demonstrated in Example 8-5.

Example 8-5. Explicit implementation

```
#region Using directives

using System;
using System.Collections.Generic;
using System.Text;

#endregion

namespace ExplicitImplementation
{
    interface IStorable
    {
        void Read();
        void Write();
    }
```

Example 8-5. Explicit implementation (continued)

```csharp
interface ITalk
{
    void Talk();
    void Read();
}

// Modify Document to implement IStorable and ITalk
public class Document : IStorable, ITalk
{
    // the document constructor
    public Document( string s )
    {
        Console.WriteLine( "Creating document with: {0}", s );

    }

    // Make read virtual
    public virtual void Read()
    {
        Console.WriteLine( "Implementing IStorable.Read" );
    }

    public void Write()
    {
        Console.WriteLine( "Implementing IStorable.Write" );

    }

    void ITalk.Read()
    {
        Console.WriteLine( "Implementing ITalk.Read" );
    }

    public void Talk()
    {
        Console.WriteLine( "Implementing ITalk.Talk" );
    }
}

public class Tester
{

    static void Main()
    {
        // create a document object
        Document theDoc = new Document( "Test Document" );
        IStorable isDoc = theDoc;
        isDoc.Read();

        ITalk itDoc = theDoc;
        itDoc.Read();
```

Example 8-5. Explicit implementation (continued)

```
        theDoc.Read();
        theDoc.Talk();
    }
  }
}
```

```
Output:
Creating document with: Test Document
Implementing IStorable.Read
Implementing ITalk.Read
Implementing IStorable.Read
Implementing ITalk.Talk
```

Selectively Exposing Interface Methods

A class designer can take advantage of the fact that when an interface is implemented through explicit implementation, the interface is not visible to clients of the implementing class except through casting.

Suppose the semantics of your Document object dictate that it implement the IStorable interface, but you don't want the Read() and Write() methods to be part of the public interface of your Document. You can use explicit implementation to ensure that they aren't available except through casting. This allows you to preserve the public API of your Document class while still having it implement IStorable. If your client wants an object that implements the IStorable interface, it can make a cast, but when using your document as a Document, the API will not include Read() and Write().

In fact, you can select which methods to make visible through explicit implementation so that you can expose some implementing methods as part of Document but not others. In Example 8-5, the Document object exposes the Talk() method as a method of Document, but the ITalk.Read() method can be obtained only through a cast. Even if IStorable didn't have a Read() method, you might choose to make Read() explicitly implemented so that you don't expose Read() as a method of Document.

Note that because explicit interface implementation prevents the use of the virtual keyword, a derived class would be forced to reimplement the method. Thus, if Note derived from Document, it would be forced to reimplement ITalk.Read() because the Document implementation of ITalk.Read() couldn't be virtual.

Member Hiding

It is possible for an interface member to become hidden. For example, suppose you have an interface IBase that has a property P:

```
interface IBase
{
```

```
    int P { get; set; }
}
```

Suppose you derive from that interface a new interface, IDerived, that hides the property P with a new method P():

```
interface IDerived : IBase
{
    new int P();
}
```

Setting aside whether this is a good idea, you have now hidden the property P in the base interface. An implementation of this derived interface will require at least one explicit interface member. You can use explicit implementation for *either* the base property or the derived method, or you can use explicit implementation for both. Thus, any of the following three versions would be legal:

```
class myClass : IDerived
{
    // explicit implementation for the base property
    int IBase.P { get {...} }

    // implicit implementation of the derived method
    public int P() {...}
}

class myClass : IDerived
{
    // implicit implementation for the base property
    public int P { get {...} }

    // explicit implementation of the derived method
    int IDerived.P() {...}
}

class myClass : IDerived
{
    // explicit implementation for the base property
    int IBase.P { get {...} }

    // explicit implementation of the derived method
    int IDerived.P() {...}
}
```

Accessing Sealed Classes and Value Types

Generally, it is preferable to access the methods of an interface through an interface cast. The exception is with value types (e.g., structs) or with sealed classes. In that case, it is preferable to invoke the interface method through the object.

When you implement an interface in a struct, you are implementing it in a value type. When you cast to an interface reference, there is an implicit boxing of the object. Unfortunately, when you use that interface to modify the object, it is the boxed object, not the original value object, that is modified. Further, if you change the value of the struct from inside the method, the boxed type will remain unchanged (this is considered quite funny when it is in *someone else's* code). Example 8-6 creates a struct that implements IStorable and illustrates the impact of implicit boxing when you cast the struct to an interface reference.

Example 8-6. References on value types

```
using System;

#region Using directives

using System;
using System.Collections.Generic;
using System.Text;

#endregion

namespace ReferencesOnValueTypes
{
// declare a simple interface
    interface IStorable
    {
        void Read();
        int Status { get;set;}

    }

// Implement through a struct
    public struct myStruct : IStorable
    {

        public void Read()
        {
            Console.WriteLine(
                "Implementing IStorable.Read" );
        }

        public int Status
        {
            get
            {
                return status;
            }
            set
            {
                status = value;
            }
        }
    }
```

Example 8-6. References on value types (continued)

```
      private int status;
   }

   public class Tester
   {

      static void Main()
      {
         // create a myStruct object
         myStruct theStruct = new myStruct();
         theStruct.Status = -1;  // initialize
         Console.WriteLine(
            "theStruct.Status: {0}", theStruct.Status );

         // Change the value
         theStruct.Status = 2;
         Console.WriteLine( "Changed object." );
         Console.WriteLine(
            "theStruct.Status: {0}", theStruct.Status );

         // cast to an IStorable
         // implicit box to a reference type
         IStorable isTemp = ( IStorable ) theStruct;

         // set the value through the interface reference
         isTemp.Status = 4;
         Console.WriteLine( "Changed interface." );
         Console.WriteLine( "theStruct.Status: {0}, isTemp: {1}",
            theStruct.Status, isTemp.Status );

         // Change the value again
         theStruct.Status = 6;
         Console.WriteLine( "Changed object." );
         Console.WriteLine( "theStruct.Status: {0}, isTemp: {1}",
            theStruct.Status, isTemp.Status );
      }
   }
}
```

```
Output:
theStruct.Status: -1
Changed object.
theStruct.Status: 2
Changed interface.
theStruct.Status: 2, isTemp: 4
Changed object.
theStruct.Status: 6, isTemp: 4
```

In Example 8-6, the IStorable interface has a method (Read) and a property (Status).

This interface is implemented by the struct named myStruct:

```
   public struct myStruct : IStorable
```

The interesting code is in Tester. Start by creating an instance of the structure and initializing its property to -1. The status value is then printed:

```
myStruct theStruct = new myStruct();
theStruct.Status = -1;  // initialize
Console.WriteLine(
    "theStruct.Status: {0}", theStruct.Status);
```

The output from this shows that the status was set properly:

```
theStruct.Status: -1
```

Next access the property to change the status, again through the value object itself:

```
// Change the value
theStruct.Status = 2;
Console.WriteLine("Changed object.");
Console.WriteLine(
    "theStruct.Status: {0}", theStruct.Status);
```

The output shows the change:

```
Changed object.
theStruct.Status: 2
```

No surprises so far. At this point, create a reference to the IStorable interface. This causes an implicit boxing of the value object theStruct. Then use that interface to change the status value to 4:

```
// cast to an IStorable
// implicit box to a reference type
IStorable isTemp = (IStorable) theStruct;

// set the value through the interface reference
isTemp.Status = 4;
Console.WriteLine("Changed interface.");
Console.WriteLine("theStruct.Status: {0}, isTemp: {1}",
    theStruct.Status, isTemp.Status);
```

Here the output can be a bit surprising:

```
Changed interface.
theStruct.Status: 2, isTemp: 4
```

Aha! The object to which the interface reference points has been changed to a status value of 4, but the struct value object is unchanged. Even more interesting, when you access the method through the object itself:

```
// Change the value again
theStruct.Status = 6;
Console.WriteLine("Changed object.");
Console.WriteLine("theStruct.Status: {0}, isTemp: {1}",
    theStruct.Status, isTemp.Status);
```

the output reveals that the value object has been changed, but the boxed reference value for the interface reference has not:

```
Changed object.
theStruct.Status: 6, isTemp: 4
```

A quick look at the MSIL code (Example 8-7) reveals what's going on under the hood.

Example 8-7. MSIL code resulting from Example 8-6

```
.method private hidebysig static void  Main() cil managed
{
  .entrypoint
  // Code size       194 (0xc2)
  .maxstack  3
  .locals init ([0] valuetype ReferencesOnValueTypes.myStruct theStruct,
           [1] class ReferencesOnValueTypes.IStorable isTemp)
  IL_0000:  ldloca.s   theStruct
  IL_0002:  initobj    ReferencesOnValueTypes.myStruct
  IL_0008:  ldloca.s   theStruct
  IL_000a:  ldc.i4.m1
  IL_000b:  call       instance void ReferencesOnValueTypes.myStruct::set_Status(int32)
  IL_0010:  ldstr      "theStruct.Status: {0}"
  IL_0015:  ldloca.s   theStruct
  IL_0017:  call       instance int32 ReferencesOnValueTypes.myStruct::get_Status()
  IL_001c:  box        [mscorlib]System.Int32
  IL_0021:  call       void [mscorlib]System.Console::WriteLine(string,
                                                          object)

  IL_0026:  nop
  IL_0027:  ldloca.s   theStruct
  IL_0029:  ldc.i4.2
  IL_002a:  call       instance void ReferencesOnValueTypes.myStruct::set_Status(int32)
  IL_002f:  ldstr      "Changed object."
  IL_0034:  call       void [mscorlib]System.Console::WriteLine(string)
  IL_0039:  nop
  IL_003a:  ldstr      "theStruct.Status: {0}"
  IL_003f:  ldloca.s   theStruct
  IL_0041:  call       instance int32 ReferencesOnValueTypes.myStruct::get_Status()
  IL_0046:  box        [mscorlib]System.Int32
  IL_004b:  call       void [mscorlib]System.Console::WriteLine(string,
                                                          object)

  IL_0050:  nop
  IL_0051:  ldloc.0
  IL_0052:  box        ReferencesOnValueTypes.myStruct
  IL_0057:  stloc.1
  IL_0058:  ldloc.1
  IL_0059:  ldc.i4.4
  IL_005a:  callvirt   instance void ReferencesOnValueTypes.IStorable::set_Status(int32)
  IL_005f:  ldstr      "Changed interface."
  IL_0064:  call       void [mscorlib]System.Console::WriteLine(string)
  IL_0069:  nop
  IL_006a:  ldstr      "theStruct.Status: {0}, isTemp: {1}"
  IL_006f:  ldloca.s   theStruct
  IL_0071:  call       instance int32 ReferencesOnValueTypes.myStruct::get_Status()
  IL_0076:  box        [mscorlib]System.Int32
  IL_007b:  ldloc.1
  IL_007c:  callvirt   instance int32 ReferencesOnValueTypes.IStorable::get_Status()
  IL_0081:  box        [mscorlib]System.Int32
```

Example 8-7. MSIL code resulting from Example 8-6 (continued)

```
IL_0086:  call       void [mscorlib]System.Console::WriteLine(string,
                                                               object,
                                                               object)

IL_008b:  nop
IL_008c:  ldloca.s   theStruct
IL_008e:  ldc.i4.6
IL_008f:  call       instance void ReferencesOnValueTypes.myStruct::set_Status(int32)
IL_0094:  ldstr      "Changed object."
IL_0099:  call       void [mscorlib]System.Console::WriteLine(string)
IL_009e:  nop
IL_009f:  ldstr      "theStruct.Status: {0}, isTemp: {1}"
IL_00a4:  ldloca.s   theStruct
IL_00a6:  call       instance int32 ReferencesOnValueTypes.myStruct::get_Status()
IL_00ab:  box        [mscorlib]System.Int32
IL_00b0:  ldloc.1
IL_00b1:  callvirt   instance int32 ReferencesOnValueTypes.IStorable::get_Status()
IL_00b6:  box        [mscorlib]System.Int32
IL_00bb:  call       void [mscorlib]System.Console::WriteLine(string,
                                                               object,
                                                               object)

IL_00c0:  nop
IL_00c1:  ret
} // end of method Tester::Main
```

On line IL_000b, set_Status() was called on the value object. We see the second call on line IL_0017. Notice that the calls to WriteLine() cause boxing of the integer value status so that the GetString() method can be called.

The key line is IL_0052 (highlighted) where the struct itself is boxed. It is that boxing that creates a reference type for the interface reference. Notice on line IL_005a that this time IStorable::set_Status is called rather than myStruct::set_Status.

The design guideline is if you are implementing an interface with a value type, be sure to access the interface members through the object rather than through an interface reference.

CHAPTER 9

Arrays, Indexers, and Collections

The .NET Framework provides a rich suite of collection classes. With the advent of generics in 2.0 most of these collection classes are now type-safe, making for a greatly enhanced programming experience. These classes include the Array, List, Dictionary, Sorted Dictionary, Queue, and Stack.

The simplest collection is the Array, the only collection type for which C# provides built-in support. In this chapter, you will learn to work with single, multidimensional, and jagged arrays. Arrays have built-in indexers, allowing you to request the *n*th member of the array. In this chapter you will also be introduced to creating your own indexers, a bit of C# syntactic sugar that makes it easier to access class properties as though the class were indexed like an array.

The .NET Framework provides a number of interfaces, such as IEnumerable and ICollection, whose implementation provides you with standard ways to interact with collections. In this chapter, you will see how to work with the most essential of these. The chapter concludes with a tour of commonly used .NET collections, including List, Dictionary, Queue, and Stack.

In previous versions of C#, the collection objects were not type-safe (you could, for example, mix strings and integers in a Dictionary). The nontype-safe versions, of List (ArrayList), Dictionary, and Queue, and Stack are still available for backward compatibility but won't be covered in this book because their use is similar to the generics-based versions and because they are obsolete and deprecated.

Arrays

An *array* is an indexed collection of objects, all of the same type. C# arrays are somewhat different from arrays in C++ because they are objects. This provides them with useful methods and properties.

C# provides native syntax for the declaration of Arrays. What is actually created, however, is an object of type System.Array.* Arrays in C# thus provide you with the best of both worlds: easy-to-use C-style syntax underpinned with an actual class definition so that instances of an array have access to the methods and properties of System.Array. These appear in Table 9-1.

Table 9-1. System.Array methods and properties

Method or property	Purpose
BinarySearch()	Overloaded public static method that searches a one-dimensional sorted array.
Clear()	Public static method that sets a range of elements in the array either to 0 or to a null reference.
Copy()	Overloaded public static method that copies a section of one array to another array.
CreateInstance()	Overloaded public static method that instantiates a new instance of an array.
IndexOf()	Overloaded public static method that returns the index (offset) of the first instance of a value in a one-dimensional array.
LastIndexOf()	Overloaded public static method that returns the index of the last instance of a value in a one-dimensional array.
Reverse()	Overloaded public static method that reverses the order of the elements in a one-dimensional array.
Sort()	Overloaded public static method that sorts the values in a one-dimensional array.
IsFixedSize	Required because Array implements ICollection. With arrays, this will always return true (all arrays are of a fixed size).
IsReadOnly	Public property (required because Array implements IList) that returns a Boolean value indicating whether the array is read-only.
IsSynchronized	Public property (required because Array implements ICollection) that returns a Boolean value indicating whether the array is thread-safe.
Length	Public property that returns the length of the array.
Rank	Public property that returns the number of dimensions of the array.
SyncRoot	Public property that returns an object that can be used to synchronize access to the array.
GetEnumerator()	Public method that returns an IEnumerator.
GetLength()	Public method that returns the length of the specified dimension in the array.
GetLowerBound()	Public method that returns the lower boundary of the specified dimension of the array.
GetUpperBound()	Public method that returns the upper boundary of the specified dimension of the array.
Initialize()	Initializes all values in a value type array by calling the default constructor for each value. With reference arrays, all elements in the array are set to null.
SetValue()	Overloaded public method that sets the specified array elements to a value.

---

* Of course, when you create an array with int[] myArray = new int[5] what you actually create in the IL code is an instance of System.int32[], but since this derives from the abstract base class System.Array, it is fair to say you've created an instance of a System.Array.

Declaring Arrays

Declare a C# array with the following syntax:

```
type[] array-name;
```

For example:

```
int[] myIntArray;
```

 You aren't actually declaring an array. Technically, you are declaring a variable (myIntArray) that will hold a reference to an array of integers. As always, we'll use the shorthand and refer to myIntArray as the array, knowing that what we really mean is that it is a variable that holds a reference to an (unnamed) array.

The square brackets ([]) tell the C# compiler that you are declaring an array, and the type specifies the type of the elements it will contain. In the previous example, myIntArray is an array of integers.

Instantiate an array using the new keyword. For example:

```
myIntArray = new int[5];
```

This declaration creates and initializes an array of five integers, all of which are initialized to the value 0.

 VB6 programmers take note: in C#, the value of the size of the array marks the number of elements in the array, not the upper bound. In fact, there is no way to set the upper or lower bounds (with the exception that you can set the lower bounds in multidimensional arrays (discussed later), but even that is not supported by the .NET Framework class library).

Thus, the first element in an array is 0. The following C# statement declares an array of 10 elements, with indices 0 through 9:

```
string myArray[10];
```

The upper bound is 9, not 10, and you can't change the size of the array (that is, there is no equivalent to the VB6 Redim function).

It is important to distinguish between the array itself (which is a collection of elements) and the elements of the array. myIntArray is the array (or, more accurately, the variable that holds the reference to the array); its elements are the five integers it holds.

C# arrays are reference types, created on the heap. Thus, the array to which myIntArray refers is allocated on the heap. The *elements* of an array are allocated based on their own type. Since integers are value types, the elements in myIntArray will be value types, *not* boxed integers, and thus all the elements will be created inside the block of memory allocated for the array.

The block of memory allocated to an array of reference types will contain references to the actual elements, which are themselves created on the heap in memory separate from that allocated for the array.

Understanding Default Values

When you create an array of value types, each element initially contains the default value for the type stored in the array (refer back to Table 4-2). The statement:

```
myIntArray = new int[5];
```

creates an array of five integers, each of whose value is set to 0, which is the default value for integer types.

Unlike with arrays of value types, the reference types in an array aren't initialized to their default value. Instead, the references held in the array are initialized to null. If you attempt to access an element in an array of reference types before you have specifically initialized the elements, you will generate an exception.

Assume you have created a Button class. Declare an array of Button objects with the following statement:

```
Button[] myButtonArray;
```

and instantiate the actual array like this:

```
myButtonArray = new Button[3];
```

You can shorten this to:

```
Button[] myButtonArray = new Button[3];
```

This statement doesn't create an array with references to three Button objects. Instead, this creates the array myButtonArray with three null references. To use this array, you must first construct and assign the Button objects for each reference in the array. You can construct the objects in a loop that adds them one by one to the array.

Accessing Array Elements

Access the elements of an array using the index operator ([]). Arrays are zero-based, which means that the index of the first element is always 0—in this case, myArray[0].

As explained previously, arrays are objects and thus have properties. One of the more useful of these is Length, which tells you how many objects are in an array. Array objects can be indexed from 0 to Length-1. That is, if there are five elements in an array, their indexes are 0,1,2,3,4.

Example 9-1 illustrates the array concepts covered so far. In this example, a class named Tester creates an array of Employees and an array of integers, populates the Employee array, and then prints the values of both.

Example 9-1. Working with an array

```
namespace Programming_CSharp
{

    // a simple class to store in the array
    public class Employee
    {

        public Employee(int empID)
        {
            this.empID = empID;
        }
        public override string ToString()
        {
            return empID.ToString();
        }
        private int empID;
    }
    public class Tester
    {
        static void Main()
        {
            int[] intArray;
            Employee[] empArray;
            intArray = new int[5];
            empArray = new Employee[3];

            // populate the array
            for (int i = 0;i<empArray.Length;i++)
            {
                empArray[i] = new Employee(i+5);
            }

            for (int i = 0;i<intArray.Length;i++)
            {
                Console.WriteLine(intArray[i].ToString());
            }

            for (int i = 0;i<empArray.Length;i++)
            {
                Console.WriteLine(empArray[i].ToString());
            }
        }
    }
}

Output:
0
0
0
0
0
```

Example 9-1. Working with an array (continued)

```
5
6
7
```

The example starts with the definition of an Employee class that implements a constructor that takes a single integer parameter. The ToString() method inherited from Object is overridden to print the value of the Employee object's employee ID.

The test method declares and then instantiates a pair of arrays. The integer array is automatically filled with integers whose values are set to 0. The Employee array contents must be constructed by hand.

Finally, the contents of the arrays are printed to ensure that they are filled as intended. The five integers print their value first, followed by the three Employee objects.

The foreach Statement

The foreach looping statement is new to the C family of languages, though it is already well-known to VB programmers. The foreach statement allows you to iterate through all the items in an array or other collection, examining each item in turn. The syntax for the foreach statement is:

```
foreach (type identifier in expression) statement
```

Thus, you might update Example 9-1 to replace the for statements that iterate over the contents of the populated array with foreach statements, as shown in Example 9-2.

Example 9-2. Using foreach

```
#region Using directives

using System;
using System.Collections.Generic;
using System.Text;

#endregion

namespace UsingForEach
{
    // a simple class to store in the array
    public class Employee
    {
        // a simple class to store in the array
        public Employee( int empID )
        {
            this.empID = empID;
        }
```

Example 9-2. Using foreach (continued)

```
    public override string ToString()
    {
        return empID.ToString();
    }
    private int empID;
}
public class Tester
{
    static void Main()
    {
        int[] intArray;
        Employee[] empArray;
        intArray = new int[5];
        empArray = new Employee[3];

        // populate the array
        for ( int i = 0; i < empArray.Length; i++ )
        {
            empArray[i] = new Employee( i + 5 );
        }

        foreach ( int i in intArray )
        {
            Console.WriteLine( i.ToString() );
        }
        foreach ( Employee e in empArray )
        {
            Console.WriteLine( e.ToString() );
        }
    }
}
```

The output for Example 9-2 is identical to Example 9-1. However, instead of creating a for statement that measures the size of the array and uses a temporary counting variable as an index into the array as in the following, we try another approach:

```
for (int i = 0; i < empArray.Length; i++)
{
    Console.WriteLine(empArray[i].ToString());
}
```

We iterate over the array with the foreach loop, which automatically extracts the next item from within the array and assigns it to the temporary object you've created in the head of the statement:

```
foreach (Employee e in empArray)
{
    Console.WriteLine(e.ToString());
}
```

The object extracted from the array is of the appropriate type; thus, you may call any public method on that object.

Initializing Array Elements

It is possible to initialize the contents of an array at the time it is instantiated by providing a list of values delimited by curly brackets ({}). C# provides a longer and a shorter syntax:

```
int[] myIntArray = new int[5] { 2, 4, 6, 8, 10 }
int[] myIntArray = { 2, 4, 6, 8, 10 }
```

There is no practical difference between these two statements, and most programmers will use the shorter syntax, but see the following note.

> The reason both syntaxes exist is that in some rare circumstances you have to use the longer syntax—specifically, if the C# compiler is unable to infer the correct type for the array.

The params Keyword

You can create a method that displays any number of integers to the console by passing in an array of integers and then iterating over the array with a foreach loop.* The params keyword allows you to pass in a variable number of parameters without necessarily explicitly creating the array.

In the next example, you create a method, DisplayVals(), that takes a variable number of integer arguments:

```
public void DisplayVals(params int[] intVals)
```

The method itself can treat the array as if an integer array were explicitly created and passed in as a parameter. You are free to iterate over the array as you would over any other array of integers:

```
foreach (int i in intVals)
{
    Console.WriteLine("DisplayVals {0}",i);
}
```

The calling method, however, need not explicitly create an array: it can simply pass in integers, and the compiler will assemble the parameters into an array for the DisplayVals() method:

```
t.DisplayVals(5,6,7,8);
```

You are free to pass in an array if you prefer:

```
int [] explicitArray = new int[5] {1,2,3,4,5};
t.DisplayVals(explicitArray);
```

---

* The lifetime of objects declared in the header of a foreach loop are scoped outside the loop, much like the objects declared in a for loop.

Example 9-3 provides the complete source code illustrating the params keyword.

Example 9-3. Using the params keyword

```
#region Using directives

using System;
using System.Collections.Generic;
using System.Text;

#endregion

namespace UsingParams
{
    public class Tester
    {
        static void Main()
        {
            Tester t = new Tester();
            t.DisplayVals(5,6,7,8);
            int [] explicitArray = new int[5] {1,2,3,4,5};
            t.DisplayVals(explicitArray);
        }

        public void DisplayVals(params int[] intVals)
        {
            foreach (int i in intVals)
            {
                Console.WriteLine("DisplayVals {0}",i);
            }
        }
    }
}

Output:
DisplayVals 5
DisplayVals 6
DisplayVals 7
DisplayVals 8
DisplayVals 1
DisplayVals 2
DisplayVals 3
DisplayVals 4
DisplayVals 5
```

Multidimensional Arrays

Arrays can be thought of as long rows of slots into which values can be placed. Once you have a picture of a row of slots, imagine 10 rows, one on top of another. This is the classic two-dimensional array of rows and columns. The rows run across the array and the columns run up and down the array.

A third dimension is possible, but somewhat harder to imagine. Make your arrays three-dimensional, with new rows stacked atop the old two-dimensional array. OK, now imagine four dimensions. Now imagine 10.

Those of you who aren't string-theory physicists have probably given up, as have I. Multidimensional arrays are useful, however, even if you can't quite picture what they would look like.

C# supports two types of multidimensional arrays: rectangular and jagged. In a rectangular array, every row is the same length. A jagged array, however, is an array of arrays, each of which can be a different length.

Rectangular arrays

A *rectangular array* is an array of two (or more) dimensions. In the classic two-dimensional array, the first dimension is the number of rows and the second dimension is the number of columns.

 Java programmers take note: rectangular arrays don't exist in Java.

To declare a two-dimensional array, use the following syntax:

```
type [,] array-name
```

For example, to declare and instantiate a two-dimensional rectangular array named myRectangularArray that contains two rows and three columns of integers, you would write:

```
int [,] myRectangularArray = new int[2,3];
```

Example 9-4 declares, instantiates, initializes, and prints the contents of a two-dimensional array. In this example, a for loop is used to initialize the elements of the array.

Example 9-4. Rectangular array

```
#region Using directives

using System;
using System.Collections.Generic;
using System.Text;

#endregion

namespace RectangularArray
{
    public class Tester
    {
        static void Main()
```

Example 9-4. Rectangular array (continued)

```csharp
    {
        const int rows = 4;
        const int columns = 3;

        // declare a 4x3 integer array
        int[,] rectangularArray = new int[rows, columns];

        // populate the array
        for ( int i = 0; i < rows; i++ )
        {
            for ( int j = 0; j < columns; j++ )
            {
                rectangularArray[i, j] = i + j;
            }
        }

        // report the contents of the array
        for ( int i = 0; i < rows; i++ )
        {
            for ( int j = 0; j < columns; j++ )
            {
                Console.WriteLine( "rectangularArray[{0},{1}] = {2}",
                    i, j, rectangularArray[i, j] );
            }
        }
    }
}
}
```

```
Output:
rectangularArray[0,0] = 0
rectangularArray[0,1] = 1
rectangularArray[0,2] = 2
rectangularArray[1,0] = 1
rectangularArray[1,1] = 2
rectangularArray[1,2] = 3
rectangularArray[2,0] = 2
rectangularArray[2,1] = 3
rectangularArray[2,2] = 4
rectangularArray[3,0] = 3
rectangularArray[3,1] = 4
rectangularArray[3,2] = 5
```

In this example, you declare a pair of constant values:

```csharp
const int rows = 4;
const int columns = 3;
```

that are then used to dimension the array:

```csharp
int[,] rectangularArray = new int[rows, columns];
```

Notice the syntax. The brackets in the int[,] declaration indicate that the type is an array of integers, and the comma indicates the array has two dimensions (two commas would indicate three dimensions, and so on). The actual instantiation of rectangularArray with new int[rows, columns] sets the size of each dimension. Here the declaration and instantiation have been combined.

The program fills the rectangle with a pair of for loops, iterating through each column in each row. Thus, the first element filled is rectangularArray[0,0], followed by rectangularArray[0,1] and rectangularArray[0,2]. Once this is done, the program moves on to the next rows: rectangularArray[1,0], rectangularArray[1,1], rectangularArray[1,2], and so forth, until all the columns in all the rows are filled.

Just as you can initialize a one-dimensional array using bracketed lists of values, you can initialize a two-dimensional array using similar syntax. Example 9-5 declares a two-dimensional array (rectangularArray), initializes its elements using bracketed lists of values, and then prints out the contents.

Example 9-5. Initializing a multidimensional array

```
#region Using directives

using System;
using System.Collections.Generic;
using System.Text;

#endregion

namespace InitializingMultiDimensionalArray
{
    public class Tester
    {
        static void Main()
        {
            const int rows = 4;
            const int columns = 3;

            // imply a 4x3 array
            int[,] rectangularArray =
            {
                {0,1,2}, {3,4,5}, {6,7,8}, {9,10,11}
            };

            for ( int i = 0; i < rows; i++ )
            {
                for ( int j = 0; j < columns; j++ )
                {
                    Console.WriteLine( "rectangularArray[{0},{1}] = {2}",
                        i, j, rectangularArray[i, j] );
                }
            }
        }
    }
```

Example 9-5. Initializing a multidimensional array (continued)

```
    }
}
```

```
Output:
rectangularArrayrectangularArray[0,0] = 0
rectangularArrayrectangularArray[0,1] = 1
rectangularArrayrectangularArray[0,2] = 2
rectangularArrayrectangularArray[1,0] = 3
rectangularArrayrectangularArray[1,1] = 4
rectangularArrayrectangularArray[1,2] = 5
rectangularArrayrectangularArray[2,0] = 6
rectangularArrayrectangularArray[2,1] = 7
rectangularArrayrectangularArray[2,2] = 8
rectangularArrayrectangularArray[3,0] = 9
rectangularArrayrectangularArray[3,1] = 10
rectangularArrayrectangularArray[3,2] = 11
```

The preceding example is similar to Example 9-4, but this time you *imply* the exact dimensions of the array by how you initialize it:

```
int[,] rectangularArrayrectangularArray =
{
    {0,1,2}, {3,4,5}, {6,7,8}, {9,10,11}
};
```

Assigning values in four bracketed lists, each consisting of three elements, implies a 4×3 array. Had you written this as:

```
int[,] rectangularArrayrectangularArray =
{
    {0,1,2,3}, {4,5,6,7}, {8,9,10,11}
};
```

you would instead have implied a 3×4 array.

You can see that the C# compiler understands the implications of your clustering, since it can access the objects with the appropriate offsets, as illustrated in the output.

You might guess that since this is a 12-element array you can just as easily access an element at rectangularArray[0,3] (the fourth element in the first row) as at rectangularArray[1,0] (the first element in the second row) This works in C++, but if you try it in C#, you will run right into an exception:

```
Exception occurred: System.IndexOutOfRangeException:
Index was outside the bounds of the array.
at Programming_CSharp.Tester.Main() in
csharp\programming csharp\listing0703.cs:line 23
```

C# arrays are smart, and they keep track of their bounds. When you imply a 4×3 array, you must treat it as such.

Jagged arrays

A *jagged array* is an array of arrays. It is called "jagged" because each row need not be the same size as all the others, and thus a graphical representation of the array would not be square.

When you create a jagged array, you declare the number of rows in your array. Each row will hold an array, which can be of any length. These arrays must each be declared. You can then fill in the values for the elements in these "inner" arrays.

In a jagged array, each dimension is a one-dimensional array. To declare a jagged array, use the following syntax, where the number of brackets indicates the number of dimensions of the array:

```
type [] []...
```

For example, you would declare a two-dimensional jagged array of integers named myJaggedArray as follows:

```
int [] [] myJaggedArray;
```

Access the fifth element of the third array by writing myJaggedArray[2][4].

Example 9-6 creates a jagged array named myJaggedArray, initializes its elements, and then prints their content. To save space, the program takes advantage of the fact that integer array elements are automatically initialized to 0, and it initializes the values of only some of the elements.

Example 9-6. Working with a jagged array

```
#region Using directives

using System;
using System.Collections.Generic;
using System.Text;

#endregion

namespace JaggedArray
{
    public class Tester
    {
        static void Main()
        {
            const int rows = 4;

            // declare the jagged array as 4 rows high
            int[][] jaggedArray = new int[rows][];

            // the first row has 5 elements
            jaggedArray[0] = new int[5];

            // a row with 2 elements
            jaggedArray[1] = new int[2];
```

Example 9-6. Working with a jagged array (continued)

```
        // a row with 3 elements
        jaggedArray[2] = new int[3];

        // the last row has 5 elements
        jaggedArray[3] = new int[5];

        // Fill some (but not all) elements of the rows
        jaggedArray[0][3] = 15;
        jaggedArray[1][1] = 12;
        jaggedArray[2][1] = 9;
        jaggedArray[2][2] = 99;
        jaggedArray[3][0] = 10;
        jaggedArray[3][1] = 11;
        jaggedArray[3][2] = 12;
        jaggedArray[3][3] = 13;
        jaggedArray[3][4] = 14;

        for ( int i = 0; i < 5; i++ )
        {
           Console.WriteLine( "jaggedArray[0][{0}] = {1}",
              i, jaggedArray[0][i] );
        }

        for ( int i = 0; i < 2; i++ )
        {
           Console.WriteLine( "jaggedArray[1][{0}] = {1}",
              i, jaggedArray[1][i] );
        }

        for ( int i = 0; i < 3; i++ )
        {
           Console.WriteLine( "jaggedArray[2][{0}] = {1}",
              i, jaggedArray[2][i] );
        }
        for ( int i = 0; i < 5; i++ )
        {
           Console.WriteLine( "jaggedArray[3][{0}] = {1}",
              i, jaggedArray[3][i] );
        }
      }
   }
}

Output:
jaggedArray[0][0] = 0
jaggedArray[0][1] = 0
jaggedArray[0][2] = 0
jaggedArray[0][3] = 15
jaggedArray[0][4] = 0
jaggedArray[1][0] = 0
jaggedArray[1][1] = 12
jaggedArray[2][0] = 0
```

Example 9-6. Working with a jagged array (continued)

```
jaggedArray[2][1] = 9
jaggedArray[2][2] = 99
jaggedArray[3][0] = 10
jaggedArray[3][1] = 11
jaggedArray[3][2] = 12
jaggedArray[3][3] = 13
jaggedArray[3][4] = 14
```

In this example, a jagged array is created with four rows:

```
int[][] jaggedArray = new int[rows][];
```

Notice that the second dimension is not specified. This is set by creating a new array for each row. Each array can have a different size:

```
// the first row has 5 elements
jaggedArray[0] = new int[5];

// a row with 2 elements
jaggedArray[1] = new int[2];

// a row with 3 elements
jaggedArray[2] = new int[3];

// the last row has 5 elements
jaggedArray[3] = new int[5];
```

Once an array is specified for each row, you need only populate the various members of each array and then print out their contents to ensure that all went as expected.

Notice that when you access the members of the rectangular array, you put the indexes all within one set of square brackets:

```
rectangularArrayrectangularArray[i,j]
```

while with a jagged array you need a pair of brackets:

```
jaggedArray[3][i]
```

You can keep this straight by thinking of the first as a single array of more than one dimension and of the jagged array as an array *of arrays*.

Array Bounds

The Array class can also be created by using the overloaded CreateInstance method. One of the overloads allows you to specify the lower bounds (starting index) of each dimension in a multidimensional array. This is a fairly obscure capability, not often used.

Briefly, here is how you do it: you call the static method CreateInstance, that returns an Array, and that takes three parameters: an object of type Type (indicating the type of object to hold in the array), an array of integers indicating the length of each dimension in the array, and a second array of integers indicating the lower bound for each dimension. Note that the two arrays of integers must have the same number of elements; that is, you must specify a lower bound for each dimension:

```
#region Using directives

using System;
using System.Collections.Generic;
using System.Text;

#endregion

namespace SettingArrayBounds
{

    public class SettingArrayBounds
    {
       public static void CreateArrayWithBounds()
       {
          // Creates and initializes a multidimensional
          // Array of type String.
          int[] lengthsArray = new int[2] { 3, 5 };
          int[] boundsArray = new int[2] { 2, 3 };
          Array multiDimensionalArray = Array.CreateInstance(
                  typeof( String ),
                  lengthsArray,
                  boundsArray );

          // Displays the lower bounds and the
          // upper bounds of each dimension.
          Console.WriteLine( "Bounds:\tLower\tUpper" );
          for ( int i = 0; i < multiDimensionalArray.Rank; i++ )
             Console.WriteLine(
             "{0}:\t{1}\t{2}",
             i,
             multiDimensionalArray.GetLowerBound( i ),
             multiDimensionalArray.GetUpperBound( i ) );
       }
       static void Main()
       {
          SettingArrayBounds.CreateArrayWithBounds();
       }
    }
}
```

Array Conversions

Conversion is possible between arrays if their dimensions are equal and if a conversion is possible between the reference element types. An implicit conversion can occur if the elements can be implicitly converted; otherwise an explicit conversion is required.

It is also possible, of course, to convert an array of derived objects to an array of base objects. Example 9-7 illustrates the conversion of an array of user-defined Employee types to an array of objects.

Example 9-7. Converting arrays

```
#region Using directives

using System;
using System.Collections.Generic;
using System.Text;

#endregion

namespace ConvertingArrays
{
    // create an object we can
    // store in the array
    public class Employee
    {
        // a simple class to store in the array
        public Employee( int empID )
        {
            this.empID = empID;
        }
        public override string ToString()
        {
            return empID.ToString();
        }
        private int empID;
    }

    public class Tester
    {
        // This method takes an array of objects.
        // We'll pass in an array of Employees
        // and then an array of strings.
        // The conversion is implicit since both Employee
        // and string derive (ultimately) from object.
        public static void PrintArray( object[] theArray )
        {
            Console.WriteLine( "Contents of the Array {0}",
                theArray.ToString() );

            // walk through the array and print
            // the values.
            foreach ( object obj in theArray )
            {
                Console.WriteLine( "Value: {0}", obj );
            }
        }
```

Example 9-7. Converting arrays (continued)

```
static void Main()
{
    // make an array of Employee objects
    Employee[] myEmployeeArray = new Employee[3];

    // initialize each Employee's value
    for ( int i = 0; i < 3; i++ )
    {
        myEmployeeArray[i] = new Employee( i + 5 );
    }

    // display the values
    PrintArray( myEmployeeArray );

    // create an array of two strings
    string[] array =
        {
            "hello", "world"
        };

    // print the value of the strings
    PrintArray( array );
    }
  }
}
```

```
Output:
Contents of the Array Programming_CSharp.Employee[]
Value: 5
Value: 6
Value: 7
Contents of the Array System.String[]
Value: hello
Value: world
```

Example 9-7 begins by creating a simple Employee class, as seen earlier in the chapter. The Tester class now contains a new static method, PrintArray(), that takes as a parameter a one-dimensional array of Objects:

```
public static void PrintArray(object[] theArray)
```

Object is the implicit base class of every object in the .NET Framework, and so is the base class of both String and Employee.

The PrintArray() method takes two actions. First, it calls the ToString() method on the array itself:

```
Console.WriteLine("Contents of the Array {0}",
    theArray.ToString());
```

System.Array overrides the ToString() method to your advantage, printing an identifying name of the array:

```
Contents of the Array Programming_CSharp. Employee []
Contents of the Array System.String[]
```

PrintArray() then goes on to call ToString() on each element in the array it receives as a parameter. Because ToString() is a virtual method in the base class Object, it is guaranteed to be available in every derived class. You have overridden this method appropriately in Employee so that the code works properly. Calling ToString() on a String object might not be necessary, but it is harmless and it allows you to treat these objects polymorphically.

Sorting Arrays

Two useful static methods of Array are Sort() and Reverse(). These are fully supported for arrays of the built-in C# types such as string. Making them work with your own classes is a bit trickier, as you must implement the IComparable interface (see the section "Implementing IComparable" later in this chapter). Example 9-8 demonstrates the use of these two methods to manipulate String objects.

Example 9-8. Using Array.Sort and Array.Reverse

```csharp
#region Using directives

using System;
using System.Collections.Generic;
using System.Text;

#endregion

namespace ArraySortAndReverse
{
    public class Tester
    {
        public static void PrintMyArray( object[] theArray )
        {

            foreach ( object obj in theArray )
            {
                Console.WriteLine( "Value: {0}", obj );
            }
            Console.WriteLine( "\n" );
        }

        static void Main()
        {
            String[] myArray =
                {
                    "Who", "is", "John", "Galt"
                };

            PrintMyArray( myArray );
            Array.Reverse( myArray );
```

Example 9-8. Using Array.Sort and Array.Reverse (continued)

```
        PrintMyArray( myArray );

        String[] myOtherArray =
            {
                "We", "Hold", "These", "Truths",
                "To", "Be", "Self","Evident",
            };

        PrintMyArray( myOtherArray );
        Array.Sort( myOtherArray );
        PrintMyArray( myOtherArray );
    }
  }
}
```

```
Output:
Value: Who
Value: is
Value: John
Value: Galt

Value: Galt
Value: John
Value: is
Value: Who

Value: We
Value: Hold
Value: These
Value: Truths
Value: To
Value: Be
Value: Self
Value: Evident

Value: Be
Value: Evident
Value: Hold
Value: Self
Value: These
Value: To
Value: Truths
Value: We
```

The example begins by creating `myArray`, an array of strings with the words:

```
"Who", "is", "John", "Galt"
```

This array is printed, and then passed to the `Array.Reverse()` method, where it is printed again to see that the array itself has been reversed:

```
Value: Galt
Value: John
```

```
Value: is
Value: Who
```

Similarly, the example creates a second array, myOtherArray, containing the words:

```
"We", "Hold", "These", "Truths",
"To", "Be", "Self", "Evident",
```

This is passed to the Array.Sort() method. Then Array.Sort() happily sorts them alphabetically:

```
Value: Be
Value: Evident
Value: Hold
Value: Self
Value: These
Value: To
Value: Truths
Value: We
```

Indexers

There are times when it is desirable to access a collection within a class as though the class itself were an array. For example, suppose you create a listbox control named myListBox that contains a list of strings stored in a one-dimensional array, a private member variable named myStrings. A listbox control contains member properties and methods in addition to its array of strings. However, it would be convenient to be able to access the listbox array with an index, just as if the listbox were an array.* For example, such a property would permit statements such as the following:

```
string theFirstString = myListBox[0];
string theLastString = myListBox[Length-1];
```

An *indexer* is a C# construct that allows you to access collections contained by a class using the familiar [ ] syntax of arrays. An indexer is a special kind of property and includes get and set accessors to specify its behavior.

You declare an indexer property within a class using the following syntax:

```
type this [type argument]{get; set;}
```

The return type determines the type of object that will be returned by the indexer, while the type argument specifies what kind of argument will be used to index into the collection that contains the target objects. Although it is common to use integers as index values, you can index a collection on other types as well, including strings. You can even provide an indexer with multiple parameters to create a multidimensional array!

---

* The actual ListBox control provided by both Windows Forms and ASP.NET has a collection called Items, and it is the Items collection that implements the indexer.

The this keyword is a reference to the object in which the indexer appears. As with a normal property, you also must define get and set accessors, which determine how the requested object is retrieved from or assigned to its collection.

Example 9-9 declares a listbox control (ListBoxTest) that contains a simple array (myStrings) and a simple indexer for accessing its contents.

 C++ programmers take note: the indexer serves much the same purpose as overloading the C++ index operator ([ ]). The index operator can't be overloaded in C#, which provides the indexer in its place.

Example 9-9. Using a simple indexer

```
#region Using directives

using System;
using System.Collections.Generic;
using System.Text;

#endregion

namespace SimpleIndexer
{
    // a simplified ListBox control
    public class ListBoxTest
    {
        private string[] strings;
        private int ctr = 0;

        // initialize the list box with strings
        public ListBoxTest( params string[] initialStrings )
        {
            // allocate space for the strings
            strings = new String[256];

            // copy the strings passed in to the constructor
            foreach ( string s in initialStrings )
            {
                strings[ctr++] = s;
            }
        }

        // add a single string to the end of the list box
        public void Add( string theString )
        {
            if ( ctr >= strings.Length )
            {
                // handle bad index
            }
            else
                strings[ctr++] = theString;
        }
```

Example 9-9. Using a simple indexer (continued)

```
        // allow array-like access

        public string this[int index]
        {
            get
            {
                if ( index < 0 || index >= strings.Length )
                {
                    // handle bad index
                }
                return strings[index];
            }
            set
            {
                // add only through the add method
                if ( index >= ctr )
                {
                    // handle error
                }
                else
                    strings[index] = value;
            }
        }

        // publish how many strings you hold
        public int GetNumEntries()
        {
            return ctr;
        }
    }

    public class Tester
    {
        static void Main()
        {
            // create a new list box and initialize
            ListBoxTest lbt =
                new ListBoxTest( "Hello", "World" );

            // add a few strings
            lbt.Add( "Who" );
            lbt.Add( "Is" );
            lbt.Add( "John" );
            lbt.Add( "Galt" );

            // test the access
            string subst = "Universe";
            lbt[1] = subst;

            // access all the strings
            for ( int i = 0; i < lbt.GetNumEntries(); i++ )
            {
```

Example 9-9. Using a simple indexer (continued)

```
            Console.WriteLine( "lbt[{0}]: {1}", i, lbt[i] );
        }
    }
}
}
```

Output:
```
lbt[0]: Hello
lbt[1]: Universe
lbt[2]: Who
lbt[3]: Is
lbt[4]: John
lbt[5]: Galt
```

To keep Example 9-9 simple, we strip the listbox control down to the few features we care about. The listing ignores everything having to do with being a user control and focuses only on the list of strings the listbox maintains and methods for manipulating them. In a real application, of course, these are a small fraction of the total methods of a listbox, whose principal job is to display the strings and enable user choice.

The first things to notice are the two private members:

```
private string[] strings;
private int ctr = 0;
```

In this program, the listbox maintains a simple array of strings: strings. Again, in a real listbox you might use a more complex and dynamic container, such as a hash table (described later in this chapter). The member variable ctr will keep track of how many strings have been added to this array.

Initialize the array in the constructor with the statement:

```
strings = new String[256];
```

The remainder of the constructor adds the parameters to the array. Again, for simplicity, add new strings to the array in the order received.

Because you can't know how many strings will be added, use the keyword params, as described earlier in this chapter.

The Add() method of ListBoxTest does nothing more than append a new string to the internal array.

The key method of ListBoxTest, however, is the indexer. An indexer is unnamed, so use the this keyword:

```
public string this[int index]
```

The syntax of the indexer is very similar to that for properties. There is either a get() method, a set() method, or both. In the case shown, the get() method endeavors to implement rudimentary bounds-checking, and assuming the index requested is acceptable, it returns the value requested:

```
get
{
    if (index < 0 || index >= strings.Length)
    {
        // handle bad index
    }
    return strings[index];
}
```

The set() method checks to make sure that the index you are setting already has a value in the listbox. If not, it treats the set as an error. (New elements can only be added using Add with this approach.) The set accessor takes advantage of the implicit parameter value that represents whatever is assigned using the index operator:

```
set
{
if (index >= ctr )
  {
      // handle error
  }
  else
      strings[index] = value;
}
```

Thus, if you write:

```
lbt[5] = "Hello World"
```

the compiler will call the indexer set() method on your object and pass in the string Hello World as an implicit parameter named value.

Indexers and Assignment

In Example 9-9, you can't assign to an index that doesn't have a value. Thus, if you write:

```
lbt[10] = "wow!";
```

you would trigger the error handler in the set() method, which would note that the index you've passed in (10) is larger than the counter (6).

Of course, you can use the set() method for assignment; you simply have to handle the indexes you receive. To do so, you might change the set() method to check the Length of the buffer rather than the current value of counter. If a value was entered for an index that did not yet have a value, you would update ctr:

```
set
{
    // add only through the add method
```

```
    if (index >= strings.Length )
    {
        // handle error
    }
    else
    {
        strings[index] = value;
        if (ctr < index+1)
            ctr = index+1;
    }
}
```

> This code is kept simple and thus is not robust. There are any number of other checks you'll want to make on the value passed in (e.g., checking that you were not passed a negative index and that it doesn't exceed the size of the underlying strings[] array).

This allows you to create a "sparse" array in which you can assign to offset 10 without ever having assigned to offset 9. Thus, if you now write:

```
lbt[10] = "wow!";
```

the output would be:

```
lbt[0]: Hello
lbt[1]: Universe
lbt[2]: Who
lbt[3]: Is
lbt[4]: John
lbt[5]: Galt
lbt[6]:
lbt[7]:
lbt[8]:
lbt[9]:
lbt[10]: wow!
```

In Main(), you create an instance of the ListBoxTest class named lbt and pass in two strings as parameters:

```
ListBoxTest lbt = new ListBoxTest("Hello", "World");
```

Then call Add() to add four more strings:

```
// add a few strings
lbt.Add("Who");
lbt.Add("Is");
lbt.Add("John");
lbt.Add("Galt");
```

Before examining the values, modify the second value (at index 1):

```
string subst = "Universe";
lbt[1] = subst;
```

Finally, display each value in a loop:

```
for (int i = 0;i<lbt.GetNumEntries();i++)
{
    Console.WriteLine("lbt[{0}]: {1}",i,lbt[i]);
}
```

Indexing on Other Values

C# doesn't require that you always use an integer value as the index to a collection. When you create a custom collection class and create your indexer, you are free to create indexers that index on strings and other types. In fact, the index value can be overloaded so that a given collection can be indexed, for example, by an integer value or by a string value, depending on the needs of the client.

In the case of our listbox, we might want to be able to index into the listbox based on a string. Example 9-10 illustrates a string index. The indexer calls findString(), which is a helper method that returns a record based on the value of the string provided. Notice that the overloaded indexer and the indexer from Example 9-9 are able to coexist.

Example 9-10. Overloading an index

```
#region Using directives

using System;
using System.Collections.Generic;
using System.Text;

#endregion

namespace OverloadedIndexer
{
    // a simplified ListBox control
    public class ListBoxTest
    {
        private string[] strings;
        private int ctr = 0;

        // initialize the list box with strings
        public ListBoxTest( params string[] initialStrings )
        {
            // allocate space for the strings
            strings = new String[256];

            // copy the strings passed in to the constructor
            foreach ( string s in initialStrings )
            {
                strings[ctr++] = s;
            }
        }
```

Example 9-10. Overloading an index (continued)

```csharp
// add a single string to the end of the list box
public void Add( string theString )
{
    strings[ctr] = theString;
    ctr++;
}

// allow array-like access
public string this[int index]
{
    get
    {
        if ( index < 0 || index >= strings.Length )
        {
            // handle bad index
        }
        return strings[index];
    }
    set
    {
        strings[index] = value;
    }
}

private int findString( string searchString )
{
    for ( int i = 0; i < strings.Length; i++ )
    {
        if ( strings[i].StartsWith( searchString ) )
        {
            return i;
        }
    }
    return -1;
}

// index on string
public string this[string index]
{
    get
    {
        if ( index.Length == 0 )
        {
            // handle bad index
        }

        return this[findString( index )];
    }
    set
    {
        strings[findString( index )] = value;
```

Example 9-10. Overloading an index (continued)

```
        }
    }

    // publish how many strings you hold
    public int GetNumEntries()
    {
        return ctr;
    }
}

public class Tester
{
    static void Main()
    {
        // create a new list box and initialize
        ListBoxTest lbt =
            new ListBoxTest( "Hello", "World" );

        // add a few strings
        lbt.Add( "Who" );
        lbt.Add( "Is" );
        lbt.Add( "John" );
        lbt.Add( "Galt" );

        // test the access
        string subst = "Universe";
        lbt[1] = subst;
        lbt["Hel"] = "GoodBye";
        // lbt["xyz"] = "oops";

        // access all the strings
        for ( int i = 0; i < lbt.GetNumEntries(); i++ )
        {
            Console.WriteLine( "lbt[{0}]: {1}", i, lbt[i] );
        }       // end for
    }           // end main
}               // end tester
}
```

```
Output:
lbt[0]: GoodBye
lbt[1]: Universe
lbt[2]: Who
lbt[3]: Is
lbt[4]: John
lbt[5]: Galt
```

Example 9-10 is identical to Example 9-9 except for the addition of an overloaded indexer, which can match a string, and the method findString, created to support that index.

The findString method simply iterates through the strings held in myStrings until it finds a string that starts with the target string we use in the index. If found, it returns the index of that string; otherwise it returns the value -1.

We see in Main() that the user passes in a string segment to the index, just as with an integer:

```
lbt["Hel"] = "GoodBye";
```

This calls the overloaded index, which does some rudimentary error-checking (in this case, making sure the string passed in has at least one letter) and then passes the value (Hel) to findString. It gets back an index and uses that index to index into myStrings:

```
return this[findString(index)];
```

The set value works in the same way:

```
myStrings[findString(index)] = value;
```

> The careful reader will note that if the string doesn't match, a value of -1 is returned, which is then used as an index into myStrings. This action then generates an exception (System.NullReferenceException), as you can see by uncommenting the following line in Main():
>
> ```
> lbt["xyz"] = "oops";
> ```
>
> The proper handling of not finding a string is, as they say, left as an exercise for the reader. You might consider displaying an error message or otherwise allowing the user to recover from the error.

Collection Interfaces

The .NET Framework provides two sets of standard interfaces for enumerating and comparing collections: the traditional (nontype-safe) and the new generic type-safe collections. This book focuses only on the new, type-safe collection interfaces as these are far preferable.

You can declare an ICollection of any specific type by substituting the *actual* type (for example, int or string) for the *generic* type in the interface declaration (<T>).

> *C++ programmers note:* C# generics are similar in syntax and usage to C++ templates. However, because the generic types are expanded to their specific type at runtime, the JIT compiler is able to share code among different instances, dramatically reducing the code bloat that you may see when using templates in C++.

The key generic collection interfaces are listed in Table 9-2.[*]

---

[*] For backward compatibility, C# also provides nongeneric interfaces (e.g., ICollection, IEnumerator), but they aren't considered here because they are obsolescent.

Table 9-2. Collection interfaces

Interface	Purpose
ICollection<T>	Base interface for generic collections.
IEnumerator<T> IEnumerable<T>	Enumerates through a collection using a `foreach` statement.
ICollection<T>	Implemented by all collections to provide the `CopyTo( )` method as well as the `Count`, `IsSynchronized`, and `SyncRoot` properties.
IComparer<T> IComparable<T>	Compares two objects held in a collection so that the collection can be sorted.
IList<T>	Used by array-indexable collections.
IDictionary<K,V>	Used for key/value-based collections such as `Dictionary`.

The IEnumerable<T> Interface

You can support the foreach statement in ListBoxTest by implementing the IEnumerable<T> interface (see Example 9-11). IEnumerable has only one method, GetEnumerator(), whose job is to return an implementation of IEnumerator<T>. The C# language provides special help in creating the enumerator, using the new keyword yield.

Example 9-11. Making a ListBox an enumerable class

```
#region Using directives

using System;
using System.Collections.Generic;
using System.Text;

#endregion

namespace Enumerable
{
    public class ListBoxTest : IEnumerable<String>
    {
        private string[] strings;
        private int ctr = 0;
        // Enumerable classes can return an enumerator
        public IEnumerator<string> GetEnumerator()
        {
            foreach ( string s in strings )
            {
                yield return s;
            }
        }

        // initialize the list box with strings
        public ListBoxTest( params string[] initialStrings )
        {
```

Example 9-11. Making a ListBox an enumerable class (continued)

```
            // allocate space for the strings
            strings = new String[8];

            // copy the strings passed in to the constructor
            foreach ( string s in initialStrings )
            {
                strings[ctr++] = s;
            }
        }

        // add a single string to the end of the list box
        public void Add( string theString )
        {
            strings[ctr] = theString;
            ctr++;
        }

        // allow array-like access
        public string this[int index]
        {
            get
            {
                if ( index < 0 || index >= strings.Length )
                {
                    // handle bad index
                }
                return strings[index];
            }
            set
            {
                strings[index] = value;
            }
        }

        // publish how many strings you hold
        public int GetNumEntries()
        {
            return ctr;
        }
    }

    public class Tester
    {
        static void Main()
        {
            // create a new list box and initialize
            ListBoxTest lbt =
                new ListBoxTest( "Hello", "World" );

            // add a few strings
            lbt.Add( "Who" );
            lbt.Add( "Is" );
```

Example 9-11. Making a ListBox an enumerable class (continued)

```
        lbt.Add( "John" );
        lbt.Add( "Galt" );

        // test the access
        string subst = "Universe";
        lbt[1] = subst;

        // access all the strings
        foreach ( string s in lbt )
        {
            Console.WriteLine( "Value: {0}", s );
        }
    }
  }
}
```

```
Output:
Value: Hello
Value: Universe
Value: Who
Value: Is
Value: John
Value: Galt
Value:
Value:
```

The program begins in Main(), creating a new ListBoxTest object and passing two strings to the constructor. When the object is created, an array of Strings is created with enough room for eight strings. Four more strings are added using the Add method, and the second string is updated, just as in the previous example.

The big change in this version of the program is that a foreach loop is called, retrieving each string in the listbox. The foreach loop automatically uses the IEnumerable<T> interface, invoking GetEnumerator().

The GetEnumerator method is declared to return an IEnumerator of string:

```
public IEnumerator<string> GetEnumerator()
```

The implementation iterates through the array of strings, yielding each in turn:

```
foreach ( string s in strings )
{
    yield return s;
}
```

All the bookkeeping for keeping track of which element is next, resetting the iterator, and so forth, is provided for you by the framework.

Constraints

There are times when you must ensure that the elements you add to a generic list meet certain constraints (e.g., they derive from a given base class, or they implement a specific interface). In the next example, we implement a simplified singly linked, sortable list. The list consists of Nodes, and each Node must be guaranteed that the types added to it implement IComparer. You do so with the following statement:

```
public class Node<T> :
    IComparable<Node<T>> where T : IComparable<T>
```

This defines a generic Node that holds a type, T. Node of T implements the IComparable<T> interface, which means that two Nodes of T can be compared. The Node class is constrained (where T :IComparable<T>) to hold only types that implement the IComparable interface. Thus, you may substitute any type for T so long as that type implements IComparable.

Example 9-12 illustrates the complete implementation, with analysis to follow.

Example 9-12. Using constraints

```
using System;
using System.Collections.Generic;

namespace UsingConstraints
{
    public class Employee : IComparable<Employee>
    {
        private string name;
        public Employee(string name)
        {
            this.name = name;
        }
        public override string ToString()
        {
            return this.name;
        }

        // implement the interface
        public int CompareTo(Employee rhs)
        {
            return this.name.CompareTo(rhs.name);
        }
        public bool Equals(Employee rhs)
        {
            return this.name == rhs.name;
        }
    }

    // node must implement IComparable of Node of T.
    // constrain Nodes to only take items that implement Icomparable
    // by using the where keyword.
```

Example 9-12. Using constraints (continued)

```
public class Node<T> :
    IComparable<Node<T>> where T : IComparable<T>
{
    // member fields
    private T data;
    private Node<T> next = null;
    private Node<T> prev = null;

    // constructor
    public Node(T data)
    {
        this.data = data;
    }

    // properties
    public T Data { get { return this.data; } }

    public Node<T> Next
    {
        get { return this.next; }
    }

    public int CompareTo(Node<T> rhs)
    {
        // this works because of the constraint
        return data.CompareTo(rhs.data);
    }

    public bool Equals(Node<T> rhs)
    {
        return this.data.Equals(rhs.data);
    }

    // methods
    public Node<T> Add(Node<T> newNode)
    {
        if (this.CompareTo(newNode) > 0) // goes before me
        {
            newNode.next = this;  // new node points to me

            // if I have a previous, set it to point to
            // the new node as its next
            if (this.prev != null)
            {
                this.prev.next = newNode;
                newNode.prev = this.prev;
            }

            // set prev in current node to point to new node
            this.prev = newNode;
```

Example 9-12. Using constraints (continued)

```
                // return the newNode in case it is the new head
                return newNode;
            }
            else            // goes after me
            {
                // if I have a next, pass the new node along for
                    // comparison
                if (this.next != null)
                {
                    this.next.Add(newNode);
                }

                // I don't have a next so set the new node
                    // to be my next and set its prev to point to me.
                else
                {
                    this.next = newNode;
                    newNode.prev = this;
                }

                return this;
            }
        }

    public override string ToString()
    {
        string output = data.ToString();

        if (next != null)
        {
            output += ", " + next.ToString();
        }

        return output;
    }
}           // end class

public class LinkedList<T> where T : IComparable<T>
{
    // member fields
    private Node<T> headNode = null;

    // properties

    // indexer
    public T this[int index]
    {
        get
        {
            int ctr = 0;
            Node<T> node = headNode;
```

Example 9-12. Using constraints (continued)

```
            while (node != null && ctr <= index)
            {
                if (ctr == index)
                {
                    return node.Data;
                }
                else
                {
                    node = node.Next;
                }

                ++ctr;
            } // end while
            throw new ArgumentOutOfRangeException();
        }       // end get
    }           // end indexer

    // constructor
    public LinkedList()
    {
    }

    // methods
    public void Add(T data)
    {
        if (headNode == null)
        {
            headNode = new Node<T>(data);
        }
        else
        {
            headNode = headNode.Add(new Node<T>(data));
        }
    }
    public override string ToString()
    {
        if (this.headNode != null)
        {
            return this.headNode.ToString();
        }
        else
        {
            return string.Empty;
        }
    }
}

// Test engine
class Test
{
    // entry point
    static void Main(string[] args)
```

Example 9-12. Using constraints (continued)

```
    {
        // make an instance, run the method
        Test t = new Test();
        t.Run();
    }

    public void Run()
    {
        LinkedList<int> myLinkedList = new LinkedList<int>();
        Random rand = new Random();
        Console.Write("Adding: ");

        for (int i = 0; i < 10; i++)
        {
            int nextInt = rand.Next(10);
            Console.Write("{0}  ", nextInt);
            myLinkedList.Add(nextInt);
        }

        LinkedList<Employee> employees = new LinkedList<Employee>();
        employees.Add(new Employee("John"));
        employees.Add(new Employee("Paul"));
        employees.Add(new Employee("George"));
        employees.Add(new Employee("Ringo"));

        Console.WriteLine("\nRetrieving collections...");

        Console.WriteLine("Integers: " + myLinkedList);
        Console.WriteLine("Employees: " + employees);
    }
  }
}
```

In this example, you begin by declaring a class that can be placed into the linked list:

```
public class Employee : IComparable<Employee>
```

This declaration indicates that Employee objects are comparable, and we see that the Employee class implements the required methods (CompareTo and Equals). Note that these methods are type-safe (they know that the parameter passed to them will be of type Employee). The LinkedList itself is declared to hold only types that implement IComparable:

```
public class LinkedList<T> where T : IComparable<T>
```

so you are guaranteed to be able to sort the list. The LinkedList holds an object of type Node. Node also implements IComparable and requires that the objects it holds as data themselves implement IComparable:

```
public class Node<T> :
    IComparable<Node<T>> where T : IComparable<T>
```

These constraints make it safe and simple to implement the CompareTo method of Node because the Node knows it will be comparing other Nodes whose data is comparable:

```
public int CompareTo(Node<T> rhs)
{
    // this works because of the constraint
    return data.CompareTo(rhs.data);
}
```

Notice that we don't have to test rhs to see if it implements IComparable; we've already constrained Node to hold only data that implements IComparable.

List<T>

The classic problem with the Array type is its fixed size. If you don't know in advance how many objects an array will hold, you run the risk of declaring either too small an array (and running out of room) or too large an array (and wasting memory).

Your program might be asking the user for input, or gathering input from a web site. As it finds objects (strings, books, values, etc.), you will add them to the array, but you have no idea how many objects you'll collect in any given session. The classic fixed-size array is not a good choice, as you can't predict how large an array you'll need.

The List class is an array whose size is dynamically increased as required. Lists provide a number of useful methods and properties for their manipulation. Some of the most important are shown in Table 9-3.

Table 9-3. List methods and properties

Method or property	Purpose
Capacity	Property to get or set the number of elements the List can contain. This value is increased automatically if count exceeds capacity. You might set this value to reduce the number of reallocations, and you may call Trim( ) to reduce this value to the actual Count.
Count	Property to get the number of elements currently in the array.
Item()	Gets or sets the element at the specified index. This is the indexer for the List class.[a]
Add()	Public method to add an object to the List.
AddRange()	Public method that adds the elements of an ICollection to the end of the List.
BinarySearch()	Overloaded public method that uses a binary search to locate a specific element in a sorted List.
Clear()	Removes all elements from the List.
Contains()	Determines if an element is in the List.
CopyTo()	Overloaded public method that copies a List to a one-dimensional array.
Exists()	Determines if an element is in the List.
Find()	Returns the first occurrence of the element in the List.
FindAll()	Returns all the specified elements in the List.
GetEnumerator()	Overloaded public method that returns an enumerator to iterate through a List.

Table 9-3. List methods and properties (continued)

Method or property	Purpose
GetRange()	Copies a range of elements to a new List.
IndexOf()	Overloaded public method that returns the index of the first occurrence of a value.
Insert()	Inserts an element into the List.
InsertRange()	Inserts the elements of a collection into the List.
LastIndexOf()	Overloaded public method that returns the index of the last occurrence of a value in the List.
Remove()	Removes the first occurrence of a specific object.
RemoveAt()	Removes the element at the specified index.
RemoveRange()	Removes a range of elements.
Reverse()	Reverses the order of elements in the List.
Sort()	Sorts the List.
ToArray()	Copies the elements of the List to a new array.
TrimToSize()	Sets the capacity of the actual number of elements in the List.

ª The idiom in the FCL is to provide an Item element for collection classes which is implemented as an indexer in C#.

When you create a List, you don't define how many objects it will contain. Add to the List using the Add() method, and the list takes care of its own internal book-keeping, as illustrated in Example 9-13.

Example 9-13. Working with List

```
#region Using directives

using System;
using System.Collections.Generic;
using System.Text;

#endregion

namespace ListCollection
{
    // a simple class to store in the List
    public class Employee
    {
        private int empID;

        public Employee( int empID )
        {
            this.empID = empID;
        }
        public override string ToString()
        {
            return empID.ToString();
        }
        public int EmpID
        {
```

Example 9-13. Working with List (continued)

```
        get
        {
            return empID;
        }
        set
        {
            empID = value;
        }
    }
}
public class Tester
{
    static void Main()
    {

        List<Employee> empList = new List<Employee>();
        List<int> intList = new List<int>();

        // populate the List
        for ( int i = 0; i < 5; i++ )
        {
            empList.Add( new Employee( i + 100 ) );
            intList.Add( i * 5 );
        }

        // print all the contents
        for ( int i = 0; i < intList.Count; i++ )
        {
            Console.Write( "{0} ", intList[i].ToString() );
        }

        Console.WriteLine( "\n" );

        // print all the contents of the Employee List
        for ( int i = 0; i < empList.Count; i++ )
        {
            Console.Write( "{0} ", empList[i].ToString() );
        }

        Console.WriteLine( "\n" );
        Console.WriteLine( "empList.Capacity: {0}",
            empList.Capacity );
    }
}
}
```

Output:
0 5 10 15 20
100 101 102 103 104
empArray.Capacity: 16

With an `Array` class, you define how many objects the array will hold. If you try to add more than that, the `Array` class will throw an exception. With a `List`, you don't declare how many objects the `List` will hold. The `List` has a property, `Capacity`, which is the number of elements the `List` is capable of storing:

```
public int Capacity { get; set; }
```

The default capacity is 16. When you add the 17th element, the capacity is automatically doubled to 32. If you change the `for` loop to:

```
for (int i = 0;i<17;i++)
```

the output looks like this:

```
0 5 10 15 20 25 30 35 40 45 50 55 60 65 70 75 80
5 6 7 8 9 10 11 12 13 14 15 16 17 18 19 20 21
empArray.Capacity: 32
```

You can manually set the capacity to any number equal to or greater than the count. If you set it to a number less than the count, the program will throw an exception of type `ArgumentOutOfRangeException`.

Implementing IComparable

Like all collections, the `List` implements the `Sort()` method, which allows you to sort any objects that implement `IComparable`. In the next example, you'll modify the `Employee` object to implement `IComparable`:

```
public class Employee : IComparable<Employee>
```

To implement the `IComparable<Employee>` interface, the `Employee` object must provide a `CompareTo()` method:

```
public int CompareTo(Employee rhs)
{
    return this.empID.CompareTo(r.empID);
}
```

The `CompareTo()` method takes an `Employee` as a parameter. We know this is an `Employee` because this is a type-safe collection. The current `Employee` object must compare itself to the `Employee` passed in as a parameter and return -1 if it is smaller than the parameter, 1 if it is greater than the parameter, and 0 if it is equal to the parameter. It is up to `Employee` to determine what `smaller than`, `greater than`, and `equal to` mean. In this example, you delegate the comparison to the `empId` member. The `empId` member is an `int` and uses the default `CompareTo()` method for integer types, which will do an integer comparison of the two values.

The `System.Int32` class implements `IComparable<Int32>`, so you may delegate the comparison responsibility to integers.

You are now ready to sort the array list of employees, empList. To see if the sort is working, you'll need to add integers and Employee instances to their respective arrays with random values. To create the random values, you'll instantiate an object of class Random; to generate the random values, you'll call the Next() method on the Random object, which returns a pseudorandom number. The Next() method is overloaded; one version allows you to pass in an integer that represents the largest random number you want. In this case, you'll pass in the value 10 to generate a random number between 0 and 10:

```
Random r = new Random();
r.Next(10);
```

Example 9-14 creates an integer array and an Employee array, populates them both with random numbers, and prints their values. It then sorts both arrays and prints the new values.

Example 9-14. Sorting an integer and an employee array

```
#region Using directives

using System;
using System.Collections.Generic;
using System.Text;

#endregion

namespace IComparable
{
    // a simple class to store in the array
    public class Employee : IComparable<Employee>
    {
        private int empID;

        public Employee( int empID )
        {
            this.empID = empID;
        }

        public override string ToString()
        {
            return empID.ToString();
        }

        public bool Equals( Employee other )
        {
            if ( this.empID == other.empID )
            {
                return true;
            }
            else
            {
                return false;
```

Example 9-14. Sorting an integer and an employee array (continued)

```
      }
   }

   // Comparer delegates back to Employee
   // Employee uses the integer's default
   // CompareTo method

   public int CompareTo( Employee rhs )
   {
      return this.empID.CompareTo( rhs.empID );
   }
}
public class Tester
{
   static void Main()
   {
      List<Employee> empArray = new List<Employee>();
      List<Int32> intArray = new List<Int32>();

      // generate random numbers for
      // both the integers and the
      // employee id's

      Random r = new Random();

      // populate the array
      for ( int i = 0; i < 5; i++ )
      {
         // add a random employee id
         empArray.Add( new Employee( r.Next( 10 ) + 100 ) );

         // add a random integer
         intArray.Add( r.Next( 10 ) );
      }

      // display all the contents of the int array
      for ( int i = 0; i < intArray.Count; i++ )
      {
         Console.Write( "{0} ", intArray[i].ToString() );
      }
      Console.WriteLine( "\n" );

      // display all the contents of the Employee array
      for ( int i = 0; i < empArray.Count; i++ )
      {
         Console.Write( "{0} ", empArray[i].ToString() );
      }
      Console.WriteLine( "\n" );

      // sort and display the int array
      intArray.Sort();
      for ( int i = 0; i < intArray.Count; i++ )
```

Example 9-14. Sorting an integer and an employee array (continued)

```
        {
            Console.Write( "{0} ", intArray[i].ToString() );
        }
        Console.WriteLine( "\n" );

        // sort and display the employee array
        empArray.Sort(c);

        empArray.Sort();

        // display all the contents of the Employee array
        for ( int i = 0; i < empArray.Count; i++ )
        {
            Console.Write( "{0} ", empArray[i].ToString() );
        }
        Console.WriteLine( "\n" );
    }
  }
}
```

```
Output:
4 5 6 5 7
108 100 101 103 103
4 5 5 6 7
100 101 103 103 108
```

The output shows that the integer array and Employee array were generated with random numbers. When sorted, the display shows the values have been ordered properly.

Implementing IComparer

When you call Sort() on the List, the default implementation of IComparer is called, which uses QuickSort to call the IComparable implementation of CompareTo() on each element in the List.

You are free to create your own implementation of IComparer, which you might want to do if you need control over how the sort ordering is defined. In the next example, you will add a second field to Employee, yearsOfSvc. You want to be able to sort the Employee objects in the List on either field, empID or yearsOfSvc.

To accomplish this, create a custom implementation of IComparer, which you pass to the Sort() method of the List. This IComparer class, EmployeeComparer, knows about Employee objects and knows how to sort them.

EmployeeComparer has the WhichComparison property, of type Employee. EmployeeComparer.ComparisonType:

```
    public Employee.EmployeeComparer.ComparisonType
        WhichComparison
```

```
{
   get{return whichComparison;}
   set{whichComparison = value;}
}
```

ComparisonType is an enumeration with two values, empID or yearsOfSvc (indicating that you want to sort by employee ID or years of service, respectively):

```
public enum ComparisonType
{
   EmpID,
   YearsOfService
};
```

Before invoking Sort(), create an instance of EmployeeComparer and set its ComparisionType property:

```
Employee.EmployeeComparer c = Employee.GetComparer();
c.WhichComparison=Employee.EmployeeComparer.ComparisonType.EmpID;
empArray.Sort(c);
```

When you invoke Sort(), the List calls the Compare method on the EmployeeComparer, which in turn delegates the comparison to the Employee.CompareTo() method, passing in its WhichComparison property:

```
public int Compare( Employee lhs, Employee rhs )
{
   return lhs.CompareTo( rhs, WhichComparison );
}
```

The Employee object must implement a custom version of CompareTo(), which takes the comparison and compares the objects accordingly:

```
public int CompareTo(
   Employee rhs,
   Employee.EmployeeComparer.ComparisonType which)
{
   switch (which)
   {
      case Employee.EmployeeComparer.ComparisonType.EmpID:
         return this.empID.CompareTo(rhs.empID);
      case Employee.EmployeeComparer.ComparisonType.Yrs:
         return this.yearsOfSvc.CompareTo(rhs.yearsOfSvc);
   }
   return 0;
}
```

The complete source for this example is shown in Example 9-15. The integer array has been removed to simplify the example, and the output of the employee's ToString() method has been enhanced to enable you to see the effects of the sort.

Example 9-15. Sorting an array by employees' IDs and years of service

```
#region Using directives

using System;
using System.Collections.Generic;
using System.Text;

#endregion

namespace IComparer
{
    public class Employee : IComparable<Employee>
    {
        private int empID;

        private int yearsOfSvc = 1;

        public Employee( int empID )
        {
            this.empID = empID;
        }

        public Employee( int empID, int yearsOfSvc )
        {
            this.empID = empID;
            this.yearsOfSvc = yearsOfSvc;
        }

        public override string ToString()
        {
            return "ID: " + empID.ToString() +
            ". Years of Svc: " + yearsOfSvc.ToString();
        }

        public bool Equals( Employee other )
        {
            if ( this.empID == other.empID )
            {
                return true;
            }
            else
            {
                return false;
            }
        }

        // static method to get a Comparer object
        public static EmployeeComparer GetComparer()
        {
            return new Employee.EmployeeComparer();
        }
```

Example 9-15. Sorting an array by employees' IDs and years of service (continued)

```
// Comparer delegates back to Employee
// Employee uses the integer's default
// CompareTo method
public int CompareTo( Employee rhs )
{
   return this.empID.CompareTo( rhs.empID );
}

// Special implementation to be called by custom comparer
public int CompareTo(
   Employee rhs,
   Employee.EmployeeComparer.ComparisonType which )
{
   switch ( which )
   {
      case Employee.EmployeeComparer.ComparisonType.EmpID:
         return this.empID.CompareTo( rhs.empID );
      case Employee.EmployeeComparer.ComparisonType.Yrs:
         return this.yearsOfSvc.CompareTo( rhs.yearsOfSvc );
   }
   return 0;

}

// nested class which implements IComparer
public class EmployeeComparer : IComparer<Employee>
{

   // private state variable
   private Employee.EmployeeComparer.ComparisonType
      whichComparison;

   // enumeration of comparison types
   public enum ComparisonType
   {
      EmpID,
      Yrs
   };

   public  bool Equals( Employee lhs, Employee rhs )
   {
      return this.Compare( lhs, rhs ) == 0;
   }

   public  int GetHashCode(Employee e)
   {
      return e.GetHashCode();
   }

   // Tell the Employee objects to compare themselves
   public int Compare( Employee lhs, Employee rhs )
   {
```

Example 9-15. Sorting an array by employees' IDs and years of service (continued)

```
                return lhs.CompareTo( rhs, WhichComparison );
        }

        public Employee.EmployeeComparer.ComparisonType
            WhichComparison
        {
            get{return whichComparison;}
            set{whichComparison = value;}
        }
    }
}
public class Tester
{
    static void Main()
    {
        List<Employee> empArray = new List<Employee>();

        // generate random numbers for
        // both the integers and the
        // employee id's
        Random r = new Random();

        // populate the array
        for ( int i = 0; i < 5; i++ )
        {
            // add a random employee id

            empArray.Add(
                new Employee(
                    r.Next( 10 ) + 100, r.Next( 20 )
                )
            );
        }

        // display all the contents of the Employee array
        for ( int i = 0; i < empArray.Count; i++ )
        {
            Console.Write( "\n{0} ", empArray[i].ToString() );
        }
        Console.WriteLine( "\n" );

        // sort and display the employee array
        Employee.EmployeeComparer c = Employee.GetComparer();
        c.WhichComparison =
            Employee.EmployeeComparer.ComparisonType.EmpID;
        empArray.Sort( c );

        // display all the contents of the Employee array
        for ( int i = 0; i < empArray.Count; i++ )
        {
            Console.Write( "\n{0} ", empArray[i].ToString() );
```

Example 9-15. Sorting an array by employees' IDs and years of service (continued)

```
        }
        Console.WriteLine( "\n" );

        c.WhichComparison = Employee.EmployeeComparer.ComparisonType.Yrs;
        empArray.Sort( c );

        for ( int i = 0; i < empArray.Count; i++ )
        {
            Console.Write( "\n{0} ", empArray[i].ToString() );
        }
        Console.WriteLine( "\n" );
    }
  }
}
```

```
Output:
ID: 103. Years of Svc: 11
ID: 108. Years of Svc: 15
ID: 107. Years of Svc: 14
ID: 108. Years of Svc: 5
ID: 102. Years of Svc: 0

ID: 102. Years of Svc: 0
ID: 103. Years of Svc: 11
ID: 107. Years of Svc: 14
ID: 108. Years of Svc: 15
ID: 108. Years of Svc: 5

ID: 102. Years of Svc: 0
ID: 108. Years of Svc: 5
ID: 103. Years of Svc: 11
ID: 107. Years of Svc: 14
ID: 108. Years of Svc: 15
```

The first block of output shows the Employee objects as they are added to the List. The employee ID values and the years of service are in random order. The second block shows the results of sorting by the employee ID, and the third block shows the results of sorting by years of service.

 If you are creating your own collection, as in Example 9-11, and wish to implement IComparer, you may need to ensure that all the types placed in the list implement IComparer (so that they may be sorted), by using constraints as described earlier.

Queues

A *queue* represents a first-in, first-out (FIFO) collection. The classic analogy is to a line (or queue if you are British) at a ticket window. The first person in line ought to be the first person to come off the line to buy a ticket.

A queue is a good collection to use when you are managing a limited resource. For example, you might want to send messages to a resource that can handle only one message at a time. You would then create a message queue so that you can say to your clients: "Your message is important to us. Messages are handled in the order in which they are received."

The Queue class has a number of member methods and properties, as shown in Table 9-4.

Table 9-4. Queue methods and properties

Method or property	Purpose
Count	Public property that gets the number of elements in the Queue.
Clear()	Removes all objects from the Queue.
Contains()	Determines if an element is in the Queue.
CopyTo()	Copies the Queue elements to an existing one-dimensional array.
Dequeue()	Removes and returns the object at the beginning of the Queue.
Enqueue()	Adds an object to the end of the Queue.
GetEnumerator()	Returns an enumerator for the Queue.
Peek()	Returns the object at the beginning of the Queue without removing it.
ToArray()	Copies the elements to a new array.

Add elements to your queue with the Enqueue command, take them off the queue with Dequeue, or examine its elements by using an enumerator. Example 9-16 illustrates.

Example 9-16. Working with a queue

```
#region Using directives

using System;
using System.Collections.Generic;
using System.Text;

#endregion

namespace Queue
{
   public class Tester
   {

      static void Main()
      {

         Queue<Int32> intQueue = new Queue<Int32>();

         // populate the array
         for ( int i = 0; i < 5; i++ )
         {
```

Example 9-16. Working with a queue (continued)

```
            intQueue.Enqueue( i * 5 );

        }

        // Display the Queue.
        Console.Write( "intQueue values:\t" );
        PrintValues( intQueue );

        // Remove an element from the queue.
        Console.WriteLine(
            "\n(Dequeue)\t{0}", intQueuee.Dequeue() );

        // Display the Queue.
        Console.Write( "intQueue values:\t" );
        PrintValues( intQueue );

        // Remove another element from the queue.
        Console.WriteLine(
            "\n(Dequeue)\t{0}", intQueuee.Dequeue() );

        // Display the Queue.
        Console.Write( "intQueue values:\t" );
        PrintValues( intQueue );

        // View the first element in the
        // Queue but do not remove.
        Console.WriteLine(
            "\n(Peek)    \t{0}", intQueuee.Peek() );

        // Display the Queue.
        Console.Write( "intQueue values:\t" );
        PrintValues( intQueue );

    }

    public static void PrintValues(IEnumerable<Int32> myCollection)
    {
        IEnumerator<Int32> myEnumerator =
            myCollection.GetEnumerator();
        while ( myEnumerator.MoveNext() )
            Console.Write( "{0} ", myEnumerator.Current );
        Console.WriteLine();
    }
  }
}
```

```
Output:
intQueue values:        0 5 10 15 20

(Dequeue)       0
intQueuee values:       5 10 15 20
```

Example 9-16. Working with a queue (continued)

```
(Dequeue)        5
intQueue values:        10 15 20

(Peek)          10
intQueue values:        10 15 20
```

In this example the List is replaced by a Queue. I've dispensed with the Employee class to save room, but of course you can Enqueue user-defined objects as well.

The output shows that queuing objects adds them to the Queue, and calls to Dequeue return the object and also remove them from the Queue. The Queue class also provides a Peek() method that allows you to see, but not remove, the first element.

Because the Queue class is enumerable, you can pass it to the PrintValues method, which is provided as an IEnumerable interface. The conversion is implicit. In the PrintValues method you call GetEnumerator, which you will remember is the single method of all IEnumerable classes. This returns an IEnumerator, which you then use to enumerate all the objects in the collection.

Stacks

A *stack* is a last-in, first-out (LIFO) collection, like a stack of dishes at a buffet table, or a stack of coins on your desk. A dish added on top is the first dish you take off the stack.

The principal methods for adding to and removing from a stack are Push() and Pop(); Stack also offers a Peek() method, very much like Queue. The significant methods and properties for Stack are shown in Table 9-5.

Table 9-5. Stack methods and properties

Method or property	Purpose
Count	Public property that gets the number of elements in the Stack.
Clear()	Removes all objects from the Stack.
Clone()	Creates a shallow copy.
Contains()	Determines if an element is in the Stack.
CopyTo()	Copies the Stack elements to an existing one-dimensional array.
GetEnumerator()	Returns an enumerator for the Stack.
Peek()	Returns the object at the top of the Stack without removing it.
Pop()	Removes and returns the object at the top of the Stack.
Push()	Inserts an object at the top of the Stack.
ToArray()	Copies the elements to a new array.

The List, Queue, and Stack types contain overloaded CopyTo() and ToArray() methods for copying their elements to an array. In the case of a Stack, the CopyTo() method will copy its elements to an existing one-dimensional array, overwriting the contents of the array beginning at the index you specify. The ToArray() method returns a new array with the contents of the stack's elements. Example 9-17 illustrates.

Example 9-17. Working with a stack

```
#region Using directives

using System;
using System.Collections.Generic;
using System.Text;

#endregion

namespace Stack
{
    public class Tester
    {
        static void Main()
        {
            Stack<Int32> intStack = new Stack<Int32>();

            // populate the stack

            for ( int i = 0; i < 8; i++ )
            {
                intStack.Push( i * 5 );
            }

            // Display the Stack.
            Console.Write( "intStack values:\t" );
            PrintValues( intStack );

            // Remove an element from the stack.
            Console.WriteLine( "\n(Pop)\t{0}",
            intStack.Pop() );

            // Display the Stack.
            Console.Write( "intStack values:\t" );
            PrintValues( intStack );

            // Remove another element from the stack.
            Console.WriteLine( "\n(Pop)\t{0}",
                intStack.Pop() );

            // Display the Stack.
            Console.Write( "intStack values:\t" );
            PrintValues( intStack );

            // View the first element in the
            // Stack but do not remove.
```

Example 9-17. Working with a stack (continued)

```
        Console.WriteLine( "\n(Peek)   \t{0}",
            intStack.Peek() );

        // Display the Stack.
        Console.Write( "intStack values:\t" );
        PrintValues( intStack );

        // declare an array object which will
        // hold 12 integers
        int[] targetArray = new int[12];

        for (int i = 0; i < targetArray.Length; i++)
        {
            targetArray[i] = i * 100 + 100;
        }
        // Display the values of the target Array instance.
        Console.WriteLine( "\nTarget array:  " );
        PrintValues( targetArray );

        // Copy the entire source Stack to the
        // target Array instance, starting at index 6.
        intStack.CopyTo( targetArray, 6 );

        // Display the values of the target Array instance.
        Console.WriteLine( "\nTarget array after copy:  " );
        PrintValues( targetArray );
    }

    public static void PrintValues(
        IEnumerable<Int32> myCollection )
    {
        IEnumerator<Int32> enumerator =
            myCollection.GetEnumerator();
        while ( enumerator.MoveNext() )
            Console.Write( "{0}  ", enumerator.Current );
        Console.WriteLine();
    }
  }
}
```

```
Output:
intStack values:        35  30  25  20  15  10  5  0

(Pop)   35
intStack values:        30  25  20  15  10  5  0

(Pop)   30
intStack values:        25  20  15  10  5  0

(Peek)          25
intStack values:        25  20  15  10  5  0
```

Example 9-17. Working with a stack (continued)

```
Target array:
100  200  300  400  500  600  700  800  900  1000 1100 1200

Target array after copy:
100  200  300  400  500  600  25  20  15  10  5  0
```

The output reflects that the items pushed onto the stack were popped in reverse order.

The effect of CopyTo( ) can be seen by examining the target array before and after calling CopyTo( ). The array elements are overwritten beginning with the index specified (6).

Dictionaries

A *dictionary* is a collection that associates a *key* to a *value*. A language dictionary, such as Webster's, associates a word (the key) with its definition (the value).

To see the value of dictionaries, start by imagining that you want to keep a list of the state capitals. One approach might be to put them in an array:

```
string[] stateCapitals = new string[50];
```

The stateCapitals array will hold 50 state capitals. Each capital is accessed as an offset into the array. For example, to access the capital for Arkansas, you need to know that Arkansas is the fourth state in alphabetical order:

```
string capitalOfArkansas = stateCapitals[3];
```

It is inconvenient, however, to access state capitals using array notation. After all, if I need the capital for Massachusetts, there is no easy way for me to determine that Massachusetts is the 21st state alphabetically.

It would be far more convenient to store the capital with the state name. A dictionary allows you to store a value (in this case, the capital) with a key (in this case, the name of the state).

A .NET Framework dictionary can associate any kind of key (string, integer, object, etc.) with any kind of value (string, integer, object, etc.). Typically, of course, the key is fairly short, the value fairly complex.

The most important attributes of a good dictionary are that it is easy to add and quick to retrieve values (see Table 9-6).

Table 9-6. Dictionary methods and properties

Method or property	Purpose
`Count`	Public property that gets the number of elements in the `Dictionary`.
`Item()`	The indexer for the `Dictionary`.
`Keys`	Public property that gets a collection containing the keys in the `Dictionary` (see also `Values`).
`Values`	Public property that gets a collection containing the values in the `Dictionary` (see also `Keys`).
`Add()`	Adds an entry with a specified `Key` and `Value`.
`Clear()`	Removes all objects from the `Dictionary`.
`ContainsKey()`	Determines whether the `Dictionary` has a specified key.
`ContainsValue()`	Determines whether the `Dictionary` has a specified value.
`GetEnumerator()`	Returns an enumerator for the `Dictionary`.
`GetObjectData()`	Implements `ISerializable` and returns the data needed to serialize the `Dictionary`.
`Remove()`	Removes the entry with the specified `Key`.

The key in a `Dictionary` can be a primitive type, or it can be an instance of a user-defined type (an object). Objects used as keys for a `Dictionary` must implement `GetHashCode()` as well as `Equals`. In most cases, you can simply use the inherited implementation from `Object`.

IDictionary<K,V>

Dictionaries implement the `IDictionary<K,V>` interface (where `K` is the key type and `V` is the value type). `IDictionary` provides a public property `Item`. The `Item` property retrieves a value with the specified key. In C#, the declaration for the `Item` property is:

```
V[K key]
{get; set;}
```

The `Item` property is implemented in C# with the index operator ([]). Thus, you access items in any `Dictionary` object using the offset syntax, as you would with an array.

Example 9-18 demonstrates adding items to a `Dictionary` and then retrieving them with the `Item` property.

Example 9-18. The Item property as offset operators

```
namespace Dictionary
{
    public class Tester
    {
        static void Main()
        {
            // Create and initialize a new Dictionary.
            Dictionary<string,string> Dictionary =
                new Dictionary<string,string>();
```

Example 9-18. The Item property as offset operators (continued)

```
        Dictionary.Add("000440312", "Jesse Liberty");
        Dictionary.Add("000123933", "Stacey Liberty");
        Dictionary.Add("000145938", "John Galt");
        Dictionary.Add("000773394", "Ayn Rand");

        // access a particular item
        Console.WriteLine("myDictionary[\"000145938\"]: {0}",
            Dictionary["000145938"]);
    }
  }
}
```

```
Output:
Dictionary["000145938"]: John Galt
```

Example 9-18 begins by instantiating a new `Dictionary`. The type of the key and of the value is declared to be `string`.

Add four key/value pairs. In this example, the Social Security number is tied to the person's full name. (Note that the Social Security numbers here are intentionally bogus.)

Once the items are added, you access a specific entry in the dictionary using the Social Security number as key.

> If you use a reference type as a key, and the type is mutable (strings are immutable), you must not change the value of the key object once you are using it in a dictionary.
>
> If, for example, you use the `Employee` object as a key, changing the employee ID creates problems if that property is used by the `Equals` or `GetHashCode` methods because the dictionary consults these methods.

CHAPTER 10

Strings and Regular Expressions

There was a time when people thought of computers exclusively as manipulating numeric values. Early computers were first used to calculate missile trajectories (though recently declassified documents suggest that some were used for code-breaking as well). In any case, there was a time that programming was taught in the math department of major universities and computer science was considered a discipline of mathematics.

Today, most programs are concerned more with strings of characters than with strings of numbers. Typically these strings are used for word processing, document manipulation, and creation of web pages.

C# provides built-in support for a fully functional `string` type. More importantly, C# treats strings as objects that encapsulate all the manipulation, sorting, and searching methods normally applied to strings of characters.

 C++ programmers take note: in C#, `string` is a first-class type, not an array of characters.

Complex string manipulation and pattern-matching are aided by the use of *regular expressions*. C# combines the power and complexity of regular expression syntax, originally found only in string manipulation languages such as awk and Perl, with a fully object-oriented design.

In this chapter, you will learn to work with the C# `string` type and the .NET Framework `System.String` class that it aliases. You will see how to extract substrings, manipulate and concatenate strings, and build new strings with the `StringBuilder` class. In addition, you will learn how to use the `RegEx` class to match strings based on complex regular expressions.

Strings

C# treats strings as first-class types that are flexible, powerful, and easy to use.

> In C# programming you typically use the C# alias for a Framework type (e.g., int for Int32) but you are always free to use the underlying type. C# programmers thus use string (lowercase) and the underlying Framework type String (uppercase) interchangeably.

The declaration of the String class is:

```
public sealed class String :
    IComparable<T>, ICloneable, IConvertible, IEnumerable<T>
```

This declaration reveals that the class is sealed, meaning that it is not possible to derive from the String class. The class also implements four system interfaces—IComparable<T>, ICloneable, IConvertible, and IEnumerable<T>—that dictate functionality that String shares with other classes in the .NET Framework.

> Each string object is an *immutable* sequence of Unicode characters. The fact that String is immutable means that methods that appear to change the string actually return a modified copy; the original string remains intact in memory until it is garbage-collected. This may have performance implications; if you plan to do significant repeated string manipulation, use a StringBuilder (described later).

As seen in Chapter 9, the IComparable<T> interface is implemented by types whose values can be ordered. Strings, for example, can be alphabetized; any given string can be compared with another string to determine which should come first in an ordered list.[*] IComparable classes implement the CompareTo method. IEnumerable, also discussed in Chapter 9, lets you use the foreach construct to enumerate a string as a collection of chars.

ICloneable objects can create new instances with the same value as the original instance. In this case, it is possible to clone a string to produce a new string with the same values (characters) as the original. ICloneable classes implement the Clone() method.

---

[*] Ordering the string is one of a number of lexical operations that act on the value of the string and take into account culture-specific information based on the explicitly declared culture or the implicit current culture. Therefore, if the current culture is U.S. English (as is assumed throughout this book), the Compare method considers 'a' less than 'A'. CompareOrdinal performs an ordinal comparison, and thus regardless of culture, 'a' is greater than 'A'.

Actually, because strings are immutable, the Clone() method on String just returns a reference to the original string. If you change the cloned string, a new String is then created:

```
string s1 = "One Two Three Four";
string sx = (string)s1.Clone();

Console.WriteLine(
    Object.ReferenceEquals(s1,sx));
sx += " Five";
Console.WriteLine(
    Object.ReferenceEquals(s1, sx));
Console.WriteLine(sx);
```

In this case, sx is created as a clone of s1. The first WriteLine statement will print the word true; the two strings variables refer to the same string in memory. When you change sx you actually create a new string from the first, and when the ReferenceEquals method returns false, the final WriteLine statement returns the contents of the original string with the word "Five" appended.

IConvertible classes provide methods to facilitate conversion to other primitive types such as ToInt32(), ToDouble(), ToDecimal(), etc.

Creating Strings

The most common way to create a string is to assign a quoted string of characters, known as a *string literal*, to a user-defined variable of type string:

```
string newString = "This is a string literal";
```

Quoted strings can include *escape characters,* such as \n or \t, which begin with a backslash character (\). The two shown are used to indicate where line breaks or tabs are to appear, respectively.

Because the backslash is the escape character, if you want to put a backslash into a string (e.g., to create a path listing), you must quote the backslash with a second backslash (\\).

Strings can also be created using *verbatim* string literals, which start with the (@) symbol. This tells the String constructor that the string should be used verbatim, even if it spans multiple lines or includes escape characters. In a verbatim string literal, backslashes and the characters that follow them are simply considered additional characters of the string. Thus, the following two definitions are equivalent:

```
string literalOne = "\\\\MySystem\\MyDirectory\\ProgrammingC#.cs";
string verbatimLiteralOne =
    @"\\MySystem\MyDirectory\ProgrammingC#.cs";
```

In the first line, a nonverbatim string literal is used, and so the backslash character (\) must be *escaped*. This means it must be preceded by a second backslash character. In the second line, a verbatim literal string is used, so the extra backslash is not needed. A second example illustrates multiline verbatim strings:

```
string literalTwo = "Line One\nLine Two";
string verbatimLiteralTwo = @"Line One
Line Two";
```

 If you have double quotes within a verbatim string, you must escape them so that the compiler knows when the verbatim string ends.

Again, these declarations are interchangeable. Which one you use is a matter of convenience and personal style.

The ToString() Method

Another common way to create a string is to call the ToString() method on an object and assign the result to a string variable. All the built-in types override this method to simplify the task of converting a value (often a numeric value) to a string representation of that value. In the following example, the ToString() method of an integer type is called to store its value in a string:

```
int myInteger = 5;
string integerString = myInteger.ToString();
```

The call to myInteger.ToString() returns a String object, which is then assigned to integerString.

The .NET String class provides a wealth of overloaded constructors that support a variety of techniques for assigning string values to string types. Some of these constructors enable you to create a string by passing in a character array or character pointer. Passing in a character array as a parameter to the constructor of the String creates a CLR-compliant new instance of a string. Passing in a character pointer requires the unsafe marker as explained in Chapter 22.

Manipulating Strings

The string class provides a host of methods for comparing, searching, and manipulating strings, the most important of which are shown in Table 10-1.

Table 10-1. Methods and fields for the string class

Method or field	Purpose
Empty	Public static field that represents the empty string.
Compare()	Overloaded public static method that compares two strings.
CompareOrdinal()	Overloaded public static method that compares two strings without regard to locale or culture.
Concat()	Overloaded public static method that creates a new string from one or more strings.

Table 10-1. Methods and fields for the string class (continued)

Method or field	Purpose
Copy()	Public static method that creates a new string by copying another.
Equals()	Overloaded public static and instance method that determines if two strings have the same value.
Format()	Overloaded public static method that formats a string using a format specification.
Join()	Overloaded public static method that concatenates a specified string between each element of a string array.
Chars	The string indexer.
Length	The number of characters in the instance.
CompareTo()	Compares this string with another.
CopyTo()	Copies the specified number of characters to an array of Unicode characters.
EndsWith()	Indicates whether the specified string matches the end of this string.
Equals()	Determines if two strings have the same value.
Insert()	Returns a new string with the specified string inserted.
LastIndexOf()	Reports the index of the last occurrence of a specified character or string within the string.
PadLeft()	Right-aligns the characters in the string, padding to the left with spaces or a specified character.
PadRight()	Left-aligns the characters in the string, padding to the right with spaces or a specified character.
Remove()	Deletes the specified number of characters.
Split()	Returns the substrings delimited by the specified characters in a string array.
StartsWith()	Indicates if the string starts with the specified characters.
Substring()	Retrieves a substring.
ToCharArray()	Copies the characters from the string to a character array.
ToLower()	Returns a copy of the string in lowercase.
ToUpper()	Returns a copy of the string in uppercase.
Trim()	Removes all occurrences of a set of specified characters from beginning and end of the string.
TrimEnd()	Behaves like Trim( ), but only at the end.
TrimStart()	Behaves like Trim( ), but only at the start.

Example 10-1 illustrates the use of some of these methods, including Compare(), Concat() (and the overloaded + operator), Copy() (and the = operator), Insert(), EndsWith(), and IndexOf().

Example 10-1. Working with strings

```
#region Using directives

using System;
using System.Collections.Generic;
using System.Text;

#endregion
```

Example 10-1. Working with strings (continued)

```
namespace WorkingWithStrings
{
    public class StringTester
    {
        static void Main()
        {
            // create some strings to work with
            string s1 = "abcd";
            string s2 = "ABCD";
            string s3 = @"Liberty Associates, Inc.
                    provides custom .NET development,
                    on-site Training and Consulting";

            int result;  // hold the results of comparisons

            // compare two strings, case sensitive
            result = string.Compare( s1, s2 );
            Console.WriteLine(
                "compare s1: {0}, s2: {1}, result: {2}\n",
                s1, s2, result );

            // overloaded compare, takes boolean "ignore case"
            //(true = ignore case)
            result = string.Compare( s1, s2, true );
            Console.WriteLine( "compare insensitive\n" );
            Console.WriteLine( "s4: {0}, s2: {1}, result: {2}\n",
                s1, s2, result );

            // concatenation method
            string s6 = string.Concat( s1, s2 );
            Console.WriteLine(
                "s6 concatenated from s1 and s2: {0}", s6 );

            // use the overloaded operator
            string s7 = s1 + s2;
            Console.WriteLine(
                "s7 concatenated from s1 + s2: {0}", s7 );

            // the string copy method
            string s8 = string.Copy( s7 );
            Console.WriteLine(
                "s8 copied from s7: {0}", s8 );

            // use the overloaded operator
            string s9 = s8;
            Console.WriteLine( "s9 = s8: {0}", s9 );

            // three ways to compare.
            Console.WriteLine(
                "\nDoes s9.Equals(s8)?: {0}",
                s9.Equals( s8 ) );
            Console.WriteLine(
```

Example 10-1. Working with strings (continued)

```
            "Does Equals(s9,s8)?: {0}",
            string.Equals( s9, s8 ) );
        Console.WriteLine(
            "Does s9==s8?: {0}", s9 == s8 );

        // Two useful properties: the index and the length
        Console.WriteLine(
            "\nString s9 is {0} characters long. ",
            s9.Length );
        Console.WriteLine(
            "The 5th character is {0}\n", s9[4] );

        // test whether a string ends with a set of characters
        Console.WriteLine( "s3:{0}\nEnds with Training?: {1}\n",
            s3,
            s3.EndsWith( "Training" ) );
        Console.WriteLine(
            "Ends with Consulting?: {0}",
            s3.EndsWith( "Consulting" ) );

        // return the index of the substring
        Console.WriteLine(
            "\nThe first occurrence of Training " );
        Console.WriteLine( "in s3 is {0}\n",
            s3.IndexOf( "Training" ) );

        // insert the word excellent before "training"
        string s10 = s3.Insert( 101, "excellent " );
        Console.WriteLine( "s10: {0}\n", s10 );

        // you can combine the two as follows:
        string s11 = s3.Insert( s3.IndexOf( "Training" ),
            "excellent " );
        Console.WriteLine( "s11: {0}\n", s11 );
    }
  }
}
```

```
Output:
compare s1: abcd, s2: ABCD, result: -1

compare insensitive

s4: abcd, s2: ABCD, result: 0

s6 concatenated from s1 and s2: abcdABCD
s7 concatenated from s1 + s2: abcdABCD
s8 copied from s7: abcdABCD
s9 = s8: abcdABCD
```

Example 10-1. Working with strings (continued)

```
Does s9.Equals(s8)?: True
Does Equals(s9,s8)?: True
Does s9==s8?: True

String s9 is 8 characters long.
The 5th character is A

s3:Liberty Associates, Inc.
                provides custom .NET development,
                on-site Training and Consulting
Ends with Training?: False

Ends with Consulting?: True

The first occurrence of Training
in s3 is 101

s10: Liberty Associates, Inc.
                provides custom .NET development,
                on-site excellent Training and Consulting

s11: Liberty Associates, Inc.
                provides custom .NET development,
                on-site excellent Training and Consulting
```

Example 10-1 begins by declaring three strings:

```
string s1 = "abcd";
string s2 = "ABCD";
string s3 = @"Liberty Associates, Inc.
    provides custom .NET development,
    on-site Training and Consulting";
```

The first two are string literals, and the third is a verbatim string literal. We begin by comparing s1 to s2. The Compare() method is a public static method of string, and it is overloaded. The first overloaded version takes two strings and compares them:

```
// compare two strings, case sensitive
result = string.Compare(s1, s2);
Console.WriteLine("compare s1: {0}, s2: {1}, result: {2}\n",
    s1, s2, result);
```

This is a case-sensitive comparison and returns different values, depending on the results of the comparison:

- A negative integer, if the first string is less than the second string
- 0, if the strings are equal
- A positive integer, if the first string is greater than the second string

In this case, the output properly indicates that s1 is "less than" s2. In Unicode (as in ASCII), a lowercase letter has a smaller value than an uppercase letter:

```
compare s1: abcd, s2: ABCD, result: -1
```

The second comparison uses an overloaded version of Compare() that takes a third, Boolean parameter, whose value determines whether case should be ignored in the comparison. If the value of this "ignore case" parameter is true, the comparison is made without regard to case, as in the following:

```
result = string.Compare(s1,s2, true);
Console.WriteLine("compare insensitive\n");
Console.WriteLine("s4: {0}, s2: {1}, result: {2}\n",
    s1, s2, result);
```

 The result is written with two WriteLine() statements to keep the lines short enough to print properly in this book.

This time the case is ignored and the result is 0, indicating that the two strings are identical (without regard to case):

```
compare insensitive

s4: abcd, s2: ABCD, result: 0
```

Example 10-1 then concatenates some strings. There are a couple of ways to accomplish this. You can use the Concat() method, which is a static public method of string:

```
string s6 = string.Concat(s1,s2);
```

or you can simply use the overloaded concatenation (+) operator:

```
string s7 = s1 + s2;
```

In both cases, the output reflects that the concatenation was successful:

```
s6 concatenated from s1 and s2: abcdABCD
s7 concatenated from s1 + s2: abcdABCD
```

Similarly, creating a new copy of a string can be accomplished in two ways. First, you can use the static Copy() method:

```
string s8 = string.Copy(s7);
```

This actually creates two separate strings with the same values. Since strings are immutable, this is wasteful. Better is either to use the overloaded assignment operator or the Clone method (mentioned earlier), both of which leave you with two variables pointing to the same string in memory:

```
string s9 = s8;
```

The .NET String class provides three ways to test for the equality of two strings. First, you can use the overloaded Equals() method and ask s9 directly whether s8 is of equal value:

```
Console.WriteLine("\nDoes s9.Equals(s8)?: {0}",
    s9.Equals(s8));
```

A second technique is to pass both strings to String's static method Equals():

```
Console.WriteLine("Does Equals(s9,s8)?: {0}",
    string.Equals(s9,s8));
```

A final method is to use the equality operator (==) of String:

```
Console.WriteLine("Does s9==s8?: {0}", s9 == s8);
```

In each case, the returned result is a Boolean value, as shown in the output:

```
Does s9.Equals(s8)?: True
Does Equals(s9,s8)?: True
Does s9==s8?: True
```

The next several lines in Example 10-1 use the index operator ([ ]) to find a particular character within a string, and use the Length property to return the length of the entire string:

```
Console.WriteLine("\nString s9 is {0} characters long.",
    s9.Length);
Console.WriteLine("The 5th character is {1}\n",
    s9.Length, s9[4]);
```

Here's the output:

```
String s9 is 8 characters long.
The 5th character is A
```

The EndsWith() method asks a string whether a substring is found at the end of the string. Thus, you might first ask s3 if it ends with Training (which it doesn't) and then if it ends with Consulting (which it does):

```
// test whether a string ends with a set of characters
Console.WriteLine("s3:{0}\nEnds with Training?: {1}\n",
    s3, s3.EndsWith("Training") );
Console.WriteLine("Ends with Consulting?: {0}",
    s3.EndsWith("Consulting"));
```

The output reflects that the first test fails and the second succeeds:

```
s3:Liberty Associates, Inc.
            provides custom .NET development,
            on-site Training and Consulting
Ends with Training?: False
Ends with Consulting?: True
```

The IndexOf() method locates a substring within our string, and the Insert() method inserts a new substring into a copy of the original string.

The following code locates the first occurrence of Training in s3:

```
Console.WriteLine("\nThe first occurrence of Training ");
Console.WriteLine ("in s3 is {0}\n",
    s3.IndexOf("Training"));
```

The output indicates that the offset is 101:

```
The first occurrence of Training
in s3 is 101
```

You can then use that value to insert the word excellent, followed by a space, into that string. Actually, the insertion is into a copy of the string returned by the Insert() method and assigned to s10:

```
string s10 = s3.Insert(101,"excellent ");
Console.WriteLine("s10: {0}\n",s10);
```

Here's the output:

```
s10: Liberty Associates, Inc.
               provides custom .NET development,
               on-site excellent Training and Consulting
```

Finally, you can combine these operations:

```
string s11 = s3.Insert(s3.IndexOf("Training"),"excellent ");
Console.WriteLine("s11: {0}\n",s11);
```

to obtain the identical output:

```
s11: Liberty Associates, Inc.
               provides custom .NET development,
               on-site excellent Training and Consulting
```

Finding Substrings

The String type provides an overloaded Substring() method for extracting substrings from within strings. Both versions take an index indicating where to begin the extraction, and one of the two versions takes a second index to indicate where to end the operation. The Substring() method is illustrated in Example 10-2.

Example 10-2. Using the Substring() method

```
#region Using directives

using System;
using System.Collections.Generic;
using System.Text;

#endregion

namespace SubString
{
   public class StringTester
   {
      static void Main()
      {
         // create some strings to work with
         string s1 = "One Two Three Four";

         int ix;

         // get the index of the last space
         ix = s1.LastIndexOf( " " );
```

Example 10-2. Using the Substring() method (continued)

```
            // get the last word.
            string s2 = s1.Substring( ix + 1 );

            // set s1 to the substring starting at 0
            // and ending at ix (the start of the last word
            // thus s1 has one two three
            s1 = s1.Substring( 0, ix );

            // find the last space in s1 (after two)
            ix = s1.LastIndexOf( " " );

            // set s3 to the substring starting at
            // ix, the space after "two" plus one more
            // thus s3 = "three"
            string s3 = s1.Substring( ix + 1 );

            // reset s1 to the substring starting at 0
            // and ending at ix, thus the string "one two"
            s1 = s1.Substring( 0, ix );

            // reset ix to the space between
            // "one" and "two"
            ix = s1.LastIndexOf( " " );

            // set s4 to the substring starting one
            // space after ix, thus the substring "two"
            string s4 = s1.Substring( ix + 1 );

            // reset s1 to the substring starting at 0
            // and ending at ix, thus "one"
            s1 = s1.Substring( 0, ix );

            // set ix to the last space, but there is
            // none so ix now = -1
            ix = s1.LastIndexOf( " " );

            // set s5 to the substring at one past
            // the last space. there was no last space
            // so this sets s5 to the substring starting
            // at zero
            string s5 = s1.Substring( ix + 1 );

            Console.WriteLine( "s2: {0}\ns3: {1}", s2, s3 );
            Console.WriteLine( "s4: {0}\ns5: {1}\n", s4, s5 );
            Console.WriteLine( "s1: {0}\n", s1 );
        }
    }
}
```

Output:
s2: Four
s3: Three

Example 10-2. Using the Substring() method (continued)

```
s4: Two
s5: One

s1: One
```

Example 10-2 is not an elegant solution to the problem of extracting words from a string, but it is a good first approximation, and it illustrates a useful technique. The example begins by creating a string, s1:

```
string s1 = "One Two Three Four";
```

Then ix is assigned the value of the *last* space in the string:

```
ix=s1.LastIndexOf(" ");
```

Then the substring that begins one space later is assigned to the new string, s2:

```
string s2 = s1.Substring(ix+1);
```

This extracts ix+1 to the end of the line, assigning to s2 the value Four.

The next step is to remove the word Four from s1. You can do this by assigning to s1 the substring of s1, which begins at 0 and ends at ix:

```
s1 = s1.Substring(0,ix);
```

Reassign ix to the last (remaining) space, which points you to the beginning of the word Three, which we then extract into string s3. Continue like this until s4 and s5 are populated. Finally, print the results:

```
s2: Four
s3: Three
s4: Two
s5: One

s1: One
```

This isn't elegant, but it works and it illustrates the use of Substring. This is not unlike using pointer arithmetic in C++, but without the pointers and unsafe code.

Splitting Strings

A more effective solution to the problem illustrated in Example 10-2 is to use the Split() method of String, whose job is to parse a string into substrings. To use Split(), pass in an array of delimiters (characters that will indicate a split in the words), and the method returns an array of substrings. Example 10-3 illustrates.

Example 10-3. Using the Split() method

```
#region Using directives

using System;
using System.Collections.Generic;
```

Example 10-3. Using the Split() method (continued)

```
using System.Text;

#endregion

namespace StringSplit
{
    public class StringTester
    {
        static void Main()
        {
            // create some strings to work with
            string s1 = "One,Two,Three Liberty Associates, Inc.";

            // constants for the space and comma characters
            const char Space = ' ';
            const char Comma = ',';

            // array of delimiters to split the sentence with
            char[] delimiters = new char[]
                {
                    Space,
                    Comma
                };

            string output = "";
            int ctr = 1;

            // split the string and then iterate over the
            // resulting array of strings
            foreach ( string subString in s1.Split( delimiters ) )
            {
                output += ctr++;
                output += ": ";
                output += subString;
                output += "\n";
            }
            Console.WriteLine( output );
        }
    }
}

Output:
1: One
2: Two
3: Three
4: Liberty
5: Associates
6:
7: Inc.
```

You start by creating a string to parse:

```
string s1 = "One,Two,Three Liberty Associates, Inc.";
```

The delimiters are set to the space and comma characters. You then call Split() on this string, and pass the results to the foreach loop:

```
foreach (string subString in s1.Split(delimiters))
```

 Because Split uses the params keyword, you can reduce your code to:

```
foreach (string subString in s1.Split(' ', ','))
```

This eliminates the declaration of the array entirely.

Start by initializing output to an empty string and then build up the output string in four steps. Concatenate the value of ctr. Next add the colon, then the substring returned by split, then the newline. With each concatenation, a new copy of the string is made, and all four steps are repeated for each substring found by Split(). This repeated copying of string is terribly inefficient.

The problem is that the string type is not designed for this kind of operation. What you want is to create a new string by appending a formatted string each time through the loop. The class you need is StringBuilder.

Manipulating Dynamic Strings

The System.Text.StringBuilder class is used for creating and modifying strings. The important members of StringBuilder are summarized in Table 10-2.

Table 10-2. StringBuilder methods

Method	Explanation
Chars	The indexer.
Length	Retrieves or assigns the length of the StringBuilder.
Append()	Overloaded public method that appends a string of characters to the end of the current StringBuilder.
AppendFormat()	Overloaded public method that replaces format specifiers with the formatted value of an object.
Insert()	Overloaded public method that inserts a string of characters at the specified position.
Remove()	Removes the specified characters.
Replace()	Overloaded public method that replaces all instances of specified characters with new characters.

Unlike String, StringBuilder is mutable; when you modify a StringBuilder, you modify the actual string, not a copy. Example 10-4 replaces the String object in Example 10-3 with a StringBuilder object.

Example 10-4. Using a StringBuilder

```
#region Using directives

using System;
using System.Collections.Generic;
```

Example 10-4. Using a StringBuilder (continued)

```
using System.Text;

#endregion

namespace UsingStringBuilder
{
    public class StringTester
    {
        static void Main()
        {
            // create some strings to work with
            string s1 = "One,Two,Three Liberty Associates, Inc.";

            // constants for the space and comma characters
            const char Space = ' ';
            const char Comma = ',';

            // array of delimiters to split the sentence with
            char[] delimiters = new char[]
            {
                Space,
                Comma
            };

            // use a StringBuilder class to build the
            // output string
            StringBuilder output = new StringBuilder();
            int ctr = 1;

            // split the string and then iterate over the
            // resulting array of strings
            foreach ( string subString in s1.Split( delimiters ) )
            {
                // AppendFormat appends a formatted string
                output.AppendFormat( "{0}: {1}\n", ctr++, subString );
            }
            Console.WriteLine( output );
        }
    }
}
```

Only the last part of the program is modified. Instead of using the concatenation operator to modify the string, use the AppendFormat() method of StringBuilder to append new, formatted strings as you create them. This is more efficient. The output is identical to that of Example 10-3:

```
1: One
2: Two
3: Three
4: Liberty
5: Associates
6:
7: Inc.
```

Regular Expressions

Regular expressions are a powerful language for describing and manipulating text. A regular expression is *applied* to a string—that is, to a set of characters. Often that string is an entire text document.

The result of applying a regular expression to a string is to find out if the string matches the regular expression or to return a substring, or to return a new string representing a modification of some part of the original string. (Remember that strings are immutable and so can't be changed by the regular expression.)

By applying a properly constructed regular expression to the following string:

```
One,Two,Three Liberty Associates, Inc.
```

you can return any or all of its substrings (e.g., Liberty or One), or modified versions of its substrings (e.g., LIBeRtY or OnE). What the regular expression *does* is determined by the syntax of the regular expression itself.

A regular expression consists of two types of characters: *literals* and *metacharacters*. A literal is a character you wish to match in the target string. A metacharacter is a special symbol that acts as a command to the regular expression parser. The parser is the engine responsible for understanding the regular expression. For example, if you create a regular expression:

```
^(From|To|Subject|Date):
```

this will match any substring with the letters "From," "To," "Subject," or "Date," so long as those letters start a new line (^) and end with a colon (:).

The caret (^) in this case indicates to the regular expression parser that the string you're searching for must begin a new line. The letters "From" and "To" are literals, and the metacharacters left and right parentheses ((,)) and vertical bar (|) are all used to group sets of literals and indicate that any of the choices should match. (Note that ^ is a metacharacter as well, used to indicate the start of the line.)

Thus, you would read this line:

```
^(From|To|Subject|Date):
```

as follows: "Match any string that begins a new line followed by any of the four literal strings From, To, Subject, or Date followed by a colon."

 A full explanation of regular expressions is beyond the scope of this book, but all the regular expressions used in the examples are explained. For a complete understanding of regular expressions, I highly recommend *Mastering Regular Expressions* (O'Reilly).

Using Regular Expressions: Regex

The .NET Framework provides an object-oriented approach to regular expression matching and replacement.

 C#'s regular expressions are based on Perl 5 *regexp*, including lazy quantifiers (??, *?, +?, {n,m}?), positive and negative look ahead, and conditional evaluation.

The namespace System.Text.RegularExpressions is the home to all the .NET Framework objects associated with regular expressions. The central class for regular expression support is Regex, which represents an immutable, compiled regular expression. Although instances of Regex can be created, the class also provides a number of useful static methods. The use of Regex is illustrated in Example 10-5.

Example 10-5. Using the Regex class for regular expressions

```
#region Using directives

using System;
using System.Collections.Generic;
using System.Text;
using System.Text.RegularExpressions;

#endregion

namespace UsingRegEx
{
    public class Tester
    {
        static void Main()
        {
            string s1 =
                "One,Two,Three Liberty Associates, Inc.";
            Regex theRegex = new Regex( " |, |," );
            StringBuilder sBuilder = new StringBuilder();
            int id = 1;

            foreach ( string subString in theRegex.Split( s1 ) )
            {
                sBuilder.AppendFormat(
```

Example 10-5. Using the Regex class for regular expressions (continued)

```
                "{0}: {1}\n", id++, subString );
            }
            Console.WriteLine( "{0}", sBuilder );
        }
    }
}
```

```
Output:
1: One
2: Two
3: Three
4: Liberty
5: Associates
6: Inc.
```

Example 10-5 begins by creating a string, s1, that is identical to the string used in Example 10-4:

```
string s1 = "One,Two,Three Liberty Associates, Inc.";
```

It also creates a regular expression, which will be used to search that string:

```
Regex theRegex = new Regex(" |,| ");
```

One of the overloaded constructors for Regex takes a regular expression string as its parameter. This is a bit confusing. In the context of a C# program, which is the regular expression? Is it the text passed in to the constructor, or the Regex object itself? It is true that the text string passed to the constructor is a regular expression in the traditional sense of the term. From an object-oriented C# point of view, however, the argument to the constructor is just a string of characters; it is theRegex that is the regular expression object.

The rest of the program proceeds like the earlier Example 10-4, except that instead of calling Split() on string s1, the Split() method of Regex is called. Regex.Split() acts in much the same way as String.Split(), returning an array of strings as a result of matching the regular expression pattern within theRegex.

Regex.Split() is overloaded. The simplest version is called on an instance of Regex, as shown in Example 10-5. There is also a static version of this method, which takes a string to search and the pattern to search with, as illustrated in Example 10-6.

Example 10-6. Using static Regex.Split()

```
#region Using directives

using System;
using System.Collections.Generic;
using System.Text;
using System.Text.RegularExpressions;

#endregion
```

Example 10-6. Using static Regex.Split() (continued)

```
namespace RegExSplit
{
    public class Tester
    {
        static void Main()
        {
            string s1 =
                "One,Two,Three Liberty Associates, Inc.";
            StringBuilder sBuilder = new StringBuilder();
            int id = 1;
            foreach ( string subStr in Regex.Split( s1, " |, |," ) )
            {
                sBuilder.AppendFormat( "{0}: {1}\n", id++, subStr );
            }
            Console.WriteLine( "{0}", sBuilder );
        }
    }
}
```

Example 10-6 is identical to Example 10-5, except that the latter example doesn't instantiate an object of type Regex. Instead, Example 10-6 uses the static version of Split(), which takes two arguments: a string to search for and a regular expression string that represents the pattern to match.

The instance method of Split() is also overloaded with versions that limit the number of times the split will occur and also determine the position within the target string where the search will begin.

Using Regex Match Collections

Two additional classes in the .NET RegularExpressions namespace allow you to search a string repeatedly, and to return the results in a collection. The collection returned is of type MatchCollection, which consists of zero or more Match objects. Two important properties of a Match object are its length and its value, each of which can be read as illustrated in Example 10-7.

Example 10-7. Using MatchCollection and Match

```
#region Using directives

using System;
using System.Collections.Generic;
using System.Text;
using System.Text.RegularExpressions;

#endregion

namespace UsingMatchCollection
{
```

Example 10-7. Using MatchCollection and Match (continued)

```
class Test
{
   public static void Main()
   {
      string string1 = "This is a test string";

      // find any nonwhitespace followed by whitespace
      Regex theReg = new Regex( @"(\S+)\s" );

      // get the collection of matches
      MatchCollection theMatches =
         theReg.Matches( string1 );

      // iterate through the collection
      foreach ( Match theMatch in theMatches )
      {
         Console.WriteLine(
            "theMatch.Length: {0}", theMatch.Length );

         if ( theMatch.Length != 0 )
         {
            Console.WriteLine( "theMatch: {0}",
               theMatch.ToString() );
         }
      }
   }
}
}
```

```
Output:
theMatch.Length: 5
theMatch: This
theMatch.Length: 3
theMatch: is
theMatch.Length: 2
theMatch: a
theMatch.Length: 5
theMatch: test
```

Example 10-7 creates a simple string to search:

```
string string1 = "This is a test string";
```

and a trivial regular expression to search it:

```
Regex theReg = new Regex(@"(\S+)\s");
```

The string \S finds nonwhitespace, and the plus sign indicates one or more. The string \s (note lowercase) indicates whitespace. Thus, together, this string looks for any nonwhitespace characters followed by whitespace.

Remember the at (@) symbol before the string creates a verbatim string, which avoids having to escape the backslash (\) character.

The output shows that the first four words were found. The final word wasn't found because it isn't followed by a space. If you insert a space after the word `string` and before the closing quotation marks, this program finds that word as well.

The `length` property is the length of the captured substring, and is discussed in the section "Using CaptureCollection," later in this chapter.

Using Regex Groups

It is often convenient to group subexpression matches together so that you can parse out pieces of the matching string. For example, you might want to match on IP addresses and group all IP addresses found anywhere within the string.

IP addresses are used to locate computers on a network, and typically have the form x.x.x.x, where x is generally any digit between 0 and 255 (such as 192.168.0.1).

The `Group` class allows you to create groups of matches based on regular expression syntax, and represents the results from a single grouping expression.

A grouping expression names a group and provides a regular expression; any substring matching the regular expression will be added to the group. For example, to create an `ip` group you might write:

```
@"(?<ip>(\d|\.)+)\s"
```

The `Match` class derives from `Group`, and has a collection called `Groups` that contains all the groups your `Match` finds.

Creation and use of the `Groups` collection and `Group` classes are illustrated in Example 10-8.

Example 10-8. Using the Group class

```
#region Using directives

using System;
using System.Collections.Generic;
using System.Text;
using System.Text.RegularExpressions;

#endregion

namespace RegExGroup
{
```

Example 10-8. Using the Group class (continued)

```
class Test
{
    public static void Main()
    {
        string string1 = "04:03:27 127.0.0.0 LibertyAssociates.com";

        // group time = one or more digits or colons followed by space
        Regex theReg = new Regex( @"(?<time>(\d|\:)+)\s" +
            // ip address = one or more digits or dots followed by  space
            @"(?<ip>(\d|\.)+)\s" +
            // site = one or more characters
            @"(?<site>\S+)" );

        // get the collection of matches
        MatchCollection theMatches = theReg.Matches( string1 );

        // iterate through the collection
        foreach ( Match theMatch in theMatches )
        {
            if ( theMatch.Length != 0 )
            {
                Console.WriteLine( "\ntheMatch: {0}",
                    theMatch.ToString() );
                Console.WriteLine( "time: {0}",
                    theMatch.Groups["time"] );
                Console.WriteLine( "ip: {0}",
                    theMatch.Groups["ip"] );
                Console.WriteLine( "site: {0}",
                    theMatch.Groups["site"] );
            }
        }
    }
}
```

Again, Example 10-8 begins by creating a string to search:

```
string string1 = "04:03:27 127.0.0.0 LibertyAssociates.com";
```

This string might be one of many recorded in a web server log file or produced as the result of a search of the database. In this simple example, there are three columns: one for the time of the log entry, one for an IP address, and one for the site, each separated by spaces. Of course, in an example solving a real-life problem, you might need to do more complex queries and choose to use other delimiters and more complex searches.

In Example 10-8, we want to create a single Regex object to search strings of this type and break them into three groups: time, ip address, and site. The regular expression string is fairly simple, so the example is easy to understand. However, keep in mind that in a real search, you would probably use only a part of the source string rather than the entire source string, as shown here.

```
// group time = one or more digits or colons
// followed by space
Regex theReg = new Regex(@"(?<time>(\d|\:)+)\s" +
// ip address = one or more digits or dots
// followed by  space
@"(?<ip>(\d|\.)+)\s" +
// site = one or more characters
@"(?<site>\S+)");
```

Let's focus on the characters that create the group:

```
(?<time>(\d|\:)
```

The parentheses create a group. Everything between the opening parenthesis (just before the question mark) and the closing parenthesis (in this case, after the + sign) is a single unnamed group.

The string ?<time> names that group time, and the group is associated with the matching text, which is the regular expression (\d|\:)+)\s". This regular expression can be interpreted as "one or more digits or colons followed by a space."

Similarly, the string ?<ip> names the ip group, and ?<site> names the site group. As Example 10-7 does, Example 10-8 asks for a collection of all the matches:

```
MatchCollection theMatches = theReg.Matches(string1);
```

Example 10-8 iterates through the Matches collection, finding each Match object.

If the Length of the Match is greater than 0, a Match was found; it prints the entire match:

```
Console.WriteLine("\ntheMatch: {0}",
    theMatch.ToString());
```

Here's the output:

```
theMatch: 04:03:27 127.0.0.0 LibertyAssociates.com
```

It then gets the time group from theMatch.Groups collection and prints that value:

```
Console.WriteLine("time: {0}",
    theMatch.Groups["time"]);
```

This produces the output:

```
time: 04:03:27
```

The code then obtains ip and site groups:

```
Console.WriteLine("ip: {0}",
    theMatch.Groups["ip"]);
Console.WriteLine("site: {0}",
    theMatch.Groups["site"]);
```

This produces the output:

```
ip: 127.0.0.0
site: LibertyAssociates.com
```

In Example 10-8, the `Matches` collection has only one `Match`. It is possible, however, to match more than one expression within a string. To see this, modify `string1` in Example 10-8 to provide several `logFile` entries instead of one, as follows:

```
string string1 = "04:03:27 127.0.0.0 LibertyAssociates.com " +
"04:03:28 127.0.0.0 foo.com " +
"04:03:29 127.0.0.0 bar.com " ;
```

This creates three matches in the `MatchCollection`, called `theMatches`. Here's the resulting output:

```
theMatch: 04:03:27 127.0.0.0 LibertyAssociates.com
time: 04:03:27
ip: 127.0.0.0
site: LibertyAssociates.com

theMatch: 04:03:28 127.0.0.0 foo.com
time: 04:03:28
ip: 127.0.0.0
site: foo.com

theMatch: 04:03:29 127.0.0.0 bar.com
time: 04:03:29
ip: 127.0.0.0
site: bar.com
```

In this example, `theMatches` contains three `Match` objects. Each time through the outer foreach loop we find the next `Match` in the collection and display its contents:

```
foreach (Match theMatch in theMatches)
```

For each `Match` item found, you can print out the entire match, various groups, or both.

Using CaptureCollection

Each time a `Regex` object matches a subexpression, a `Capture` instance is created and added to a `CaptureCollection` collection. Each `Capture` object represents a single capture. Each group has its own capture collection of the matches for the subexpression associated with the group.

A key property of the `Capture` object is its `length,` which is the length of the captured substring. When you ask `Match` for its length, it is `Capture.Length` that you retrieve because `Match` derives from `Group`, which in turn derives from `Capture`.

> The regular expression inheritance scheme in .NET allows `Match` to include in its interface the methods and properties of these parent classes. In a sense, a `Group` *is-a* capture: it is a capture that encapsulates the idea of grouping subexpressions. A `Match`, in turn, *is-a* `Group`: it is the encapsulation of all the groups of subexpressions making up the entire match for this regular expression. (See Chapter 5 for more about the *is-a* relationship and other relationships.)

Typically, you will find only a single Capture in a CaptureCollection, but that need not be so. Consider what would happen if you were parsing a string in which the company name might occur in either of two positions. To group these together in a single match, create the ?<company> group in two places in your regular expression pattern:

```
Regex theReg = new Regex(@"(?<time>(\d|\:)+)\s" +
@"(?<company>\S+)\s" +
@"(?<ip>(\d|\.)+)\s" +
@"(?<company>\S+)\s");
```

This regular expression group captures any matching string of characters that follows time, and also any matching string of characters that follows ip. Given this regular expression, you are ready to parse the following string:

```
string string1 = "04:03:27 Jesse 0.0.0.127 Liberty ";
```

The string includes names in both the positions specified. Here is the result:

```
theMatch: 04:03:27 Jesse 0.0.0.127 Liberty
time: 04:03:27
ip: 0.0.0.127
Company: Liberty
```

What happened? Why is the Company group showing Liberty? Where is the first term, which also matched? The answer is that the second term overwrote the first. The group, however, has captured both. Its Captures collection can demonstrate, as illustrated in Example 10-9.

Example 10-9. Examining the Captures collection

```
#region Using directives

using System;
using System.Collections.Generic;
using System.Text;
using System.Text.RegularExpressions;

#endregion

namespace CaptureCollection
{
    class Test
    {
        public static void Main()
        {
            // the string to parse
            // note that names appear in both
            // searchable positions
            string string1 =
                "04:03:27 Jesse 0.0.0.127 Liberty ";

            // regular expression which groups company twice
            Regex theReg = new Regex( @"(?<time>(\d|\:)+)\s" +
```

Example 10-9. Examining the Captures collection (continued)

```
            @"(?<company>\S+)\s" +
            @"(?<ip>(\d|\.)+)\s" +
            @"(?<company>\S+)\s" );

     // get the collection of matches
     MatchCollection theMatches =
        theReg.Matches( string1 );

     // iterate through the collection
     foreach ( Match theMatch in theMatches )
     {
        if ( theMatch.Length != 0 )
        {
           Console.WriteLine( "theMatch: {0}",
              theMatch.ToString() );
           Console.WriteLine( "time: {0}",
              theMatch.Groups["time"] );
           Console.WriteLine( "ip: {0}",
              theMatch.Groups["ip"] );
           Console.WriteLine( "Company: {0}",
              theMatch.Groups["company"] );

           // iterate over the captures collection
           // in the company group within the
           // groups collection in the match

           foreach ( Capture cap in
              theMatch.Groups["company"].Captures )
           {
              Console.WriteLine( "cap: {0}", cap.ToString() );
           }
        }
     }
  }
}
```

```
Output:
theMatch: 04:03:27 Jesse 0.0.0.127 Liberty
time: 04:03:27
ip: 0.0.0.127
Company: Liberty
cap: Jesse
cap: Liberty
```

The code in bold iterates through the Captures collection for the Company group:

```
foreach (Capture cap in
   theMatch.Groups["company"].Captures)
```

Let's review how this line is parsed. The compiler begins by finding the collection that it will iterate over. theMatch is an object that has a collection named Groups. The

Groups collection has an indexer that takes a string and returns a single Group object. Thus, the following line returns a single Group object:

```
theMatch.Groups["company"]
```

The Group object has a collection named Captures. Thus, the following line returns a Captures collection for the Group stored at Groups["company"] within the theMatch object:

```
theMatch.Groups["company"].Captures
```

The foreach loop iterates over the Captures collection, extracting each element in turn and assigning it to the local variable cap, which is of type Capture. You can see from the output that there are two capture elements: Jesse and Liberty. The second one overwrites the first in the group, and so the displayed value is just Liberty. However, by examining the Captures collection, you can find both values that were captured.

Handling Exceptions

Like many object-oriented languages, C# handles errors and abnormal conditions with *exceptions*. An exception is an object that encapsulates information about an unusual program occurrence.

It is important to distinguish between bugs, errors, and exceptions. A *bug* is a programmer mistake that should be fixed before the code is shipped. Exceptions aren't a protection against bugs. Although a bug might cause an exception to be thrown, you should not rely on exceptions to handle your bugs. Rather, you should fix the bugs.

An *error* is caused by user action. For example, the user might enter a number where a letter is expected. Once again, an error might cause an exception, but you can prevent that by catching errors with validation code. Whenever possible, errors should be anticipated and prevented.

Even if you remove all bugs and anticipate all user errors, you will still run into predictable but unpreventable problems, such as running out of memory or attempting to open a file that no longer exists. You can't prevent exceptions, but you can handle them so that they don't bring down your program.

When your program encounters an exceptional circumstance, such as running out of memory, it *throws* (or "raises") an exception. When an exception is thrown, execution of the current function halts and the stack is unwound until an appropriate exception handler is found.

This means that if the currently running function doesn't handle the exception, the current function will terminate and the calling function will get a chance to handle the exception. If none of the calling functions handles it, the exception will ultimately be handled by the CLR, which will abruptly terminate your program.

An *exception handler* is a block of code designed to handle the exception you've thrown. Exception handlers are implemented as catch statements. Ideally, if the exception is caught and handled, the program can fix the problem and continue. Even if your program can't continue, by catching the exception, you have an opportunity to print a meaningful error message and terminate gracefully.

If there is code in your function that must run regardless of whether an exception is encountered (e.g., to release resources you've allocated), you can place that code in a finally block, where it is certain to run, even in the presence of exceptions.

Throwing and Catching Exceptions

In C#, you can throw only objects of type System.Exception, or objects derived from that type. The CLR System namespace includes a number of exception types that your program can use. These exception types include ArgumentNullException, InvalidCastException, and OverflowException, as well as many others.

 C++ programmers take note: in C#, not just any object can be thrown—it must be derived from System.Exception.

The throw Statement

To signal an abnormal condition in a C# class, you throw an exception. To do this, use the keyword throw. This line of code creates a new instance of System.Exception and then throws it:

```
throw new System.Exception();
```

Throwing an exception immediately halts execution while the CLR searches for an exception handler. If an exception handler can't be found in the current method, the runtime unwinds the stack, popping up through the calling methods until a handler is found. If the runtime returns all the way through Main() without finding a handler, it terminates the program. Example 11-1 illustrates.

Example 11-1. Throwing an exception

```
namespace Programming_CSharp
{
    using System;

    public class Test
    {
        public static void Main()
        {
            Console.WriteLine("Enter Main...");
            Test t = new Test();
            t.Func1();
            Console.WriteLine("Exit Main...");

        }

        public void Func1()
        {
            Console.WriteLine("Enter Func1...");
```

Example 11-1. Throwing an exception (continued)

```
            Func2();
            Console.WriteLine("Exit Func1...");
        }

        public void Func2()
        {
            Console.WriteLine("Enter Func2...");
            throw new System.Exception();
            Console.WriteLine("Exit Func2...");
        }
    }
}

Output:
Enter Main...
Enter Func1...
Enter Func2...
```

When you run this program in debug mode, an "Exception was unhandled" message box comes up, as shown in Figure 11-1.

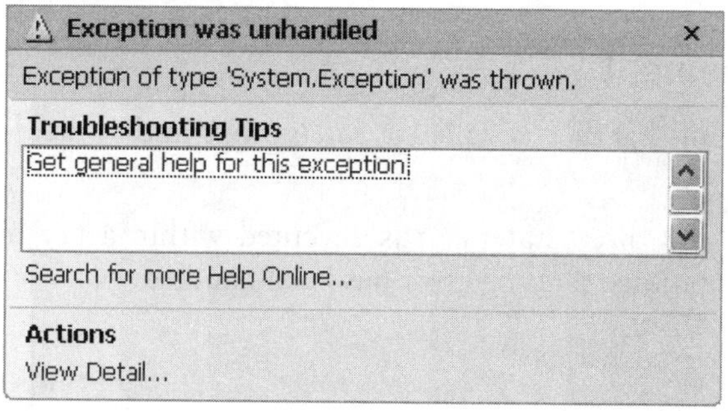

Figure 11-1. Unhandled exception

If you click View Detail, you find the details of the unhandled exception, as shown in Figure 11-2.

This simple example writes to the console as it enters and exits each method. Main() creates an instance of type Test and call Func1(). After printing out the Enter Func1 message, Func1() immediately calls Func2(). Func2() prints out the first message and throws an object of type System.Exception.

Execution immediately stops, and the CLR looks to see if there is a handler in Func2(). There is not, and so the runtime unwinds the stack (never printing the exit statement) to Func1(). Again, there is no handler, and the runtime unwinds the stack back to Main(). With no exception handler there, the default handler is called, which opens the exception message box.

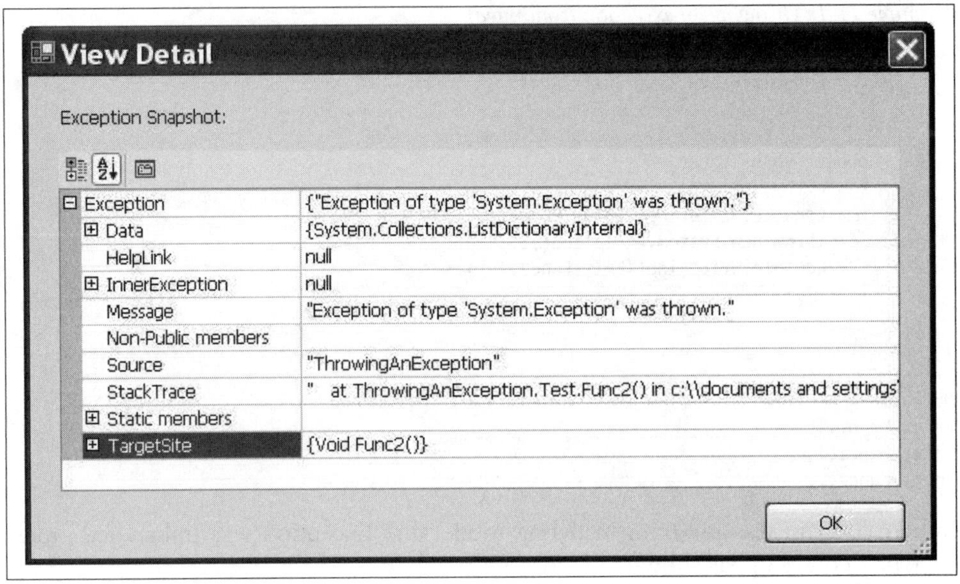

Figure 11-2. Exception details

The catch Statement

In C#, an exception handler is called a *catch block* and is created with the catch keyword.

In Example 11-2, the throw statement is executed within a try block, and a catch block is used to announce that the error has been handled.

Example 11-2. Catching an exception

```
#region Using directives

using System;
using System.Collections.Generic;
using System.Text;

#endregion

namespace CatchingAnException
{
   public class Test
   {
      public static void Main()
      {
         Console.WriteLine( "Enter Main..." );
         Test t = new Test();
         t.Func1();
         Console.WriteLine( "Exit Main..." );
```

Example 11-2. Catching an exception (continued)

```
      }

      public void Func1()
      {
         Console.WriteLine( "Enter Func1..." );
         Func2();
         Console.WriteLine( "Exit Func1..." );
      }

      public void Func2()
      {
         Console.WriteLine( "Enter Func2..." );

         try
         {
            Console.WriteLine( "Entering try block..." );
            throw new System.Exception();
            Console.WriteLine( "Exiting try block..." );
         }
         catch
         {
            Console.WriteLine(
               "Exception caught and handled." );
         }

         Console.WriteLine( "Exit Func2..." );
      }
   }
}
```

```
Output:
Enter Main...
Enter Func1...
Enter Func2...
Entering try block...
Exception caught and handled.
Exit Func2...
Exit Func1...
Exit Main...
```

Example 11-2 is identical to Example 11-1 except that now the program includes a try/catch block. You would typically put the try block around a potentially "dangerous" statement, such as accessing a file, allocating large blocks of memory, etc.

Following the try statement is a generic catch statement. The catch statement in Example 11-2 is generic because you haven't specified what kind of exceptions to catch. In this case, the statement will catch any exceptions that are thrown. Using catch statements to catch specific types of exceptions is discussed later in this chapter.

Taking corrective action

In Example 11-2, the catch statement simply reports that the exception has been caught and handled. In a real-world example, you might take corrective action to fix the problem that caused an exception to be thrown. For example, if the user is trying to open a read-only file, you might invoke a method that allows the user to change the attributes of the file. If the program has run out of memory, you might give the user an opportunity to close other applications. If all else fails, the catch block can print an error message so the user knows what went wrong.

Unwinding the call stack

Examine the output of Example 11-2 carefully. You see the code enter Main(), Func1(), Func2(), and the try block. You never see it exit the try block, though it does exit Func2(), Func1(), and Main(). What happened?

When the exception is thrown, execution halts immediately and is handed to the catch block. It *never* returns to the original code path. It never gets to the line that prints the exit statement for the try block. The catch block handles the error, and then execution falls through to the code following catch.

Without catch the call stack unwinds, but with catch it doesn't unwind, as a result of the exception. The exception is now handled; there are no more problems, and the program continues. This becomes a bit clearer if you move the try/catch blocks up to Func1(), as shown in Example 11-3.

Example 11-3. Catch in a calling function

```csharp
#region Using directives

using System;
using System.Collections.Generic;
using System.Text;

#endregion

namespace CatchingExceptionInCallingFunc
{
    public class Test
    {
        public static void Main()
        {
            Console.WriteLine( "Enter Main..." );
            Test t = new Test();
            t.Func1();
            Console.WriteLine( "Exit Main..." );

        }

        public void Func1()
        {
```

Example 11-3. Catch in a calling function (continued)

```
        Console.WriteLine( "Enter Func1..." );

        try
        {
           Console.WriteLine( "Entering try block..." );
           Func2();
           Console.WriteLine( "Exiting try block..." );
        }
        catch
        {
           Console.WriteLine(
              "Exception caught and handled." );
        }

        Console.WriteLine( "Exit Func1..." );
     }

     public void Func2()
     {
        Console.WriteLine( "Enter Func2..." );
        throw new System.Exception();
        Console.WriteLine( "Exit Func2..." );
     }
  }
}
```

```
Output:
Enter Main...
Enter Func1...
Entering try block...
Enter Func2...
Exception caught and handled.
Exit Func1...
Exit Main...
```

This time the exception is not handled in Func2(), it is handled in Func1(). When Func2() is called, it prints the Enter statement and then throws an exception. Execution halts and the runtime looks for a handler, but there isn't one. The stack unwinds, and the runtime finds a handler in Func1(). The catch statement is called, and execution resumes immediately following the catch statement, printing the Exit statement for Func1() and then for Main().

Make sure you are comfortable with why the Exiting Try Block statement and the Exit Func2 statement aren't printed. This is a classic case where putting the code into a debugger and then stepping through it can make things very clear.

Creating dedicated catch statements

So far, you've been working only with generic catch statements. You can create dedicated catch statements that handle only some exceptions and not others, based on the type of exception thrown. Example 11-4 illustrates how to specify which exception you'd like to handle.

Example 11-4. Specifying the exception to catch

```csharp
#region Using directives

using System;
using System.Collections.Generic;
using System.Text;

#endregion

namespace SpecifyingCaughtException
{
    public class Test
    {
        public static void Main()
        {
            Test t = new Test();
            t.TestFunc();
        }

        // try to divide two numbers
        // handle possible exceptions
        public void TestFunc()
        {
            try
            {
                double a = 5;
                double b = 0;
                Console.WriteLine( "{0} / {1} = {2}",
                    a, b, DoDivide( a, b ) );
            }

            // most derived exception type first
            catch ( System.DivideByZeroException )
            {
                Console.WriteLine(
                    "DivideByZeroException caught!" );
            }
            catch ( System.ArithmeticException )
            {
                Console.WriteLine(
                    "ArithmeticException caught!" );
            }

            // generic exception type last
            catch
            {
                Console.WriteLine(
                    "Unknown exception caught" );
```

Example 11-4. Specifying the exception to catch (continued)

```
        }
    }

    // do the division if legal
    public double DoDivide( double a, double b )
    {
        if ( b == 0 )
            throw new System.DivideByZeroException();
        if ( a == 0 )
            throw new System.ArithmeticException();
        return a / b;
    }
  }
}
```

```
Output:
DivideByZeroException caught!
```

In this example, the DoDivide() method doesn't let you divide 0 by another number, nor does it let you divide a number by 0. It throws an instance of DivideByZeroException if you try to divide by 0. If you try to divide 0 by another number, there is no appropriate exception; dividing 0 by another number is a legal mathematical operation and shouldn't throw an exception at all. For the sake of this example, assume you don't want 0 to be divided by any number and throw an ArithmeticException.

When the exception is thrown, the runtime examines each exception handler *in order* and matches the first one it can. When you run this with a=5 and b=7, the output is:

```
    5 / 7 = 0.7142857142857143
```

As you'd expect, no exception is thrown. However, when you change the value of a to 0, the output is:

```
    ArithmeticException caught!
```

The exception is thrown, and the runtime examines the first exception, Divide-ByZeroException. Because this doesn't match, it goes on to the next handler, ArithmeticException, which does match.

In a final pass through, suppose you change a to 7 and b to 0. This throws the DivideByZeroException.

You have to be particularly careful with the order of the catch statements because the `DivideByZeroException` is derived from `ArithmeticException`. If you reverse the catch statements, the `DivideByZeroException` matches the `ArithmeticException` handler, and the exception won't get to the `DivideByZeroException` handler. In fact, if their order is reversed, it's impossible for *any* exception to reach the `DivideByZeroException` handler. The compiler recognizes that the `DivideByZeroException` handler can't be reached and reports a compile error!

It is possible to distribute your try/catch statements, catching some specific exceptions in one function and more generic exceptions in higher, calling functions. Your design goals should dictate the exact design.

Assume you have a method A that calls another method B, which in turn calls method C. Method C calls method D, which then calls method E. Method E is deep in your code; methods B and A are higher up. If you anticipate that method E might throw an exception, you should create a try/catch block deep in your code to catch that exception as close as possible to the place where the problem arises. You might also want to create more general exception handlers higher up in the code in case unanticipated exceptions slip by.

The finally Statement

In some instances, throwing an exception and unwinding the stack can create a problem. For example, if you have opened a file or otherwise committed a resource, you might need an opportunity to close the file or flush the buffer.

In the event, however, that there is some action you must take regardless of whether an exception is thrown (such as closing a file) you have two strategies to choose from. One approach is to enclose the dangerous action in a try block and then to close the file in both the catch and try blocks. However, this is an ugly duplication of code, and it's error-prone. C# provides a better alternative in the finally block.

The code in the finally block is guaranteed to be executed regardless of whether an exception is thrown.* The TestFunc() method in Example 11-5 simulates opening a file as its first action. The method undertakes some mathematical operations, and the file is closed. It is possible that some time between opening and closing the file an exception will be thrown. If this were to occur, it would be possible for the file to remain open. The developer knows that no matter what happens, at the end of this method the file should be closed, so the file close function call is moved to a finally block, where it will be executed regardless of whether an exception is thrown.

---

* If you throw an exception from within your finally block, there is no guarantee that your finally block will complete execution.

Example 11-5. Using a finally block

```csharp
#region Using directives

using System;
using System.Collections.Generic;
using System.Text;

#endregion

namespace UsingFinally
{
   public class Test
   {
      public static void Main()
      {
         Test t = new Test();
         t.TestFunc();
      }

      // try to divide two numbers
      // handle possible exceptions
      public void TestFunc()
      {
         try
         {
            Console.WriteLine( "Open file here" );
            double a = 5;
            double b = 0;
            Console.WriteLine( "{0} / {1} = {2}",
                a, b, DoDivide( a, b ) );
            Console.WriteLine(
                "This line may or may not print" );
         }

         // most derived exception type first
         catch ( System.DivideByZeroException )
         {
            Console.WriteLine(
                "DivideByZeroException caught!" );
         }
         catch
         {
            Console.WriteLine( "Unknown exception caught" );
         }

         finally
         {
            Console.WriteLine( "Close file here." );
         }
      }

      // do the division if legal
      public double DoDivide( double a, double b )
```

Example 11-5. Using a finally block (continued)

```
        {
            if ( b == 0 )
                throw new System.DivideByZeroException();
            if ( a == 0 )
                throw new System.ArithmeticException();
            return a / b;
        }
    }
}
```

```
Output:
Open file here
DivideByZeroException caught!
Close file here.

Output when b = 12:
Open file here
5 / 12 = 0.416666666666667
This line may or may not print
Close file here.
```

In this example, one of the catch blocks is eliminated to save space, and a finally block is added. Whether or not an exception is thrown, the finally block is executed, and in both output examples you see the message Close file here.

 A finally block can be created with or without catch blocks, but a finally block requires a try block to execute. It is an error to exit a finally block with break, continue, return, or goto.

Exception Objects

So far you've been using the exception as a sentinel—that is, the presence of the exception signals the error—but you haven't touched or examined the Exception object itself. The System.Exception object provides a number of useful methods and properties. The Message property provides information about the exception, such as why it was thrown. The Message property is read-only; the code throwing the exception can set the Message property as an argument to the exception constructor.

The HelpLink property provides a link to the help file associated with the exception. This property is read/write.

VB6 programmers take note: in C#, you need to be careful when declaring and instantiating object variables on the same line of code. If there is a possibility that an error could be thrown in the constructor method, you might be tempted to put the variable declaration and instantiation inside the try block. But if you do that, the variable will only be scoped within the try block, and it can't be referenced within the catch or finally blocks. The best approach is to *declare* the object variable *before* the try block and *instantiate* it *within* the try block.

The StackTrace property is read-only and is set by the runtime. In Example 11-6, the Exception.HelpLink property is set and retrieved to provide information to the user about the DivideByZeroException. The StackTrace property of the exception can provide a stack trace for the error statement. A stack trace displays the *call stack*: the series of method calls that lead to the method in which the exception was thrown.

Example 11-6. Working with an exception object

```
#region Using directives

using System;
using System.Collections.Generic;
using System.Text;

#endregion

namespace ExceptionObject
{
   public class Test
   {
      public static void Main()
      {
         Test t = new Test();
         t.TestFunc();
      }

      // try to divide two numbers
      // handle possible exceptions
      public void TestFunc()
      {
         try
         {
            Console.WriteLine( "Open file here" );
            double a = 12;
            double b = 0;
            Console.WriteLine( "{0} / {1} = {2}",
               a, b, DoDivide( a, b ) );
            Console.WriteLine(
               "This line may or may not print" );
         }
```

Example 11-6. Working with an exception object (continued)

```
            // most derived exception type first
            catch ( System.DivideByZeroException e )
            {
                Console.WriteLine(
                    "\nDivideByZeroException! Msg: {0}",
                    e.Message );
                Console.WriteLine(
                    "\nHelpLink: {0}", e.HelpLink );
                Console.WriteLine(
                    "\nHere's a stack trace: {0}\n",
                    e.StackTrace );
            }
            catch (System.Exception e)
            {
                Console.WriteLine(
                    "Unknown exception caught" + e.Message );
            }
            finally
            {
                Console.WriteLine(
                    "Close file here." );
            }
        }

        // do the division if legal
        public double DoDivide( double a, double b )
        {
            if ( b == 0 )
            {
                DivideByZeroException e =
                    new DivideByZeroException();
                e.HelpLink =
                    "http://www.libertyassociates.com";
                throw e;
            }
            if ( a == 0 )
                throw new ArithmeticException();
            return a / b;
        }
    }
}

Output:
Open file here

DivideByZeroException! Msg: Attempted to divide by zero.

HelpLink: http://www.libertyassociates.com

Here's a stack trace:
at Programming_CSharp.Test.DoDivide(Double a, Double b)
 in c:\...exception06.cs:line 56
```

Example 11-6. Working with an exception object (continued)

```
at Programming_CSharp.Test.TestFunc()
in...exception06.cs:line 22
```

```
Close file here.
```

In the output, the stack trace lists the methods in the reverse order in which they were called; that is, it shows that the error occurred in DoDivide(), which was called by TestFunc(). When methods are deeply nested, the stack trace can help you understand the order of method calls.

In this example, rather than simply throwing a DivideByZeroException, you create a new instance of the exception:

```
DivideByZeroException e = new DivideByZeroException();
```

You don't pass in a custom message, and so the default message will be printed:

```
DivideByZeroException! Msg: Attempted to divide by zero.
```

You can modify this line of code to pass in a default message:

```
new DivideByZeroException(
    "You tried to divide by zero which is not meaningful");
```

In this case, the output message will reflect the custom message:

```
DivideByZeroException! Msg:
You tried to divide by zero which is not
meaningful
```

Before throwing the exception, set the HelpLink property:

```
e.HelpLink = "http://www.libertyassociates.com";
```

When this exception is caught, the program prints the message and the HelpLink:

```
catch (System.DivideByZeroException e)
{
    Console.WriteLine("\nDivideByZeroException! Msg: {0}",
        e.Message);
    Console.WriteLine("\nHelpLink: {0}", e.HelpLink);
```

This allows you to provide useful information to the user. In addition, it prints the StackTrace by getting the StackTrace property of the exception object:

```
Console.WriteLine("\nHere's a stack trace: {0}\n",
    e.StackTrace);
```

The output of this call reflects a full StackTrace leading to the moment the exception was thrown:

```
Here's a stack trace:
at Programming_CSharp.Test.DoDivide(Double a, Double b)
 in c:\...exception06.cs:line 56
at Programming_CSharp.Test.TestFunc()
in...exception06.cs:line 22
```

Note that I've abbreviated the pathnames, so your printout might look different.

Custom Exceptions

The intrinsic exception types the CLR provides, coupled with the custom messages shown in the previous example, will often be all you need to provide extensive information to a catch block when an exception is thrown.

There will be times, however, when you will want to have separate exception handlers based on what caused the exception. To do so, you will want to create your own custom exception types (and thus, you can create specialized handlers). Your custom exception types can add additional information or capabilities, but often their principle reason for existing is just to be a different type that the catch block can differentiate.

 Microsoft recommends that you never throw a base Exception or even an ApplicationException object; it is best to treat these as abstract types.

It is a simple matter to create your own *custom exception* class; the only restriction is that it must derive (directly or indirectly) from System.ApplicationException. Example 11-7 illustrates the creation of a custom exception.

Example 11-7. Creating a custom exception

```
#region Using directives

using System;
using System.Collections.Generic;
using System.Text;

#endregion

namespace CustomExceptions
{
    public class MyCustomException :
        System.ApplicationException
    {
        public MyCustomException( string message ):
            base(message)
        {

        }
    }

    public class Test
    {
        public static void Main()
        {
```

Example 11-7. Creating a custom exception (continued)

```
      Test t = new Test();
      t.TestFunc();
   }

   // try to divide two numbers
   // handle possible exceptions
   public void TestFunc()
   {
      try
      {
         Console.WriteLine( "Open file here" );
         double a = 0;
         double b = 5;
         Console.WriteLine( "{0} / {1} = {2}",
            a, b, DoDivide( a, b ) );
         Console.WriteLine(
            "This line may or may not print" );
      }

      // most derived exception type first
      catch ( System.DivideByZeroException e )
      {
         Console.WriteLine(
            "\nDivideByZeroException! Msg: {0}",
            e.Message );
         Console.WriteLine(
            "\nHelpLink: {0}\n", e.HelpLink );
      }
      catch ( MyCustomException e )
      {
         Console.WriteLine(
            "\nMyCustomException! Msg: {0}",
            e.Message );
         Console.WriteLine(
            "\nHelpLink: {0}\n", e.HelpLink );
      }
      catch
      {
         Console.WriteLine(
            "Unknown exception caught" );
      }
      finally
      {
         Console.WriteLine( "Close file here." );
      }
   }

   // do the division if legal
   public double DoDivide( double a, double b )
   {
      if ( b == 0 )
      {
```

Example 11-7. Creating a custom exception (continued)

```
                DivideByZeroException e =
                    new DivideByZeroException();
                e.HelpLink =
                    "http://www.libertyassociates.com";
                throw e;
            }
            if ( a == 0 )
            {
                MyCustomException e =
                    new MyCustomException(
                        "Can't have zero dividend" );
                e.HelpLink =
                "http://www.libertyassociates.com/NoZeroDivisor.htm";
                throw e;
            }
            return a / b;
        }
    }
}
```

MyCustomException is derived from System.ApplicationException and consists of nothing more than a constructor that takes a string message that it passes to its base class, as described in Chapter 4. In this case, the advantage of creating this custom exception class is that it better reflects the particular design of the Test class, in which it is not legal to have a zero divisor. Using the ArithmeticException rather than a custom exception would work as well, but it might confuse other programmers because a zero divisor wouldn't normally be considered an arithmetic error.

Rethrowing Exceptions

You might want your catch block to take some initial corrective action and then rethrow the exception to an outer try block (in a calling function). It might rethrow the *same* exception, or it might throw a different one. If it throws a different one, it may want to embed the original exception inside the new one so that the calling method can understand the exception history. The InnerException property of the new exception retrieves the original exception.

Some exceptions make any sense only in the context in which they were thrown. This is particularly the case with, for example, the NullReferenceException, which may result from bad user input. In cases where you can't anticipate this by checking input in advance, you should catch the exception, and rethrow an ArgumentException to provide the caller with a better indication of the cause of the problem.

It can sometimes be a good idea to put a catch handler at the boundary of a component or design layer, to trap unexpected exceptions. In this case you might throw a custom InternalErrorException signaling the client code that something went wrong within your component.

Because the `InnerException` is also an exception, it too might have an inner exception. Thus, an entire chain of exceptions can be nested one within the other, much like *Matryoshka* dolls* are contained one within the other. Example 11-8 illustrates.

Example 11-8. Rethrowing inner exceptions

```
#region Using directives

using System;
using System.Collections.Generic;
using System.Text;

#endregion

namespace RethrowingExceptions
{
   public class MyCustomException : System.ApplicationException
   {
      public MyCustomException(
         string message, Exception inner ):
         base(message,inner)
      {

      }
   }

   public class Test
   {
      public static void Main()
      {
         Test t = new Test();
         t.TestFunc();
      }

      public void TestFunc()
      {
         try
         {
            DangerousFunc1();
         }

         // if you catch a custom exception
            // print the exception history
         catch ( MyCustomException e )
         {
            Console.WriteLine( "\n{0}", e.Message );
            Console.WriteLine(
```

---

* In earlier editions I referred to nested Ukrainian dolls. Many readers have written to say that they are *Russian* dolls. The dolls I refer to are properly called *Matryoshka* dolls and, according to Internet sources, are associated with both Russia and the Ukraine. As an interesting additional note, there is evidence of nested dolls as far back as 11th century China.

Example 11-8. Rethrowing inner exceptions (continued)

```
            "Retrieving exception history..." );
         Exception inner =
            e.InnerException;
         while ( inner != null )
         {
            Console.WriteLine(
               "{0}", inner.Message );
            inner =
               inner.InnerException;
         }
      }
   }
}

public void DangerousFunc1()
{
   try
   {
      DangerousFunc2();
   }

   // if you catch any exception here
      // throw a custom exception
   catch ( System.Exception e )
   {
      MyCustomException ex =
         new MyCustomException(
            "E3 - Custom Exception Situation!", e );
      throw ex;
   }
}

public void DangerousFunc2()
{
   try
   {
      DangerousFunc3();
   }

   // if you catch a DivideByZeroException take some
      // corrective action and then throw a general exception
   catch ( System.DivideByZeroException e )
   {
      Exception ex =
         new Exception(
            "E2 - Func2 caught divide by zero", e );
      throw ex;
   }
}

public void DangerousFunc3()
{
   try
```

Example 11-8. Rethrowing inner exceptions (continued)

```
            {
                DangerousFunc4();
            }
            catch ( System.ArithmeticException )
            {
                Console.WriteLine("Arithmetic exception caught in DF3,
                        and rethrown...");
                    throw;
            }

            catch ( System.Exception )
            {
                Console.WriteLine(
                    "Exception handled here." );
            }
        }

        public void DangerousFunc4()
        {
            throw new DivideByZeroException( "E1 - DivideByZero Exception" );
        }
    }
}
```

```
Output:
Arithmetic exception caught in DF3, and rethrown...
E3 - Custom Exception Situation!
Retrieving exception history...
E2 - Func2 caught divide by zero
E1 - DivideByZeroException
```

Because this code has been stripped to the essentials, the output might leave you scratching your head.* The best way to see how this code works is to use the debugger to step through it.

Begin by calling DangerousFunc1() in a try block:

```
    try
    {
        DangerousFunc1();
    }
```

DangerousFunc1() calls DangerousFunc2(), which calls DangerousFunc3(), which in turn calls DangerousFunc4(). All these calls are in their own try blocks. At the end, DangerousFunc4() throws a DivideByZeroException. System.DivideByZeroException normally has its own error message, but you are free to pass in a custom message. Here, to make it easier to identify the sequence of events, the custom message E1 - DivideByZeroException is passed in.

---

* In Beta 2, a stack trace is shown as well.

The exception thrown in DangerousFunc4() is caught in the catch block in DangerousFunc3(). The logic in DangerousFunc3() is that if any ArithmeticException is caught (such as DivideByZeroException), it writes a message to the console and then rethrows the exception:

```
catch (System.ArithmeticException)
{
        Console.WriteLine("Arithmetic exception caught in DF3,
            and rethrown...");
    throw;
}
```

The syntax to rethrow the exact same exception (without modifying it) is just the word throw.

The exception is thus rethrown to DangerousFunc2(), which catches it, takes some corrective action, and throws a new exception of type Exception. In the constructor to that new exception, DangerousFunc2() passes in a custom message (E2 - Func2 caught divide by zero) *and the original exception.* Thus, the original exception (E1) becomes the InnerException for the new exception (E2). DangerousFunc2() then throws this new E2 exception to DangerousFunc1().

DangerousFunc1() catches the exception, does some work, and creates a new exception of type MyCustomException. It passes a new string (E3 - Custom Exception Situation!) to the constructor as well as the exception it just caught (E2). Remember, the exception it just caught is the exception with a DivideByZeroException (E1) as its inner exception. At this point, you have an exception of type MyCustomException (E3), with an inner exception of type Exception (E2), which in turn has an inner exception of type DivideByZeroException (E1). All this is then thrown to the test function, where it is caught.

When the catch function runs, it prints the message:

```
E3 - Custom Exception Situation!
```

and then drills down through the layers of inner exceptions, printing their messages:

```
while (inner != null)
{
    Console.WriteLine("{0}",inner.Message);
    inner = inner.InnerException;
}
```

The output reflects the chain of exceptions thrown and caught:

```
Retrieving exception history...
E2 - Func2 caught divide by zero
E1 - DivideByZero Exception
```

As an alternative, you can call ToString() on the exception:

```
Console.Write(e.ToString());
```

The output reflects the entire stack of messages and the call stacks associated with them:

```
RethrowingExceptions.MyCustomException: E3 - Custom Exception Situation!
---> System.Exception: E2 - Func2 caught divide by zero ---> System.
DivideByZeroException: E1 - DivideByZero Exception
   at RethrowingExceptions.Test.DangerousFunc4() in c:\rethrowingexceptions\
rethrowingexceptions.cs:line 114
   at RethrowingExceptions.Test.DangerousFunc3() in c:\rethrowingexceptions\
rethrowingexceptions.cs:line 102
   at RethrowingExceptions.Test.DangerousFunc2() in c:\rethrowingexceptions\
rethrowingexceptions.cs:line 79
   --- End of inner exception stack trace ---
   at RethrowingExceptions.Test.DangerousFunc2() in c:\rethrowingexceptions\
rethrowingexceptions.cs:line 89
   at RethrowingExceptions.Test.DangerousFunc1() in c:\rethrowingexceptions\
rethrowingexceptions.cs:line 61
   --- End of inner exception stack trace ---
   at RethrowingExceptions.Test.DangerousFunc1() in c:\rethrowingexceptions\
rethrowingexceptions.cs:line 71
   at RethrowingExceptions.Test.TestFunc() in c:\rethrowingexceptions\
rethrowingexceptions.cs:line 33
```

CHAPTER 12

Delegates and Events

When a head of state dies, the president of the United States typically doesn't have time to attend the funeral personally. Instead, he dispatches a delegate. Often this delegate is the vice president, but sometimes the VP is unavailable and the president must send someone else, such as the secretary of state or even the first lady. He doesn't want to "hardwire" his delegated authority to a single person; he might delegate this responsibility to anyone who is able to execute the correct international protocol.

The president defines in advance what responsibility will be delegated (attend the funeral), what parameters will be passed (condolences, kind words), and what value he hopes to get back (good will). He then assigns a particular person to that delegated responsibility at "runtime" as the course of his presidency progresses.

In programming, you are often faced with situations where you need to execute a particular action, but you don't know in advance which method, or even which object, you'll want to call upon to execute it. For example, a button might know that it must notify some object when it is pushed, but it might not know which object or objects need to be notified. Instead of wiring the button to a particular object, you will connect the button to a *delegate* and then resolve that delegate to a particular method when the program executes.

In the early, dark, and primitive days of computing, a program would begin execution and then proceed through its steps until it completed. If the user was involved, the interaction was strictly controlled and limited to filling in fields.

Today's GUI programming model requires a different approach, known as *event-driven programming*. A modern program presents the user interface and waits for the user to take an action. The user might take many different actions, such as choosing among menu selections, pushing buttons, updating text fields, clicking icons, and so forth. Each action causes an event to be raised. Other events can be raised without direct user action, such as events that correspond to timer ticks of the internal clock, email being received, file-copy operations completing, etc.

An event is the encapsulation of the idea that "something happened" to which the program must respond. Events and delegates are tightly coupled concepts because flexible event handling requires that the response to the event be dispatched to the appropriate event handler. An event handler is typically implemented in C# via a delegate.

Delegates are also used as callbacks so that one class can say to another "do this work and when you're done, let me know."

Delegates

In C#, delegates are first-class objects, fully supported by the language. Technically, a delegate is a reference type used to encapsulate a method with a specific signature and return type.* You can encapsulate any matching method in that delegate.

 In C++ and many other languages, you can to some degree accomplish this requirement with function pointers and pointers to member functions.

A delegate is created with the delegate keyword, followed by a return type and the signature of the methods that can be delegated to it, as in the following:

```
public delegate int WhichIsFirst(object obj1, object obj2);
```

This declaration defines a delegate named WhichIsFirst, which will encapsulate any method that takes two objects as parameters and that returns an int.

Once the delegate is defined, you can encapsulate a member method with that delegate by instantiating the delegate, passing in a method that matches the return type and signature. As an alternative, you can use anonymous methods as described later. In either case, the delegate can then be used to invoke that encapsulated method.

Using Delegates to Specify Methods at Runtime

Delegates *decouple* the class that declares the delegate from the class that uses the delegate. For example, suppose that you want to create a simple generic container class called a Pair that can hold and sort any two objects passed to it. You can't know in advance what kind of objects a Pair will hold, but by creating methods within those objects to which the sorting task can be delegated, you can delegate responsibility for determining their order to the objects themselves.

Different objects will sort differently (for example, a Pair of Counter objects might sort in numeric order, while a Pair of Buttons might sort alphabetically by their

---

* If the method is an instance method, the delegate encapsulates the target object as well.

name). As the author of the Pair class, you want the objects in the pair to have the responsibility of knowing which should be first and which should be second. To accomplish this, you will insist that the objects to be stored in the Pair must provide a method that tells you how to sort the objects.

You can define this requirement with interfaces, as well. Delegates are smaller and of finer granularity than interfaces. The Pair class doesn't need to implement an entire interface, it just needs to define the signature and return type of the method it wants to invoke. That is what delegates are for: they define the return type and signature of methods that can be invoked through the interface.

In this case, the Pair class will declare a delegate named WhichIsFirst. When the Pair needs to know how to order its objects, it will invoke the delegate passing in its two member objects as parameters. The responsibility for deciding which of the two objects comes first is delegated to the method encapsulated by the delegate:

```
public delegate Comparison
    WhichIsFirst( T obj1, T obj2 )
```

In this definition, WhichIsFirst is defined to encapsulate a method that takes two objects as parameters, and that returns an object of type Comparison. Comparison turns out to be an enumeration you will define:

```
public enum Comparison
{
    theFirstComesFirst = 1,
    theSecondComesFirst = 2
}
```

To test the delegate, you will create two classes, a Dog class and a Student class. Dogs and Students have little in common, except that they both implement methods that can be encapsulated by WhichComesFirst, and thus both Dog objects and Student objects are eligible to be held within Pair objects.

In the test program, you will create a couple of Students and a couple of Dogs, and store them each in a Pair. You will then create instances of WhichIsFirst to encapsulate their respective methods that will determine which Student or which Dog object should be first, and which second. Let's take this step by step.

You begin by creating a Pair constructor that takes two objects and stashes them away in a private array:

```
public Pair(
    T firstObject,
    T secondObject )
{
    thePair[0] = firstObject;
    thePair[1] = secondObject;
}
```

Next, you override ToString() to obtain the string value of the two objects:

```
public override string ToString()
{
    return thePair [0].ToString() + ", " +
        thePair[1].ToString();
}
```

You now have two objects in your Pair and you can print out their values. You're ready to sort them and print the results of the sort. You can't know in advance what kind of objects you will have, so you delegate the responsibility of deciding which object comes first in the sorted Pair to the objects themselves.

Both the Dog class and the Student class implement methods that can be encapsulated by WhichIsFirst. Any method that takes two objects and returns a Comparison can be encapsulated by this delegate at runtime.

You can now define the Sort() method for the Pair class:

```
public void Sort(WhichIsFirst theDelegatedFunc)
{
    if (theDelegatedFunc(thePair[0],thePair[1]) ==
        Comparison.theSecondComesFirst)
    {
        T temp = thePair[0];
        thePair[0] = thePair[1];
        thePair[1] = temp;
    }
}
```

This method takes a parameter: a delegate of type WhichIsFirst named the-DelegatedFunc. The Sort() method delegates responsibility for deciding which of the two objects in the Pair comes first to the method encapsulated by that delegate. In the body of the Sort() method, it invokes the delegated method and examines the return value, which will be one of the two enumerated values of Comparison.

If the value returned is theSecondComesFirst, the objects within the pair are swapped; otherwise no action is taken.

This is analogous to how the other parameters work. If you had a method that took an int as a parameter:

```
int SomeMethod (int myParam){//...}
```

the parameter name is myParam, but you can pass in any int value or variable. Similarly, the parameter name in the delegate example is theDelegatedFunc, but you can pass in any method that meets the return value and signature defined by the delegate WhichIsFirst.

Imagine you are sorting Students by name. You write a method that returns the-FirstComesFirst if the first student's name comes first, and theSecondComesFirst if the second student's name does. If you pass in "Amy, Beth" the method returns theFirstComesFirst, and if you pass in "Beth, Amy" it returns theSecondComesFirst. If you get back theSecondComesFirst, the Sort() method reverses the items in its array, setting Amy to the first position and Beth to the second.

Now add one more method, ReverseSort(), which forces the items in the array into the reverse of their normal order:

```
public void ReverseSort(WhichIsFirst theDelegatedFunc)
{
    if (theDelegatedFunc(thePair[0], thePair[1]) ==
            Comparison.theFirstComesFirst)
    {
        T temp = thePair[0];
        thePair[0] = thePair[1];
        thePair[1] = temp;
    }
}
```

The logic here is identical to Sort(), except that this method performs the swap if the delegated method says that the first item comes first. Because the delegated function thinks the first item comes first, and this is a reverse sort, the result you want is for the second item to come first. This time if you pass in "Amy, Beth," the delegated function returns theFirstComesFirst (i.e., Amy should come first), but because this is a *reverse* sort, it swaps the values, setting Beth first. This allows you to use the same delegated function as you used with Sort(), without forcing the object to support a function that returns the reverse sorted value.

Now all you need are some objects to sort. You'll create two absurdly simple classes: Student and Dog. Assign Student objects a name at creation:

```
public class Student
{
    public Student(string name)
    {
        this.name = name;
    }
```

The Student class requires two methods: one to override ToString() and the other to be encapsulated as the delegated method.

Student must override ToString() so that the ToString() method in Pair, which invokes ToString() on the contained objects, will work properly; the implementation does nothing more than return the student's name (which is already a string object):

```
public override string ToString()
{
    return name;
}
```

It must also implement a method to which Pair.Sort() can delegate the responsibility of determining which of two objects comes first:

```
        return (String.Compare(s1.name, s2.name) < 0 ?
            Comparison.theFirstComesFirst :
            Comparison.theSecondComesFirst);
```

String.Compare() is a .NET Framework method on the String class that compares two strings and returns less than zero if the first is smaller, greater than zero if the second is smaller, and zero if they are the same. This method was discussed in some detail in Chapter 10. Notice that the logic here returns theFirstComesFirst only if the first string is smaller; if they are the same or the second is larger, this method returns theSecondComesFirst.

Notice that the WhichStudentComesFirst() method takes two objects as parameters and returns a Comparison. This qualifies it to be a Pair.WhichIsFirst delegated method, whose signature and return value it matches.

The second class is Dog. For our purposes, Dog objects will be sorted by weight, lighter dogs before heavier. Here's the complete declaration of Dog:

```
public class Dog
{
    public Dog(int weight)
    {
        this.weight=weight;
    }

    // dogs are ordered by weight
    public static Comparison WhichDogComesFirst(
        Object o1, Object o2)
    {
        Dog d1 = (Dog) o1;
        Dog d2 = (Dog) o2;
        return d1.weight > d2.weight ?
          Comparison.theSecondComesFirst :
            Comparison.theFirstComesFirst;
    }
    public override string ToString()
    {
        return weight.ToString();
    }
    private int weight;
}
```

The Dog class also overrides ToString and implements a static method with the correct signature for the delegate. Notice also that the Dog and Student delegate methods don't have the same name. They don't need to have the same name, as they will be assigned to the delegate dynamically at runtime.

You can call your delegated method names anything you like, but creating parallel names (for example, WhichStudentComesFirst and WhichDogComesFirst) makes the code easier to read, understand, and maintain.

Example 12-1 is the complete program, which illustrates how the delegate methods are invoked.

Example 12-1. Working with delegates

```
#region Using directives

using System;
using System.Collections.Generic;
using System.Text;

#endregion

namespace Delegates
{
    public enum Comparison
    {
        theFirstComesFirst = 1,
        theSecondComesFirst = 2
    }

    // a simple collection to hold 2 items
    public class Pair<T>
    {

        // private array to hold the two objects
        private T[] thePair = new T[2];

        // the delegate declaration
        public delegate Comparison
            WhichIsFirst( T obj1, T obj2 );

        // passed in constructor take two objects,
        // added in order received
        public Pair(
            T firstObject,
            T secondObject )
        {
            thePair[0] = firstObject;
            thePair[1] = secondObject;
        }

        // public method which orders the two objects
        // by whatever criteria the object likes!
        public void Sort(
            WhichIsFirst theDelegatedFunc )
        {
            if ( theDelegatedFunc( thePair[0], thePair[1] )
                == Comparison.theSecondComesFirst )
            {
                T temp = thePair[0];
                thePair[0] = thePair[1];
                thePair[1] = temp;
```

Example 12-1. Working with delegates (continued)

```
        }
    }

    // public method which orders the two objects
    // by the reverse of whatever criteria the object likes!
    public void ReverseSort(
        WhichIsFirst theDelegatedFunc )
    {
        if ( theDelegatedFunc( thePair[0], thePair[1] ) ==
            Comparison.theFirstComesFirst )
        {
            T temp = thePair[0];
            thePair[0] = thePair[1];
            thePair[1] = temp;
        }
    }

    // ask the two objects to give their string value
    public override string ToString()
    {
        return thePair[0].ToString() + ", "
            + thePair[1].ToString();
    }
}        // end class Pair

public class Dog
{
    private int weight;

    public Dog( int weight )
    {
        this.weight = weight;
    }

    // dogs are ordered by weight
    public static Comparison WhichDogComesFirst(
        Dog d1, Dog d2 )
    {
        return d1.weight > d2.weight ?
            Comparison.theSecondComesFirst :
            Comparison.theFirstComesFirst;
    }
    public override string ToString()
    {
        return weight.ToString();
    }
}        // end class Dog

public class Student
{
    private string name;
```

Example 12-1. Working with delegates (continued)

```csharp
   public Student( string name )
   {
      this.name = name;
   }

   // students are ordered alphabetically
   public static Comparison
      WhichStudentComesFirst( Student s1, Student s2 )
   {
      return ( String.Compare( s1.name, s2.name ) < 0 ?
         Comparison.theFirstComesFirst :
         Comparison.theSecondComesFirst );
   }

   public override string ToString()
   {
      return name;
   }
}         // end class Student

public class Test
{
   public static void Main()
   {
      // create two students and two dogs
      // and add them to Pair objects
      Student Jesse = new Student( "Jesse" );
      Student Stacey = new Student( "Stacey" );
      Dog Milo = new Dog( 65 );
      Dog Fred = new Dog( 12 );

      Pair<Student> studentPair = new Pair<Student>( Jesse, Stacey );
      Pair<Dog> dogPair = new Pair<Dog>( Milo, Fred );
      Console.WriteLine( "studentPair\t\t\t: {0}",
         studentPair.ToString() );
      Console.WriteLine( "dogPair\t\t\t\t: {0}",
         dogPair.ToString() );

      // Instantiate  the delegates
      Pair<Student>.WhichIsFirst theStudentDelegate =
         new Pair<Student>.WhichIsFirst(
         Student.WhichStudentComesFirst );

      Pair<Dog>.WhichIsFirst theDogDelegate =
         new Pair<Dog>.WhichIsFirst(
         Dog.WhichDogComesFirst );

      // sort using the delegates
      studentPair.Sort( theStudentDelegate );
      Console.WriteLine( "After Sort studentPair\t\t: {0}",
         studentPair.ToString() );
      studentPair.ReverseSort( theStudentDelegate );
```

Example 12-1. Working with delegates (continued)

```
        Console.WriteLine( "After ReverseSort studentPair\t: {0}",
            studentPair.ToString() );

        dogPair.Sort( theDogDelegate );
        Console.WriteLine( "After Sort dogPair\t\t: {0}",
            dogPair.ToString() );
        dogPair.ReverseSort( theDogDelegate );
        Console.WriteLine( "After ReverseSort dogPair\t: {0}",
            dogPair.ToString() );
    }
  }
}
```

```
Output:
studentPair                : Jesse, Stacey
dogPair                    : 65, 12
After Sort studentPair     : Jesse, Stacey
After ReverseSort studentPair  : Stacey, Jesse
After Sort dogPair         : 12, 65
After ReverseSort dogPair  : 65, 12
```

The Test program creates two Student objects and two Dog objects and then adds them to Pair containers. The student constructor takes a string for the student's name and the dog constructor takes an int for the dog's weight:

```
Student Jesse = new Student( "Jesse" );
Student Stacey = new Student( "Stacey" );
Dog Milo = new Dog( 65 );
Dog Fred = new Dog( 12 );

Pair<Student> studentPair = new Pair<Student>( Jesse, Stacey );
Pair<Dog> dogPair = new Pair<Dog>( Milo, Fred );
Console.WriteLine( "studentPair\t\t\t: {0}",
    studentPair.ToString() );
Console.WriteLine( "dogPair\t\t\t\t: {0}",
    dogPair.ToString() );
```

It then prints the contents of the two Pair containers to see the order of the objects. The output looks like this:

```
studentPair          : Jesse, Stacey
dogPair              : 65, 12
```

As expected, the objects are in the order in which they were added to the Pair containers. We next instantiate two delegate objects:

```
Pair<Student>.WhichIsFirst theStudentDelegate =
    new Pair<Student>.WhichIsFirst(
    Student.WhichStudentComesFirst );

Pair<Dog>.WhichIsFirst theDogDelegate =
    new Pair<Dog>.WhichIsFirst(
    Dog.WhichDogComesFirst );
```

The first delegate, theStudentDelegate, is created by passing in the appropriate static method from the Student class. The second delegate, theDogDelegate, is passed a static method from the Dog class.

The delegates are now objects that can be passed to methods. You pass the delegates first to the Sort() method of the Pair object, and then to the ReverseSort() method. The results are printed to the console:

```
After Sort studentPair         : Jesse, Stacey
After ReverseSort studentPair  : Stacey, Jesse
After Sort dogPair             : 12, 65
After ReverseSort dogPair      : 65, 12
```

Delegates and Instance Methods

In Example 12-1, the delegates encapsulate static methods, as in the following:

```
public static Comparison
    WhichStudentComesFirst(Student s1, Student s2)
```

The delegate is then instantiated using the class rather than an instance:

```
Pair<Student>.WhichIsFirst  theStudentDelegate =
    new Pair.WhichIsFirst(
    Student.WhichStudentComesFirst);
```

You can just as easily encapsulate instance methods:

```
public Comparison
    WhichStudentComesFirst(Student s1, Student s2)
```

in which case you will instantiate the delegate by passing in the instance method as invoked through an instance of the class, rather than through the class itself:

```
Pair<Student>.WhichIsFirst  theStudentDelegate =
    new Pair<Student>.WhichIsFirst(
    Jesse.WhichStudentComesFirst);
```

Static Delegates

One disadvantage of Example 12-1 is that it forces the calling class (in this case Test) to instantiate the delegates it needs to sort the objects in a Pair. It would be nice to get the delegate from the Student or Dog class itself. You can do this by giving each class its own static delegate. Thus, you can modify Student to add this:

```
public static readonly Pair<Student>.WhichIsFirst OrderStudents =
    new Pair<Student>.WhichIsFirst( Student.WhichStudentComesFirst );
```

This creates a static, read-only delegate field named OrderStudents.

Marking OrderStudents read-only denotes that once this static field is created, it isn't modified.

You can create a similar delegate within the Dog class:

```
public static readonly Pair<Dog>.WhichIsFirst OrderDogs =
    new Pair<Dog>.WhichIsFirst( Dog.WhichDogComesFirst );
```

These are now static fields of their respective classes. Each is prewired to the appropriate method within the class. You can invoke delegates without declaring a local delegate instance. You just pass in the static delegate of the class:

```
studentPair.Sort(Student.OrderStudents);
Console.WriteLine("After Sort studentPair\t\t: {0}",
    studentPair.ToString());
studentPair.ReverseSort(Student.OrderStudents);
Console.WriteLine("After ReverseSort studentPair\t: {0}",
    studentPair.ToString());

dogPair.Sort(Dog.OrderDogs);
Console.WriteLine("After Sort dogPair\t\t: {0}",
    dogPair.ToString());
dogPair.ReverseSort(Dog.OrderDogs);
Console.WriteLine("After ReverseSort dogPair\t: {0}",
    dogPair.ToString());
```

The output after these changes is identical to Example 12-1.

Delegates as Properties

The problem with static delegates is that they must be instantiated, whether or not they are ever used, as with Student and Dog in Example 12-1. If you are creating hundreds of delegates you might consider implementing the static delegate fields as properties.

For Student, you take out the declaration:

```
public static readonly Pair<Student>.WhichIsFirst OrderStudents =
    new Pair<Student>.WhichIsFirst( Student.WhichStudentComesFirst );
```

and replace it with:

```
public static Pair<Student>.WhichIsFirst OrderStudents
{
    get
    {
        return new Pair<Student>.WhichIsFirst( WhichStudentComesFirst );
    }
}
```

Similarly, you replace the static Dog field with:

```
public static Pair<Dog>.WhichIsFirst OrderDogs
{
   get
   {
      return new Pair<Dog>.WhichIsFirst( WhichDogComesFirst );
   }
}
```

The assignment of the delegates is unchanged:

```
studentPair.Sort(Student.OrderStudents);
dogPair.Sort(Dog.OrderDogs);
```

When the OrderStudent property is accessed, the delegate is created:

```
return new Pair.WhichIsFirst(WhichStudentComesFirst);
```

The key advantage is that the delegate is not created until it is requested. This allows the test class to determine when it needs a delegate, but still allows the details of the creation of the delegate to be the responsibility of the Student (or Dog) class.

Multicasting

At times, it is desirable to call two (or more) implementing methods through a single delegate. This becomes particularly important when handling events (discussed later in this chapter).

The goal is to have a single delegate that invokes more than one method. For example, when a button is pressed, you might want to take more than one action.

Two delegates can be combined with the addition operator (+). The result is a new multicast delegate that invokes both of the original implementing methods. For example, assuming Writer and Logger are delegates, the following line will combine them and produce a new multicast delegate named myMulticastDelegate:

```
myMulticastDelegate = Writer + Logger;
```

You can add delegates to a multicast delegate using the plus-equals (+=) operator. This operator adds the delegate on the right side of the operator to the multicast delegate on the left. For example, assuming Transmitter and myMulticastDelegate are delegates, the following line adds Transmitter to myMulticastDelegate:

```
myMulticastDelegate += Transmitter;
```

To see how multicast delegates are created and used, let's walk through a complete example. In Example 12-2, you will create a class called MyClassWithDelegate that defines a delegate that takes a string as a parameter and returns void:

```
public delegate void StringDelegate(string s);
```

You then define a class called MyImplementingClass that has three methods, all of which return void and take a string as a parameter: WriteString, LogString, and

---

TransmitString. The first writes the string to standard output, the second simulates writing to a log file, and the third simulates transmitting the string across the Internet. You instantiate the delegates to invoke the appropriate methods:

```
Writer("String passed to Writer\n");
Logger("String passed to Logger\n");
Transmitter("String passed to Transmitter\n");
```

To see how to combine delegates, you create another delegate instance:

```
MyClassWithDelegate.StringDelegate myMulticastDelegate;
```

and assign to it the result of "adding" two existing delegates:

```
myMulticastDelegate = Writer + Logger;
```

You add to this delegate an additional delegate using the += operator:

```
myMulticastDelegate += Transmitter;
```

Finally, you selectively remove delegates using the -= operator:

```
myMulticastDelegate -= Logger;
```

Example 12-2 shows how to combine delegates in this way.

Example 12-2. Combining delegates

```
#region Using directives

using System;
using System.Collections.Generic;
using System.Text;

#endregion

namespace MulticastDelegates
{
    public class MyClassWithDelegate
    {
        // the delegate declaration
        public delegate void StringDelegate( string s );

    }

    public class MyImplementingClass
    {
        public static void WriteString( string s )
        {
            Console.WriteLine( "Writing string {0}", s );
        }

        public static void LogString( string s )
        {
            Console.WriteLine( "Logging string {0}", s );
        }
```

Example 12-2. Combining delegates (continued)

```
    public static void TransmitString( string s )
    {
        Console.WriteLine( "Transmitting string {0}", s );
    }
}

public class Test
{
    public static void Main()
    {
        // define three StringDelegate objects
        MyClassWithDelegate.StringDelegate
            Writer, Logger, Transmitter;

        // define another StringDelegate
        // to act as the multicast delegate
        MyClassWithDelegate.StringDelegate
            myMulticastDelegate;

        // Instantiate the first three delegates,
        // passing in methods to encapsulate
        Writer = new MyClassWithDelegate.StringDelegate(
            MyImplementingClass.WriteString );
        Logger = new MyClassWithDelegate.StringDelegate(
            MyImplementingClass.LogString );
        Transmitter =
            new MyClassWithDelegate.StringDelegate(
            MyImplementingClass.TransmitString );

        // Invoke the Writer delegate method
        Writer( "String passed to Writer\n" );

        // Invoke the Logger delegate method
        Logger( "String passed to Logger\n" );

        // Invoke the Transmitter delegate method
        Transmitter( "String passed to Transmitter\n" );

        // Tell the user you are about to combine
        // two delegates into the multicast delegate
        Console.WriteLine(
            "myMulticastDelegate = Writer + Logger" );

        // combine the two delegates, the result is
        // assigned to myMulticast Delegate
        myMulticastDelegate = Writer + Logger;

        // Call the delegated methods, two methods
        // will be invoked
        myMulticastDelegate(
            "First string passed to Collector" );
```

Example 12-2. Combining delegates (continued)

```
                // Tell the user you are about to add
                // a third delegate to the multicast
                Console.WriteLine(
                    "\nmyMulticastDelegate += Transmitter" );

                // add the third delegate
                myMulticastDelegate += Transmitter;

                // invoke the three delegated methods
                myMulticastDelegate(
                    "Second string passed to Collector" );

                // tell the user you are about to remove
                // the logger delegate
                Console.WriteLine(
                    "\nmyMulticastDelegate -= Logger" );

                // remove the logger delegate
                myMulticastDelegate -= Logger;

                // invoke the two remaining
                // delegated methods
                myMulticastDelegate(
                    "Third string passed to Collector" );
        }
    }
}
```

```
Output:
Writing string String passed to Writer

Logging string String passed to Logger

Transmitting string String passed to Transmitter

myMulticastDelegate = Writer + Logger
Writing string First string passed to Collector
Logging string First string passed to Collector

myMulticastDelegate += Transmitter
Writing string Second string passed to Collector
Logging string Second string passed to Collector
Transmitting string Second string passed to Collector

myMulticastDelegate -= Logger
Writing string Third string passed to Collector
Transmitting string Third string passed to Collector
```

In the Test portion of Example 12-2, the delegate instances are defined and the first three (Writer, Logger, and Transmitter) are invoked. The fourth delegate, myMulticastDelegate, is then assigned the combination of the first two, and it is invoked, causing both delegated methods to be called. The third delegate is added, and when `myMulticastDelegate` is invoked, all three delegated methods are called. Finally, `Logger` is removed, and when `myMulticastDelegate` is invoked, only the two remaining methods are called.

The power of multicast delegates is best understood in terms of events, discussed in the next section. When an event such as a button press occurs, an associated multicast delegate can invoke a series of event handler methods that will respond to the event.

Events

GUIs, such as Microsoft Windows and web browsers, require that programs respond to *events*. An event might be a button push, a menu selection, the completion of a file transfer, and so forth. In short, something happens and you must respond to it. You can't predict the order in which events will arise. The system is quiescent until the event, and then springs into action to handle it.

In a GUI environment, any number of widgets can *raise* an event. For example, when you click a button, it might raise the `Click` event. When you add to a drop-down list, it might raise a `ListChanged` event.

Other classes will be interested in responding to these events. How they respond is not of interest to the class raising the event. The button says, "I was clicked," and the responding classes react appropriately.

Publishing and Subscribing

In C#, any object can *publish* a set of events to which other classes can *subscribe*. When the publishing class raises an event, all the subscribed classes are notified. With this mechanism, your object can say, "Here are things I can notify you about," and other classes might sign up, saying, "Yes, let me know when that happens." For example, a button might notify any number of interested observers when it is clicked. The button is called the *publisher* because the button publishes the `Click` event and the other classes are the *subscribers* because they subscribe to the `Click` event.

This design implements the Publish/Subscribe (Observer) Pattern described in the seminal work *Design Patterns* (Addison Wesley). Gamma describes the intent of this pattern: "Define a one to many dependency between objects so that when one object changes state, all its dependents are notified and updated automatically."

Note that the publishing class doesn't know or care who (if anyone) subscribes; it just raises the event. Who responds to that event, and how they respond, isn't the concern of the publishing class.

As a second example, a `Clock` might notify interested classes whenever the time changes by one second. The `Clock` class could itself be responsible for the User

Interface representation of the time, instead of raising an event, so why bother with the indirection of using delegates? The advantage of the publish/subscribe idiom is that the Clock class need not know how its information will be used; the monitoring of the time is thus decoupled from the representation of that information. In addition, any number of classes can be notified when an event is raised. The subscribing classes don't need to know how the Clock works, and the Clock doesn't need to know what they are going to do in response to the event.

The publisher and the subscribers are decoupled by the delegate. This is highly desirable; it makes for more flexible and robust code. The Clock can change how it detects time without breaking any of the subscribing classes. The subscribing classes can change how they respond to time changes without breaking the Clock. The two classes spin independently of one another, and that makes for code that is easier to maintain.

Events and Delegates

Events in C# are implemented with delegates. The publishing class defines a delegate. The subscribing class does two things: first it creates a method that matches the signature of the delegate, and then it creates an instance of that delegate type encapsulating that method. When the event is raised, the subscribing class's methods are invoked through the delegate.

A method that handles an event is called an *event handler*. You can declare your event handlers as you would any other delegate.

By convention, event handlers in the .NET Framework return void and take two parameters. The first parameter is the "source" of the event (that is, the publishing object). The second parameter is an object derived from EventArgs. It is recommended that your event handlers follow this design pattern.

 VB6 programmers take note: C# doesn't put restrictions on the names of the methods that handle events. Also, the .NET implementation of the publish/subscribe model lets you have a single method that subscribes to multiple events.

EventArgs is the base class for all event data. Other than its constructor, the EventArgs class inherits all its methods from Object, though it does add a public static field named empty, which represents an event with no state (to allow for the efficient use of events with no state). The EventArgs derived class contains information about the event.

Suppose you want to create a Clock class that uses delegates to notify potential subscribers whenever the local time changes value by one second. Call this delegate SecondChangeHandler.

The declaration for the SecondChangeHandler delegate is:

```
public delegate void SecondChangeHandler(
    object clock,
    TimeInfoEventArgs timeInformation
    );
```

This delegate will encapsulate any method that returns void and that takes two parameters. The first parameter is an object that represents the clock (the object raising the event), and the second parameter is an object of type TimeInfoEventArgs that will contain useful information for anyone interested in this event. TimeInfoEventArgs is defined as follows:

```
public class TimeInfoEventArgs : EventArgs
{
    public TimeInfoEventArgs(int hour, int minute, int second)
    {
        this.hour = hour;
        this.minute = minute;
        this.second = second;
    }
    public readonly int hour;
    public readonly int minute;
    public readonly int second;
}
```

The TimeInfoEventArgs object will have information about the current hour, minute, and second. It defines a constructor and three public, read-only integer variables.

In addition to its delegate, a Clock has three member variables—hour, minute, and second—as well as a single method, Run():

```
public void Run()
{
    for(;;)
    {
        // sleep 10 milliseconds
        Thread.Sleep(10);

        // get the current time
        System.DateTime dt = System.DateTime.Now;

        // if the second has changed
        // notify the subscribers
        if (dt.Second != second)
        {
            // create the TimeInfoEventArgs object
            // to pass to the subscriber
    TimeInfoEventArgs timeInformation =
      new TimeInfoEventArgs(
      dt.Hour,dt.Minute,dt.Second);

            // if anyone has subscribed, notify them
            if (OnSecondChange != null)
```

```
            {
                OnSecondChange(this,timeInformation);
            }
        }
        // update the state
        this.second = dt.Second;
        this.minute = dt.Minute;
        this.hour = dt.Hour;
    }
}
```

Run() creates an infinite for loop that periodically checks the system time. If the time has changed from the Clock object's current time, it notifies all its subscribers and then updates its own state.

The first step is to sleep for 10 milliseconds:

```
Thread.Sleep(10);
```

This makes use of a static method of the Thread class from the System.Threading namespace, which will be covered in some detail in Chapter 20. The call to Sleep() prevents the loop from running so tightly that little else on the computer gets done.

After sleeping for 10 milliseconds, the method checks the current time:

```
System.DateTime dt = System.DateTime.Now;
```

About every 100 times it checks, the second will have incremented. The method notices that change and notifies its subscribers. To do so, it first creates a new TimeInfoEventArgs object:

```
if (dt.Second != second)
{
    // create the TimeInfoEventArgs object
    // to pass to the subscriber
    TimeInfoEventArgs timeInformation =
        new TimeInfoEventArgs(dt.Hour,dt.Minute,dt.Second);
```

It then notifies the subscribers by firing the OnSecondChange event:

```
    // if anyone has subscribed, notify them
    if (OnSecondChange != null)
    {
        OnSecondChange(this,timeInformation);
    }
}
```

If an event has no subscribers registered, it evaluates to null. The preceding test checks that the value isn't null, ensuring that there are subscribers before calling OnSecondChange.

Remember that OnSecondChange takes two arguments: the source of the event and the object derived from EventArgs. In the snippet, you see that the clock's this reference is passed because the clock is the source of the event. The second parameter is the TimeInfoEventArgs object, timeInformation, created on the line above.

Raising the event invokes whatever methods have been registered with the Clock class through the delegate. We'll examine this in a moment.

Once the event is raised, update the state of the Clock class:

```
this.second = dt.Second;
this.minute = dt.Minute;
this.hour = dt.Hour;
```

 No attempt has been made to make this code thread-safe. Thread safety and synchronization are discussed in Chapter 20.

All that is left is to create classes that can subscribe to this event. You create two. First is the DisplayClock class. The job of DisplayClock isn't to keep track of time, but rather, to display the current time to the console.

The example simplifies this class down to two methods. The first is a helper method named Subscribe() that subscribes to the clock's OnSecondChange delegate. The second method is the event handler TimeHasChanged():

```
public class DisplayClock
{
    public void Subscribe(Clock theClock)
    {
        theClock.OnSecondChange +=
            new Clock.SecondChangeHandler(TimeHasChanged);
    }

    public void TimeHasChanged(
        object theClock, TimeInfoEventArgs ti)
    {
            Console.WriteLine("Current Time: {0}:{1}:{2}",
                ti.hour.ToString(),
                ti.minute.ToString(),
                ti.second.ToString());
    }
}
```

When the first method, Subscribe(), is invoked, it creates a new Second-ChangeHandler delegate, passing in its event handler method, TimeHasChanged(). It then registers that delegate with the OnSecondChange event of Clock.

Now create a second class that also responds to this event, LogCurrentTime. This class normally logs the event to a file, but for our demonstration purposes, it logs to the standard console:

```
public class LogCurrentTime
{
    public void Subscribe(Clock theClock)
    {
        theClock.OnSecondChange +=
```

```
                new Clock.SecondChangeHandler(WriteLogEntry);
        }

        // This method should write to a file.
        // We write to the console to see the effect.
        // This object keeps no state.
        public void WriteLogEntry(
            object theClock, TimeInfoEventArgs ti)
        {
            Console.WriteLine("Logging to file: {0}:{1}:{2}",
                ti.hour.ToString(),
                ti.minute.ToString(),
                ti.second.ToString());
        }
    }
```

Although in this example these two classes are very similar, in a production program any number of disparate classes might subscribe to an event.

All that remains is to create a Clock class, create the DisplayClock class, and tell it to subscribe to the event. You then create a LogCurrentTime class and tell it to subscribe as well. Finally, tell the Clock to run. All this is shown in Example 12-3 (you need to press Ctrl-C to terminate this application).

Example 12-3. Implementing events with delegates

```
#region Using directives

using System;
using System.Collections.Generic;
using System.Text;
using System.Threading;

#endregion

namespace EventsWithDelegates
{
    // a class to hold the information about the event
    // in this case it will hold only information
    // available in the clock class, but could hold
    // additional state information
    public class TimeInfoEventArgs : EventArgs
    {
        public TimeInfoEventArgs( int hour, int minute, int second )
        {
            this.hour = hour;
            this.minute = minute;
            this.second = second;
        }
        public readonly int hour;
        public readonly int minute;
        public readonly int second;
    }
```

Example 12-3. Implementing events with delegates (continued)

```
// our subject -- it is this class that other classes
// will observe. This class publishes one delegate:
// OnSecondChange.
public class Clock
{
   private int hour;
   private int minute;
   private int second;

   // the delegate the subscribers must implement
   public delegate void SecondChangeHandler
     (
        object clock,
        TimeInfoEventArgs timeInformation
     );

   // an instance of the delegate
   public SecondChangeHandler OnSecondChange;

   // set the clock running
   // it will raise an event for each new second
   public void Run()
   {

      for ( ; ; )
      {
         // sleep 10 milliseconds
         Thread.Sleep( 10 );

         // get the current time
         System.DateTime dt = System.DateTime.Now;

         // if the second has changed
         // notify the subscribers
         if ( dt.Second != second )
         {
            // create the TimeInfoEventArgs object
            // to pass to the subscriber
            TimeInfoEventArgs timeInformation =
              new TimeInfoEventArgs(
              dt.Hour, dt.Minute, dt.Second );

            // if anyone has subscribed, notify them
            if ( OnSecondChange != null )
            {
               OnSecondChange(
                  this, timeInformation );
            }
         }

         // update the state
         this.second = dt.Second;
```

Example 12-3. Implementing events with delegates (continued)

```
            this.minute = dt.Minute;
            this.hour = dt.Hour;
        }
    }
}

// an observer. DisplayClock subscribes to the
// clock's events. The job of DisplayClock is
// to display the current time
public class DisplayClock
{
    // given a clock, subscribe to
    // its SecondChangeHandler event
    public void Subscribe( Clock theClock )
    {
        theClock.OnSecondChange +=
            new Clock.SecondChangeHandler( TimeHasChanged );
    }

    // the method that implements the
    // delegated functionality
    public void TimeHasChanged(
        object theClock, TimeInfoEventArgs ti )
    {
        Console.WriteLine( "Current Time: {0}:{1}:{2}",
            ti.hour.ToString(),
            ti.minute.ToString(),
            ti.second.ToString() );
    }
}

// a second subscriber whose job is to write to a file
public class LogCurrentTime
{
    public void Subscribe( Clock theClock )
    {
        theClock.OnSecondChange +=
            new Clock.SecondChangeHandler( WriteLogEntry );
    }

    // This method should write to a file.
    // We write to the console to see the effect.
    // This object keeps no state.
    public void WriteLogEntry(
        object theClock, TimeInfoEventArgs ti )
    {
        Console.WriteLine( "Logging to file: {0}:{1}:{2}",
            ti.hour.ToString(),
            ti.minute.ToString(),
            ti.second.ToString() );
    }
}
```

Example 12-3. Implementing events with delegates (continued)

```
public class Test
{
    public static void Main()
    {
        // create a new clock
        Clock theClock = new Clock();

        // create the display and tell it to
        // subscribe to the clock just created
        DisplayClock dc = new DisplayClock();
        dc.Subscribe( theClock );

        // create a Log object and tell it
        // to subscribe to the clock
        LogCurrentTime lct = new LogCurrentTime();
        lct.Subscribe( theClock );

        // Get the clock started
        theClock.Run();
    }
}
}
```

```
Output:
Current Time: 14:53:56
Logging to file: 14:53:56
Current Time: 14:53:57
Logging to file: 14:53:57
Current Time: 14:53:58
Logging to file: 14:53:58
Current Time: 14:53:59
Logging to file: 14:53:59
Current Time: 14:54:0
Logging to file: 14:54:0
```

The net effect of this code is to create two classes, DisplayClock and LogCurrentTime, both of which subscribe to a third class' event (Clock.OnSecondChange).

OnSecondChange is a multicast delegate field, initially referring to nothing. In time it refers to a single delegate, and then later to multiple delegates. When the observer classes wish to be notified, they create an instance of the delegate and then add these delegates to OnSecondChange. For example, in DisplayClock's Subscribe() method, you see this line of code:

```
theClock.OnSecondChange +=
    new Clock.SecondChangeHandler(TimeHasChanged);
```

It turns out that the LogCurrentTime class also wants to be notified. In its Subscribe() method is very similar code:

```
public void Subscribe(Clock theClock)
{
```

```
    theClock.OnSecondChange +=
        new Clock.SecondChangeHandler(WriteLogEntry);
}
```

Solving Delegate Problems with Events

There is a problem with Example 12-3, however. What if the LogCurrentTime class was not so considerate, and it used the assignment operator (=) rather than the subscribe operator (+=), as in the following:

```
public void Subscribe(Clock theClock)
{
    theClock.OnSecondChange =
        new Clock.SecondChangeHandler(WriteLogEntry);
}
```

If you make that one tiny change to the example, you'll find that the Logger() method is called, but the DisplayClock method is *not* called. The assignment operator *replaced* the delegate held in the OnSecondChange multicast delegate. This isn't good.

A second problem is that other methods can call SecondChangeHandler directly. For example, you might add the following code to the Main() method of your Test class:

```
Console.WriteLine("Calling the method directly!");
System.DateTime dt = System.DateTime.Now.AddHours(2);

TimeInfoEventArgs timeInformation =
    new TimeInfoEventArgs(
    dt.Hour,dt.Minute,dt.Second);

theClock.OnSecondChange(theClock, timeInformation);
```

Here Main() has created its own TimeInfoEventArgs object and invoked OnSecondChange directly. This runs fine, even though it is not what the designer of the Clock class intended. Here is the output:

```
Calling the method directly!
Current Time: 18:36:7
Logging to file: 18:36:7
Current Time: 16:36:7
Logging to file: 16:36:7
```

The problem is that the designer of the Clock class intended the methods encapsulated by the delegate to be invoked only when the event is fired. Here Main() has gone around through the back door and invoked those methods itself. What is more, it has passed in bogus data (passing in a time construct set to two hours into the future!).

How can you, as the designer of the Clock class, ensure that no one calls the delegated method directly? You can make the delegate private, but then it won't be possible for clients to register with your delegate at all. What's needed is a way to say,

"This delegate is designed for event handling: you may subscribe and unsubscribe, but you may not invoke it directly."

The event Keyword

The solution to this dilemma is to use the event keyword. The event keyword indicates to the compiler that the delegate can be invoked only by the defining class, and that other classes can only subscribe to and unsubscribe from the delegate using the appropriate += and -= operators, respectively.

To fix your program, change your definition of OnSecondChange from:

```
public SecondChangeHandler OnSecondChange;
```

to the following:

```
public event SecondChangeHandler OnSecondChange;
```

Adding the event keyword fixes both problems. Classes can no longer attempt to subscribe to the event using the assignment operator (=), as they could previously, nor can they invoke the event directly, as was done in Main() in the preceding example. Either of these attempts will now generate a compile error:

```
The event 'Programming_CSharp.Clock.OnSecondChange' can only appear on
the left hand side of += or -= (except when used from within the type 'Programming_
CSharp.Clock')
```

There are two ways of looking at OnSecondChange now that you've modified it. In one sense, it is simply a delegate instance to which you've restricted access using the keyword event. In another, more important sense, OnSecondChange *is* an event, implemented by a delegate of type SecondChangeHandler. These two statements mean the same thing, but the latter is a more object-oriented way of looking at it, and better reflects the intent of this keyword: to create an event that your object can raise, and to which other objects can respond.

The complete source, modified to use the event rather than the unrestricted delegate, is shown in Example 12-4.

Example 12-4. Using the event keyword

```
#region Using directives

using System;
using System.Collections.Generic;
using System.Text;
using System.Threading;

#endregion

namespace EventKeyword
{
```

Example 12-4. Using the event keyword (continued)

```csharp
// a class to hold the information about the event
// in this case it will hold only information
// available in the clock class, but could hold
// additional state information
public class TimeInfoEventArgs : EventArgs
{
 public readonly int hour;
 public readonly int minute;
 public readonly int second;
 public TimeInfoEventArgs(int hour, int minute, int second)
  {
    this.hour = hour;
    this.minute = minute;
    this.second = second;
  }
}

// our subject -- it is this class that other classes
// will observe. This class publishes one event:
// OnSecondChange. The observers subscribe to that event
public class Clock
{
  private int hour;
  private int minute;
  private int second;

   // the delegate the subscribers must implement
  public delegate void SecondChangeHandler
    (
    object clock,
    TimeInfoEventArgs timeInformation
    );

  // the keyword event controls access to the delegate
  public event SecondChangeHandler OnSecondChange;

  // set the clock running
  // it will raise an event for each new second
  public void Run()
  {

    for(;;)
    {
      // sleep 10 milliseconds
      Thread.Sleep(10);

      // get the current time
      System.DateTime dt = System.DateTime.Now;

      // if the second has changed
      // notify the subscribers
      if (dt.Second != second)
```

Example 12-4. Using the event keyword (continued)

```
      {
        // create the TimeInfoEventArgs object
        // to pass to the subscriber
        TimeInfoEventArgs timeInformation =
          new TimeInfoEventArgs(
          dt.Hour,dt.Minute,dt.Second);

        // if anyone has subscribed, notify them
        if (OnSecondChange != null)
        {
          OnSecondChange(
            this,timeInformation);
        }
      }

      // update the state
      this.second = dt.Second;
      this.minute = dt.Minute;
      this.hour = dt.Hour;
    }
  }
}

// an observer. DisplayClock subscribes to the
// clock's events. The job of DisplayClock is
// to display the current time
public class DisplayClock
{
  // given a clock, subscribe to
  // its SecondChangeHandler event
  public void Subscribe(Clock theClock)
  {
    theClock.OnSecondChange +=
      new Clock.SecondChangeHandler(TimeHasChanged);
  }

  // the method that implements the
  // delegated functionality
  public void TimeHasChanged(
    object theClock, TimeInfoEventArgs ti)
  {
    Console.WriteLine("Current Time: {0}:{1}:{2}",
      ti.hour.ToString(),
      ti.minute.ToString(),
      ti.second.ToString());
  }
}

// a second subscriber whose job is to write to a file
public class LogCurrentTime
{
  public void Subscribe(Clock theClock)
```

Example 12-4. Using the event keyword (continued)

```
    {
        theClock.OnSecondChange +=
            new Clock.SecondChangeHandler(WriteLogEntry);
    }

    // This method should write to a file.
    // We write to the console to see the effect.
    // This object keeps no state.
    public void WriteLogEntry(
        object theClock, TimeInfoEventArgs ti)
    {
        Console.WriteLine("Logging to file: {0}:{1}:{2}",
            ti.hour.ToString(),
            ti.minute.ToString(),
            ti.second.ToString());
    }
}

public class Test
{
    public static void Main()
    {
        // create a new clock
        Clock theClock = new Clock();

        // create the display and tell it to
        // subscribe to the clock just created
        DisplayClock dc = new DisplayClock();
        dc.Subscribe( theClock );

        // create a Log object and tell it
        // to subscribe to the clock
        LogCurrentTime lct = new LogCurrentTime();
        lct.Subscribe( theClock );

        // Get the clock started
        theClock.Run();
    }
}
}
```

Using Anonymous Methods

In the previous example, you subscribed to the event by invoking a new instance of the delegate, passing in the name of a method that implements the event:

```
theClock.OnSecondChange +=
    new Clock.SecondChangeHandler(TimeHasChanged);
```

You can also assign this delegate by writing the shortened version:

theClock.OnSecondChange += TimeHasChanged

Later in the code, you must define TimeHasChanged as a method that matches the signature of the SecondChangeHandler delegate:

```
public void TimeHasChanged(
  object theClock, TimeInfoEventArgs ti)
{
  Console.WriteLine("Current Time: {0}:{1}:{2}",
    ti.hour.ToString(),
    ti.minute.ToString(),
    ti.second.ToString());
}
```

Anonymous methods allow you to pass a code block rather than the name of the method. This can make for more efficient and easier-to-maintain code, and the anonymous method has access to the variables in the scope in which they are defined:

```
clock.OnSecondChange += delegate( object theClock, TimeInfoEventArgs ti )
{
  Console.WriteLine( "Current Time: {0}:{1}:{2}",
  ti.hour.ToString(),
  ti.minute.ToString(),
  ti.second.ToString() );
};
```

Notice that instead of registering an instance of a delegate, you use the keyword delegate, followed by the parameters that would be passed to your method, followed by the body of your method encased in braces and terminated by a semicolon.

This "method" has no name, hence it is anonymous. You can invoke the method only through the delegate; but that is exactly what you want.

Retrieving Values from Multicast Delegates

In most situations, the methods you'll encapsulate with a multicast delegate will return void. In fact, the most common use of multicast delegates is with events, and you will remember that by convention, all events are implemented by delegates that encapsulate methods that return void (and also take two parameters: the sender and an EventArgs object).

It is possible, however, to create multicast delegates for methods that don't return void. In the next example, you will create a very simple test class with a delegate that encapsulates any method that takes no parameters but returns an integer:

```
public class ClassWithDelegate
{
  public delegate int DelegateThatReturnsInt();
  public DelegateThatReturnsInt theDelegate;
```

To test this, you implement two classes that subscribe to your delegate. The first encapsulates a method that increments a counter and returns that value as an integer:

```
public class FirstSubscriber
{
  private int myCounter = 0;

  public void Subscribe(ClassWithDelegate theClassWithDelegate)
  {
    theClassWithDelegate.theDelegate +=
      new ClassWithDelegate.DelegateThatReturnsInt(DisplayCounter);
  }

  public int DisplayCounter()
  {
    return ++myCounter;
  }
}
```

The second class also maintains a counter, but its delegated method adds two to the counter and returns that doubled value:

```
public class SecondSubscriber
{
  private int myCounter = 0;

  public void Subscribe(ClassWithDelegate theClassWithDelegate)
  {
    theClassWithDelegate.theDelegate +=
      new ClassWithDelegate.DelegateThatReturnsInt(Doubler);
  }

  public int Doubler()
  {
    return myCounter += 2;
  }
}
```

When you fire this delegate, each encapsulated method is called in turn, and each returns a value:

```
int result = theDelegate();
Console.WriteLine(
  "Delegates fired! Returned result: {0}",
  result);
```

The problem is that as each method returns its value, it overwrites the value assigned to result. The output looks like this:

```
Delegates fired! Returned result: 2
Delegates fired! Returned result: 4
Delegates fired! Returned result: 6
Delegates fired! Returned result: 8
Delegates fired! Returned result: 10
```

The first method, DisplayCounter() (which was called by FirstSubscriber), returned the values 1,2,3,4,5, but these values were overwritten by the values returned by the second method.

Your goal is to display the result of each method invocation in turn. To do so, you must take over the responsibility of invoking the methods encapsulated by your multicast delegate. You do so by obtaining the invocation list from your delegate and explicitly invoking each encapsulated method in turn:

```
foreach (
  DelegateThatReturnsInt del in
    theDelegate.GetInvocationList() )
{
  int result = del();
  Console.WriteLine(
    "Delegates fired! Returned result: {0}",
    result);
}
Console.WriteLine();
```

This time, result is assigned the value of each invocation, and that value is displayed before invoking the next method. The output reflects this change:

```
Delegates fired! Returned result: 1
Delegates fired! Returned result: 2

Delegates fired! Returned result: 2
Delegates fired! Returned result: 4

Delegates fired! Returned result: 3
Delegates fired! Returned result: 6

Delegates fired! Returned result: 4
Delegates fired! Returned result: 8

Delegates fired! Returned result: 5
Delegates fired! Returned result: 10
```

The first delegated method is counting up (1,2,3,4,5) while the second is doubling (2,4,6,8,10). The complete source is shown in Example 12-5.

Example 12-5. Invoking delegated methods manually

```
#region Using directives

using System;
using System.Collections.Generic;
using System.Text;
using System.Threading;

#endregion

namespace InvokingDelegatedMethodsManually
{
```

Example 12-5. Invoking delegated methods manually (continued)

```
public class ClassWithDelegate
{
   // a multicast delegate that encapsulates a method
   // that returns an int
   public delegate int DelegateThatReturnsInt();
   public DelegateThatReturnsInt theDelegate;

   public void Run()
   {
      for ( ; ; )
      {
         // sleep for a half second
         Thread.Sleep( 500 );

         if ( theDelegate != null )
         {
            // explicitly invoke each delegated method
            foreach (
              DelegateThatReturnsInt del in
                theDelegate.GetInvocationList() )
            {
               int result = del();
               Console.WriteLine(
                 "Delegates fired! Returned result: {0}",
                 result );
            }  // end foreach
            Console.WriteLine();
         }    // end if
      }       // end for ;;
   }          // end run
}             // end class

public class FirstSubscriber
{
   private int myCounter = 0;

   public void Subscribe( ClassWithDelegate theClassWithDelegate )
   {
      theClassWithDelegate.theDelegate +=
        new ClassWithDelegate.DelegateThatReturnsInt( DisplayCounter );
   }

   public int DisplayCounter()
   {
      return ++myCounter;
   }
}

public class SecondSubscriber
{
   private int myCounter = 0;
```

Example 12-5. Invoking delegated methods manually (continued)

```
   public void Subscribe( ClassWithDelegate theClassWithDelegate )
   {
      theClassWithDelegate.theDelegate +=
         new ClassWithDelegate.DelegateThatReturnsInt( Doubler );
   }

   public int Doubler()
   {
      return myCounter += 2;
   }
}

public class Test
{
   public static void Main()
   {
      ClassWithDelegate theClassWithDelegate =
         new ClassWithDelegate();

      FirstSubscriber fs = new FirstSubscriber();
      fs.Subscribe( theClassWithDelegate );

      SecondSubscriber ss = new SecondSubscriber();
      ss.Subscribe( theClassWithDelegate );

      theClassWithDelegate.Run();
   }
}
}
```

Invoking Events Asynchronously

It may turn out that the event handlers take longer than you like to respond to the event. In that case, it may take a while to notify later handlers, while you wait for results from earlier handlers. For example, suppose the DisplayCounter() method in FirstSubscriber needs to do a lot of work to compute the return result. This would create a delay before SecondSubscriber was notified of the event. You can simulate this by adding a few lines to DisplayCounter:

```
   public int DisplayCounter()
   {
     Console.WriteLine("Busy in DisplayCounter...");
     Thread.Sleep(4000);
     Console.WriteLine("Done with work in DisplayCounter...");
     return ++myCounter;
   }
```

When you run the program, you can see the four-second delay each time First-Subscriber is notified. An alternative to invoking each method through the delegates (as shown earlier) is to call the BeginInvoke() method on each delegate. This will cause the methods to be invoked asynchronously, and you can get on with your work, without waiting for the method you invoke to return.

Unlike Invoke(), BeginInvoke() returns immediately. It creates a separate thread in which its own work is done.* (For more information about threads, see Chapter 20.)

This presents a problem, however, since you do want to get the results from the methods you invoke. You have two choices. First, you can constantly poll each delegated method, asking if it has a result yet. This would be like asking your assistant to do some work for you and then telephoning every five seconds saying, "Is it done yet?" (a waste of everybody's time). What you want to do is to turn to your assistant and say, "Do this work, and call me when you have a result."

Callback Methods

You accomplish this goal of delegating work and being called back when it is done with a callback, which you implement with (surprise!) a delegate. The .NET Framework provides a callback mechanism by defining the ASyncCallBack delegate:

```
[Serializable]
public delegate void AsyncCallback(
    IAsyncResult ar
);
```

The attribute (Serializable) is covered in Chapter 18. You can see here, however, that AsyncCallBack is a delegate for a method that returns void and takes a single argument, an object of type IAsyncResult. This interface is defined by the Framework, and the CLR will be calling your method with an object that implements the interface, so you don't need to know the details of the interface; you can just use the object provided to you.

Here's how it works. You will ask the delegate for its invocation list, and you will call BeginInvoke on each delegate in that list. BeginInvoke will take two parameters. The first will be a delegate of type AsyncCallBack, and the second will be your own delegate that invokes the method you want to call:

```
del.BeginInvoke(new AsyncCallback(ResultsReturned),del);
```

In the line of code shown here, you are calling the method encapsulated by del (e.g., DisplayCounter) and when that method completes, you want to be notified via your method ResultsReturned.

The method to be called back (ResultsReturned) must match the return type and signature of the AsyncCallback delegate: it must return void and must take an object of type IAsyncResult:

```
private void ResultsReturned(IAsyncResult iar)
{
```

---

* .NET provides thread pooling, and the "new" thread will typically be pulled from the pool.

When that method is called back, the IAsyncResult object is passed in by the .NET Framework. The second parameter to BeginInvoke is your delegate, and that delegate is stashed away for you in the AsyncState property of the IAsyncResult as an Object. Inside the ResultsReturned callback method, you can extract that Object and cast it to its original type:

```
DelegateThatReturnsInt del = (DelegateThatReturnsInt)iar.AsyncState;
```

You can now use that delegate to call the EndInvoke() method, passing in the IAsyncResult object you received as a parameter:

```
int result = del.EndInvoke(iar);
```

EndInvoke() returns the value of the called (and now completed) method, which you assign to a local variable named result, and which you are now free to display to the user.

The net effect is that in Run(), you get each registered method in turn (first FirstSubscriber.DisplayCounter and then SecondSubscriber.Doubler), and you invoke each asynchronously. There is no delay between the call to the first and the call to the second, as you aren't waiting for DisplayCounter to return.

When DisplayCounter (or Doubler) has results, your callback method (ResultsReturned) is invoked, and you use the IAsyncResult object provided as a parameter to get the actual results back from these methods. The complete implementation is shown in Example 12-6.

Example 12-6. Asynchronous invocation of delegates

```
#region Using directives

using System;
using System.Collections.Generic;
using System.Text;
using System.Threading;

#endregion

namespace AsynchDelegates
{
    public class ClassWithDelegate
    {
        // a multicast delegate that encapsulates a method
        // that returns an int
        public delegate int DelegateThatReturnsInt();
        public event DelegateThatReturnsInt theDelegate;

        public void Run()
        {
            for ( ; ; )
            {
                // sleep for a half second
```

Example 12-6. Asynchronous invocation of delegates (continued)

```
            Thread.Sleep( 500 );

            if ( theDelegate != null )
            {
              // explicitly invoke each delegated method
              foreach (
                DelegateThatReturnsInt del in
                  theDelegate.GetInvocationList() )
              {
                // invoke asynchronously
                // pass the delegate in as a state object
                del.BeginInvoke( new AsyncCallback( ResultsReturned ),
                    del );

              } // end foreach
          }     // end if
        }       // end for ;;
      }         // end run

    // call back method to capture results
    private void ResultsReturned( IAsyncResult iar )
    {
      // cast the state object back to the delegate type
      DelegateThatReturnsInt del =
        ( DelegateThatReturnsInt ) iar.AsyncState;

      // call EndInvoke on the delegate to get the results
      int result = del.EndInvoke( iar );

      // display the results
      Console.WriteLine( "Delegate returned result: {0}", result );
    }
  }           // end class

public class FirstSubscriber
{
    private int myCounter = 0;

    public void Subscribe( ClassWithDelegate theClassWithDelegate )
    {
      theClassWithDelegate.theDelegate +=
        new ClassWithDelegate.DelegateThatReturnsInt( DisplayCounter );
    }

    public int DisplayCounter()
    {
      Console.WriteLine( "Busy in DisplayCounter..." );
      Thread.Sleep( 10000 );
      Console.WriteLine( "Done with work in DisplayCounter..." );
      return ++myCounter;
    }
}
```

Example 12-6. Asynchronous invocation of delegates (continued)

```
public class SecondSubscriber
{
    private int myCounter = 0;

    public void Subscribe( ClassWithDelegate theClassWithDelegate )
    {
        theClassWithDelegate.theDelegate +=
          new ClassWithDelegate.DelegateThatReturnsInt( Doubler );
    }

    public int Doubler()
    {
        return myCounter += 2;
    }
}

public class Test
{
    public static void Main()
    {
        ClassWithDelegate theClassWithDelegate =
          new ClassWithDelegate();

        FirstSubscriber fs = new FirstSubscriber();
        fs.Subscribe( theClassWithDelegate );

        SecondSubscriber ss = new SecondSubscriber();
        ss.Subscribe( theClassWithDelegate );

        theClassWithDelegate.Run();
    }
}
```

PART II

Programming with C#

CHAPTER 13

Building Windows Applications

The previous chapters have used console applications to demonstrate C# and the CLR. Although console applications can be implemented simply, it is time to turn your attention to the reason you're learning the C# language in the first place: building Windows and web applications.

In the early days of Windows computing, an application ran on a desktop, in splendid isolation. Over time, developers found it beneficial to spread their applications across a network, with the user interface on one computer and a database on another. This division of responsibilities, or partitioning of an application, came to be called two-tier or client-server application development. Later, three-tier or *n*-tier approaches emerged as developers began to use web servers to host business objects that could handle the database access on behalf of clients.

When the Web first came along, there was a clear distinction between Windows applications and web applications. Windows applications ran on the desktop or a local area network (LAN), and web applications ran on a distant server and were accessed by a browser. This distinction is now being blurred somewhat as Windows applications reach out to the Web for services. Many new applications consist of logic running on a client, a database server, and remote third-party computers located on the Web. Traditional desktop applications such as Excel or Outlook are now able to integrate data retrieved through web connections seamlessly, and web applications can distribute some of their processing to client-side components.

The primary remaining distinction between a Windows application and a web application might be this: who owns the user interface. Will your application use a browser to display its user interface, or will the UI be built into the executable running on the desktop?

 Even the distinction of "who owns the user interface" is somewhat arbitrary, as browser-based interfaces can have components running locally and desktop-based applications can have embedded web browsers!

There are enormous advantages to web applications, starting with the obvious: they can be accessed from any browser that can connect to the server. In addition, updates can be made at the server, without the need to distribute new DLLs to your customers.

On the other hand, if your application derives no benefit from being on the Web, you might find that you can achieve greater control over the look and feel of your application or that you can achieve better performance by building a desktop application.

.NET offers closely related, but distinguishable, suites of tools for building Windows or web applications. Both are based on the premise that many applications have user interfaces centered on interacting with the user through forms and controls, such as buttons, listboxes, text, and so forth.

The tools for creating web applications are called Web Forms and are considered in Chapter 15. The tools for creating Windows applications are called Windows Forms and are the subject of this chapter.

On the following pages, you will learn how to create Windows applications using the tools provided by Visual Studio. This application will bring together a number of C# techniques taught in earlier chapters.

Creating a Simple Windows Form

A Windows Form is a tool for building a Windows application. The .NET Framework offers extensive support for Windows application development, the centerpiece of which is the Windows Forms framework. Not surprisingly, Windows Forms use the metaphor of a form. This idea was borrowed from the wildly successful VB environment and supports RAD. Arguably, C# is the first development environment to marry the RAD tools of VB with the object-oriented and high-performance characteristics of a C-family language.

Using the Visual Studio Designer

While it is possible to build a Windows application using any editor (even Notepad!) and compiling from the command line, it is senseless to do so, when Visual Studio.NET makes life so much easier.

To begin work on a new Windows application, first open Visual Studio and choose File → New → Project. In the New Project window, create a new C# Windows application and name it ProgCSharpWindowsForm, as shown in Figure 13-1.

Visual Studio responds by creating a Windows Form application and, best of all, putting you into a design environment, as shown in Figure 13-2.

The Design window displays a blank Windows Form (Form1). A Toolbox window is also available, with a selection of Windows widgets and controls. If the Toolbox is

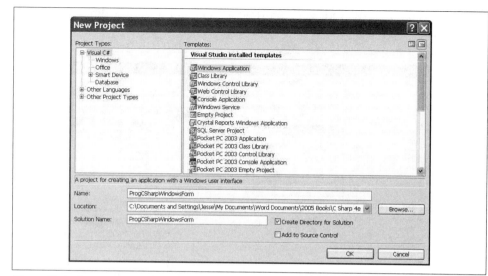

Figure 13-1. Creating a Windows Form application

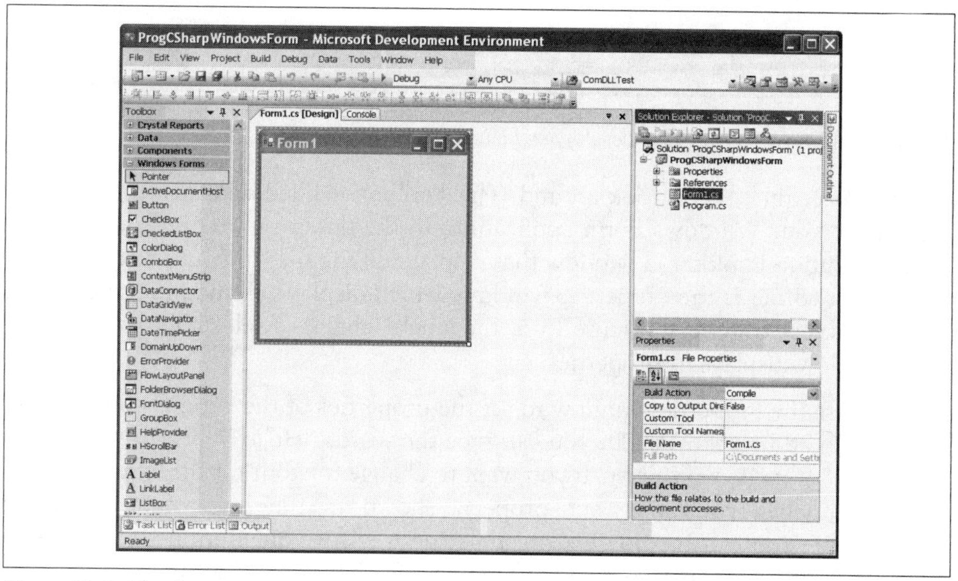

Figure 13-2. The design environment

not displayed, try clicking the word "Toolbox," or selecting View → Toolbox on the
Visual Studio menu. You can also use the keyboard shortcut Ctrl-Alt-X to display the
Toolbox.*

---

* Visual Studio allows a great deal of personalization; please check all the keyboard shortcuts to ensure that
  they work as expected in your environment.

With the Toolbox displayed, you can drag a label and a button directly onto the form, as shown in Figure 13-3.

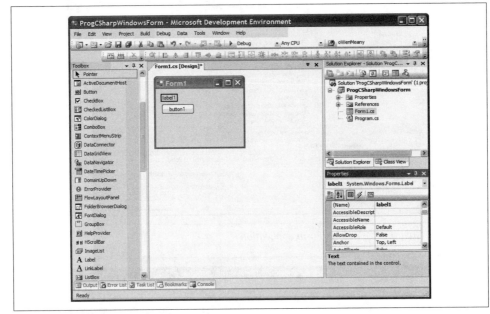

Figure 13-3. The Windows Form development environment

Before proceeding, take a look around. The Toolbox is filled with controls that you can add to your Windows Form application. In the upper-right corner, you should see the Solution Explorer, a window that displays all the files in your projects. In the lower-right corner is the Properties window, which displays all the properties of the currently selected item. In Figure 13-3, the label (label1) is selected, and the Properties window displays *its* properties.

You can use the Properties window to set the properties of the various controls. For example, to add text to label1, you can type the words "Hello World" into the box to the right of its Text property. If you want to change the font for the lettering in the HelloWorld label, click the Font property shown in the lower-right corner of Figure 13-4. (You can provide text in the same way for your button—button1—by selecting it in the Properties window and typing the word "Cancel" into its Text property.)

Any one of these steps is often easier than modifying these properties in code (though that is certainly possible).

Once you have the form laid out the way you want, all that remains is to create the click handler for the Cancel button. Double-clicking the Cancel button will create the event handler, register it, and put you on the *code* page (the page that holds the

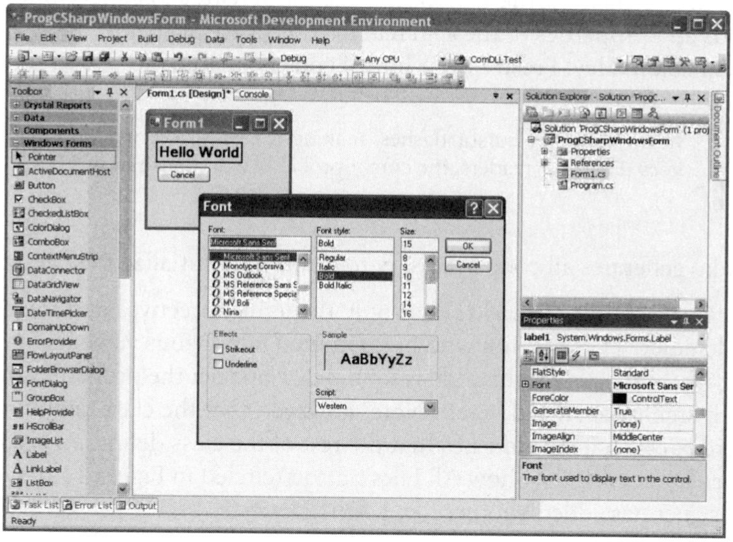

Figure 13-4. Modifying the font

source code for this form), in which you can enter the event-handling logic, as shown in Figure 13-5.

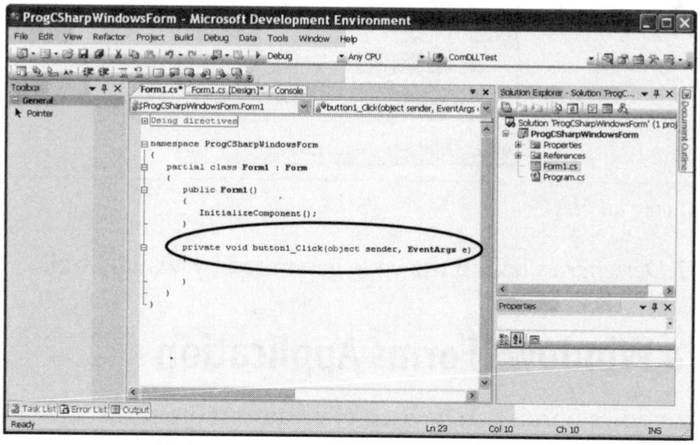

Figure 13-5. After double-clicking the Cancel button

The cursor is already in place; you have only to enter one line of code:

```
Application.Exit();
```

You'll find that as you try to enter this code, Intellisense tries to help you. When you type A, the first possible object that begins with A is shown. Continue typing through Appl and then hit the period: the class `Application` is filled in for you,[*] and the methods and properties of the `Application` object are available. Type Ex and then type the semicolon. Hey! Presto! Your line of code is written.

 In the IDE, the cursor flashes, making it easy to see where the code goes. For most readers, the cursor probably won't flash in this book.

Visual Studio generates all code necessary to create and initialize the components.

Note that your code file (*Form1.cs*) has only the using directives and the constructor and event handler. Those of you who programmed in previous versions of C# may be wondering where the rest of the code is to initialize and set the properties of your controls (which aren't even listed here!). Note, however, that the class definition contains the keyword `partial`. This indicates that the rest of the class definition is contained in another file. If you click the Show All Files button (circled in Figure 13-6), you will see that the designer has added another file, *Form1.Designer.cs*.

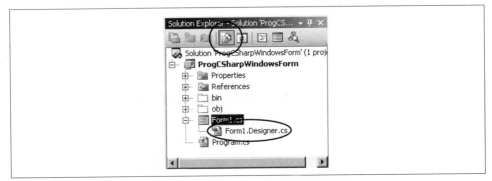

Figure 13-6. Showing all files

The file *Form1.Designer.cs* has all the code generated by Visual Studio.

Creating a Windows Forms Application

To see how Windows Forms can be used to create a more realistic Windows application, in this section you'll build a utility named `FileCopier` that copies all files from a group of directories selected by the user to a single target directory or device, such as a floppy or backup hard drive on the company network. Although you won't implement every possible feature, you can imagine programming this application so that you can mark dozens of files and have them copied to multiple disks, packing them

---

[*] Note that Intellisense will remember your most recent choice and start with that; usually this is a great convenience.

as tightly as possible. You might even extend the application to compress the files. The true goal of this example is for you to exercise many of the C# skills learned in earlier chapters and to explore the Windows.Forms namespace.

For the purposes of this example and to keep the code simple, focus on the user interface and the steps needed to wire up its various controls. The final application UI is shown in Figure 13-7.

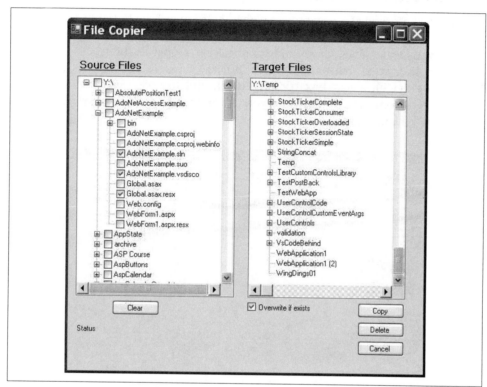

Figure 13-7. The File Copier user interface

The user interface for FileCopier consists of the following controls:

- Labels (Source Files and Target Files)
- Buttons (Clear, Copy, Delete, and Cancel)
- An "Overwrite if exists" checkbox
- A text box displaying the path of the selected target directory
- Two large tree-view controls, one for available source directories and one for available target devices and directories

The goal is to allow the user to check files (or entire directories) in the left tree view (source). If the user clicks the Copy button, the files checked on the left side will be copied to the Target Files specified in the right-side control. If the user clicks Delete, the checked files will be deleted.

The rest of this chapter implements a number of FileCopier features to demonstrate the fundamental features of Windows Forms.

Creating the Basic UI Form

The first task is to open a new project named FileCopier. The IDE puts you into the Designer, in which you can drag widgets onto the form. You can expand the form to the size you want. Drag, drop, and set the Name properties of labels (lblSource, lblTarget, lblStatus), buttons (btnClear, btnCopy, btnDelete, btnCancel), a checkbox (chkOverwrite), a text box (txtTargetDir), and tree-view controls (tvwSource, tvwTargetDir) from the Toolbox onto your form until it looks more or less like the one shown in Figure 13-8.

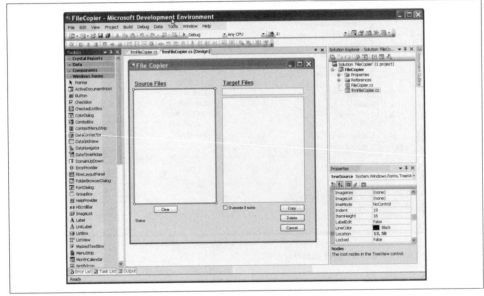

Figure 13-8. Creating the form in the Designer

You want checkboxes next to the directories and files in the source selection window but not in the target (where only one directory will be chosen). Set the Check-Boxes property on the left TreeView control, tvwSource, to true, and set the property on the right TreeView control, tvwTargetDir, to false. To do so, click each control in turn and adjust the values in the Properties window.

Once this is done, double-click the Cancel button to create its event handler; when you double-click a control, Visual Studio creates an event handler for that object.

Each object has a "default" event that Visual Studio will use if you double-click the object. For buttons, the default event is Click.

```
protected void btnCancel_Click (object sender, System.EventArgs e)
{
    Application.Exit();
}
```

You can handle many different events for the various controls. An easy way to do so is by clicking the Events button in the Properties window. From there you can create new handlers, just by filling in a new event-handler method name or picking one of the existing event handlers. Visual Studio registers the event handler and opens the editor for the code, where it creates the header and puts the cursor in an empty method body.

So much for the easy part. Visual Studio generates code to set up the form and initializes all the controls, but it doesn't fill the TreeView controls. That you must do by hand.

.NET Windows Forms Tips for VB6 Programmers

It's great that the basic .NET Windows controls have a lot in common with their VB6 ancestors. But there are some changes that could catch you off guard. Keep these tips in mind when designing forms.

In VB6, some controls display text using the Text property and some use the Caption property. With .NET, all text-related properties are now simply called Text.

VB6 CommandButtons use the properties Default and Cancel so that the user could effectively select them by pressing the Enter or the Escape key. With .NET, these properties are now part of the Form object. The AcceptButton and CancelButton properties are used to reference which button on the form assumes each responsibility.

Displaying a VB6 form is done by calling the Show() method. If you want the form to be displayed as a modal dialog box, you pass the vbModal enumerator to the Show() method. In .NET these two functions have been separated into two different method calls: Show() and ShowModal().

Populating the TreeView Controls

The two TreeView controls work identically, except that the left control, tvwSource, lists the directories and files, whereas the right control, tvwTargetDir, lists only directories. The CheckBoxes property on tvwSource is set to true, and on tvwTargetDir it is set to false. Also, although tvwSource will allow multiselect, which is the default for TreeView controls, you will enforce single selection for tvwTargetDir.

You'll factor the common code for both TreeView controls into a shared method FillDirectoryTree and pass in the control with a flag indicating whether to get the files. You'll call this method from the Form's constructor, once for each of the two controls:

```
FillDirectoryTree(tvwSource, true);
FillDirectoryTree(tvwTargetDir, false);
```

The FillDirectoryTree implementation names the TreeView parameter tvw. This will represent the source TreeView and the destination TreeView in turn. You'll need some classes from System.IO, so add a using System.IO; statement at the top of Form1.cs. Next, add the method declaration to Form1.cs:

```
private void FillDirectoryTree(TreeView tvw, bool isSource)
```

TreeNode objects

The TreeView control has a property, Nodes, which gets a TreeNodeCollection object. The TreeNodeCollection is a collection of TreeNode objects, each of which represents a node in the tree. Start by emptying that collection:

```
tvw.Nodes.Clear();
```

You are ready to fill the TreeView's Nodes collection by recursing through the directories of all the drives. First, get all the logical drives on the system. To do so, call a static method of the Environment object, GetLogicalDrives(). The Environment class provides information about and access to the current platform environment. You can use the Environment object to get the machine name, OS version, system directory, and so forth, from the computer on which you are running your program.

```
string[] strDrives = Environment.GetLogicalDrives();
```

GetLogicalDrives() returns an array of strings, each of which represents the root directory of one of the logical drives. You will iterate over that collection, adding nodes to the TreeView control as you go.

```
foreach (string rootDirectoryName in strDrives)
{
```

You process each drive within the foreach loop.

The very first thing you need to determine is whether the drive is ready. My hack for that is to get the list of top-level directories from the drive by calling GetDirectories() on a DirectoryInfo object I created for the root directory:

```
DirectoryInfo dir = new DirectoryInfo(rootDirectoryName);
dir.GetDirectories();
```

The DirectoryInfo class exposes instance methods for creating, moving, and enumerating through directories, their files, and their subdirectories. The DirectoryInfo class is covered in detail in Chapter 21.

The GetDirectories() method returns a list of directories, but actually, this code throws the list away. You are calling it here only to generate an exception if the drive is not ready.

Wrap the call in a try block and take no action in the catch block. The effect is that if an exception is thrown, the drive is skipped.

Once you know that the drive is ready, create a TreeNode to hold the root directory of the drive and add that node to the TreeView control:

```
TreeNode ndRoot = new TreeNode(rootDirectoryName);
tvw.Nodes.Add(ndRoot);
```

To get the + signs right in the TreeView, you must find at least two levels of directories (so that the TreeView knows which directories have subdirectories and can write the + sign next to them). You don't want to recurse through all the subdirectories, however, because that would be too slow.

The job of the GetSubDirectoryNodes()method is to recurse two levels deep, passing in the root node, the name of the root directory, a flag indicating whether you want files, and the current level (you always start at level 1):

```
if ( isSource )
{

    GetSubDirectoryNodes(
        ndRoot, ndRoot.Text, true,1 );
}
else
{
    GetSubDirectoryNodes(
        ndRoot, ndRoot.Text, false,1 );
}
```

You are probably wondering why you need to pass in ndRoot.Text if you're already passing in ndRoot. Patience—you will see why this is needed when you recurse back into GetSubDirectoryNodes. You are now finished with FillDirectoryTree(). See Example 13-1 later in this chapter for a complete listing of this method.

Recursing through the subdirectories

GetSubDirectoryNodes() begins by once again calling GetDirectories(), this time stashing away the resulting array of DirectoryInfo objects:

```
private void GetSubDireoctoryNodes(
    TreeNode parentNode, string fullName, bool getFileNames,
        int level)
{
    DirectoryInfo dir = new DirectoryInfo(fullName);
    DirectoryInfo[] dirSubs = dir.GetDirectories();
```

Notice that the node passed in is named parentNode. The current level of nodes will be considered children to the node passed in. This is how you map the directory structure to the hierarchy of the tree view.

Iterate over each subdirectory, skipping any that are marked Hidden:

```
foreach (DirectoryInfo dirSub in dirSubs)
{
    if ( (dirSub.Attributes &
        FileAttributes.Hidden) != 0 )
    {
        continue;
    }
}
```

FileAttributes is an enum; other possible values include Archive, Compressed, Directory, Encrypted, Hidden, Normal, ReadOnly, etc.

 The property dirSub.Attributes is the bit pattern of the current attributes of the directory. If you logically AND that value with the bit pattern FileAttributes.Hidden, a bit is set if the file has the hidden attribute; otherwise all the bits are cleared. You can check for any hidden bit by testing whether the resulting int is something other than 0.

Create a TreeNode with the directory name and add it to the Nodes collection of the node passed in to the method (parentNode):

```
TreeNode subNode = new TreeNode(dirSub.Name);
parentNode.Nodes.Add(subNode);
```

Now you check the current level (passed in by the calling method) against a constant defined for the class:

```
private const int MaxLevel = 2;
```

so as to recurse only two levels deep:

```
if ( level < MaxLevel )
{
    GetSubDirectoryNodes(
        subNode, dirSub.FullName, getFileNames, level+1 );
}
```

You pass in the node you just created as the new parent, the full path as the full name of the parent, and the flag you received, along with one greater than the current level (thus, if you started at level one, this next call will set the level to two).

The call to the TreeNode constructor uses the Name property of the DirectoryInfo object, while the call to GetSubDirectoryNodes() uses the FullName property. If your directory is *C:\Windows\Media\Sounds*, the FullName property returns the full path, while the Name property returns just Sounds. Pass in only the name to the node because that is what you want displayed in the tree view. Pass in the full name with the path to the GetSubDirectoryNodes() method so that the method can locate all the subdirectories on the disk. This answers the question asked earlier as to why you need to pass in the root node's name the first time you call this method. What is passed in isn't the name of the node; it is the full path to the directory represented by the node!

Getting the files in the directory

Once you've recursed through the subdirectories, it is time to get the files for the directory if the getFileNames flag is true. To do so, call the GetFiles() method on the DirectoryInfo object. An array of FileInfo objects is returned:

```
if (getFileNames)
{
    // Get any files for this node.
    FileInfo[] files = dir.GetFiles();
```

The FileInfo class (covered in Chapter 21) provides instance methods for manipulating files.

You can now iterate over this collection, accessing the Name property of the FileInfo object and passing that name to the constructor of a TreeNode, which you then add to the parent node's Nodes collection (thus creating a child node). There is no recursion this time because files don't have subdirectories:

```
foreach (FileInfo file in files)
{
    TreeNode fileNode = new TreeNode(file.Name);
    parentNode.Nodes.Add(fileNode);
}
```

That's all it takes to fill the two tree views. See Example 13-1 for a complete listing of this method.

If you found any of this confusing, I highly recommend putting the code into your debugger and stepping through the recursion; you can watch the TreeView build its nodes.

Handling TreeView Events

You must handle a number of events in this example. First, the user might click Cancel, Copy, Clear, or Delete. Second, the user might click one of the checkboxes in the left TreeView, one of the nodes in the right TreeView, or one of the + signs in either view.

Let's consider the clicks on the TreeViews first, as they are the more interesting, and potentially the more challenging.

Clicking the source TreeView

There are two TreeView objects, each with its own event handler. Consider the source TreeView object first. The user checks the files and directories he wants to copy from. Each time the user clicks the checkbox indicating a file or directory, a number of events are raised. The event you must handle is AfterCheck.

To do so, implement a custom event-handler method you will create and name tvwSource_AfterCheck(). Visual Studio will wire this to the event handler, or if you aren't using the IDE, you must do so yourself.

```
tvwSource.AfterCheck +=
new System.Windows.Forms.TreeViewEventHandler
  (this.tvwSource_AfterCheck);
```

The implementation of AfterCheck() delegates the work to a recursable method named SetCheck() that you'll also write. The SetCheck method will recursively set the check mark for all the contained folders.

To add the AfterCheck event, select the tvwSource control, click the Events icon in the Properties window, then double-click AfterCheck. This will add the event, wire it up, and place you in the code editor where you can add the body of the method:

```
private void tvwSource_AfterCheck (
object sender, System.Windows.Forms.TreeViewEventArgs e)
{
    SetCheck(e.Node,e.Node.Checked);
}
```

The event handler passes in the sender object and an object of type TreeView-EventArgs. It turns out that you can get the node from this TreeViewEventArgs object (e). Call SetCheck(), passing in the node and the state of whether the node has been checked.

Each node has a Nodes property, which gets a TreeNodeCollection containing all the subnodes. SetCheck() recurses through the current node's Nodes collection, setting each subnode's check mark to match that of the node that was checked. In other words, when you check a directory, all its files and subdirectories are checked, recursively, all the way down.

For each TreeNode in the Nodes collection, check to see if it is a leaf. A node is a leaf if its own Nodes collection has a count of 0. If it is a leaf, set its check property to whatever was passed in as a parameter. If it isn't a leaf, recurse:

```
private void SetCheck(TreeNode node, bool check)
{
    // find all the child nodes from this node
    foreach (TreeNode n in node.Nodes)
    {
        n.Checked = check;    // check the node

        // if this is a node in the tree, recurse
        if (n.Nodes.Count != 0)
        {
            SetCheck(n,check);
        }
    }
}
```

This propagates the check mark (or clears the check mark) down through the entire structure. In this way, the user can indicate that he wants to select all the files in all the subdirectories by clicking a single directory.

Expanding a directory

Each time you click a + sign next to a directory in the source (or in the target), you want to expand that directory. To do so, you'll need an event handler for the BeforeExpand event. Since the event handlers will be identical for both the source and the target tree views, you'll create a shared event handler (assigning the same event handler to both):

```
private void tvwExpand(object sender, TreeViewCancelEventArgs e)
{

    TreeView tvw = ( TreeView ) sender;
    bool getFiles = tvw == tvwSource;
    TreeNode currentNode = e.Node;
    string fullName = currentNode.FullPath;
    currentNode.Nodes.Clear();
    GetSubDirectoryNodes( currentNode, fullName, getFiles, 1 );

}
```

The first line of this code casts the object passed in by the delegate from `object` to `TreeView`, which is safe since you know that only a `TreeView` can trigger this event.

Your second task is to determine whether you want to get the files in the directory you are opening, and you do only if the name of the `TreeView` that triggered the event is `tvwSource`.

You determine which node's + sign was checked by getting the `Node` property from the `TreeViewCancelEventArgs` that is passed in by the event:

```
TreeNode currentNode = e.Node;
```

Once you have the current node you get its full pathname (which you will need as a parameter to `GetSubDirectoryNodes`) and then you must clear its collection of subnodes, because you are going to refill that collection by calling in to `GetSubDirectoryNodes`:

```
currentNode.Nodes.Clear();
```

Why do you clear the subnodes and then refill them? Because this time you will go another level deep so that the subnodes know if *they* in turn have subnodes, and thus will know if they should draw a + sign next to their subdirectories.

Clicking the target TreeView

The second event handler for the target `TreeView` (in addition to `BeforeExpand`) is somewhat trickier. The event itself is `AfterSelect`. (Remember that the target `TreeView` doesn't have checkboxes.) This time, you want to take the one directory chosen and put its full path into the text box at the upper-left corner of the form.

To do so, you must work your way up through the nodes, finding the name of each parent directory and building the full path:

```
private void tvwTargetDir_AfterSelect (
    object sender, System.Windows.Forms.TreeViewEventArgs e)
{

    string theFullPath = GetParentString(e.Node);
```

We'll look at `GetParentString()` in just a moment. Once you have the full path, you must lop off the backslash (if any) on the end, and then you can fill the text box:

```
if (theFullPath.EndsWith("\\"))
{
    theFullPath =
        theFullPath.Substring(0,theFullPath.Length-1);
}
txtTargetDir.Text = theFullPath;
```

The `GetParentString()` method takes a node and returns a string with the full path. To do so, it recurses upward through the path, adding the backslash after any node that is not a leaf:

```
private string GetParentString(TreeNode node)
{
```

```
if(node.Parent == null)
{
    return node.Text;
}
else
{
    return GetParentString(node.Parent) + node.Text +
        (node.Nodes.Count == 0  ? "" : "\\");
}
}
```

> The conditional operator (?) is the only ternary operator in C# (a ter-
> nary operator takes three terms). The logic is "test whether node.
> Nodes.Count is 0; if so, return the value before the colon (in this case,
> an empty string). Otherwise return the value after the colon (in this
> case, a backslash)."

The recursion stops when there is no parent; that is, when you hit the root directory.

Handling the Clear button event

Given the SetCheck() method developed earlier, handling the Clear button's Click
event is trivial:

```
protected void btnClear_Click (object sender, System.EventArgs e)
{
    foreach (TreeNode node in tvwSource.Nodes)
    {
        SetCheck(node, false);
    }
}
```

Just call the SetCheck() method on the root nodes and tell them to recursively
uncheck all their contained nodes.

Implementing the Copy Button Event

Now that you can check the files and pick the target directory, you're ready to handle the Copy button-click event. The very first thing you need to do is to get a list of
which files were selected. What you want is an array of FileInfo objects, but you
have no idea how many objects will be in the list. This is a perfect job for ArrayList.
Delegate responsibility for filling the list to a method called GetFileList():

```
private void btnCopy_Click (
        object sender, System.EventArgs e)
{
    List<FileInfo> fileList = GetFileList();
```

Let's pick that method apart before returning to the event handler.

Getting the selected files

Start by instantiating a new List object to hold the strings representing the names of all the files selected:

```
private List<FileInfo> GetFileList()
{
    // create an unsorted array list of the full file names
        List<string> fileNames = new List<string>();
```

To get the selected filenames, you can walk through the source TreeView control:

```
foreach (TreeNode theNode in tvwSource.Nodes)
{
    GetCheckedFiles(theNode, fileNames);
}
```

To see how this works, step into the GetCheckedFiles() method. This method is pretty simple: it examines the node it was handed. If that node has no children (node.Nodes.Count == 0), it is a leaf. If that leaf is checked, get the full path (by calling GetParentString() on the node) and add it to the ArrayList passed in as a parameter:

```
private void GetCheckedFiles( TreeNode node,
    List<string> fileNames )
{
    // if this is a leaf...
    if ( node.Nodes.Count == 0 )
    {
        // if the node was checked...
        if ( node.Checked )
        {
            // get the full path and add it to the arrayList
            string fullPath = GetParentString( node );
            fileNames.Add( fullPath );
        }
    }
}
```

If the node is *not* a leaf, recurse down the tree, finding the child nodes:

```
else
{
    foreach (TreeNode n in node.Nodes)
    {
        GetCheckedFiles(n,fileNames);
    }
}
}
```

This returns the List filled with all the filenames. Back in GetFileList(), use this List of filenames to create a second List, this time to hold the actual FileInfo objects:

```
List<FileInfo> fileList = new List<FileInfo>();
```

Notice the use of type-safe List objects to ensure that the compiler flags any objects added to the collection that aren't of type FileInfo.

You can now iterate through the filenames in fileList, picking out each name and instantiating a FileInfo object with it. You can detect if it is a file or a directory by calling the Exists property, which will return false if the File object you created is actually a directory. If it is a File, you can add it to the new ArrayList:

```
foreach (string fileName in fileNames)
{
    FileInfo file = new FileInfo(fileName);

    if (file.Exists)
    {
        fileList.Add(file);
    }
}
```

Sorting the list of selected files

You want to work your way through the list of selected files in large to small order so that you can pack the target disk as tightly as possible. You must therefore sort the ArrayList. You can call its Sort() method, but how will it know how to sort FileInfo objects?

To solve this, you must pass in an IComparer<T> interface. We'll create a class called FileComparer that will implement this generic interface for FileInfo objects:

```
public class FileComparer : IComparer<FileInfo>
{
```

This class has only one method, Compare(), which takes two FileInfo objects as arguments:

```
public int Compare(FileInfo file1, FileInfo file2){
```

The normal approach is to return 1 if the first object (file1) is larger than the second (file2), to return -1 if the opposite is true, and to return 0 if they are equal. In this case, however, you want the list sorted from big to small, so you should reverse the return values.

 Because this is the only use of the compare method, it is reasonable to put this special knowledge that the sort is from big to small right into the compare method itself. The alternative is to sort small to big, and have the *calling* method reverse the results, as you saw in Example 12-1.

To test the length of the FileInfo object, you must cast the Object parameters to FileInfo objects (which is safe because you know this method will never receive anything else):

```
if (file1.Length > file2.Length)
{
    return -1;
```

```
        }
        if (file1.Length < file2.Length)
        {
            return 1;
        }
        return 0;
    }
}
```

Returning to GetFileList(), you were about to instantiate the IComparer reference and pass it to the Sort() method of fileList:

```
IComparer<FileInfo> comparer = ( IComparer<FileInfo> ) new FileComparer();
fileList.Sort(comparer);
```

That done, you can return fileList to the calling method:

```
return fileList;
```

The calling method was btnCopy_Click. Remember, you went off to GetFileList() in the first line of the event handler!

```
protected void btnCopy_Click (object sender, System.EventArgs e)
{
    List<FileInfo> fileList = GetFileList();
```

At this point, you've returned with a sorted list of File objects, each representing a file selected in the source TreeView.

You can now iterate through the list, copying the files and updating the UI:

```
foreach (FileInfo file in fileList)
{
    try
    {
        lblStatus.Text = "Copying " +
            txtTargetDir.Text + "\\" +
                file.Name + "...";
        Application.DoEvents();

        file.CopyTo(txtTargetDir.Text + "\\" +
            file.Name,chkOverwrite.Checked);
    }

    catch (Exception ex)
    {
        MessageBox.Show(ex.Message);
    }
}
lblStatus.Text = "Done.";
```

As you go, write the progress to the lblStatus label and call Application.DoEvents() to give the UI an opportunity to redraw. Then call CopyTo() on the file, passing in the target directory obtained from the text field, and a Boolean flag indicating whether the file should be overwritten if it already exists.

You'll notice that the flag you pass in is the value of the chkOverWrite checkbox. The Checked property evaluates true if the checkbox is checked and false if not.

The copy is wrapped in a try block because you can anticipate any number of things going wrong when copying files. For now, handle all exceptions by popping up a dialog box with the error; you might want to take corrective action in a commercial application.

That's it; you've implemented file copying!

Handling the Delete Button Event

The code to handle the Delete event is even simpler. The very first thing you do is ask the user if she is sure she wants to delete the files:

```
protected void btnDelete_Click
(object sender, System.EventArgs e)
{
System.Windows.Forms.DialogResult result =
   MessageBox.Show(
   "Are you quite sure?",                // msg
   "Delete Files",                       // caption
   MessageBoxButtons.OKCancel,           // buttons
   MessageBoxIcon.Exclamation,           // icons
   MessageBoxDefaultButton.Button2);  // default button
```

You can use the MessageBox static Show() method, passing in the message you want to display, the title "Delete Files" as a string, and flags, as follows:

- MessageBox.OKCancel asks for two buttons: OK and Cancel.

- MessageBox.IconExclamation indicates that you want to display an exclamation mark icon.

- MessageBox.DefaultButton.Button2 sets the second button (Cancel) as the default choice.

When the user chooses OK or Cancel, the result is passed back as a System.Windows. Forms.DialogResult enumerated value. You can test this value to see if the user selected OK:

```
if (result == System.Windows.Forms.DialogResult.OK)
{
```

If so, you can get the list of fileNames and iterate through it, deleting each as you go:

```
ArrayList fileNames = GetFileList();

foreach (FileInfo file in fileNames)
{
    try
    {
        lblStatus.Text = "Deleting " +
            txtTargetDir.Text + "\\" +
```

```
              file.Name + "...";
         Application.DoEvents();

              file.Delete();
     }

     catch (Exception ex)
     {
              MessageBox.Show(ex.Message);
     }
 }
 lblStatus.Text = "Done.";
 Application.DoEvents();
```

This code is identical to the copy code, except that the method that is called on the file is Delete().

Example 13-1 provides the commented source code for this example.

Example 13-1. FileCopier source code

```
#region Using directives

using System;
using System.Collections;
using System.Collections.Generic;
using System.ComponentModel;
using System.Data;
using System.Drawing;
using System.IO;
using System.Windows.Forms;

#endregion

/// <remarks>
///     File Copier - Windows Forms demonstration program
///     (c) Copyright 2005 Liberty Associates, Inc.
/// </remarks>
namespace FileCopier
{

    /// <summary>
    /// Form demonstrating Windows Forms implementation
    /// </summary>
    partial class frmFileCopier : Form
    {
        private const int MaxLevel = 2;
        public frmFileCopier()
        {
            InitializeComponent();
            FillDirectoryTree( tvwSource, true );
            FillDirectoryTree( tvwTarget, false );
        }
```

Example 13-1. FileCopier source code (continued)

```
/// <summary>
///     nested class which knows how to compare
///     two files we want to sort large to small,
///     so reverse the normal return values.
/// </summary>
public class FileComparer : IComparer<FileInfo>
{

    public int Compare(FileInfo file1, FileInfo file2)
    {

      if ( file1.Length > file2.Length )
      {
         return -1;
      }
      if ( file1.Length < file2.Length )
      {
         return 1;
      }
      return 0;
   }

    public bool Equals(FileInfo x, FileInfo y) {
      throw new NotImplementedException();
    }
    public int GetHashCode(FileInfo x) {
      throw new NotImplementedException();
    }
}

private void FillDirectoryTree( TreeView tvw, bool isSource )
{
   // Populate tvwSource, the Source TreeView,
   // with the contents of
   // the local hard drive.
   // First clear all the nodes.
   tvw.Nodes.Clear();

   // Get the logical drives and put them into the
   // root nodes. Fill an array with all the
   // logical drives on the machine.
   string[] strDrives = Environment.GetLogicalDrives();

   // Iterate through the drives, adding them to the tree.
   // Use a try/catch block, so if a drive is not ready,
   // e.g. an empty floppy or CD,
   //    it will not be added to the tree.
   foreach ( string rootDirectoryName in strDrives )
   {

      try
      {
```

Example 13-1. FileCopier source code (continued)

```
            // Fill an array with all the first level
            // subdirectories. If the drive is
            // not ready, this will throw an exception.
            DirectoryInfo dir =
                new DirectoryInfo( rootDirectoryName );

            dir.GetDirectories(); // force exception if drive not ready

            TreeNode ndRoot = new TreeNode( rootDirectoryName );

            // Add a node for each root directory.
            tvw.Nodes.Add( ndRoot );

            // Add subdirectory nodes.
            // If Treeview is the source,
            // then also get the filenames.
            if ( isSource )
            {

                GetSubDirectoryNodes(
                    ndRoot, ndRoot.Text, true,1 );
            }
            else
            {
                GetSubDirectoryNodes(
                    ndRoot, ndRoot.Text, false,1 );
            }
        }
        // Catch any errors such as
            // Drive not ready.
        catch
        {
        }
        Application.DoEvents();
    }
} // close for FillSourceDirectoryTree

/// <summary>
/// Gets all the subdirectories below the
/// passed in directory node.
/// Adds to the directory tree.
/// The parameters passed in are the parent node
/// for this subdirectory,
/// the full path name of this subdirectory,
/// and a Boolean to indicate
/// whether or not to get the files in the subdirectory.
/// </summary>
private void GetSubDirectoryNodes(
    TreeNode parentNode, string fullName, bool getFileNames,
        int level )
{
```

Example 13-1. FileCopier source code (continued)

```
DirectoryInfo dir = new DirectoryInfo( fullName );
DirectoryInfo[] dirSubs = dir.GetDirectories();

// Add a child node for each subdirectory.
foreach ( DirectoryInfo dirSub in dirSubs )
{

    // do not show hidden folders
    if ( ( dirSub.Attributes & FileAttributes.Hidden )
       != 0 )
    {
       continue;
    }

    /// <summary>
    ///     Each directory contains the full path.
    ///     We need to split it on the backslashes,
    ///     and only use
    ///     the last node in the tree.
    ///     Need to double the backslash since it
    ///     is normally
    ///     an escape character
    /// </summary>
    TreeNode subNode = new TreeNode( dirSub.Name );
    parentNode.Nodes.Add( subNode );

    // Call GetSubDirectoryNodes recursively.

    if ( level < MaxLevel )
    {
       GetSubDirectoryNodes(
          subNode, dirSub.FullName, getFileNames, level+1 );
    }
}
if ( getFileNames )
{
    // Get any files for this node.
    FileInfo[] files = dir.GetFiles();

    // After placing the nodes,
    // now place the files in that subdirectory.
    foreach ( FileInfo file in files )
    {
       TreeNode fileNode = new TreeNode( file.Name );
       parentNode.Nodes.Add( fileNode );
    }
}
}

/// <summary>
///     Create an ordered list of all
///     the selected files, copy to the
```

Example 13-1. FileCopier source code (continued)

```csharp
///     target directory
/// </summary>
private void btnCopy_Click( object sender,
    System.EventArgs e )
{
    // get the list

    List<FileInfo> fileList = GetFileList();

    // copy the files
    foreach ( FileInfo file in fileList )
    {
        try
        {
            // update the label to show progress
            lblStatus.Text = "Copying " + txtTargetDir.Text +
                "\\" + file.Name + "...";
            Application.DoEvents();

            // copy the file to its destination location
            file.CopyTo( txtTargetDir.Text + "\\" +
                file.Name, chkOverwrite.Checked );
        }

        catch ( Exception ex )
        {
            // you may want to do more than
            // just show the message
            MessageBox.Show( ex.Message );
        }
    }
    lblStatus.Text = "Done.";
    Application.DoEvents();

}

/// <summary>
///     Tell the root of each tree to uncheck
///     all the nodes below
/// </summary>
private void btnClear_Click( object sender, System.EventArgs e )
{
    // get the top most node for each drive
    // and tell it to clear recursively
    foreach ( TreeNode node in tvwSource.Nodes )
    {
        SetCheck( node, false );
    }
}

/// <summary>
///     on cancel, exit
```

Example 13-1. FileCopier source code (continued)

```
/// </summary>
private void btnCancel_Click(object sender, EventArgs e)
{
    Application.Exit();
}

/// <summary>
///     Given a node and an array list
///     fill the list with the names of
///     all the checked files
/// </summary>
// Fill the ArrayList with the full paths of
// all the files checked
private void GetCheckedFiles( TreeNode node,
    List<string> fileNames )
{
    // if this is a leaf...
    if ( node.Nodes.Count == 0 )
    {
        // if the node was checked...
        if ( node.Checked )
        {
            // get the full path and add it to the arrayList
            string fullPath = GetParentString( node );
            fileNames.Add( fullPath );
        }
    }
    else  // if this node is not a leaf
    {
        // if this node is not a leaf
        foreach ( TreeNode n in node.Nodes )
        {
            GetCheckedFiles( n, fileNames );
        }
    }
}

/// <summary>
///     Given a node, return the
///     full path name
/// </summary>
private string GetParentString( TreeNode node )
{
    // if this is the root node (c:\) return the text
    if ( node.Parent == null )
    {
        return node.Text;
    }
    else
    {
        // recurse up and get the path then
        // add this node and a slash
```

Example 13-1. FileCopier source code (continued)

```
            // if this node is the leaf, don't add the slash
            return GetParentString( node.Parent ) + node.Text +
                ( node.Nodes.Count == 0 ? "" : "\\" );
        }
    }


    /// <summary>
    ///     shared by delete and copy
    ///     creates an ordered list of all
    ///     the selected files
    /// </summary>
    private List<FileInfo> GetFileList()
    {
        // create an unsorted array list of the full file names
        List<string> fileNames = new List<string>();

        // ArrayList fileNames = new ArrayList();

        // fill the fileNames ArrayList with the
        // full path of each file to copy
        foreach ( TreeNode theNode in tvwSource.Nodes )
        {
            GetCheckedFiles( theNode, fileNames );
        }

        // Create a list to hold the FileInfo objects
        List<FileInfo> fileList = new List<FileInfo>();
         // ArrayList fileList = new ArrayList();

        // for each of the file names we have in our unsorted list
        // if the name corresponds to a file (and not a directory)
        // add it to the file list
        foreach ( string fileName in fileNames )
        {
            // create a file with the name
            FileInfo file = new FileInfo( fileName );

            // see if it exists on the disk
            // this fails if it was a directory
            if ( file.Exists )
            {
                // both the key and the value are the file
                // would it be easier to have an empty value?
                fileList.Add( file );
            }
        }

        // Create an instance of the IComparer interface
        IComparer<FileInfo> comparer = ( IComparer<FileInfo> )
            new FileComparer();
```

Example 13-1. FileCopier source code (continued)

```csharp
            // pass the comparer to the sort method so that the list
            // is sorted by the compare method of comparer.
            fileList.Sort( comparer );
            return fileList;
        }

        /// <summary>
        ///     check that the user does want to delete
        ///     Make a list and delete each in turn
        /// </summary>
        private void btnDelete_Click( object sender, System.EventArgs e )
        {
            // ask them if they are sure
            System.Windows.Forms.DialogResult result =
                MessageBox.Show(
                "Are you quite sure?",              // msg
                "Delete Files",                     // caption
                MessageBoxButtons.OKCancel,         // buttons
                MessageBoxIcon.Exclamation,         // icons
                MessageBoxDefaultButton.Button2 );  // default button

            // if they are sure...
            if ( result == System.Windows.Forms.DialogResult.OK )
            {
                // iterate through the list and delete them.
                // get the list of selected files
                List<FileInfo> fileNames = GetFileList();

                foreach ( FileInfo file in fileNames )
                {
                    try
                    {
                        // update the label to show progress
                        lblStatus.Text = "Deleting " +
                            file.Name + "...";
                        Application.DoEvents();

                        // Danger Will Robinson!
                        file.Delete();
                    }

                    catch ( Exception ex )
                    {
                        // you may want to do more than
                        // just show the message
                        MessageBox.Show( ex.Message );
                    }
                }
                lblStatus.Text = "Done.";
                Application.DoEvents();
            }
        }
```

Example 13-1. FileCopier source code (continued)

```
/// <summary>
///    Get the full path of the chosen directory
///    copy it to txtTargetDir
/// </summary>
private void tvwTargetDir_AfterSelect(
    object sender,
    System.Windows.Forms.TreeViewEventArgs e )
{
    // get the full path for the selected directory
    string theFullPath = GetParentString( e.Node );

    // if it is not a leaf, it will end with a back slash
    // remove the backslash
    if ( theFullPath.EndsWith( "\\" ) )
    {
        theFullPath =
            theFullPath.Substring( 0, theFullPath.Length - 1 );
    }
    // insert the path in the text box
    txtTargetDir.Text = theFullPath;
}


/// <summary>
///    Mark each node below the current
///    one with the current value of checked
/// </summary>
private void tvwSource_AfterCheck( object sender,
    System.Windows.Forms.TreeViewEventArgs e )
{
    // Call a recursible method.
    // e.node is the node which was checked by the user.
    // The state of the check mark is already
    // changed by the time you get here.
    // Therefore, we want to pass along
    // the state of e.node.Checked.
    if(e.Action != TreeViewAction.Unknown)
    {
        SetCheck(e.Node, e.Node.Checked );
    }
}

/// <summary>
/// recursively set or clear check marks
/// </summary>
private void SetCheck( TreeNode node, bool check )
{
    // find all the child nodes from this node
    foreach ( TreeNode n in node.Nodes )
    {
        n.Checked = check;    // check the node

        // if this is a node in the tree, recurse
        if ( n.Nodes.Count != 0 )
```

Example 13-1. FileCopier source code (continued)

```
            {
                SetCheck( n, check );
            }
        }
    }

    private void tvwExpand(object sender, TreeViewCancelEventArgs e)
    {

        TreeView tvw = ( TreeView ) sender;
        bool getFiles = tvw == tvwSource;
        TreeNode currentNode = e.Node;
        string fullName = currentNode.FullPath;
        currentNode.Nodes.Clear();
        GetSubDirectoryNodes( currentNode, fullName, getFiles, 1 );
    }
  }
}
```

XML Documentation Comments

C# supports a new *documentation comment* style, with three slash marks (///). You can see these comments sprinkled throughout Example 13-1. The Visual Studio editor recognizes these comments and helps format them properly.

The C# compiler processes these comments into an XML file. You can create this file by using the */doc* command-line switch. For example, you might compile the program in Example 13-1 with this command line:

```
csc Form1.cs /doc:XMLDoc.XML
```

You can accomplish this same operation in Visual Studio by clicking the FileCopier project icon in the Solution Explorer window, selecting View Property Pages on the Visual Studio menu, and then clicking Build property page. Click the XMLDocumentation File checkbox and type in a name for the XML file you want to produce, e.g., Filecopier.XML.

An excerpt of the file that's produced for the FileCopier application of the previous section is shown in Example 13-2.

Example 13-2. The XML output (excerpt) for file copy

```
<doc>
    <assembly>
        <name>FileCopier</name>
    </assembly>
    <members>
        <member name="T:FileCopier.frmFileCopier">
            <summary>
            Form demonstrating Windows Forms implementation
```

Example 13-2. The XML output (excerpt) for file copy (continued)

```
      </summary>
  </member>
  <member name="F:FileCopier.frmFileCopier.components">
      <summary>
      Required designer variable.
      </summary>
  </member>
  <member name="M:FileCopier.frmFileCopier.Dispose(System.Boolean)">
      <summary>
      Clean up any resources being used.
      </summary>
  </member>
  <member name="M:FileCopier.frmFileCopier.InitializeComponent">
      <summary>
      Required method for Designer support - do not modify
      the contents of this method with the code editor.
      </summary>
  </member>
  <member name="M:FileCopier.frmFileCopier.GetSubDirectoryNodes
    (System.Windows.Forms.TreeNode,System.String,System.Boolean,System.Int32)">
      <summary>
      Gets all the subdirectories below the
      passed in directory node.
      Adds to the directory tree.
      The parameters passed in are the parent node
      for this subdirectory,
      the full path name of this subdirectory,
      and a Boolean to indicate
      whether or not to get the files in the subdirectory.
      </summary>
  </member>
  <member name="M:FileCopier.frmFileCopier.btnCopy_Click
          (System.Object,System.EventArgs)">
      <summary>
        Create an ordered list of all
        the selected files, copy to the
        target directory
      </summary>
  </member>
```

The file is quite long, and although it can be read by humans, it isn't especially useful in that format. You could, however, write an XSLT file to translate the XML into HTML, or you could read the XML document into a database of documentation. You can also drag the file from File Explorer into Windows Explorer, which provides a nice interface for reading the XML, as shown in Figure 13-9.

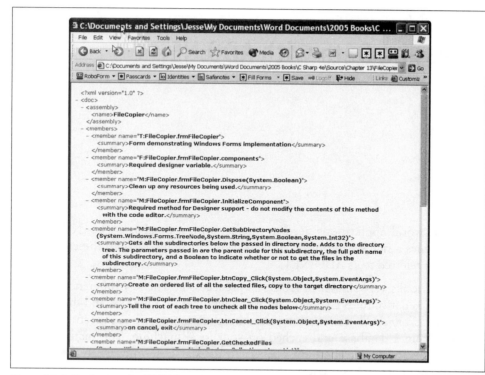

Figure 13-9. Reviewing the XML documentation in Internet Explorer

CHAPTER 14

Accessing Data with ADO.NET

Many real-world applications need to interact with a database. The .NET Framework provides a rich set of objects to manage database interaction; these classes are collectively referred to as ADO.NET.

ADO.NET looks very similar to ADO, its predecessor. The key differences are that ADO.NET is native to .NET (and isn't just a wrapper on OLEDB) and that it is primarily a *disconnected* data architecture. In a disconnected architecture, data is retrieved from a database and cached on your local machine. You manipulate the data on your local computer and connect to the database only when you wish to alter records or acquire new data.

There are significant advantages to disconnecting your data architecture from your database. The biggest advantage is that your application, whether running on the Web or on a local machine, will create a reduced burden on the database server which may help your application to scale well. Database connections are resource-intensive, and it is difficult to have thousands (or hundreds of thousands) of simultaneous continuous connections. A disconnected architecture is resource-frugal.

ADO.NET typically connects to the database to retrieve data, and connects again to update data when you've made changes. Most applications spend most of their time simply reading through data and displaying it; ADO.NET provides a disconnected subset of the data for your use, while reading and displaying.

Relational Databases and SQL

Although one can certainly write an entire book on relational databases, and another on SQL, the essentials of these technologies aren't hard to understand. A *database* is a repository of data. A *relational database* organizes your data into tables. Consider the Northwind database provided with Microsoft SQL Server and Microsoft Access.

Tables, Records, and Columns

The Northwind database describes a fictional company buying and selling food products. The data for Northwind is divided into 13 tables, including Customers, Employees, Orders, Order Details, Products, and so forth.

Every table in a relational database is organized into rows, where each row represents a single record. The rows are organized into columns. All the rows in a table have the same column structure. For example, the Orders table has these columns: `OrderID`, `CustomerID`, `EmployeeID`, `OrderDate`, etc.

For any given order, you need to know the customer's name, address, contact name, and so forth. You could store that information with each order, but that would be very inefficient. Instead, you use a second table called Customers, in which each row represents a single customer. In the Customers table is a column for the `CustomerID`. Each customer has a unique ID, and that field is marked as the *primary key* for that table. A primary key is the column or combination of columns that uniquely identifies a record in a given table.

For VB6 Programmers Moving to ADO.NET

ADO.NET is somewhat different from ADO. While learning how to implement the new functionality found in ADO.NET, you are probably going to keep asking yourself things like: "Where is the `MoveNext()` method?" and "How do I test for the end-of-file?"

In ADO.NET, the functionality that was in Record Sets now resides in two places. Navigation and retrieval are in the `IDataReader` interface, and support for disconnected operation is in the (tremendously more powerful) `DataSet` and `DataTables`.

`DataTables` can be thought of as an array of `DataRows`. Calling the `MoveFirst()` method in ADO.NET would be the same as going to the first index of the array. Testing for the end-of-file is the same as testing whether the current index matches the array's upper bound. Want to set a bookmark for a particular record? Just create a variable and assign it the index of the current record—you don't need a special `BookMark` property.

The Orders table uses the `CustomerID` as a *foreign key*. A foreign key is a column (or combination of columns) that is a primary (or otherwise unique) key from a different table. The Orders table uses the `CustomerID` (the primary key used in the Customers table) to identify which customer has placed the order. To determine the address for the order, you can use the `CustomerID` to look up the customer record in the Customers table.

This use of foreign keys is particularly helpful in representing one-to-many or many-to-one relationships between tables. By separating information into tables that are linked by foreign keys, you avoid having to repeat information in records. A single customer, for example, can have multiple orders, but it is inefficient to place the same customer information (name, phone number, credit limit, and so on) in every order record. The process of removing redundant information from your records and shifting it to separate tables is called *normalization*.

Normalization

Normalization not only makes your use of the database more efficient, but also it reduces the likelihood of data corruption. If you kept the customer's name in both the Customers table and the Orders table, you would run the risk that a change in one table might not be reflected in the other. Thus, if you changed the customer's address in the Customers table, that change might not be reflected in every row in the Orders table (and a lot of work would be necessary to make sure that it was reflected). By keeping only the CustomerID in Orders, you are free to change the address in Customers, and the change is automatically reflected for each order.

Just as C# programmers want the compiler to catch bugs at compile time rather than at runtime, database programmers want the database to help them avoid data corruption. The compiler helps avoid bugs in C# by enforcing the rules of the language (for example, you can't use a variable you've not defined). SQL Server and other modern relational databases avoid bugs by enforcing constraints that you request. For example, the Customers database marks the CustomerID as a primary key. This creates a primary key constraint in the database, which ensures that each CustomerID is unique. If you were to enter a customer named Liberty Associates, Inc. with the CustomerID of LIBE, and then tried to add Liberty Mutual Funds with a CustomerID of LIBE, the database would reject the second record because of the primary key constraint.

Declarative Referential Integrity

Relational databases use *Declarative Referential Integrity* (DRI) to establish constraints on the relationships among the various tables. For example, you might declare a constraint on the Orders table that dictates that no order can have a CustomerID unless that CustomerID represents a valid record in Customers. This helps avoid two types of mistakes. First, you can't enter a record with an invalid CustomerID. Second, you can't delete a Customer record if that CustomerID is used in any order. The integrity of your data and its relationships is thus protected.

SQL

The most popular language for querying and manipulating databases is SQL, usually pronounced "sequel." SQL is a declarative language, as opposed to a procedural language, and it can take a while to get used to working with a declarative language when you are used to languages such as C#.

The heart of SQL is the *query*. A query is a statement that returns a set of records from the database.

For example, you might like to see all the CompanyNames and CustomerIDs of every record in the Customers table in which the customer's address is in London. To do so, write:

```
Select CustomerID, CompanyName from Customers where city = 'London'
```

This returns the following six records as output:

```
CustomerID CompanyName
---------- -----------------------------------------
AROUT      Around the Horn
BSBEV      B's Beverages
CONSH      Consolidated Holdings
EASTC      Eastern Connection
NORTS      North/South
SEVES      Seven Seas Imports
```

SQL is capable of much more powerful queries. For example, suppose the Northwind manager would like to know what products were purchased in July of 1996 by the customer "Vins et alcools Chevalier." This turns out to be somewhat complicated. The Order Details table knows the ProductID for all the products in any given order. The Orders table knows which CustomerIDs are associated with an order. The Customers table knows the CustomerID for a customer, and the Products table knows the product name for the ProductID. How do you tie all this together? Here's the query:

```
select  o.OrderID, productName
from [Order Details] od
join orders o on o.OrderID = od.OrderID
join products p on p.ProductID = od.ProductID
join customers c on o.CustomerID = c.CustomerID
where c.CompanyName = 'Vins et alcools Chevalier'
and orderDate >= '7/1/1996' and orderDate <= '7/31/1996'
```

This asks the database to get the OrderID and the product name from the relevant tables. First, look at Order Details (which we've called od for short), then join that with the Orders table for every record in which the OrderID in the Order Details table is the same as the OrderID in the Orders table.

When you join two tables, you can say either "Get every record that exists in either table" (this is called an *outer join*), or as I've done here, "Get only those records that exist in both tables" (called an *inner join*). That is, an inner join states to get only the records in Orders that match the records in Order Details by having the same value in the OrderID field (on o.Orderid = od.Orderid).

SQL joins are inner joins by default. Writing join orders is the same as writing inner join orders.

The SQL statement goes on to ask the database to create an inner join with Products, getting every row in which the ProductID in the Products table is the same as the ProductID in the Order Details table.

Then create an inner join with customers for those rows where the CustomerID is the same in both the Orders table and the Customers table.

Finally, tell the database to constrain the results to only those rows in which the CompanyName is the one you want, and the dates are in July.

The collection of constraints finds only three records that match:

```
OrderID      ProductName
-----------  ----------------------------------------
10248        Queso Cabrales
10248        Singaporean Hokkien Fried Mee
10248        Mozzarella di Giovanni
```

This output shows that there was only one order (10248) in which the customer had the right ID and in which the date of the order was July 1996. That order produced three records in the Order Details table, and using the product IDs in these three records, you got the product names from the Products table.

You can use SQL not only for searching for and retrieving data, but also for creating, updating, and deleting tables, and generally managing and manipulating both the content and the structure of the database.

For a full explanation of SQL and tips on how to put it to best use, I recommend *Transact SQL Programming* (O'Reilly). If you are using a SQL database that is not SQL Server, you'll want to consult O'Reilly's *SQL Pocket Guide* because each provider may use a slightly different "dialect" of SQL.

The ADO.NET Object Model

The ADO.NET object model is rich, but at its heart it is a fairly straightforward set of classes. The most important of these is the DataSet. The DataSet represents a subset of the entire database, cached on your machine without a continuous connection to the database.

Periodically, you'll reconnect the DataSet to its parent database, update the database with changes you've made to the DataSet, and update the DataSet with changes in the database made by other processes.

This is highly efficient, but to be effective the DataSet must be a robust subset of the database, capturing not just a few rows from a single table, but also a set of tables with all the metadata necessary to represent the relationships and constraints of the original database. This is, not surprisingly, what ADO.NET provides.

The DataSet is composed of DataTable objects as well as DataRelation objects. These are accessed as properties of the DataSet object. The Tables property returns a DataTableCollection, which in turn contains all the DataTable objects.

DataTables and DataColumns

The DataTable can be created programmatically or as a result of a query against the database. The DataTable has a number of public properties, including the Columns collection, which returns the DataColumnCollection object, which in turn consists of DataColumn objects. Each DataColumn object represents a column in a table.

DataRelations

In addition to the Tables collection, the DataSet has a Relations property, which returns a DataRelationCollection consisting of DataRelation objects. Each DataRelation represents a relationship between two tables through DataColumn objects. For example, in the Northwind database the Customers table is in a relationship with the Orders table through the CustomerID column.

The nature of the relationship is one-to-many, or parent-to-child. For any given order, there will be exactly one customer, but any given customer might be represented in any number of orders.

Rows

DataTable's Rows collection returns a set of rows for that table. Use this collection to examine the results of queries against the database, iterating through the rows to examine each record in turn. Programmers experienced with ADO are often confused by the absence of the RecordSet with its moveNext and movePrevious commands. With ADO.NET, you don't iterate through the DataSet; instead, access the table you need, and then you can iterate through the Rows collection, typically with a foreach loop. You'll see this in the first example in this chapter.

Data Adapter

The DataSet is an abstraction of a relational database. ADO.NET uses a DataAdapter as a bridge between the DataSet and the data source, which is the underlying database. DataAdapter provides the Fill() method to retrieve data from the database and populate the DataSet.

DBCommand and DBConnection

The DBConnection object represents a connection to a data source. This connection can be shared among different command objects. The DBCommand object allows you to send a command (typically a SQL statement or a stored procedure) to the database. Often these objects are implicitly created when you create a DataAdapter, but you can explicitly access these objects, as you'll see in a subsequent example.

DataAdapter

Instead of tying the DataSet object too closely to your database architecture, ADO. NET uses a DataAdapter object to mediate between the DataSet object and the database. This decouples the DataSet from the database and allows a single DataSet to represent more than one database or other data source.

DataReader

An alternative to creating a DataSet (and DataAdapter) is to create a DataReader. The DataReader provides connected, forward-only, read-only access to a collection of tables, by executing either a SQL statement or stored procedures. DataReaders are lightweight objects that are ideally suited for filling controls with data and then breaking the connection to the backend database.

Getting Started with ADO.NET

Enough theory! Let's write some code and see how this works. Working with ADO. NET can be complex, but for many queries, the model is surprisingly simple.

In this example, create a simple Windows Form, with a single listbox in it called lbCustomers. Populate this listbox with bits of information from the Customers table in the Northwind database.

Begin by creating a DataAdapter object:

```
SqlDataAdapter DataAdapter =
new SqlDataAdapter(
commandString, connectionString);
```

The two parameters are commandString and connectionString. The commandString is the SQL statement that will generate the data you want in your DataSet:

```
string commandString =
    "Select CompanyName, ContactName from Customers";
```

The connectionString is whatever string is needed to connect to the database. In my case, I'm running SQL Server on my development machine where I have a trusted connection to the database:

```
string connectionString =
    "server=localhost; trusted_connection=true; database=northwind";
```

If you don't have SQL Server installed, select Quickstart Tutorials from the Microsoft .NET Framework SDK program group (you must have selected this option when you installed Visual Studio or the .NET Framework SDK). A web page appears, giving you the option to install the Microsoft SQL Server Desktop Engine (MSDE). After you install MSDE, set up the QuickStarts (this will create the Northwind sample database). To use this database, you need this connection string:

```
"server=(local)\\NetSDK; Trusted_Connection=yes; database=northwind"
```

With the DataAdapter in hand, you're ready to create the DataSet and fill it with the data that you obtain from the SQL select statement:

```
DataSet DataSet = new DataSet();
DataAdapter.Fill(DataSet,"Customers");
```

That's it. You now have a DataSet, and you can query, manipulate, and otherwise manage the data. The DataSet has a collection of tables; you care only about the first one because you've retrieved only a single table:

```
DataTable dataTable = DataSet.Tables[0];
```

You can extract the rows you've retrieved with the SQL statement and add the data to the listbox:

```
foreach (DataRow dataRow in dataTable.Rows)
{
    lbCustomers.Items.Add(
        dataRow["CompanyName"] +
        " (" + dataRow["ContactName"] + ")" );
}
```

The listbox is filled with the company name and contact name from the table in the database, according to the SQL statement we passed in. Example 14-1 contains the complete source code for this example.

Example 14-1. Working with ADO.NET

```
#region Using directives

using System;
using System.Collections.Generic;
using System.ComponentModel;
using System.Data;
using System.Data.SqlClient;
using System.Drawing;
using System.Windows.Forms;

#endregion

namespace WorkingWithADONET
{
    partial class ADONetForm1 : Form
    {
        public ADONetForm1()
```

Example 14-1. Working with ADO.NET (continued)

```
    {
        InitializeComponent();

        // connect to my local server, northwind db

        string connectionString = "server=localhost;" +
            "Trusted_Connection=yes; database=northwind";

        // get records from the customers table
        string commandString =
        "Select CompanyName, ContactName from Customers";

        // create the data set command object
        // and the DataSet
        SqlDataAdapter DataAdapter =
        new SqlDataAdapter(
        commandString, connectionString );

        DataSet DataSet = new DataSet();

        // fill the data set object
        DataAdapter.Fill( DataSet, "Customers" );

        // Get the one table from the DataSet
        DataTable dataTable = DataSet.Tables[0];

        // for each row in the table, display the info
        foreach ( DataRow dataRow in dataTable.Rows )
        {
            lbCustomers.Items.Add(
                dataRow["CompanyName"] +
                " (" + dataRow["ContactName"] + ")" );
        }
    }
  }
}
```

With just a few lines of code, you have extracted a set of data from the database and displayed it in the listbox, as shown in Figure 14-1.

The eight lines of code accomplish the following tasks:

- Create the string for the connection:

```
string connectionString = "server=localhost;" +
    "Trusted_Connection=yes; database=northwind";
```

- Create the string for the select statement:

```
string commandString =
"Select CompanyName, ContactName from Customers";
```

Figure 14-1. Output from Example 14-1

- Create the DataAdapter and pass in the select and connection strings:

```
SqlDataAdapter DataAdapter =
new SqlDataAdapter(
commandString, connectionString);
```

- Create a new DataSet object:

```
DataSet DataSet = new DataSet();
```

- Fill the DataSet from the Customers table using the DataAdapter:

```
DataAdapter.Fill(DataSet,"Customers");
```

- Extract the DataTable from the DataSet:

```
DataTable dataTable = DataSet.Tables[0];
```

- Use the DataTable to fill the listbox:

```
foreach (DataRow dataRow in dataTable.Rows)
{
   lbCustomers.Items.Add(
      dataRow["CompanyName"] +
      " (" + dataRow["ContactName"] + ")" );
}
```

Using OLE DB Managed Providers

Four managed providers are currently available with ADO.NET: the SQL Server Managed Provider, the OLE DB Managed Provider, the ODBC Managed Provider, and a managed provider for Oracle. The previous example used the SQL Server Managed Provider, which is optimized for SQL Server and is restricted to working with SQL Server databases. The more general solution is the OLE DB Managed Provider, which will connect to any OLE DB provider, including Access.

You can rewrite Example 14-1 to work with the Northwind database using Access rather than SQL Server with just a few small changes. First, you need to change the connection string:

```
string connectionString =
    "provider=Microsoft.JET.OLEDB.4.0; "
    + "data source = c:\\nwind.mdb";
```

This query connects to the Northwind database on the C: drive. (Your exact path might be different.)

Next, change the DataAdapter object to an OLEDBDataAdapter rather than a SqlDataAdapter:

```
OleDbDataAdapter DataAdapter =
    new OleDbDataAdapter (commandString, connectionString);
```

Also be sure to add a using statement for the OleDb namespace:

```
using System.Data.OleDb;
```

This design pattern continues throughout the two Managed Providers; for every object whose class name begins with "Sql," there is a corresponding class beginning with "OleDb." Example 14-2 illustrates the complete OLE DB version of Example 14-1.

Example 14-2. Using the ADO Managed Provider

```
#region Using directives

using System;
using System.Collections.Generic;
using System.ComponentModel;
using System.Data;
using System.Data.OleDb;
using System.Drawing;
using System.Windows.Forms;

#endregion

namespace UsingADOManagedProvider
{
    partial class ADONetForm1 : Form
    {
        public ADONetForm1()
        {
            InitializeComponent();
            // connect to Northwind Access database

            string connectionString =
                "provider=Microsoft.JET.OLEDB.4.0; "
                + "data source = c:\\nwind.mdb";
```

Example 14-2. Using the ADO Managed Provider (continued)

```
            // get records from the customers table
            string commandString =
            "Select CompanyName, ContactName from Customers";

            // create the data set command object
            // and the DataSet

            OleDbDataAdapter DataAdapter =
            new OleDbDataAdapter(
            commandString, connectionString );

            DataSet DataSet = new DataSet();

            // fill the data set object
            DataAdapter.Fill( DataSet, "Customers" );

            // Get the one table from the DataSet
            DataTable dataTable = DataSet.Tables[0];

            // for each row in the table, display the info
            foreach ( DataRow dataRow in dataTable.Rows )
            {
                lbCustomers.Items.Add(
                    dataRow["CompanyName"] +
                    " (" + dataRow["ContactName"] + ")" );
            }
        }
    }
}
```

The output from this is identical to that from the previous example, as shown in Figure 14-2.

The OLE DB Managed Provider is more general than the SQL Managed Provider and can, in fact, be used to connect to SQL Server as well as to any other OLE DB object. Because the SQL Server Provider is optimized for SQL Server, it is more efficient to use the SQL Server-specific provider when working with SQL Server. In time, any number of specialized managed providers will be available.

Working with Data-Bound Controls

Let's try a different, somewhat more declarative approach. Create a new Windows Forms Solution (call it DeclarativeDataDisplay). Begin by enlarging the form, and renaming it to DeclarativeDB.cs and retitling it to Declarative Data Base. Drag a DataGridView onto the form.

Once it is in place, an Action menu will appear. Click the drop down to choose a data source. Click Add Project Data Source to open the Data Source Configuration Wizard. Click Next to choose your datatype, as shown in Figure 14-3.

Figure 14-2. Using the ADO Managed Provider

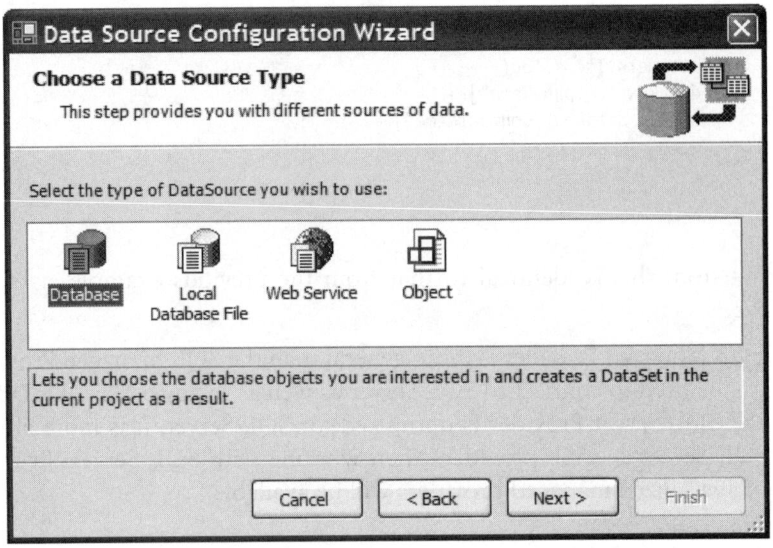

Figure 14-3. The Data Source Configuration Wizard

Click Database and click Next. This brings you to the Data Source Configuration Wizard, where you can click New Connection, as shown in Figure 14-4.

Fill in the appropriate information for the Connection Properties, as shown in Figure 14-5.

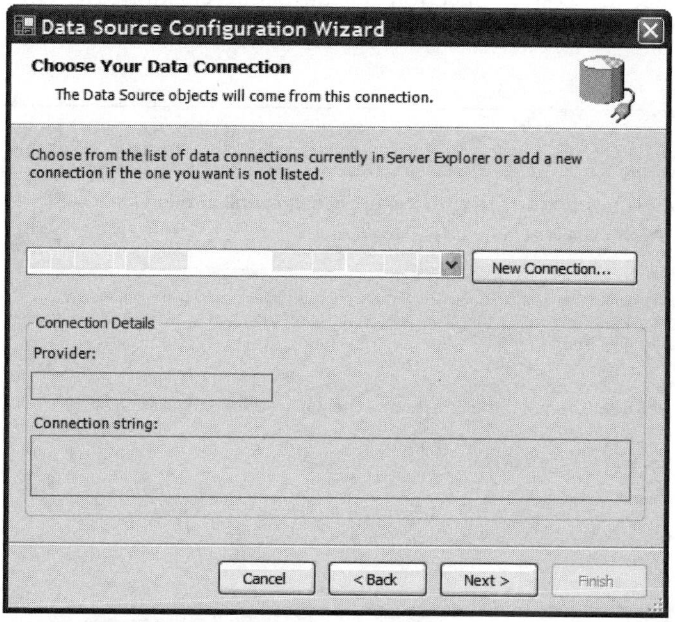

Figure 14-4. Choosing a data connection

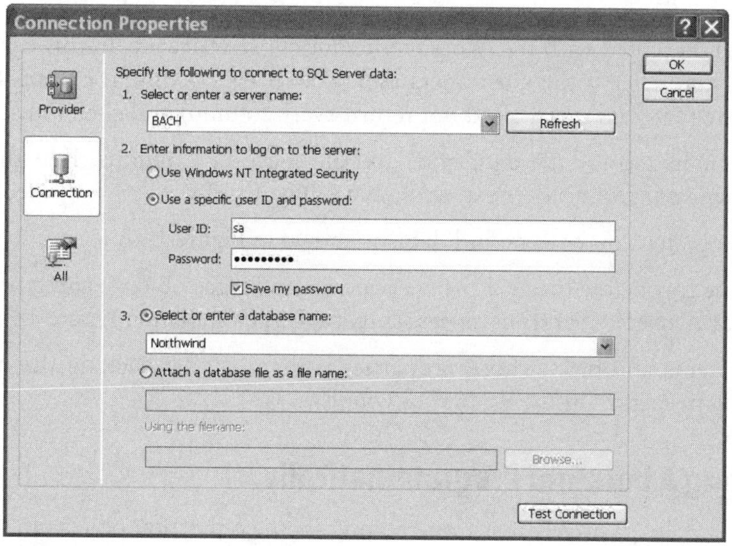

Figure 14-5. Setting the connection properties

Be sure to click the Test Connection button before clicking OK. On the next tab, click both "Yes, save the connection as" and "Include sensitive data," as shown in Figure 14-6.

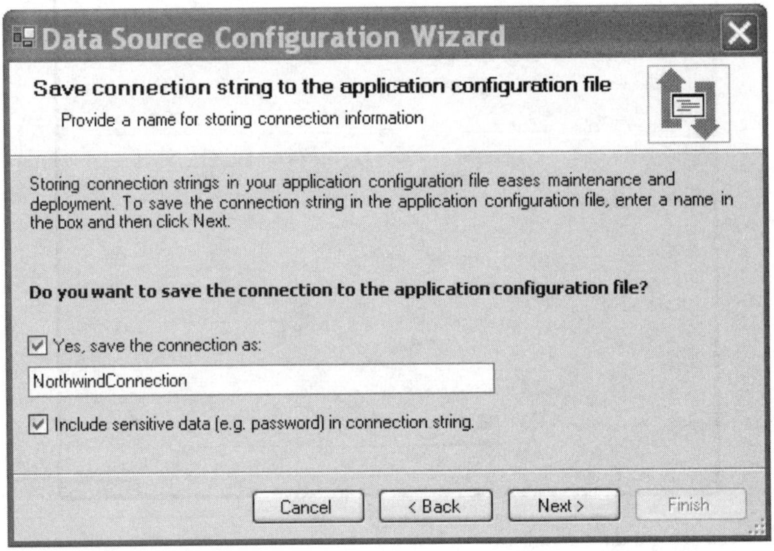

Figure 14-6. Saving sensitive data

You will be presented with the contents of your chosen DataSet. In this case, expand the tables, and expand the Customers table. Select every column except Region (to demonstrate that your query need not return every column) and click Finish.

Click the smart tab for the data grid, and choose Edit Columns. Edit the column headers to meaningful header text, as shown in Figure 14-7.

Run the program. You have bound data, as shown in Figure 14-8.

Examine the tray below the grid, where you will find three objects: northwindDataSet, CustomerDataConnector, and customersTableAdapter, as shown in Figure 14-9.

Each represents an object whose properties you can set by clicking the object and then setting properties in the Properties window.

Populating a DataGrid Programmatically

If you absolutely, positively insist on creating these connection objects by hand, you can certainly do so, and you can manually wire them up to your data grid as well.

Create a new project called ProgrammaticDataDisplay. Rename the *.cs* file and the form and set the title appropriately. Drag a DataGridView in place, but ignore the action menu.

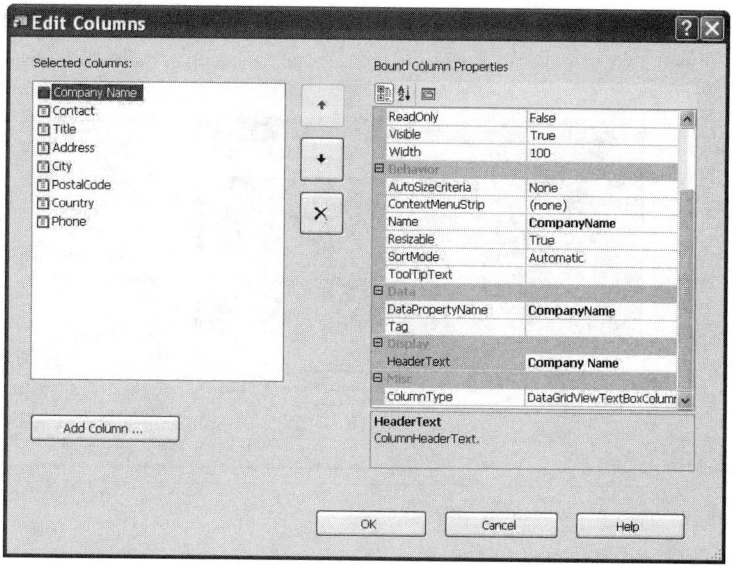

Figure 14-7. Editing columns

Figure 14-8. The data grid in action

Right-click the form and choose View Code. Add these lines to the constructor:

```
string connectionString = "server=localhost;" +
"Trusted_Connection=yes; database=northwind";
string commandString =
    "Select CompanyName, ContactName, ContactTitle, "
    + "Phone, Fax from Customers";

// create a data set and fill it
SqlDataAdapter DataAdapter =
    new SqlDataAdapter( commandString, connectionString );
```

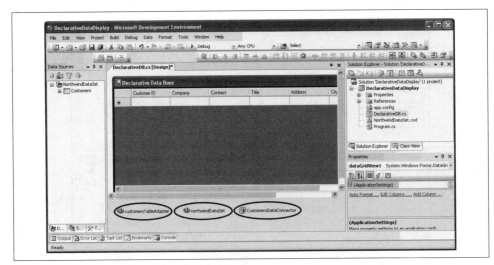

Figure 14-9. Examining the objects in the tray

```
DataSet DataSet = new DataSet();
DataAdapter.Fill( DataSet, "Customers" );

// bind the DataSet to the grid
dataGridView1.DataSource =
    DataSet.Tables["Customers"].DefaultView;
```

In this case, you are setting the connection string and command string by hand, and then creating a SqlDataAdapter and DataSet to retrieve the data. You then bind the dataGridView's DataSource property to the Default view of the Customers table you retrieved.

You are free to set the DataGridView's properties programmatically or declaratively, and you can mix and match approaches. But clearly, Microsoft has gone a long way to allowing you to just drag and drop database connection controls onto your form to make interacting with ADO.NET much simpler.

Customizing the DataSet

It is possible to control precisely every aspect of creating the DataSet, instead of using the default settings. You may do so declaratively or programmatically.

In the previous example, when you created the DataSet, you passed in a commandString and a connectionString:

```
SqlDataAdapter DataAdapter =
    new SqlDataAdapter(commandString, connectionString);
```

These were assigned internally to a SqlCommand object and a SqlConnection object, respectively. You can instead explicitly create these objects.

In this next example, you'll give the class four new members:

```
private System.Data.SqlClient.SqlConnection myConnection;
private System.Data.DataSet myDataSet;
private System.Data.SqlClient.SqlCommand myCommand;
private System.Data.SqlClient.SqlDataAdapter DataAdapter;
```

The connection is created by instantiating a SqlConnection object with the connection string:

```
string connectionString = "server=(local)\\NetSDK;" +
    "Trusted_Connection=yes; database=northwind";
myConnection = new System.Data.SqlClient.SqlConnection(connectionString);
```

and then it is opened explicitly:

```
myConnection.Open();
```

By hanging on to this connection, you can reuse it (as you'll see in a subsequent example) and you can also use its transaction support if needed.

 You can also allow the DataAdapter to create your connection, and then explicitly open it or even maintain a reference to it by using code such as:

```
SqlConnection myConnection = myAdapter.Connection
```

Next, explicitly create the DataSet object and set one of its properties:

```
myDataSet = new System.Data.DataSet();
myDataSet.CaseSensitive=true;
```

Setting CaseSensitive to true indicates that string comparisons within DataTable objects are case-sensitive.

Next, explicitly create the SqlCommand object and give that new command object the connection object and the text for the command:

```
myCommand = new System.Data.SqlClient.SqlCommand()
myCommand.Connection=myConnection;
myCommand.CommandText = "Select * from Customers";
```

Finally, create the SqlDataAdapter object and assign to it the SqlCommand object you just established. Then tell the DataAdapter how to map the table columns, using the table you're searching, and instruct the SqlDataAdapter to fill the DataSet object:

```
DataAdapter = new System.Data.SqlClient.SqlDataAdapter();
DataAdapter.SelectCommand= myCommand;
DataAdapter.TableMappings.Add("Table","Customers");
DataAdapter.Fill(myDataSet);
```

With that done, you're ready to fill the DataGridView (note that this time I've used the default name for the DataGrid):

```
dataGrid1.DataSource=
    myDataSet.Tables["Customers"].DefaultView;
```

Example 14-3 provides the complete source code.

Example 14-3. Customizing a DataSet

```csharp
#region Using directives

using System;
using System.Collections.Generic;
using System.ComponentModel;
using System.Data;
using System.Data.SqlClient;
using System.Drawing;
using System.Windows.Forms;

#endregion

namespace CustomizedDataSet
{
    partial class CustomizedDataSet : Form
    {
        private System.Data.SqlClient.SqlConnection myConnection;
        private System.Data.DataSet myDataSet;
        private System.Data.SqlClient.SqlCommand myCommand;
        private System.Data.SqlClient.SqlDataAdapter DataAdapter;

        public CustomizedDataSet()
        {
            InitializeComponent();
            string connectionString = "server=localhost;" +
                "Trusted_Connection=yes; database=northwind";
            myConnection = new
                System.Data.SqlClient.SqlConnection( connectionString );
            myConnection.Open();

            // create the DataSet and set a property
            myDataSet = new System.Data.DataSet();
            myDataSet.CaseSensitive = true;

            // create the SqlCommand  object and assign the
            // connection and the select statement
            myCommand = new System.Data.SqlClient.SqlCommand();
            myCommand.Connection = myConnection;
            myCommand.CommandText = "Select * from Customers";

            // create the DataAdapter object and pass in the
            // SQL Command object and establish the table mappings
            DataAdapter = new System.Data.SqlClient.SqlDataAdapter();
            DataAdapter.SelectCommand = myCommand;
            DataAdapter.TableMappings.Add( "Table", "Customers" );

            // Tell the DataAdapter object to fill the DataSet
            DataAdapter.Fill( myDataSet );
```

Example 14-3. Customizing a DataSet (continued)

```
        // display it in the grid
        dataGridView1.DataSource =
            myDataSet.Tables["Customers"].DefaultView;
    }
  }
}
```

CHAPTER 15

Programming ASP.NET Applications and Web Services

Developers are writing more and more of their applications to run over the Web.

There are many obvious advantages. For one, you don't have to create as much of the user interface; you can let Internet Explorer and other browsers handle a lot of the work for you. Another, perhaps bigger, advantage is that distribution of the application and of revisions is faster, easier, and less expensive. Most important, a web application can be run on any platform by any user at any location; this is harder to do (though not impossible) with smart-client applications.

The third advantage of web applications is distributed processing, though smart-client applications are making inroads. With a web-based application, it is easy to provide server-side processing, and the Web provides standardized protocols (e.g., HTTP, HTML, and XML) to facilitate building *n*-tier applications.

The .NET technology for building web applications (and dynamic web sites) is ASP. NET 2.0, which provides a rich collection of types for building web applications in its System.Web and System.Web.UI namespaces. There is a great deal to learn about ASP.NET, but much of it is language-independent. ASP.NET offers a rich suite of controls and related tools, including tools to validate data, display dates, present advertisements, interact with users, and so forth. Most of these require no coding whatsoever.

The focus of this chapter is where ASP.NET and C# programming intersect: the creation of Web Forms and web services. The role of the C# programmer in ASP.NET development is in writing the event handlers that respond to user interaction. Many of the event handlers will either add data to a database or retrieve data and make it available to the controls. For coverage of ASP.NET alone, see my book (co-written with Dan Hurwitz), *Programming ASP.NET* (O'Reilly).

Web Forms bring RAD techniques (such as those used in Windows Forms) to the development of web applications. As with Windows Forms, you drag-and-drop controls onto a form and write the supporting code either inline or in *code-behind* pages.

With Web Forms, however, the application is deployed to a web server, and users interact with the application through a standard browser.

.NET web services expand on the concept of distributed processing to build components whose methods can be invoked across the Internet using industry-wide standard protocols. These components can be built in any .NET language,* and they communicate using open protocols that are platform-independent. For example, a stock exchange server might provide a web service method that takes a stock ticker symbol as a parameter and returns a quote. An application might combine that service with another service from a different company that also takes a stock symbol but that returns background data about the company. The application developer can concentrate on adding value to these services, instead of duplicating the same service for his own application.

This chapter demonstrates Web Forms and web services programming using C#.

Understanding Web Forms

ASP.NET 2.0 Web Forms are the successor to the enormously successful ASP.NET 1.x Web Forms, which in turn were the successor to ASP pages. The goal of ASP.NET 2.0 was to reduce the amount of coding by 70% compared to ASP 1.x. This means that web programming is increasingly *declarative* rather than *programmatic*—that is, you declare controls on your Web Form rather than writing (and rewriting) boilerplate code.

You still have the option of writing code (you can always write code), but for the vast majority of web programming, you'll write a lot less code with ASP.NET 2.0 than you did with 1.x.

Web Forms implement a programming model in which web pages are dynamically generated on a web server for delivery to a browser over the Internet. With Web Forms, you create an ASPX page with more or less static content consisting of HTML and web controls, and you write C# code to add additional dynamic content. The C# code *runs on the server*, and the data produced is integrated with the declared objects on your page to create an HTML page that is sent to the browser.

There are three critical points to pick up from the previous paragraph, and which should be kept in mind for this entire chapter:

- Web pages can have both HTML and web controls (described later).
- All processing is done on the server (you can have client-side processing with scripting languages, but that isn't part of ASP.NET).

---

* Web services can, of course, be written in any language on any platform; the point of web services is that they are platform-independent. For the purposes of this book, however, we will focus on creating and consuming web services using .NET.

- If you use ASP.NET web controls, what the browser sees is just HTML (there is an exception to this; with up-level browsers some script may be sent as well).

In short, Web Forms are designed to be viewed through any browser, with the server generating the correct browser-compliant HTML. You can do the programming for the logic of the Web Form in any .NET language. I will of course use C#. Just as with Windows Forms, you *can* create Web Forms in Notepad (or another editor of your choice) rather than in Visual Studio. Many developers will choose to do so, but Visual Studio makes the process of designing and testing Web Forms *much* easier.

Web Forms divide the user interface into two parts: the visual part or user interface (UI), and the logic that lies behind it. This is very similar to developing Windows Forms as shown in Chapter 13. This is called *code separation*; all examples in this book use code separation, though it is possible to write the C# code in the same file with the user interface.

 In Version 2.0 of ASP.NET, Visual Studio takes advantage of partial classes, allowing the code-separation page to be far simpler than it was in 1.x. Because the code-separation and declarative pages are part of the same class, there is no longer a need to have protected variables to reference the controls of the page, and the designer can hide its initialization code in a separate file.

The UI page is stored in a file with the extension *.aspx*. When you run the form, the server generates HTML sent to the client browser. This code uses the rich Web Forms types found in the System.Web and System.Web.UI namespaces of the .NET FCL.

With Visual Studio, Web Forms programming couldn't be simpler: open a form, drag some controls onto it, and write the code to handle events. Presto! You've written a web application.

On the other hand, even with Visual Studio, writing a robust and complete web application can be a daunting task. Web Forms offer a very rich UI; the number and complexity of web controls have greatly multiplied in recent years, and user expectations about the look and feel of web applications have risen accordingly.

In addition, web applications are inherently distributed. Typically, the client will not be in the same building as the server. For most web applications, you must take network latency, bandwidth, and network server performance into account when creating the UI; a round trip from client to host might take a few seconds.

Web Form Events

Web Forms are event-driven. An *event* represents the idea that "something happened" (see Chapter 12 for a full discussion of events).

An event is generated (or *raised*) when the user clicks a button, or selects from a list-box, or otherwise interacts with the UI. Events can also be generated by the system starting or finishing work. For example, open a file for reading, and the system raises an event when the file has been read into memory.

The method that responds to the event is called the *event handler*. Event handlers are written in C# and are associated with controls in the HTML page through control attributes.

By convention, ASP.NET event handlers return void and take two parameters. The first parameter represents the object raising the event. The second, called the *event argument*, contains information specific to the event, if any. For most events, the event argument is of type EventArgs, which doesn't expose any properties. For some controls, the event argument might be of a type derived from EventArgs that can expose properties specific to that event type.

In web applications, most events are typically handled on the server and, therefore, require a round trip. ASP.NET supports only a limited set of events, such as button clicks and text changes. These are events that the user might expect to cause a significant change, as opposed to Windows events (such as mouse-over) that might happen many times during a single user-driven task.

Postback versus nonpostback events

Postback events are those that cause the form to be posted back to the server immediately. These include click-type events, such as the Button Click event. In contrast, many events (typically change events) are considered *nonpostback* in that the form isn't posted back to the server immediately. Instead, these events are cached by the control until the next time a postback event occurs.

You can force controls with nonpostback events to behave in a post-back manner by setting their AutoPostBack property to true.

State

A web application's *state* is the current value of all the controls and variables for the current user in the current session. The Web is inherently a "stateless" environment. This means that every post to the server loses the state from previous posts, unless the developer takes great pains to preserve this session knowledge. ASP.NET, however, provides support for maintaining the state of a user's session.

Whenever a page is posted to the server, it is re-created by the server from scratch before it is returned to the browser. ASP.NET provides a mechanism that automatically maintains state for server controls (ViewState) independent of the HTTP session. Thus, if you provide a list and the user has made a selection, that selection is preserved after the page is posted back to the server and redrawn on the client.

The HTTP session maintains the illusion of a connection between the user and the web application, despite the fact that the Web is a stateless, connectionless environment.

Web Form Life Cycle

Every request for a page made to a web server causes a chain of events at the server. These events, from beginning to end, constitute the *life cycle* of the page and all its components. The life cycle begins with a request for the page, which causes the server to load it. When the request is complete, the page is unloaded. From one end of the life cycle to the other, the goal is to render appropriate HTML output back to the requesting browser. The life cycle of a page is marked by the following events, each of which you can handle yourself or leave to default handling by the ASP.NET server:

Initialize
> Initialize is the first phase in the life cycle for any page or control. It is here that any settings needed for the duration of the incoming request are initialized.

Load ViewState
> The ViewState property of the control is populated. The ViewState information comes from a hidden variable on the control, used to persist the state across round trips to the server. The input string from this hidden variable is parsed by the page framework, and the ViewState property is set. This can be modified via the LoadViewState() method. This allows ASP.NET to manage the state of your control across page loads so that each control isn't reset to its default state each time the page is posted.

Process Postback Data
> During this phase, the data sent to the server in the posting is processed. If any of this data results in a requirement to update the ViewState, that update is performed via the LoadPostData() method.

Load
> CreateChildControls() is called, if necessary, to create and initialize server controls in the control tree. State is restored, and the form controls contain client-side data. You can modify the load phase by handling the Load event with the OnLoad() method.

Send Postback Change Modifications
> If there are any state changes between the current state and the previous state, change events are raised via the RaisePostDataChangedEvent() method.

Handle Postback Events
> The client-side event that caused the postback is handled.

PreRender

> This is your last chance to modify the output prior to rendering using the `OnPreRender()` method.

Save State

> Near the beginning of the life cycle, the persisted view state was loaded from the hidden variable. Now it is saved back to the hidden variable, persisting as a string object that will complete the round trip to the client. You can override this using the `SaveViewState()` method.

Render

> This is where the output to be sent back to the client browser is generated. You can override it using the `Render` method. `CreateChildControls()` is called, if necessary, to create and initialize server controls in the control tree.

Dispose

> This is the last phase of the life cycle. It gives you an opportunity to do any final cleanup and release references to any expensive resources, such as database connections. You can modify it using the `Dispose()` method.

Creating a Web Form

To create the simple Web Form that will be used in the next example, start up Visual Studio .NET and select File → New Web Site. In the New Web Site menu, choose C# as your language, and choose ASP.NET Web Site as the template to use. Finally, locate your web site somewhere on your disk (at the bottom of the dialog), as shown in Figure 15-1.

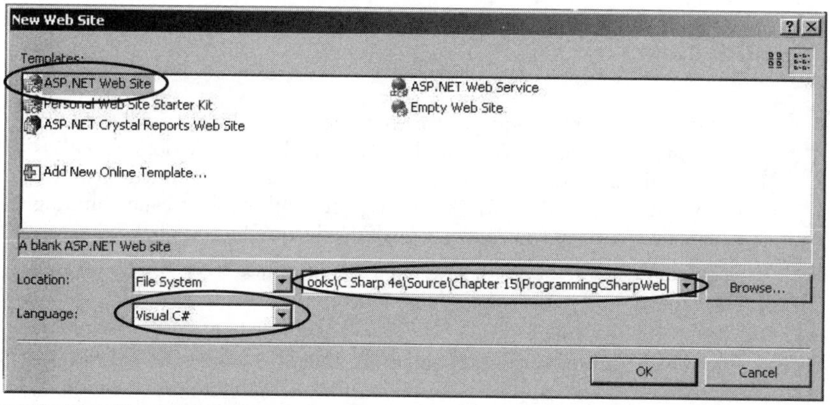

Figure 15-1. Creating a new web site

Visual Studio creates a folder named ProgrammingCSharpWeb in the directory you've indicated, and within that directory it creates your *Default.aspx* page (for the

User interface), *Default.aspx.cs* (for your code), and a *Data* directory (currently empty but often used to hold *.mdb* files or other data-specific files).

 While Visual Studio no longer uses projects for web applications, it does keep solution files to allow you to quickly return to a web site or desktop application you've been developing. The solution files are kept in a directory you may designate through the Tools → Options window, as shown in Figure 15-2.

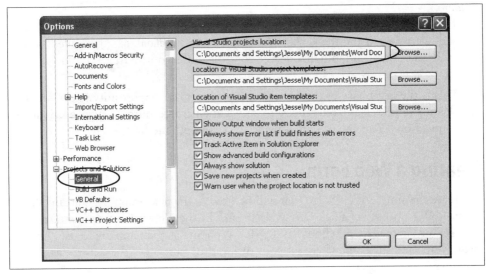

Figure 15-2. Saving a solution

Code-Behind Files

 ASP.NET 1.1 programmers take note: the code-behind model for ASP. NET has changed. In Versions 1.x, the code-behind file defined a class that derived from Page. This code-behind class contained instance variables for all the controls on the page, with explicit event binding using delegates and the *.aspx* page derived from the code-behind class.

In Version 2.0, ASP.NET generates a single class from the combined *.aspx* page and partial class definitions in the code-behind file.

ASP.NET can infer the control instances and derive event bindings from the markup during compilation; thus, the new code-behind file includes only the application code you need, such as event handlers, and doesn't need to include instance variables or explicit event binding. The new code-behind files are simpler, easier to maintain, and always in sync with the *.aspx* page.

Let's take a closer look at the *.aspx* and code-behind files that Visual Studio creates. Start by renaming *Default.aspx* to *HelloWeb.aspx*. To do this, close *Default.aspx*, and

---

then right-click its name in the Solution Explorer. Choose Rename and enter the name HelloWeb.aspx. That renames the file, but not the class. To rename the class, right-click the *.aspx* page and choose View Code in the code page, then rename the class HelloWeb_aspx. You'll see a small line next to the name. Click it and you'll open the smart tag that allows you to rename the class. Click "Rename 'Default_aspx' to 'HelloWeb_aspx'" and Visual Studio ensures that every occurrence of Default_aspx is replaced with its real name, as shown in Figure 15-3.

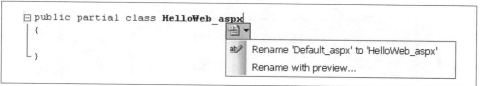

Figure 15-3. Renaming the class

Unfortunately, (at least in Beta) the name of the class isn't changed in *HelloWeb.aspx*, so go back to the *HelloWeb.aspx* file and change the page directive's `ClassName` attribute to HelloWeb_aspx:

```
<%@ Page Language="C#" CompileWith="HelloWeb.aspx.cs"
    ClassName="HelloWeb_aspx" %>
```

Within the HTML view of *HelloWeb.aspx*, you see that a form has been specified in the body of the page using the standard HTML form tag:

```
<form id="Form1" runat="server">
```

Web Forms assumes that you need at least one form to manage the user interaction, and creates one when you open a project. The attribute `runat="server"` is the key to the server-side magic. Any tag that includes this attribute is considered a server-side control to be executed by the ASP.NET framework on the server. Within the form, Visual Studio has opened `div` tags to facilitate placing your controls and text.

Having created an empty Web Form, the first thing you might want to do is add some text to the page. By switching to HTML view, you can add script and HTML directly to the file just as you could with classic ASP. Adding the following line to the body segment of the HTML page will cause it to display a greeting and the current local time:

```
Hello World! It is now <% = DateTime.Now.ToString() %>
```

The `<%` and `%>` marks work just as they did in classic ASP, indicating that code falls between them (in this case, C#). The `=` sign immediately following the opening tag causes ASP.NET to display the value, just like a call to `Response.Write()`. You could just as easily write the line as:

```
Hello World! It is now
<% Response.Write(DateTime.Now.ToString()); %>
```

Run the page by pressing F5 (or save it and navigate to it in your browser). You should see the string printed to the browser, as in Figure 15-4.

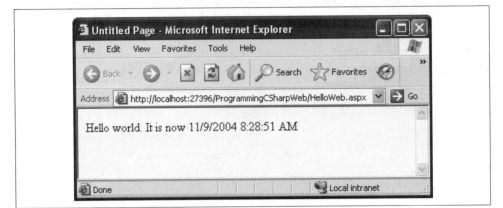

Figure 15-4. Hello World from ASP.NET 2.0

Enabling Debugging

When you press F5, you begin the debugger. It's likely that Visual Studio will notice that you don't have a *Web.config* file for this application (which is required for debugging), and the Debugging Not Enabled dialog box will appear, as shown in Figure 15-5.

The default in this dialog box is to modify (and if needed, create) the *Web.config* file. Go ahead, and press OK to enable debugging for your application.

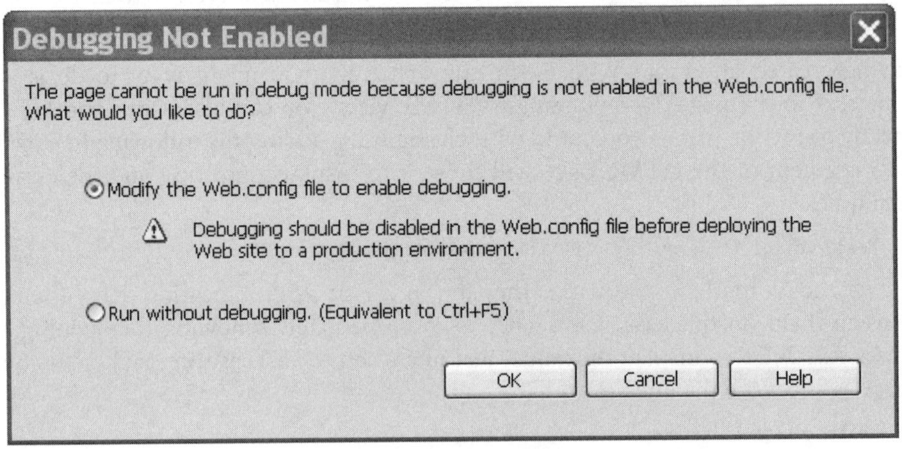

Figure 15-5. You'll see this if you start debugging before you have a Web.config file

Adding Controls

You can add server-side controls to a Web Form in three ways: by writing HTML into the HTML page, by dragging controls from the toolbox to the Design page, or by programmatically adding them at runtime. For example, suppose you want to use buttons to let the user choose one of three shippers provided in the Northwind database. You can write the following HTML into the `<form>` element in the HTML window:

```
<asp:RadioButton GroupName="Shipper" id="Speedy"
    text = "Speedy Express" Checked="True" runat="server">
</asp:RadioButton>
<asp:RadioButton GroupName="Shipper" id="United"
    text = "United Package" runat="server">
</asp:RadioButton>
<asp:RadioButton GroupName="Shipper" id="Federal"
    text = "Federal Shipping" runat="server">
</asp:RadioButton>
```

The asp tags declare server-side ASP.NET controls that are replaced with normal HTML when the server processes the page. When you run the application, the browser displays three radio buttons in a button group; pressing one deselects the others.

You can create the same effect more easily by dragging three buttons from the Visual Studio toolbox onto the Form, or, to make life even easier, you can drag a Radio Button List onto the form, which will manage a set of radio buttons declaratively. When you do, the smart tag is opened, and you are prompted to choose a Data Source (which allows you to bind to a collection; perhaps one you've obtained from a database) or to Edit Items. Clicking Edit Items opens the ListItem Collection Editor, where you can add three radio buttons.

Each radio button is given the default name ListItem, but you may edit its text and value in the ListItem properties, where you can also decide which of the radio buttons is selected, as shown in Figure 15-6.

 You can add controls to a page in one of two modes. The default mode is FlowLayout. With FlowLayout, the controls are added to the form from top to bottom, as in a Microsoft Word document. The alternative is GridLayout, in which the controls are arranged in the browser using absolute positioning (x and y coordinates).

To change from Grid to Layout or back, change the pageLayout property of the document in Visual Studio .NET.

You can improve the look of your radio button list by changing properties in the Properties window, including the font, colors, number of columns, repeat direction (vertical is the default), and so forth.

Click back and forth between Design and Source mode to see the effect of your changes, as shown in Figure 15-7.

ListItem Collection Editor

Members:

```
0  Speedy Express
1  United Package
2  Federal Shipping
```

Speedy Express Properties:

⊟ Misc	
Enabled	True
Selected	**True**
Text	**Speedy Express**
Value	**Speedy Express**

[Add]   [Remove]

[OK]   [Cancel]   [Help]

Figure 15-6. Editing a collection of ListItems

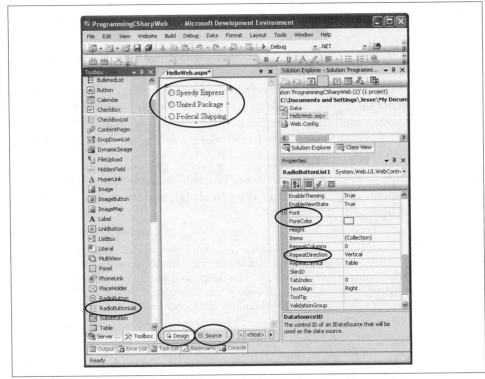

Figure 15-7. Switching between Design and Source mode after adding a radio group

Server Controls

Web Forms offer two types of server-side controls. The first is server-side HTML controls. These are HTML controls that you tag with the attribute runat=Server.

The alternative to marking HTML controls as server-side controls is to use ASP.NET Server Controls, also called ASP controls or web controls. ASP controls have been designed to augment and replace the standard HTML controls. ASP controls provide a more consistent object model and more consistently named attributes. For example, with HTML controls, there are myriad ways to handle input:

```
<input type="radio">
<input type="checkbox">
<input type="button">
<input type="text">
<textarea>
```

Each behaves differently and takes different attributes. The ASP controls try to normalize the set of controls, using attributes consistently throughout the ASP control object model. The ASP controls that correspond to the preceding HTML server-side controls are:

```
<asp:RadioButton>
<asp:CheckBox>
<asp:Button>
<asp:TextBox rows="1">
<asp:TextBox rows="5">
```

The remainder of this chapter focuses on ASP controls.

Data Binding

Various technologies have offered programmers the opportunity to bind controls to data so that as the data was modified, the controls responded automatically. As Rocky used to say to Bullwinkle, "But that trick never works." Bound controls often provided the developer with severe limitations in how the control looked and performed.

The ASP.NET designers set out to solve these problems and provide a suite of robust data-bound controls, which simplify display and modification of data, sacrificing neither performance nor control over the UI. In Version 2.0 they have expanded the list of bindable controls and provided even more out-of-the-box functionality.

In the previous section, you hardcoded radio buttons onto a form, one for each of three shippers in the Northwind database. That can't be the best way to do it; if you change the shippers in the database, you have to go back and rewire the controls. This section shows how you can create these controls dynamically and then bind them to data in the database.

You might want to create the radio buttons based on data in the database because you can't know at design time what text the buttons will have, or even how many buttons you'll need. To accomplish this, you'll bind your RadioButtonList to a data source.

Create a new web site called DisplayShippers and drag a RadioButtonList onto the form. This time, instead of choosing EditItems from the Common RadioButtonList Tasks, click Choose Data Source.... The Choose Data Source dialog opens, as shown in Figure 15-8.

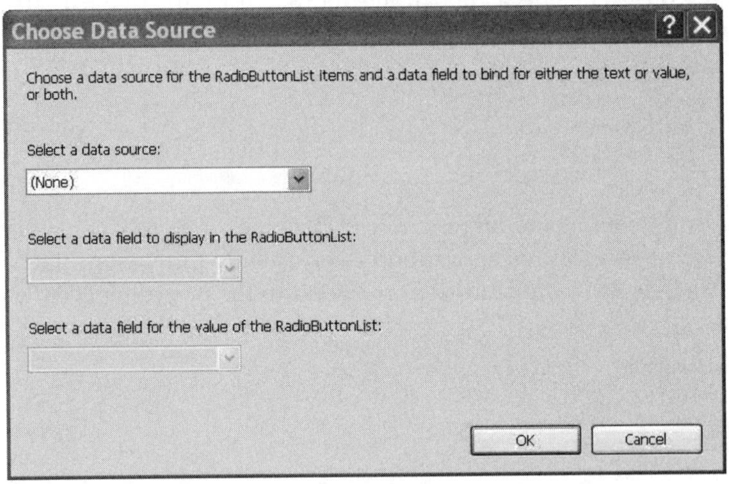

Figure 15-8. Choosing a data source

Drop down the Select a data source menu, and choose <New Data Source>. You are then prompted to choose a data source from the datatypes on your machine. Select Database, and the Configure Data Source dialog box opens, as shown in Figure 15-9.

Choose New to configure a new data source, and the Connection Properties Dialog opens. Fill in the fields: choose your server name, how you want to log into the server, and the name of the database. Be sure to click Test Connection to test the connection. When everything is working, click OK as shown in Figure 15-10.

After clicking OK, the connection properties will be filled in for the Configure Data Source dialog. Review them and if they are OK, click Next. On the next wizard page, name your connection (e.g., NorthWindConnectionString) if you want to save it to a configuration file that can be reused.

When you click Next, you'll have the opportunity to specify the columns you want to retrieve, or to specify a custom SQL statement or stored procedure for retrieving the data.

Drop the Table list and scroll down to shippers. Select the ShipperID and CompanyName fields, as shown in Figure 15-11.

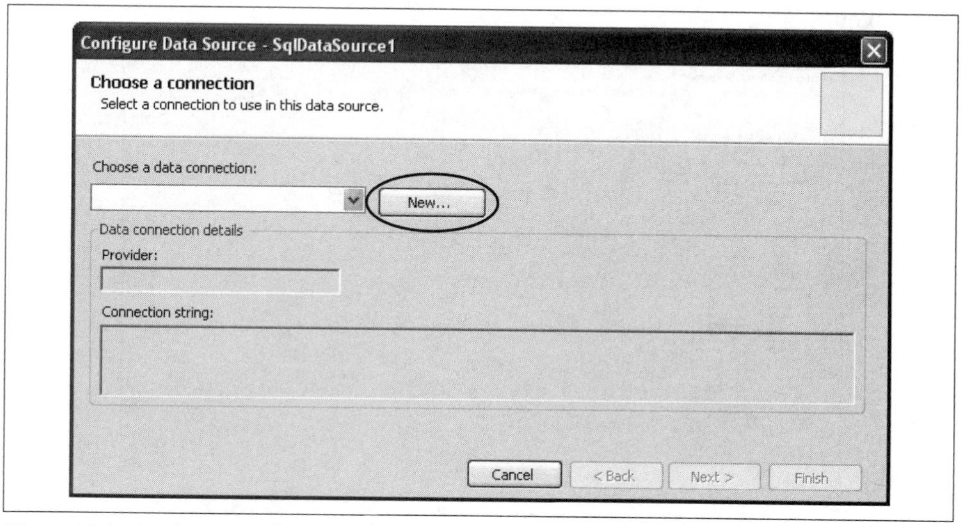

Figure 15-9. Configuring a data source

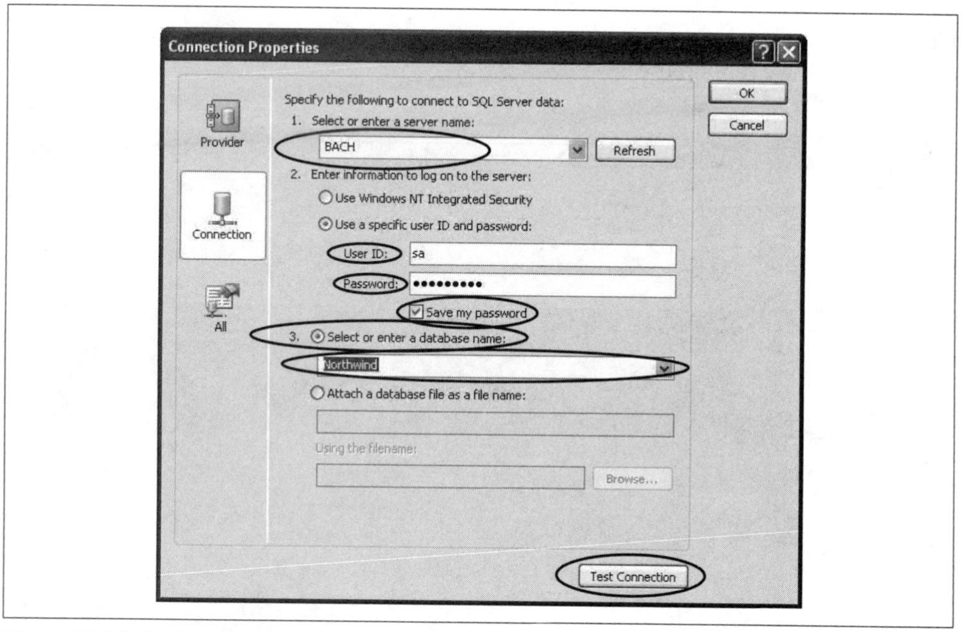

Figure 15-10. Setting the connection properties

 While you are here you may want to click the AdvancedOptions button just to see what other options are available to you.

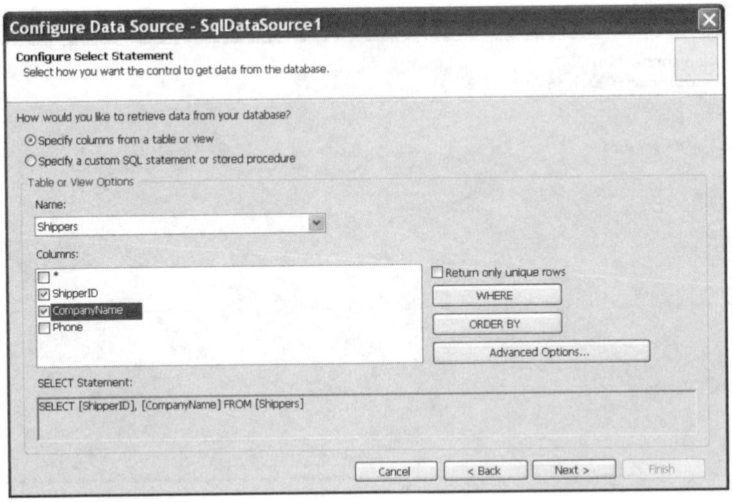

Figure 15-11. Configuring the data source

Click Next and test your query to see that you are getting back the values you expected, as shown in Figure 15-12.

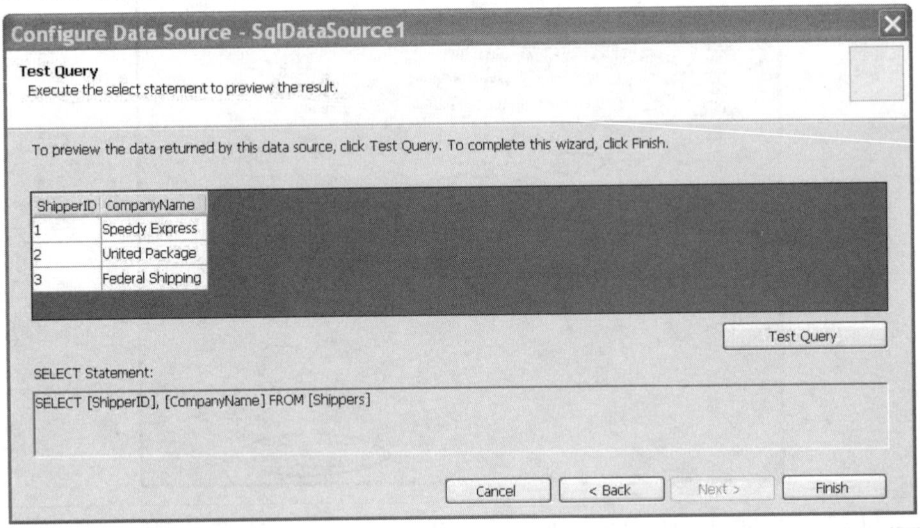

Figure 15-12. Testing the query

It is now time to attach the data source you've just built to the RadioButtonList. A RadioButtonList (like most lists) distinguishes between the value to display (e.g., the name of the delivery service) and the value of that selection (e.g., the delivery service ID). Set these fields in the wizard, using the drop down, as shown in Figure 15-13.

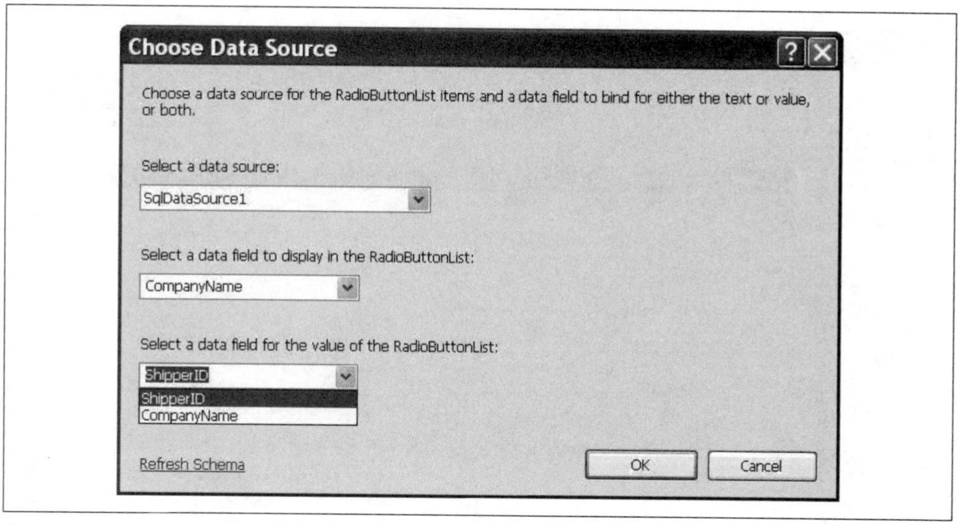

Figure 15-13. Binding fields to the radio button control

You can improve the look and feel of the radio buttons by binding to the Shippers table, clicking the Radio Button list, and then setting the list's properties in the Properties window.

Examining the Code

Before moving on, there are a few things to notice. When you press F5 to run this application, it appears in a web browser, and the radio buttons come up as expected. Choose View → Source and you'll see that what is being sent to the browser is simple HTML, as shown in Figure 15-14.

Notice that the HTML has no `RadioButtonList`; it has a table, with cells, within which are standard HTML input objects and labels. ASP.NET has translated the developer controls to HTML understandable by any browser.

 A malicious user may create a message that looks like a valid post from your form, but in which he has set a value for a field you never provided in your form. This may enable him to choose an option not properly available (e.g., a Premier-customer option) or even to launch a SQL injection attack. You want to be especially careful about exposing important data such as primary keys in your HTML, and take care that what you receive from the user may not be restricted to what you provide in your form. For more information on secure coding in .NET, see *http://msdn.microsoft.com/security/*.

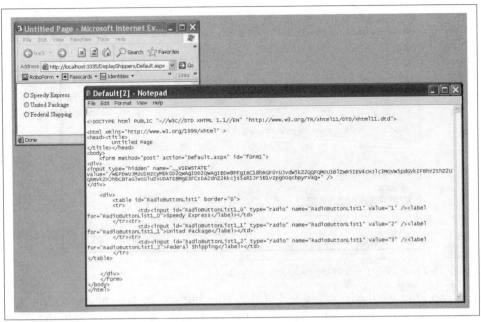

Figure 15-14. Examining the HTML that ASP.NET sends your browser

Adding Controls and Events

By adding just a few more controls, you can create a complete form with which users can interact. You will do this by adding a more appropriate greeting ("Welcome to Northwind"), a text box to accept the name of the user, two new buttons (Order and Cancel), and text that provides feedback to the user. Figure 15-15 shows the finished form.

This form won't win any awards for design, but its use will illustrate a number of key points about Web Forms.

 I've never known a developer who didn't think he could design a perfectly fine UI. At the same time, I never knew one who actually could. UI design is one of those skills (such as teaching) that we all think we possess, but only a few very talented folks are good at it. As a developer, I know my limitations: I write the code, and someone else lays it out on the page and ensures that usability issues are reviewed.

Example 15-1 is the complete HTML for the *.aspx* file.

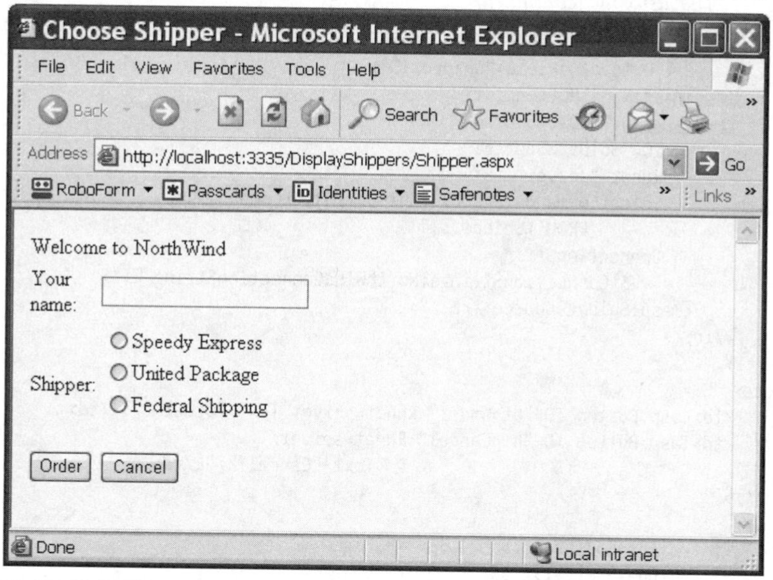

Figure 15-15. The completed shipper form

Example 15-1. The .aspx file

```
<%@ Page Language="C#" CompileWith="Shipper.aspx.cs"
  ClassName="Shipper_aspx" %>

<!DOCTYPE html PUBLIC "-//W3C//DTD XHTML 1.1//EN"
  "http://www.w3.org/TR/xhtml11/DTD/xhtml11.dtd">

<html xmlns="http://www.w3.org/1999/xhtml" >
<head runat="server">
    <title>Choose Shipper</title>
</head>
<body>
    <form id="form1" runat="server">
    <table style="width: 166px; height: 33px">
        <tr>
            <td colspan="2" style="height: 20px">Welcome to NorthWind</td>
        </tr>
        <tr>
            <td>Your name:</td>
            <td><asp:TextBox ID="txtName" Runat=server></asp:TextBox></td>
        </tr>
        <tr>
            <td>Shipper:</td>
            <td>
                <asp:RadioButtonList
                    ID="RadioButtonList1"
                    Runat="server"
                    DataSourceID="SqlDataSource1"
```

Example 15-1. The .aspx file (continued)

```
                DataTextField="CompanyName"
                DataValueField="ShipperID">
            </asp:RadioButtonList>
            <asp:SqlDataSource
            ID="SqlDataSource1"
            Runat="server"
            SelectCommand="SELECT [ShipperID], [CompanyName]
                    FROM [Shippers]"
            ConnectionString=
            "<%$ ConnectionStrings:NorthWindConnectionString %>">
            </asp:SqlDataSource> <br />
        </td>
    </tr>
    <tr>
        <td><asp:Button ID="btnOrder" Runat=server Text="Order" /></td>
        <td><asp:Button ID="btnCancel" Runat=server
                                    Text="Cancel" /></td>
    </tr>
    <tr>
        <td colspan="2"><asp:Label id="lblMsg"
            runat=server></asp:Label></td>
    </tr>
    </table>
    </form>
</body>
</html>
```

When the user clicks the Order button, you'll check that the user has filled in his name, and you'll also provide feedback on which shipper was chosen. Remember, at design time you can't know the name of the shipper (this is obtained from the database), so you'll have to ask the listbox for the chosen name (and ID).

To accomplish all of this, switch to Design mode and double-click the Order button. Visual Studio will put you in the code-behind page, and will create an event handler for the button's Click event.

 To simplify this code we will not validate that the user has entered a name in the text box. For more on the validation controls that make this simple, please see *Programming ASP.NET* (O'Reilly).

You add the event-handling code, setting the text of the label to pick up the text from the text box and the text and value from the RadioButtonList:

```
void btnOrder_Click( object sender, EventArgs e )
{

    lblMsg.Text = "Thank you " + txtName.Text.Trim() + ".  You chose " +
        rblShippers.SelectedItem.Text.ToString() + " whose ID is " +
        rblShippers.SelectedValue.ToString();
}
```

When you run this program you'll notice that none of the radio buttons is selected. Binding the list did not specify which one is the default. There are a number of ways around this, but the simplest is to override the OnLoad event and set the first radio button to be selected.

Return to *Shipper.aspx.cs* and type protected override. You will see a scrolling list of all the overrideable methods, properties, etc., as shown in Figure 15-16.

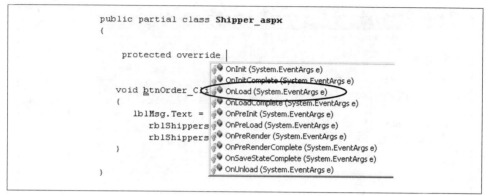

Figure 15-16. Overriding OnLoad

Start typing OnLoad; when it is highlighted press Tab. The stub for the overridden method is created, but its default body throws the NotImplementedException.

Delete the exception and replace it with this code:

```
rblShippers.SelectedIndex = 0;
```

This sets the RadioButtonList's first radio button to selected. The problem with this solution is subtle. If you run the application, you'll see that the first button is selected, but if you choose the second (or third) button and click OK, you'll find that the first button is reset. You can't seem to choose any but the first selection. This is because each time the page is loaded, the OnLoad event is run, and in that event handler you are (re-)setting the selected index.

The fact is that you only want to set this button the first time the page is selected, not when it is posted back to the browser as a result of the OK button being clicked.

To solve this, wrap the setting in an if statement that tests if the page has been posted back:

```
protected override void  OnLoad(EventArgs e)
{
    if ( !IsPostBack )
    {
        rblShippers.SelectedIndex = 0;
    }
}
```

When you run the page the IsPostBack property is checked. The first time the page is posted, this value is false and the radio button is set. If you click a radio button and then click OK, the page is sent to the server for processing (where the btnOrder_Click handler is run) and then the page is posted back to the user. This time the IsPostBack property is true, and thus the code within the if statement isn't run, and the user's choice is preserved, as shown in Figure 15-17.

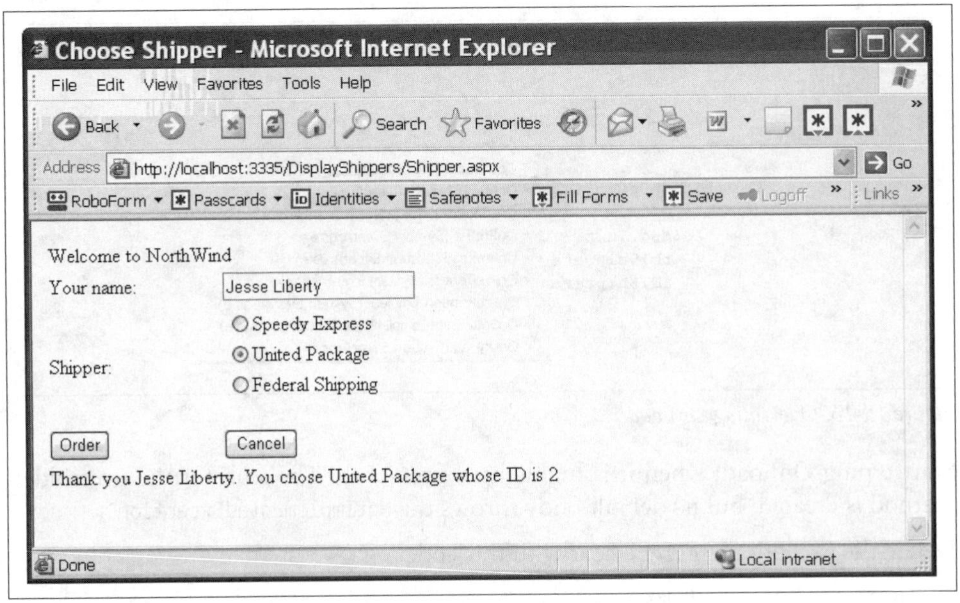

Figure 15-17. The user's choice is preserved on postback

The complete code-behind form is shown in Example 15-2.

Example 15-2. Code-behind form for Shipper.aspx.cs

```
using System;
using System.Data;
using System.Configuration;
using System.Text;
using System.Web;
using System.Web.Security;
using System.Web.UI;
using System.Web.UI.WebControls;
using System.Web.UI.WebControls.WebParts;
using System.Web.UI.HtmlControls;

public partial class Shipper_aspx
{

    protected override void OnLoad(EventArgs e)
    {
        if ( !IsPostBack )
```

Example 15-2. Code-behind form for Shipper.aspx.cs (continued)

```
    {
        rblShippers.SelectedIndex = 0;
    }
}

void btnOrder_Click( object sender, EventArgs e )
{
    lblMsg.Text = "Thank you " + txtName.Text.Trim() + ".  You chose " +
        rblShippers.SelectedItem.Text.ToString() + " whose ID is " +
        rblShippers.SelectedValue.ToString();
}
}
```

 ASP 1.1 programmers take note: as mentioned earlier, the *aspx.cs* file is now greatly simplified. You can refer to items on the page (e.g., lblMsg) without declaring protected members, and all the designer-generated code is hidden, allowing you to focus exclusively on the logic of your application.

Web Services

.NET web services help you write components whose methods can be invoked across the Internet using any .NET programming language. Developers who are creating web services can build one upon another, taking advantage of the connectivity that is at the heart of the Web. Adding value takes precedence over reinventing the wheel.

The list of web services that might be useful to developers and end users seems boundless. A bookstore might provide a web service that takes an ISBN and returns the price and availability of a title. A hotel's web service might take a date range and number of guests and return a reservation. Another web service might take a telephone number and return a name and address. Yet another might provide information about the weather or shuttle launches.

A single application might draw on and stitch together the services of hundreds of small web services distributed all over the world. This takes the Web to an entirely new dimension: not only is information retrieved and exchanged, but also methods are invoked and applications are executed.

SOAP, WSDL, and Discovery

What is needed to make web services possible is a simple, universally accepted protocol for exposing and invoking web service functions.* In 1999, Simple Object Access Protocol (SOAP) was proposed to the World Wide Web Consortium. SOAP has the advantages of being based on XML and of using standard Internet communications protocols.

 Since 1999 SOAP ceased to stand for anything, on the grounds that having "object" in there was misleading because SOAP isn't about objects; rather, it is about messaging. The second, more recent change was a new reverse-engineered term: the Service Oriented Architecture Protocol.

SOAP is a lightweight, message-based protocol built on XML, HTTP, and SMTP. Two other protocols are desirable, but not required, for a client to use a SOAP-enabled web service: a description of the methods provided by a particular service that can be understood and acted upon by clients, and a description of all such services available at a particular site or URL. The first of these is provided in .NET by the Web Service Description Language (WSDL), jointly developed by Microsoft, IBM, and others.

WSDL is an XML schema used to describe the available methods—the interface—of a web service.

Server-Side Support

The plumbing necessary to create web services is integrated into the .NET Framework and provided by classes within the System.Web.Services namespace. Creating a web service requires no special programming on your part; you need only write the implementing code, add the [WebMethod] attribute, and let the server do the rest. You can read about attributes in detail in Chapter 18.

Client-Side Support

You make use of a web service by writing client code that acts as though it were communicating directly with a local object, but in reality communicates with a host server through a *proxy*. The job of the proxy is to represent the server on the client machine, to bundle client requests into SOAP messages that are sent on to the server, and to retrieve the responses that contain the result.

---

* This is a very Remote-Procedure-Call-oriented view of SOAP because that is how .NET encourages the developer to use SOAP. In reality, SOAP is designed to pass messages; but the .NET architecture implements that message-passing to invoke methods and access properties on a remote object.

Building a Web Service

To illustrate the techniques used to implement a web service in C# using the services classes of the .NET Framework, build a simple calculator and then make use of its functions over the Web.

Begin by specifying the web service. To do so, define a class that inherits from System.Web.Services.WebService. The easiest way to create this class is to open Visual Studio and create a new C# web site. In the Templates section choose ASP.NET Web Service and name your web service CalculatorWS, as shown in Figure 15-18.

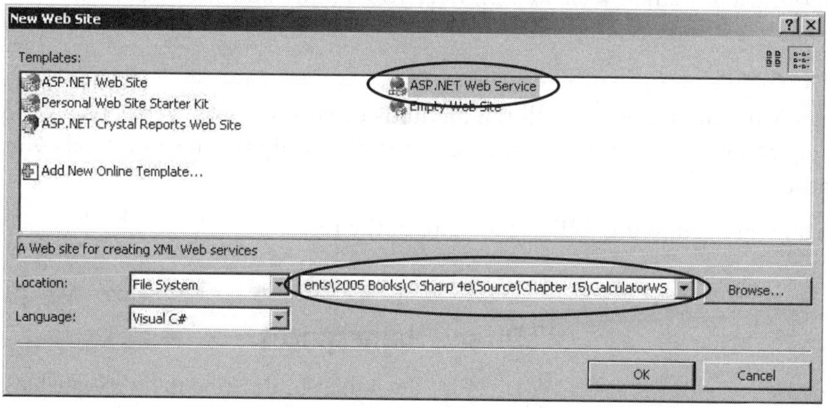

Figure 15-18. Creating a web service

Visual Studio .NET creates a skeleton web service and even provides a web service example method for you to replace with your own code, as shown in Example 15-3.

Example 15-3. Skeleton web class generated by Visual Studio .NET

```
using System.Web;
using System.Web.Services;
using System.Web.Services.Protocols;

[WebServiceBinding(ConformanceClaims=WsiClaims.BP10,EmitConformanceClaims = true)]
public class Service : System.Web.Services.WebService {

    [WebMethod]
    public string HelloWorld() {
        return "Hello World";
    }
}
```

To flesh out the calculator, replace the HelloWorld method with five other methods: Add(), Sub(), Mult(), Div(), and Pow(). Each takes two parameters of type double, performs the requested operation, and then returns a value of the same type. For example, here is the code for raising a number to some specified power:

```
public double Pow(double x, double y)
{
    double retVal = x;
    for (int i = 0;i < y-1;i++)
    {
        retVal *= x;
    }
    return retVal;
}
```

To expose each method as a web service, you simply add the [WebMethod] attribute before each method declaration:

```
[WebMethod]
```

You aren't required to expose all the methods of your class as web services. You can pick and choose, adding the [WebMethod] attribute only to those methods you want to expose.

That's all you need to do; .NET takes care of the rest.

WSDL and Namespaces

Your web service will use a WSDL XML document to describe the web-callable end points. Within any WSDL document, an XML namespace must be used to ensure that the end points have unique names. The default XML namespace is *http://tempuri.org*, but you will want to modify this before making your web service publicly available.

You can change the XML namespace by using the WebService attribute:

```
[WebService(Namespace=
        "http://www.LibertyAssociates.com/webServices/")]
```

There is no expectation that there will be a document at this URL; URLs are used because they are a convenient source of unique names.

Example 15-4 shows the complete source code for the calculator web service.

Example 15-4. Calculator web service program

```
using System.Web;
using System.Web.Services;
using System.Web.Services.Protocols;

[WebServiceBinding(ConformanceClaims=WsiClaims.BP10,EmitConformanceClaims = true)]
public class Service : System.Web.Services.WebService {

    [WebMethod]
```

Example 15-4. Calculator web service program (continued)

```
    public double Add( double x, double y )
    {
        return x + y;
    }

    [WebMethod]
    public double Sub( double x, double y )
    {
        return x - y;
    }
    [WebMethod]
    public double Mult( double x, double y )
    {
        return x * y;
    }
    [WebMethod]
    public double Div( double x, double y )
    {
        return x / y;
    }
    [WebMethod]
    public double Pow( double x, double y )
    {
        double retVal = x;
        for ( int i = 0; i < y - 1; i++ )
        {
            retVal *= x;
        }
        return retVal;
    }
}
```

Testing Your Web Service

If you invoke the browser by running the program in Visual Studio .NET, you will see an automatically generated, server-side web page that describes the web service, as shown in Figure 15-19. This page offers a good way to test your web service.

Clicking a method brings you to a page that describes the method and allows you to invoke it by typing in parameters and pressing the Clicking button. Figure 15-20 illustrates.

If you type 3 into the first value field, 4 into the second field, and click Invoke, you will have asked the web service to raise 3 to the fourth power. The result is an XML page describing the output, as shown in Figure 15-21.

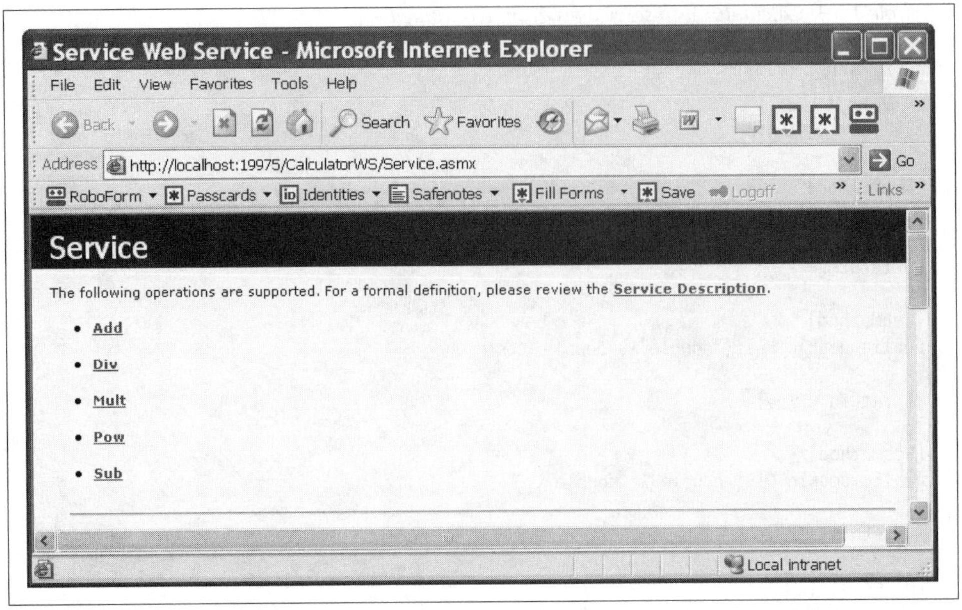

Figure 15-19. Viewing the web service test page

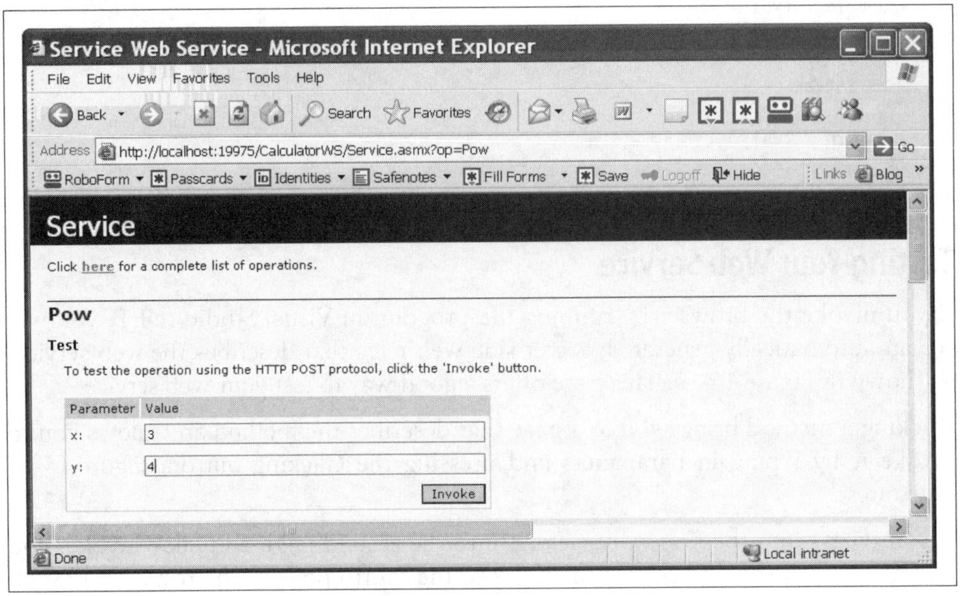

Figure 15-20. Testing the Pow( ) web service method

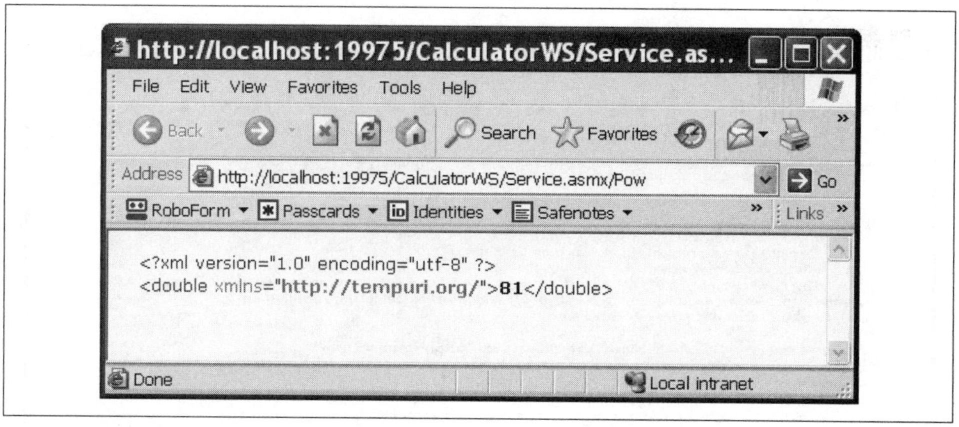

Figure 15-21. Invoking the Pow( ) method

Viewing the WSDL Contract

A lot of work is being done for you automatically. HTML pages describing your web service and its methods are generated, and these pages include links to pages in which the methods can be tested.

All web services can be described in WSDL files. You can see the WSDL document by appending ?WSDL to the web service URL, like this:

```
http://localhost:19975/CalculatorWS/Service.asmx?wsdl
```

The browser displays the WSDL document, as shown in Figure 15-22.

The details of the WSDL document are beyond the scope of this book, but you can see that each method is fully described in a structured XML format. This is the information used by SOAP to allow the client browser to invoke your web service methods on the server.

Creating the Proxy

Before you can create a client application to interact with the calculator web service, you will first create a proxy class. Once again, you can do this by hand, but that would be hard work. The folks at Microsoft have provided a tool called *wsdl* that generates the source code for the proxy based on the information in the WSDL file.

To create the proxy, enter wsdl at the Visual Studio command-line prompt, followed by the path to the WSDL contract. For example, you might enter:

```
wsdl http://localhost:19975/CalculatorWS/Service.asmx?wsdl
```

The result is the creation of a C# client file named *Service1.cs*, an excerpt of which appears in Example 15-5.

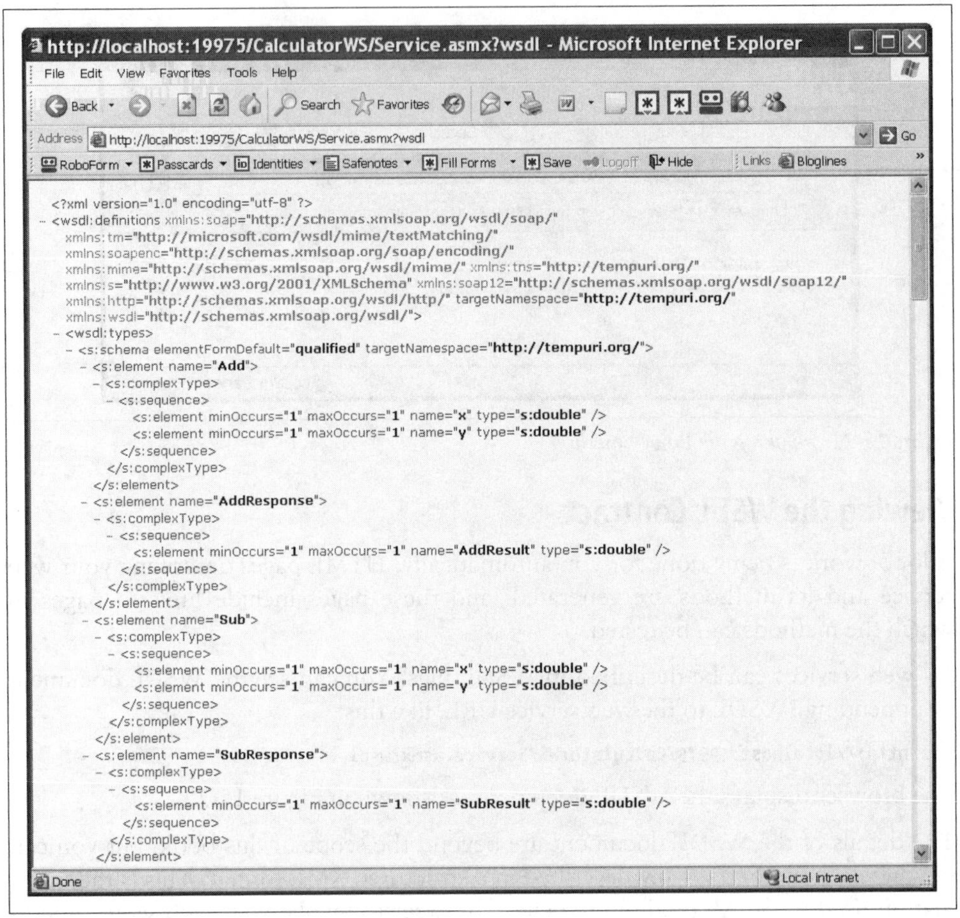

Figure 15-22. Viewing the WSDL

Example 15-5. Sample client code to access the calculator web service

```
//------------------------------------------------------------------
// <autogenerated>
//      This code was generated by a tool.
//      Runtime Version:2.0.40607.16
//
//      Changes to this file may cause incorrect behavior and
//      will be lost if the code is regenerated.
// </autogenerated>
//------------------------------------------------------------------

using System;
using System.ComponentModel;
using System.Diagnostics;
using System.Web.Services;
using System.Web.Services.Protocols;
using System.Xml.Serialization;
```

Example 15-5. Sample client code to access the calculator web service (continued)

```
//
// This source code was auto-generated by wsdl, Version=2.0.40607.16.
//

/// <remarks/>
[System.Diagnostics.DebuggerStepThroughAttribute()]
[System.ComponentModel.DesignerCategoryAttribute("code")]
[System.Web.Services.WebServiceBindingAttribute(Name="ServiceSoap",
Namespace="http://tempuri.org/")]

public class Service : System.Web.Services.Protocols.SoapHttpClientProtocol
{

    private System.Threading.SendOrPostCallback AddOperationCompleted;

    private System.Threading.SendOrPostCallback SubOperationCompleted;

    private System.Threading.SendOrPostCallback MultOperationCompleted;

    private System.Threading.SendOrPostCallback DivOperationCompleted;

    private System.Threading.SendOrPostCallback PowOperationCompleted;

    /// <remarks/>
    public Service() {
        this.Url = "http://localhost:19975/CalculatorWS/Service.asmx";
    }

    /// <remarks/>
    public event AddCompletedEventHandler AddCompleted;

    /// <remarks/>
    public event SubCompletedEventHandler SubCompleted;

    /// <remarks/>
    public event MultCompletedEventHandler MultCompleted;

    /// <remarks/>
    public event DivCompletedEventHandler DivCompleted;

    /// <remarks/>
    public event PowCompletedEventHandler PowCompleted;

    /// <remarks/>
    [System.Web.Services.Protocols.SoapDocumentMethodAttribute
    ("http://tempuri.org/Add", RequestNamespace="http://tempuri.org/",
    ResponseNamespace="http://tempuri.org/",
    Use=System.Web.Services.Description.SoapBindingUse.Literal,
    ParameterStyle=System.Web.Services.Protocols.SoapParameterStyle.Wrapped)]
    public double Add(double x, double y) {
        object[] results = this.Invoke("Add", new object[] {
```

```
                      x,
                      y});
        return ((double)(results[0]));
    }


    /// <remarks/>
    public System.IAsyncResult BeginAdd(double x, double y, System.AsyncCallback callback,
object asyncState) {
        return this.BeginInvoke("Add", new object[] {
                    x,
                    y}, callback, asyncState);
    }


    /// <remarks/>
    public double EndAdd(System.IAsyncResult asyncResult) {
        object[] results = this.EndInvoke(asyncResult);
        return ((double)(results[0]));
    }


    /// <remarks/>
    public void AddAsync(double x, double y) {
        this.AddAsync(x, y, null);
    }


    /// <remarks/>
    public void AddAsync(double x, double y, object userState) {
        if ((this.AddOperationCompleted == null)) {
            this.AddOperationCompleted = new
              System.Threading.SendOrPostCallback(
                this.OnAddOperationCompleted);
        }
        this.InvokeAsync("Add", new object[] {
                    x,
                    y}, this.AddOperationCompleted, userState);
    }


    private void OnAddOperationCompleted(object arg) {
        if ((this.AddCompleted != null)) {
            System.Web.Services.Protocols.
              InvokeCompletedEventArgs invokeArgs =
              ((System.Web.Services.Protocols.InvokeCompletedEventArgs)
              (arg));

            this.AddCompleted(this,
              new AddCompletedEventArgs(invokeArgs.Results,
              invokeArgs.Error, invokeArgs.Cancelled,
              invokeArgs.UserState));
        }
    }


    /// <remarks/>
    //...
```

This complex code is produced by the WSDL tool to build the proxy DLL you will need when you build your client. The file uses attributes extensively, but with your working knowledge of C# you can extrapolate at least how some of it works.

The file starts by declaring the Service1 class that derives from the SoapHttp-ClientProtocol class, which occurs in the namespace called System.Web.Services.Protocols:

```
public class Service1 :
    System.Web.Services.Protocols.SoapHttpClientProtocol
```

The constructor sets the URL property inherited from SoapHttpClientProtocol to the URL of the *.asmx* page you created earlier.

The Add() method is declared with a host of attributes that provide the SOAP plumbing to make the remote invocation work.

The WSDL application has also provided asynchronous support for your methods. For example, for the Add() method, it also created BeginAdd() and EndAdd(). This allows you to interact with a web service without performance penalties.

Testing the Web Service

To test the web service, create a simple C# console application. Right-click the project, and add the *Service1.cs* file you created from the console window. Visual Studio will create a proxy for you named theWebSvc.

This done, you can invoke the Pow() method as if it were a method on a locally available object:

```
for (int i = 2;i<10; i++)
    for (int j = 1;j <10;j++)
    {
        Console.WriteLine(
          "{0} to the power of {1} = {2}", i, j,
          theWebSvc.Pow(i, j));
    }
```

This simple loop creates a table of the powers of the numbers 2 through 9, displaying for each the powers 1 through 9. The complete source code and an excerpt of the output is shown in Example 15-6.

Example 15-6. A client program to test the calculator web service

```
#region Using directives

using System;
using System.Collections.Generic;
using System.Text;

#endregion
```

Example 15-6. A client program to test the calculator web service (continued)

```
namespace CalculatorTest
{
   class Program
   {
// driver program to test the web service
      public class Tester
      {
         public static void Main()
         {
            Tester t = new Tester();
            t.Run();
         }

         public void Run()
         {
            int var1 = 5;
            int var2 = 7;

            // instantiate the web service proxy
            Service theWebSvc = new Service();

            // call the add method
            Console.WriteLine( "{0} + {1} = {2}", var1, var2,
               theWebSvc.Add( var1, var2 ) );

            // build a table by repeatedly calling the pow method
            for ( int i = 2; i < 10; i++ )
               for ( int j = 1; j < 10; j++ )
               {
                  Console.WriteLine( "{0} to the power of {1} = {2}",
                     i, j, theWebSvc.Pow( i, j ) );
               }
         }
      }
   }
}

Output (excerpt):
5 + 7 = 12
2 to the power of 1 = 2
2 to the power of 2 = 4
2 to the power of 3 = 8
2 to the power of 4 = 16
2 to the power of 5 = 32
2 to the power of 6 = 64
2 to the power of 7 = 128
2 to the power of 8 = 256
2 to the power of 9 = 512
3 to the power of 1 = 3
3 to the power of 2 = 9
3 to the power of 3 = 27
3 to the power of 4 = 81
```

Example 15-6. A client program to test the calculator web service (continued)

```
3 to the power of 5 = 243
3 to the power of 6 = 729
3 to the power of 7 = 2187
3 to the power of 8 = 6561
3 to the power of 9 = 19683
```

CHAPTER 16

Putting It All Together

In this chapter, you will use many of the skills acquired so far to build a set of integrated applications. The goal of these applications is to track the relative Amazon.com sales standings of my books on C#, ASP.NET, and VB.NET.

The Overall Design

To see how various technologies work together you will actually build two independent applications (a desktop application web services client and an ASP.NET application) tied together by a backend database. Specifically, you'll create a desktop application that obtains data from Amazon's web service and stores it in a table in a SQL Server database, and then you'll display that data in your ASP.NET application.*

The SQL Server database is very simple. It is named AmazonSalesRanks and consists of a single table, BookInfo, as shown in Figure 16-1.

 All the fields in this table are allowed to be null because you can't control what information may or may not be available from Amazon at any particular moment. To make this design more robust, you might consider making the ISBN a primary key and rejecting any data that returns without an ISBN. This is left, as they say, as an exercise for the reader.

Creating the Web Services Client

In an effort to make its information available to developers and "Amazon Associates" (sites that allow its users to purchase books through Amazon.com), Amazon

---

* Content on Amazon is copyrighted and can't be used without written permission. Such permission was graciously provided for this book and for use on my web site, *http://www.LibertyAssociates.com*.

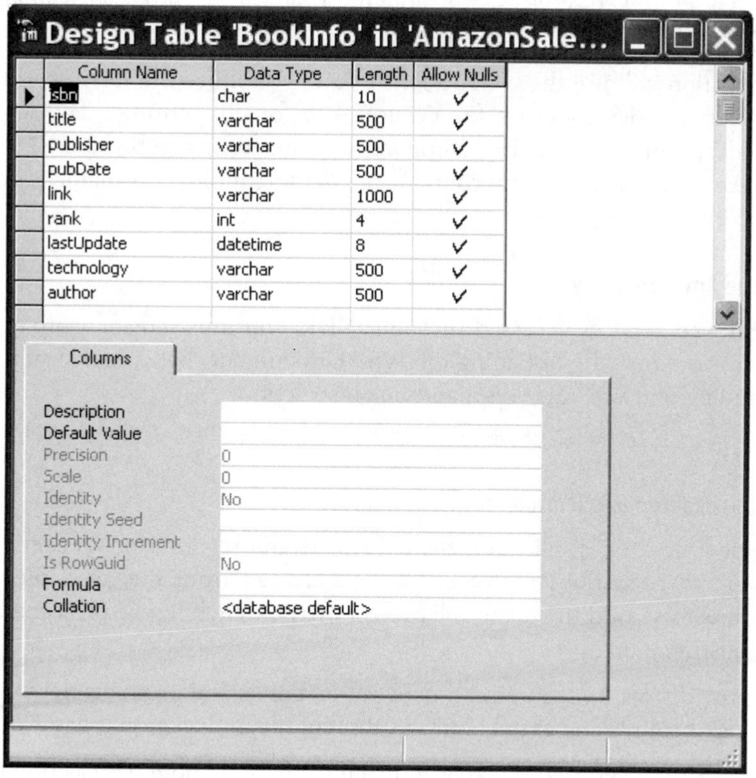

Figure 16-1. Designing the BookInfo table

The Screen-Scraper Application

In previous editions of this book, we first implemented the desktop application as a screen-scraper that downloaded data from Amazon.com.

At that time, I pointed out that screen-scraping works great as long as Amazon always lists the rank in exactly this way, but if it doesn't, the parsing will fail. Each time Amazon changes its pages, you must upgrade this program. In addition, I pointed out that the data on Amazon's pages is copyrighted, and so there are serious legal and ethical issues about scraping Amazon's pages.

Since the publication of the previous edition, Amazon has instituted security on its site that blocks simple screen-scraping applications. Since it also provides extensive support for web services, this chapter will implement the application using those web services, and we'll cover screen-scraping in Chapter 21, where we'll (legally and ethically) scrape screens from my own web site.

has created a set of web services. For more information, see *http://www.amazon.com/gp/aws/landing.html*.

Your application will use these web services, and you'll need to download the Amazon Web Services developer kit for Version 4 (as of this writing). The three things you'll need are an associatesTag (supplied by Amazon), a subscriberID (also supplied by Amazon), and the appropriate *.wsdl* file (publicly available through the Amazon Web Services pages).

Creating the Amazon proxy

As with all web services accessed through .NET, you must create a proxy class for your client. You do so by obtaining the WSDL document that Amazon supplies, and then compiling that with the command-line instruction:

```
wsdl /o:Amazon.cs AmazonWebServices.wsdl
```

Creating the desktop application

Create a new desktop application named (for example) AmazonWebServiceClient, and be sure to copy the *Amazon.cs* file you created from the *.wsdl* file into that project's directory. Add the file to the project by right-clicking the project and choosing Add Existing Item.

Amazon provides far more information about its books and products than we'll need, so we'll keep it simple and extract only a subset of the information it has available.

In addition, it provides methods that return information about a collection of books, but for now we'll greatly simplify the process (while sacrificing performance) by looking up each book one by one.

To do so you'll create a set of XML files to contain the ISBNs of the books you want to track. I've divided these by technology so that I have a *CSharpISBN.xml* file, a *VBNETISBN.xml* file, and an *ASPNET_ISBN.xml* file.

Example 16-1 shows an excerpt from one of these files.

Example 16-1. CSharpISBN.xml

```
<isbns>
 <isbn>193183654X</isbn>
 <isbn>0130461334</isbn>
 <isbn>1893115593</isbn>
 <isbn>0130622214</isbn>
 <isbn>1861007043</isbn>
 <isbn>1861004982</isbn>
 <isbn>0672320711</isbn>
 <isbn>0596001819</isbn>
 <isbn>0735612897</isbn>
 <isbn>0735612900</isbn>
 <isbn>0596003099</isbn>
```

Example 16-1. CSharpISBN.xml (continued)

```
<isbn>0596003765</isbn>
<isbn>0072133295</isbn>
<isbn>0672322358</isbn>
<isbn>0072193794</isbn>
<isbn>067232122X</isbn>
<isbn>1588801926</isbn>
<isbn>0672321521</isbn>
<isbn>0735615683</isbn>
<isbn>0201729555</isbn>
</isbns>
```

 The problem, of course, is that these files are often out of date (some books go out of print, new books become available). We'll solve that problem later in this chapter.

As each ISBN is read, the relevant values (title, publisher, rank) are found on the Amazon web site and stored in the Database table. A simple listbox is then updated to indicate progress. Once all the books are recorded, the system becomes dormant while a timer ticks down the remaining time between sessions. You can force a new session by clicking the Now button. This UI was intentionally created to be as simple as possible.

Example 16-2 is the complete desktop application, with analysis to follow.

Example 16-2. SalesRankDBWebServices

```csharp
#region Using directives

using System;
using System.Collections.Generic;
using System.ComponentModel;
using System.Data;
using System.Drawing;
using System.Windows.Forms;

#endregion

namespace AmazonWebServiceClient
{
    partial class AmazonWebServiceClient : Form
    {
        private int timeRemaining;
        const int WaitTime = 900; // 15 minutes
        private string connectionString;
        private System.Data.SqlClient.SqlConnection connection;
        private System.Data.SqlClient.SqlCommand command;

        public AmazonWebServiceClient()
        {
```

Example 16-2. SalesRankDBWebServices (continued)

```
      InitializeComponent();
   }

   private void AmazonWebServiceClient_Load( object sender, EventArgs e )
   {
      // connection string to connect to the Sales Rank Database
      connectionString =
"server=localhost;Trusted_Connection=true;database=AmazonSalesRanks";

      // Create connection object, initialize with
      // connection string.
      connection =
         new System.Data.SqlClient.SqlConnection( connectionString );

      // Create a SqlCommand object and assign the connection
      command =
         new System.Data.SqlClient.SqlCommand();

      command.Connection = connection;
      timeRemaining = 1;  // when you first start up, get the info.
      UpdateButton();

   }

   private void btnStart_Click( object sender, EventArgs e )
   {
      // toggle the timer
      updateTimer.Enabled = updateTimer.Enabled ? false : true;
      UpdateButton();

   }

   private void btnNow_Click( object sender, EventArgs e )
   {
      timeRemaining = 2;
   }

   private void UpdateButton()
   {
      btnStart.Text = updateTimer.Enabled ? "Stop" : "Start";
   }

   private void updateTimer_Tick( object sender, EventArgs e )
   {

      if ( updateTimer.Enabled )
         txtClock.Text = ( --timeRemaining ).ToString() + " seconds";
      else
         txtClock.Text = "Stopped";

      // hi ho, hi ho, it's off to work we go...
      if ( timeRemaining < 1 )
```

Example 16-2. SalesRankDBWebServices (continued)

```
    {
        timeRemaining = WaitTime;   // reset the clock

        // create data set based on xml file
        DataSet BookData = new DataSet();
        BookData.ReadXml( "aspnet_isbn.xml" );

        // iterate through, calling GetInfoFromISBN for
        // each isbn found in file
        foreach ( DataRow Book in BookData.Tables[0].Rows )
        {
            string isbn = Book[0].ToString();
            GetInfoFromISBN( isbn, "ASPNET" );
        }

        BookData = new DataSet();
        BookData.ReadXml( "csharpIsbn.xml" );
        foreach ( DataRow Book in BookData.Tables[0].Rows )
        {
            string isbn = Book[0].ToString();
            GetInfoFromISBN( isbn, "CSHARP" );
        }

        BookData = new DataSet();
        BookData.ReadXml( "VBnetIsbn.xml" );
        foreach ( DataRow Book in BookData.Tables[0].Rows )
        {
            string isbn = Book[0].ToString();
            GetInfoFromISBN( isbn, "VBNET" );
        }
    }
}

private void GetInfoFromISBN( string isbn, string technology )
{
    if ( isbn.Length != 10 )
        return;


    AWSProductData productData = new AWSProductData();
    ItemLookup lookup = null;
    try
    {
        ItemLookupRequest req = new ItemLookupRequest();
        req.IdType = ItemLookupRequestIdType.ASIN;
        req.ItemId = new string[1];
        req.ItemId[0] = isbn;
        // req.SearchIndex = "Books";

        lookup = new ItemLookup();
        lookup.AssociateTag = "libertyassocia00A";
        lookup.SubscriptionId = "0SD959SZV6KXV3BKE2R2";
```

Example 16-2. SalesRankDBWebServices (continued)

```
        lookup.Request = new ItemLookupRequest[1];
        lookup.Request[0] = req;
    }
    catch ( System.Exception e )
    {
        lblStatus.Text = e.Message;
    }

    ItemLookupResponse response;
    Items info;
    Item[] items;
    Item item;

    int salesRank = -1;
    string author = string.Empty;
    string pubDate = string.Empty;
    string publisher = string.Empty;
    string title = string.Empty;
    string strURL = string.Empty;

    try
    {
        response = productData.ItemLookup( lookup );
        info = response.Items[0];
        items = info.Item;
        item = items[0];
        salesRank = item.SalesRank == null
          ? -1 : Convert.ToInt32(item.SalesRank);
        author = FixQuotes( item.ItemAttributes.Author[0] );
        pubDate =   FixQuotes(item.ItemAttributes.PublicationDate);
        publisher = FixQuotes(item.ItemAttributes.Publisher);
        title = FixQuotes(item.ItemAttributes.Title);
        strURL = item.DetailPageURL;
    }
    catch ( System.Exception ex)
    {
        lblStatus.Text = ex.Message;
    }

    // update the list box
    string results = title + " by " + author + ": " +
        publisher + ", " + pubDate + ". Rank: " + salesRank;
    lbOutput.Items.Add( results );
    lbOutput.SelectedIndex = lbOutput.Items.Count - 1;

    // update the database
    string commandString = @"Update BookInfo set isbn = '" +
        isbn + "', title = '" + title + "', publisher = '" +
        publisher + "', pubDate = '" + pubDate + "', rank = " +
        salesRank + ", link = '" + strURL + "', lastUpdate = '" +
        System.DateTime.Now + "', technology = '" +
        technology + "', author = '" +
```

Example 16-2. SalesRankDBWebServices (continued)

```
             author + "' where isbn = '" +
             isbn + "'";

      command.CommandText = commandString;
      try
      {
         // if no rows were affected, this is a new record
         connection.Open();
         int numRowsAffected = command.ExecuteNonQuery();
         if ( numRowsAffected == 0 )
         {
            commandString = @"Insert into BookInfo values ('" +
               isbn + "', '" + title + "', '" + publisher + "', '" +
               pubDate + "', '" + FixQuotes( strURL ) + "', " +
               salesRank + ", '" +
               System.DateTime.Now +
               "', '" + technology + "', '" + author + "')";

            command.CommandText = commandString;
            command.ExecuteNonQuery();
         }
      }
      catch ( Exception ex )
      {
         lblStatus.Text = ex.Message;
         lbOutput.Items.Add( "Unable to update database!" );
         lbOutput.SelectedIndex = lbOutput.Items.Count - 1;
      }
      finally
      {
         connection.Close();        // clean up
      }
   }     // close for GetInfoFromISBN

   private string FixQuotes( string s )
   {
      if ( s == null )
         return string.Empty;
      return s.Replace( "'", "''" );

   }
} // end class
} // end name space
```

The program declares a connection string, along with SQLConnection and SQLCommand objects which will be initialized when the form is loaded:

```
private string connectionString;
private System.Data.SqlClient.SqlConnection connection;
private System.Data.SqlClient.SqlCommand command;
```

You can set the Load event by clicking the form and switching from Properties to Events. Double-click the Load event and the skeleton for the load event handler is created for you. Within that event handler, you'll create your connection string (this example uses a trusted connection; you may need to provide a username and password depending on how your database is configured), and the connection and command objects are configured:

```
private void AmazonWebServiceClient_Load( object sender, EventArgs e )
{
   connectionString =
     "server=localhost;Trusted_Connection=true;database=AmazonSalesRanks";
   connection =
      new System.Data.SqlClient.SqlConnection( connectionString );
   command =
      new System.Data.SqlClient.SqlCommand();

   command.Connection = connection;
```

The member variable timeRemaining is initialized to one second, and the buttons are updated to set the text on the Start button:

```
   timeRemaining = 1;  // when you first start up, get the info.
   UpdateButton();


}
```

Each time the timer clicks, the updateTimer_Tick method is called. If the timer is enabled (the user has not clicked Stop), the timeRemaining member variable is decremented, and when it hits 0 it is time to process the books:

```
if ( updateTimer.Enabled )
   txtClock.Text = ( --timeRemaining ).ToString() + " seconds";
else
   txtClock.Text = "Stopped";

// hi ho, hi ho, it's off to work we go...
if ( timeRemaining < 1 )
{
```

The first step is to reset the timer to WaitTime (a constant equivalent to 15 minutes) and then to process the *.xml* files:

```
timeRemaining = WaitTime;  // reset the clock
DataSet BookData = new DataSet();
try
{
   BookData.ReadXml( "aspnet_isbn.xml" );
}
```

This creates a dataset, in which each row represents an entry in the XML file. Once the books are read, you extract each ISBN in turn, and call the helper method GetInfoFromISBN, passing in the ISBN and the "technology" under which this ISBN will be stored in the database:

```
foreach ( DataRow Book in BookData.Tables[0].Rows )
{
    string isbn = Book[0].ToString();
    GetInfoFromISBN( isbn, "ASPNET" );
}
```

GetInfoFromISBN is the heart of the program; it is here that you contact the Amazon Web Service.

The first step is to ensure that the length of the ISBN is exactly 10 (a full check would use a regular expression to ensure that the ISBN is 9 integers followed by either an integer or the letter X, and then to perform a checksum on the ISBN [the final digit represents the checksum value], but that is left as an exercise for the reader).

The *Amazon.cs* file defines a number of useful objects. The ones we'll use for this example include the AWSProductData, the ItemLookup and ItemLookupRequest, as well as the Item objects and collections. Here are the steps:

1. Declare a new instance of the AWSProductData, which acts as the proxy to the Amazon web service.

2. Call the ItemLookup method on the AWSProductData instance, passing in a properly initialized instance of ItemLookup.

3. Get back an ItemLookupResponse object.

4. Extract the Items array and from that get the first object (offset 0), an object of type Items.

5. Ask that Items object for its Item property, which is an array of Items objects.

6. Get the first Item in the array and from that Item, get all the information about the book you've requested.

To make this work, you must first create an instance of ItemLookupRequest and set its IDType property to the enumerated type ItemLookupRequestIdType.ASIN:

```
ItemLookupRequest req = new ItemLookupRequest();
req.IdType = ItemLookupRequestIdType.ASIN;
```

Initialize its ItemID array to hold one string, and set that string to the ISBN you are looking for:

```
req.ItemId = new string[1];
req.ItemId[0] = isbn;
```

Next, instantiate an ItemLookup object, and set its AssociateTag and SubscriptionID properties:

```
lookup.AssociateTag = "libertyassocia00A";
lookup.SubscriptionId = "Your ID Here";
```

Initialize its Request property to be an array of one object, and set that object to the ItemLookupRequest object you created earlier:

```
lookup.Request = new ItemLookupRequest[1];
lookup.Request[0] = req;
```

Note that we're using the method-invocation idiom as .NET assumes, but what is really going on is that we're using SOAP to exchange messages with Amazon. We send "tell me about this book" and Amazon returns "here is information about the book."

You're ready to make your request. Do so in a try block to catch any exceptions that might be thrown in the process. Begin by invoking the ItemLookup method:

```
response = productData.ItemLookup( lookup );
```

Response should now be non-null. You might add error checking to handle a null response from Amazon (left out here to simplify the code). The Item property returns an object of type Items, which is an array of Item objects. You will extract the first Item object, which will contain information about the book you've requested:

```
info = response.Items[0];
items = info.Item;
item = items[0];
```

You can now set local variables to hold the values you've retrieved. The FixQuotes method is a helper method to convert single quotes in any string you receive so that they will not cause problems for the database:

```
salesRank = item.SalesRank == null ? -1 : Convert.ToInt32(item.SalesRank);
author = FixQuotes( item.ItemAttributes.Author[0] );
pubDate =   FixQuotes(item.ItemAttributes.PublicationDate);
publisher = FixQuotes(item.ItemAttributes.Publisher);
title = FixQuotes(item.ItemAttributes.Title);
strURL = item.DetailPageURL;
```

With this information in hand, you are ready to update the listbox and, more important, to update the database.

When updating the database, you'll first try an Update statement. If the number of rows affected is 0, the row doesn't yet exist in the database, so you'll insert the values.

This program would be more secure if it used parameterized queries. The query is left in-line to keep the example simple.

With that done, you're ready to move on to the next ISBN.

Displaying the Output

This time, we'll create a new ASP.NET web site, called AmazonSalesRanks, to display the information returned from Amazon. Drag three GridView objects onto the form, but don't set up their data-binding; we'll do so by hand. Example 16-3 shows the complete *.aspx* page, including the message printed above the grids, the titles for the grids, the last update label, and the text box used to decide how many rows to show in each grid.

Example 16-3. Displaying the output

```
<%@ Page Language="C#" CompileWith="Default.aspx.cs" ClassName="Default_aspx" %>

<!DOCTYPE html PUBLIC "-//W3C//DTD XHTML 1.1//EN"
                      "http://www.w3.org/TR/xhtml11/DTD/xhtml11.dtd">

<html xmlns="http://www.w3.org/1999/xhtml" >
<head runat="server">
    <title>Sales Ranks</title>
</head>
<body>
    <form id="form1" runat="server">
    <div>
        The data found here is from the Amazon Web Service and
        is stored in a local database. The data is updated every 15
        <br />
        minutes. This is a work in progress.<br />
         <br />
        <b>ASP Titles</b>
        <asp:GridView ID="gvASP" Runat="server"
        OnRowDataBound="RowDataBound"
        AutoGenerateColumns="false"
        HeaderStyle-BackColor="PapayaWhip"
        BorderColor="#000099"
        AlternatingRowStyle-BackColor="LightGrey"
        HeaderStyle-Font-Bold=true
        Width="900">
            <Columns>
                <asp:TemplateField HeaderStyle-Width ="10">
                    <HeaderTemplate>
                        Position
                    </HeaderTemplate>
                    <ItemTemplate>
                        <asp:Label Runat="server" ID="Label1">
                          <%# rowNumber %></asp:Label>
                    </ItemTemplate>
                </asp:TemplateField>
                <asp:TemplateField>
                    <HeaderTemplate>
                        Title
                    </HeaderTemplate>
                    <ItemTemplate>
                    <a href="http://www.amazon.com/exec/obidos/ASIN/<%#
                           Eval("isbn")%>/" target="_blank"><%# Eval("title") %></a>
                    </ItemTemplate>
                </asp:TemplateField>
                <asp:BoundField HeaderText="Author"
                    ReadOnly="true" DataField="Author" />
                <asp:BoundField HeaderText="Publisher"
```

Example 16-3. Displaying the output (continued)

```
                ReadOnly="true" DataField="Publisher" />
        <asp:BoundField HeaderText="Publish Date"
            ReadOnly="true" DataField="pubDate" />
        <asp:BoundField HeaderText="Rank"
            ReadOnly="true" DataField="Rank"
            DataFormatString="{0:N0}"
            ItemStyle-HorizontalAlign="right" />
    </Columns>
</asp:GridView>
<br />
<b>ASP Titles</b>
<asp:GridView ID="gvCSharp" Runat="server"
OnRowDataBound="RowDataBound"
AutoGenerateColumns="false"
HeaderStyle-BackColor="PapayaWhip"
BorderColor="#000099"
AlternatingRowStyle-BackColor="LightGrey"
HeaderStyle-Font-Bold=true
Width="900">
    <Columns>
        <asp:TemplateField HeaderStyle-Width ="10">
            <HeaderTemplate>
                Position
            </HeaderTemplate>
            <ItemTemplate>
                <asp:Label Runat="server" ID="Label2">
                  <%# rowNumber %></asp:Label>
            </ItemTemplate>
        </asp:TemplateField>
        <asp:TemplateField>
            <HeaderTemplate>
                Title
            </HeaderTemplate>
            <ItemTemplate>
              <a href="http://www.amazon.com/exec/obidos/ASIN/<%#
                  Eval("isbn")%>/" target="_blank"><%# Eval("title") %></a>
            </ItemTemplate>
        </asp:TemplateField>
        <asp:BoundField HeaderText="Author"
          ReadOnly="true" DataField="Author" />
        <asp:BoundField HeaderText="Publisher"
          ReadOnly="true" DataField="Publisher" />
        <asp:BoundField HeaderText="Publish Date"
          ReadOnly="true" DataField="pubDate" />
        <asp:BoundField HeaderText="Rank"
          ReadOnly="true" DataField="Rank"
          DataFormatString="{0:N0}"
          ItemStyle-HorizontalAlign="right" />
    </Columns>
</asp:GridView>
<br />
```

Example 16-3. Displaying the output (continued)

```
        <b>VB Titles</b>
        <asp:GridView ID="gvVBNet" Runat="server"
        OnRowDataBound="RowDataBound"
        AutoGenerateColumns="false"
        HeaderStyle-BackColor="PapayaWhip"
        BorderColor="#000099"
        AlternatingRowStyle-BackColor="LightGrey"
        HeaderStyle-Font-Bold=true
        Width="900">
            <Columns>
                <asp:TemplateField HeaderStyle-Width ="10">
                    <HeaderTemplate>
                        Position
                    </HeaderTemplate>
                    <ItemTemplate>
                        <asp:Label Runat="server" ID="Label3">
                          <%# rowNumber %></asp:Label>
                    </ItemTemplate>
                </asp:TemplateField>
                <asp:TemplateField>
                    <HeaderTemplate>
                        Title
                    </HeaderTemplate>
                    <ItemTemplate>
                      <a href="http://www.amazon.com/exec/obidos/ASIN/<%#
                            Eval("isbn")%>/" target="_blank"><%# Eval("title") %></a>
                    </ItemTemplate>
                </asp:TemplateField>
                <asp:BoundField HeaderText="Author"
                  ReadOnly="true" DataField="Author" />
                <asp:BoundField HeaderText="Publisher"
                  ReadOnly="true" DataField="Publisher" />
                <asp:BoundField HeaderText="Publish Date"
                  ReadOnly="true" DataField="pubDate" />
                <asp:BoundField HeaderText="Rank"
                  ReadOnly="true" DataField="Rank"
                  DataFormatString="{0:N0}"
                  ItemStyle-HorizontalAlign="right" />
            </Columns>
        </asp:GridView>
        <asp:Label ID="lblLastUpdate" Runat="server"
          Text="Last Update"></asp:Label>
        <br />
        Number to show in grid:
        <asp:TextBox ID="txtShowRecords" Runat="server"
          Width="48px" Height="22px"
          AutoPostBack="True"></asp:TextBox>
    </div>
    </form>
</body>
</html>
```

The key aspect of the HTML is the creation of three GridViews. They each work the same way, so we'll focus on the first:

```
<asp:GridView ID="gvASP" Runat="server"
OnRowDataBound="RowDataBound"
AutoGenerateColumns="false"
HeaderStyle-BackColor="PapayaWhip"
BorderColor="#000099"
AlternatingRowStyle-BackColor="LightGrey"
HeaderStyle-Font-Bold=true
Width="900">
```

The GridView is named gvASP. A few properties are set, the most important of which is the event handler for the OnRowDataBound event and the Boolean property AutoGenerateColumns, which is set to False. This allows you to take direct control of the columns, which you do by creating a columns element:

```
<columns>
   ...
</columns>
```

The first column within the columns element is a *template field column* element. A template field column allows you to insert controls into the column. In the first instance, you'll insert a Headertemplate (used to create a column header) with the text Position, and an asp:label control. That label will display, as its text, a row number. The mechanism for generating this row number is discussed in "Handling the RowDataBound Event," later in this chapter.

```
<asp:TemplateField HeaderStyle-Width ="10">
    <HeaderTemplate>
        Position
    </HeaderTemplate>
    <ItemTemplate>
        <asp:Label Runat="server" ID="Label1"><%# rowNumber %></asp:Label>
    </ItemTemplate>
```

 For a full explanation of template fields and the other elements used in this page, please see *Programming ASP.NET* (O'Reilly).

The second column is also a template field, this time with the column heading Title. The title itself is displayed by evaluating the title column in the current row in the data set to which this GridView is bound, and surrounding that title with a link to the appropriate page on Amazon.com. This makes the title a hyperlink the user can click.

```
<asp:TemplateField>
    <HeaderTemplate>
        Title
    </HeaderTemplate>
    <ItemTemplate>
```

```
        <a href="http://www.amazon.com/exec/obidos/ASIN/<%# Eval("isbn")%>/"
    target="_blank"><%# Eval("title") %></a>
        </ItemTemplate>
    </asp:TemplateField>
```

Let's take this apart. The first element is the template field:

```
<asp:TemplateField>
</asp:TemplateField>
```

Within the template field are two template elements: the header and the item. The header is pretty straightforward. It has simple text (though it could have any kind of HTML):

```
<headertemplate>
    Title
</headertemplate>
```

The item template is a bit trickier:

```
<itemtemplate>
    <a href="http://www.amazon.com/exec/obidos/ASIN/<%# Eval("isbn")%>/"
        target="_blank"><%# Eval("title") %></a>
</itemtemplate>
```

 Note that you'll want to test the title (and all other strings) to ensure that it is valid HTML.

We'll evaluate this one from the outside in. The first thing to notice is the start of a normal hyperlink:

```
<a href="http://www.amazon.com/exec/obidos/ASIN/
```

However, the hyperlink is then appended with the result of evaluating the ISBN from the bound data:

```
<%# Eval("isbn") %>/"
```

This hyperlink tag has an attribute:

```
target="_blank"
```

That attribute causes the link to open a new instance of the browser. The body of the link (the displayed text of the link) is also an evaluated value:

```
Eval("title")
```

If the bound data has the title *Programming Visual Basic .NET,* Second Edition, and the ISBN 0596004389, this item emits the following HTML:

```
<a href=http://www.amazon.com/exec/obidos/ASIN/0596004389/
    target="_ blank">Programming Visual Basic .NET 2nd Edition </a>
```

The first two columns are tricky. The first is tricky because we need to do some work to create the rowNumber (see the code that follows), and the second because we need to wrap the bound value (the ISBN and the title) inside a hyperlink. The next four columns are easier; they are just bound to the data.

The first bound column has the header text Author, is marked as readOnly, and is bound to the author column in the row of the DataSet table to which this GridView is bound:

```
<asp:BoundColumn HeaderText="Author"
    ReadOnly="true"
    DataField="author"/>
```

Notice that this is a self-closing element, as are the next three bound columns:

```
<asp:BoundColumn HeaderText="Publisher"
    ReadOnly="true"
    DataField="publisher"/>
<asp:BoundColumn HeaderText="Publish Date"
    ReadOnly="true"
    DataField="pubdate"/>
<asp:BoundColumn HeaderText="Rank"
    ReadOnly="true"
    DataField="Rank" DataFormatString="{0:N0}"
    ItemStyle-HorizontalAlign="Right"/>
```

Implementing the Grid

The complete source code for the code-behind file is shown in Example 16-4, followed by the analysis.

Example 16-4. Code-behind file for SalesDisplay

```
using System;
using System.Data;
using System.Data.SqlClient;
using System.Configuration;
using System.Web;
using System.Web.Security;
using System.Web.UI;
using System.Web.UI.WebControls;
using System.Web.UI.WebControls.WebParts;
using System.Web.UI.HtmlControls;

public partial class Default_aspx
{
    protected int showRecords;
    protected int totalASP;
    protected int totalCSharp;
    protected int rowNumber = 0;

    protected override void OnLoad( EventArgs e )
    {
        // initialize number of records to show to 7
        if ( !IsPostBack )
```

Example 16-4. Code-behind file for SalesDisplay (continued)

```
   {
      showRecords = 7;
   }
   // if it is a post back, get the number
   // from the text box
   else
   {
      showRecords = Convert.ToInt32( txtShowRecords.Text );
   }

   // connect to the db
   string connectionString =
   "server=localhost;Trusted_Connection=true;database=AmazonSalesRanks";

   // pick records to display
   string commandString =
      @"Select top " + showRecords +
      " * from BookInfo where technology = 'ASPNET' order by rank";
   SqlDataAdapter dataAdapter =
      new SqlDataAdapter( commandString, connectionString );
   DataSet dataSet = new DataSet();
   dataAdapter.Fill( dataSet, "aspBookInfo" ); // first table

   commandString = @"Select top " + showRecords + " *
                        from BookInfo where technology = 'CSHARP' order by rank";
   dataAdapter = new SqlDataAdapter( commandString, connectionString );
   dataAdapter.Fill( dataSet, "csBookInfo" ); // second table

   commandString = @"Select top " + showRecords +
      " * from BookInfo where technology = 'VBNET' order by rank";
   dataAdapter = new SqlDataAdapter( commandString,
      connectionString );
   dataAdapter.Fill( dataSet, "vbBookInfo" ); // third table

   // create the data view and bind to the grid
   DataView aspDataView =
      dataSet.Tables[0].DefaultView;
   gvASP.DataSource = aspDataView;
   gvASP.DataBind();

   rowNumber = 0;

   DataView csDataView = dataSet.Tables[1].DefaultView;
   gvCSharp.DataSource = csDataView;
   gvCSharp.DataBind();

   rowNumber = 0;

   DataView vbDataView = dataSet.Tables[2].DefaultView;
   this.gvVBNet.DataSource = vbDataView;
   gvVBNet.DataBind();
```

Example 16-4. Code-behind file for SalesDisplay (continued)

```
    // txtShowRecords.DataBind();
    lblLastUpdate.Text = "Last updated: " +
      dataSet.Tables[2].Rows[0]["lastUpdate"].ToString();

  }
  void RowDataBound( object sender, GridViewRowEventArgs e )
  {
    this.rowNumber++;
  }
}
```

The program begins by declaring a number of local variables, the most important of which is the rowNumber, which is initialized to 0:

```
protected int rowNumber = 0;
```

The showRecords member variable is used to keep track of how many records to display, and when the page is first displayed, showRecords is set to 7 (a safe and reasonable default). On subsequent postbacks of the page, that value is set to whatever is in the text box:

```
private void Page_Load(object sender, System.EventArgs e)
{
   if (! IsPostBack )
   {
      showRecords = 7;
   }
   else
   {
      showRecords = Convert.ToInt32(txtShowRecords.Text);
   }
```

Continuing in the page-load event handler, the database connection is made and the database is searched, based on the "technology" (i.e., ASP.NET versus C# versus VB.NET):

```
string connectionString =
   "server=localhost;Trusted_Connection=true;database=AmazonSalesRanks";

string commandString =
   @"Select top " + showRecords +
   " * from BookInfo where technology = 'ASPNET' order by rank";
SqlDataAdapter dataAdapter =
   new SqlDataAdapter(commandString, connectionString);
DataSet dataSet = new DataSet();
dataAdapter.Fill(dataSet,"aspBookInfo"); // first table
```

The same is done for each of the other queries. Once the tables in the data set are created, a data view is created for the first table. This represents a view of the ASP.NET results:

```
DataView aspDataView =
   dataSet.Tables[0].DefaultView;
```

It is to this data view that the GridView is bound:

```
gvASP.DataSource = aspDataView;
gvASP.DataBind();
```

Once this is done, the rowNumber member variable is set back to zero (we'll discuss how it moves from zero in a bit), and the next data view is created and bound to its respective GridView:

```
rowNumber = 0;
DataView csDataView = dataSet.Tables[1].DefaultView;
gvCSharp.DataSource = csDataView;
gvCSharp.DataBind();
```

This is done one final time for the third table:

```
rowNumber = 0;
DataView vbDataView = dataSet.Tables[2].DefaultView;
this.gvVBNet.DataSource = vbDataView;
gvVBNet.DataBind();
```

Finally, the label lblLastUpdate is set from the lastUpdate field in the table:

```
lblLastUpdate.Text = "Last updated: " + dataSet.Tables[2].Rows[0]["lastUpdate"].
ToString();
```

Handling the RowDataBound Event

You will remember that when you created the GridView, you bound the RowDataBound event to the RowDataBound method. As a matter of fact, you did this for all three GridViews. Whenever an item is bound on any grid, it is handled in this method. All the method does is to increment the row counter, rowNumber:

```
public void Item_Bound(Object sender, GridViewItemEventArgs e)
{
    rowNumber++;
}
```

The net effect is that each time an item is bound to the GridView, the rowNumber is incremented and then displayed in the first templated column, giving you a relative ranking within the GridView.

Searching by Category

Making a web service method call for each ISBN you want to check is by far not the most efficient approach possible. Not only does it involve multiple round trips to the Amazon service, but it is likely that the ISBNs you list will become out of date almost immediately as new competitors come on the market, and others go out of print.

Fortunately, Amazon can search by category. In the next (and final) iteration of this program, you'll dispense with your XML files with ISBNs and instead simply ask Amazon for all the books in the ASP.NET, C#, and VB.NET categories.

To keep the example simple, you'll use the default of retrieving just 10 books in each category. Amazon Web Services allow a great deal of tailoring of your request, but for this example, we'll go with the minimal properties required.

Create a copy of the SalesRankDBWebServices project and name it AmazonWebServiceClientSearching. You'll modify it as shown in Example 16-5.

Example 16-5. SalesRankDBWebServices02

```csharp
#region Using directives

using System;
using System.Collections.Generic;
using System.ComponentModel;
using System.Data;
using System.Drawing;
using System.Windows.Forms;

#endregion

namespace AmazonWebServiceClient
{
    partial class AmazonWebServiceClient : Form
    {
        private int timeRemaining;
        const int WaitTime = 900; // 15 minutes
        private string connectionString;
        private System.Data.SqlClient.SqlConnection connection;
        private System.Data.SqlClient.SqlCommand command;

        public AmazonWebServiceClient()
        {
            InitializeComponent();
        }

        private void AmazonWebServiceClient_Load( object sender,
            EventArgs e )
        {
            // connection string to connect to the Sales Rank Database
            connectionString =
"server=localhost;Trusted_Connection=true;database=AmazonSalesRanks";

            // Create connection object, initialize with
            // connection string.
            connection =
                new System.Data.SqlClient.SqlConnection( connectionString );

            // Create a SqlCommand object and assign the connection
            command =
                new System.Data.SqlClient.SqlCommand();
```

Example 16-5. SalesRankDBWebServices02 (continued)

```csharp
      command.Connection = connection;
      timeRemaining = 1;   // when you first start up, get the info.
      UpdateButton();

   }

   private void btnStart_Click( object sender, EventArgs e )
   {
      // toggle the timer
      updateTimer.Enabled = updateTimer.Enabled ? false : true;
      UpdateButton();

   }

   private void btnNow_Click( object sender, EventArgs e )
   {
      timeRemaining = 2;
   }

   private void UpdateButton()
   {
      btnStart.Text = updateTimer.Enabled ? "Stop" : "Start";
   }

   private void updateTimer_Tick( object sender, EventArgs e )
   {

      if ( updateTimer.Enabled )
         txtClock.Text = ( --timeRemaining ).ToString() + " seconds";
      else
         txtClock.Text = "Stopped";

      // hi ho, hi ho, it's off to work we go...
      if ( timeRemaining < 1 )
      {
         timeRemaining = WaitTime;   // reset the clock
         timeRemaining = WaitTime;
         GetInfoFromAmazon( "ASP.NET", "ASPNET" );
         GetInfoFromAmazon( "C#", "CSHARP" );
         GetInfoFromAmazon( "VB.NET", "VBNET" );
      }
   }

   private void GetInfoFromAmazon( string keyword, string technology )
   {

      AWSProductData productData = new AWSProductData();

      ItemSearch srch = null;
      try
      {
```

Example 16-5. SalesRankDBWebServices02 (continued)

```
        ItemSearchRequest req = new ItemSearchRequest();
        req.Keywords = keyword;
        req.SearchIndex = "Books";

        srch = new ItemSearch();
        srch.AssociateTag = "libertyassocia00A";
        srch.SubscriptionId = " Your Subscription ID ";
        srch.Request = new ItemSearchRequest[1];
        srch.Request[0] = req;

    }
    catch ( System.Exception e )
    {
        lblStatus.Text = e.Message;
    }

    ItemSearchResponse response;

    int salesRank = -1;
    string isbn = string.Empty;
    string author = string.Empty;
    string pubDate = string.Empty;
    string publisher = string.Empty;
    string title = string.Empty;
    string strURL = string.Empty;

    Items[] responseItems = null;
    try
    {
        // get back ItemSearchResponse
        response = productData.ItemSearch( srch );

        // Items returns array of Items
        responseItems = response.Items;

        foreach ( Items items in responseItems )
        {
            // Item property of Items is an array of Item objects
            Item[] arrayOfItem = items.Item;

            foreach ( Item item in arrayOfItem )
            {
                isbn = FixQuotes( item.ItemAttributes.ISBN );
                salesRank = item.SalesRank ==
                    null ? -1 : Convert.ToInt32( item.SalesRank );
                author = FixQuotes( item.ItemAttributes.Author[0] );
                pubDate = FixQuotes(
                    item.ItemAttributes.PublicationDate);
                publisher = FixQuotes( item.ItemAttributes.Publisher );
                title = FixQuotes( item.ItemAttributes.Title );
                strURL = item.DetailPageURL;
                // update the list box
```

Example 16-5. SalesRankDBWebServices02 (continued)

```
            string results = title + " by " + author + ": " +
                publisher + ", " + pubDate + ". Rank: " + salesRank;
            lbOutput.Items.Add( results );
            lbOutput.SelectedIndex = lbOutput.Items.Count - 1;

            // update the database
            string commandString = @"Update BookInfo set isbn = '" +
                isbn + "', title = '" + title + "', publisher = '" +
                publisher + "', pubDate = '" +
                pubDate + "', rank = " +
                salesRank + ", link = '" +
                strURL + "', lastUpdate = '" +
                System.DateTime.Now + "', technology = '" +
                technology + "', author = '" +
                author + "' where isbn = '" +
                isbn + "'";

        command.CommandText = commandString;
        try
        {
            // if no rows were affected, this is a new record
            connection.Open();
            int numRowsAffected = command.ExecuteNonQuery();
            if ( numRowsAffected == 0 )
            {
                commandString = @"Insert into BookInfo values ('" +
                    isbn + "', '" + title + "', '" + publisher +
                    "', '" +
                    pubDate + "', '" + FixQuotes( strURL ) + "', "
                    + salesRank + ", '" +
                    System.DateTime.Now +
                    "', '" + technology + "', '" + author + "')";

                command.CommandText = commandString;
                command.ExecuteNonQuery();
            }
        }
        catch ( Exception ex )
        {
            lblStatus.Text = ex.Message;
            lbOutput.Items.Add( "Unable to update database!" );
            lbOutput.SelectedIndex = lbOutput.Items.Count - 1;
        }
        finally
        {
            connection.Close();         // clean up
        }
        Application.DoEvents();          // update the UI
    }
  }
}
catch ( System.Exception ex)
```

Example 16-5. SalesRankDBWebServices02 (continued)

```
        {
            lblStatus.Text = ex.Message;
        }

    }       // close for GetInfoFromAmazon

    private string FixQuotes( string s )
    {
        if ( s == null )
            return string.Empty;
        return s.Replace( "'", "''" );

    }
  } // end class
} // end name space
```

In this version, all the code to manipulate the XML files is removed. The method GetInfoFromISBN is replaced by GetInfoFromAmazon. Instead of creating an ItemLookupRequest object, you create a KeywordRequest object:

```
    private void GetInfoFromAmazon( string keyword, string technology )
    {

        AWSProductData productData = new AWSProductData();

        ItemSearch srch = null;
        try
        {
            ItemSearchRequest req = new ItemSearchRequest();
            req.Keywords = keyword;
            req.SearchIndex = "Books";

            srch = new ItemSearch();
            srch.AssociateTag = "libertyassocia00A";
            srch.SubscriptionId = "Your Subscription ID";
            srch.Request = new ItemSearchRequest[1];
            srch.Request[0] = req;

        }
```

Notice that the keyword property has been assigned the keyword parameter passed in (i.e., C#, ASP.NET, or VB.NET). The SearchIndex property limits the search to books (rather than, for example, records).

Once the ItemSearchRequest object is created, you embed it in an ItemSearch object that holds the AssociateTag and the SubscriptionID.

What you get back is an ItemSearchResponse object. The Items property of this object is an array of Item objects. Each Item object has an Item property which, not surprisingly, is an array of Item objects. It is in these Item objects that you'll find the information about the matching books.

PART III

The CLR and the .NET Framework

CHAPTER 17

Assemblies and Versioning

The basic unit of .NET deployment is the *assembly*. An assembly is a collection of files that appear to be a single DLL or executable (EXE). As noted earlier, DLLs are collections of classes and methods that are linked into your running program only when they are needed.

Assemblies are the .NET unit of reuse, versioning, security, and deployment. This chapter discusses assemblies in detail, including the architecture and contents of assemblies, private assemblies, and shared assemblies.

In addition to the object code for the application, assemblies contain resources such as *.gif* files, type definitions for each class you define, as well as other metadata about the code and data.

PE Files

On disk, assemblies are Portable Executable (PE) files. PE files aren't new. The format of a .NET PE file is exactly the same as a normal Windows PE file. PE files are implemented as DLLs or EXEs.

Physically, assemblies consist of one or more *modules*. Modules are the constituent pieces of assemblies. Standing alone, modules can't be executed; they must be combined into assemblies to be useful.

You will deploy and reuse the entire contents of an assembly as a unit. Assemblies are loaded on demand, and will not be loaded if not needed.

Metadata

Metadata is information stored in the assembly that describes the types and methods of the assembly and provides other useful information about the assembly. Assemblies are said to be *self-describing* because the metadata fully describes the contents of each module. Metadata is discussed in detail in Chapter 18.

Security Boundary

Assemblies form security boundaries as well as type boundaries. That is, an assembly is the scope boundary for the types it contains, and type definitions can't cross assemblies. You can, of course, refer to types across assembly boundaries by adding a reference to the required assembly, either in the IDE or on the command line, at compile time. What you can't do is have the definition of a type span two assemblies.

The internal access modifier limits access (for a method, for example) to the current assembly.

Manifests

As part of its metadata, every assembly has a *manifest*. This describes what is in the assembly: identification information (name, version, etc.), a list of the types and resources in the assembly, a list of modules, a map to connect public types with the implementing code, and a list of assemblies referenced by this assembly.

Even the simplest program has a manifest. You can examine that manifest using ILDasm, which is provided as part of your development environment. When you open the manifest in ILDasm, the EXE program created by Example 12-3 looks like Figure 17-1.

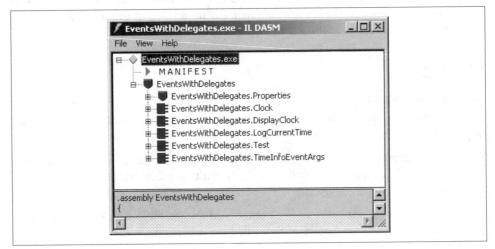

Figure 17-1. ILDasm of Example 12-3

Notice the manifest (second line from the top). Double-clicking the manifest opens a Manifest window, as shown in Figure 17-2.

This file serves as a map of the contents of the assembly. You can see in the first line the reference to the mscorlib assembly, which is referenced by this and every .NET

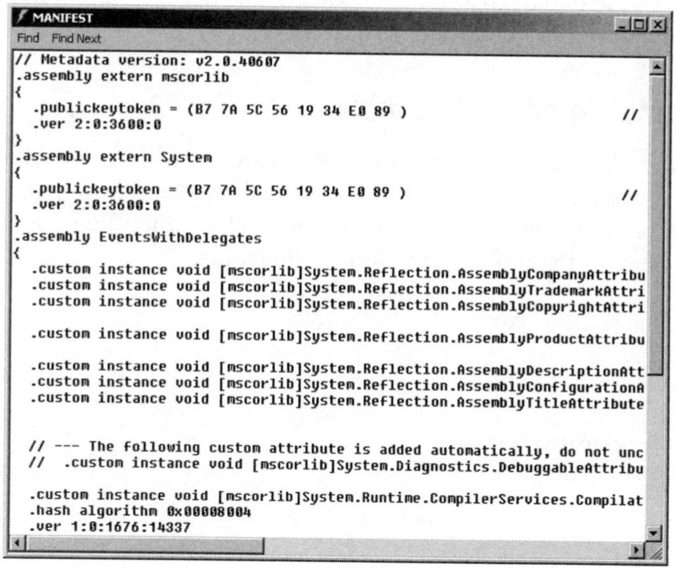

Figure 17-2. The Manifest window

application. The `mscorlib` assembly is the core library assembly for .NET and is available on every .NET platform.

The next assembly line is a reference to the assembly from Example 12-3. You can also see that this assembly consists of a single module. You can ignore the rest of the metadata for now.

Multimodule Assemblies

Assemblies can consist of more than one module, though this isn't supported by Visual Studio 2005.

A single-module assembly has a single file that can be an EXE or DLL file. This single module contains all the types and implementations for the application. The assembly manifest is embedded within this module.

Each module has a manifest of its own that is separate from the assembly manifest. The module manifest lists the assemblies referenced by that particular module. In addition, if the module declares any types, these are listed in the manifest along with the code to implement the module. A module can also contain resources, such as the images needed by that module.

A multimodule assembly consists of multiple files (zero or one EXE and zero or more DLL files, though you must have at least one EXE or DLL). The assembly manifest in this case can reside in a standalone file, or it can be embedded in one of the modules.

When the assembly is referenced, the runtime loads the file containing the manifest and then loads the required modules as needed.

Building a Multimodule Assembly

To demonstrate the use of multimodule assemblies, the following example creates a couple of very simple modules that you can then combine into a single assembly. The first module is a Fraction class. This simple class will allow you to create and manipulate common fractions. Example 17-1 illustrates.

Example 17-1. The Fraction class

```
#region Using directives

using System;
using System.Collections.Generic;
using System.Text;

#endregion

namespace ProgCS
{
    public class Fraction
    {
        private int numerator;
        private int denominator;

        public Fraction( int numerator, int denominator )
        {
            this.numerator = numerator;
            this.denominator = denominator;
        }

        public Fraction Add( Fraction rhs )
        {
            if ( rhs.denominator != this.denominator )
            {
                return new Fraction(
                    rhs.denominator * numerator +
                    rhs.numerator * denominator,
                    denominator * rhs.denominator);
            }

            return new Fraction(
                this.numerator + rhs.numerator,
                    this.denominator );
        }

        public override string ToString()
        {
```

Example 17-1. The Fraction class (continued)

```
        return numerator + "/" + denominator;
    }
  }
}
```

Notice that the Fraction class is in the ProgCS namespace. The full name for the class is ProgCS.Fraction.

The Fraction class takes two values in its constructor: a numerator and a denominator. There is also an Add() method, which takes a second Fraction and returns the sum, assuming the two share a common denominator. This class is simplistic, but it will demonstrate the functionality necessary for this example.

The second class is the MyCalc class, which stands in for a robust calculator. Example 17-2 illustrates.

Example 17-2. The calculator

```
#region Using directives

using System;
using System.Collections.Generic;
using System.Text;

#endregion

namespace ProgCS
{
    public class MyCalc
    {
        public int Add( int val1, int val2 )
        {
            return val1 + val2;
        }
        public int Mult( int val1, int val2 )
        {
            return val1 * val2;
        }
    }
}
```

Once again, MyCalc is a very stripped-down class to keep things simple. Notice that MyCalc is also in the ProgCS namespace.

This is sufficient to create an assembly. Use an *AssemblyInfo.cs* file to add some metadata to the assembly. The use of metadata is covered in Chapter 18.

You can write your own *AssemblyInfo.cs* file, but the simplest approach is to let Visual Studio generate one for you automatically.

Visual Studio creates only single-module assemblies.

You can create a multimodule resource with the /addModules command-line option. The easiest way to compile and build a multimodule assembly is with a makefile, which you can create with Notepad or any text editor.

If you are unfamiliar with makefiles, don't worry; this is the only example that needs a makefile, and that is just to get around the current limitation of Visual Studio creating only single-module assemblies. If necessary, you can just use the makefile as offered without fully understanding every line. For more information, see *Managing Projects with make* (O'Reilly).

Example 17-3 shows the complete makefile (which is explained in detail immediately afterward). To run this example, put the makefile (with the name *makefile*) in a directory together with a copy of *Calc.cs*, *Fraction.cs*, and *AssemblyInfo.cs*. Start up a .NET command window and cd to that directory. Invoke *nmake* without any command switch. You will find the *SharedAssembly.dll* in the *bin* subdirectory.

Example 17-3. The complete makefile for a multimodule assembly

```
ASSEMBLY= MySharedAssembly.dll

BIN=.\bin
SRC=.
DEST=.\bin

CSC=csc /nologo /debug+ /d:DEBUG /d:TRACE

MODULETARGET=/t:module
LIBTARGET=/t:library
EXETARGET=/t:exe

REFERENCES=System.dll

MODULES=$(DEST)\Fraction.dll $(DEST)\Calc.dll
METADATA=$(SRC)\AssemblyInfo.cs

all: $(DEST)\MySharedAssembly.dll

# Assembly metadata placed in same module as manifest
$(DEST)\$(ASSEMBLY): $(METADATA) $(MODULES) $(DEST)
    $(CSC) $(LIBTARGET) /addmodule:$(MODULES: =;) /out:$@ %s
```

Example 17-3. The complete makefile for a multimodule assembly (continued)

```
# Add Calc.dll module to this dependency list
$(DEST)\Calc.dll: Calc.cs $(DEST)
    $(CSC) $(MODULETARGET) /r:$(REFERENCES: =;) /out:$@ %s

# Add Fraction
$(DEST)\Fraction.dll: Fraction.cs $(DEST)
    $(CSC) $(MODULETARGET) /r:$(REFERENCES: =;) /out:$@ %s

$(DEST)::
!if !EXISTS($(DEST))
    mkdir $(DEST)
!endif
```

The makefile begins by defining the assembly you want to build:

```
ASSEMBLY= MySharedAssembly.dll
```

It then defines the directories you'll use, putting the output in a *bin* directory beneath the current directory and retrieving the source code from the current directory:

```
SRC=.
DEST=.\bin
```

Build the assembly as follows:

```
$(DEST)\$(ASSEMBLY): $(METADATA) $(MODULES) $(DEST)
    $(CSC) $(LIBTARGET) /addmodule:$(MODULES: =;) /out:$@ %s
```

This places the assembly (*MySharedAssembly.dll*) in the destination directory (*bin*). It tells *nmake* (the program that executes the makefile) that the $(DEST)\$(ASSEMBLY) build target depends upon the three other build targets listed, and it provides the command line required to build the assembly.

The metadata is defined earlier as:

```
METADATA=$(SRC)\AssemblyInfo.cs
```

The modules are defined as the two DLLs:

```
MODULES=$(DEST)\Fraction.dll $(DEST)\Calc.dll
```

The compile line builds the library and adds the modules, putting the output into the assembly file *MySharedAssembly.dll*:

```
$(DEST)\$(ASSEMBLY): $(METADATA) $(MODULES) $(DEST)
    $(CSC) $(LIBTARGET) /addmodule:$(MODULES: =;) /out:$@ %s
```

To accomplish this, *nmake* needs to know how to make the modules. Start by telling *nmake* how to create *Calc.dll*. You need the *Calc.cs* source file for this; tell *nmake* the command line to build that DLL:

```
$(DEST)\Calc.dll: Calc.cs $(DEST)
    $(CSC) $(MODULETARGET) /r:$(REFERENCES: =;) /out:$@ %s
```

Then do the same thing for *Fraction.dll*:

```
$(DEST)\Fraction.dll: Fraction.cs $(DEST)
    $(CSC) $(MODULETARGET) /r:$(REFERENCES: =;) /out:$@ %s
```

The result of running *nmake* on this makefile is to create three DLLs: *Fraction.dll*, *Calc.dll*, and *MySharedAssembly.dll*. If you open *MySharedAssembly.dll* with ILDasm, you'll find that it consists of nothing but a manifest, as shown in Figure 17-3.

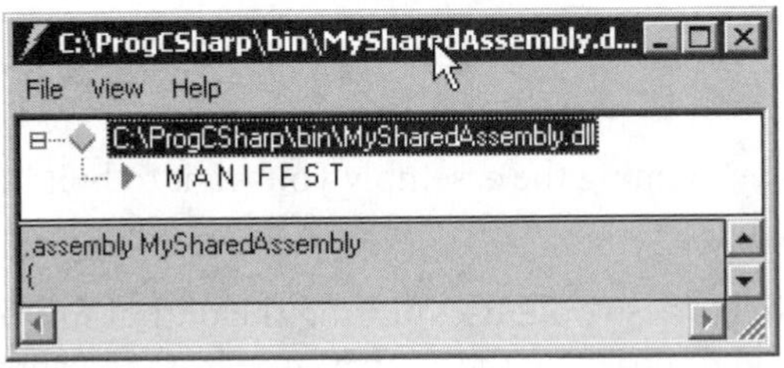

Figure 17-3. MySharedAssembly.dll

If you examine the manifest, you see the metadata for the libraries you created, as shown in Figure 17-4.

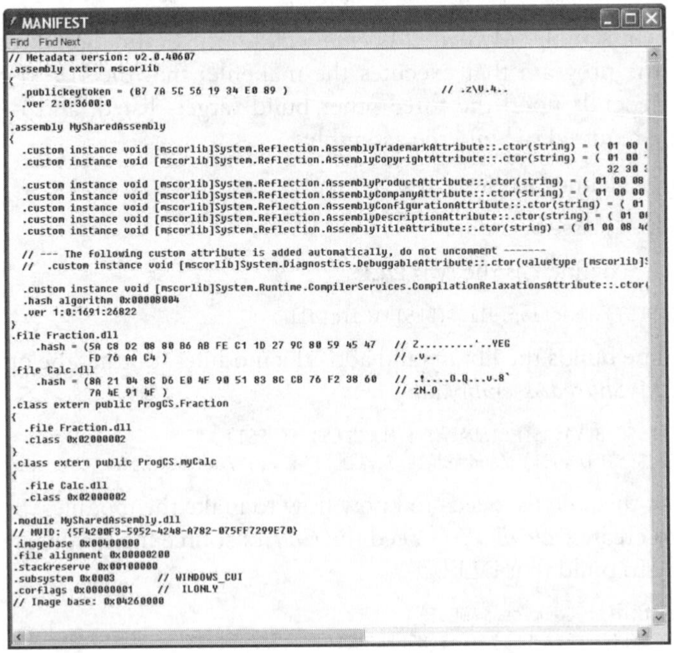

Figure 17-4. The manifest for MySharedAssembly.dll

You first see an external assembly for the core library (mscorlib), followed by the two modules, ProgCS.Fraction and ProgCS.myCalc.

You now have an assembly that consists of three DLL files: *MySharedAssembly.dll* with the manifest, and *Calc.dll* and *Fraction.dll* with the types and implementation needed.

Testing the assembly

To use these modules, you'll create a driver program. Example 17-4 illustrates. Save this program as *Test.cs* in the same directory as the other modules. Add a reference to the assembly (Project Menu → Add Reference → *MySharedAssembly.dll*).

Example 17-4. A module test-driver

```
namespace Programming_CSharp
{
    using System;

    public class Test
    {
        // main will not load the shared assembly
        static void Main()
        {
            Test t = new Test();
            t.UseCS();
            t.UseFraction();

        }

        // calling this loads the myCalc assembly
        // and the mySharedAssembly assembly as well
        public void UseCS()
        {
            ProgCS.myCalc calc = new ProgCS.myCalc();
            Console.WriteLine("3+5 = {0}\n3*5 = {1}",
                calc.Add(3,5), calc.Mult(3,5));
        }

        // calling this adds the Fraction assembly
        public void UseFraction()
        {
            ProgCS.Fraction frac1 = new ProgCS.Fraction(3,5);
            ProgCS.Fraction frac2 = new ProgCS.Fraction(1,5);
            ProgCS.Fraction frac3 = frac1.Add(frac2);
            Console.WriteLine("{0} + {1} = {2}",
                frac1, frac2, frac3);
        }
    }
}
```

Example 17-4. A module test-driver (continued)

```
Output:
3+5 = 8
3*5 = 15
3/5 + 1/5 = 4/5
```

For the purposes of this demonstration, it is important not to put any code in Main() that depends on your modules. You don't want the modules loaded when Main() loads, and so no Fraction or Calc objects are placed in Main(). When you call into UseFraction and UseCalc, you'll be able to see that the modules are individually loaded.

Loading the assembly

An assembly is loaded into its application by the AssemblyResolver through a process called *probing*. The assembly resolver is called by the .NET Framework automatically; you don't call it explicitly. Its job is to load your program.

 The three DLLs produced earlier must be in the directory in which Example 17-4 executes or in a subdirectory of that directory that is in the binpath (the user-defined list of subdirectories under the root location that is specified in the application configuration file).

Put a breakpoint on the second line in Main(), as shown in Figure 17-5.

```
Programming_CSharp.Test                                    Main()
        namespace Programming_CSharp
        {
            using System;

            public class Test
            {
                // main will not load the shared assembly
                static void Main()
                {
                    Test t = new Test();
                    t.UseCS();
                    t.UseFraction();
```

Figure 17-5. A breakpoint in Main( )

Execute to the breakpoint and open the Modules window. Only two of our modules are loaded, as shown in Figure 17-6.

Name	Path	Optimized	My Code	Symbol Status	Symbol File	Or...	Version	Timestamp
mscorlib.dll	C:\WINDOWS\assembly\GAC_3...	Yes	No	No symbols loa...		1	2.0.4060...	7/7/2004 7:04 PM
vshostutil.dll	C:\WINDOWS\assembly\GAC_M...	Yes	No	No symbols loa...		2	8.0.4060...	7/25/2004 9:06 ...
System.Windows.Forms.dll	C:\WINDOWS\assembly\GAC_M...	Yes	No	No symbols loa...		3	2.0.4060...	7/7/2004 7:04 PM
System.dll	C:\WINDOWS\assembly\GAC_M...	Yes	No	No symbols loa...		4	2.0.4060...	7/7/2004 7:04 PM
System.Drawing.dll	C:\WINDOWS\assembly\GAC_M...	Yes	No	No symbols loa...		5	2.0.4060...	7/7/2004 7:04 PM
ModuleTestDriver.vshost.exe	C:\Documents and Settings\Jes...	Yes	No	No symbols loa...		6	8.0.4060...	6/25/2004 6:08 PM
System.Data.dll	C:\WINDOWS\assembly\GAC_3...	Yes	No	No symbols loa...		7	2.0.4060...	7/7/2004 7:04 PM
System.Xml.dll	C:\WINDOWS\assembly\GAC_M...	Yes	No	No symbols loa...		8	2.0.4060...	7/7/2004 7:04 PM
ModuleTestDriver.exe	C:\Documents and Settings\Jes...	No	Yes	Symbols loaded.	C:\Documents and Setti...	9	1.0.1691....	8/18/2004 4:05 PM

```
namespace ModuleTestDriver
{
    public class Test
    {
        // main will not load the shared assembly
        static void Main()
        {
            Test t = new Test();
            t.UseCS();
            t.UseFraction();
        }

        // calling this loads the myCalc assembly
```

Figure 17-6. Only two modules loaded

> If you didn't develop *Test.cs* as part of a Visual Studio .NET solution, put a call to System.Diagnostics.Debugger.Launch() just before the second line in Main(). This lets you choose which debugger to use. (Make sure to compile *Test.cs* with the options /debug and /r: MySharedAssembly.dll.)

Step into the first method call and watch the Modules window. As soon as you step into UseCS, the AssemblyLoader recognizes that it needs a module from *MySharedAssembly.dll*. The DLL is loaded, and from that assembly's manifest the AssemblyLoader finds that it needs *Calc.dll*, which is loaded as well, as shown in Figure 17-7.

When you step into Fraction, the final DLL is loaded.

Private Assemblies

Assemblies come in two flavors: *private* and *shared*. Private assemblies are intended to be used by only one application; shared assemblies are intended to be shared among many applications.

All the assemblies you've built so far are private. By default, when you compile a C# application, a private assembly is created. The files for a private assembly are all kept in the same folder (or in a tree of subfolders). This tree of folders is isolated from the rest of the system, as nothing other than the one application depends on it, and you can redeploy this application to another machine just by copying the folder and its subfolders.

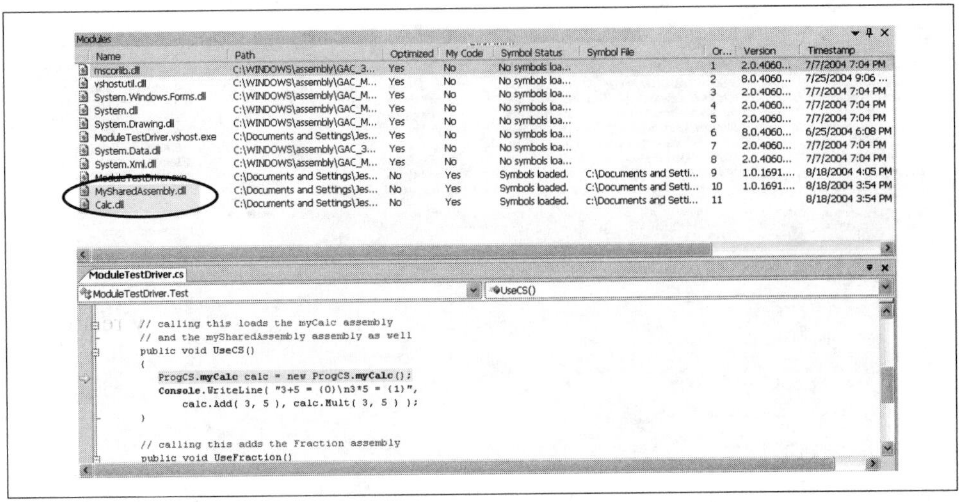

Figure 17-7. Modules loaded on demand

A private assembly can have any name you choose. It doesn't matter if that name clashes with assemblies in another application; the names are local only to a single application.

In the past, DLLs were installed on a machine and (for COM DLLs) an entry was made in the Windows Registry. It was difficult to avoid polluting the Registry with useless cruft. In any case, reinstalling the program on another machine was nontrivial. With assemblies, all of that goes away. With private assemblies, installing is as simple as copying the files to the appropriate directory (called *xcopy deployment*). Period.

Shared Assemblies

You can create assemblies that can be shared by other applications. You might want to do this if you have written a generic control or a class that might be used by other developers. If you want to share your assembly, it must meet certain stringent requirements.

First, your assembly must have a *strong name*. Strong names are globally unique.

> No one else can generate the same strong name as you because an assembly generated with one private key is guaranteed to have a different name than any assembly generated with another private key.

Second, your shared assembly must be protected against newer versions trampling over it, and so each new version you release must have a new version number.

Finally, to share your assembly, place it in the *Global Assembly Cache* (GAC) (pronounced "gak"). This is an area of the filesystem set aside by the CLR to hold shared assemblies.

The End of DLL Hell

Assemblies mark the end of DLL Hell. Remember this scenario: you install Application A on your machine, and it loads a number of DLLs into your Windows directory. It works great for months. You then install Application B on your machine, and suddenly, unexpectedly, Application A breaks. Application B is in no way related to Application A. So what happened? It turns out, you later learn, that Application B replaced a DLL that Application A needed, and suddenly Application A began to stagger about, blind and senseless.

When DLLs were invented, disk space was at a premium and reusing DLLs seemed like a good idea. The theory was that DLLs would be backward-compatible, so automatically upgrading to the new DLL would be painless and safe. As my old boss Pat Johnson used to say, "In theory, theory and practice are the same. But in practice, they never are."

When the new DLL was added to the computer, the old application, which was happily minding its own business in another corner of your machine, suddenly linked to a DLL that was incompatible with its expectations and hey! Presto! It went into the dance of death. This phenomenon led customers to be justifiably leery of installing new software, or even of upgrading existing programs, and it is one of the reasons Windows machines are perceived to be unstable. With assemblies, this entire nightmare goes away.

Versions

Shared assemblies in .NET are uniquely identified by their names and their versions. The GAC allows for "side-by-side" versions in which an older version of an assembly is available alongside a newer version.

 Side-by-side versioning applies only to items in the GAC. Private assemblies don't need this feature and don't have it.

A version number for an assembly might look like this: 1:0:2204:21 (four numbers, separated by colons). The first two numbers (1:0) are the major and minor versions. The third number (2204) is the build, and the fourth (21) is the revision.

When two assemblies have different major or minor numbers, they are considered by convention to be incompatible. When they have different build numbers, they might or might not be compatible, and when they have different revision numbers, they are considered *definitely* compatible with each other. This is great in theory, but the CLR assembly resolver ignores this convention and it serves only to remind the developer; it isn't enforced at runtime.

Strong Names

To use a shared assembly, you must meet two requirements:

- You need to be able to specify the exact assembly you want to load.
- You need to ensure that the assembly has not been tampered with and that the assembly being loaded is the one authored by the actual creator of the assembly. To do so, your assembly needs a digital signature when it is built.

Both of these requirements are met by strong names. Strong names must be globally unique and use public key encryption. A strong name is a string of hexadecimal digits and isn't meant to be human-readable.

To create a strong name, a public-private key pair is generated for one or more assemblies. A hash is taken of the names and contents of the files in the assembly. The hash is then encrypted with the private key for the assembly, and the public key token (an 8-byte hash of the full key) is placed in the manifest along with the public key. This is known as *signing the assembly*.

Public Key Encryption

Strong names are based on public key encryption technology. The essence of public key encryption is this: you create two keys. Data encrypted with the first key can only be decrypted with the second. Data encrypted with the second key can only be decrypted with the first.

Distribute your first key as a *public key* that anyone can have. Keep your second key as a *private key* that no one but you can have access to.

The reciprocal relationship between the keys allows anyone to encrypt data with your public key, and then you can decrypt it with your private key. No one else has access to the data once it is encrypted, including the person who encrypted it.

Similarly, you can encrypt data with your private key, and then anyone can decrypt that data with your public key. Although this makes the data freely available, it ensures that only you could have created it. This is called a *digital signature*.

When an application loads the assembly, the CLR uses the public key to decode the hash of the files in the assembly to ensure that they have not been tampered with. This also protects against name clashes.

You can create a strong name with the sn utility:

```
sn -k c:\myStrongName.snk
```

The -k flag indicates that you want a new key pair written to the specified file. You can call the file anything you like. Remember, a strong name is a string of bytes and isn't meant to be human-readable.

You can associate this strong name with your assembly by using an attribute:

```
using System.Runtime.CompilerServices;
[assembly: AssemblyKeyFile("c:\\myStrongName.key")]
```

Attributes are covered in detail in Chapter 18. For now, you can just put this code at the top of your file to associate the strong name you generated with your assembly.

The Global Assembly Cache

Once you've created your strong name and associated it with your assembly, all that remains is to place the assembly in the GAC. You can do so with the gacutil utility:

```
gacutil /i MySharedAssembly.dll
```

Or you can open your File Explorer and drag your assembly into the GAC. To see the GAC, open the File Explorer and navigate to *%SystemRoot%\assembly*; Explorer turns into a GAC utility.

Building a Shared Assembly

The best way to understand shared assemblies is to build one. Let's return to the earlier multimodule project (see Examples 17-1 through 17-4) and navigate to the directory that contains the files *Calc.cs* and *Fraction.cs*.

Try this experiment: locate the *bin* directory for the driver program and make sure that you don't have a local copy of the *MySharedAssembly* DLL files.

 The referenced assembly (MySharedAssembly) should have its CopyLocal property set to false.

Run the program. It should fail with an exception saying it can't load the assembly:

```
Unhandled Exception: System.IO.FileNotFoundException: File or assembly name
MySharedAssembly, or one of its dependencies, was not found.
File name: "MySharedAssembly"
   at Programming_CSharp.Test.UseCS()
   at Programming_CSharp.Test.Main()
```

Now copy the DLLs into the driver program's directory tree, run it again, and this time you should find that it works fine.

Let's make the MySharedAssembly into a shared assembly. This is done in two steps. First, create a strong name for the assembly, and then put the assembly into the GAC (of course, you are also free to just use this strongly named assembly via xcopy deployment if you choose).

Step 1: Create a strong name

Create a key pair by opening a command window and entering:

```
sn -k keyFile.snk
```

Now open the *AssemblyInfo.cs* file in the project for the *MySharedAssembly.dll* and modify this line:

```
[assembly: AssemblyKeyFile("")]
```

as follows:

```
[assembly: AssemblyKeyFile("keyFile.snk")]
```

This sets the key file for the assembly. Rebuild with the same makefile as earlier, and then open the resulting DLL in ILDasm and open the manifest. You should see a public key, as shown in Figure 17-8.

```
.publickey = (00 24 00 00 04 80 00 00 94 00 00 00 06 02 00 00   // .$..............
              00 24 00 00 52 53 41 31 00 04 00 00 01 00 01 00   // .$..RSA1........
              11 13 95 3C 41 19 2B 41 28 29 E8 AF DE 8C A2 04   // ...<A.+A()......
              88 22 BD 4F A9 E1 F5 57 2C 2D E2 43 CF C3 68 4E   // ."..O...W.-.C..hN
              F7 C7 72 E8 55 94 85 11 EA 66 30 F6 D4 22 DB 0D   // ..r.U....f0.."..
              6E D6 A6 0D 6D 58 28 10 E9 75 D8 BF CC 82 2A EB   // n...mX(..u....*.
              04 19 D5 C1 86 B0 CF D5 CB E6 5C 58 43 08 0D E9   // ..........\XC...
              20 8F 9B DC 29 AC 46 A3 CD 7A 87 3C F8 92 7A 84   // ....).F..z.<..z.
              E3 47 84 AD 56 73 3E 0D AD 1D C0 A2 FA 15 14 A3   // .G..Vs>.........
              88 17 01 AC F3 A3 7A F8 59 BC 3A 16 CB AB 34 C5 ) // ......z.Y.:...4.
```

Figure 17-8. The manifest of MySharedAssembly.dll

By adding the strong name, you have signed this assembly (your exact values will be different). To illustrate that the names match in the GAC and in the reference in the client manifest, you'll want to get the strong name from the DLL. To do this, navigate to the directory with the DLL and enter the following at a command prompt:

```
sn -T MySharedAssembly.dll
```

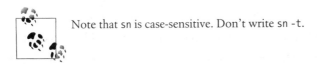 Note that sn is case-sensitive. Don't write sn -t.

The response should be something like this:

```
Public key token is 01fad8e0f0941a4d
```

This value is an abbreviated version of the assembly's public key, called the *public key token*.

Remove the DLLs from the test program's directory structure and run it again. It should fail again. Although you've given this assembly a strong name, you haven't yet registered it in the GAC.

Step 2: Put the shared assembly in the GAC

The next step is to drag the library into the GAC. To do so, open an Explorer window and navigate to the *%SystemRoot%* directory. When you double-click the *Assembly* subdirectory, Explorer turns into a GAC viewer.

You can drag and drop into the GAC viewer, or you can invoke this command-line utility:

```
Gacutil /i mySharedAssembly.dll
```

Just to close the circle, you might want to check that your assembly was loaded into the GAC, and that the public key token shown in the GAC viewer matches the value you got back from sn:

```
Public key token is 01fad8e0f0941a4d
```

This is illustrated in Figure 17-9.

Assembly Name	Version	Culture	Public Key Token
Microsoft.StdFormat	7.0.3300.0		b03f5f7f11d50a3a
Microsoft.VisualBasic	8.0.1200.0		b03f5f7f11d50a3a
Microsoft.VisualBasic.Compatibility	8.0.1200.0		b03f5f7f11d50a3a
Microsoft.VisualBasic.Compatibility.Data	8.0.1200.0		b03f5f7f11d50a3a
Microsoft.VisualBasic.Vsa	8.0.1200.0		b03f5f7f11d50a3a
Microsoft.VisualC	8.0.1200.0		b03f5f7f11d50a3a
Microsoft.VisualC.ApplicationVerifier	1.0.0.0		b03f5f7f11d50a3a
Microsoft.VisualC.VSCodeParser	8.0.1200.0		b03f5f7f11d50a3a
Microsoft.VisualC.VSCodeProvider	8.0.1200.0		b03f5f7f11d50a3a
Microsoft.VisualStudio	2.0.3600.0		b03f5f7f11d50a3a
Microsoft.VisualStudio.CommandBars	8.0.0.0		b03f5f7f11d50a3a
Microsoft.VisualStudio.Configuration	2.0.3600.0		b03f5f7f11d50a3a

Figure 17-9. The GAC

Once this is done, you have a shared assembly that can be accessed by any client. Refresh the client by building it again, and look at its manifest, as shown in Figure 17-10.

```
.assembly extern MySharedAssembly
{
  .publickeytoken = (A5 92 9F 01 02 E0 C4 73 )
  .ver 1:0:535:29377
}
```

Figure 17-10. The manifest

There's `MySharedAssembly`, listed as an external assembly, and the public key now matches the value shown in the GAC. Very nice; time to try it.

Close ILDasm, and run your code. It should work fine, even though there are no DLLs for this library in its immediate path. You've just created and used a shared assembly.

Other Required Assemblies

The assembly manifest also contains references to other assemblies. Each such reference includes the name of the other assembly, the version number and required culture, and optionally, the other assembly's public key token (a digital signature).

Culture is a string representing the language and national display characteristics for the person using your program. It is culture that determines, for example, whether dates are in month/date/year format or date/month/year format.

CHAPTER 18

Attributes and Reflection

Throughout this book, I have emphasized that a .NET application contains code, data, and metadata. *Metadata* is information about the data—that is, information about the types, code, assembly, and so forth—stored along with your program. This chapter explores how some of that metadata is created and used.

Attributes are a mechanism for adding metadata, such as compiler instructions and other data about your data, methods, and classes, to the program itself. Attributes are inserted into the metadata and are visible through ILDasm and other metadata-reading tools.

Reflection is the process by which a program can read its own metadata or metadata from another program. A program is said to reflect on itself or on another program, extracting metadata from the reflected assembly and using that metadata either to inform the user or to modify the program's behavior.

Attributes

An attribute is an object that represents data you want to associate with an element in your program. The element to which you attach an attribute is referred to as the *target* of that attribute. For example, the attribute:

```
[NoIDispatch]
```

is associated with a class or an interface to indicate that the target class should derive from IUnknown rather than IDispatch when exporting to COM. COM interface programming is discussed in detail in Chapter 22.

In Chapter 17, you saw this attribute:

```
[assembly: AssemblyKeyFile("c:\\myStrongName.key")]
```

This inserts metadata into the assembly to designate the program's strong name.[*]

Attributes

Some attributes are supplied as part of the CLR, or by the framework. In addition, you are free to create your own custom attributes for your own purposes.

Most programmers will use only the attributes provided by the framework, though creating your own custom attributes can be a powerful tool when combined with reflection, described later in this chapter.

Attribute targets

If you search through the CLR, you'll find a great many attributes. Some attributes are applied to an assembly, others to a class or interface, and some, such as [Web-Method], are applied to class members. These are called the *attribute targets*. The possible attributes are declared in the AttributeTargets enumeration and are detailed in Table 18-1.

Table 18-1. Possible attribute targets

Member name	Usage
All	Applied to any of the following elements: assembly, class, constructor, delegate, enum, event, field, interface, method, module, parameter, property, return value, or struct
Assembly	Applied to the assembly itself
Class	Applied to a class
Constructor	Applied to a given constructor
Delegate	Applied to a delegate
Enum	Applied to an enumeration
Event	Applied to an event
Field	Applied to a field
Interface	Applied to an interface
Method	Applied to a method
Module	Applied to a single module
Parameter	Applied to a parameter of a method
Property	Applied to a property (both get and set, if implemented)
ReturnValue	Applied to a return value
Struct	Applied to a struct

[*] Actually the assembly attribute does more than just insert metadata. The C# compiler watches for this particular attribute (as well as several others) and triggers special behavior; in this case, it reads the key file and uses it to sign the assembly. Typically, however, attributes are just static metadata inserted in the assembly.

Applying attributes

Apply attributes to their targets by placing them in square brackets immediately before the target item (except in the case of assemblies, in which case you place them at the top of the file).

You can combine attributes by stacking one on top of another:

```
[assembly: AssemblyDelaySign(false)]
[assembly: AssemblyKeyFile(".\\keyFile.snk")]
```

This can also be done by separating the attributes with commas:

```
[assembly: AssemblyDelaySign(false),
    assembly: AssemblyKeyFile(".\\keyFile.snk")]
```

 You must place assembly attributes after all using statements and before any code.

Many attributes are used for interoperating with COM, as discussed in detail in Chapter 22. You've already seen use of one attribute ([WebMethod]) in Chapter 16. You'll see other attributes, such as the [Serializable] attribute, used in the discussion of serialization in Chapter 19.

The System.Reflection namespace offers a number of attributes, including attributes for assemblies (such as the AssemblyKeyFileAttribute), for configuration, and for version attributes.

One of the attributes you are most likely to use in your everyday C# programming (if you aren't interacting with COM) is [Serializable]. As you'll see in Chapter 19, all you need to do to ensure that your class can be serialized to disk or to the Internet is add the [Serializable] attribute to the class:

```
[Serializable]
class MySerializableClass
```

The attribute tag is put in square brackets immediately before its target—in this case, the class declaration.

The key fact about attributes is that you know when you need them; the task will dictate their use.

Custom Attributes

You are free to create your own custom attributes and use them at runtime as you see fit. Suppose, for example, that your development organization wants to keep track of bug fixes. You already keep a database of all your bugs, but you'd like to tie your bug reports to specific fixes in the code.

You might add comments to your code along the lines of:

```
// Bug 323 fixed by Jesse Liberty 1/1/2005.
```

This would make it easy to see in your source code, but there is no enforced connection to Bug 323 in the database. A custom attribute might be just what you need. You would replace your comment with something like this:

```
[BugFixAttribute(323,"Jesse Liberty","1/1/2005",
Comment="Off by one error")]
```

You could then write a program to read through the metadata to find these bug-fix notations and update the database. The attribute would serve the purposes of a comment, but would also allow you to retrieve the information programmatically through tools you'd create.

 This may be a somewhat artificial example, however, because these attributes would be compiled into the shipping code.

Declaring an attribute

Attributes, like most things in C#, are embodied in classes. To create a custom attribute, derive your new custom attribute class from `System.Attribute`:

```
public class BugFixAttribute : System.Attribute
```

You need to tell the compiler which kinds of elements this attribute can be used with (the attribute target). Specify this with (what else?) an attribute:

```
[AttributeUsage(AttributeTargets.Class |
    AttributeTargets.Constructor |
    AttributeTargets.Field |
    AttributeTargets.Method |
    AttributeTargets.Property,
    AllowMultiple = true)]
```

`AttributeUsage` is an attribute applied to attributes: a *meta-attribute*. It provides, if you will, meta-metadata—that is, data about the metadata. For the `AttributeUsage` attribute constructor, you pass two arguments. The first argument is a set of flags that indicate the target—in this case, the class and its constructor, fields, methods, and properties. The second argument is a flag that indicates whether a given element might receive more than one such attribute. In this example, `AllowMultiple` is set to true, indicating that class members can have more than one `BugFixAttribute` assigned.

Naming an attribute

The new custom attribute in this example is named `BugFixAttribute`. The convention is to append the word Attribute to your attribute name. The compiler supports this by allowing you to call the attribute with the shorter version of the name. Thus, you can write:

```
[BugFix(123, "Jesse Liberty", "01/01/05", Comment="Off by one")]
```

The compiler will first look for an attribute named `BugFix` and, if it doesn't find that, will then look for `BugFixAttribute`.

Constructing an attribute

Attributes take two types of parameters: *positional* and *named*. In the `BugFix` example, the programmer's name, the bug ID, and the date are positional parameters, and `comment` is a named parameter. Positional parameters are passed in through the constructor and must be passed in the order declared in the constructor:

```
public BugFixAttribute(int bugID, string programmer,
string date)
{
    this.bugID = bugID;
    this.programmer = programmer;
    this.date = date;
}
```

Named parameters are implemented as fields or as properties:

```
public string Comment
{
    get
    {
        return comment;
    }
    set
    {
        comment = value;
    }
}
```

It is common to create read-only properties for the positional parameters:

```
public int BugID
{
    get
    {
        return bugID;
    }
}
```

Using an attribute

Once you have defined an attribute, you can put it to work by placing it immediately before its target. To test the `BugFixAttribute` of the preceding example, the following program creates a simple class named MyMath and gives it two functions. Assign BugFixAttributes to the class to record its code-maintenance history:

```
[BugFixAttribute(121,"Jesse Liberty","01/03/05")]
[BugFixAttribute(107,"Jesse Liberty","01/04/05",
    Comment="Fixed off by one errors")]
public class MyMath
```

These attributes are stored with the metadata. Example 18-1 shows the complete program.

Example 18-1. Working with custom attributes

```csharp
#region Using directives

using System;
using System.Collections.Generic;
using System.Text;

#endregion

namespace CustomAttributes
{
    // create custom attribute to be assigned to class members
    [AttributeUsage( AttributeTargets.Class |
        AttributeTargets.Constructor |
        AttributeTargets.Field |
        AttributeTargets.Method |
        AttributeTargets.Property,
        AllowMultiple = true )]
    public class BugFixAttribute : System.Attribute
    {

        // private member data
        private int bugID;
        private string comment;
        private string date;
        private string programmer;

        // attribute constructor for
        // positional parameters
        public BugFixAttribute
            ( int bugID,
              string programmer,
              string date )
        {
            this.bugID = bugID;
            this.programmer = programmer;
            this.date = date;
        }

        // accessor
        public int BugID
        {
```

Example 18-1. Working with custom attributes (continued)

```
      get
      {
         return bugID;
      }
   }

   // property for named parameter
   public string Comment
   {
      get
      {
         return comment;
      }
      set
      {
         comment = value;
      }
   }

   // accessor
   public string Date
   {
      get
      {
         return date;
      }
   }

   // accessor
   public string Programmer
   {
      get
      {
         return programmer;
      }
   }
}

// ********* assign the attributes to the class ********

[BugFixAttribute( 121, "Jesse Liberty", "01/03/05" )]
[BugFixAttribute( 107, "Jesse Liberty", "01/04/05",
   Comment = "Fixed off by one errors" )]
public class MyMath
{

   public double DoFunc1( double param1 )
   {
      return param1 + DoFunc2( param1 );
   }

   public double DoFunc2( double param1 )
```

Example 18-1. Working with custom attributes (continued)

```
        {
            return param1 / 3;
        }
    }

    public class Tester
    {
        public static void Main()
        {
            MyMath mm = new MyMath();
            Console.WriteLine( "Calling DoFunc(7). Result: {0}",
                mm.DoFunc1( 7 ) );
        }
    }
}
```

```
Output:
Calling DoFunc(7). Result: 9.3333333333333333
```

As you can see, the attributes had absolutely no impact on the output. In fact, for the moment, you have only my word that the attributes exist at all. A quick look at the metadata using ILDasm does reveal that the attributes are in place, however, as shown in Figure 18-1. You'll see how to get at this metadata and use it in your program in the next section.

Reflection

For the attributes in the metadata to be useful, you need a way to access them, ideally during runtime. The classes in the Reflection namespace, along with the System. Type class, provide support for examining and interacting with the metadata.

Reflection is generally used for any of four tasks.

Viewing metadata
> This might be used by tools and utilities that wish to display metadata.

Performing type discovery
> This allows you to examine the types in an assembly and interact with or instantiate those types. This can be useful in creating custom scripts. For example, you might want to allow your users to interact with your program using a script language, such as JavaScript, or a scripting language you create yourself.

Late binding to methods and properties
> This allows the programmer to invoke properties and methods on objects dynamically instantiated, based on type discovery. This is also known as *dynamic invocation*.

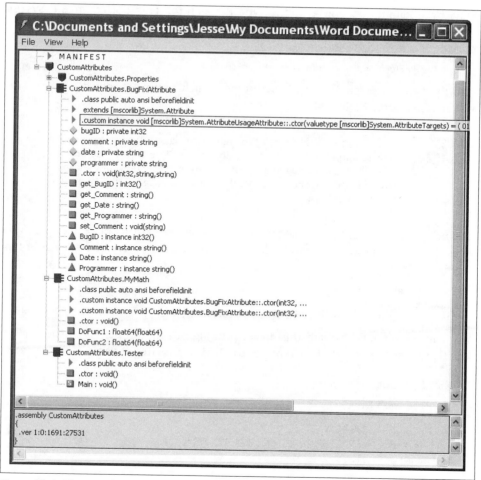

Figure 18-1. The metadata in the assembly

Creating types at runtime (reflection emit)

The ultimate use of reflection is to create new types at runtime and then to use those types to perform tasks. You might do this when a custom class, created at runtime, will run significantly faster than more generic code created at compile time.

Viewing Metadata

In this section, you will use the C# reflection support to read the metadata in the MyMath class.

Start by obtaining an object of the type MemberInfo. This object, in the System. Reflection namespace, is provided to discover the attributes of a member and to provide access to the metadata:

```
System.Reflection.MemberInfo inf = typeof(MyMath);
```

Call the typeof operator on the MyMath type, which returns an object of type Type, which derives from MemberInfo.

 The Type class is the heart of the reflection classes. Type encapsulates a representation of the type of an object. The Type class is the primary way to access metadata. Type derives from MemberInfo and encapsulates information about the members of a class (e.g., methods, properties, fields, events, etc.).

The next step is to call GetCustomAttributes on this MemberInfo object, passing in the type of the attribute you want to find. You get back an array of objects, each of type BugFixAttribute:

```
object[] attributes;
attributes =
    inf.GetCustomAttributes(typeof(BugFixAttribute),false);
```

You can now iterate through this array, printing out the properties of the BugFix-Attribute object. Example 18-2 replaces the Tester class from Example 18-1.

Example 18-2. Using reflection

```
public static void Main()
{
    MyMath mm = new MyMath();
    Console.WriteLine("Calling DoFunc(7). Result: {0}",
        mm.DoFunc1(7));

    // get the member information and use it to
    // retrieve the custom attributes
    System.Reflection.MemberInfo inf = typeof(MyMath);
    object[] attributes;
    attributes =
        inf.GetCustomAttributes(
            typeof(BugFixAttribute), false);

    // iterate through the attributes, retrieving the
    // properties
    foreach(Object attribute in attributes)
    {
        BugFixAttribute bfa = (BugFixAttribute) attribute;
        Console.WriteLine("\nBugID: {0}", bfa.BugID);
        Console.WriteLine("Programmer: {0}", bfa.Programmer);
        Console.WriteLine("Date: {0}", bfa.Date);
```

Example 18-2. Using reflection (continued)

```
        Console.WriteLine("Comment: {0}", bfa.Comment);
    }
}
```

```
Output:
Calling DoFunc(7). Result: 9.3333333333333333
```

```
BugID: 121
Programmer: Jesse Liberty
Date: 01/03/05
Comment:
```

```
BugID: 107
Programmer: Jesse Liberty
Date: 01/04/05
Comment: Fixed off by one errors
```

When you put this replacement code into Example 18-1 and run it, you can see the metadata printed as you'd expect.

Type Discovery

You can use reflection to explore and examine the contents of an assembly. You can find the types associated with a module; the methods, fields, properties, and events associated with a type, as well as the signatures of each of the type's methods; the interfaces supported by the type; and the type's base class.

To start, load an assembly dynamically with the Assembly.Load() static method. The Assembly class encapsulates the actual assembly itself, for purposes of reflection. One signature for the Load method is:

```
    public static Assembly.Load(AssemblyName)
```

For the next example, pass in the core library to the Load() method. *Mscorlib.dll* has the core classes of the .NET Framework:

```
    Assembly a = Assembly.Load("Mscorlib");
```

Once the assembly is loaded, you can call GetTypes() to return an array of Type objects. The Type object is the heart of reflection. Type represents type declarations (classes, interfaces, arrays, values, and enumerations):

```
    Type[] types = a.GetTypes();
```

The assembly returns an array of types that you can display in a foreach loop, as shown in Example 18-3. Because this example uses the Type class, you will want to add a using directive for the System.Reflection namespace.

Example 18-3. Reflecting on an assembly

```
#region Using directives

using System;
using System.Collections.Generic;
using System.Reflection;
using System.Text;

#endregion

namespace ReflectingAnAssembly
{
    public class Tester
    {
        public static void Main()
        {
            // what is in the assembly
            Assembly a = Assembly.Load( "Mscorlib" );
            Type[] types = a.GetTypes();
            foreach ( Type t in types )
            {
                Console.WriteLine( "Type is {0}", t );
            }
            Console.WriteLine(
                "{0} types found", types.Length );
        }
    }
}
```

The output from this would fill many pages. Here is a short excerpt:

```
Type is System.Object
Type is ThisAssembly
Type is AssemblyRef
Type is System.ICloneable
Type is System.Collections.IEnumerable
Type is System.Collections.ICollection
Type is System.Collections.IList
Type is System.Array
2373 types found
```

This example obtained an array filled with the types from the core library and printed them one by one. The array contained 2,373 entries on my machine.

 In Version 1.1, I found 1,426 entries on my machine. Microsoft has been busy!

Reflecting on a Type

You can reflect on a single type in the Mscorlib assembly as well. To do so, extract a type from the assembly with either typeOf or the GetType() method, as shown in Example 18-4.

Example 18-4. Reflecting on a type

```
#region Using directives

using System;
using System.Collections.Generic;
using System.Reflection;
using System.Text;

#endregion

namespace ReflectingOnAType
{
    public class Tester
    {
        public static void Main()
        {
            // examine a type
            Type theType =
                Type.GetType(
                    "System.Reflection.Assembly" );
            Console.WriteLine(
                "\nSingle Type is {0}\n", theType );
        }
    }
}
```

```
Output:
Single Type is System.Reflection.Assembly
```

Finding all type members

You can ask the Assembly type for all its members using the GetMembers() method of the Type class, which lists all the methods, properties, and fields, as shown in Example 18-5.

Example 18-5. Reflecting on the members of a type

```
#region Using directives

using System;
using System.Collections.Generic;
using System.Reflection;
using System.Text;

#endregion
```

Example 18-5. Reflecting on the members of a type (continued)

```
namespace ReflectingOnMembersOfAType
{
   public class Tester
   {
      public static void Main()
      {
         // examine a single object
         Type theType =
            Type.GetType(
               "System.Reflection.Assembly" );
         Console.WriteLine(
            "\nSingle Type is {0}\n", theType );

         // get all the members
         MemberInfo[] mbrInfoArray =
            theType.GetMembers();
         foreach ( MemberInfo mbrInfo in mbrInfoArray )
         {
            Console.WriteLine( "{0} is a {1}",
               mbrInfo, mbrInfo.MemberType );
         }
      }
   }
}
```

Once again, the output is quite lengthy, but within the output you see fields, methods, constructors, and properties, as shown in this excerpt:

```
System.Type GetType(System.String, Boolean, Boolean) is a Method
System.Type[] GetExportedTypes() is a Method
System.Reflection.Module GetModule(System.String) is a Method
System.String get_FullName() is a Method
```

Finding type methods

You might want to focus on methods only, excluding the fields, properties, and so forth. To do so, remove the call to GetMembers():

```
MemberInfo[] mbrInfoArray =
   theType.GetMembers();
```

and add a call to GetMethods():

```
mbrInfoArray = theType.GetMethods();
```

The output now is nothing but the methods:

```
Output (excerpt):
Boolean Equals(System.Object) is a Method
System.String ToString() is a Method
System.String CreateQualifiedName(
      System.String, System.String) is a Method
Boolean get_GlobalAssemblyCache() is a Method
```

Finding particular type members

Finally, to narrow it down even further, you can use the `FindMembers` method to find particular members of the type. For example, you can narrow your search to methods whose names begin with the letters Get.

To narrow the search, use the `FindMembers` method, which takes four parameters:

MemberTypes

> A `MemberTypes` object that indicates the type of the member to search for. These include `All`, `Constructor`, `Custom`, `Event`, `Field`, `Method`, `Nestedtype`, `Property`, and `TypeInfo`. You will also use the `MemberTypes.Method` to find a method.

BindingFlags

> An enumeration that controls the way searches are conducted by reflection. There are a great many `BindingFlags` values, including `IgnoreCase`, `Instance`, `Public`, `Static`, and so forth.

MemberFilter

> A delegate (see Chapter 12) that filters the list of members in the `MemberInfo` array of objects. You use a `Type.FilterName` filter, which is a field of the `Type` class that filters on a name.

Object

> A string value used by the filter. In this case you pass in Get* to match only those methods that begin with the letters Get.

The complete listing for filtering on these methods is shown in Example 18-6.

Example 18-6. Finding particular members

```
#region Using directives

using System;
using System.Collections.Generic;
using System.Reflection;
using System.Text;

#endregion

namespace FindingParticularMembers
{
    public class Tester
    {
        public static void Main()
        {
            // examine a single object
            Type theType = Type.GetType(
                "System.Reflection.Assembly" );

            // just members which are methods beginning with Get
            MemberInfo[] mbrInfoArray =
                theType.FindMembers( MemberTypes.Method,
```

Example 18-6. Finding particular members (continued)

```
            BindingFlags.Public |
            BindingFlags.Static |
            BindingFlags.NonPublic |
            BindingFlags.Instance |
            BindingFlags.DeclaredOnly,
            Type.FilterName, "Get*" );
    foreach ( MemberInfo mbrInfo in mbrInfoArray )
    {
        Console.WriteLine( "{0} is a {1}",
            mbrInfo, mbrInfo.MemberType );
    }
        }
    }
}
```

```
Output (excerpt):
System.Type GetType(System.String, Boolean, Boolean) is a Method
System.Type[] GetExportedTypes() is a Method
System.Reflection.Module GetModule(System.String) is a Method
System.Reflection.AssemblyName[] GetReferencedAssemblies() is a Method
Int64 GetHostContext() is a Method
System.String GetLocation() is a Method
System.String GetFullName() is a Method
```

Late Binding

Once you find a method, it's possible to invoke it using reflection. For example, you might like to invoke the Cos() method of System.Math, which returns the cosine of an angle.

> You can, of course, call Cos() in the normal course of your code, but reflection allows you to bind to that method at runtime. This is called *late binding* and offers the flexibility of choosing at runtime which object to bind to and invoking it programmatically. This can be useful when creating a custom script to be run by the user or when working with objects that might not be available at compile time. For example, by using late binding, your program can interact with the spellchecker or other components of a running commercial word processing program such as Microsoft Word.

To invoke Cos(), first get the Type information for the System.Math class:

```
Type theMathType = Type.GetType("System.Math");
```

With that type information, you can dynamically load an instance of a class using a static method of the Activator class. Because Cos() is static, you don't need to construct an instance of System.Math (and you can't because System.Math has no public constructor).

The Activator class contains four methods, all static, that you can use to create objects locally or remotely, or to obtain references to existing objects. The four methods are as follows.

CreateComInstanceFrom
> Creates instances of COM objects.

CreateInstanceFrom
> Creates a reference to an object from a particular assembly and type name.

GetObject
> Used when marshaling objects. Marshaling is discussed in detail in Chapter 19.

CreateInstance
> Creates local or remote instances of an object. For example:
> ```
> Object theObj = Activator.CreateInstance(someType);
> ```

Back to the Cos() example, you now have one object in hand: a Type object named theMathType, which you created by calling GetType.

Before you can invoke a method on the object, you must get the method you need from the Type object, theMathType. To do so, you'll call GetMethod(), and you'll pass in the signature of the Cos method.

The signature, you will remember, is the name of the method (Cos) and its parameter types. In the case of Cos(), there is only one parameter: a double. However, Type.GetMethod takes two parameters. The first represents the name of the method you want, and the second represents the parameters. The name is passed as a string; the parameters are passed as an array of types:

```
MethodInfo CosineInfo =
    theMathType.GetMethod("Cos",paramTypes);
```

Before calling GetMethod(), you must prepare the array of types:

```
Type[] paramTypes = new Type[1];
paramTypes[0]= Type.GetType("System.Double");
```

This code declares the array of Type objects and then fills the first element (paramTypes[0]) with a type representing a double. Obtain the type representing a double by calling the static method Type.GetType(), and passing in the string System.Double.

You now have an object of type MethodInfo on which you can invoke the method. To do so, you must pass in the object to invoke the method on and the actual value of the parameters, again in an array. Since this is a static method, pass in theMathType. (If Cos() were an instance method, you could use theObj instead of theMathType.)

```
Object[] parameters = new Object[1];
parameters[0] = 45 * (Math.PI/180); // 45 degrees in radians
Object returnVal = CosineInfo.Invoke(theMathType,parameters);
```

Note that you've created two arrays. The first, paramTypes, holds the type of the parameters. The second, parameters, holds the actual value. If the method had taken two arguments, you'd have declared these arrays to hold two values. If the method didn't take any values, you can still create the array, but you give it a size of zero!

```
Type[] paramTypes = new Type[0];
```

Odd as this looks, it is correct.

Example 18-7 illustrates dynamically calling the Cos() method.

Example 18-7. Dynamically invoking a method

```
#region Using directives

using System;
using System.Collections.Generic;
using System.Reflection;
using System.Text;

#endregion

namespace DynamicallyInvokingAMethod
{
    public class Tester
    {
        public static void Main()
        {
            Type theMathType = Type.GetType( "System.Math" );
            // Since System.Math has no public constructor, this
            // would throw an exception.
            //Object theObj =
            //    Activator.CreateInstance(theMathType);

            // array with one member
            Type[] paramTypes = new Type[1];
            paramTypes[0] = Type.GetType( "System.Double" );

            // Get method info for Cos()
            MethodInfo CosineInfo =
                theMathType.GetMethod( "Cos", paramTypes );

            // fill an array with the actual parameters
            Object[] parameters = new Object[1];
            parameters[0] = 45 * ( Math.PI / 180 ); // 45 degrees in radians
            Object returnVal =
                CosineInfo.Invoke( theMathType, parameters );
            Console.WriteLine(
                "The cosine of a 45 degree angle {0}",
                returnVal );
        }
    }
}
```

Example 18-7. Dynamically invoking a method (continued)

```
Output:
The cosine of a 45 degree angle 0.707106781186548
```

That was a lot of work just to invoke a single method. The power, however, is that you can use reflection to discover an assembly on the user's machine, to query what methods are available, and to invoke one of those members dynamically.

CHAPTER 19

Marshaling and Remoting

The days of integrated programs all running in a single process on a single machine are, if not dead, at least seriously wounded. Today's programs consist of complex components running in multiple processes, often across the network. The Web has facilitated distributed applications in a way that was unthinkable even a few years ago, and the trend is toward distribution of responsibility.

A second trend is toward centralizing business logic on large servers. Although these trends appear to be contradictory, in fact they are synergistic: business objects are being centralized while the user interface and even some middleware are being distributed.

The net effect is that objects need to be able to talk with one another at a distance. Objects running on a server handling the web user interface need to be able to interact with business objects living on centralized servers at corporate headquarters.

The process of moving an object across a boundary is called *marshal by value*. Boundaries exist at various levels of abstraction in your program. The most obvious boundary is between objects running on different machines.

The process of preparing an object to be remoted is called *marshaling*. On a single machine, objects might need to be marshaled across context, app domain, or process boundaries.

A *process* is essentially a running application. If an object in your word processor wants to interact with an object in your spreadsheet, they must communicate across process boundaries.

Processes are divided into *application domains* (often called *app domains*); these in turn are divided into various *contexts*. App domains act like lightweight processes, and contexts create boundaries that objects with similar rules can be contained within. At times, objects will be marshaled across both context and app domain boundaries, as well as across process and machine boundaries.

When an object is marshaled by value, it appears to be sent through the wire from one computer to another, much like Captain Kirk being teleported down to the surface of a planet some miles below the orbiting USS Enterprise.

In *Star Trek*, Kirk was actually sent to the planet, but in the .NET edition, it is all an illusion. If you are standing on the surface of the planet, you might think you are seeing and talking with the real Kirk, but you aren't talking to Kirk at all: you are talking to a proxy, perhaps a hologram, whose job is to take your message up to the Enterprise where it is relayed to the real Kirk.

Between you and Kirk there are also a number of "sinks." A *sink* is an object whose job is to enforce policy. For example, if Kirk tries to tell you something that might influence the development of your civilization, the prime-directive sink might disallow the transmission.

When the real Kirk responds, he passes his response through various sinks until it gets to the proxy and the proxy tells you. It seems to you as though Kirk is really there, but he's actually sneaking up behind you to thwart your nefarious plans. Alas, it turns out that it was Mr. Sulu who was controlling the hologram the whole time. Better luck next episode.

The actual transmission of your message is done by a *channel*. The channel's job is to know how to move the message from the Enterprise to the planet. The channel works with a *formatter*. The formatter makes sure the message is in the right format. Perhaps you speak only Vulcan, and the poor Captain doesn't. The formatter can translate your message into Federation Standard, and translate Kirk's response from Federation Standard back to Vulcan. You appear to be talking with one another, but the formatter (known as the *universal translator* in the Star Trek universe) is silently facilitating the communication.

This chapter demonstrates how your objects can be marshaled across various boundaries, and how proxies and stubs can create the illusion that your object has been squeezed through the network cable to a machine across the office or around the world. In addition, this chapter explains the role of formatters, channels, and sinks, and how to apply these concepts to your programming.

Application Domains

A process is, essentially, a running application. Each .NET application runs in its own process. If you have Word, Excel, and Visual Studio open, you have three processes running. If you open Outlook, another process starts up. Each process is subdivided into one or more application domains. An app domain acts like a process but uses fewer resources.

App domains can be independently started and halted. They are secure, lightweight, and versatile. An app domain can provide fault tolerance; if you start an object in a second app domain and it crashes, it will bring down the app domain but not your entire program. You can imagine that web servers might use app domains for running users' code; if the code has a problem, the web server can maintain operations.

An app domain is encapsulated by an instance of the AppDomain class, which offers a number of methods and properties. A few of the most important are listed in Table 19-1.

Table 19-1. Methods and properties of the AppDomain class

Method or property	Details
CurrentDomain	Public static property that returns the application domain for the current thread
CreateDomain()	Overloaded public static method that creates a new application domain
GetCurrentThreadID()	Public static method that returns the current thread identifier
Unload()	Public static method that removes the specified app domain
FriendlyName	Public property that returns the friendly name for this app domain
DefineDynamicAssembly()	Overloaded public method that defines a dynamic assembly in the current app domain
ExecuteAssembly()	Public method that executes the designated assembly
GetData()	Public method that gets the value stored in the current application domain given a key
Load()	Public method that loads an assembly into the current app domain
SetAppDomainPolicy()	Public method that sets the security policy for the current app domain
SetData()	Public method that puts data into the specified app domain property

App domains also support a variety of events—including AssemblyLoad, AssemblyResolve, ProcessExit, and ResourceResolve—that are fired as assemblies are found, loaded, run, and unloaded.

Every process has an initial app domain, and can have additional app domains as you create them. Each app domain exists in exactly one process. Until now, all the programs in this book have been in a single app domain: the default app domain. Each process has its own default app domain. In many, perhaps in most of the programs you write, the default app domain will be all that you'll need.

However, there are times when a single domain is insufficient. You might create a second app domain if you need to run a library written by another programmer. Perhaps you don't trust the library, and want to isolate it in its own domain so that if a method in the library crashes the program, only the isolated domain will be affected. If you were the author of Internet Information Server (IIS), Microsoft's web hosting software), you might spin up a new app domain for each plug-in application or each virtual directory you host. This would provide fault tolerance so that if one web application crashed, it would not bring down the web server.

It is also possible that the other library might require a different security environment; creating a second app domain allows the two security environments to coexist.

Each app domain has its own security, and the app domain serves as a security boundary.

App domains aren't threads and should be distinguished from threads. A Win32 thread exists in one app domain at a time, and a thread can access (and report) which app domain it is executing in. App domains are used to isolate applications; within an app domain there might be multiple threads operating at any given moment (see Chapter 20).

To see how app domains work, let's set up an example. Suppose you wish your program to instantiate a Shape class, but in a second app domain.

 There is no good reason for this Shape class to be put in a second app domain, except to illustrate how these techniques work. It is possible, however, that more complex objects might need a second app domain to provide a different security environment. Further, if you are creating classes that might engage in risky behavior, you might like the protection of starting them in a second app domain.

Normally, you'd load the Shape class from a separate assembly, but to keep this example simple, you'll just put the definition of the Shape class into the same source file as all the other code in this example (see Chapter 17). Further, in a production environment, you might run the Shape class methods in a separate thread, but for simplicity, you'll ignore threading for now. (Threading is covered in detail in Chapter 20.) By sidestepping these ancillary issues, you can keep the example straightforward and focus on the details of creating and using application domains and marshaling objects across app domain boundaries.

Creating and Using App Domains

Create a new app domain by calling the static method CreateDomain() on the AppDomain class:

```
AppDomain ad2 =
    AppDomain.CreateDomain("Shape Domain");
```

This creates a new app domain with the *friendly name* Shape Domain. The friendly name is a convenience to the programmer; it is a way to interact with the domain programmatically without knowing the internal representation of the domain. You can check the friendly name of the domain you're working in with the property System.AppDomain.CurrentDomain.FriendlyName.

Once you have instantiated an AppDomain object, you can create instances of classes, interfaces, and so forth, using its CreateInstance() method. Here's the signature:

```
public ObjectHandle CreateInstance(
    string assemblyName,
    string typeName,
```

```
        bool ignoreCase,
        BindingFlags bindingAttr,
        Binder binder,
        object[] args,
        CultureInfo culture,
        object[] activationAttributes,
        Evidence securityAttributes
    );
```

And here's how to use it:

```
ObjectHandle oh = ad2.CreateInstance(
"ProgCSharp",                                       // the assembly name
"ProgCSharp.Shape",                                 // the type name with namespace
false,                                              // ignore case
System.Reflection.BindingFlags.CreateInstance,      // flag
null,                                               // binder
new object[] {3, 5},                                // args
null,                                               // culture
null,                                               // activation attributes
null );                                             // security attributes
```

The first parameter (ProgCSharp) is the name of the assembly, and the second (ProgCSharp.Shape) is the name of the class. The class name must be fully qualified by namespaces.

A *binder* is an object that enables dynamic binding of an assembly at runtime. Its job is to allow you to pass in information about the object you want to create, to create that object for you, and to bind your reference to that object. In the vast majority of cases, including this example, you'll use the default binder, which is accomplished by passing in null.

It is possible, of course, to write your own binder that might, for example, check your ID against special permissions in a database and reroute the binding to a different object, based on your identity or your privileges.

 Binding typically refers to attaching an object name to an object. *Dynamic binding* refers to the ability to make that attachment when the program is running, as opposed to when it is compiled. In this example, the Shape object is bound to the instance variable at runtime, through the app domain's CreateInstance() method.

Binding flags help the binder fine-tune its behavior at binding time. In this example, use the BindingFlags enumeration value CreateInstance. The default binder normally looks at public classes only for binding, but you can add flags to have it look at private classes if you have the right permissions.

When you bind an assembly at runtime, don't specify the assembly to load at compile time; rather, determine which assembly you want programmatically, and bind your variable to that assembly when the program is running.

The constructor you're calling takes two integers, which must be put into an object array (new object[] {3, 5}). You can send null for the culture because you'll use the default (en) culture and won't specify activation attributes or security attributes.

You get back an *object handle*, which is a type that is used to pass an object (in a wrapped state) between multiple app domains without loading the metadata for the wrapped object in each object through which the ObjectHandle travels. You can get the actual object itself by calling Unwrap() on the object handle, and casting the resulting object to the actual type—in this case, Shape.

The CreateInstance() method provides an opportunity to create the object in a new app domain. If you were to create the object with new, it would be created in the current app domain.

Marshaling Across App Domain Boundaries

You've created a Shape object in the Shape domain, but you're accessing it through a Shape object in the original domain. To access the shape object in another domain, you must marshal the object across the domain boundary.

Marshaling is the process of preparing an object to move across a boundary; once again, like Captain Kirk transporting to the planet's surface. Marshaling is accomplished in two ways: *by value* or *by reference*. When an object is marshaled by value, a copy is made. It is as if I called you on the phone and asked you to send me your calculator, and you called up the office supply store and had them send me one that is identical to yours. I can use the copy just as I would the original, but entering numbers on my copy has no effect on your original.

Marshaling by reference is almost like sending me your own calculator. Here's how it works. You don't actually give me the original, but instead keep it in your house. You do send me a proxy. The proxy is very smart: when I press a button on my proxy calculator, it sends a signal to your original calculator, and the number appears over there. Pressing buttons on the proxy looks and feels to me just like I touched your original calculator.

Understanding marshaling with proxies

The Captain Kirk and calculator analogies are fine as far as analogies go, but what actually happens when you marshal by reference? The CLR provides your calling object with a *transparent proxy* (TP).

The job of the TP is to take everything known about your method call (the return value, the parameters, etc.) off of the stack and stuff it into an object that implements the IMessage interface. That IMessage is passed to a RealProxy object.

RealProxy is an abstract base class from which all proxies derive. You can implement your own real proxy, or any of the other objects in this process except for the transparent proxy. The default real proxy will hand the IMessage to a series of sink objects.

Any number of sinks can be used depending on the number of policies you wish to enforce, but the last sink in a chain will put the IMessage into a channel. Channels are split into client-side and server-side channels, and their job is to move the message across the boundary. Channels are responsible for understanding the transport protocol. The actual format of a message as it moves across the boundary is managed by a formatter. The .NET Framework provides two formatters: a SOAP formatter, which is the default for HTTP channels, and a Binary formatter, which is the default for TCP/IP channels. You are free to create your own formatters and, if you are truly a glutton for punishment, your own channels.

Once a message is passed across a boundary, it is received by the server-side channel and formatter, which reconstitute the IMessage and pass it to one or more sinks on the server side. The final sink in a sink chain is the StackBuilder, whose job is to take the IMessage and turn it back into a stack frame so that it appears to be a function call to the server.

Specifying the marshaling method

To illustrate the distinction between marshaling by value and marshaling by reference, in the next example you'll tell the Shape object to marshal by reference but give it a member variable of type Point, which you'll specify as a marshal by value.

Note that each time you create a class that might be used across a boundary, you must choose how it will be marshaled. Normally, objects can't be marshaled at all; you must take action to indicate that an object can be marshaled, either by value or by reference.

The easiest way to make an object marshal by value is to mark it with the Serializable attribute:

```
[Serializable]
public class Point
```

When an object is serialized, its internal state is written out to a stream, either for marshaling or for storage. The details of serialization are covered in Chapter 21.

The easiest way to make an object marshal by reference is to derive its class from MarshalByRefObject:

```
public class Shape : MarshalByRefObject
```

The Shape class will have just one member variable, upperLeft. This variable will be a Point object, which holds the coordinates of the upper-left corner of the shape.

The constructor for Shape will initialize its Point member:

```
public Shape(int upperLeftX, int upperLeftY)
{
```

```
        Console.WriteLine( "[{0}] Event{1}",
            System.AppDomain.CurrentDomain.FriendlyName,
            "Shape constructor");
        upperLeft = new Point(upperLeftX, upperLeftY);
    }
```

Provide Shape with a method for displaying its position:

```
public void ShowUpperLeft()
{
    Console.WriteLine( "[{0}] Upper left: {1},{2}",
        System.AppDomain.CurrentDomain.FriendlyName,
        upperLeft.X, upperLeft.Y);
}
```

Also provide a second method for returning its upperLeft member variable:

```
public Point GetUpperLeft()
{
    return upperLeft;
}
```

The Point class is very simple as well. It has a constructor that initializes its two member variables and accessors to get their value.

Once you create the Shape, ask it for its coordinates:

```
s1.ShowUpperLeft();      // ask the object to display
```

Then ask it to return its upperLeft coordinate as a Point object that you'll change:

```
Point localPoint = s1.GetUpperLeft();

localPoint.X = 500;
localPoint.Y = 600;
```

Ask that Point to print its coordinates, and then ask the Shape to print *its* coordinates. So, will the change to the local Point object be reflected in the Shape? That depends on how the Point object is marshaled. If it is marshaled by value, the localPoint object will be a copy, and the Shape object will be unaffected by changing the localPoint variables' values. If, on the other hand, you change the Point object to marshal by reference, you'll have a proxy to the actual upperLeft variable, and changing that *will* change the Shape. Example 19-1 illustrates this point. Make sure you build Example 19-1 in a project named ProgCSharp. When Main() instantiates the Shape object, the method is looking for *ProgCSharp.exe*.

Example 19-1. Marshaling across app domain boundaries

```
#region Using directives

using System;
using System.Collections.Generic;
using System.Runtime.Remoting;
using System.Reflection;
using System.Text;
```

Example 19-1. Marshaling across app domain boundaries (continued)

```
#endregion

namespace Marshaling
{
    // for marshal by reference comment out
    // the attribute and uncomment the base class
    [Serializable]
    public class Point   // : MarshalByRefObject
    {
        private int x;
        private int y;

        public Point (int x, int y)
        {
            Console.WriteLine( "[{0}] {1}",
                System.AppDomain.CurrentDomain.FriendlyName,
                "Point constructor");

            this.x = x;
            this.y = y;
        }

        public int X
        {
            get
            {
                Console.WriteLine( "[{0}] {1}",
                    System.AppDomain.CurrentDomain.FriendlyName,
                    "Point x.get");

                return this.x;
            }

            set
            {
                Console.WriteLine( "[{0}] {1}",
                    System.AppDomain.CurrentDomain.FriendlyName,
                    "Point x.set");
                this.x = value;
            }
        }

        public int Y
        {
            get
            {
                Console.WriteLine( "[{0}] {1}",
                    System.AppDomain.CurrentDomain.FriendlyName,
                    "Point y.get");
                return this.y;
            }
```

Example 19-1. Marshaling across app domain boundaries (continued)

```
        set
        {
            Console.WriteLine( "[{0}] {1}",
                System.AppDomain.CurrentDomain.FriendlyName,
                "Point y.set");
            this.y = value;
        }
    }
}

// the shape class marshals by reference
public class Shape : MarshalByRefObject
{
    private Point upperLeft;

    public Shape(int upperLeftX, int upperLeftY)
    {
        Console.WriteLine( "[{0}] {1}",
            System.AppDomain.CurrentDomain.FriendlyName,
            "Shape constructor");

        upperLeft = new Point(upperLeftX, upperLeftY);
    }
    public Point GetUpperLeft()
    {
        return upperLeft;
    }

    public void ShowUpperLeft()
    {
        Console.WriteLine( "[{0}] Upper left: {1},{2}",
            System.AppDomain.CurrentDomain.FriendlyName,
            upperLeft.X, upperLeft.Y);
    }
}
public class Tester
{
    public static void Main()
    {

        Console.WriteLine( "[{0}] {1}",
            System.AppDomain.CurrentDomain.FriendlyName,
            "Entered Main");

        // create the new app domain
        AppDomain ad2 =
            AppDomain.CreateDomain("Shape Domain");

        //  Assembly a = Assembly.LoadFrom("ProgCSharp.exe");
        //  Object theShape = a.CreateInstance("Shape");
        // instantiate a Shape object
        ObjectHandle oh = ad2.CreateInstance(
```

Example 19-1. Marshaling across app domain boundaries (continued)

```
            "Marshaling",
            "Marshaling.Shape", false,
            System.Reflection.BindingFlags.CreateInstance,
            null, new object[] {3, 5},
            null, null, null );

        Shape s1 = (Shape) oh.Unwrap();

        s1.ShowUpperLeft();        // ask the object to display

        // get a local copy? proxy?
        Point localPoint = s1.GetUpperLeft();

        // assign new values
        localPoint.X = 500;
        localPoint.Y = 600;

        // display the value of the local Point object
        Console.WriteLine( "[{0}] localPoint: {1}, {2}",
            System.AppDomain.CurrentDomain.FriendlyName,
            localPoint.X, localPoint.Y);

        s1.ShowUpperLeft();        // show the value once more
        }
    }
}
```

```
Output:
[[Marshaling.vshost.exe] Entered Main
[Shape Domain] Shape constructor
[Shape Domain] Point constructor
[Shape Domain] Point x.get
[Shape Domain] Point y.get
[Shape Domain] Upper left: 3,5
[Marshaling.vshost.exe] Point x.set
[Marshaling.vshost.exe] Point y.set
[Marshaling.vshost.exe] Point x.get
[Marshaling.vshost.exe] Point y.get
[Marshaling.vshost.exe] localPoint: 500, 600
[Shape Domain] Point x.get
[Shape Domain] Point y.get
[Shape Domain] Upper left: 3,5
```

Read through the code, or better yet, put it in your debugger and step through it. The output reveals that the Shape and Point constructors run in the Shape domain, as does the access of the values of the Point object in the Shape.

The property is set in the original app domain, setting the local copy of the Point object to 500 and 600. Because Point is marshaled by value, however, you are setting a *copy* of the Point object. When you ask the Shape to display its upperLeft member variable, it is unchanged.

To complete the experiment, comment out the attribute at the top of the Point declaration and uncomment the base class:

```
// [serializable]
public class Point    : MarshalByRefObject
```

Now run the program again. The output is quite different:

```
[Marshaling.vshost.exe] Entered Main
[Shape Domain] Shape constructor
[Shape Domain] Point constructor
[Shape Domain] Point x.get
[Shape Domain] Point y.get
[Shape Domain] Upper left: 3,5
[Shape Domain] Point x.set
[Shape Domain] Point y.set
[Shape Domain] Point x.get
[Shape Domain] Point y.get
[Marshaling.vshost.exe] localPoint: 500, 600
[Shape Domain] Point x.get
[Shape Domain] Point y.get
[Shape Domain] Upper left: 500,600
```

This time you get a proxy for the Point object and the properties are set through the proxy on the original Point member variable. Thus, the changes are reflected within the Shape itself.

Context

App domains themselves are subdivided into contexts. Contexts can be thought of as boundaries within which objects share usage rules. These usage rules include synchronization transactions (see Chapter 20), and so forth.

Context-Bound and Context-Agile Objects

Objects are either *context-bound* or *context-agile*. If they are context-bound, they exist in a context, and to interact with them, the message must be marshaled. If they are context-agile, they act within the context of the calling object: their methods execute in the context of the object that invokes the method and so marshaling isn't required.

Suppose you have an object A that interacts with the database and so is marked to support transactions. This creates a context. All method calls on A occur within the context of the protection afforded by the transaction. Object A can decide to roll back the transaction, and all actions taken since the last commit are undone.

Suppose that you have another object, B, which is context-agile. Now suppose that object A passes a database reference to object B and then calls methods on B. Perhaps A and B are in a callback relationship, in which B will do some work and then call A back with the results. Because B is context-agile, B's method operates in the context of the calling object; thus it will be afforded the transaction protection of object A. The changes B makes to the database will be undone if A rolls back the transaction because B's methods execute within the context of the caller. So far, so good.

Should B be context-agile or context-bound? In the case examined so far, B worked fine being agile. Suppose one more class exists: C. C doesn't have transactions, and it calls a method on B that changes the database. Now A tries to roll back, but unfortunately, the work B did for C was in C's context and thus was not afforded the support of transactions. Uh-oh: that work can't be undone.

If B was marked context-bound when A created it, B would have inherited A's context. In that case, when C invoked a method on B, it would have to be marshaled across the context boundary, but then when B executed the method, it would have been in the context of A's transaction. Much better.

This would work if B were context-bound but without attributes. B of course could have its own context attributes, and these might force B to be in a different context from A. For example, B might have a transaction attribute marked RequiresNew. In this case, when B is created, it gets a new context, and thus can't be in A's context. Thus, when A rolled back, B's work could not be undone. You might mark B with the RequiresNew enumeration value because B is an audit function. When A takes an action on the database, it informs B, which updates an audit trail. You don't want B's work undone when A undoes its transaction. You want B to be in its own transaction context, rolling back only its own mistakes, not A's.

An object thus has three choices. The first option is to be context-agile. A context-agile object operates in the context of its caller. Option two is to be context-bound (accomplished by deriving from ContextBoundObject but having no attributes, and thus operating in the context of the creator). Option three is to be context-bound with context attributes, and thus operate only in the context that matches the attributes.

Which you decide upon depends on how your object will be used. If your object is a simple calculator that can't possibly need synchronization or transactions or any context support, it is more efficient to be context-agile. If your object should use the context of the object that creates it, you should make that object context-bound with no attributes. Finally, if your object has its own context requirements, you should give it the appropriate attributes.

Marshaling Across Context Boundaries

No proxy is needed when accessing context-agile objects within a single app domain. When an object in one context accesses a context-bound object in a second context, it does so through a proxy, and at that time the two context policies are enforced. It is in this sense that a context creates a boundary; the policy is enforced at the boundary between contexts.

For example, when you mark a context-bound object with the System.EnterpriseServices.Synchronization attribute, you indicate that you want the system to manage synchronization for that object. All objects outside that context must pass through the context boundary to touch one of the objects, and at that time the policy of synchronization will be applied.

 Strictly speaking, marking two classes with the Synchronization attribute doesn't guarantee that they will end up in the same context. Each attribute gets to vote on whether it is happy with the current context at activation. If two objects are marked for synchronization, but one is pooled, they will be forced into different contexts.

Objects are marshaled differently across context boundaries, depending on how they are created:

- Typical objects aren't marshaled at all; within app domains they are context-agile.

- Objects marked with the Serializable attribute are marshaled by value across app domains and are context-agile.

- Objects that derive from MarshalByRefObject are marshaled by reference across app domains and are context-agile.

- Objects derived from ContextBoundObject are marshaled by reference across app domains as well as by reference across context boundaries.

Remoting

In addition to being marshaled across context and app domain boundaries, objects can be marshaled across process boundaries, and even across machine boundaries. When an object is marshaled, either by value or by proxy, across a process or machine boundary, it is said to be *remoted*.

Understanding Server Object Types

There are two types of server objects supported for remoting in .NET: *well-known* and *client-activated*. The communication with well-known objects is established each time a message is sent by the client. There is no permanent connection with a well-known object, as there is with client-activated objects.

Well-known objects come in two varieties: *singleton* and *single-call*. With a well-known singleton object, all messages for the object, from all clients, are dispatched to a single object running on the server. The object is created the first time a client attempts to connect to it, and is there to provide service to any client that can reach it. Well-known objects must have a parameterless constructor.

With a well-known single-call object, each new message from a client is handled by a new object. This is highly advantageous on server farms, where a series of messages from a given client might be handled in turn by different machines depending on load balancing.

Client-activated objects are typically used by programmers who are creating dedicated servers, which provide services to a client they are also writing. In this scenario, the client and the server create a connection, and they maintain that connection until the needs of the client are fulfilled.*

Specifying a Server with an Interface

The best way to understand remoting is to walk through an example. Here, build a simple four-function Calculator class, like the one used in an earlier discussion on web services (see Chapter 15) that implements the interface shown in Example 19-2.

Example 19-2. The Calculator interface

```
#region Using directives

using System;
using System.Collections.Generic;
using System.Text;

#endregion

namespace Calculator
{
    public interface ICalc
    {
        double Add( double x, double y );
        double Sub( double x, double y );
        double Mult( double x, double y );
        double Div( double x, double y );
    }
}
```

Save this in a file named *ICalc.cs* and compile it into a file named *Calculator.dll*. To create and compile the source file in Visual Studio, create a new project of type C# Class Library, enter the interface definition in the Edit window, and then select Build on the Visual Studio menu bar. Alternatively, if you have entered the source code

---

* Client-activated objects can be less robust. If a call fails to a client-activated object, the developer must assume that the object has been lost on the server and must regenerate the object from scratch.

using Notepad or another text editor, you can compile the file at the command line by entering:

```
csc /t:library ICalc.cs
```

There are tremendous advantages to implementing a server through an interface. If you implement the calculator as a class, the client must link to that class to declare instances on the client. This greatly diminishes the advantages of remoting because changes to the server require the class definition to be updated on the client. In other words, the client and server would be *tightly coupled*. Interfaces help decouple the two objects; in fact, you can later update that implementation on the server, and as long as the server still fulfills the contract implied by the interface, the client need not change at all.

Building a Server

To build the server used in Example 19-3, create *CalculatorServer.cs* in a new project of type C# Console Application (be sure to include a reference to *Calculator.dll*) and then compile it by selecting Build on the Visual Studio menu bar.

The CalculatorServer class implements ICalc. It derives from MarshalByRefObject so that it will deliver a proxy of the calculator to the client application:

```
class CalculatorServer : MarshalByRefObject, Calculator.ICalc
```

The implementation consists of little more than a constructor and simple methods to implement the four functions.

In Example 19-3, you'll put the logic for the server into the Main() method of *CalculatorServer.cs*.

Your first task is to create a *channel*. Use HTTP as the transport mechanism. You can use the HTTPChannel type provided by .NET:

```
HTTPChannel chan = new HTTPChannel(65100);
```

Notice that you register the channel on TCP/IP port 65100 (see the discussion of port numbers in Chapter 21).

Next, register the channel with the CLR *ChannelServices* using the static method RegisterChannel:

```
ChannelServices.RegisterChannel(chan);
```

This step informs .NET that you will be providing HTTP services on port 65100, much as IIS does on port 80. Because you've registered an HTTP channel and not provided your own formatter, your method calls will use the SOAP formatter by default.

Now you're ready to ask the RemotingConfiguration class to register your well-known object. You must pass in the type of the object you want to register, along with an endpoint. An *endpoint* is a name that RemotingConfiguration will associate with your type. It completes the address. If the IP address identifies the machine and the port identifies the channel, the endpoint indicates the exact service. To get the type of the object, you can use typeof, which returns a Type object. Pass in the full name of the object whose type you want:

```
Type calcType =
    typeof( "CalculatorServerNS.CalculatorServer" );
```

Also, pass in the enumerated type that indicates whether you are registering a SingleCall or Singleton:

```
RemotingConfiguration.RegisterWellKnownServiceType
    ( calcType, "theEndPoint",WellKnownObjectMode.Singleton );
```

The call to RegisterWellKnownServiceType creates the server-side sink chain. Now you're ready to rock and roll. Example 19-3 provides the entire source code for the server.

Example 19-3. The Calculator server

```
#region Using directives

using System;
using System.Collections.Generic;
using System.Runtime.Remoting;
using System.Runtime.Remoting.Channels;
using System.Runtime.Remoting.Channels.Http;
using System.Text;

#endregion

namespace CalculatorServerNS
{
    class CalculatorServer : MarshalByRefObject, Calculator.ICalc
    {
        public CalculatorServer()
        {
            Console.WriteLine( "CalculatorServer constructor" );
        }
        // implement the four functions
        public double Add( double x, double y )
        {
            Console.WriteLine( "Add {0} + {1}", x, y );
            return x + y;
        }
        public double Sub( double x, double y )
        {
            Console.WriteLine( "Sub {0} - {1}", x, y );
            return x - y;
        }
        public double Mult( double x, double y )
        {
            Console.WriteLine( "Mult {0} * {1}", x, y );
            return x * y;
```

Example 19-3. The Calculator server (continued)

```
    }
    public double Div( double x, double y )
    {
        Console.WriteLine( "Div {0} / {1}", x, y );
        return x / y;
    }
}

public class ServerTest
{
    public static void Main()
    {
        // create a channel and register it
        HttpChannel chan = new HttpChannel( 65100 );
        ChannelServices.RegisterChannel( chan );

        Type calcType =
            Type.GetType( "CalculatorServerNS.CalculatorServer" );

        // register our well-known type and tell the server
        // to connect the type to the endpoint "theEndPoint"
        RemotingConfiguration.RegisterWellKnownServiceType
            ( calcType,
                "theEndPoint",
                WellKnownObjectMode.Singleton );

        //  "They also serve who only stand and wait." (Milton)
        Console.WriteLine( "Press [enter] to exit..." );
        Console.ReadLine();
    }
}
}
```

When you run this program, it prints its self-deprecating message:

```
Press [enter] to exit...
```

and then waits for a client to ask for service.

Building the Client

While the CLR will preregister the TCP and HTTP channel, you will need to register a channel on the client if you want to receive callbacks or you are using a nonstandard channel. For this example, you can use channel 0:

```
HTTPChannel chan = new HTTPChannel(0);
ChannelServices.RegisterChannel(chan);
```

The client now need only connect through the remoting services, passing a Type object representing the type of the object it needs (in our case, the ICalc interface) and the Uniform Resource Identifier (URI) of the service.

```
Object obj =
    RemotingServices.Connect
        (typeof(Programming_CSharp.ICalc),
        "http://localhost:65100/theEndPoint");
```

In this case, the server is assumed to be running on your local machine, so the URI is http://localhost, followed by the port for the server (65100), followed in turn by the endpoint you declared in the server (theEndPoint).

The remoting service should return an object representing the interface you've requested. You can then cast that object to the interface and begin using it. Because remoting can't be guaranteed (the network might be down, the host machine may not be available, and so forth), you should wrap the usage in a try block:

```
try
{
    Programming_CSharp.ICalc calc =
        obj as Programming_CSharp.ICalc;

    double sum = calc.Add(3,4);
```

You now have a proxy of the calculator operating on the server, but usable on the client, across the process boundary and, if you like, across the machine boundary. Example 19-4 shows the entire client (to compile it, you must include a reference to *Calculator.dll* as you did with *CalcServer.cs*).

Example 19-4. The remoting Calculator client

```
#region Using directives

using System;
using System.Collections.Generic;
using System.Runtime.Remoting;
using System.Runtime.Remoting.Channels;
using System.Runtime.Remoting.Channels.Http;
using System.Text;

#endregion

namespace CalculatorClient
{
    class CalcClient
    {

        public static void Main()
        {
            int[] myIntArray = new int[3];

            Console.WriteLine("Watson, come here I need you...");

            // create an Http channel and register it
            // uses port 0 to indicate won't be listening
```

Example 19-4. The remoting Calculator client (continued)

```
        HttpChannel chan = new HttpChannel(0);
        ChannelServices.RegisterChannel(chan);

        Object obj = RemotingServices.Connect
            (typeof(Calculator.ICalc),
            "http://localhost:65100/theEndPoint");

        try
        {
            // cast the object to our interface
            Calculator.ICalc calc = obj as Calculator.ICalc;

            // use the interface to call methods
            double sum = calc.Add(3.0,4.0);
            double difference = calc.Sub(3,4);
            double product = calc.Mult(3,4);
            double quotient = calc.Div(3,4);

            // print the results
            Console.WriteLine("3+4 = {0}", sum);
            Console.WriteLine("3-4 = {0}", difference);
            Console.WriteLine("3*4 = {0}", product);
            Console.WriteLine("3/4 = {0}", quotient);
        }
        catch( System.Exception ex )
        {
            Console.WriteLine("Exception caught: ");
            Console.WriteLine(ex.Message);
        }
      }
   }
}

Output on client:
Watson, come here I need you...
3+4 = 7
3-4 = -1
3*4 = 12
3/4 = 0.75

Output on server:
Calculator constructor
Press [enter] to exit...
Add 3 + 4
Sub 3 - 4
Mult 3 * 4
Div 3 / 4
```

The server starts up and waits for the user to press Enter to signal that it can shut down. The client starts and displays a message to the console. The client then calls each of the four operations. You see the server printing its message as each method is called, and then the results are printed on the client.

It is as simple as that; you now have code running on the server and providing services to your client.

Using SingleCall

To see the difference that SingleCall makes versus Singleton, change one line in the server's Main() method. Here's the existing code:

```
RemotingConfiguration.RegisterWellKnownServiceType
    ( calcType,
      "theEndPoint",
      WellKnownObjectMode.Singleton );
```

Change the object to SingleCall:

```
RemotingConfiguration.RegisterWellKnownServiceType
    ( calcType,
      "theEndPoint",
      WellKnownObjectMode.SingleCall);
```

The output reflects that a new object is created to handle each request:

```
Calculator constructor
Press [enter] to exit...
Calculator constructor
Add 3 + 4
Calculator constructor
Sub 3 - 4
Calculator constructor
Mult 3 * 4
Calculator constructor
Div 3 / 4
```

Understanding RegisterWellKnownServiceType

When you called the RegisterWellKnownServiceType() method on the server, what actually happened? Remember that you obtain a Type object for the Calculator class:

```
Type.GetType("CalculatorServerNS.CalculatorServer");
```

You then called RegisterWellKnownServiceType(), passing in that Type object along with the endpoint and the Singleton enumeration. This signals the CLR to instantiate your Calculator and then to associate it with an endpoint.

To do that work yourself, you would need to modify Example 19-3, changing Main() to instantiate a Calculator and then passing that Calculator to the Marshal() method of RemotingServices with the endpoint to which you want to associate that instance of Calculator. The modified Main() is shown in Example 19-5 and, as you can see, its output is identical to that of Example 19-3.

Example 19-5. Manually instantiating and associating Calculator with an endpoint

```
public static void Main()
{
   HttpChannel chan = new HttpChannel( 65100 );
   ChannelServices.RegisterChannel( chan );

   CalculatorServerNS.CalculatorServer  calculator =
      new CalculatorServer();
    RemotingServices.Marshal( calculator, "theEndPoint" );

   //  "They also serve who only stand and wait." (Milton)
   Console.WriteLine( "Press [enter] to exit..." );
   Console.ReadLine();
}
```

The net effect is that you have instantiated a Calculator object and associated a proxy for remoting with the endpoint you've specified (see the "Understanding End-points," section later in this chapter).

You can take that file to your client and reconstitute it on the client machine. To do so, again create a channel and register it. This time, however, open a fileStream on the file you just copied from the server:

```
FileStream fileStream =
        new FileStream ("calculatorSoap.txt", FileMode.Open);
```

Then instantiate a SoapFormatter and call Deserialize() on the formatter, passing in the filename and getting back an ICalc:

```
SoapFormatter soapFormatter =
   new SoapFormatter ();
try
{
    ICalc calc=
        (ICalc) soapFormatter.Deserialize (fileStream);
```

You are now free to invoke methods on the server through that ICalc, which acts as a proxy to the Calculator object running on the server that you described in the *calculatorSoap.txt* file. The complete replacement for the client's Main() method is shown in Example 19-6. You also need to add two using statements to this example.

Example 19-6. Replacement of Main() from Example 19-4 (the client)

```
using System.IO;
using System.Runtime.Serialization.Formatters.Soap;

// ...

public static void Main()
{

   int[] myIntArray = new int[3];
```

```
Console.WriteLine("Watson, come here I need you...");

// create an Http channel and register it
// uses port 0 to indicate you won't be listening
HttpChannel chan = new HttpChannel(0);
ChannelServices.RegisterChannel(chan);

FileStream fileStream =
    new FileStream ("calculatorSoap.txt", FileMode.Open);
SoapFormatter soapFormatter =
    new SoapFormatter ();

try
{
    ICalc calc=
        (ICalc) soapFormatter.Deserialize (fileStream);

    // use the interface to call methods
    double sum = calc.Add(3.0,4.0);
    double difference = calc.Sub(3,4);
    double product = calc.Mult(3,4);
    double quotient = calc.Div(3,4);

    // print the results
    Console.WriteLine("3+4 = {0}", sum);
    Console.WriteLine("3-4 = {0}", difference);
    Console.WriteLine("3*4 = {0}", product);
    Console.WriteLine("3/4 = {0}", quotient);
}
catch( System.Exception ex )
{
    Console.WriteLine("Exception caught: ");
    Console.WriteLine(ex.Message);
}
}
```

When the client starts up, the file is read from the disk and the proxy is unmarshaled. This is the mirror operation to marshaling and serializing the object on the server. Once you have unmarshaled the proxy, you are able to invoke the methods on the Calculator object running on the server.

Understanding Endpoints

What is going on when you register the endpoint in Example 19-5 (the server)? Clearly, the server is associating that endpoint with the type. When the client connects, that endpoint is used as an index into a table so that the server can provide a proxy to the correct object (in this case, the calculator).

If you don't provide an endpoint for the client to talk to, you can instead write all the information about your Calculator object to a file and physically give that file to your client. For example, you could send it to your buddy by email, and he could load it on his local computer.

The client can deserialize the object and reconstitute a proxy, which it can then use to access the calculator on your server! (The following example was suggested to me by Mike Woodring, formerly of DevelopMentor, who uses a similar example to drive home the idea that the endpoint is simply a convenience for accessing a marshaled object remotely.)

To see how you can invoke an object without a known endpoint, modify the `Main()` method of Example 19-3 once again. This time, instead of calling `Marshal()` with an endpoint, just pass in the object:

```
ObjRef objRef = RemotingServices.Marshal(calculator)
```

`Marshal()` returns an `ObjRef` object. An `ObjRef` object stores all the information required to activate and communicate with a remote object. When you do supply an endpoint, the server creates a table that associates the endpoint with an `objRef` so that the server can create the proxy when a client asks for it. `ObjRef` contains all the information needed by the client to build a proxy, and `objRef` itself is serializable.

Open a file stream for writing to a new file and create a new SOAP formatter. You can serialize your `ObjRef` to that file by invoking the `Serialize()` method on the formatter, passing in the file stream and the `ObjRef` you got back from `Marshal`. Presto! You have all the information you need to create a proxy to your object written out to a disk file. The complete replacement for Example 19-5's `Main()` is shown in Example 19-7. You'll also need to add three using statements to *CalcServer.cs,* as shown.

Example 19-7. Marshaling an object without a well-known endpoint

```
using System;
using System.IO;
using System.Runtime.Serialization.Formatters.Soap;

public static void Main()
{
    // create a channel and register it
    HttpChannel chan = new HttpChannel(65100);
    ChannelServices.RegisterChannel(chan);
    // make your own instance and call Marshal directly
    Calculator calculator = new Calculator();

    ObjRef objRef = RemotingServices.Marshal(calculator);

    FileStream fileStream =
        new FileStream("calculatorSoap.txt",FileMode.Create);

    SoapFormatter soapFormatter = new SoapFormatter();

    soapFormatter.Serialize(fileStream,objRef);
    fileStream.Close();
```

```
    //  "They also serve who only stand and wait." (Milton)
    Console.WriteLine(
      "Exported to CalculatorSoap.txt. Press ENTER to exit...");
    Console.ReadLine();
}
```

When you run the server, it writes the file *calculatorSoap.txt* to the filesystem. The server then waits for the client to connect. It might have a long wait. (Though after about 10 minutes, it shuts itself down.)

CHAPTER 20

Threads and Synchronization

Threads are responsible for multitasking within a single application. The System.
Threading namespace provides a wealth of classes and interfaces to manage multithreaded programming. The majority of programmers might never need to manage
threads explicitly, however, because the CLR abstracts much of the threading support into classes that simplify most threading tasks. For example, in Chapter 21 you
will see how to create multithreaded reading and writing streams without resorting
to managing the threads yourself.

The first part of this chapter shows you how to create, manage, and kill threads.
Even if you don't create your own threads explicitly, you'll want to ensure that your
code can handle multiple threads if it's run in a multithreading environment. This
concern is especially important if you are creating components that might be used by
other programmers in a program that supports multithreading. It is particularly significant to remoting and web services developers. Although web services (covered in
Chapter 15) have many attributes of desktop applications, they are run on the server,
generally lack a user interface, and force the developer to think about server-side
issues such as efficiency and multithreading.

The second part of this chapter focuses on synchronization. When you have a limited resource (such as a database connection), you may need to restrict access to that
resource to one thread at a time. A classic analogy is to a restroom on an airplane.
You want to allow access to the restroom for only one person at a time. This is done
by putting a lock on the door. When passengers want to use the restroom, they try
the door handle; if it is locked, they either go away and do something else, or wait
patiently in line with others who want access to the resource. When the resource
becomes free, one person is taken off the line and given the resource, which is then
locked again.

At times, various threads might want to access a resource in your program, such as a
file. It might be important to ensure that only one thread has access to your resource
at a time, and so you will lock the resource, allow a thread access, and then unlock

the resource. Programming locks can be fairly sophisticated, ensuring a fair distribution of resources.

Threads

Threads are typically created when you want a program to do two things at once. For example, assume you are calculating *pi* (3.141592653589...) to the 10 billionth place. The processor will happily begin computing this, but nothing will write to the user interface while it is working. Because computing *pi* to the 10 billionth place will take a few weeks, you might like the processor to provide an update as it goes. In addition, you might want to provide a Stop button so that the user can cancel the operation at any time. To allow the program to handle the click on the Stop button, you will need a second thread of execution.

Another common place to use threading is when you must wait for an event, such as user input, a read from a file, or receipt of data over the network. Freeing the processor to turn its attention to another task while you wait (such as computing another 10,000 values of *pi*) is a good idea, and it makes your program appear to run more quickly.

On the flip side, note that in some circumstances, threading can actually slow you down. Assume that in addition to calculating *pi*, you also want to calculate the Fibonacci series (1,1,2,3,5,8,13,21...). If you have a multiprocessor machine, this will run faster if each computation is in its own thread. If you have a single-processor machine (as most users do), computing these values in multiple threads will certainly run *slower* than computing one and then the other in a single thread because the processor must switch back and forth between the two threads. This incurs some overhead.

Starting Threads

The simplest way to create a thread is to create a new instance of the Thread class. The Thread constructor takes a single argument: a delegate instance. The CLR provides the ThreadStart delegate class specifically for this purpose, which points to a method you designate. This allows you to construct a thread and to say to it, "When you start, run this method." The ThreadStart delegate declaration is:

```
public delegate void ThreadStart();
```

As you can see, the method you attach to this delegate must take no parameters and must return void. Thus, you might create a new thread like this:

```
Thread myThread = new Thread( new ThreadStart(myFunc) );
```

For example, you might create two worker threads, one that counts up from zero:

```
public void Incrementer()
{
```

```
        for (int i =0;i<1000;i++)
        {
            Console.WriteLine("Incrementer: {0}", i);
        }
    }
```

and one that counts down from 1,000:

```
    public void Decrementer()
    {
        for (int i = 1000;i>=0;i--)
        {
            Console.WriteLine("Decrementer: {0}", i);
        }
    }
```

To run these in threads, create two new threads, each initialized with a ThreadStart delegate. These in turn would be initialized to the respective member functions:

```
    Thread t1 = new Thread( new ThreadStart(Incrementer) );
    Thread t2 = new Thread( new ThreadStart(Decrementer) );
```

Instantiating these threads doesn't start them running. To do so you must call the Start method on the Thread object itself:

```
    t1.Start();
    t2.Start();
```

 If you don't take further action, the thread stops when the function returns. You'll see how to stop a thread before the function ends later in this chapter.

Example 20-1 is the full program and its output. You will need to add a using statement for System.Threading to make the compiler aware of the Thread class. Notice the output, where you can see the processor switching from t1 to t2.

Example 20-1. Using threads

```
#region Using directives

using System;
using System.Collections.Generic;
using System.Text;
using System.Threading;

#endregion

namespace UsingThreads
{
    class Tester
    {
        static void Main()
        {
```

Example 20-1. Using threads (continued)

```
            // make an instance of this class
            Tester t = new Tester();

            Console.WriteLine( "Hello" );
            // run outside static Main
            t.DoTest();
        }

    public void DoTest()
    {
        // create a thread for the Incrementer
        // pass in a ThreadStart delegate
        // with the address of Incrementer
        Thread t1 =
            new Thread(
                new ThreadStart( Incrementer ) );

        // create a thread for the Decrementer
        // pass in a ThreadStart delegate
        // with the address of Decrementer
        Thread t2 =
            new Thread(
                new ThreadStart( Decrementer ) );

        // start the threads
        t1.Start();
        t2.Start();
    }

    // demo function, counts up to 1K
    public void Incrementer()
    {
        for ( int i = 0; i < 1000; i++ )
        {

            System.Console.WriteLine(
                "Incrementer: {0}", i );
        }
    }

    // demo function, counts down from 1k
    public void Decrementer()
    {
        for ( int i = 1000; i >= 0; i-- )
        {
            System.Console.WriteLine(
                "Decrementer: {0}", i );
        }
    }
    }
}
```

Example 20-1. Using threads (continued)

```
Output (excerpt):
Incrementer: 102
Incrementer: 103
Incrementer: 104
Incrementer: 105
Incrementer: 106
Decrementer: 1000
Decrementer: 999
Decrementer: 998
Decrementer: 997
```

The processor allows the first thread to run long enough to count up to 106. Then, the second thread kicks in, counting down from 1,000 for a while. Then the first thread is allowed to run. When I run this with larger numbers, I notice that each thread is allowed to run for about 100 numbers before switching.

 The actual amount of time devoted to any given thread is handled by the thread scheduler and depends on many factors, such as the processor speed, demands on the processor from other programs, etc.

Joining Threads

When you tell a thread to stop processing and wait until a second thread completes its work, you are said to be joining the first thread to the second. It is as if you tied the tip of the first thread on to the tail of the second—hence "joining" them.

To join thread 1 (t1) onto thread 2 (t2), write:

```
t2.Join();
```

If this statement is executed in a method in thread t1, t1 will halt and wait until t2 completes and exits. For example, you might ask the thread in which Main() executes to wait for all our other threads to end before it writes its concluding message. In this next code snippet, assume you've created a collection of threads named myThreads. Iterate over the collection, joining the current thread to each thread in the collection in turn:

```
foreach (Thread myThread in myThreads)
{
    myThread.Join();
}

Console.WriteLine("All my threads are done.");
```

The final message All my threads are done isn't be printed until all the threads have ended. In a production environment, you might start up a series of threads to accomplish some task (e.g., printing, updating the display, etc.) and not want to continue the main thread of execution until the worker threads are completed.

Blocking Threads with Sleep

At times, you want to suspend your thread for a short while. You might, for example, like your clock thread to suspend for about a second in between testing the system time. This lets you display the new time about once a second without devoting hundreds of millions of machine cycles to the effort.

The Thread class offers a public static method, Sleep, for just this purpose. The method is overloaded; one version takes an int, the other a timeSpan object. Each represents the number of milliseconds you want the thread suspended for, expressed either as an int (e.g., 2,000 = 2,000 milliseconds or 2 seconds) or as a timeSpan.

Although timeSpan objects can measure *ticks* (100 nanoseconds), the Sleep() method's granularity is in milliseconds (1,000,000 nanoseconds).

To cause your thread to sleep for one second, you can invoke the static method of Thread.Sleep, which suspends the thread in which it is invoked:

```
Thread.Sleep(1000);
```

At times, you'll pass zero for the amount of time to sleep; this signals the thread scheduler that you'd like your thread to yield to another thread, even if the thread scheduler might otherwise give your thread a bit more time.

If you modify Example 20-1 to add a Thread.Sleep(1) statement after each WriteLine(), the output changes significantly:

```
for (int i =0;i<1000;i++)
{
    Console.WriteLine(
        "Incrementer: {0}", i);
    Thread.Sleep(1);
}
```

This small change is sufficient to give each thread an opportunity to run once the other thread prints one value. The output reflects this change:

```
Incrementer: 0
Incrementer: 1
Decrementer: 1000
Incrementer: 2
Decrementer: 999
Incrementer: 3
Decrementer: 998
Incrementer: 4
Decrementer: 997
Incrementer: 5
Decrementer: 996
Incrementer: 6
Decrementer: 995
```

Killing Threads

Typically, threads die after running their course. You can, however, ask a thread to kill itself. The cleanest way is to set a KeepAlive Boolean flag that the thread can check periodically. When the flag changes state (e.g., goes from true to false) the thread can stop itself.

An alternative is to call Thread.Interrupt which asks the thread to kill itself. Finally, in desperation, and if you are shutting down your application in any case, you may call Thread.Abort. This causes a ThreadAbortException exception to be thrown, which the thread can catch.

The thread ought to treat the ThreadAbortException exception as a signal that it is time to exit immediately. In any case, you don't so much kill a thread as politely request that it commit suicide.

You might wish to kill a thread in reaction to an event, such as the user clicking the Cancel button. The event handler for the Cancel button might be in thread t1, and the event it is canceling might be in thread t2. In your event handler, you can call Abort on t2:

```
t2.abort();
```

An exception will be raised in t1's currently running method that t1 can catch.

In Example 20-2, three threads are created and stored in an array of Thread objects. Before the Threads are started, the IsBackground property is set to true (background threads are exactly like foreground threads, except that they don't stop a process from terminating). Each thread is then started and named (e.g., Thread1, Thread2, etc.). A message is displayed indicating that the thread is started, and then the main thread sleeps for 50 milliseconds before starting up the next thread.

After all three threads are started and another 50 milliseconds have passed, the first thread is aborted by calling Abort(). The main thread then joins all three of the running threads. The effect of this is that the main thread will not resume until all the other threads have completed. When they do complete, the main thread prints a message: All my threads are done. The complete source is displayed in Example 20-2.

Example 20-2. Interrupting a thread

```
#region Using directives

using System;
using System.Collections.Generic;
using System.Text;
using System.Threading;

#endregion

namespace InterruptingThreads
{
```

Example 20-2. Interrupting a thread (continued)

```csharp
class Tester
{
    static void Main()
    {
        // make an instance of this class
        Tester t = new Tester();

        // run outside static Main
        t.DoTest();
    }

    public void DoTest()
    {
        // create an array of unnamed threads
        Thread[] myThreads =
        {
          new Thread( new ThreadStart(Decrementer) ),
          new Thread( new ThreadStart(Incrementer) ),
          new Thread( new ThreadStart(Decrementer) ),
          new Thread( new ThreadStart(Incrementer) )
        };

        // start each thread
        int ctr = 1;
        foreach (Thread myThread in myThreads)
        {
            myThread.IsBackground = true;
            myThread.Start();
            myThread.Name = "Thread" + ctr.ToString();
            ctr++;
            Console.WriteLine("Started thread {0}", myThread.Name);
            Thread.Sleep(50);
        }

        // ask the first thread to stop
        myThreads[0].Interrupt();

        // tell the second thread to abort immediately
        myThreads[1].Abort();

        // wait for all threads to end before continuing
        foreach (Thread myThread in myThreads)
        {
            myThread.Join();
        }

        // after all threads end, print a message
        Console.WriteLine("All my threads are done.");
    }

    // demo function, counts down from 100
    public void Decrementer()
```

Example 20-2. Interrupting a thread (continued)

```
    {
        try
        {
            for (int i = 100; i >= 0; i--)
            {
                Console.WriteLine(
                    "Thread {0}. Decrementer: {1}",
                    Thread.CurrentThread.Name,
                    i);
                Thread.Sleep(1);
            }
        }
        catch (ThreadAbortException)
        {
            Console.WriteLine(
                "Thread {0} aborted! Cleaning up...",
                Thread.CurrentThread.Name);
        }
        catch (System.Exception e)
        {
            Console.WriteLine("Thread has been interrupted ");
        }
        finally
        {
            Console.WriteLine(
                "Thread {0} Exiting. ",
                Thread.CurrentThread.Name);
        }
    }

    // demo function, counts up to 100
    public void Incrementer()
    {
        try
        {
            for (int i = 0; i < 100; i++)
            {
                Console.WriteLine(
                    "Thread {0}. Incrementer: {1}",
                    Thread.CurrentThread.Name,
                    i);
                Thread.Sleep(1);
            }
        }
        catch (ThreadAbortException)
        {
            Console.WriteLine(
                "Thread {0} aborted!",
                Thread.CurrentThread.Name);
        }
        catch (System.Exception e)
        {
```

Example 20-2. Interrupting a thread (continued)

```
                Console.WriteLine("Thread has been interrupted");
            }
            finally
            {
                Console.WriteLine(
                    "Thread {0} Exiting. ",
                    Thread.CurrentThread.Name);
            }
        }
    }
}
```

```
Output (excerpt):
Started thread Thread1
Thread Thread1. Decrementer: 100
Thread Thread1. Decrementer: 99
Started thread Thread2
Thread Thread2. Incrementer: 0
Thread Thread1. Decrementer: 98
Started thread Thread3
Thread Thread3. Decrementer: 100
Thread Thread1. Decrementer: 97
Thread Thread2. Incrementer: 1
Started thread Thread4
Thread Thread4. Incrementer: 0
Thread Thread2 aborted!
Thread Thread3. Decrementer: 99
Thread Thread2 Exiting.
Thread has been interrupted
Thread Thread3. Decrementer: 98
Thread Thread4. Incrementer: 1
Thread Thread1 Exiting.
Thread Thread3. Decrementer: 97
Thread Thread3. Decrementer: 1
Thread Thread4. Incrementer: 98
Thread Thread3. Decrementer: 0
Thread Thread4. Incrementer: 99
Thread Thread3 Exiting.
Thread Thread4 Exiting.
All my threads are done.
```

You see the first thread start and decrement from 100 to 99. The second thread starts, and the two threads are interleaved for a while until the third and fourth threads start. After a short while, however, Thread2 reports that it has been aborted, and then it reports that it is exiting. A little while later, Thread1 reports that it was interrupted. Because the interrupt waits for the thread to be in a wait state, this can be a bit less immediate than a call to Abort. The two remaining threads continue until they are done. They then exit naturally, and the main thread, which was joined on all three, resumes to print its exit message.

Synchronization

At times, you might want to control access to a resource, such as an object's properties or methods, so that only one thread at a time can modify or use that resource. Your object is similar to the airplane restroom discussed earlier, and the various threads are like the people waiting in line. Synchronization is provided by a lock on the object, which helps the developer avoid having a second thread barge in on your object until the first thread is finished with it.

This section examines three synchronization mechanisms: the Interlock class, the C# lock statement, and the Monitor class. But first, you need to create a shared resource, (often a file or printer); in this case a simple integer variable: counter. You will increment counter from each of two threads.

To start, declare the member variable and initialize it to 0:

```
int counter = 0;
```

Modify the Incrementer method to increment the counter member variable:

```
public void Incrementer()
{
   try
   {
      while (counter < 1000)
      {
         int temp = counter;
         temp++; // increment

         // simulate some work in this method
         Thread.Sleep(1);

         // assign the Incremented value
         // to the counter variable
         // and display the results
         counter = temp;
         Console.WriteLine(
            "Thread {0}. Incrementer: {1}",
            Thread.CurrentThread.Name,
            counter);
      }
   }
}
```

The idea here is to simulate the work that might be done with a controlled resource. Just as you might open a file, manipulate its contents, and then close it, here you read the value of counter into a temporary variable, increment the temporary variable, sleep for one millisecond to simulate work, and then assign the incremented value back to counter.

The problem is that your first thread reads the value of counter (0) and assigns that to a temporary variable. It then increments the temporary variable. While it is doing its work, the second thread reads the value of counter (still 0) and assigns that value to a temporary variable. The first thread finishes its work, then assigns the temporary value (1) back to counter and displays it. The second thread does the same. What is printed is 1,1. In the next go around, the same thing happens. Rather than having the two threads count 1,2,3,4, you'll see 1,2,3,3,4,4. Example 20-3 shows the complete source code and output for this example.

Example 20-3. Simulating a shared resource

```
#region Using directives

using System;
using System.Collections.Generic;
using System.Text;
using System.Threading;

#endregion

namespace SharedResource
{
    class Tester
    {
        private int counter = 0;

        static void Main()
        {
            // make an instance of this class
            Tester t = new Tester();

            // run outside static Main
            t.DoTest();
        }

        public void DoTest()
        {
            Thread t1 = new Thread( new ThreadStart( Incrementer ) );
            t1.IsBackground = true;
            t1.Name = "ThreadOne";
            t1.Start();
            Console.WriteLine( "Started thread {0}",
                t1.Name );

            Thread t2 = new Thread( new ThreadStart( Incrementer ) );
            t2.IsBackground = true;
            t2.Name = "ThreadTwo";
            t2.Start();
            Console.WriteLine( "Started thread {0}",
                t2.Name );
            t1.Join();
            t2.Join();

            // after all threads end, print a message
            Console.WriteLine( "All my threads are done." );
        }
```

Example 20-3. Simulating a shared resource (continued)

```
        // demo function, counts up to 1K
        public void Incrementer()
        {
            try
            {
                while ( counter < 1000 )
                {
                    int temp = counter;
                    temp++; // increment

                    // simulate some work in this method
                    Thread.Sleep( 1 );

                    // assign the decremented value
                    // and display the results
                    counter = temp;
                    Console.WriteLine(
                        "Thread {0}. Incrementer: {1}",
                        Thread.CurrentThread.Name,
                        counter );
                }
            }
            catch ( ThreadInterruptedException )
            {
                Console.WriteLine(
                    "Thread {0} interrupted! Cleaning up...",
                    Thread.CurrentThread.Name );
            }
            finally
            {
                Console.WriteLine(
                    "Thread {0} Exiting. ",
                    Thread.CurrentThread.Name );
            }
        }
    }
}
```

```
Output:
Started thread ThreadOne
Started thread ThreadTwo
Thread ThreadOne. Incrementer: 1
Thread ThreadOne. Incrementer: 2
Thread ThreadOne. Incrementer: 3
Thread ThreadTwo. Incrementer: 3
Thread ThreadTwo. Incrementer: 4
Thread ThreadOne. Incrementer: 4
Thread ThreadTwo. Incrementer: 5
Thread ThreadOne. Incrementer: 5
Thread ThreadTwo. Incrementer: 6
Thread ThreadOne. Incrementer: 6
```

Using Interlocked

The CLR provides a number of synchronization mechanisms. These include the common synchronization tools such as critical sections (called *locks* in .NET), as well as the Monitor class. Each is discussed later in this chapter.

Incrementing and decrementing a value is such a common programming pattern, and one which so often needs synchronization protection, that the CLR offers a special class, Interlocked, just for this purpose. Interlocked has two methods, Increment and Decrement, which not only increment or decrement a value, but also do so under synchronization control.

Modify the Incrementer method from Example 20-3 as follows:

```
public void Incrementer()
{
    try
    {
        while (counter < 1000)
        {
            int temp = Interlocked.Increment(ref counter);

            // simulate some work in this method
            Thread.Sleep(0);

            // display the incremented value
            Console.WriteLine(
                "Thread {0}. Incrementer: {1}",
                Thread.CurrentThread.Name,
                temp);
        }
    }
}
```

The catch and finally blocks and the remainder of the program are unchanged from the previous example.

Interlocked.Increment() expects a single parameter: a reference to an int. Because int values are passed by value, use the ref keyword, as described in Chapter 4.

> The Increment() method is overloaded and can take a reference to a long rather than to an int, if that is what you need.

Once this change is made, access to the counter member is synchronized, and the output is what we'd expect:

```
Output (excerpts):
Started thread ThreadOne
Started thread ThreadTwo
Thread ThreadOne. Incrementer: 1
Thread ThreadTwo. Incrementer: 2
```

```
Thread ThreadOne. Incrementer: 3
Thread ThreadTwo. Incrementer: 4
Thread ThreadOne. Incrementer: 5
Thread ThreadTwo. Incrementer: 6
Thread ThreadOne. Incrementer: 7
Thread ThreadTwo. Incrementer: 8
Thread ThreadOne. Incrementer: 9
Thread ThreadTwo. Incrementer: 10
Thread ThreadOne. Incrementer: 11
Thread ThreadTwo. Incrementer: 12
Thread ThreadOne. Incrementer: 13
Thread ThreadTwo. Incrementer: 14
Thread ThreadOne. Incrementer: 15
Thread ThreadTwo. Incrementer: 16
Thread ThreadOne. Incrementer: 17
Thread ThreadTwo. Incrementer: 18
Thread ThreadOne. Incrementer: 19
Thread ThreadTwo. Incrementer: 20
```

Using Locks

Although the Interlocked object is fine if you want to increment or decrement a value, there will be times when you want to control access to other objects as well. What is needed is a more general synchronization mechanism. This is provided by the C# lock feature.

A lock marks a critical section of your code, providing synchronization to an object you designate while the lock is in effect. The syntax of using a lock is to request a lock on an object and then to execute a statement or block of statements. The lock is removed at the end of the statement block.

C# provides direct support for locks through the lock keyword. Pass in a reference to an object, and follow the keyword with a statement block:

```
lock(expression) statement-block
```

For example, you can modify Incrementer again to use a lock statement, as follows:

```
public void Incrementer()
{
   try
   {
      while (counter < 1000)
      {
         int temp;
         lock (this)
         {
            temp = counter;
            temp ++;
            Thread.Sleep(1);
            counter = temp;
         }
```

```
            // assign the decremented value
            // and display the results
            Console.WriteLine(
                "Thread {0}. Incrementer: {1}",
                Thread.CurrentThread.Name,
                temp);
        }
    }
```

The catch and finally blocks and the remainder of the program are unchanged from the previous example.

The output from this code is identical to that produced using Interlocked.

Using Monitors

The objects used so far will be sufficient for most needs. For the most sophisticated control over resources, you might want to use a *monitor*. A monitor lets you decide when to enter and exit the synchronization, and it lets you wait for another area of your code to become free.

When you want to begin synchronization, call the Enter() method of the monitor, passing in the object you want to lock:

```
    Monitor.Enter(this);
```

If the monitor is unavailable, the object protected by the monitor is presumed to be in use. You can do other work while you wait for the monitor to become available and then try again. You can also explicitly choose to Wait(), suspending your thread until the moment the monitor is free and the developer calls Pulse (discussed in a bit). Wait() helps you control thread ordering.

For example, suppose you are downloading and printing an article from the Web. For efficiency, you'd like to print in a background thread, but you want to ensure that at least 10 pages have downloaded before you begin.

Your printing thread will wait until the get-file thread signals that enough of the file has been read. You don't want to Join the get-file thread because the file might be hundreds of pages. You don't want to wait until it has completely finished downloading, but you do want to ensure that at least 10 pages have been read before your print thread begins. The Wait() method is just the ticket.

To simulate this, rewrite Tester, and add back the decrementer method. Your incrementer counts up to 10. The decrementer method counts down to zero. It turns out you don't want to start decrementing unless the value of counter is at least 5.

In decrementer, call Enter on the monitor. Then check the value of counter, and if it is less than 5, call Wait on the monitor:

```
if (counter < 5)
{
    Monitor.Wait(this);
}
```

This call to Wait() frees the monitor, but signals the CLR that you want the monitor back the next time it is free. Waiting threads are notified of a chance to run again if the active thread calls Pulse():

```
Monitor.Pulse(this);
```

Pulse() signals the CLR that there has been a change in state that might free a thread that is waiting.

When a thread is finished with the monitor, it must mark the end of its controlled area of code with a call to Exit():

```
Monitor.Exit(this);
```

Example 20-4 continues the simulation, providing synchronized access to a counter variable using a Monitor.

Example 20-4. Using a Monitor object

```
#region Using directives

using System;
using System.Collections.Generic;
using System.Text;
using System.Threading;

#endregion

namespace UsingAMonitor
{
    class Tester
    {
        private long counter = 0;

        static void Main()
        {
            // make an instance of this class
            Tester t = new Tester();

            // run outside static Main
            t.DoTest();
        }

        public void DoTest()
        {
            // create an array of unnamed threads
            Thread[] myThreads =
                {
```

Example 20-4. Using a Monitor object (continued)

```
           new Thread( new ThreadStart(Decrementer) ),
           new Thread( new ThreadStart(Incrementer) )
        };

    // start each thread
    int ctr = 1;
    foreach ( Thread myThread in myThreads )
    {
        myThread.IsBackground = true;
        myThread.Start();
        myThread.Name = "Thread" + ctr.ToString();
        ctr++;
        Console.WriteLine( "Started thread {0}", myThread.Name );
        Thread.Sleep( 50 );
    }

    // wait for all threads to end before continuing
    foreach ( Thread myThread in myThreads )
    {
        myThread.Join();
    }

    // after all threads end, print a message
    Console.WriteLine( "All my threads are done." );
}

void Decrementer()
{
    try
    {
        // synchronize this area of code
        Monitor.Enter( this );

        // if counter is not yet 10
        // then free the monitor to other waiting
        // threads, but wait in line for your turn
        if ( counter < 10 )
        {
            Console.WriteLine(
                "[{0}] In Decrementer. Counter: {1}. Gotta Wait!",
                Thread.CurrentThread.Name, counter );
            Monitor.Wait( this );
        }

        while ( counter > 0 )
        {
            long temp = counter;
            temp--;
            Thread.Sleep( 1 );
            counter = temp;
            Console.WriteLine(
```

Example 20-4. Using a Monitor object (continued)

```
                        "[{0}] In Decrementer. Counter: {1}. ",
                        Thread.CurrentThread.Name, counter );
                }
            }
            finally
            {
                Monitor.Exit( this );
            }
        }

        void Incrementer()
        {
            try
            {
                Monitor.Enter( this );
                while ( counter < 10 )
                {
                    long temp = counter;
                    temp++;
                    Thread.Sleep( 1 );
                    counter = temp;
                    Console.WriteLine(
                        "[{0}] In Incrementer. Counter: {1}",
                        Thread.CurrentThread.Name, counter );
                }

                // I'm done incrementing for now, let another
                // thread have the Monitor
                Monitor.Pulse( this );
            }
            finally
            {
                Console.WriteLine( "[{0}] Exiting...",
                    Thread.CurrentThread.Name );
                Monitor.Exit( this );
            }
        }
    }
}
```

```
Output:
Started thread Thread1
[Thread1] In Decrementer. Counter: 0. Gotta Wait!
Started thread Thread2
[Thread2] In Incrementer. Counter: 1
[Thread2] In Incrementer. Counter: 2
[Thread2] In Incrementer. Counter: 3
[Thread2] In Incrementer. Counter: 4
[Thread2] In Incrementer. Counter: 5
[Thread2] In Incrementer. Counter: 6
[Thread2] In Incrementer. Counter: 7
[Thread2] In Incrementer. Counter: 8
```

Example 20-4. Using a Monitor object (continued)

```
[Thread2] In Incrementer. Counter: 9
[Thread2] In Incrementer. Counter: 10
[Thread2] Exiting...
[Thread1] In Decrementer. Counter: 9.
[Thread1] In Decrementer. Counter: 8.
[Thread1] In Decrementer. Counter: 7.
[Thread1] In Decrementer. Counter: 6.
[Thread1] In Decrementer. Counter: 5.
[Thread1] In Decrementer. Counter: 4.
[Thread1] In Decrementer. Counter: 3.
[Thread1] In Decrementer. Counter: 2.
[Thread1] In Decrementer. Counter: 1.
[Thread1] In Decrementer. Counter: 0.
All my threads are done.
```

In this example, decrementer is started first. In the output you see Thread1 (the decre-menter) start up and then realize that it has to wait. You then see Thread2 start up. Only when Thread2 pulses does Thread1 begin its work.

Try some experiments with this code. First, comment out the call to Pulse(). You'll find that Thread1 never resumes. Without Pulse(), there is no signal to the waiting threads.

As a second experiment, rewrite Incrementer to pulse and exit the monitor after each increment:

```
void Incrementer()
{
    try
    {
        while (counter < 10)
        {
          Monitor.Enter(this);
            long temp = counter;
            temp++;
            Thread.Sleep(1);
            counter = temp;
            Console.WriteLine(
                "[{0}] In Incrementer. Counter: {1}",
                Thread.CurrentThread.Name, counter);
            Monitor.Pulse(this);
            Monitor.Exit(this);
        }
```

Rewrite Decrementer as well, changing the if statement to a while statement and knocking down the value from 10 to 5:

```
//if (counter < 10)
while (counter < 5)
```

The net effect of these two changes is to cause Thread2, the Incrementer, to pulse the Decrementer after each increment. While the value is smaller than five, the

---

Decrementer must continue to wait; once the value goes over five, the Decrementer runs to completion. When it is done, the Incrementer thread can run again. The output is shown here:

```
[Thread2] In Incrementer. Counter: 2
[Thread1] In Decrementer. Counter: 2. Gotta Wait!
[Thread2] In Incrementer. Counter: 3
[Thread1] In Decrementer. Counter: 3. Gotta Wait!
[Thread2] In Incrementer. Counter: 4
[Thread1] In Decrementer. Counter: 4. Gotta Wait!
[Thread2] In Incrementer. Counter: 5
[Thread1] In Decrementer. Counter: 4.
[Thread1] In Decrementer. Counter: 3.
[Thread1] In Decrementer. Counter: 2.
[Thread1] In Decrementer. Counter: 1.
[Thread1] In Decrementer. Counter: 0.
[Thread2] In Incrementer. Counter: 1
[Thread2] In Incrementer. Counter: 2
[Thread2] In Incrementer. Counter: 3
[Thread2] In Incrementer. Counter: 4
[Thread2] In Incrementer. Counter: 5
[Thread2] In Incrementer. Counter: 6
[Thread2] In Incrementer. Counter: 7
[Thread2] In Incrementer. Counter: 8
[Thread2] In Incrementer. Counter: 9
[Thread2] In Incrementer. Counter: 10
```

Race Conditions and Deadlocks

The .NET library provides sufficient thread support that you will rarely find yourself creating your own threads and managing synchronization manually.

Thread synchronization can be tricky, especially in complex programs. If you do decide to create your own threads, you must confront and solve all the traditional problems of thread synchronization, such as race conditions and deadlock.

Race Conditions

A race condition exists when the success of your program depends on the uncontrolled order of completion of two independent threads.

Suppose, for example, that you have two threads—one is responsible for opening a file and the other is responsible for writing to the file. It is important that you control the second thread so that it's assured that the first thread has opened the file. If not, under some conditions, the first thread will open the file and the second thread will work fine; under other unpredictable conditions, the first thread won't finish opening the file before the second thread tries to write to it, and you'll throw an exception (or worse, your program will simply seize up and die). This is a race condition, and race conditions can be very difficult to debug.

You can't leave these two threads to operate independently; you must ensure that Thread1 will have completed before Thread2 begins. To accomplish this, you might Join() Thread2 on Thread1. As an alternative, you can use a Monitor and Wait() for the appropriate conditions before resuming Thread2.

Deadlock

When you wait for a resource to become free, you are at risk of *deadlock*, also called a *deadly embrace*. In a deadlock, two or more threads are waiting for each other, and neither can become free.

Suppose you have two threads, ThreadA and ThreadB. ThreadA locks down an Employee object and then tries to get a lock on a row in the database. It turns out that ThreadB already has that row locked, so ThreadA waits.

Unfortunately, ThreadB can't update the row until it locks down the Employee object, which is already locked down by ThreadA. Neither thread can proceed, and neither thread will unlock its own resource. They are waiting for each other in a deadly embrace.

As described, the deadlock is fairly easy to spot—and to correct. In a program running many threads, deadlock can be very difficult to diagnose, let alone solve. One guideline is to get all the locks you need or to release all the locks you have. That is, as soon as ThreadA realizes that it can't lock the Row, it should release its lock on the Employee object. Similarly, when ThreadB can't lock the Employee, it should release the Row. A second important guideline is to lock as small a section of code as possible and to hold the lock as briefly as possible.

CHAPTER 21

Streams

For many applications, data is held in memory and accessed as if it were a three-dimensional solid; when you need to access a variable or an object, use its name—and, presto, it is available to you. When you want to move your data into or out of a file, across the network, or over the Internet, however, your data must be *streamed.*[*] In a *stream*, data flows much like bubbles in a stream of water.

Typically, the endpoint of a stream is a backing store. The backing store provides a source for the stream, like a lake provides a source for a river. Typically, the backing store is a file, but it is also possible for the backing store to be a network or web connection.

Files and directories are abstracted by classes in the .NET Framework. These classes provide methods and properties for creating, naming, manipulating, and deleting files and directories on your disk.

The .NET Framework provides both buffered and unbuffered streams, as well as classes for asynchronous I/O. With asynchronous I/O you can instruct the .NET classes to read your file; while they are busy getting the bits off the disk, your program can be working on other tasks. The asynchronous I/O tasks notify you when their work is done. The asynchronous classes are sufficiently powerful and robust that you might be able to avoid creating threads explicitly (see Chapter 20).

Streaming into and out of files is no different from streaming across the network, and the second part of this chapter will describe streaming using both TCP/IP and web protocols.

To create a stream of data, your object will typically be *serialized*, or written to the stream as a series of bits. You have already encountered serialization in Chapter 19. The .NET Framework provides extensive support for serialization, and the final part

---

[*] Internet data may also be sent in datagrams.

of this chapter walks you through the details of taking control of the serialization of your object.

Files and Directories

Before looking at how you can get data into and out of files, let's start by examining the support provided for file and directory manipulation.

The classes you need are in the System.IO namespace. These include the File class, which represents a file on disk, and the Directory class, which represents a directory (also known in Windows as a *folder*).

Working with Directories

The Directory class exposes static methods for creating, moving, and exploring directories. All the methods of the Directory class are static, and therefore you can call them all without having an instance of the class.

The DirectoryInfo class is a similar class, but one which has nothing but instance members (i.e., no static members at all). DirectoryInfo derives from FileSystemInfo, which in turn derives from MarshalByRefObject. The FileSystemInfo class has a number of properties and methods that provide information about a file or directory.

Table 21-1 lists the principal methods of the Directory class, and Table 21-2 lists the principal methods of the DirectoryInfo class, including important properties and methods inherited from FileSystemInfo.

Table 21-1. Principal methods of the Directory class

Method	Use
CreateDirectory()	Creates all directories and subdirectories specified by its path parameter.
GetCreationTime()	Returns and sets the time the specified directory was created.
GetDirectories()	Gets named directories.
GetLogicalDrives()	Returns the names of all the logical drives in the form <drive>:\.
GetFiles()	Returns the names of files matching a pattern.
GetParent()	Returns the parent directory for the specified path.
Move()	Moves a directory and its contents to a specified path.

Table 21-2. Principal methods and properties of the DirectoryInfo class

Method or property	Use
Attributes	Inherits from FileSystemInfo; gets or sets the attributes of the current file.
CreationTime	Inherits from FileSystemInfo; gets or sets the creation time of the current file.
Exists	Public property Boolean value, which is true if the directory exists.
Extension	Public property inherited from FileSystemInfo; i.e., the file extension.

Table 21-2. Principal methods and properties of the DirectoryInfo class (continued)

Method or property	Use
FullName	Public property inherited from FileSystemInfo; i.e., the full path of the file or directory.
LastAccessTime	Public property inherited from FileSystemInfo; gets or sets the last access time.
LastWriteTime	Public property inherited from FileSystemInfo; gets or sets the time when the current file or directory was last written to.
Name	Public property name of this instance of DirectoryInfo.
Parent	Public property parent directory of the specified directory.
Root	Public property root portion of the path.
Create()	Public method that creates a directory.
CreateSubdirectory()	Public method that creates a subdirectory on the specified path.
Delete()	Public method that deletes a DirectoryInfo and its contents from the path.
GetDirectories()	Public method that returns a DirectoryInfo array with subdirectories.
GetFiles()	Public method that returns a list of files in the directory.
GetFileSystemIn fos()	Public method that retrieves an array of FileSystemInfo objects.
MoveTo()	Public method that moves a DirectoryInfo and its contents to a new path.
Refresh()	Public method inherited from FileSystemInfo; refreshes the state of the object.

Creating a DirectoryInfo Object

To explore a directory hierarchy, you need to instantiate a DirectoryInfo object. The DirectoryInfo class provides methods for getting not just the names of contained files and directories, but also FileInfo and DirectoryInfo objects, allowing you to dive into the hierarchical structure, extracting subdirectories and exploring these recursively.

Instantiate a DirectoryInfo object with the name of the directory you want to explore:

```
string path = Environment.GetEnvironmentVariable("SystemRoot");
DirectoryInfo dir = new DirectoryInfo(path);
```

 Remember that the @ sign before a string creates a verbatim string literal in which it isn't necessary to escape characters such as the backslash. This was covered in Chapter 10.

You can ask that DirectoryInfo object for information about itself, including its name, full path, attributes, the time it was last accessed, and so forth. To explore the subdirectory hierarchy, ask the current directory for its list of subdirectories:

```
DirectoryInfo[] directories = dir.GetDirectories();
```

This returns an array of DirectoryInfo objects, each of which represents a directory. You can then recurse into the same method, passing in each DirectoryInfo object in turn:

```
foreach (DirectoryInfo newDir in directories)
{
    dirCounter++;
    ExploreDirectory(newDir);
}
```

The dirCounter static int member variable keeps track of how many subdirectories have been found altogether. To make the display more interesting, add a second static int member variable indentLevel that will be incremented each time you recurse into a subdirectory, and will be decremented when you pop out. This will allow you to display the subdirectories indented under the parent directories. The complete listing is shown in Example 21-1.

Example 21-1. Recursing through subdirectories

```
#region Using directives

using System;
using System.Collections.Generic;
using System.IO;
using System.Text;

#endregion

namespace RecursingDirectories
{
    class Tester
    {

        // static member variables to keep track of totals
        // and indentation level
        static int dirCounter = 1;
        static int indentLevel = -1; // so first push = 0

        public static void Main()
        {
            Tester t = new Tester();

            // choose the initial subdirectory
            string theDirectory =
                Environment.GetEnvironmentVariable( "SystemRoot" );
            // Mono and Shared Source CLI users on Linux, Unix or
            // Mac OS X should comment out the preceding two lines
            // of code and uncomment the following:
            //string theDirectory = "/tmp";

            // call the method to explore the directory,
            // displaying its access date and all
            // subdirectories
```

Example 21-1. Recursing through subdirectories (continued)

```
        DirectoryInfo dir = new DirectoryInfo( theDirectory );

        t.ExploreDirectory( dir );

        // completed. print the statistics
        Console.WriteLine(
           "\n\n{0} directories found.\n",
           dirCounter );
     }

     // Set it running with a directoryInfo object
     // for each directory it finds, it will call
     // itself recursively

     private void ExploreDirectory( DirectoryInfo dir )
     {
        indentLevel++;  // push a directory level

        // create indentation for subdirectories
        for ( int i = 0; i < indentLevel; i++ )
           Console.Write( "  " ); // two spaces per level

        // print the directory and the time last accessed
        Console.WriteLine( "[{0}] {1} [{2}]\n",
           indentLevel, dir.Name, dir.LastAccessTime );

        // get all the directories in the current directory
        // and call this method recursively on each
        DirectoryInfo[] directories = dir.GetDirectories();
        foreach ( DirectoryInfo newDir in directories )
        {
           dirCounter++;  // increment the counter
           ExploreDirectory( newDir );
        }
        indentLevel--; // pop a directory level
     }
   }
}
```

Output (excerpt):

```
   [2] logiscan [5/1/2001 3:06:41 PM]

   [2] miitwain [5/1/2001 3:06:41 PM]

  [1] Web [5/1/2001 3:06:41 PM]

   [2] printers [5/1/2001 3:06:41 PM]

    [3] images [5/1/2001 3:06:41 PM]
```

Example 21-1. Recursing through subdirectories (continued)

```
[2] Wallpaper [5/1/2001 3:06:41 PM]
```

363 directories found.

 You must add using System.IO; to the top of your file; Visual Studio 2005 doesn't do this automatically.

The program begins by identifying a directory (*SystemRoot*, usually *C:\WinNT* or *C:\Windows*) and creating a DirectoryInfo object for that directory. It then calls ExploreDirectory, passing in that DirectoryInfo object. ExploreDirectory displays information about the directory and then retrieves all the subdirectories.

The list of all the subdirectories of the current directory is obtained by calling Get-Directories. This returns an array of DirectoryInfo objects. ExploreDirectory is the recursive method; each DirectoryInfo object is passed into ExploreDirectory in turn. The effect is to push recursively into each subdirectory, and then pop back out to explore sister directories until all the subdirectories of *%SystemRoot%* are displayed. When ExploreDirectory finally returns, the calling method prints a summary.

Working with Files

The DirectoryInfo object can also return a collection of all the files in each subdirectory found. The GetFiles() method returns an array of FileInfo objects, each of which describes a file in that directory. The FileInfo and File objects relate to one another, much as DirectoryInfo and Directory do. Like the methods of Directory, all the File methods are static; like DirectoryInfo, all the methods of FileInfo are instance methods.

Table 21-3 lists the principal methods of the File class; Table 21-4 lists the important members of the FileInfo class.

Table 21-3. Principal public static methods of the File class

Method	Use
AppendText()	Creates a StreamWriter that appends text to the specified file.
Copy()	Copies an existing file to a new file.
Create()	Creates a file in the specified path.
CreateText()	Creates a StreamWriter that writes a new text file to the specified file.
Delete()	Deletes the specified file.
Exists()	Returns true if the specified file exists.
GetAttributes(), SetAttributes()	Gets and sets the FileAttributes of the specified file.

Method	Use
GetCreationTime(), SetCreationTime()	Returns and sets the creation date and time of the file.
GetLastAccessTime(), SetLastAccessTime()	Returns and sets the last time the specified file was accessed.
GetLastWriteTime(), SetLastWriteTime()	Returns and sets the last time the specified file was written to.
Move()	Moves a file to a new location; can be used to rename a file.
OpenRead()	Public static method that opens a FileStream on the file.
OpenWrite()	Creates a read/write Stream on the specified path.

Table 21-4. Methods and properties of the FileInfo class

Method or property	Use
Attributes()	Inherits from FileSystemInfo; gets or sets the attributes of the current file.
CreationTime	Inherits from FileSystemInfo; gets or sets the creation time of the current file.
Directory	Public property that gets an instance of the parent directory.
Exists	Public property Boolean value that is true if the directory exists.
Extension	Public property inherited from FileSystemInfo; i.e., the file extension.
FullName	Public property inherited from FileSystemInfo; i.e., the full path of the file or directory.
LastAccessTime	Public property inherited from FileSystemInfo; gets or sets the last access time.
LastWriteTime	Public property inherited from FileSystemInfo; gets or sets the time when the current file or directory was last written to.
Length	Public property that gets the size of the current file.
Name	Public property Name of this DirectoryInfo instance.
AppendText()	Public method that creates a StreamWriter that appends text to a file.
CopyTo()	Public method that copies an existing file to a new file.
Create()	Public method that creates a new file.
Delete()	Public method that permanently deletes a file.
MoveTo()	Public method to move a file to a new location; can be used to rename a file.
Open()	Public method that opens a file with various read/write and sharing privileges.
OpenRead()	Public method that creates a read-only FileStream.
OpenText()	Public method that creates a StreamReader that reads from an existing text file.
OpenWrite()	Public method that creates a write-only FileStream.

Example 21-2 modifies Example 21-1, adding code to get a FileInfo object for each file in each subdirectory. That object is used to display the name of the file, along with its length and the date and time it was last accessed.

Example 21-2. Exploring files and subdirectories

```csharp
#region Using directives

using System;
using System.Collections.Generic;
using System.IO;
using System.Text;

#endregion

namespace ExploringFilesAndSubdirectories
{
    class Tester
    {

        // static member variables to keep track of totals
        // and indentation level
        static int dirCounter = 1;
        static int indentLevel = -1; // so first push = 0

        static int fileCounter = 0;

        public static void Main()
        {
            Tester t = new Tester();

            // choose the initial subdirectory
            string theDirectory =
                Environment.GetEnvironmentVariable( "SystemRoot" );
            // Mono and Shared Source CLI users on Linux, Unix or
            // Mac OS X should comment out the preceding two lines
            // of code and uncomment the following:
            //string theDirectory = "/tmp";

            // call the method to explore the directory,
            // displaying its access date and all
            // subdirectories
            DirectoryInfo dir = new DirectoryInfo( theDirectory );

            t.ExploreDirectory( dir );

            // completed. print the statistics

            Console.WriteLine(
                "\n\n{0} files in {1}  directories found.\n",
                fileCounter, dirCounter );
        }

        // Set it running with a directoryInfo object
        // for each directory it finds, it will call
        // itself recursively
        private void ExploreDirectory( DirectoryInfo dir )
        {
```

Example 21-2. Exploring files and subdirectories (continued)

```
         indentLevel++;  // push a directory level

         // create indentation for subdirectories
         for ( int i = 0; i < indentLevel; i++ )
            Console.Write( "  " ); // two spaces per level

         // print the directory and the time last accessed
         Console.WriteLine( "[{0}] {1} [{2}]\n",
            indentLevel, dir.Name, dir.LastAccessTime );

         // get all the files in the directory and
         // print their name, last access time, and size
         FileInfo[] filesInDir = dir.GetFiles();
         foreach ( FileInfo file in filesInDir )
         {
            // indent once extra to put files
            // under their directory
            for ( int i = 0; i < indentLevel + 1; i++ )
               Console.Write( "  " ); // two spaces per level

            Console.WriteLine( "{0} [{1}] Size: {2} bytes",
               file.Name,
               file.LastWriteTime,
               file.Length );
            fileCounter++;
         }

         // get all the directories in the current directory
         // and call this method recursively on each
         DirectoryInfo[] directories = dir.GetDirectories();
         foreach ( DirectoryInfo newDir in directories )
         {
            dirCounter++;  // increment the counter
            ExploreDirectory( newDir );
         }
         indentLevel--; // pop a directory level
      }
   }
}

Output (excerpt):
[0] WINDOWS [9/4/2004 8:37:13 AM]

  0.LOG [8/30/2004 8:26:05 PM] Size: 0 bytes
  AC3API.INI [1/14/1999 2:04:06 PM] Size: 231 bytes
  actsetup.log [7/1/2004 11:13:11 AM] Size: 3848 bytes
  Blue Lace 16.bmp [8/29/2002 6:00:00 AM] Size: 1272 bytes
  BOOTSTAT.DAT [8/30/2004 8:25:03 PM] Size: 2048 bytes
12630 files in 1444  directories found.
```

The example is initialized with the name of the *SystemRoot* directory. It prints information about all the files in that directory and then recursively explores all the subdirectories and all their subdirectories (your output might differ). This can take quite a while to run because the *SystemRoot* directory tree is rather large (1,444 subdirectories on my machine, as shown in the output).

Modifying Files

As you can see from Tables 21-3 and 21-4, it's possible to use the `FileInfo` class to create, copy, rename, and delete files. The next example creates a new subdirectory, copies files in, renames some, deletes others, and then deletes the entire directory.

 To set up these examples, create a *test* directory and copy the media directory from WinNT or Windows into the *test* directory. Don't work on files in the system root directly; when working with system files you want to be extraordinarily careful.

The first step is to create a `DirectoryInfo` object for the test directory (adjust theDirectory appropriately if you are on a Mac OS X, Linux, or Unix system):

```
string theDirectory = @"c:\test\media";
DirectoryInfo dir = new DirectoryInfo(theDirectory);
```

Next, create a subdirectory within the test directory by calling `CreateSubDirectory` on the `DirectoryInfo` object. You get back a new `DirectoryInfo` object, representing the newly created subdirectory:

```
string newDirectory = "newTest";
DirectoryInfo newSubDir =
    dir.CreateSubdirectory(newDirectory);
```

You can now iterate over the test and copy files to the newly created subdirectory:

```
FileInfo[] filesInDir = dir.GetFiles();
foreach (FileInfo file in filesInDir)
{
    string fullName = newSubDir.FullName +
        "\\" + file.Name;
    file.CopyTo(fullName);
    Console.WriteLine("{0} copied to newTest",
        file.FullName);
}
```

Notice the syntax of the `CopyTo` method. This is a method of the `FileInfo` object. Pass in the full path of the new file, including its full name and extension.

Once you've copied the files, you can get a list of the files in the new subdirectory and work with them directly:

```
filesInDir = newSubDir.GetFiles();
foreach (FileInfo file in filesInDir)
{
```

Create a simple integer variable named counter and use it to rename every other file:

```
if (counter++ %2 == 0)
{
    file.MoveTo(fullName + ".bak");
    Console.WriteLine("{0} renamed to {1}",
        fullName,file.FullName);
}
```

You rename a file by "moving" it to the same directory, but with a new name. You can, of course, move a file to a new directory with its original name, or you can move and rename at the same time.

Rename every other file, and delete the ones you don't rename:

```
file.Delete();
Console.WriteLine("{0} deleted.",
    fullName);
```

Once you're done manipulating the files, you can clean up by deleting the entire subdirectory:

```
newSubDir.Delete(true);
```

The Boolean parameter determines whether this is a recursive delete. If you pass in false, and if this directory has subdirectories with files in it, it throws an exception.

Example 21-3 lists the source code for the complete program. Be careful when running this: when it is done, the subdirectory is gone. To see the renaming and deletions, either put a breakpoint on the last line or remove the last line.

Example 21-3. Creating a subdirectory and manipulating files

```
#region Using directives

using System;
using System.Collections.Generic;
using System.IO;
using System.Text;

#endregion

namespace CreatingSubdirectoryManipulatingFile
{
    class Tester
    {
        public static void Main()
        {
            // make an instance and run it
            Tester t = new Tester();
            string theDirectory = @"c:\test\media";
            DirectoryInfo dir = new DirectoryInfo( theDirectory );
            t.ExploreDirectory( dir );
        }
```

Example 21-3. Creating a subdirectory and manipulating files (continued)

```
        // Set it running with a directory name
        private void ExploreDirectory( DirectoryInfo dir )
        {

            // make a new subdirectory
            string newDirectory = "newTest";
            DirectoryInfo newSubDir =
                dir.CreateSubdirectory( newDirectory );

            // get all the files in the directory and
            // copy them to the new directory
            FileInfo[] filesInDir = dir.GetFiles();
            foreach ( FileInfo file in filesInDir )
            {
                string fullName = newSubDir.FullName +
                    "\\" + file.Name;
                file.CopyTo( fullName );
                Console.WriteLine( "{0} copied to newTest",
                    file.FullName );
            }

            // get a collection of the files copied in
            filesInDir = newSubDir.GetFiles();

            // delete some and rename others
            int counter = 0;
            foreach ( FileInfo file in filesInDir )
            {
                string fullName = file.FullName;

                if ( counter++ % 2 == 0 )
                {
                    file.MoveTo( fullName + ".bak" );
                    Console.WriteLine( "{0} renamed to {1}",
                        fullName, file.FullName );
                }
                else
                {
                    file.Delete();
                    Console.WriteLine( "{0} deleted.",
                        fullName );
                }
            }

            newSubDir.Delete( true ); // delete the subdirectory
        }
    }
}
```

Example 21-3. Creating a subdirectory and manipulating files (continued)

```
Output (excerpts):
c:\test\media\Bach's Brandenburg Concerto No. 3.RMI
        copied to newTest
c:\test\media\Beethoven's 5th Symphony.RMI copied to newTest
c:\test\media\Beethoven's Fur Elise.RMI copied to newTest
c:\test\media\canyon.mid copied to newTest
c:\test\media\newTest\Bach's Brandenburg Concerto
        No. 3.RMI renamed to
c:\test\media\newTest\Bach's Brandenburg Concerto
        No. 3.RMI.bak
c:\test\media\newTest\Beethoven's 5th Symphony.RMI deleted.
c:\test\media\newTest\Beethoven's Fur Elise.RMI renamed to
c:\test\media\newTest\Beethoven's Fur Elise.RMI.bak
c:\test\media\newTest\canyon.mid deleted.
```

Reading and Writing Data

Reading and writing data is accomplished with the Stream class. Remember streams? This is a chapter about streams.*

Stream supports synchronous and asynchronous reads and writes. The .NET Framework provides a number of classes derived from Stream, including FileStream, MemoryStream, and NetworkStream. In addition, there is a BufferedStream class that provides buffered I/O and can be used with any of the other stream classes. The principal classes involved with I/O are summarized in Table 21-5.

Table 21-5. Principal I/O classes of the .NET Framework

Class	Use
Stream	Abstract class that supports reading and writing bytes.
BinaryReader/BinaryWriter	Read and write encoded strings and primitive datatypes to and from streams.
File, FileInfo, Directory, DirectoryInfo	Provide implementations for the abstract FileSystemInfo classes, including creating, moving, renaming, and deleting files and directories.
FileStream	For reading to and from File objects; supports random access to files. Opens files synchronously by default; supports asynchronous file access.
TextReader, TextWriter, StringReader, StringWriter	TextReader and TextWriter are abstract classes designed for Unicode character I/O. StringReader and StringWriter write to and from strings, allowing your input and output to be either a stream or a string.
BufferedStream	A stream that adds buffering to another stream such as a NetworkStream. BufferedStreams can improve performance of the stream to which they are attached, but note that FileStream has buffering built in.

---

* With a tip of the hat to Arlo Guthrie.

Table 21-5. Principal I/O classes of the .NET Framework (continued)

Class	Use
MemoryStream	A nonbuffered stream whose encapsulated data is directly accessible in memory, and is most useful as a temporary buffer.
NetworkStream	A stream over a network connection.

Binary Files

This section starts by using the basic Stream class to perform a binary read of a file. The term *binary read* is used to distinguish from a *text read*. If you don't know for certain that a file is just text, it is safest to treat it as a stream of bytes, known as a *binary* file.

The Stream class is chock-a-block with methods, but the most important are Read(), Write(), BeginRead(), BeginWrite(), and Flush(). All of these are covered in the next few sections.

To perform a binary read, begin by creating a pair of Stream objects, one for reading and one for writing:

```
Stream inputStream = File.OpenRead(
    @"C:\test\source\test1.cs");

Stream outputStream = File.OpenWrite(
    @"C:\test\source\test1.bak");
```

To open the files to read and write, use the static OpenRead() and OpenWrite() methods of the File class. The static overload of these methods takes the path for the file as an argument, as shown previously.

Binary reads work by reading into a buffer. A buffer is just an array of bytes that will hold the data read by the Read() method.

Pass in the buffer, the offset in the buffer at which to begin storing the data read in, and the number of bytes to read. InputStream.Read reads bytes from the backing store into the buffer and returns the total number of bytes read.

It continues reading until no more bytes remain:

```
while ( (bytesRead =
    inputStream.Read(buffer,0,SIZE_BUFF)) > 0 )
{
    outputStream.Write(buffer,0,bytesRead);
}
```

Each bufferful of bytes is written to the output file. The arguments to Write() are the buffer from which to read, the offset into that buffer at which to start reading, and the number of bytes to write. Notice that you write the same number of bytes as you just read.

Example 21-4 provides the complete listing.

Example 21-4. Implementing a binary read and write to a file

```
#region Using directives

using System;
using System.Collections.Generic;
using System.IO;
using System.Text;

#endregion

namespace ImplementingBinaryReadWriteToFile
{
    class Tester
    {
        const int SizeBuff = 1024;

        public static void Main()
        {
            // make an instance and run it
            Tester t = new Tester();
            t.Run();
        }

        // Set it running with a directory name
        private void Run()
        {
            // the file to read from
            Stream inputStream = File.OpenRead(
                @"C:\test\source\test1.cs" );

            // the file to write to
            Stream outputStream = File.OpenWrite(
                @"C:\test\source\test1.bak" );

            // create a buffer to hold the bytes
            byte[] buffer = new Byte[SizeBuff];
            int bytesRead;

            // while the read method returns bytes
            // keep writing them to the output stream
            while ( ( bytesRead =
                inputStream.Read( buffer, 0, SizeBuff ) ) > 0 )
            {
                outputStream.Write( buffer, 0, bytesRead );
            }

            // tidy up before exiting
            inputStream.Close();
            outputStream.Close();
        }
    }
}
```

Before you run this program, create the *C:\test\source* subdirectory and add a file (containing the source to this program) named *test1.cs*. As with previous examples, Unix, Linux, and Mac OS X readers should adjust the paths appropriately.

The result of running this program is that a copy of the input file (*test1.cs*) is made in the same directory and named *test1.bak*. You can compare these files using your favorite file comparison tool; they are identical, as shown in Figure 21-1.*

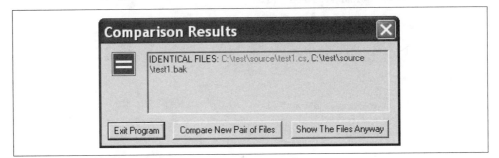

Figure 21-1. File comparison showing the two files are identical

Buffered Streams

In the previous example, you created a buffer to read into. When you called Read(), a bufferful was read from disk. It might be, however, that the operating system can be much more efficient if it reads a larger (or smaller) number of bytes at once.

A *buffered stream* object creates an internal buffer, and reads bytes to and from the backing store in whatever increments it thinks are most efficient. It will still fill your buffer in the increments you dictate, but your buffer is filled from the in-memory buffer, not from the backing store. The net effect is that the input and output are more efficient and thus faster.

A BufferedStream object is composed around an existing Stream object that you already have created. To use a BufferedStream, start by creating a normal stream class as you did in Example 21-4:

```
Stream inputStream = File.OpenRead(
    @"C:\test\source\folder3.cs");

Stream outputStream = File.OpenWrite(
    @"C:\test\source\folder3.bak");
```

---

* My personal favorite file comparison utility, as shown here, is ExamDiff Pro (*http://www.prestosoft.com/ps. asp?page=edp_examdiffpro*).

Once you have the normal stream, pass that stream object to the buffered stream's constructor:

```
BufferedStream bufferedInput =
    new BufferedStream(inputStream);

BufferedStream bufferedOutput =
    new BufferedStream(outputStream);
```

You can then use the BufferedStream as a normal stream, calling Read() and Write() just as you did before. The operating system handles the buffering:

```
while ( (bytesRead =
    bufferedInput.Read(buffer,0,SIZE_BUFF)) > 0 )
{
    bufferedOutput.Write(buffer,0,bytesRead);
}
```

Remember to *flush* the buffer when you want to ensure that the data is written out to the file:

```
bufferedOutput.Flush();
```

This essentially tells the in-memory buffer to flush out its contents.

 Note that all streams should be closed, though the finalizer will eventually close them for you if you just let them go out of scope. In a robust program, you should always explicitly close the buffer.

Example 21-5 provides the complete listing.

Example 21-5. Implementing buffered I/O

```
namespace Programming_CSharp
{
    using System;
    using System.IO;

    class Tester
    {
        const int SizeBuff = 1024;

        public static void Main()
        {
            // make an instance and run it
            Tester t = new Tester();
            t.Run();
        }

        // Set it running with a directory name
        private void Run()
        {
            // create binary streams
```

Example 21-5. Implementing buffered I/O (continued)

```
        Stream inputStream = File.OpenRead(
            @"C:\test\source\folder3.cs");

        Stream outputStream = File.OpenWrite(
            @"C:\test\source\folder3.bak");

        // add buffered streams on top of the
        // binary streams
        BufferedStream bufferedInput =
            new BufferedStream(inputStream);

        BufferedStream bufferedOutput =
            new BufferedStream(outputStream);
        byte[] buffer = new Byte[SizeBuff];
        int bytesRead;

        while ( (bytesRead =
            bufferedInput.Read(buffer,0,SizeBuff)) > 0 )
        {
            bufferedOutput.Write(buffer,0,bytesRead);
        }

        bufferedOutput.Flush();
        bufferedInput.Close();
        bufferedOutput.Close();
    }
  }
}
```

With larger files, this example should run more quickly than Example 21-4 did.

Working with Text Files

If you know that the file you are reading (and writing) contains nothing but text, you might want to use the StreamReader and StreamWriter classes. These classes are designed to make manipulation of text easier. For example, they support the ReadLine() and WriteLine() methods that read and write a line of text at a time. You've already used WriteLine() with the Console object.

To create a StreamReader instance, start by creating a FileInfo object and then call the OpenText() method on that object:

```
    FileInfo theSourceFile =
        new FileInfo (@"C:\test\source\test1.cs");

    StreamReader stream = theSourceFile.OpenText();
```

OpenText() returns a StreamReader for the file. With the StreamReader in hand, you can now read the file, line by line:

```
    do
    {
        text = stream.ReadLine();
    } while (text != null);
```

ReadLine() reads a line at a time until it reaches the end of the file. The StreamReader will return null at the end of the file.

To create the StreamWriter class, call the StreamWriter constructor, passing in the full name of the file you want to write to:

```
StreamWriter writer = new
StreamWriter(@"C:\test\source\folder3.bak",false);
```

The second parameter is the Boolean argument append. If the file already exists, true will cause the new data to be appended to the end of the file, and false will cause the file to be overwritten. In this case, pass in false, overwriting the file if it exists.

You can now create a loop to write out the contents of each line of the old file into the new file, and while you're at it, to print the line to the console as well:

```
    do
    {
        text = reader.ReadLine();
        writer.WriteLine(text);
        Console.WriteLine(text);
    } while (text != null);
```

Example 21-6 provides the complete source code.

Example 21-6. Reading and writing to a text file

```
#region Using directives

using System;
using System.Collections.Generic;
using System.IO;
using System.Text;

#endregion

namespace ReadingWritingToTextFile
{
    class Tester
    {
        public static void Main()
        {
            // make an instance and run it
            Tester t = new Tester();
            t.Run();
        }

        // Set it running with a directory name
        private void Run()
        {
```

Example 21-6. Reading and writing to a text file (continued)

```
    // open a file
    FileInfo theSourceFile = new FileInfo(
        @"C:\test\source\test.cs" );

    // create a text reader for that file
    StreamReader reader = theSourceFile.OpenText();

    // create a text writer to the new file
    StreamWriter writer = new StreamWriter(
        @"C:\test\source\test.bak", false );

    // create a text variable to hold each line
    string text;

    // walk the file and read every line
    // writing both to the console
    // and to the file
    do
    {
        text = reader.ReadLine();
        writer.WriteLine( text );
        Console.WriteLine( text );
    } while ( text != null );

    // tidy up
    reader.Close();
    writer.Close();
    }
  }
}
```

When this program is run, the contents of the original file are written both to the screen and to the new file. Notice the syntax for writing to the console:

```
Console.WriteLine(text);
```

This syntax is nearly identical to that used to write to the file:

```
writer.WriteLine(text);
```

The key difference is that the WriteLine() method of Console is static, while the WriteLine() method of StreamWriter, which is inherited from TextWriter, is an instance method, and thus must be called on an object rather than on the class itself.

Asynchronous I/O

All the programs you've looked at so far perform *synchronous I/O*, meaning that while your program is reading or writing, all other activity is stopped. It can take a long time (relatively speaking) to read data to or from the backing store, especially if the backing store is a slow disk or (horrors!) a source on the Internet.

With large files, or when reading or writing across the network, you'll want *asynchronous I/O*, which allows you to begin a read and then turn your attention to other matters while the CLR fulfills your request. The .NET Framework provides asynchronous I/O through the BeginRead() and BeginWrite() methods of Stream.

The sequence is to call BeginRead() on your file and then to go on to other, unrelated work while the read continues, possibly in another thread. When the read completes, you are notified via a callback method. You can then process the data that was read, kick off another read, and then go back to your other work.

In addition to the three parameters you've used in the binary read (the buffer, the offset, and how many bytes to read), BeginRead() asks for a *delegate* and a *state object*.

 This is an instance of the more general async pattern seen throughout .NET (e.g., async stream I/O, async socket operations, async delegate invocation, etc.).

The delegate is an optional callback method, which, if provided, is called when the data is read. The state object is also optional. In this example, pass in null for the state object. The state of the object is kept in the member variables of the test class.

You are free to put any object you like in the state parameter, and you can retrieve it when you are called back. Typically (as you might guess from the name), you stash away state values that you'll need on retrieval. The state parameter can be used by the developer to hold the state of the call (paused, pending, running, etc.).

In this example, create the buffer and the Stream object as private member variables of the class:

```
public class AsynchIOTester
{
    private Stream inputStream;
    private byte[] buffer;
    const int BufferSize = 256;
```

In addition, create your delegate as a private member of the class:

```
private AsyncCallback myCallBack; // delegated method
```

The delegate is declared to be of type AsyncCallback, which is what the BeginRead() method of Stream expects.

An AsyncCallBack delegate is declared in the System namespace as follows:

```
public delegate void AsyncCallback (IAsyncResult ar);
```

Thus, this delegate can be associated with any method that returns void and that takes an IAsyncResult interface as a parameter. The CLR will pass in the IAsyncResult interface object at runtime when the method is called. You only have to declare the method:

```
void OnCompletedRead(IAsyncResult asyncResult)
```

and then hook up the delegate in the constructor:

```
AsynchIOTester()
{
    //...
    myCallBack = new AsyncCallback(this.OnCompletedRead);
}
```

Here's how it works, step by step. In Main(), create an instance of the class and tell it to run:

```
public static void Main()
{
    AsynchIOTester theApp = new AsynchIOTester();
    theApp.Run();
}
```

The call to new invokes the constructor. In the constructor, open a file and get a Stream object back. Then allocate space in the buffer, and hook up the callback mechanism:

```
AsynchIOTester()
{
    inputStream = File.OpenRead(@"C:\test\source\AskTim.txt");
    buffer = new byte[BufferSize];
    myCallBack = new AsyncCallback(this.OnCompletedRead);
}
```

 This example needs a large text file. I've copied a column written by Tim O'Reilly ("Ask Tim") from *http://www.oreilly.com* into a text file named *AskTim.txt*. I placed that in a subdirectory *test\source* on my C: drive. You can use any text file in any subdirectory.

In the Run() method, call BeginRead(), which causes an asynchronous read of the file:

```
inputStream.BeginRead(
    buffer,          // where to put the results
    0,               // offset
    buffer.Length,   // BufferSize
    myCallBack,      // call back delegate
    null);           // local state object
```

Then go on to do other work. In this case, simulate useful work by counting up to 500,000, displaying your progress every 1,000 iterations:

```
for (long i = 0; i < 500000; i++)
{
    if (i%1000 == 0)
    {
        Console.WriteLine("i: {0}", i);
    }
}
```

When the read completes, the CLR will call your callback method:

```
void OnCompletedRead(IAsyncResult asyncResult)
{
```

The first thing to do when notified that the read has completed is to find out how many bytes were actually read. Do so by calling the EndRead() method of the Stream object, passing in the IAsyncResult interface object passed in by the CLR:

```
int bytesRead = inputStream.EndRead(asyncResult);
```

EndRead() returns the number of bytes read. If the number is greater than zero, you'll convert the buffer into a string and write it to the console, and then call BeginRead() again, for another asynchronous read:

```
if (bytesRead > 0)
{
    String s =
    Encoding.ASCII.GetString (buffer, 0, bytesRead);
    Console.WriteLine(s);
    inputStream.BeginRead(
    buffer, 0, buffer.Length,
    myCallBack, null);
}
```

The effect is that you can do other work while the reads are taking place, but you can handle the read data (in this case, by outputting it to the console) each time a bufferful is ready. Example 21-7 provides the complete program.

Example 21-7. Implementing asynchronous I/O

```
#region Using directives

using System;
using System.Collections.Generic;
using System.IO;
using System.Text;

#endregion

namespace AsynchronousIO
{
    public class AsynchIOTester
    {
        private Stream inputStream;

        // delegated method
        private AsyncCallback myCallBack;

        // buffer to hold the read data
        private byte[] buffer;

        // the size of the buffer
        const int BufferSize = 256;
```

Example 21-7. Implementing asynchronous I/O (continued)

```csharp
// constructor
AsynchIOTester()
{
   // open the input stream
   inputStream =
      File.OpenRead(
      @"C:\test\source\AskTim.txt" );

   // allocate a buffer
   buffer = new byte[BufferSize];

   // assign the call back
   myCallBack =
      new AsyncCallback( this.OnCompletedRead );
}

public static void Main()
{
   // create an instance of AsynchIOTester
   // which invokes the constructor
   AsynchIOTester theApp =
      new AsynchIOTester();

   // call the instance method
   theApp.Run();
}

void Run()
{
   inputStream.BeginRead(
      buffer,              // holds the results
      0,                   // offset
      buffer.Length,       // (BufferSize)
      myCallBack,          // call back delegate
      null );              // local state object

   // do some work while data is read
   for ( long i = 0; i < 500000; i++ )
   {
      if ( i % 1000 == 0 )
      {
         Console.WriteLine( "i: {0}", i );
      }
   }
}

// call back method
void OnCompletedRead( IAsyncResult asyncResult )
{
   int bytesRead =
      inputStream.EndRead( asyncResult );
```

Example 21-7. Implementing asynchronous I/O (continued)

```
                // if we got bytes, make them a string
                // and display them, then start up again.
                // Otherwise, we're done.
                if ( bytesRead > 0 )
                {
                    String s =
                        Encoding.ASCII.GetString( buffer, 0, bytesRead );
                    Console.WriteLine( s );
                    inputStream.BeginRead(
                        buffer, 0, buffer.Length, myCallBack, null );
                }
            }
        }
    }
}

Output (excerpt):
i: 47000
i: 48000
i: 49000
Date: January 2001
From: Dave Heisler
To: Ask Tim
Subject: Questions About O'Reilly
Dear Tim,
I've been a programmer for about ten years. I had heard of
O'Reilly books,then...
Dave,
You might be amazed at how many requests for help with
school projects I get;
i: 50000
i: 51000
i: 52000
```

The output reveals that the program is working on the two threads concurrently. The reads are done in the background while the other thread is counting and printing out every thousanth iteration. As the reads complete, they are printed to the console, and then you go back to counting. (I've shortened the listings to illustrate the output.)

In a real-world application, you might process user requests or compute values while the asynchronous I/O is busy retrieving or storing to a file or database.

Network I/O

Writing to a remote object on the Internet isn't very different from writing to a file on your local machine. You might want to do this if your program needs to store its data to a file on a machine on your network, or if you are creating a program that displays information on a monitor connected to another computer on your network.

Network I/O is based on the use of streams created with sockets. Sockets are very useful for client/server applications, peer to peer (P2P), and when making remote procedure calls.

A socket is an object that represents an endpoint for communication between processes communicating across a network. Sockets can work with various protocols, including UDP and TCP. In this section, we create a TCP/IP connection between a server and a client. TCP/IP is a connection-based stream-like protocol for network communication. Connection-based means that with TCP/IP, once a connection is made, the two processes can talk with one another as if they were connected by a direct phone line.

 Although TCP/IP is designed to talk across a network, you can simulate network communication by running the two processes on the same machine.

It is possible for more than one application on a given computer to be talking to various clients all at the same time (e.g., you might be running a web server, an FTP server, and a program that provides calculation support). Therefore, each application must have a unique ID so that the client can indicate which application it is looking for. That ID is known as a *port*. Think of the IP address as a phone number and the port as an extension.

The server instantiates a `TcpListener` and tells the listener to listen for connections on a specific port. The constructor for the `TcpListener` has two parameters, an IP address and an `int` representing the port on which that listener should listen.

Client applications connect to a specific IP address. For example, Yahoo's IP address is 66.94.234.13. Clients must also connect to a specific port. All web browsers connect to port 80 by default. Port numbers range from 0 to 65,535 (e.g., 216); however, some numbers are reserved.*

 Ports are divided into the following ranges:

- 0–1023: well-known ports
- 1024–49151: registered ports
- 49152–65535: dynamic and/or private ports

For a list of all the well-known and registered ports, look at *http://www.iana.org/assignments/port-numbers*.

Once the listener is created, call `Start()` on it, telling the listener to begin accepting network connections. When the server is ready to start responding to calls from

---

* If you run your program on a network with a firewall, talk to your network administrator about which ports are closed.

clients, call AcceptSocket(). The thread in which you've called AcceptSocket() blocks (waiting sadly by the phone, wringing its virtual hands, hoping for a call).

You can imagine creating the world's simplest listener. It waits patiently for a client to call. When it gets a call, it interacts with that client to the exclusion of all other clients. The next few clients to call will connect, but they will automatically be put on hold. While they are listening to the music and being told their call is important and will be handled in the order received, they will block in their own threads. Once the backlog (hold) queue fills, subsequent callers will get the equivalent of a busy signal. They must hang up and wait for our simple socket to finish with its current client. This model works fine for servers that take only one or two requests a week, but it doesn't scale well for real-world applications. Most servers need to handle thousands, even tens of thousands of connections a minute!

To handle a high volume of connections, applications use asynchronous I/O to accept a call and create a socket with the connection to the client. The original listener then returns to listening, waiting for the next client. This way your application can handle many calls; each time a call is accepted, a new socket is created.

The client is unaware of this sleight of hand in which a new socket is created. As far as the client is concerned, he has connected with the IP address and port he requested. Note that the new socket establishes a connection with the client. This is quite different from UDP, which uses a connectionless protocol. With TCP/IP, once the connection is made, the client and server know how to talk with each other without having to readdress each packet.

Creating a Network Streaming Server

To create a network server for TCP/IP streaming, start by creating a TcpListener object to listen to the TCP/IP port you've chosen. I've arbitrarily chosen port 65000 from the available port IDs:

```
IPAddress localAddr = IPAddress.Parse("127.0.0.1");
TcpListener tcpListener = new TcpListener(localAddr, 65000);
```

Once the TcpListener object is constructed, you can ask it to start listening:

```
tcpListener.Start();
```

Now wait for a client to request a connection:

```
Socket socketForClient = tcpListener.AcceptSocket();
```

The AcceptSocket method of the TcpListener object returns a Socket object that represents a *Berkeley socket interface* and is bound to a specific endpoint. AcceptSocket() is a synchronous method that will not return until it receives a connection request.

Because the model is widely accepted by computer vendors, *Berkeley sockets* simplify the task of porting existing socket-based source code from both Windows and Unix environments.

Once you have a socket you're ready to send the file to the client. Create a NetworkStream class, passing the socket into the constructor:

```
NetworkStream networkStream = new NetworkStream(socketForClient);
```

Then create a StreamWriter object much as you did before, except this time not on a file, but rather, on the NetworkStream you just created:

```
System.IO.StreamWriter streamWriter = new
    System.IO.StreamWriter(networkStream);
```

When you write to this stream, the stream is sent over the network to the client. Example 21-8 shows the entire server. (I've stripped this server down to its bare essentials. With a production server, you almost certainly would run the request processing code in a thread, and you'd want to enclose the logic in try blocks to handle network problems.)

Example 21-8. Implementing a network streaming server

```
#region Using directives

using System;
using System.Collections.Generic;
using System.Net;
using System.Net.Sockets;
using System.Text;

#endregion

namespace NetworkStreamingServer
{
    public class NetworkIOServer
    {

        public static void Main()
        {
            NetworkIOServer app =
                new NetworkIOServer();
            app.Run();
        }

        private void Run()
        {
            // create a new TcpListener and start it up
            // listening on port 65000
```

Example 21-8. Implementing a network streaming server (continued)

```
        IPAddress localAddr = IPAddress.Parse( "127.0.0.1" );
        TcpListener tcpListener = new TcpListener( localAddr, 65000 );
        tcpListener.Start();

        // keep listening until you send the file
        for ( ; ; )
        {
            // if a client connects, accept the connection
            // and return a new socket named socketForClient
            // while tcpListener keeps listening
            Socket socketForClient =
                tcpListener.AcceptSocket();
            Console.WriteLine( "Client connected" );

            // call the helper method to send the file
            SendFileToClient( socketForClient );

            Console.WriteLine(
                    "Disconnecting from client..." );

            // clean up and go home
            socketForClient.Close();
            Console.WriteLine( "Exiting..." );
                break;
        }
    }

    // helper method to send the file
    private void SendFileToClient(
        Socket socketForClient )
    {
        // create a network stream and a stream writer
        // on that network stream
        NetworkStream networkStream =
            new NetworkStream( socketForClient );
        System.IO.StreamWriter streamWriter =
            new System.IO.StreamWriter( networkStream );

        // create a stream reader for the file
        System.IO.StreamReader streamReader =
            new System.IO.StreamReader(
                @"C:\test\source\myTest.txt" );

        string theString;

        // iterate through the file, sending it
        // line-by-line to the client
        do
        {
            theString = streamReader.ReadLine();
```

Example 21-8. Implementing a network streaming server (continued)

```
        if ( theString != null )
        {
            Console.WriteLine(
                "Sending {0}", theString );
            streamWriter.WriteLine( theString );
            streamWriter.Flush();
        }
    }
    while ( theString != null );

    // tidy up
    streamReader.Close();
    networkStream.Close();
    streamWriter.Close();
        }
    }
}
```

Creating a Streaming Network Client

The client instantiates a TcpClient class, which represents a TCP/IP client connection to a host:

```
TcpClient socketForServer;
socketForServer = new TcpClient("localHost", 65000);
```

With this TcpClient, you can create a NetworkStream, and on that stream you can create a StreamReader:

```
NetworkStream networkStream = socketForServer.GetStream();
System.IO.StreamReader streamReader =
    new System.IO.StreamReader(networkStream);
```

Now read the stream as long as there is data on it, outputting the results to the console:

```
do
{
    outputString = streamReader.ReadLine();

    if( outputString != null )
    {
        Console.WriteLine(outputString);
    }
}
while( outputString != null );
```

Example 21-9 is the complete client.

Example 21-9. Implementing a network streaming client

```
#region Using directives

using System;
using System.Collections.Generic;
using System.Net.Sockets;
using System.Text;

#endregion

namespace NetworkStreamingClient
{
    public class Client
    {

        static public void Main( string[] Args )
        {

            // create a TcpClient to talk to the server
            TcpClient socketForServer;

            try
            {
                socketForServer =
                    new TcpClient( "localHost", 65000 );
            }
            catch
            {
                Console.WriteLine(
                    "Failed to connect to server at {0}:65000",
                        "localhost" );
                return;
            }

            // create the Network Stream and the Stream Reader object
            NetworkStream networkStream =
                    socketForServer.GetStream();
            System.IO.StreamReader streamReader =
                new System.IO.StreamReader( networkStream );

            try
            {
                string outputString;

                // read the data from the host and display it
                do
                {
                    outputString = streamReader.ReadLine();

                    if ( outputString != null )
                    {
                        Console.WriteLine( outputString );
                    }
```

Example 21-9. Implementing a network streaming client (continued)

```
            }
            while ( outputString != null );
        }
        catch
        {
            Console.WriteLine(
                "Exception reading from Server" );
        }

        // tidy up
        networkStream.Close();
    }
  }
}
```

To test this, I created a simple test file named *myText.txt*:

```
This is line one
This is line two
This is line three
This is line four
```

Here is the output from the server and the client:

```
Output (Server):

Client connected
Sending This is line one
Sending This is line two
Sending This is line three
Sending This is line four
Disconnecting from client...
Exiting...
Output (Client):

This is line one
This is line two
This is line three
This is line four
Press any key to continue
```

 If you are testing this on a single machine, run the client and server in separate command windows or individual instances of the development environment. You need to start the server first, or the client will fail, saying it can't connect. If you aren't running this on a single machine, you need to replace occurrences of 127.0.0.1 and localhost to the IP address of the machine running the server. If you are running Windows XP Service Pack 2 with the default settings, you will get a Windows Security Alert asking if you want to unblock the port.

Handling Multiple Connections

As mentioned earlier, this example doesn't scale well. Each client demands the entire attention of the server. A server is needed that can accept the connection and then pass the connection to overlapped I/O, providing the same asynchronous solution that you used earlier for reading from a file.

To manage this, create a new server, AsynchNetworkServer, which will nest within it a new class, ClientHandler. When your AsynchNetworkServer receives a client connection, it instantiates a ClientHandler and passes the socket to that ClientHandler instance.

The ClientHandler constructor will create a copy of the socket and a buffer and open a new NetworkStream on that socket. It then uses overlapped I/O to asynchronously read and write to that socket. For this demonstration, it simply echoes whatever text the client sends, back to the client and also to the console.

To create the asynchronous I/O, ClientHandler defines two delegate methods, OnReadComplete() and OnWriteComplete(), that manages the overlapped I/O of the strings sent by the client.

The body of the Run() method for the server is very similar to what you saw in Example 21-8. First, create a listener and then call Start(). Then create a forever loop and call AcceptSocket(). Once the socket is connected, instead of handling the connection, create a new ClientHandler and call StartRead() on that object.

The complete source for the server is shown in Example 21-10.

Example 21-10. Implementing an asynchronous network streaming server

```
#region Using directives

using System;
using System.Collections.Generic;
using System.Net;
using System.Net.Sockets;
using System.Text;

#endregion

namespace AsynchNetworkServer
{
    public class AsynchNetworkServer
    {

        class ClientHandler
        {
            private byte[] buffer;
            private Socket socket;
            private NetworkStream networkStream;
```

Example 21-10. Implementing an asynchronous network streaming server (continued)

```
private AsyncCallback callbackRead;
private AsyncCallback callbackWrite;

public ClientHandler( Socket socketForClient )
{
   socket = socketForClient;
   buffer = new byte[256];
   networkStream =
      new NetworkStream( socketForClient );

   callbackRead =
      new AsyncCallback( this.OnReadComplete );

   callbackWrite =
      new AsyncCallback( this.OnWriteComplete );
}

// begin reading the string from the client
public void StartRead()
{
   networkStream.BeginRead(
      buffer, 0, buffer.Length,
      callbackRead, null );
}

// when called back by the read, display the string
// and echo it back to the client
private void OnReadComplete( IAsyncResult ar )
{
   int bytesRead = networkStream.EndRead( ar );

   if ( bytesRead > 0 )
   {
      string s =
         System.Text.Encoding.ASCII.GetString(
            buffer, 0, bytesRead );
      Console.Write(
            "Received {0} bytes from client: {1}",
            bytesRead, s );
      networkStream.BeginWrite(
         buffer, 0, bytesRead, callbackWrite, null );
   }
   else
   {
      Console.WriteLine( "Read connection dropped" );
      networkStream.Close();
      socket.Close();
      networkStream = null;
      socket = null;
   }
}
```

```
    // after writing the string, print a message and resume reading
    private void OnWriteComplete( IAsyncResult ar )
    {
        networkStream.EndWrite( ar );
        Console.WriteLine( "Write complete" );
        networkStream.BeginRead(
            buffer, 0, buffer.Length,
            callbackRead, null );
    }
}

public static void Main()
{
    AsynchNetworkServer app =
        new AsynchNetworkServer();
    app.Run();
}

private void Run()
{
    // create a new TcpListener and start it up
    // listening on port 65000

    IPAddress localAddr = IPAddress.Parse( "127.0.0.1" );
    TcpListener tcpListener = new TcpListener( localAddr, 65000 );
    tcpListener.Start();

    // keep listening until you send the file
    for ( ; ; )
    {
        // if a client connects, accept the connection
        // and return a new socket named socketForClient
        // while tcpListener keeps listening
        Socket socketForClient =
            tcpListener.AcceptSocket();
        Console.WriteLine( "Client connected" );
        ClientHandler handler =
            new ClientHandler( socketForClient );
        handler.StartRead();
    }
}
```

The server starts up and listens to port 65000. If a client connects, the server will instantiate a ClientHandler that will manage the I/O with the client while the server listens for the next client.

In this example, you write the string received from the client to the console in `OnReadComplete()` and `OnWriteComplete()`. Writing to the console can block your thread until the write completes. In a production program, you don't want to take any blocking action in these methods because you are using a pooled thread. If you block in `OnReadComplete()` or `OnWriteComplete()`, you may cause more threads to be added to the thread pool, which is inefficient and will harm performance and scalability.

The client code is very simple. The client creates a `tcpSocket` for the port on which the server will listen (65000) and creates a `NetworkStream` object for that socket. It then writes a message to that stream and flushes the buffer. The client creates a `StreamReader` to read on that stream and writes whatever it receives to the console. The complete source for the client is shown in Example 21-11.

Example 21-11. Implementing a client for asynchronous network I/O

```
#region Using directives

using System;
using System.Collections.Generic;
using System.Net.Sockets;
using System.Text;

#endregion

namespace AsynchNetworkClient
{
    public class AsynchNetworkClient
    {
        private NetworkStream streamToServer;

        static public int Main()
        {

            AsynchNetworkClient client =
                new AsynchNetworkClient();
            return client.Run();
        }

        AsynchNetworkClient()
        {
            string serverName = "localhost";
            Console.WriteLine( "Connecting to {0}", serverName );
            TcpClient tcpSocket = new TcpClient( serverName, 65000 );
            streamToServer = tcpSocket.GetStream();
        }

        private int Run()
        {
            string message = "Hello Programming C#";
```

Example 21-11. Implementing a client for asynchronous network I/O (continued)

```
            Console.WriteLine(
                "Sending {0} to server.", message );

            // create a streamWriter and use it to
            // write a string to the server
            System.IO.StreamWriter writer =
                new System.IO.StreamWriter( streamToServer );
            writer.WriteLine( message );
            writer.Flush();

            // Read response
            System.IO.StreamReader reader =
                new System.IO.StreamReader( streamToServer );
            string strResponse = reader.ReadLine();
            Console.WriteLine( "Received: {0}", strResponse );
            streamToServer.Close();
            return 0;
        }
    }
}
```

```
Output (Server):
Client connected
Received 22 bytes from client: Hello Programming C#
Write complete
Read connection dropped

Output (Client):
Connecting to localhost
Sending Hello Programming C# to server.
Received: Hello Programming C#
```

In this example, the network server doesn't block while it is handling client connections, but rather, it delegates the management of those connections to instances of ClientHandler. Clients should not experience a delay waiting for the server to handle their connections.

Asynchronous Network File Streaming

You can now combine the skills learned for asynchronous file reads with asynchronous network streaming, to produce a program that serves a file to a client on demand.

Your server will begin with an asynchronous read on the socket, waiting to get a filename from the client. Once you have the filename, you can kick off an asynchronous read of that file on the server. As each bufferful of the file becomes available, you can begin an asynchronous write back to the client. When the asynchronous write to the client finishes, you can kick off another read of the file; in this way you ping-pong back and forth, filling the buffer from the file and writing the buffer out to the client. The client need do nothing but read the stream from the server. In the next example, the client will write the contents of the file to the console, but you could easily begin an asynchronous write to a new file on the client, thereby creating a network-based file copy program.

The structure of the server isn't unlike that shown in Example 21-10. Once again you will create a `ClientHandler` class, but this time add an `AsyncCallBack` named `myFileCallBack`, which you initialize in the constructor along with the callbacks for the network read and write:

```
myFileCallBack =
    new AsyncCallback(this.OnFileCompletedRead);

callbackRead =
    new AsyncCallback(this.OnReadComplete);

callbackWrite =
    new AsyncCallback(this.OnWriteComplete);
```

The `Run()` function of the outer class, now named `AsynchNetworkFileServer`, is unchanged. Once again you create and start the `TcpListener` class as well as create a forever loop in which you call `AcceptSocket()`. If you have a socket, instantiate the `ClientHandler` and call `StartRead()`. As in the previous example, `StartRead()` kicks off a `BeginRead()`, passing in the buffer and the delegate to `OnReadComplete`.

When the read from the network stream completes, your delegated method `OnReadComplete()` is called and it retrieves the filename from the buffer. If text is returned, `OnReadComplete()` retrieves a string from the buffer using the static `System.Text.Encoding.ASCII.GetString()` method:

```
if( bytesRead > 0 )
{
    string fileName =
        System.Text.Encoding.ASCII.GetString(
        buffer, 0, bytesRead);
```

You now have a filename; with that, you can open a stream to the file and use the exact same asynchronous file read used in Example 21-7:

```
inputStream =
    File.OpenRead(fileName);

inputStream.BeginRead(
    buffer,             // holds the results
    0,                  // offset
    buffer.Length,      // Buffer Size
    myFileCallBack,     // call back delegate
    null);              // local state object
```

This read of the file has its own callback that will be invoked when the input stream has read a bufferful from the file on the server disk drive.

As noted earlier, you normally shouldn't take any action in an overlapped I/O method that might block the thread for any appreciable time. The call to open the file and begin reading it is normally pushed off to a helper thread, instead of doing this work in OnReadComplete(). It has been simplified for this example to avoid distracting from the issues at hand.

When the buffer is full, OnFileCompletedRead() is called, which checks to see if any bytes were read from the file. If so, it begins an asynchronous write to the network:

```
if (bytesRead > 0)
{
    // write it out to the client
    networkStream.BeginWrite(
        buffer, 0, bytesRead, callbackWrite, null);
}
```

If OnFileCompletedRead was called and no bytes were read, this signifies that the entire file has been sent. The server reacts by closing the NetworkStream and socket, thus letting the client know that the transaction is complete:

```
networkStream.Close();
socket.Close();
networkStream = null;
socket = null;
```

When the network write completes, the OnWriteComplete() method is called, and this kicks off another read from the file:

```
private void OnWriteComplete( IAsyncResult ar )
{
    networkStream.EndWrite(ar);
    Console.WriteLine( "Write complete");

    inputStream.BeginRead(
        buffer,              // holds the results
        0,                   // offset
        buffer.Length,       // (BufferSize)
        myFileCallBack,      // call back delegate
        null);               // local state object

}
```

The cycle begins again with another read of the file, and the cycle continues until the file has been completely read and transmitted to the client. The client code simply writes a filename to the network stream to kick off the file read:

```
string message = @"C:\test\source\AskTim.txt";
System.IO.StreamWriter writer =
    new System.IO.StreamWriter(streamToServer);
writer.Write(message);
writer.Flush();
```

The client then begins a loop, reading from the network stream until no bytes are sent by the server. When the server is done, the network stream is closed. Start by initializing a Boolean value to false and creating a buffer to hold the bytes sent by the server:

```
bool fQuit = false;
while (!fQuit)
{
    char[] buffer = new char[BufferSize];
```

You are now ready to create a new `StreamReader` from the `NetworkStream` member variable streamToServer:

```
System.IO.StreamReader reader =
    new System.IO.StreamReader(streamToServer);
```

The call to `Read()` takes three parameters: the buffer, the offset at which to begin reading, and the size of the buffer:

```
int bytesRead = reader.Read(buffer,0, BufferSize);
```

Check to see if the `Read()` returned any bytes; if not, you are done and you can set the Boolean value fQuit to true, causing the loop to terminate:

```
if (bytesRead == 0)
    fQuit = true;
```

If you did receive bytes, you can write them to the console, or write them to a file, or do whatever it is you will do with the values sent from the server:

```
    else
    {
        string theString = new String(buffer);
        Console.WriteLine(theString);
    }
}
```

Once you break out of the loop, close the `NetworkStream`:

```
streamToServer.Close();
```

The complete annotated source for the server is shown in Example 21-12, with the client following in Example 21-13.

Example 21-12. Implementing an asynchronous network file server

```
#region Using directives

using System;
using System.Collections.Generic;
using System.IO;
using System.Net;
using System.Net.Sockets;
using System.Text;
```

Example 21-12. Implementing an asynchronous network file server (continued)

```
#endregion

namespace AsynchNetworkFileServer
{
    public class AsynchNetworkFileServer
    {

        class ClientHandler
        {
            private const int BufferSize = 256;
            private byte[] buffer;
            private Socket socket;
            private NetworkStream networkStream;
            private Stream inputStream;
            private AsyncCallback callbackRead;
            private AsyncCallback callbackWrite;
            private AsyncCallback myFileCallBack;

            // constructor
            public ClientHandler(
                Socket socketForClient )
            {
                // initialize member variable
                socket = socketForClient;

                // initialize buffer to hold
                // contents of file
                buffer = new byte[256];

                // create the network stream
                networkStream =
                    new NetworkStream( socketForClient );

                // set the file callback for reading
                // the file
                myFileCallBack =
                    new AsyncCallback( this.OnFileCompletedRead );

                // set the callback for reading from the
                // network stream
                callbackRead =
                    new AsyncCallback( this.OnReadComplete );

                // set the callback for writing to the
                // network stream
                callbackWrite =
                    new AsyncCallback( this.OnWriteComplete );
            }

            // begin reading the string from the client
            public void StartRead()
            {
```

```
        // read from the network
        // get a filename
        networkStream.BeginRead(
            buffer, 0, buffer.Length,
            callbackRead, null );
    }

    // when called back by the read, display the string
    // and echo it back to the client
    private void OnReadComplete( IAsyncResult ar )
    {
        int bytesRead = networkStream.EndRead( ar );

        // if you got a string
        if ( bytesRead > 0 )
        {
            // turn the string to a file name
            string fileName =
                System.Text.Encoding.ASCII.GetString(
                buffer, 0, bytesRead );

            // update the console
            Console.Write(
                "Opening file {0}", fileName );

            // open the file input stream
            inputStream =
                File.OpenRead( fileName );

            // begin reading the file
            inputStream.BeginRead(
                buffer,              // holds the results
                0,                   // offset
                buffer.Length,       // BufferSize
                myFileCallBack,      // call back delegate
                null );              // local state object

        }
        else
        {
            Console.WriteLine( "Read connection dropped" );
            networkStream.Close();
            socket.Close();
            networkStream = null;
            socket = null;
        }
    }

    // when you have a bufferful of the file
    void OnFileCompletedRead( IAsyncResult asyncResult )
    {
```

```
        int bytesRead =
           inputStream.EndRead( asyncResult );

        // if you read some file
        if ( bytesRead > 0 )
        {
           // write it out to the client
           networkStream.BeginWrite(
              buffer, 0, bytesRead, callbackWrite, null );
        }
        else
        {
           Console.WriteLine( "Finished." );
           networkStream.Close();
           socket.Close();
           networkStream = null;
           socket = null;
        }
     }

     // after writing the string, get more of the file
     private void OnWriteComplete( IAsyncResult ar )
     {
        networkStream.EndWrite( ar );
        Console.WriteLine( "Write complete" );

        // begin reading more of the file
        inputStream.BeginRead(
           buffer,              // holds the results
           0,                   // offset
           buffer.Length,       // (BufferSize)
           myFileCallBack,          // call back delegate
           null );              // local state object
     }
  }

  public static void Main()
  {
     AsynchNetworkFileServer app =
        new AsynchNetworkFileServer();
     app.Run();
  }

  private void Run()
  {
     // create a new TcpListener and start it up
     // listening on port 65000

     IPAddress localAddr = IPAddress.Parse( "127.0.0.1" );
     TcpListener tcpListener = new TcpListener( localAddr, 65000 );
     tcpListener.Start();
```

Example 21-12. Implementing an asynchronous network file server (continued)

```
            // keep listening until you send the file
            for ( ; ; )
            {
                // if a client connects, accept the connection
                // and return a new socket named socketForClient
                // while tcpListener keeps listening
                Socket socketForClient =
                    tcpListener.AcceptSocket();
                if ( socketForClient.Connected )
                {
                    Console.WriteLine( "Client connected" );
                    ClientHandler handler =
                        new ClientHandler( socketForClient );
                    handler.StartRead();
                }
            }
        }
    }
}
```

Example 21-13. Implementing a client for an asynchronous network file server

```
using System;
using System.Net.Sockets;
using System.Threading;
using System.Text;

public class AsynchNetworkClient
{
    private const int BufferSize = 256;
    private NetworkStream    streamToServer;

    static public int Main()
    {

        AsynchNetworkClient client =
            new AsynchNetworkClient();
        return client.Run();
    }

    AsynchNetworkClient()
    {
        string serverName = "localhost";
        Console.WriteLine("Connecting to {0}", serverName);
        TcpClient tcpSocket = new TcpClient(serverName, 65000);
        streamToServer = tcpSocket.GetStream();
    }

    private int Run()
    {
```

```
    string message = @"C:\test\source\AskTim.txt";
    Console.Write(
        "Sending {0} to server.", message);

    // create a streamWriter and use it to
    // write a string to the server
    System.IO.StreamWriter writer =
        new System.IO.StreamWriter(streamToServer);
    writer.Write(message);
    writer.Flush();

    bool fQuit = false;

    // while there is data coming
    // from the server, keep reading
    while (!fQuit)
    {
        // buffer to hold the response
        char[] buffer = new char[BufferSize];

        // Read response
        System.IO.StreamReader reader =
            new System.IO.StreamReader(streamToServer);

        // see how many bytes are
        // retrieved to the buffer
        int bytesRead =
            reader.Read(buffer,0,BufferSize);
        if (bytesRead == 0)  // none? quite
            fQuit = true;
        else                 // got some?
        {
            // display it as a string
            string theString = new String(buffer);
            Console.WriteLine(theString);
        }
    }
    streamToServer.Close(); // tidy up
    return 0;
    }
}
```

By combining the asynchronous file read with the asynchronous network read, you have created a scalable application that can handle requests from a number of clients.

Web Streams

Instead of reading from a stream provided by a custom server, you can just as easily read from any web page on the Internet.

A WebRequest is an object that requests a resource identified by a URI such as the URL for a web page. You can use a WebRequest object to create a WebResponse object that will encapsulate the object pointed to by the URI. That is, you can call GetResponse() on your WebRequest object to get access to the object pointed to by the URI. What is returned is encapsulated in a WebResponse object. You can then ask that WebResponse object for a Stream object by calling GetResponseStream(). GetResponseStream() returns a stream that encapsulates the contents of the web object (e.g., a stream with the web page).

The next example retrieves the contents of a web page as a stream. To get a web page, you'll want to use HttpWebRequest. HttpWebRequest derives from WebRequest and provides additional support for interacting with the HTTP protocol.

To create the HttpWebRequest, cast the WebRequest returned from the static Create() method of the WebRequestFactory:

```
HttpWebRequest webRequest =
    (HttpWebRequest) WebRequest.Create
    ("http://www.libertyassociates.com/book_edit.htm");
```

Create() is a static method of WebRequest. When you pass in a URI, an instance of HttpWebRequest is created.

 The method is overloaded on the type of the parameter. It returns different derived types depending on what is passed in. For example, if you pass in a URI, an object of type HttpWebRequest is created. The return type, however, is WebRequest, and so you must cast the returned value to HttpWebRequest.

Creating the HttpWebRequest establishes a connection to a page on your web site. What you get back from the host is encapsulated in an HttpWebResponse object, which is an HTTP protocol-specific subclass of the more general WebResponse class:

```
HttpWebResponse webResponse =
    (HttpWebResponse) webRequest.GetResponse();
```

You can now open a StreamReader on that page by calling the GetResponseStream() method of the WebResponse object:

```
StreamReader streamReader = new StreamReader(
    webResponse.GetResponseStream(), Encoding.ASCII);
```

You can read from that stream exactly as you read from the network stream. Example 21-14 shows the complete listing.

Example 21-14. Reading a web page as an HTML stream

```
#region Using directives

using System;
using System.Collections.Generic;
```

Example 21-14. Reading a web page as an HTML stream (continued)

```
using System.IO;
using System.Net;
using System.Net.Sockets;
using System.Text;

#endregion

namespace ReadingWebPageAsHTML
{
    public class Client
    {

        static public void Main( string[] Args )
        {

            // create a webRequest for a particular page
            HttpWebRequest webRequest =
                ( HttpWebRequest ) WebRequest.Create
                ( "http://www.libertyassociates.com/");

            // ask the web request for a webResponse encapsulating
            // that page
            HttpWebResponse webResponse =
                ( HttpWebResponse ) webRequest.GetResponse();

            // get the streamReader from the response
            StreamReader streamReader = new StreamReader(
                webResponse.GetResponseStream(), Encoding.ASCII );

            try
            {
                string outputString;
                outputString = streamReader.ReadToEnd();
                Console.WriteLine( outputString );
            }
            catch
            {
                Console.WriteLine( "Exception reading from web page" );
            }
            streamReader.Close();
        }
    }
}

Output (excerpt):
<html>
<head>
<title>Liberty Associates</title>
<meta http-equiv="Content-Type" content="text/html; charset=iso-8859-1">
<script language="JavaScript">
<!--
isNS=(navigator.appName=="Netscape");
```

Example 21-14. Reading a web page as an HTML stream (continued)

```
activeMenu="";
activeIndex=-1;
activeImg="";

window.onError = null;

function setImage(imgName,index) {
 if(activeImg==imgName)
   return true;
 document.images[imgName].src = rolloverImg[index].src;
 return true;
}

rolloverImg=new Array();
```

The output shows that what is sent through the stream is the HTML of the page you requested. You might use this capability for *screen scraping*: reading a page from a site into a buffer and then extracting the information you need.

 All examples of screen scraping in this book assume that you are reading a site for which you have copyright permission.

Serialization

When an object is streamed to disk, its various member data must be *serialized*—that is, written out to the stream as a series of bytes. The object will also be serialized when stored in a database or when marshaled across a context, app domain, process, or machine boundary.

The CLR provides support for serializing an *object graph*—an object and all the member data of that object. As noted in Chapter 19, by default, types aren't serializable. To be able to serialize an object, you must explicitly mark it with the [Serializable] attribute.

The CLR will do the work of serializing your object for you. Because the CLR knows how to serialize all the primitive types, if your object consists of nothing but primitive types (all your member data consists of integers, longs, strings, etc.), you're all set. If your object consists of other user-defined types (classes), you must ensure that these types are also serializable. The CLR will try to serialize each object contained by your object (and all their contained objects as well), but these objects themselves must be either primitive types or serializable, or else they will not be serialized.

This was also evident in Chapter 19 when you marshaled a Shape object that contained a Point object as member data. The Point object in turn consisted of primitive data. To serialize (and thus marshal) the Shape object, its constituent member, the Point object, also had to be marked as serializable.

When an object is marshaled, either by value or by reference, it must be serialized. The difference is only whether a copy is made or a proxy is provided to the client. Objects marked with the [Serializable] attribute are marshaled by value; those that derive from MarshalByRefObject are marshaled by reference, but both are serialized. See Chapter 19 for more information.

Using a Formatter

When data is serialized, it is eventually read, by either the same program or another program on the same or a different computer. In any case, the code reading the data expects that data to be in a particular format. Most of the time in a .NET application, the expected format is either native binary format or SOAP.

SOAP is a simple, lightweight, XML-based protocol for exchanging information across the Web. SOAP is highly modular and very extensible. It also leverages existing Internet technologies, such as HTTP and SMTP.

When data is serialized, the format of the serialization is determined by the formatter you apply. In Chapter 19, you used formatters with channels when communicating with a remote object. Formatter classes implement the interface IFormatter; you are also free to create your own formatter, though very few programmers will ever need or want to! The CLR provides both a SoapFormatter for use with web services and a BinaryFormatter that is useful for fast local storage or remoting.

You can instantiate these objects with their default constructors:

```
BinaryFormatter binaryFormatter =
    new BinaryFormatter();
```

Once you have an instance of a formatter, you can invoke its Serialize() method, passing in a stream and an object to serialize. You'll see how this is done in the next example.

Working with Serialization

To see serialization at work, you need a sample class that you can serialize and then deserialize. You can start by creating a class named SumOf. SumOf has three member variables:

```
private int startNumber = 1;
private int endNumber;
private int[] theSums;
```

The member array theSums represents the value of the sums of all the numbers from startNumber through endNumber. Thus, if startNumber is 1 and endNumber is 10, the array will have the values:

```
1,3,6,10,15,21,28,36,45,55
```

Each value is the sum of the previous value plus the next in the series. Thus if the series is 1,2,3,4, the first value in theSums will be 1. The second value is the previous value (1) plus the next in the series (2); thus, theSums[1] will hold the value 3. Likewise, the third value is the previous value (3) plus the next in the series, so theSums[2] is 6. Finally, the fourth value in theSums is the previous value (6) plus the next in the series (4), for a value of 10.

The constructor for the SumOf object takes two integers: the starting number and the ending number. It assigns these to the local values and then calls a helper function to compute the contents of the array:

```
public SumOf(int start, int end)
{
    startNumber = start;
    endNumber = end;
    ComputeSums();
```

The ComputeSums helper function fills in the contents of the array by computing the sums in the series from startNumber through endNumber:

```
private void ComputeSums()
{
    int count = endNumber - startNumber + 1;
    theSums = new int[count];
    theSums[0] = startNumber;
    for (int i=1,j=startNumber + 1;i<count;i++,j++)
    {
        theSums[i] =  j + theSums[i-1];
    }
}
```

You can display the contents of the array at any time by using a foreach loop:

```
private void DisplaySums()
{
    foreach(int i in theSums)
    {
        Console.WriteLine("{0}, ",i);
    }
}
```

Serializing the object

Now, mark the class as eligible for serialization with the [Serializable] attribute:

```
[Serializable]
class SumOf
```

To invoke serialization, you first need a fileStream object into which you'll serialize the SumOf object:

```
FileStream fileStream =
    new FileStream("DoSum.out",FileMode.Create);
```

You are now ready to call the formatter's Serialize() method, passing in the stream and the object to serialize. Because this is done in a method of SumOf, you can pass in the this object, which points to the current object:

```
binaryFormatter.Serialize(fileStream,this);
```

This serializes the SumOf object to disk.

Deserializing the object

To reconstitute the object, open the file and ask a binary formatter to DeSerialize it:

```
public static SumOf DeSerialize()
{
    FileStream fileStream =
        new FileStream("DoSum.out",FileMode.Open);
    BinaryFormatter binaryFormatter =
        new BinaryFormatter();
    SumOf retVal = (SumOf) binaryFormatter.Deserialize(fileStream);
        fileStream.Close();
        return retVal;
}
```

To make sure all this works, first instantiate a new object of type SumOf and tell it to serialize itself. Then create a new instance of type SumOf by calling the static deserializer and asking it to display its values:

```
public static void Main()
{
    Console.WriteLine("Creating first one with new...");
    SumOf app = new SumOf(1,10);

    Console.WriteLine(
        "Creating second one with deserialize...");
    SumOf newInstance = SumOf.DeSerialize();
    newInstance.DisplaySums();
}
```

Example 21-15 provides the complete source code to illustrate serialization and deserialization.

Example 21-15. Serializing and deserializing an object

```
#region Using directives

using System;
using System.Collections.Generic;
using System.IO;
using System.Runtime.Serialization;
```

Example 21-15. Serializing and deserializing an object (continued)

```
using System.Runtime.Serialization.Formatters.Binary;
using System.Text;

#endregion

namespace SerializingDeserialingAnObject
{
    [Serializable]
    class SumOf
    {
        private int startNumber = 1;
        private int endNumber;
        private int[] theSums;

        public static void Main()
        {
            Console.WriteLine( "Creating first one with new..." );
            SumOf app = new SumOf( 1, 10 );

            Console.WriteLine( "Creating second one with deserialize..." );
            SumOf newInstance = SumOf.DeSerialize();
            newInstance.DisplaySums();
        }

        public SumOf( int start, int end )
        {
            startNumber = start;
            endNumber = end;
            ComputeSums();
            DisplaySums();
            Serialize();
        }

        private void ComputeSums()
        {
            int count = endNumber - startNumber + 1;
            theSums = new int[count];
            theSums[0] = startNumber;
            for ( int i = 1, j = startNumber + 1; i < count; i++, j++ )
            {
                theSums[i] = j + theSums[i - 1];
            }
        }

        private void DisplaySums()
        {
            foreach ( int i in theSums )
            {
                Console.WriteLine( "{0}, ", i );
            }
        }
```

Example 21-15. Serializing and deserializing an object (continued)

```
    private void Serialize()
    {
        Console.Write( "Serializing..." );
        // create a file stream to write the file
        FileStream fileStream =
            new FileStream( "DoSum.out", FileMode.Create );
        // use the CLR binary formatter
        BinaryFormatter binaryFormatter =
            new BinaryFormatter();
        // serialize to disk
        binaryFormatter.Serialize( fileStream, this );
        Console.WriteLine( "...completed" );
        fileStream.Close();
    }

    public static SumOf DeSerialize()
    {
        FileStream fileStream =
            new FileStream( "DoSum.out", FileMode.Open );
        BinaryFormatter binaryFormatter =
            new BinaryFormatter();
        SumOf retVal = ( SumOf ) binaryFormatter.Deserialize( fileStream );
        fileStream.Close();
        return retVal;
    }
  }
}
```

```
Output:
Creating first one with new...
1,
3,
6,
10,
15,
21,
28,
36,
45,
55,
Serializing......completed
Creating second one with deserialize...
1,
3,
6,
10,
15,
21,
28,
36,
45,
55,
```

The output shows that the object was created, displayed, and then serialized. The object was then deserialized and output again, with no loss of data.

Handling Transient Data

In some ways, the approach to serialization demonstrated in Example 21-15 is very wasteful. Because you can compute the contents of the array given its starting and ending numbers, there really is no reason to store its elements to disk. Although the operation might be inexpensive with a small array, it could become costly with a very large one.

You can tell the serializer not to serialize some data by marking it with the [NonSerialized] attribute:

```
[NonSerialized] private int[] theSums;
```

If you don't serialize the array, however, the object you create will not be correct when you deserialize it. The array will be empty. Remember, when you deserialize the object, you simply read it up from its serialized form; no methods are run.

To fix the object before you return it to the caller, implement the IDeserializationCallback interface:

```
[Serializable]
class SumOf : IDeserializationCallback
```

Also implement the one method of this interface: OnDeserialization(). The CLR promises that if you implement this interface, your class's OnDeserialization() method will be called when the entire object graph has been deserialized. This is just what you want: the CLR will reconstitute what you've serialized, and then you have the opportunity to fix up the parts that were not serialized.

This implementation can be very simple. Just ask the object to recompute the series:

```
public virtual void OnDeserialization (Object sender)
{
    ComputeSums();
}
```

This is a classic space/time trade-off; by not serializing the array, you may make deserialization somewhat slower (because you must take the time to recompute the array), and you make the file somewhat smaller. To see if not serializing the array had any effect, I ran the program with the digits 1 to 5,000. Before setting [NonSerialized] on the array, the serialized file was 20K. After setting [NonSerialized], the file was 1K. Not bad. Example 21-16 shows the source code using the digits 1 to 5 as input (to simplify the output).

Example 21-16. Working with a nonserialized object

```
#region Using directives

using System;
using System.Collections.Generic;
using System.IO;
using System.Runtime.Serialization;
using System.Runtime.Serialization.Formatters.Binary;
using System.Text;

#endregion

namespace WorkingWithNonSerializedObject
{
    [Serializable]
    class SumOf : IDeserializationCallback
    {
        private int startNumber = 1;
        private int endNumber;
        [NonSerialized]
        private int[] theSums;

        public static void Main()
        {
            Console.WriteLine("Creating first one with new...");
            SumOf app = new SumOf(1,5);

            Console.WriteLine("Creating second one with deserialize...");
            SumOf newInstance = SumOf.DeSerialize();
            newInstance.DisplaySums();
        }

        public SumOf(int start, int end)
        {
            startNumber = start;
            endNumber = end;
            ComputeSums();
            DisplaySums();
            Serialize();
        }

        private void ComputeSums()
        {
            int count = endNumber - startNumber + 1;
            theSums = new int[count];
            theSums[0] = startNumber;
            for (int i=1,j=startNumber + 1;i<count;i++,j++)
            {
                theSums[i] =  j + theSums[i-1];
            }
        }
```

Example 21-16. Working with a nonserialized object (continued)

```
    private void DisplaySums()
    {
        foreach(int i in theSums)
        {
            Console.WriteLine("{0}, ",i);
        }
    }

    private void Serialize()
    {
        Console.Write("Serializing...");
        // create a file stream to write the file
        FileStream fileStream =
            new FileStream("DoSum.out",FileMode.Create);
        // use the CLR binary formatter
        BinaryFormatter binaryFormatter =
            new BinaryFormatter();
        // serialize to disk
        binaryFormatter.Serialize(fileStream,this);
        Console.WriteLine("...completed");
        fileStream.Close();
    }

    public static SumOf DeSerialize()
    {
        FileStream fileStream =
            new FileStream("DoSum.out",FileMode.Open);
        BinaryFormatter binaryFormatter =
            new BinaryFormatter();
        SumOf retVal = (SumOf) binaryFormatter.Deserialize(fileStream);
        fileStream.Close();
        return retVal;
    }

    // fix up the nonserialized data

    public virtual void OnDeserialization
        (Object sender)
    {
        ComputeSums();
    }
    }
}

Output:
Creating first one with new...
1,
3,
6,
10,
15,
Serializing......completed
```

Example 21-16. Working with a nonserialized object (continued)

```
Creating second one with deserialize...
1,
3,
6,
10,
15,
```

You can see in the output that the data was successfully serialized to disk and then reconstituted by deserialization. The trade-off of disk storage space versus time doesn't make a lot of sense with five values, but it makes a great deal of sense with five million values.

So far you've streamed your data to disk for storage and across the network for easy communication with distant programs. There is one other time you might create a stream: to store permanent configuration and status data on a per-user basis. For this purpose, the .NET Framework offers *isolated storage*.

Isolated Storage

The .NET CLR provides isolated storage to allow the application developer to store data on a *per-user* basis. Isolated storage provides much of the functionality of traditional Windows *.ini* files or the more recent HKEY_CURRENT_USER key in the Windows Registry.

Applications save data to a unique *data compartment* associated with the application. The CLR implements the data compartment with a *data store*, which is typically a directory on the filesystem.

Administrators are free to limit how much isolated storage individual applications can use. They can also use security so that less-trusted code can't call more highly trusted code to write to isolated storage.

What is important about isolated storage is that the CLR provides a standard place to store your application's data, but it doesn't impose (or support) any particular layout or syntax for that data. In short, you can store anything you like in isolated storage.

Typically, you will store text, often in the form of name-value pairs. Isolated storage is a good mechanism for saving user configuration information such as login name, the position of various windows and widgets, and other application-specific, user-specific information. The data is stored in a separate file for each user, but the files can be isolated even further by distinguishing among different aspects of the identity of the code (by assembly or by originating application domain).

Using isolated storage is fairly straightforward. To write to isolated storage, create an instance of an IsolatedStorageFileStream, which you initialize with a filename and a file mode (create, append, etc.).

```
IsolatedStorageFileStream configFile =
    new IsolatedStorageFileStream
    ("Tester.cfg",FileMode.Create);
```

Now create a StreamWriter on that file:

```
StreamWriter writer =
    new StreamWriter(configFile);
```

Then write to that stream as you would to any other. Example 21-17 illustrates.

Example 21-17. Writing to isolated storage

```
#region Using directives

using System;
using System.Collections.Generic;
using System.IO;
using System.IO.IsolatedStorage;
using System.Text;

#endregion

namespace WritingToIsolatedStorage
{
    public class Tester
    {

        public static void Main()
        {
            Tester app = new Tester();
            app.Run();
        }

        private void Run()
        {
            // create the configuration file stream
            IsolatedStorageFileStream configFile =
                new IsolatedStorageFileStream
                ( "Tester.cfg", FileMode.Create );

            // create a writer to write to the stream
            StreamWriter writer =
                new StreamWriter( configFile );

            // write some data to the config. file
            String output;
            System.DateTime currentTime = System.DateTime.Now;
            output = "Last access: " + currentTime.ToString();
            writer.WriteLine( output );
            output = "Last position = 27,35";
            writer.WriteLine( output );
```

Example 21-17. Writing to isolated storage (continued)

```
        // flush the buffer and clean up
        writer.Close();
        configFile.Close();
      }
    }
}
```

After running this code, search your hard disk for *Tester.cfg*. On my machine, this file is found in:

```
C:\Documents and Settings\Jesse\Local Settings\Application Data\IsolatedStorage\
mipjwcsz.iir\2hzvpjcc.p0y\StrongName.mwoxzllzqpx3u0taclp1dti11kpddwyo\Url.
a2f4v2g3ytucslmvlpt2wmdxhrhqg1pz\Files
```

You can read this file with Notepad if what you've written is just text:

```
Last access: 5/2/2001 10:00:57 AM
Last position = 27,35
```

Or, you can access this data programmatically. To do so, reopen the file:

```
IsolatedStorageFileStream configFile =
    new IsolatedStorageFileStream
    ("Tester.cfg",FileMode.Open);
```

Create a `StreamReader` object:

```
StreamReader reader =
    new StreamReader(configFile);
```

Use the standard stream idiom to read through the file:

```
string theEntry;
do
{
    theEntry = reader.ReadLine();
    Console.WriteLine(theEntry);
} while (theEntry != null);
Console.WriteLine(theEntry);
```

Isolated storage is scoped by assembly (so if you shut down your program and start it later, you can read the configuration file you created, but you can't read the configuration of any other assembly). Example 21-18 provides the method needed to read the file. Replace the `Run()` method in the previous example, recompile it, and run it (but don't change its name, or it won't be able to access the isolated storage you created previously).

Example 21-18. Reading from isolated storage

```
    private void Run()
    {
        // open the configuration file stream
        IsolatedStorageFileStream configFile =
            new IsolatedStorageFileStream
            ("Tester.cfg",FileMode.Open);
```

Example 21-18. Reading from isolated storage (continued)

```
            // create a standard stream reader
            StreamReader reader =
                new StreamReader(configFile);

            // read through the file and display
            string theEntry;
            do
            {
                theEntry = reader.ReadLine();
                Console.WriteLine(theEntry);
            } while (theEntry != null);

            reader.Close();
            configFile.Close();
        }
```

Output:
Last access: 5/2/2001 10:00:57 AM
Last position = 27,35

CHAPTER 22

Programming .NET and COM

Programmers love a clean slate. Although it would be nice if we could throw away all the code we've ever written and start over, this typically isn't a viable option for most companies. Over the past decade, many development organizations have made a substantial investment in developing and purchasing COM components and ActiveX controls. Microsoft has made a commitment to ensure that these legacy components are usable from within .NET applications, and (perhaps less important) .NET components are easily callable from COM.

This chapter describes the support .NET provides for importing ActiveX controls and COM components into your application, for exposing .NET classes to COM-based applications, and for making direct calls to Win32 APIs. You will also learn about C# pointers and keywords for accessing memory directly, a technique that may be crucial in some applications.

Importing ActiveX Controls

ActiveX controls are COM components typically dropped into a form, which might or might not have a user interface. When Microsoft developed the OCX standard, which allowed developers to build ActiveX controls in VB and use them with C++ (and vice versa), the ActiveX control revolution began. Over the past few years, thousands of such controls have been developed, sold, and used. They are small, easy to work with, and an effective example of binary reuse.

Importing ActiveX controls into .NET is surprisingly easy, considering how different COM objects are from .NET objects. Visual Studio 2005 is able to import ActiveX controls automagically. As an alternative to using Visual Studio, Microsoft has developed a command-line utility, AxImp, that will create the assemblies necessary for the control to be used in a .NET application.

Creating an ActiveX Control

To demonstrate the ability to use classic ActiveX controls in a .NET application, first develop a simple four-function calculator as an ActiveX control and then invoke that ActiveX control from within a C# application. Build the control in VB6, and test it in a VB6 application. If you don't have VB6 or don't want to bother creating the control, you can download the control from my web site (*http://www.LibertyAssociates. com*).

Once the control is working in the standard Windows environment, you'll import it into your Windows Forms application.

To create the control, open VB6 and choose ActiveX Control as the new project type. Make the project form as small as possible because this control will not have a user interface. Right-click UserControl1 and choose Properties. Rename it Calculator in the Properties window. Click the Project in the Project Explorer, and in the Properties window, rename it CalcControl. Immediately save the project and name both the file and the project CalcControl, as shown in Figure 22-1.

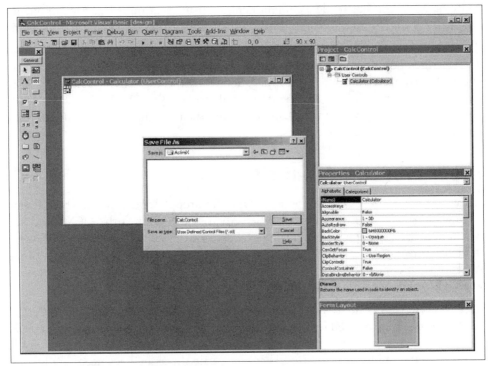

Figure 22-1. Creating a VB ActiveX control

Now you can add the four calculator functions by right-clicking the CalcControl form, selecting View Code from the pop-up menu, and typing in the VB code shown in Example 22-1.

Example 22-1. Implementing the CalcControl ActiveX control

```
Public Function _
Add(left As Double, right As Double) _
As Double
    Add = left + right
End Function

Public Function _
Subtract(left As Double, right As Double) _
As Double
    Subtract = left - right
End Function

Public Function _
Multiply(left As Double, right As Double) _
As Double
    Multiply = left * right
End Function

Public Function _
Divide(left As Double, right As Double) _
As Double
    Divide = left / right
End Function
```

This is the entire code for the control. Compile this to the *CalcControl.ocx* file by choosing File → Make CalcControl.ocx on the VB6 menu bar.

Next, open a second project in VB as a standard executable (EXE). Name the form TestForm and name the project CalcTest. Save the file and project as CalcTest.

Add the ActiveX control as a component by pressing Ctrl-T and choosing CalcControl from the Controls tab, as shown in Figure 22-2.

This action puts a new control on the toolbox, as shown circled in Figure 22-3.

Drag the new control onto the form TestForm and name it CalcControl. Note that the new control will not be visible; this control has no user interface. Add two text boxes, four buttons, and one label, as shown in Figure 22-4.

Name the buttons btnAdd, btnSubtract, btnMultiply, and btnDivide. All that is left is for you to implement methods for handling the button-click events of the calculator buttons. Each time a button is clicked, you want to get the values in the two text boxes, cast them to double (as required by CalcControl) using the VB6 CDbl function, invoke a CalcControl function, and print the result in the label control. Example 22-2 provides the complete source code.

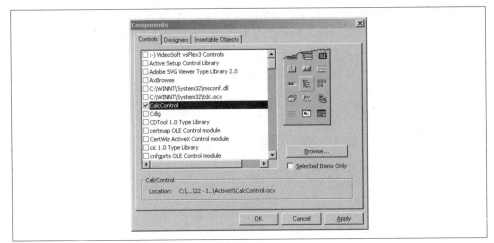

Figure 22-2. Adding the CalcControl to the VB6 toolbox

Figure 22-3. Locating CalcControl in the VB 6 toolbox

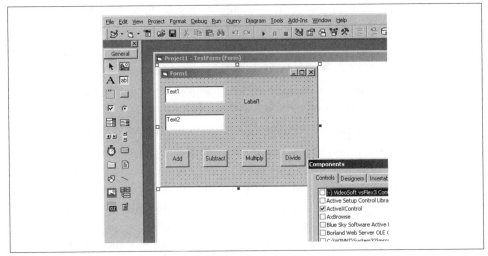

Figure 22-4. Building the TestForm user interface

Example 22-2. Using the CalcControl ActiveX control in a VB program (TestForm)

```
Private Sub btnAdd_Click()
    Label1.Caption = _
        calcControl.Add(CDbl(Text1.Text), _
            CDbl(Text2.Text))
End Sub

Private Sub btnDivide_Click()
    Label1.Caption = _
        calcControl.Divide(CDbl(Text1.Text), _
            CDbl(Text2.Text))
End Sub

Private Sub btnMultiply_Click()
    Label1.Caption = _
        calcControl.Multiply(CDbl(Text1.Text), _
            CDbl(Text2.Text))
End Sub

Private Sub btnSubtract_Click()
    Label1.Caption = _
        calcControl.Subtract(CDbl(Text1.Text), _
            CDbl(Text2.Text))
End Sub
```

Importing a Control in .NET

Now that you've shown that the CalcControl ActiveX control is working, you can copy the *CalcControl.ocx* file to your .NET development environment. Once you have copied it, remember that the *CalcControl.ocx* file requires that you register it using Regsvr32. You're now ready to build a test program in .NET to use the calculator:

```
Regsvr32 CalcControl.ocx
```

To get started, create a Visual C# Windows application in Visual Studio 2005 (see Chapter 13), name the application InteropTest, and design a form (such as the TestForm form you created in VB in the preceding section) by dragging and dropping controls onto it. Name the form TestForm. A complete sample form is shown in Figure 22-5.

Importing a control

There are two ways to import an ActiveX control into the Visual Studio 2005 development environment: you can use the Visual Studio 2005 tools themselves, or you can import the control manually using the aximp utility that ships with the .NET SDK Framework. To use Visual Studio 2005, choose Tools → Choose Toolbox Items from the menu. This opens a dialog box. On the COM Components tab, find the CalcControl.Calculator object you just registered, as shown in Figure 22-6.

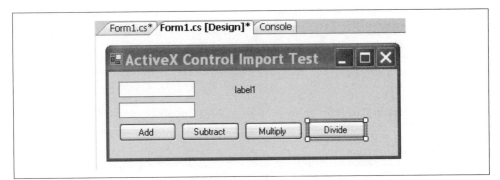

Figure 22-5. Building a Windows Form to test the CalcControl ActiveX control

```
Choose Toolbox Items                                          [?][X]

 .NET Framework Components  COM Components

  Name                              Path                         Library
  ☐ AxListViewCtrl Class            C:\PROGRA~1\NORTON~1\NAVComUI...  NAVComUI 1.0 T...
  ☑ CalcControl.Calculator          C:\Documents and Settings\Jesse\My ...  CalcControl
  ☐ Calendar Control 11.0           C:\Program Files\Microsoft Office\OFFIC...  Microsoft Calenda...
  ☐ CDDBControl Class               C:\Program Files\Creative\Shared Files\...  CDDBControl 1.0 ...
  ☐ CDDBControl Class               C:\Program Files\Real\RealOne Player\C...
  ☐ CDDBRoxioControl Class          C:\WINDOWS\System32\CDDBControl...  CDDBControl(Rox...
  ☐ CDToolCtrl Class                C:\WINDOWS\System32\cdtool.dll     CDTool 1.0 Type...
  ☐ ColorBvr Class                  C:\WINDOWS\System32\lmrt.dll
  ☐ COMNSView Class                 C:\WINDOWS\System32\comsnap.dll    ComSnap 1.0 Ty...
  ☐ Cr Behavior Factory             C:\WINDOWS\System32\lmrt.dll
  ☐ Crystal ActiveX Report Viewer Contr...  C:\Program Files\Common Files\Crystal ...  Crystal ActiveX R...

  :-) VideoSoft FlexArray Control                                  [ Browse... ]
       Language:     Language Neutral
       Version:      3.0

                                    [ OK ]   [ Cancel ]   [ Reset ]
```

Figure 22-6. Importing the CalcControl ActiveX control

Because CalcControl is registered on your .NET machine, the Visual Studio 2005
Choose Toolbox Items dialog (on the Tools menu) is able to find it. When you select
the control from this dialog box, it is imported into your application; Visual Studio
takes care of the details, including adding it to your toolbar.

Manually importing the control

Alternatively, you can open a command box and import the control manually using
the axing.exe utility, as shown in Figure 22-7.

axing.exe takes one argument, the ActiveX control you want to import (*CalcControl.
ocx*). It produces three files:

Figure 22-7. Running aximp

AxCalcControl.dll
>   A .NET Windows control

CalcControl.dll
>   A proxy .NET class library

AxCalcControl.pdb
>   A debug file

Once this is done, you can return to the Choose Toolbox Items window, but this time select .NET Framework Components. You can now browse to the location at which the .NET Windows control *AxCalcControl.dll* was generated and import that file into the toolbox, as shown in Figure 22-8.

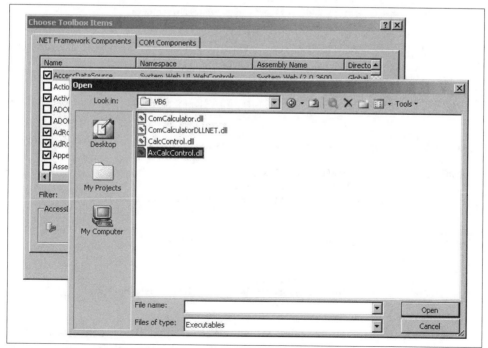

Figure 22-8. Browsing for the imported control

Adding the control to the form

Once imported, the control appears on the toolbox menu, as shown in Figure 22-9. Note that the control may appear at the bottom of the toolbox.

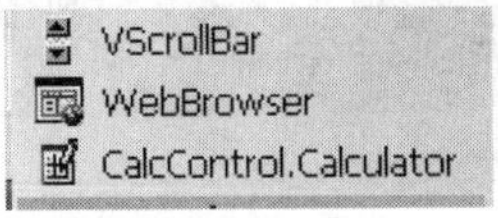

Figure 22-9. Viewing the AxCalcControl calculator after importing it into the toolbox

Now you can drag this control onto your Windows Form and make use of its functions, just as you did in the VB6 example.

Add event handlers for each of the four buttons. The event handlers will delegate their work to the ActiveX control you wrote in VB6 and imported into .NET.

The source code for the event handlers is shown in Example 22-3.

Example 22-3. Implementing event handlers for the test Windows Form

```
private void btnAdd_Click(object sender, System.EventArgs e)
{
    double left = double.Parse(textBox1.Text);
    double right = double.Parse(textBox2.Text);
    label1.Text = axCalculator1.Add( ref left, ref right).ToString();
}

private void btnDivide_Click(object sender, System.EventArgs e)
{
    double left = double.Parse(textBox1.Text);
    double right = double.Parse(textBox2.Text);
    label1.Text = axCalculator1.Divide(ref left, ref right).ToString();
}

private void btnMultiply_Click(object sender, System.EventArgs e)
{
    double left = double.Parse(textBox1.Text);
    double right = double.Parse(textBox2.Text);
    label1.Text = axCalculator1.Multiply(ref left, ref right).ToString();
}

private void btnSubtract_Click(object sender, System.EventArgs e)
{
    double left = double.Parse(textBox1.Text);
    double right = double.Parse(textBox2.Text);
    label1.Text = axCalculator1.Subtract(ref left, ref right).ToString();
}
```

Each implementing method obtains the values in the text fields, converts them to double using the static method `double.Parse()`, and passes those values to the calculator's methods. The results are cast back to a string and inserted in the label, as shown in Figure 22-10.

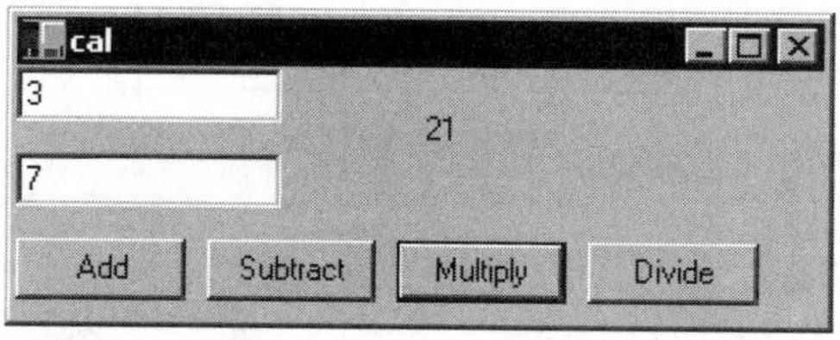

Figure 22-10. Running the imported ActiveX control in a Windows Form

Importing COM Components

Importing ActiveX controls turns out to be fairly straightforward. Many of the COM components that companies develop aren't ActiveX controls, however: they are standard COM DLL files. To see how to use these with .NET, return to VB6 and create a COM business object that will act exactly as the component from the previous section did.

The first step is to create a new ActiveX DLL project. This is how VB6 creates standard COM DLLs. Name the class ComCalc and name the project ComCalculator. Save the file and project. Copy the methods from Example 22-4 into the code window.

Example 22-4. Implementing the methods for ComCalc

```
Public Function _
Add(left As Double, right As Double) _
As Double
    Add = left + right
End Function

Public Function _
Subtract(left As Double, right As Double) _
As Double
    Subtract = left - right
End Function

Public Function _
Multiply(left As Double, right As Double) _
As Double
    Multiply = left * right
End Function

Public Function _
Divide(left As Double, right As Double) _
As Double
    Divide = left / right
End Function
```

Build the DLL by using the menu sequence File → Make ComCalculator.dll. You can test this by returning to your earlier test program and removing the Calculator control from the form. Add the new DLL by opening the project reference window and navigating to the ComCalculator, as shown in Figure 22-11.

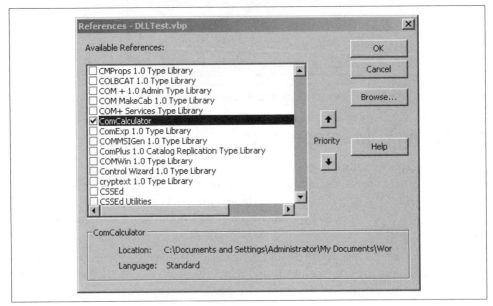

Figure 22-11. Adding a reference to ComCalculator.dll

Coding the COMTestForm Program

The code to exercise the COM component is very similar to the earlier example. This time, however, you instantiate a ComCalc object and call its methods, as shown in Example 22-5.

Example 22-5. The driver program for ComCalc.dll

```
Private Sub btnAdd_Click()
    Dim theCalc As New ComCalc
    Label1.Caption = _
        theCalc.Add(CDbl(Text1.Text), _
            CDbl(Text2.Text))
End Sub

Private Sub btnDivide_Click()
    Dim theCalc As New ComCalc
    Label1.Caption = _
        theCalc.Divide(CDbl(Text1.Text), _
            CDbl(Text2.Text))
End Sub
```

Example 22-5. The driver program for ComCalc.dll (continued)

```
Private Sub btnMultiply_Click()
    Dim theCalc As New ComCalc
    Label1.Caption = _
        theCalc.Multiply(CDbl(Text1.Text), _
            CDbl(Text2.Text))
End Sub

Private Sub btnSubtract_Click()
    Dim theCalc As New ComCalc
    Label1.Caption = _
        theCalc.Subtract(CDbl(Text1.Text), _
            CDbl(Text2.Text))
End Sub
```

Importing the COM .DLL to .NET

Now that you have a working ComCalc DLL, you can import it to .NET. Before you can import it, however, you must choose between early and late binding. When the client calls a method on the server, the address of the server's method in memory must be resolved. That process is called *binding*.

With *early binding*, the resolution of the address of a method on the server occurs when the client project is compiled and metadata is added to the client .NET module. With *late binding*, the resolution doesn't happen until runtime, when COM explores the server to see if it supports the method.

Early binding has many advantages. The most significant is performance. Early-bound methods are invoked more quickly than late-bound methods. For the compiler to perform early binding, it must interrogate the COM object. If the compiler is going to interrogate the server's type library, it must first be imported into .NET.

Importing the Type Library

The VB6-created COM DLL has a type library within it, but the format of a COM type library can't be used by a .NET application. To solve this problem, you must import the COM type library into an assembly. Once again, you have two ways of doing this: you can allow the IDE to import the class by registering the component, as shown in the following section, or you can import the type library manually by using the standalone program *TlbImp.exe*.

TlbImp.exe will produce an interop assembly. The .NET object that wraps the COM object is called a *Runtime Callable Wrapper* (RCW). The .NET client will use the RCW to bind to the methods in the COM object, as shown in the following section.

Importing Manually

Start by copying the *ComCalculator.dll* file to your .NET environment and register-ing it with Regsvr32. Then you're ready to import the COM object into .NET, by running *TlbImp.exe*. The syntax is to enter the name of the COM component, fol-lowed by an optional name for the filename produced, as shown in Figure 22-12.

Figure 22-12. Running TlbImp.exe

Creating a Test Program

Now it's time to create a driver program to test the COM object, which you'll name COMDllTest.

If you decide not to import the library manually, you import it through the IDE. To do so, select the COM tab on the Add Reference dialog box and select the registered COM object, as shown in Figure 22-13.

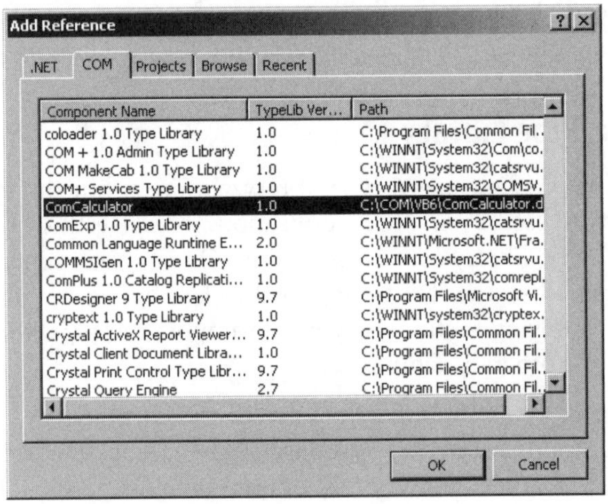

Figure 22-13. Adding a reference to ComCalculator

This will invoke *TlbImp* for you and will copy the resulting RCW to *C:\Documents and Settings\Administrator\Application Data\Microsoft\VisualStudio\RCW*.

You'll have to be careful, however, because the DLL it produces has the same name as the COM DLL.

If you do use *TlbImp.exe*, you can add the reference from the Projects tab. Browse to the directory in which *ComCalculatorDLLNET.dll* was created, and add it to the references.

In either case, you can now create the user interface, which is, again, similar to that used for testing the ActiveX control, as shown in Figure 22-14.

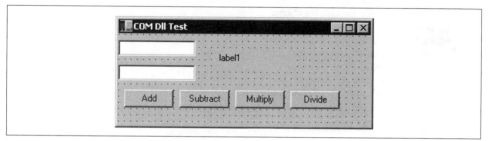

Figure 22-14. The form for testing the COM object

All that is left is to write the event handlers for the four buttons, as shown in Example 22-6.

Example 22-6. Implementing event handlers for the VB6 COM DLL test form

```
#region Using directives

using System;
using System.Collections.Generic;
using System.ComponentModel;
using System.Data;
using System.Drawing;
using System.Windows.Forms;

#endregion

namespace ComDLLTest
{
    partial class Form1 : Form
    {
        public Form1()
        {
            InitializeComponent();
        }

        private void btnAdd_Click(
            object sender, System.EventArgs e )
```

```
   {
      Double left, right, result;
      left = Double.Parse( textBox1.Text );
      right = Double.Parse( textBox2.Text );

      ComCalculatorDLLNET.ComCalc theCalc =
        new ComCalculatorDLLNET.ComCalc();
      result = theCalc.Add( ref left, ref right );
      label1.Text = result.ToString();
   }

   private void btnSubtract_Click(
      object sender, System.EventArgs e )
   {
      Double left, right, result;
      left = Double.Parse(textBox1.Text);
      right = Double.Parse(textBox2.Text);
      ComCalculatorDLLNET.ComCalc theCalc =
        new ComCalculatorDLLNET.ComCalc();
      result = theCalc.Subtract(ref left, ref right);
      label1.Text = result.ToString();
   }

   private void btnMultiply_Click(
      object sender, System.EventArgs e )
   {
      Double left, right, result;
      left = Double.Parse( textBox1.Text );
      right = Double.Parse( textBox2.Text );
      ComCalculatorDLLNET.ComCalc theCalc =
         new ComCalculatorDLLNET.ComCalc();
      result = theCalc.Multiply( ref left, ref right );
      label1.Text = result.ToString();
   }

   private void btnDivide_Click(
      object sender, System.EventArgs e )
   {
      Double left, right, result;
      left = Double.Parse( textBox1.Text );
      right = Double.Parse( textBox2.Text );
      ComCalculatorDLLNET.ComCalc theCalc =
        new ComCalculatorDLLNET.ComCalc();
      result = theCalc.Divide( ref left, ref right );
      label1.Text = result.ToString();
   }
  }
}
```

Instead of referring to an ActiveX control that is on the form, you must instantiate the ComCalculatorDLLNET.ComCalc object. The COM object is then available for use as

had been created in a .NET assembly, and the running program works as expected, as shown in Figure 22-15.

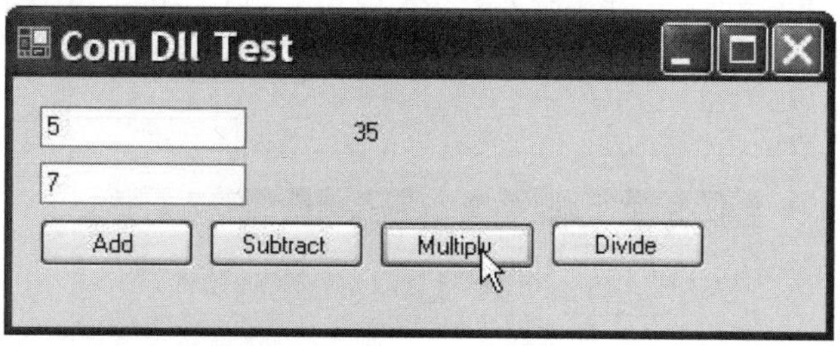

Figure 22-15. The test-driver program in action

Using Late Binding and Reflection

If you don't have a type library file for your third-party COM object, you must use late binding with reflection. In Chapter 18, you saw how to invoke methods dynamically in .NET assemblies; the process with COM objects isn't terribly different.

To see how to do this, start with the application shown in Example 22-6, but remove the reference to the imported library. The four button handlers must now be rewritten. You can no longer instantiate a ComCalculator.comCalc object, so instead you must invoke its methods dynamically.

Just as you saw in Chapter 18, you begin by creating a Type object to hold information about the comCalc type:

```
Type comCalcType;
comCalcType = Type.GetTypeFromProgID("ComCalculator.ComCalc");
```

The call to GetTypeFromProgID instructs the .NET Framework to open the registered COM DLL and retrieve the necessary type information for the specified object. This is the equivalent to calling GetType, as you did in Chapter 18:

```
Type theMathType = Type.GetType("System.Math");
```

You can now proceed exactly as you would if you were invoking this method on a class described in a .NET assembly. Start by calling CreateInstance to get back an instance of the comCalc object:

```
object comCalcObject = Activator.CreateInstance(comCalcType);
```

Next create an array to hold the arguments, and then invoke the method using InvokeMember, passing in the method you want to invoke as a string, a binder flag, a null binder, the object returned by CreateInstance, and the input argument array:

```
object[] inputArguments = {left, right };
result = (Double) comCalcType.InvokeMember(
    "Subtract",                    // the method to invoke
    BindingFlags.InvokeMethod,     // how to bind
```

```
            null,                          // binder
            comCalcObject,                 // the COM object
            inputArguments);               // the method arguments
```

The results of this invocation are cast to Double and stored in the local variable result. You can then display this result in the user interface, as shown in Figure 22-16.

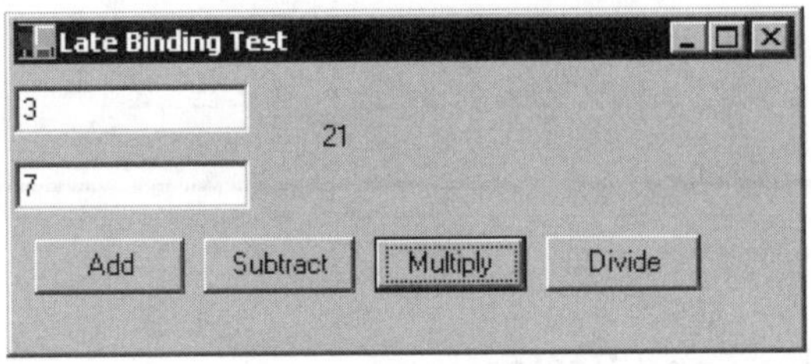

Figure 22-16. Late Binding Test

Because all four event handlers must replicate this work, differing only in the method they call, you'll factor the common code to a private helper method named Invoke, as shown in Example 22-7. You also need to add a using statement for System. Reflection in the source code.

Example 22-7. Late binding of COM objects

```
#region Using directives

using System;
using System.Collections.Generic;
using System.ComponentModel;
using System.Data;
using System.Drawing;
using System.Reflection;
using System.Windows.Forms;

#endregion

namespace LateBinding
{
    partial class Form1 : Form
    {
        public Form1()
        {
            InitializeComponent();
        }

        private void btnAdd_Click(
            object sender, System.EventArgs e )
        {
            Invoke( "Add" );
```

Example 22-7. Late binding of COM objects (continued)

```csharp
    }

    private void btnSubtract_Click(
        object sender, System.EventArgs e )
    {
        Invoke( "Subtract" );
    }

    private void btnMultiply_Click(
        object sender, System.EventArgs e )
    {
        Invoke( "Multiply" );
    }

    private void btnDivide_Click(
        object sender, System.EventArgs e )
    {
        Invoke( "Divide" );
    }

    private void Invoke( string whichMethod )
    {
        Double left, right, result;
        left = Double.Parse( textBox1.Text );
        right = Double.Parse( textBox2.Text );

        // create a Type object to hold type information
        Type comCalcType;

        // an array for the arguments
        object[] inputArguments =
    { left, right };

        // get the type info from the COM object
        comCalcType =
            Type.GetTypeFromProgID(
                "ComCalculator.ComCalc" );

        // create an instance
        object comCalcObject =
            Activator.CreateInstance( comCalcType );

        // invoke the method dynamically and
        // cast the result to Double
        result = ( Double ) comCalcType.InvokeMember(
            whichMethod,                  // the method to invoke
            BindingFlags.InvokeMethod,    // how to bind
            null,                         // binder
            comCalcObject,                // the COM object
            inputArguments );             // the method arguments
```

Example 22-7. Late binding of COM objects (continued)

```
        label1.Text = result.ToString();
    }
  }
}
```

Exporting .NET Components

You can export your .NET class for use with existing COM components. The Regasm tool will register the metadata from your component in the System Registry.

Invoke Regasm with the name of the DLL, which must be installed in the GAC (see Chapter 17). For example:

```
Regasm myAssembly.dll
```

This will export your component's metadata to the Registry. For example, you can create a new C# DLL project in which you recreate your four-function calculator, as shown in Example 22-8.

Example 22-8. The four-function calculator in a DLL

```
using System;
using System.Reflection;

[assembly: AssemblyKeyFile("test.key")]
namespace Programming_CSharp
{
    public class Calculator
    {
        public Calculator()
        {

        }
        public Double Add (Double left, Double right)
        {
            return left + right;
        }
        public Double Subtract (Double left, Double right)
        {
            return left - right;
        }
        public Double Multiply (Double left, Double right)
        {
            return left * right;
        }
        public Double Divide (Double left, Double right)
        {
            return left / right;
        }
    }
}
```

Save this to a file named *Calculator.cs* in a project named ProgrammingCSharpDLL. To create a strong name, click Project → ProgrammingCSharpDLL Properties. Choose the Signing tab and sign the assembly, as shown in Figure 22-17.

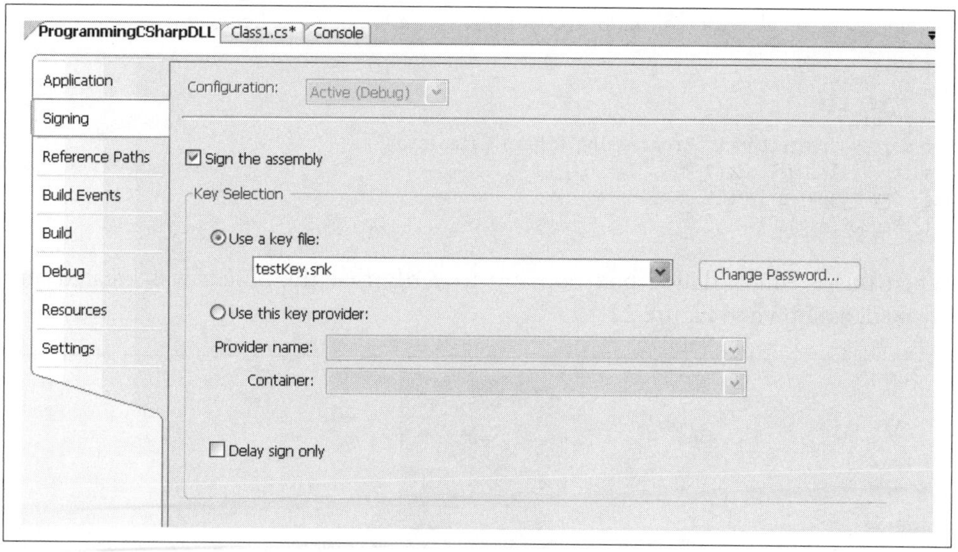

Figure 22-17. Creating a key within Visual Studio

This will open the Create Key dialog, as shown in Figure 22-18.

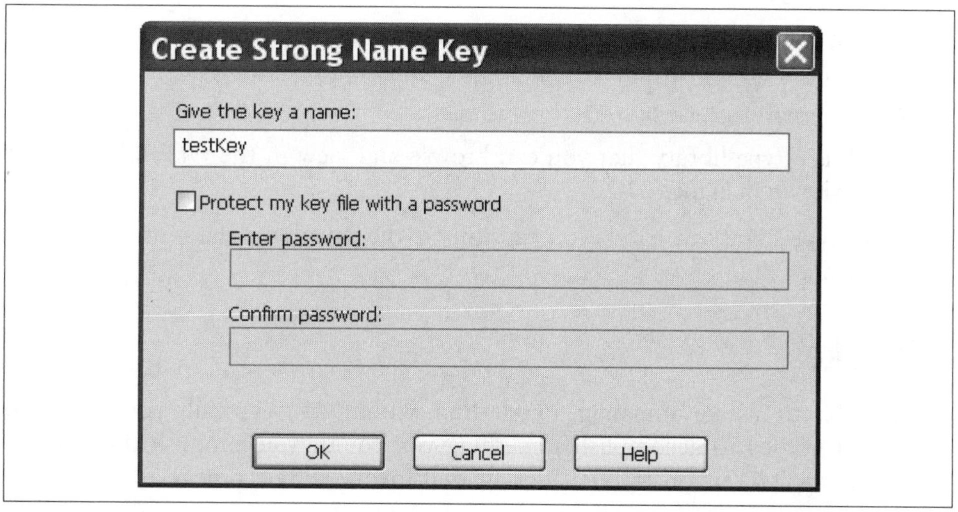

Figure 22-18. Creating a strong name key

Add your program to the GAC, and register it:

```
gacutil /i ProgrammingCSharpDLL.dll
Regasm ProgrammingCSharpDLL.dll
```

You can now invoke the four-function calculator as a COM object using standard VBScript. For example, you can create a tiny Windows-script host file, as shown in Example 22-9.

Example 22-9. Invoking the calculator COM object with a Windows-scripting host file

```
dim calc
dim msg
dim result
set calc = CreateObject("Programming_CSharp.Calculator")
result = calc.Multiply(7,3)
msg = "7 * 3 =" & result & "."
Call MsgBox(msg)
```

When this is run, a dialog box pops up to verify that the object was created and invoked, as shown in Figure 22-19.

Figure 22-19. Late binding via COM

Creating a Type Library

If you wish to use early binding with your .NET DLL, you'll typically create a type library. You can do so with the TlbExp (Type Library Export) utility, by writing:

```
TlbExp ProgrammingCSharpDLL.dll /out:Calc.tlb
```

The result is a type library that you can browse and view in the OLE/COM object viewer, as shown in Figure 22-20.

With this type library in hand, you can import the calculator class into any COM environment.

P/Invoke

It is possible to invoke unmanaged code from within C#. Typically you would do this if you needed to accomplish something you couldn't accomplish through the FCL. With the 2.0 version of .NET, the use of P/Invoke will become relatively rare.

The .NET *platform invoke facility (P/Invoke)* was originally intended only to provide access to the Windows API, but you can use it to call functions in any DLL.

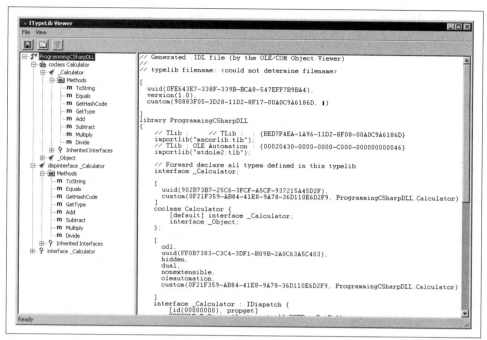

Figure 22-20. Viewing the type library contents

To see how this works, let's revisit Example 21-3. You will recall that you used the FileInfo class to rename files by invoking the MoveTo() method:

```
file.MoveTo(fullName + ".bak");
```

You can accomplish the same thing by using Windows' *kernel32.dll* and invoking the MoveFile method.* To do so, you need to declare the method as a static extern and use the DllImport attribute:

```
[DllImport("kernel32.dll", EntryPoint="MoveFile",
    ExactSpelling=false, CharSet=CharSet.Unicode,
    SetLastError=true)]
static extern bool MoveFile(
  string sourceFile, string destinationFile);
```

The DllImport attribute class is used to indicate that an unmanaged method will be invoked through P/Invoke. The parameters are as follows:

DLL name

The name of the DLL you are invoking.

EntryPoint

Indicates the name of the DLL entry point (the method) to call.

---

* In fact, this is what Fileinfo.Move() is doing itself.

ExactSpelling
> Allows the CLR to match methods with slightly different names based on the CLR's knowledge of naming conventions.

CharSet
> Indicates how the string arguments to the method should be marshaled.

SetLastError
> Setting this to true allows you to call `Marshal.GetLastWin32 Error`, and check whether an error occurred when invoking this method.

The rest of the code is virtually unchanged, except for the invocation of the `MoveFile()` method itself. Notice that `MoveFile()` is declared to be a static method of the class, so use static method semantics:

```
Tester.MoveFile(file.FullName,file.FullName + ".bak");
```

Pass in the original filename and the new name and the file is moved, just as it was when calling `file.MoveTo()`. In this example, there is no advantage—and actually considerable disadvantage—to using P/Invoke. You have left managed code, and the result is that you've abandoned type safety and your code will no longer run in "partial-trusted" scenarios. Example 22-10 shows the complete source code for using P/Invoke to move the files.

Example 22-10. Using P/Invoke to call a Win32 API method

```csharp
#region Using directives

using System;
using System.Collections.Generic;
using System.IO;
using System.Runtime.InteropServices;
using System.Text;

#endregion

namespace UsingPInvoke
{
    class Tester
    {

        // declare the WinAPI method you wish to P/Invoke
        [DllImport( "kernel32.dll", EntryPoint = "MoveFile",
            ExactSpelling = false, CharSet = CharSet.Unicode,
            SetLastError = true )]
        static extern bool MoveFile(
            string sourceFile, string destinationFile );

        public static void Main()
        {
            // make an instance and run it
            Tester t = new Tester();
            string theDirectory = @"c:\test\media";
```

Example 22-10. Using P/Invoke to call a Win32 API method (continued)

```
        DirectoryInfo dir =
            new DirectoryInfo( theDirectory );
        t.ExploreDirectory( dir );
}

// Set it running with a directory name
private void ExploreDirectory( DirectoryInfo dir )
{

    // make a new subdirectory
    string newDirectory = "newTest";
    DirectoryInfo newSubDir =
        dir.CreateSubdirectory( newDirectory );

    // get all the files in the directory and
    // copy them to the new directory
    FileInfo[] filesInDir = dir.GetFiles();
    foreach ( FileInfo file in filesInDir )
    {
        string fullName = newSubDir.FullName +
            "\\" + file.Name;
        file.CopyTo( fullName );
        Console.WriteLine( "{0} copied to newTest",
            file.FullName );
    }

    // get a collection of the files copied in
    filesInDir = newSubDir.GetFiles();

    // delete some and rename others
    int counter = 0;
    foreach ( FileInfo file in filesInDir )
    {
        string fullName = file.FullName;

        if ( counter++ % 2 == 0 )
        {
            // P/Invoke the Win API
            Tester.MoveFile( fullName, fullName + ".bak" );

            Console.WriteLine( "{0} renamed to {1}",
                fullName, file.FullName );
        }
        else
        {
            file.Delete();
            Console.WriteLine( "{0} deleted.",
                fullName );
        }
    }
    // delete the subdirectory
    newSubDir.Delete( true );
```

Example 22-10. Using P/Invoke to call a Win32 API method (continued)

```
      }
    }
}
```

```
Output (excerpt):
c:\test\media\newTest\recycle.wav renamed to
    c:\test\media\newTest\recycle.wav
c:\test\media\newTest\ringin.wav renamed to
    c:\test\media\newTest\ringin.wav
```

Pointers

Until now you've seen no code using C/C++ style pointers. Only here, in the final paragraphs of the final pages of the book, does this topic arise, even though pointers are central to the C family of languages. In C#, pointers are relegated to unusual and advanced programming; typically they are used only with P/Invoke.

C# supports the usual C pointer operators, listed in Table 22-1.

Table 22-1. C# pointer operators

Operator	Meaning
&	The address-of operator returns a pointer to the address of a value.
*	The dereference operator returns the value at the address of a pointer.
->	The member access operator is used to access the members of a type.

The use of pointers is almost never required, and is nearly always discouraged. When you do use pointers, you must mark your code with the C# unsafe modifier. The code is marked unsafe because you can manipulate memory locations directly with pointers. This is a feat that is otherwise impossible within a C# program. In unsafe code you can directly access memory, perform conversions between pointers and integral types, take the address of variables, and so forth. In exchange, you give up garbage collection and protection against uninitialized variables, dangling pointers, and accessing memory beyond the bounds of an array. In essence, unsafe code creates an island of C++ code within your otherwise safe C# application, and your code will not work in partial-trust scenarios.

As an example of when this might be useful, read a file to the console by invoking two Win32 API calls: CreateFile and ReadFile. ReadFile takes, as its second parameter, a pointer to a buffer. The declaration of the two imported methods isn't unlike those shown in Example 22-11.

Example 22-11. Declaring Win32 API methods for import into a C# program

```
[DllImport("kernel32", SetLastError=true)]
static extern unsafe int CreateFile(
```

```
    string filename,
    uint desiredAccess,
    uint shareMode,
    uint attributes,
    uint creationDisposition,
    uint flagsAndAttributes,
    uint templateFile);

[DllImport("kernel32", SetLastError=true)]
static extern unsafe bool ReadFile(
    int hFile,
    void* lpBuffer,
    int nBytesToRead,
    int* nBytesRead,
    int overlapped);
```

You will create a new class, APIFileReader, whose constructor will invoke the
CreateFile() method. The constructor takes a filename as a parameter, and passes
that filename to the CreateFile() method:

```
public APIFileReader(string filename)
{
    fileHandle = CreateFile(
        filename,        // filename
        GenericRead,     // desiredAccess
        UseDefault,      // shareMode
        UseDefault,      // attributes
        OpenExisting,    // creationDisposition
        UseDefault,      // flagsAndAttributes
        UseDefault);     // templateFile
}
```

The APIFileReader class implements only one other method, Read(), which invokes
ReadFile(). It passes in the file handle created in the class constructor, along with a
pointer into a buffer, a count of bytes to retrieve, and a reference to a variable that
will hold the number of bytes read. It is the pointer to the buffer that is of interest to
us here. To invoke this API call, you must use a pointer.

Because you will access it with a pointer, the buffer needs to be pinned in memory;
the .NET Framework can't be allowed to move the buffer during garbage collection.
To accomplish this, use the C# fixed keyword. fixed allows you to get a pointer to
the memory used by the buffer, and also to mark that instance so that the garbage
collector won't move it.

The block of statements following the fixed keyword creates a scope, within which
the memory will be pinned. At the end of the fixed block, the instance will be un-
marked so that it can be moved. This is known as *declarative pinning*:

```
public unsafe int Read(byte[] buffer, int index, int count)
{
    int bytesRead = 0;
```

```
      fixed (byte* bytePointer = buffer)
      {
         ReadFile(
            fileHandle,
            bytePointer +      index,
            count,
            &bytesRead, 0);
      }
      return bytesRead;
   }
```

Notice that the method must be marked with the unsafe keyword. This creates an unsafe context and allows you to create pointers. To compile this you must use the /unsafe compiler option. The easiest way to do so is to open the project properties, click the Build tab, and check the Allow Unsafe Code checkbox, as shown in Figure 22-21.

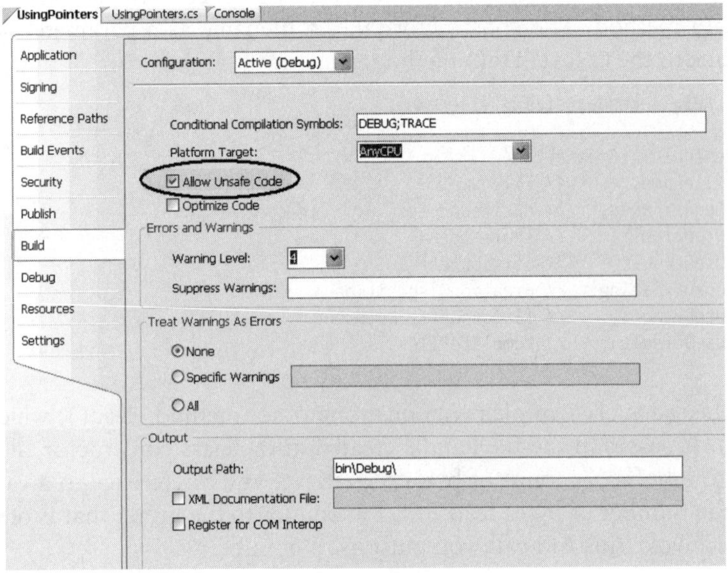

Figure 22-21. Allowing unsafe code

The test program instantiates the APIFileReader and an ASCIIEncoding object. It passes the filename to the constructor of the APIFileReader and then creates a loop to repeatedly fill its buffer by calling the Read() method, which invokes the ReadFile API call. An array of bytes is returned, which is converted to a string using the ASCIIEncoding object's GetString() method. That string is passed to the Console. Write() method, to be displayed on the console. The complete source is shown in Example 22-12.

Example 22-12. Using pointers in a C# program

```
#region Using directives

using System;
using System.Collections.Generic;
using System.Runtime.InteropServices;
using System.Text;

#endregion

namespace UsingPointers
{
   class APIFileReader
   {
      const uint GenericRead = 0x80000000;
      const uint OpenExisting = 3;
      const uint UseDefault = 0;
      int fileHandle;

      [DllImport( "kernel32", SetLastError = true )]
      static extern unsafe int CreateFile(
         string filename,
         uint desiredAccess,
         uint shareMode,
         uint attributes,
         uint creationDisposition,
         uint flagsAndAttributes,
         uint templateFile );

      [DllImport( "kernel32", SetLastError = true )]
      static extern unsafe bool ReadFile(
         int hFile,
         void* lpBuffer,
         int nBytesToRead,
         int* nBytesRead,
         int overlapped );

      // constructor opens an existing file
      // and sets the file handle member
      public APIFileReader( string filename )
      {
         fileHandle = CreateFile(
            filename,        // filename
            GenericRead,     // desiredAccess
            UseDefault,      // shareMode
            UseDefault,      // attributes
            OpenExisting,    // creationDisposition
            UseDefault,      // flagsAndAttributes
            UseDefault );    // templateFile
      }

      public unsafe int Read( byte[] buffer, int index, int count )
      {
```

Example 22-12. Using pointers in a C# program (continued)

```
      int bytesRead = 0;
      fixed ( byte* bytePointer = buffer )
      {
         ReadFile(
            fileHandle,            // hfile
            bytePointer + index,   // lpBuffer
            count,                 // nBytesToRead
            &bytesRead,            // nBytesRead
            0 );                   // overlapped
      }
      return bytesRead;
   }
}

class Test
{
   public static void Main()
   {
      // create an instance of the APIFileReader,
      // pass in the name of an existing file
      APIFileReader fileReader =
         new APIFileReader( "myTestFile.txt" );

      // create a buffer and an ASCII coder
      const int BuffSize = 128;
      byte[] buffer = new byte[BuffSize];
      ASCIIEncoding asciiEncoder = new ASCIIEncoding();

      // read the file into the buffer and display to console
      while ( fileReader.Read( buffer, 0, BuffSize ) != 0 )
      {
         Console.Write( "{0}", asciiEncoder.GetString( buffer ) );
      }
   }
}
```

The key section of code where you create a pointer to the buffer and fix that buffer in memory using the fixed keyword is shown in bold. You need to use a pointer here because the API call demands it.

C# Keywords

abstract
: A class modifier that specifies that the class must be derived from to be instantiated.

as A binary-operator type that casts the left operand to the type specified by the right operand, and that returns null instead of throwing an exception if the cast fails.

base
: A variable with the same meaning as this, except it accesses a base class implementation of a member.

bool
: A logical datatype that can be true or false.

break
: A jump statement that exits a loop or switch statement block.

byte
: A one-byte unsigned integral datatype.

case
: A selection statement that defines a particular choice in a switch statement.

catch
: The part of a try statement that catches exceptions of a specific type defined in the catch clause.

char
: A two-byte Unicode character datatype.

checked
: A statement or operator that enforces arithmetic bounds checking on an expression or statement block.

class
: An extendable reference type that combines data and functionality into one unit.

const

A modifier for a local variable or field declaration that indicates the value is a constant. A `const` is evaluated at compile time and can only be a predefined type.

continue

A jump statement that skips the remaining statements in a statement block and continues to the next iteration in a loop.

decimal

A 16-byte precise decimal datatype.

default

A marker in a `switch` statement specifying the action to take when no case statements match the `switch` expression.

delegate

A type for defining a method signature so that delegate instances can hold and invoke a method or list of methods that match its signature.

do A loop statement to iterate a statement block until an expression at the end of the loop evaluates to `false`.

double

An eight-byte floating-point datatype.

else

A conditional statement that defines the action to take when a preceding `if` expression evaluates to `false`.

enum

A value type that defines a group of named numeric constants.

event

A member modifier for a delegate field or property that indicates only the `+=` and `-=` methods of the delegate can be accessed.

explicit

An operator that defines an explicit conversion.

extern

A method modifier that indicates the method is implemented with unmanaged code.

false

A Boolean literal.

finally

The part of a try statement that is always executed when control leaves the scope of the try block.

fixed

A statement to pin down a reference type so that the garbage collector won't move it during pointer arithmetic operations.

float
> A four-byte floating-point datatype.

for A loop statement that combines an initialization statement, stopping condition, and iterative statement into one statement.

foreach
> A loop statement that iterates over collections that implement IEnumerable.

get The name of the accessor that returns the value of a property.

goto
> A jump statement that jumps to a label within the same method and same scope as the jump point.

if A conditional statement that executes its statement block if its expression evaluates to true.

implicit
> An operator that defines an implicit conversion.

in The operator between a type and an IEnumerable in a foreach statement.

int A four-byte signed integral datatype.

interface
> A contract that specifies the members a class or struct can implement to receive generic services for that type.

internal
> An access modifier that indicates a type or type member is accessible only to other types in the same assembly.

is A relational operator that evaluates to true if the left operand's type matches, is derived from, or implements the type specified by the right operand.

lock
> A statement that acquires a lock on a reference-type object to help multiple threads cooperate.

long
> An eight-byte signed integral datatype.

namespace
> Maps a set of types to a common name.

new An operator that calls a constructor on a type, allocating a new object on the heap if the type is a reference type, or initializing the object if the type is a value type. The keyword is overloaded to hide an inherited member.

null
> A reference-type literal that indicates no object is referenced.

object
> The type all other types derive from.

operator
: A method modifier that overloads operators.

out A parameter modifier that specifies the parameter is passed by reference and must be assigned by the method being called.

override
: A method modifier that indicates that a method of a class overrides a virtual method of a class or interface.

params
: A parameter modifier that specifies that the last parameter of a method can accept multiple parameters of the same type.

private
: An access modifier that indicates that only the containing type can access the member.

protected
: An access modifier that indicates that only the containing type or derived types can access the member.

public
: An access modifier that indicates that a type or type member is accessible to all other types.

readonly
: A field modifier specifying that a field can be assigned only once, in either its declaration or its containing type's constructor.

ref A parameter modifier that specifies that the parameter is passed by reference and is assigned before being passed to the method.

return
: A jump statement that exits a method, specifying a return value when the method is nonvoid.

sbyte
: A one-byte signed integral datatype.

sealed
: A class modifier that indicates a class cannot be derived from.

set The name of the accessor that sets the value of a property.

short
: A two-byte signed integral datatype.

sizeof
: An operator that returns the size, in bytes, of a struct.

stackalloc
: An operator that returns a pointer to a specified number of value types allocated on the stack.

static
A type member modifier that indicates that the member applies to the type rather than an instance of the type.

string
A predefined reference type that represents an immutable sequence of Unicode characters.

struct
A value type that combines data and functionality in one unit.

switch
A selection statement that allows a selection of choices to be made based on the value of a predefined type.

this
A variable that references the current instance of a class or struct.

throw
A jump statement that throws an exception when an abnormal condition has occurred.

true
A Boolean literal.

try A statement that provides a way to handle an exception or a premature exit in a statement block.

typeof
An operator that returns the type of an object as a System.Type object.

uint
A four-byte unsigned integral datatype.

ulong
An eight-byte unsigned integral datatype.

unchecked
A statement or operator that prevents arithmetic bounds from checking on an expression.

unsafe
A method modifier or statement that permits pointer arithmetic to be performed within a particular block.

ushort
A two-byte unsigned integral datatype.

using
Specifies that types in a particular namespace can be referred to without requiring their fully qualified type names. The using statement defines a scope. At the end of the scope, the object is disposed.

value
> The name of the implicit variable set by the set accessor of a property.

virtual
> A class-method modifier that indicates that a method can be overridden by a derived class.

void
> A keyword used in place of a type, for methods that don't have a return value.

volatile
> Indicates that a field may be modified by the operating system or another thread.

while
> A loop statement to iterate a statement block until an expression at the start of each iteration evaluates to false.

Index

Symbols

{ } (braces)
  class properties and behaviors,
      defining, 10
  surrounding statement blocks, 42
  whitespace and, 52
( ) (parentheses)
  grouping in regular expressions, 258
  nesting for proper order of operations, 62
  regular expression metacharacters, 251
<< >> (shift) operator, 61
+= (addition assignment) operator, 57
+ (addition) operator, 55
  overloading, 127
& (ampersand)
  & (logical AND) operator, 61
<% and %>, indicating code between, 387
&& (AND) operator, 60, 61
= (assignment) operator, 54
@ (at) symbol in verbatim string
      literals, 237, 256
  DirectoryInfo object, creating, 527
\ (backslash) escape character, 237
[] (brackets)
  [] (index) operator, 109, 179
    C#, overloading not supported, 198
    finding particular character in a
      string, 244
  accessing array members, 191
  array declarations, 178
^ (caret)
  in regular expressions, 251
, (comma), in array declarations, 187

? (conditional) operator, 343
|| (conditional OR) operator, 61
-- (decrement) operator, 57
* (dereference operator), 608
/= (division assignment) operator, 57
/ (division) operator, 55
. (dot) operator, 13
  for member access and namespaces, 13
  invoking a method, 12
== (equals) operator, 59
  assignment operator (=) vs., 43
  overloading, 129
  testing string equality, 244
> (greater than) operator, 59
>= (greater than or equals) operator, 59
++ (increment) operator, 57
< (less than) operator, 59
<= less than or equals operator, 59
& (logical AND) operator
  as an address-of C++ operator, 608
^ (logical XOR) operator, 61
-> (member access) operator, 608
. (member access) operator
  writing text to the monitor, 12
%= (modulus assignment) operator, 57
% (modulus) operator, 55
*= (multiplication assignment) operator, 57
* (multiplication) operator, 55
!= (not equal) operator, 59
! (not) operator, 60
(pound sign), in preprocessor
      directives, 63
:: (scope resolution) operator, C++, 13

We'd like to hear your suggestions for improving our indexes. Send email to *index@oreilly.com*.

B

background threads, 509
backing store, 525
backslash (see \, under Symbols)
base class, 107
    abstract classes as, 115
    constructors, calling, 112
    Object class as root of all classes, 119
    virtual method, overriding, 108
base keyword, 613
base type (underlying type) for
        enumerations, 34
BeginRead( ) method, 546
    (Stream class), 538, 545
BeginWrite( ) method (Stream class), 538,
    545
Berkeley socket interface, 551
binary files, 538–540
Binary formatter, 484
binary operators, 128
binary read (of a file), 538
BinaryFormatter, 573
BinaryReader class, 537
BinarySearch( ) method
    List class, 215
    (System.Array), 177
BinaryWriter class, 537
binders, 482
binding, 482
    importing the COM DLL to .NET, 595
    late (see late binding)
BindingFlags parameter, 473
bool types, 613
Boolean expressions, 40
boolean value type, C and C++ programmers
        note, 26
boxing types, 26, 121–124
    interface reference, 170, 173
    structs, 139
branch keywords
    conditional branching, 40
    unconditional branching, 39
branching (see conditional branching;
        unconditional branching)
break statements, 39, 52–54, 613
    use with switch statements, 44
breakpoints
    compiling and running programs, 21
    setting, 21
browsers
    IP addresses and, 550
    Web Forms, running on, 382

buffered streams, 540–542
BufferedStream class, 537, 540
buffers, 538
    pinned in memory, 609, 612
bugs, defined, 263
built-in types, 25–29
    char, 28
    choosing, 27
    converting, 28
    Object as root, 121
    value types, listing of, 26
buttons
    data binding and, 391
    (see also controls)
byte type, 613

C

C#
    class definitions, 7
    collections, strongly typed, 25
    command-line compiler, compiling Hello
        World program, 19
    keywords, 613–618
    language
        ASP.NET and, 380
        fundamentals, 24–66
        overview, 7
    lock statement, 513
    Web Forms, using with, 381
C and C++ programmers notes
    abstract classes, limitations in C#, 118
    binary operators, 128
    boolean value type, 26
    case statements, 46
    conditional expressions, 40
    copy constructor, 78
    delete operator, 27
    destructors, 85
    enum types, 36
    exceptions, throwing, 264
    generics (C#) vs. C++ templates, 206
    implicit keyword, 130
    indexers, 198
    inheritance, 119
    Main( ) method, 10
    namespaces, 13
    operator overloading, logical pairs, 129
    preprocessor, 63
    private or protected inheritance, 107
    reference parameters, 94
    reference types, 25
    semicolons, 10, 68

directories, 526–537
    DirectoryInfo object, creating, 527–530
        recursing through
            subdirectories, 528–530
    expanding, 341
    recursing through subdirectories, 337
    working with, 526
Directory class, 526, 537
    methods, 526
Directory property (FileInfo class), 531
DirectoryInfo class, 526, 537
    creating instance of, 527–530, 534
    GetFiles( ) method, 530
    methods, 526
DirectoryInfo objects, 336
dirSub.Attributes property, 338
disconnected data architecture, 360
discovery (type), 466, 469
Dispose( ) method, 86, 385
    invoked by Close( ), 87
    invoked by using statement, 87
Distributed interNet Applications (DNA)
        architecture, 4
Div( ) method, 403
DivideByZeroException, 272
division (/) operator, 55
DllImportAttribute class, 605
DLLs (dynamic link libraries)
    assemblies and, 441
    calling functions with P/Invoke, 604–608
    COM components, importing, 593–602
    multimodule assemblies and, 443
    shared assemblies and, 453
DNA (Distributed interNet Applications)
        architecture, 4
do statements, 38, 614
do...while loops, 49
documentation comments, 357–359
DoEvents( ) method (Application), 346
dot operator (see under Symbols)
double type, 27, 614
DrawWindow( ) method, 23
    calling on array of Control objects, 109
    Control class
        abstract class and method, 116–118
    Control class, marking as virtual, 108
DRI (Declarative Referential Integrity), 362
dynamic binding, 482
dynamic strings, 249–251
    delimiter limitations, 251

E

early binding
    defined, 595
    .NET DLL, using with, 604
editing Hello World program, 17
elements of an array, 178
#elif statement, 65
#else statement, 64, 65
else statement, 614
Emacs, editing programs with, 16
Empty field (String), 238
encapsulating data with properties, 97–101
encryption technology for strong names, 454
#endif statement, 64, 65
end-of-line (Visual Basic programmers
        note), 38
endpoints, 493, 498
    manually associating service with, 498
    sockets as, 550
    of a stream, 525
    understanding, 500
EndRead( ) method, 547
#endregion statement, 65
EndsWith( ) method (String), 239, 244
Enqueue( ) method (Queue), 227
Enter( ) method (Monitor), 518
EntryPoint parameter, 605
Enum attribute target, 460
enum keyword, 34
enumerations, 32, 34–36
    converting between enum and integral
        type, 36
    declaring, 34
    enum statement, 35
    enum types, 614
    (see also IEnumerable interface;
        IEnumerator interface)
enumerator list, 34, 35
Environment class, 336
Equals( ) method, 119, 214
    dictionary key objects, 233
    overriding virtual, 129
    (String), 239, 243
equals operator (==), 59
    assignment operator (=) vs., 43
    overloading, 129
errors, defined, 263
escape characters, 237
    common, 28
Event attribute target, 460
event handlers, 383
    defined, 303

GetObject( ) method (Activator), 475
GetObjectData( ) method (Dictionary), 233
GetParent( ) method (Directory class), 526
GetParentString( ) method, 342, 344
GetRange( ) method (List class), 216
GetResponse( ) method, 570
GetResponseStream( ) method
        (WebResponse), 570
GetString( ) method, 610
GetSubDirectoryNodes( ) method, 337, 339
GetType( ) method, 119, 471
    (Type), 475, 498
GetUpperBound( ) method
        (System.Array), 177
.gif files, 441
Global Assembly Cache (GAC), 453, 455
global methods, 81
goto statements, 39, 47, 615
    switch statement, use in, 44
    switch statement, using with, 46
graphical user interface (GUI)
        design tools, 12
greater than operator (>), 59
greater than or equals (>=) operator, 59
GridLayout mode, adding controls to Web
        Forms, 389
GridViews, creating, 428
Group class (Regex), 256–259
GUI (graphical user interface) design
        tools, 12

H

handles (object), 483
heap
    allocation of array elements, 178
    defined, 27
Hejlsberg, Anders, 7
Hello World program, 9–23
    classes, objects, and types, 9–16
    compiling and running, 18–20
    developing, 16
    editing, 17
    sample code, 9
    Visual Studio .NET debugger,
        using, 21–23
HelpLink property (Exception), 274
hidden bits, 338
hidden interface members, 169
HTML
    adding to Web Forms, 387
    controls, adding to Web Forms, 389
    creation of three GridViews, 428

developer controls translated to, 395
server-side controls, 391
stream, reading web page as, 570
WSDL contract, viewing with, 407
HTTP sessions, 383
HTTPChannel type, 493
HttpWebRequest, 570
HttpWebResponse object, 570
Hungarian notation, 37

I

IAsyncResult interface, 545
ICalc interface, 493, 495
ICloneable interface, 78
ICloneable objects, strings and, 236
ICollection interface, 207
IComparable interface, 207, 210–215
    implementing, 218–221
    strings and, 236
IComparer interface, 207, 345
    implementing, 221–226
        constraints, 226
IConvertible classes, 237
IDataReader interface, 361
IDE (Integrated Development
        Environment), 16
identifiers, 36
    defining, 63
    undefining, 64
IDeserializationCallback interface, 578
IDictionary interface, 207, 233
IDisposable interface, 86
IDL (Interface Definition Language), 7
IEnumerable interface, 207–209, 229
    strings and, 236
IEnumerator interface, 207, 229
#if statement, 64
if statements, 615
    nested, 41–43
        switch statement as alternative, 44
if...else statements, 40
Iformatter interface, 573
IL files (see MSIL files)
ILDasm, 442
IList interface, 207
IMessage interface, 483
immutability of strings, 236
implements relationship, 145
implicit conversions, 28, 130
    boxing, 122
implicit operator, 615

About the Author

Jesse Liberty is the author of a dozen books, including *Programming ASP.NET* from O'Reilly. Jesse is the president of Liberty Associates, Inc. (*http://www.LibertyAssociates.com*), where he provides .NET training, contract programming, and consulting. He is a former vice president of electronic delivery for Citibank, and a former distinguished software engineer and architect for AT&T, Ziff Davis, Xerox, and PBS.

Colophon

Our look is the result of reader comments, our own experimentation, and feedback from distribution channels. Distinctive covers complement our distinctive approach to technical topics, breathing personality and life into potentially dry subjects.

The animal on the cover of *Programming C#*, Fourth Edition, is an African crowned crane. This tall, skinny bird wanders the marshes and grasslands of west and east Africa (the Western and Eastern African crowned cranes, *Balearica pavonia pavonia* and *Balearica regulorum gibbericeps*, respectively).

Adult birds stand about three feet tall and weigh six to nine pounds. Inside their long necks is a five-foot long windpipe—part of which is coiled inside their breastbone—giving voice to loud calls that can carry for miles. They live for about 22 years, spending most of their waking hours looking for the various plants, small animals, and insects they like to eat. (One crowned crane food-finding technique, perfected during the 38 to 54 million years these birds have existed, is to stamp their feet as they walk, flushing out tasty bugs.) They are the only type of crane to perch in trees, which they do at night when sleeping.

Social and talkative, African crowned cranes group together in pairs or families, and the smaller groups band together in flocks of more than 100 birds. Their elaborate mating dance has served as a model for some of the dances of local people.

Mary Anne Weeks Mayo was the production editor, and Audrey Doyle was the copyeditor for *Programming C#*, Fourth Edition. Jamie Peppard, Matt Hutchinson, and Claire Cloutier provided quality control. Lydia Onofrei and Keith Fahlgren provided production assistance. Ellen Troutman Zaig wrote the index.

Ellie Volckhausen designed the cover of this book, based on a series design by Edie Freedman. The cover image is an original engraving from the 19th century. Emma Colby produced the cover layout with Adobe InDesign CS using Adobe's ITC Garamond font.

David Futato designed the interior layout. This book was converted by Julie Hawks to FrameMaker 5.5.6 with a format conversion tool created by Erik Ray, Jason McIntosh, Neil Walls, and Mike Sierra that uses Perl and XML technologies. The text font is Linotype Birka; the heading font is Adobe Myriad Condensed; and the code font is LucasFont's TheSans Mono Condensed. The illustrations that appear in the book were produced by Robert Romano, Jessamyn Read, and Lesley Borash using Macromedia FreeHand MX and Adobe Photoshop CS. The tip and warning icons were drawn by Christopher Bing. This colophon was written by Leanne Soylemez.

Better than e-books

Search
over 2000 top
tech books

Download
whole chapters

Cut and Paste
code examples

Find
answers fast

Read books from cover
to cover. Or, simply click
to the page you need.

**Search Safari! The premier electronic reference
library for programmers and IT professionals**

Related Titles Available from O'Reilly

.NET

.NET and XML

.NET Compact Framework Pocket Guide

.NET Framework Essentials, *3rd Edition*

.NET Windows Forms in a Nutshell

ADO.NET in a Nutshell

ADO.NET Cookbook

C# Essentials, *2nd Edition*

C# Cookbook

C# Language Pocket Guide

Learning C#

Learning Visual Basic.NET

Mastering Visual Studio.NET

Mono: A Developer's Notebook

Object Oriented Programming with Visual Basic .NET

Programming .NET Components

Programming .NET Security

Programming .NET Web Services

Programming ASP.NET, *2nd Edition*

Programming Visual Basic .NET, *2nd Edition*

VB.NET Core Classes in a Nutshell

VB.NET Language in a Nutshell, *2nd Edition*

VB.NET Language Pocket Reference

O'REILLY®

Our books are available at most retail and online bookstores.
To order direct: 1-800-998-9938 • *order@oreilly.com* • *www.oreilly.com*
Online editions of most O'Reilly titles are available by subscription at *safari.oreilly.com*

Keep in touch with O'Reilly

1. Download examples from our books

To find example files for a book, go to:

www.oreilly.com/catalog

select the book, and follow the "Examples" link.

2. Register your O'Reilly books

Register your book at *register.oreilly.com*

Why register your books?
Once you've registered your O'Reilly books you can:

- Win O'Reilly books, T-shirts or discount coupons in our monthly drawing.
- Get special offers available only to registered O'Reilly customers.
- Get catalogs announcing new books (US and UK only).
- Get email notification of new editions of the O'Reilly books you own.

3. Join our email lists

Sign up to get topic-specific email announcements of new books and conferences, special offers, and O'Reilly Network technology newsletters at:

elists.oreilly.com

It's easy to customize your free elists subscription so you'll get exactly the O'Reilly news you want.

4. Get the latest news, tips, and tools

www.oreilly.com

- "Top 100 Sites on the Web"—PC Magazine
- CIO Magazine's Web Business 50 Awards

Our web site contains a library of comprehensive product information (including book excerpts and tables of contents), downloadable software, background articles, interviews with technology leaders, links to relevant sites, book cover art, and more.

5. Work for O'Reilly

Check out our web site for current employment opportunities:

jobs.oreilly.com

6. Contact us

O'Reilly & Associates
1005 Gravenstein Hwy North
Sebastopol, CA 95472 USA

TEL: 707-827-7000 or 800-998-9938
(6am to 5pm PST)

FAX: 707-829-0104

order@oreilly.com
For answers to problems regarding your order or our products. To place a book order online, visit:

www.oreilly.com/order_new

catalog@oreilly.com
To request a copy of our latest catalog.

booktech@oreilly.com
For book content technical questions or corrections.

corporate@oreilly.com
For educational, library, government, and corporate sales.

proposals@oreilly.com
To submit new book proposals to our editors and product managers.

international@oreilly.com
For information about our international distributors or translation queries. For a list of our distributors outside of North America check out:

international.oreilly.com/distributors.html

adoption@oreilly.com
For information about academic use of O'Reilly books, visit:

academic.oreilly.com

O'REILLY®

Our books are available at most retail and online bookstores.
To order direct: 1-800-998-9938 • order@oreilly.com • www.oreilly.com
Online editions of most O'Reilly titles are available by subscription at *safari.oreilly.com*